Political Social Work

Shannon R. Lane · Suzanne Pritzker

Political Social Work

Using Power to Create Social Change

Foreword by Charles E. Lewis, Jr.

 Springer

Shannon R. Lane
School of Social Work
Adelphi University
Garden City, NY, USA

Suzanne Pritzker
Graduate College of Social Work
University of Houston
Houston, TX, USA

ISBN 978-3-319-68587-8   (hardcover)   ISBN 978-3-319-68588-5   (eBook)
ISBN 978-3-030-00789-8   (softcover)
https://doi.org/10.1007/978-3-319-68588-5

Library of Congress Control Number: 2017955959

Printed on acid-free paper

This Springer imprint is published by Springer Nature
The registered company is Springer International Publishing AG
The registered company address is: Gewerbestrasse 11, 6330 Cham, Switzerland

Dedicated to the many social workers who pursue social change everyday, and to Caroline, Kathleen, Matan, and Mori, who we hope grow up in a more just world as a result.

Foreword

This new textbook, *Political Social Work: Using Power to Create Social Change*, is an important milestone that will further institutionalize political social work as an accepted practice in the social work profession. Political social work is fast becoming a critical method needed to advance the profession's pursuit of social and economic justice. The knowledge, skills and values social workers bring to the political arena are profoundly needed, particularly in today's caustic climate. Shannon Lane and Suzanne Pritzker have meticulously crafted the missing manual that will help guide the development of political social work's curriculum and practice knowledge and skills in future years. Each has been researching political participation and how social workers, in particular, participate in the political arena for nearly 15 years.

Dr. Lane served as a political social worker in the United States Senate, working for then-Senate Majority Leader Tom Daschle. She worked with Dr. Nancy A. Humphreys at the University of Connecticut School of Social Work where she earned her Ph.D. and continues to coordinate research with the Nancy A. Humphreys Institute for Political Social Work. She examined the political careers of more than 400 social workers who have sought local, state or federal elected office, the largest number of politically active social work office seekers currently known. Her research is designed to increase the political involvement of social workers and underserved populations, and improve policy and political content within social work education. She has served on the social work faculties of Adelphi University and Sacred Heart University.

Dr. Pritzker earned her Ph.D. at the prestigious George Warren Brown School of Social Work at Washington University in St. Louis, known for its outstanding policy education and practice. She served as a policy advisor for the Virginia Secretary of Education and as an analyst with the Virginia General Assembly. At the University of Houston Graduate College of Social Work, known for its longstanding commitment to political social work, Dr. Pritzker leads political social work education and programming and directs an intensive state legislative placement for graduate social work students. Her research has largely focused on the civic engagement of young people and finding ways to encourage their active participation in political activity. She sees political engagement as fundamental to the empowerment of communities—particularly under-resourced communities that lack political clout.

Combining their knowledge, skills and experience, they make a powerful team. The inaugural edition of this textbook covers political social work from soup to nuts. *Political Social Work: Using Power to Create Social Change* provides a comprehensive overview of the history of political social work, its various contexts for practice, a thorough review of the many ethical challenges for social workers in the political arena, and a wealth of strategies and techniques that will aid social workers opting to engage in the political arena. *Political Social Work: Using Power to Create Social Change* will help to elevate political social work to its needed place in the profession and the world of policy and politics.

As the book fully describes, social workers have a long and proud history of political participation in all levels of government. From school boards to local and state legislative bodies, and in many components of the federal government including the Congress, social workers serve in a myriad of roles with various responsibilities. Students who are entertaining the idea of pursuing political social work will find Chap. 15 appealing as it provides a road map for engagement. Following the tradition of Jane Addams, social workers and students will discover that they can not only help those with whom they work navigate the world shaped by policies and politics, but also be change agents to make theirs a more just and equitable society.

If this textbook had existed several years ago, it would had made my path into political social work much smoother. Growing up in Brooklyn, New York, the son of a politically active pastor, I was engaged in political activity at an early age. My father, Rev. Dr. Charles E. Lewis, Sr., lost an election in 1964 for a seat on the New York State Assembly to Shirley Chisholm, who would ultimately become the first black woman in Congress. I later worked at the Brooklyn Borough President's Office in the 1980s where I met former Congressman Edolphus "Ed" Towns, a social worker, who was then serving as Brooklyn's first black Deputy Borough President. I worked on his successful 1982 Congressional campaign and years later would become his Deputy Chief of Staff and Communications Director and assist him in creating the Congressional Social Work Caucus. During the intervening years, I entered the social work profession and completed a Ph.D. in policy at Columbia University. While on the Hill, I met Dr. Nancy A. Humphreys, who formally introduced me to political social work. At that time, political social work was little discussed outside of the University of Houston Graduate College of Social Work, where Bob Fischer and colleagues had developed a political social work specialization, and the University of Connecticut, where Dr. Humphreys had developed the Nancy A. Humphreys Institute for Political Social Work.

There are many challenges facing society today, from global warming to economic and social inequality, inadequate affordable healthcare and housing, and wage stagnation, that are begging for solutions. The *12 Grand Challenges for Social Work*, under the auspices of the American Academy for Social Work and Social Welfare, is providing an incubator where research, practice, and policy can work together to find solutions for some of these problems. At the Congressional Research Institute for Social Work and Policy, we endeavor to contribute to significant social change. Political social work will enable our profession to turn these ideas into legislation and active policy.

Washington, DC   Charles E. Lewis, Jr., M.S.W., Ph.D.

Preface

Both authors come to this book after many years both of professional practice in the political arena and of teaching and researching about political engagement. Shannon pursued a political social work career for over a decade at the federal level in the U.S. Senate. Suzanne began her career in policy at the state level in Virginia before entering the field of social work, in order to be a part of a profession that is committed to creating a more accessible and inclusive policy environment where more diverse voices are represented. We have both continued to advocate for social change at the state and federal level throughout our academic careers. While our backgrounds and professional experiences in policy and politics are different, we share a strong commitment to the power of political engagement to bring about more responsive and more just policies. We are both firmly convinced that social workers can and should be at the forefront of efforts to expand political engagement and to bring about political change.

Building on that commitment, this book discusses the many opportunities for social workers to participate and lead in the political arena. This book marries the social work profession's ethical imperative to pursue political action, individual social workers' passion for the populations and communities with whom we work, and effective strategies and tools to move both our ethical imperative and our passions into action. Combining the generalist skills and knowledge that social workers develop through their education and practice with political knowledge and skills lays the groundwork for strong and effective efforts to influence and shape policy.

We have written this book to support both social work students and professional social workers in expanding their own political participation. We identify and explore five domains of political social work practice—each of which social workers may engage in either as full-time political social work practitioners *or* as complementary to their social work practice in clinical, community, or administrative settings. In our classrooms and in the field, we have frequently heard students and practitioners ask for examples and models of what political social work practice might look like. We incorporate profiles of real-life social workers whose work has inspired us, and who offer models of political social work practice in each domain.

In this book, we place the political environment front and center, focusing on knowledge and skills necessary to navigate the often-challenging contexts for political action. Throughout the book, we describe the incredible array of political contexts in which U.S. social workers practice. Social workers work within very ideologically distinct contexts, and across communities with vast differences in political structures and resources. You will read about small towns where citizens come together in town halls to voice their opinions and vote on town budgets and policies, and large cities where fewer than ten percent of citizens ever vote, much less voice their opinions on municipal candidates or issues. We describe communities where information about the policies our elected officials are considering is immediately available online, and communities where the local government does not even have a website. We consider communities represented by politicians earning full-time salaries who can afford to focus solely on their political responsibilities, and communities represented by politicians who earn just $300 a year for their civic work and who must hold other full-time commitments in order to make ends meet. We identify and provide illustrative examples of this diversity in order to help readers learn how to better navigate their own political contexts.

This book is divided into four parts, highlighting steps in the process of political social work. You will see many parallels between these steps and the process of social work in other practice arenas. In Part I, *Social Work in Politics*, Chaps. 1 and 2 introduce readers to political social work and to the five domains of political social work practice. These chapters also provide readers with the opportunity to assess their own orientations to political engagement. Chapters 3 and 4 introduce central theories, as well as critical concepts of power, empowerment, and conflict, that underlie political social work practice. In Part II, *Assessing and Planning Effective Political Social Work Strategies*, readers learn to strategically plan political change efforts. Core concepts of political assessment and strategy development are introduced in Chap. 5. Chapter 6 applies these concepts to the unique characteristics involved in developing advocacy strategy, while Chap. 7 applies these concepts to the steps of developing a winning electoral campaign strategy. Chapter 8 explores strategy in an often under-appreciated aspect of political social work: identifying ways to educate and empower voters.

Part III, *Engaging and Intervening with Effective Political Social Work Strategies*, takes readers through the nuts and bolts of engaging with individual community members, staff, policymakers, and the media in order to implement political change efforts. Readers will learn about and practice ways to effectively incorporate professional use of self and strategic communications skills to communicate effectively with voters, policymakers, and the media in Chap. 9. Chapter 10 focuses on engaging with staff and volunteers, critical to managing or participating in any political change effort. Strategic attention to both fundraising and budgeting is essential to implementing strategy in political social work; therefore, Chaps. 11 and 12 focus on managing financial resources in a political context. Finally, Part IV, *Evaluating Political Social Work and Planning for the Future*, calls on readers to reflect on ways to continue to strengthen their political social work practice as they move forward in their careers. In Chap. 13, readers consider both the challenges and opportunities involved in evaluating practice in political settings. Chapter 14 asks readers to consider how they can utilize the National Association of Social Workers' Code of Ethics to navigate the many ethical challenges that political social work may entail throughout their careers. Chapter 15 provides resources to help social workers prepare and market themselves for careers that incorporate political social work practice. The book concludes with a discussion critical for all political social workers: how to consider and plan for self-care as you pursue your political change efforts.

Throughout the four parts to this book, we focus heavily on the knowledge, skills, and critical thinking essential for practicing social work in political settings. Readers will find interactive and reflective exercises throughout the book (titled: *Build Your Knowledge*, *Apply Your Skills*, *Self-Assessment*, *Explore Your Values*, and *Further Reflection*). Whether you are reading this book in a classroom setting or on your own, we hope that these exercises help make this content useful as you apply it directly to your own political context.

We hope this book prepares you to use the political process in order to create social change that is meaningful to you. We encourage you to use the knowledge and skills here to take your current political involvement to the next level, empower those around you to use their voices, and use collective power to work for social justice.

Garden City, NY, USA
Houston, TX, USA

Shannon R. Lane
Suzanne Pritzker

Acknowledgments

We are thankful for the many individuals who have helped us in writing this book. In particular, we would like to gratefully acknowledge the contributions of the following generous, talented people.

The M.S.W. and Ph.D. students who have supported our work and contributed to this book's content: Samantha Heinly, Jenna Powers, Cristin Sauter, and Gardenia Garza. Thank you for your tireless work, good humor, and encouragement. You are the future of political social work.

The amazing political social workers who have lent their stories to this book through our profiles and case studies: Jane Addams, Nancy Amidei, Berenice Hernandez Becerra, Constance Brooks, Joanne Cannon, Nathaniel Cindrich, Richard Cloward, Susan Collins, Sheryl Grossman, Kara Hahn, Susan Hoechstetter, Chenelle Hammonds, Juliana Cruz Kerker, Steve Kornell, Stephanie Mace, Barbara Mikulski, Jessica J. Mitchell, Melanie Pang, Rebecca Phillips, Natalie Powell, Torey Powell, Jeannette Rankin, Katie Richards-Schuster, Ana Rodriguez, Tanya Rhodes Smith, Sally Tamarkin, and honorary political social worker Frances Fox Piven. Thank you for allowing us to tell your stories, and for all that each of you has done to further social change.

There are many other advocates and activists whose efforts are described in this book. We want to particularly mention Beth Caldwell, an activist, advocate, and friend, whose advocacy to increase funding for metastatic breast cancer is described in this book. Beth died due to her cancer in 2017, but not before making a huge difference in the issues that were dear to her heart and we hope this book contributes in some small way to her message being heard.

Many people gave of their time and knowledge to review chapters, answer questions, and in general, help us minimize the number of mistakes in this book. Heather Kanenberg and Jenna Powers were kind enough to read and provide feedback on the entire book. Christina Chiarelli-Helminiak, Mae Flexer, Ellen Graham, Katharine Hill, Mary Hylton, Elizabeth Kanick, Cara Lane, Sheila Lane, Sacha Klein, Jessica J. Mitchell, Jason Ostrander, Danielle Parrish, Carolyn Peabody, Stephanie Podewell, Lauren Prause, Laura Quiros, Addie Sandler, Tanya Rhodes Smith, and Todd Vanidestine reviewed individual chapters and provided significant expertise, encouragement, and thoughtful ideas.

Thank you to those who have contributed ideas or suggestions incorporated throughout, including many of our colleagues at the University of Houston and

Adelphi University, as well as Laura Bartok, Tom Felke, Jillian Gilchrest, Peter Hanson, Amber Huus, Lirio Negroni, Rebecca Lane, Neela Lockel, Laura Quiros, Cristina Mogro Wilson, and Rani Varghese. All of you and many others who have discussed and debated the concepts here over the last 2 years have added a depth of insight and variety of perspectives to our writing. Likewise, we thank our students over the years with whom we have practiced many of the exercises presented here. They have helped us refine many of our ideas about how to write and teach about political social work content and how to better support the career development of future political social workers. As our former students have graduated and moved into their social work practice, they continue to inspire us to prepare more political social workers to join them in their social change efforts.

We want to acknowledge the work of Charles Lewis of the Congressional Research Institute for Social Work and Policy. Charles has elevated political social work within the national conversation, and we appreciate his contribution to this book through the forward.

Thank you to our editor, Jennifer Hadley, and the supportive staff at Springer Social and Behavioral Sciences for turning the idea of this book into a reality.

From Shannon:

In 1993, I began an internship with Senator Tom Daschle that would turn into a 10-year career on Capitol Hill, as well as a lifelong commitment to social change in the political arena. Thank you to Senator Daschle and Daschleland. Thank you also to John Tropman, my advisor at the University of Michigan School of Social Work, who inspired me to connect my political work with my social work education, and to consider academia as an option. I owe a huge debt of gratitude to Dr. Nancy A. Humphreys, the founder of the Nancy A. Humphreys Institute for Political Social Work at the University of Connecticut, current director Tanya Rhodes Smith, the community of political social workers at the University of Connecticut School of Social Work, and Kate Coyne-McCoy, who has trained hundreds of social workers to run for political office through the UConn Campaign School for Social Workers and other venues. The incredible knowledge and expertise of Nancy, Tanya, Kate, and the Institute alumni are the foundation for my understanding of political social work and an inspiration always.

Thank you to my husband, Michael Kapralos, daughters Caroline and Kathleen, and the rest of my family and support network who have encouraged me, helped me with classes, entertained my children, or helped with other responsibilities to make time for writing. And thank you to Suzanne for being the best co-author possible.

From Suzanne:

Thank you to Robert Schneider, professor emeritus at Virginia Commonwealth University and founder of social work's national Influencing State Policy organization (now known as Influencing Social Policy), and Steve Harms, who both recruited me into the social work profession and introduced me to the power that social workers have to impact political systems and to shape inclusive and responsive policy. Thank you to Amanda Moore McBride who encouraged my commitment to political engagement scholarship as a doctoral student and whose national leadership on social work and civic engagement continues to inspire my work. I am especially appreciative of the faculty members at the University of Houston Graduate College of Social Work who, long before my time on faculty, set an example for the integral nature of political social work and its emphasis on navigating power to every aspect of social work practice, and to Ira Colby who hired me into my first faculty position in order to continue building on this critical tradition.

Thank you to my husband Andy Love and to my sons Matan and Mori, who have gone above and beyond to support me in writing this "chapter book," as they call it. And thank you to Shannon, from whom I have learned so much—about political social work, collaboration, and so much more. I am so grateful that we decide to embark on this project together years ago.

Contents

Part I

Social Work in Politics

"Politics is social work with power."

–Senator Barbara Mikulski, MSW

Consider Yourself Asked: Introduction to Political Social Work

1

Table of Contents

© Springer International Publishing AG 2018
S.R. Lane, S. Pritzker, *Political Social Work*,
https://doi.org/10.1007/978-3-319-68588-5_1

Section 1: Overview

Political social work is social work practice that explicitly attends to power dynamics in policy-making and to political mechanisms for eliciting social change. Political social work includes expanding political participation, influencing policy agendas, working on campaigns or in electoral offices, and holding elected office. It is a form of practice, as well as related research and theory, through which social workers fulfill their ethical responsibility to engage in social and political action for social justice and human rights.

Social work has a long, rich history of courageous individuals and groups using power and the political system to promote social justice, equality, and self-determination. This book describes these highlights of our profession's history, as well as many missed opportunities, such as the experience of US social workers who chose not to act and therefore helped facilitate the internment of Japanese-Americans during World War II. You will meet trailblazing social workers like United States Congresswoman Jeannette Rankin, the first woman to be elected to a national representative body anywhere in the world. You will be introduced to the interrelationships between social work and political activity and the various ways that the guiding documents of the social work profession, including the National Association of Social Workers (NASW) Code of Ethics, encourage and guide political social work practice through the core values of the profession.

Developing Social Work Competency
The Council on Social Work Education establishes educational standards for all social work programs in the USA. Content in this chapter supports building competency in the following areas that are considered core to the practice of social work:
COMPETENCY 1: Demonstrate Ethical and Professional Behavior
COMPETENCY 5: Engage in Policy Practice

Section 2: Consider Yourself Asked

A leading framework for understanding political participation, discussed in depth later in this book, suggests that three key factors precede people's involvement in activities that influence politics and policy: knowing how and what to do (knowledge and skills), feeling like you want to—and are capable of—participating (interest and efficacy), and being asked or encouraged to participate. This book is specifically designed to help you build your political knowledge, skills, interest, and efficacy. However, we want to take this opportunity at the beginning of this book to directly *ask* you for your participation.

You may have spent your whole life interested in influencing policy, or you may be questioning why policy is relevant to a social work career. You may have always seen yourself with a rightful place in the political arena, or you may have been told throughout your life—either explicitly or implicitly—that politics is not the place for you. The authors of this book have worked with many students and social workers who have been told directly by their parents, their friends, their community, or even the broader society that politics is not something they need to concern themselves with, that it is unimportant or someone else's domain. You may have heard some of these messages. As a woman, you may have been told by family members that politics and policy are a man's domain. As a person of color, you may have gotten the message that your voice is not needed or welcomed in political discussions. As a Millennial, you may have endured a constant refrain of negative media attention and headlines like one that appeared in *The Washington Post* in January 2016 stating "Why #Millennials don't matter much in American politics" (Bump 2016).

What we want to say to you is that *you do have a place in the world of politics and policy-making; your voice does belong*. As a person, as a social worker, as you, with all the experiences and identities you bring with you—you have a valuable voice to bring to policy-making, and we want to encourage you to use it. You came to social work because of a desire to help people, especially those who are vulnerable, marginalized, and often invisible to the larger society. These people need your direct assistance, but they also need you to help them and their concerns become visible in policy-making, as very few other people do. You, as a social worker who sees and understands the challenges that your clients face *and* who understands how larger structures contribute to these challenges, are exactly who our political arena needs. So, consider yourself asked to participate, to become a **political social worker**, a social worker who effectively navigates power dynamics and political strategies in order to bring about social justice and social change.

POLITICAL SOCIAL WORKER PROFILE: Barbara Mikulski, MSW
US Representative 1977–1987, US Senator 1987–2017 (D-MD) (Fig. 1.1).

Fig. 1.1 Barbara
Mikulski, MSW

"Politics is social work with power." These words were spoken by a force within the political and social work world, Sen. Barbara Mikulski. She was the second woman (first female Democrat) to be elected to the US Senate, without replacing a deceased spouse, and in 2012 was elected to chair the powerful Senate Appropriations committee. The first woman to chair this committee, her position allowed her to oversee bills appropriating federal

(continued)

funds and to ensure that federal spending was consistent with values that reflected equity and equal opportunity. She is a self-proclaimed "social worker with power," someone whose grit and perseverance consistently met push-back from some colleagues as she defended spending on federal social welfare programs such as food stamps and Temporary Assistance for Needy Families (Weigel 2013). During her Senate career, she was widely regarded with respect and was tenacious in her pursuit of creating bipartisan solutions. Her intention was to focus solely on the best manner of appropriating funds, rather than feeding into partisan political games.

To hold such staunch beliefs and remain unwavering in the face of opposition requires unbelievable fortitude, especially in a male-dominated political arena. How did Sen. Mikulski supersede the onslaught of difficulties she faced in public office? How was she able to not only survive in the political world, but also thrive, all while maintaining her social work core? Growing up in a working-class family, completing her MSW, and engaging in coalition building as a community organizer grounded her political work. As a community organizer, she led the way for diverse populations to join together in protest to fight against highway building through their neighborhoods (Archives of Maryland n.d.).

Her community organizing led her to her first elected seat, on the Baltimore City Council. "I thought, 'Gee, why should I be out there knocking on doors trying to get inside?' Why not run for City Council and be inside, opening the doors for the people?" She led in a way that was seen as strong and direct, even amidst assumptions that as a woman and as a social worker, such approaches would be difficult to carry out. As Fisher and Johnson (2015) note, she blazed a trail for social workers and women in the political world, and chose to retire by posing the question "Do I spend my time raising money? Or do I spend my time raising hell?"

FURTHER REFLECTION: Barbara Mikulski and a Social Worker's Path to Politics
Watch the first 5 minutes of this interview on C-SPAN with former Senator Barbara Mikulski (D-MD): https://www.c-span.org/video/?10419-1/life-career-barbara-mikulski. What are your initial thoughts as you listen to her discuss her path to politics? What connections, if any, do you personally see between social work and politics?

Section 3: Why Political Social Work?

Social workers and those who laid the foundation for the social work profession have long navigated power dynamics, engaging with and challenging the political system to promote social justice, equality, and self-determination. Despite incredible changes in social work, in our communities, and in the world since the profession's inception, social work's call to improve society, advocate for social justice, and fight for equality remains constant. The National Association of Social Workers' (2017) Code of Ethics requires social workers to "engage in social and political action" to "expand choice and opportunity" and "promote policies and practices that … safeguard the rights of and confirm equity and social justice for all people." Through its focus on influencing power and political dynamics, **political social work** practice is a central way in which social workers can meet these ethical obligations.

Above, you read about former Senator Barbara Mikulski's work and the impact she has had over her long political social work career. When she retired from the US Senate in 2016, she described herself as "a social worker with power" who wanted "to serve people with their day-to-day needs" (Fisher and Johnson 2015). Through her example, she shows us that social workers have social workers have both the capacity and perspectives necessary for navigating power dynamics on behalf of their clients and constituencies. Political social work practice provides a framework for social workers to effect change in the political process. Through political social work, we impact the contexts in which policies are made, thereby shaping the content of these policies. We are guided by our professional values and ethics to change the voices represented in policy-making and to shape how issues and policies are framed.

The skill discussions in this book are designed to prepare readers to engage in political social work at all levels of practice, including leadership roles within a social work career. This book is designed to help social workers develop the skills necessary for all stages of political social work including assessing the political environment, engaging with social workers and nonsocial workers around political issues, implementing successful advocacy and electoral campaigns, and evaluating practice in the political arena.

Section 4: What Does Political Social Work Look Like?

"Political social work" emerged as a term in the early 1990s, calling the profession's attention to the importance of training social workers to effectively navigate power and political dynamics to further social change. Two discrete definitions were promoted in the term's early years. Nancy A. Humphreys, founder of the University of Connecticut Humphreys Institute for Political Social Work, defined political social work as a subset of macro-focused policy practice, through which specialist social workers work full time in political arenas (NASW 2003). Political social work was instead defined as part of social work across all practice methods by Robert Fisher (1995) and his University of Houston colleagues. Through this view, all social work is political, requiring engaging with power and politics.

Contemporary political social work includes social work practice, research, and theory construction that explicitly attends to power dynamics in policy-making and political mechanisms used for eliciting social change. Political social work requires social workers to understand political strategies and to be skilled in implementing these strategies in all levels of systems. Political social workers must also be able to communicate political and policy information to the clients and client systems they work with in order to create opportunities for empowerment. Through political social work practice, social work values and ethics can be injected into policy-making. Ultimately, political social workers accomplish this by contributing to political leadership, leading change movements, and empowering clients to choose to leverage their political voices.

What Are Political Social Work Strategies?

We identify five domains in which political social work commonly takes place. Social workers may practice in each of these domains as full-time political social work practitioners or as complementary to their practice in clinical, community, or administrative settings. We use this five-domain framework throughout the book to guide discussion of the various ways in which social workers can pursue social change through political means.

Domains of Political Social Work	
1. Engaging individuals and communities in political processes	◄
2. Influencing policy agendas and decision-making	◄
3. Holding professional and political positions	◄
4. Engaging with electoral campaigns	◄
5. Seeking and holding elected office	◄

Within each of these five domains, social workers can use specific strategies to effect change in each of these domains. These specific strategies include the following:

Domain 1: Engaging individuals and communities in political processes

- Performing outreach to increase voting on the part of underrepresented groups
- Educating underrepresented groups to increase political awareness and engagement
- Registering eligible members of client systems to vote
- Advocating for expanded political power to underrepresented groups, including increased voting rights and more just and responsive electoral processes

Domain 2: Influencing policy agendas and decision-making

- Influencing the policy agendas of candidates
- Influencing policy agendas and policy decision-making by elected officials
- Influencing policy agendas and policy decision-making by government agencies

Domain 3: Holding professional and political staff positions

- Working on policy through civil service or other professional positions
- Serving as political appointees in a range of government offices
- Working in the offices of elected officials

Domain 4: Engaging with electoral campaigns

- Working on campaigns as a volunteer or paid staff
- Seeking passage or defeat of ballot initiatives or referenda
- Educating voters about policy issues that are part of candidate or issue campaigns
- Influencing which candidates run for elected office

Domain 5: Seeking and holding elected office

- Running for elected office
- Serving in elected office

In What Settings Do Political Social Workers Practice?

To advance the profession of social work, address the many challenges society faces, and ensure that social work's values and principles help guide our policy process, all social workers, regardless of field of practice or method, require core political knowledge and skills. As Reisch (2000) argues, the social work profession needs both social workers who can lead political efforts *and* a larger group who engage in political action "with purpose, conviction, perseverance, and even with relish" (p. 293).

While *all* social workers can and should engage in political practice to fulfill our ethical mandate, political knowledge and skills are consistently used and advanced by full-time macro-oriented political social workers, whom we refer to as **specialists**. These social workers hold jobs that require continual interaction with political and policy processes. They call upon these skills to provide leadership to their organizations, communities, and profession. Specialist political social workers practice in a wide range of politically oriented settings. As we describe in more depth throughout this book, these settings include advocacy or lobbying organizations, political action committees, grassroots community organizations, political campaigns, offices of local, state, or national elected officials, and in elected positions.

A wider group of social workers are what we refer to as **generalists**, those who integrate political work into broader social work practice. These social workers may not engage with the political process on a daily basis, but they understand policy-making and political process and they engage that system and its specialists when needed in order to create change for their clients, communities, or agencies. Generalist social workers work or volunteer in many of the same settings as specialist social workers. They volunteer for political campaigns, influence political party agendas, and attend political fundraisers. Within their fields of practice, generalist social workers empower their clients to leverage their own political voices, implement voter registration drives, and build community coalitions that engage politicians around issues, candidates, and political processes.

Because political social work requires explicit attention to power and political dynamics inherent in the policy process, these two groups of social workers must work together to ensure that the experiences and needs of clients and communities are represented within the political process and resulting policies. The expertise of each social work group's complements the expertise of the other. Specialists may have a deeper understanding of the process, players, and mechanisms of change, while generalists may have a deeper understanding of the needs of particular populations. Both sets of social workers can use core social work skills to help craft policy. For example, social workers who develop strong political relationships are able to bring their expertise to policy-makers both as consultants behind the scenes and by testifying or providing public comments throughout the policy process. While all social workers may engage in these types of advocacy efforts, social workers who consistently focus on the importance of human relationships in their political social work practice will be well situated to impact policy outcomes.

Section 5: History of Political Social Work

A review of social work's "grand accomplishments" reveals that social workers have played important roles throughout history in eliciting fundamental societal change through governmental institutions, including—at crucial times—through political leadership (AASWSW 2013). Involvement by social workers in politics began in a small but significant way in the profession's early years (Mahaffey 1987). In 1896, James B. Reynolds wrote the first known article urging social workers to go into politics. He also analyzed the political process as it related to neighborhood residents' problems.

As the profession began to develop, social workers focused on causes. Gradually, social work began to develop an emphasis on the interrelationship between individuals and their environment. Social workers began to articulate the value that all people are entitled to the resources necessary to meet their basic human needs and achieve their maximum potential in a democratic society (Mahaffey 1987). Early social workers involved in activism included Lillian Wald, Florence Kelly, Paul Kellogg, and most famously Jane Addams (Huff n.d.). Many of these early activists came out of the settlement house movement (Davis 1964a). These social workers argued that money spent properly on social reform would end poverty and social conflict. They advocated for higher wages, shorter working hours, better working conditions, a minimum wage, ending child labor, universal pensions, and unions.

At the same time, a second perspective within social work held that an impartial approach to the political world, clean and above the fray, was necessary for social work to obtain and maintain a professional status (Mahaffey 1987). Those with this perspective raised concerns about social workers' involvement in political activity. They were apprehensive that social workers who became involved in politics would risk the unbiased image of the new profession. Their view of the role of social workers was that members of the profession should make their expertise available for legislators working on social policy, but should not be involved firsthand in making political decisions. Social workers holding this view, such as Edward Devine, worked to inform legislators and helped create new social policy organizations, but strongly believed that nonpartisanship was crucial for professionalism. Under this perspective, social workers should supply information to be used for public policy, but go no further (Mahaffey and Hanks 1982).

A third perspective was exemplified by caseworkers such as Mary Richmond, who thought that poverty was rooted in individual and moral failings (Mahaffey 1987). Richmond stated that social workers should focus on helping people on a case-by-case basis, rather than focusing on social legislation. Richmond and others with this viewpoint argued that reform movements did not represent genuine social work. They maintained that when a social worker engaged in political activities, such as being elected to office, that person was leaving the field of social work. They were concerned that political efforts would divert attention and resources from practice (Mahaffey and Hanks 1982).

This conflict between social workers' involvement in policy-level change and microlevel practice was underscored when Miriam Van Waters spoke out against the involvement of social workers in politics in a 1930 speech to the National Conference of Social Welfare (Mahaffey 1987), and has remained a long-standing challenge within the profession. As president of the organization, Van Waters maintained that concentrating on legislative and constitutional reform would result in a neglect of the concept of personality and individual responsibility, thus concluding that reform movements did not represent genuine social work. However, her contemporary, Francis McLean, a leader in family social work, disagreed. McLean countered that good casework demanded caseworkers be active in working for the development of a more sensible economic system. Along these lines, the American Association of Social Workers (AASW) proposed a "radical program" in 1933 that stressed the importance of redistribution of wealth and power through reconstruction of socio-economic institutions. The organization endorsed a permanent government welfare system and praised other New Deal programs.

Such rifts in the profession occasionally brought about consequences for those social workers whom it judged to have crossed a line in regard to political action. Bertha Capen Reynolds' social views, including her support for unions and for Marxism, found her blacklisted during and after World War II (Leighninger 1999). Addams and Wald were both ostracized by many for their activism, particularly for activities such as those related to unions and peace causes, which were seen by some as radical (Mahaffey 1987).

Efforts by social work organizations to engage social workers in political activity began to grow in the latter half of the twentieth century. When the NASW Code of Ethics was adopted in 1960, it specifically established that responsibility to the community and broader society is a professional obligation for social workers. In 1979, NASW took an even stronger stance on behalf of political action, introducing specific responsibilities to society, including a responsibility to advocate for policy change. In 1996, NASW went even further, adding an explicit call to *all* social workers "to engage in social and political action" that remains in place today (NASW n.d.).

Involvement of professional social work organizations in politics was first formalized in the 1970s when the National Association of Social Workers (NASW) began to lobby and influence partisan elections on the state and federal level (Dempsey 2003). At the national and state levels, Education Legislative Action Network (ELAN) committees were developed for social workers to learn about legislation, disseminate related information to chapter members, and influence policy (Alexander 1982). As early as 1981, political activity figured prominently in the social work literature, with the profession's premier journal, *Social Work*, devoting the editorial page and five articles to social workers' political activity. It was determined on the floor of the NASW Delegate Assembly in 1993 that the profession should strengthen its focus on political action (Dr. Nancy A. Humphreys, personal communication, January 15, 2007).

In 1945, Pray argued that social workers should limit political action to work needed to help an agency function (Alexander 1982). While opposition to social workers' political activity is weaker today, the debate has not entirely concluded. Writing from Israel, Shamai and Boehm (2001) suggest that politically oriented social work intervention may be possible for many social workers, but caution against allowing an unprofessional "political debate" into the process. Despite these concerns, social workers and social work organizations have increasingly embraced and furthered the expansion of social workers' political engagement.

The following section highlights the history of political social work within each of the domains previously described in Section 4 of this chapter.

History: Engaging Individuals and Communities in Political Processes (Domain 1)

Social work historically has sought to expand political power among populations traditionally underrepresented. In fact, this is codified in the NASW (2017) Code of Ethics, with the call for social workers to enhance "meaningful participation in decision making for all people." Two critical mechanisms for doing this are voter registration and voter education. One of the largest innovations in expanding voter registration in the USA was led by social worker Richard Cloward, profiled in Chap. 8. Cloward cofounded a national coalition, Human SERVE (Service Employees Registration and Voter Education), to expand **suffrage**, the right to vote. Among the accomplishments of this coalition were voter registration drives organized across the USA and their work toward passage of the federal National Voter Registration Act in 1993. This coalition's advocacy resulted in the development of federal and state motor-voter programs in order to increase the accessibility of voter registration (Piven and Minnite 2013).

Efforts to integrate voter engagement into social work education emerged in the early twenty-first century. Innovative programs at the University of Connecticut and the University of Nevada Reno involve social work students registering voters at their field placements. Two policy-focused social work organizations, Influencing Social Policy (ISP) and the Congressional Research Institute for Social Work and Policy (CRISP), joined together in advance of the 2016 Presidential Election to sponsor a nonpartisan Voter Empowerment Campaign (Lewis 2015). This national campaign developed and disseminated social work-specific tools designed to facilitate voter registration and education.

History: Influencing Policy Agendas and Decision-Making (Domain 2)

From social work's earliest years, practitioners have influenced the policy agendas of both candidates and elected officials. Many social workers, including Alice Paul, Lucy Burns, and Mary Church Terrell, actively sought to expand women's right to vote by influencing elected officials to put this on their agendas and move it through the policy process. Jane Addams and Jeanette Rankin sought to influence policies surrounding war and peace through their participation in early-twentieth-century peace movements.

NASW has been active in lobbying and influencing the decision-making of elected officials on the state and federal levels since the 1970s. Their involvement began with development of Education Legislative Action Network (ELAN) committees (Alexander 1982). Then and now, these ELAN committees attached to state NASW chapters and at the federal level educate policy-makers about issues key to social work and the communities we serve, and ensure that those issues stay on the legislative agenda. Social workers also have sought to influence local policy, from Jane Addams' early days seeking to change garbage collection in Chicago to the present day. Social workers in Houston, Texas, showed leadership regarding expanding rights for the LGBTQ community in Houston by joining in a community effort to advocate for an ordinance to expand nondiscrimination protections (Guerra 2015). This effort is discussed in more detail in Chap. 9's profile of Melanie Pang.

History: Holding Professional and Political Staff Positions (Domain 3)

Social workers serve in both professional and political staff positions. One category of political appointees are those employees who are appointed to their positions by chief executives (presidents, vice presidents, governors, or other appointees). Social worker Frances Perkins was the first woman ever appointed by a President to his cabinet. Perkins served as President Franklin Roosevelt's Secretary of Labor from 1933 to 1945. In this position, she was actively involved in developing the Social Security Act. Social workers Harry Hopkins and John Collier also were appointed to federal leadership posts by Roosevelt. During the Depression, Hopkins led federal work relief programs including the Federal Emergency Relief Administration and the Works Progress Administration. As Commissioner for the Bureau of Indian Affairs, Collier designed the "Indian New Deal" (AASWSW 2013). Another significant social worker and political appointee was Wilbur Cohen, appointed by President Lyndon Johnson as Secretary of Health, Education, and Welfare to guide the passage of Medicare. In a more recent example, Jared Bernstein was appointed by Vice President Joseph Biden as his Chief Economist and Economic Adviser under President Barack Obama.

Local, state, and federal legislators also hire staff who typically share their political orientations. Social worker Gabe Zimmerman served as the community outreach director for former Congresswoman Gabrielle Giffords. In this role, he organized the outreach event at which he lost his life, when a gunman targeted Giffords (NASW 2011). Working for legislators is a setting in which some students begin their political social work careers. For example, the University of Houston runs a legislative internship program; through this program, students participate in a full-time block placement as legislative staffers during Texas' biennial legislative session. After graduation, some of these social work interns come back to the legislature to hold positions such as chief of staff or legislative director.

Social workers also work in professional positions as **civil servants**, employees hired through merit-based procedures separate from the political system. Social workers may be employed in executive branch agencies. They also may work for the legislature as part of nonpartisan offices, such as the federal Congressional Budget Office.

History: Engaging with Electoral Campaigns (Domain 4)

In the early years of the twentieth century, social workers, often direct practitioners, played an active role in electoral politics. As early as 1901, social worker and public health nurse Lillian Wald supported the New York City mayoral campaign of Seth Low. When Mayor Low was elected, he honored his campaign promise to Wald to increase the number of public health nurses in the city.

Jane Addams and other social workers sought to "apply the principles and techniques of social work and research to the organization of a political party" (Davis 1964b). They developed a National Progressive Service and engaged in developing a political platform and voter education. This work supported the Progressive Party. They served on its executive boards, and took on roles as active campaigners, voter registrars, and delegates to the party's 1912 convention. Following Roosevelt's decision to run on the Progressive Party third-party ticket in 1912, Addams seconded his nomination for president at that year's Progressive Party convention, the first time in US history that a woman presented a nominating or seconding speech at a party's national convention (Dempsey 2003; Leighninger 2004).

Social work organizations became involved in endorsing and donating to candidates in the second half of the twenty-first century. NASW formed the PACE (Political Action for Candidate Election) committee as a national political action committee (PAC), and it was authorized by the 1976 Delegate Assembly (Dempsey

1999). PACE endorses and contributes to federal candidates, mobilizes NASW members to vote for endorsed candidates, hires field organizers to increase voter turnout in targeted races, compiles voting records for elected officials, and maintains information on social workers who currently hold political office at all levels. With parallel purposes, the first state PACE committee was formed in Florida in 1978 (Mathews 1983). Development of other state PACE committees followed in subsequent years. Notably, less than one-third of state PACE committees endorse candidates in local elections (Scanlon et al. 2006). Through its annual Campaign School, the Humphreys Institute for Political Social Work prepares social work students to volunteer for and lead electoral campaigns (Ostrander et al. 2017). We also continue to see social workers' involvement in issue-based electoral campaigns. For example, following the efforts mentioned above to strengthen Houston's nondiscrimination protections, social workers became actively involved in efforts to pass an Equal Rights Ordinance referendum placed on the city's ballot (Guerra 2015).

History: Seeking and Holding Elected Office (Domain 5)

Social worker Jeannette Rankin was the first woman in the USA elected to Congress in 1916, and was elected again in 1940. In 1971, Ron Dellums became the second social worker elected to the US House of Representatives. Dellums was known for his peace activities, his radicalism, founding the Congressional Black Caucus, and serving on the Armed Services Committee (Dellums and Halterman 2000). When Dellums retired in 1998, his chief of staff, Barbara Lee, also a social worker, replaced him. During the 1970s, at a time when the profession was becoming more politically active, the number of social workers in Congress doubled with the election of Barbara Mikulski (D-MD) in 1976 (Mikulski et al. 2000). Mikulski retired in 2016 as the most senior female in the US Senate (Davis 1964b).

In 1979, 51 social workers holding elected state legislative offices in the USA were identified (Mahaffey 1987). In 2007, the National Association of Social Workers had information about 10 social workers serving in the federal legislature and 192 in state and local offices (Lane and Humphreys 2011). As of 2008, Lane and Humphreys (2011) had identified 467 social workers who had run for elective office. Nine social workers held office during the 115th Congress (January 2017–January 2019): one in the Senate (Sen. Debbie Stabenow from Michigan) and eight in the House of Representatives (Personal communication, D. Kastner, January 3, 2017). Social workers also serve as elected officials at the state level, and most commonly in local government positions, as elected members of commissions, councils, and boards. Holding municipal office is a strong fit for social workers who can use political strategies to address the basic needs of local communities (Rose 1999). Social workers can receive social work-specific training for running for office. The Humphreys Institute Campaign School mentioned above has included training on running for elected office for over 20 years; more recently, CRISP has offered a Political Boot Camp.

POLITICAL SOCIAL WORKER PROFILE: Jeanette Rankin
US Representative 1917–1919; 1941–1943

Jeanette Rankin was a pioneer in political social work. She began her social work career doing casework with orphans in a group facility in Spokane, Washington. She soon became discouraged with casework. She was frustrated with hoping for benefits to be distributed to people in need, and decided that it would be better to educate and motivate the public. She joined the successful women's suffrage campaign in Washington state and then continued to work as part of successful women's suffrage efforts in California, New York, Ohio, Wisconsin, and Montana (Davidson 1994; Josephson 1974).

On November 6, 1916, Rankin was able to vote in Montana for the first time in her life. She voted in this election—for herself. She was the first woman to run for the US Congress. With her victory, Rankin became the first woman elected to Congress and, in fact, to any national representative body in the world.

Once in the US House, she was one of only a few votes against the US entrance into World War I. She is often remembered for this vote, an example of where social work and peace movements intersected in the profession's early years (Simon 2002). In office, she fought for economic justice, women's rights, civil rights, and election reform, and was a sponsor of the first mother-and-child health bill proposed to Congress (Josephson 1974). After one term, she lost her bid for election to the Senate, and spent the next two decades as a lobbyist.

On November 5, 1940, Rankin was once again elected to the US House of Representatives from Montana. Once again, she had the opportunity to vote against US entry into a war. After Pearl Harbor, she stood alone as the only member of Congress to vote against US entry into World War II (Josephson 1974). After two separate terms in office and two separate votes against entry into a world war, Rankin chose not to run for election.

SELF-ASSESSMENT: Social Work and Politics
Answer the following questions created by Rome and Hoechstetter (2010). Check the box in the first column if you plan to do this in the future, and the box in the second column if you think social workers should do this action. Tally your answers for each column. Discuss your answers with a fellow social worker.

Activity	I *plan* to do this in the future	Social workers *should* do this
Vote in federal elections	☐	☐
Work for pay on campaigns for candidates of my choice	☐	☐
Encourage others to vote on election day	☐	☐
Share my political opinions with others	☐	☐
Take an active role in relation to issues that affect me personally	☐	☐

(continued)

Activity	I _plan_ to do this in the future	Social workers _should_ do this
Vote in state elections	☐	☐
Read, listen to, or watch the news	☐	☐
Refuse to vote to demonstrate dissatisfaction with certain elements of the political system	☐	☐
Volunteer for political campaigns	☐	☐
Donate money to causes that are important to me	☐	☐
Follow the progress of legislation that interests me	☐	☐
Volunteer with interest groups (NASW, EMILY's List, NRA), civic organizations (local nonprofit, community group), or a political party (Republican, Democrat)	☐	☐
Keep track of how my legislators vote on issues that interest me	☐	☐
Participate in political rallies, marches, protests, etc.	☐	☐
Voice my opinion on policy issues to media markets (radio, newspapers, TV, etc.)	☐	☐
Take an active role in relation to issues that affect my clients	☐	☐
Participate in civil disobedience when unjust laws or policies are enacted	☐	☐
Contact elected officials about issues that affect my clients	☐	☐
Use social media (Facebook, Twitter, blogs) to organize and engage in politics	☐	☐
Write/deliver testimony to elected and/or appointed political bodies	☐	☐
Vote in local elections	☐	☐
Donate money to political campaigns and/or parties	☐	☐
Discuss current policy issues with others	☐	☐
Take part in concerts or supporting events that are associated with a cause (such as "Race for a Cure") and raise awareness and donations	☐	☐
Choose to spend my money on products, organizations, or businesses that support my personal beliefs	☐	☐
Contact my local elected official(s) about issues that concern me	☐	☐
Contact my state elected official(s) about issues that concern me	☐	☐
Contact my federal elected official(s) about issues that concern me	☐	☐
Encourage and/or help others register to vote	☐	☐
Been appointed/seek appointment to a political position or government office (i.e., local commission, government board)?	☐	☐
Run for local office	☐	☐
Run for state office	☐	☐
Run for federal office	☐	☐
Total (0–33)		

Section 6: The Importance of Political Social Work in Social Work Ethics and Values

Since 1996, the Code of Ethics has explicitly required *all* social workers "to engage in social and political action" (NASW n.d.). It does not stop with that statement, however. It calls on social workers to specifically "expand choice and opportunity" and "promote policies and practices that … safeguard the rights of and confirm equity and social justice for all people" (6.04) (NASW 2017). Such statements clearly underscore the ethical obligation of social workers to promote social justice and further social change.

Political social work practice is an essential component to promoting social justice. If social workers want to influence the content of policies that impact vulnerable and oppressed populations, we also must influence *who* possesses the power to make policy decisions. By engaging in political social work practice, we can skillfully navigate the power and political dynamics inherent in political processes in order to be impactful.

Through political social work, we also can expand representation in politics from both social workers and vulnerable populations with whom we work. Research finds that when policy-making bodies are representative of diverse gender, racial, or ethnic communities, policy priorities differ from the status quo. For example, elected bodies that include women place greater emphasis on education, medical issues, and human welfare than do other policy-making bodies (Thomas 1994; Smith 2013). A similar dynamic takes place when legislative bodies include representation from a variety of racial and ethnic backgrounds (Kittilson and Tate 2005). Evidence suggests that the composition of policy-making bodies also impacts the language used to frame policy issues. For example, when women are part of policy-making, they are more likely to discuss reproductive rights through the lens of women's health than of morality (Levy et al. 2001).

We want to emphasize that the discussion of political action in the Code of Ethics is not limited to how social workers participate. The Code also emphasizes political empowerment, calling on social workers to promote meaningful and informed public participation in policy decision-making. Throughout this book, we discuss political social work strategies that can be used in engaging social work clients and constituencies in political processes.

Section 7: What Will Readers Be Able to Do at the End of this Book?

By the end of this text, readers will be able to accomplish the following:

- Identify the diverse array of political social work career opportunities
- Increase self-awareness of personal ideology, knowledge, skills, and efficacy
- Describe political social work theories, models, and legal issues
- Identify power, ways to assess it, and ways to engage with it productively
- Apply social work assessment skills in political contexts
- Design effective strategies for electoral and advocacy campaigns

- Use critical thinking skills to identify campaign targets and effective ways to reach them
- Identify key strategies for empowering communities through voter engagement
- Demonstrate persuasive political communication skills, including interpersonal communication, framing, and effective use of language
- Develop skills for hiring and managing volunteers and staff members in political settings
- Understand rules and concepts of raising money on political efforts
- Understand rules and concepts of spending money on political efforts
- Learn how to monitor and evaluate success within a political context
- Develop skills in evaluating and navigating ethical dilemmas in the context of political practice
- Create an individualized roadmap for a political social work career, as a generalist or specialist
- Increase the social work profession's presence and power in the political arena

---

FURTHER REFLECTION: US Social Workers and the Internment of Japanese-Americans During World War II
Read the article "Facilitating Injustice: Tracing the Role of Social Workers in the World War II Internment of Japanese Americans" by Yoosun Park (2008). What actions by social workers in this situation would have honored the value of social justice? What political skills might have been useful in taking those actions?

The article can be accessed either though a university or college online library database, or you may read it online for free by going to this link and creating a free "MyJSTOR" account: http://www.jstor.org/stable/pdf/10.1086/592361.pdf.

Review of Key Terms and Concepts

Civil servants: government employees vetted through merit-based procedures designed to be separate from the political system.

Generalists: a wider group of social workers compared to specialists (see below), who integrate political work into broader social work practice. These social workers may not engage with the political process on a daily basis, but they understand policy-making and political process, and they engage that system and its specialists when needed in order to create change for their clients, communities, or agencies.

Political social work: social work practice that explicitly attends to power dynamics in policy-making and to political mechanisms for eliciting social change.

Political social worker: a social worker who effectively navigates power dynamics and political strategies in order to bring about social justice and social change.

Specialists: full-time macro-oriented political social workers who are in jobs that require continual interaction with the political or policy process and call upon these skills to provide leadership to their organizations, communities, and profession.

Suffrage: the right to vote.

Resources

Article

Rome, S. H., & Hoechstetter, S. (2010). Social work and civic engagement: The political participation of professional social workers. *Journal of Sociology and Social Welfare, 37*, 107–129.

Websites

Congressional Research Institute for Social Work and Policy (CRISP): http://www.crispinc.org
Nancy A. Humphreys Institute for Political Social Work, University of Connecticut: http://www.politicalinstitute.uconn.edu
University of Houston, Austin Legislative Internship Program: http://www.uh.edu/socialwork/academics/msw/specializations/political-specializations/austin-legislative-internship/index.php

References

Alexander, C. A. (1982). Professional social workers and political responsibility. In M. Mahaffey & J. W. Hanks (Eds.), *Practical politics: Social work and political responsibility* (pp. 15–31). Silver Spring, MD: NASW Press.

American Academy of Social Work and Social Welfare. (2013). *Grand accomplishments in social work*. Grand challenges for social work initiative, Working Paper No. 2. Baltimore, MD: American Academy of Social Work and Social Welfare.

Archives of Maryland (n.d.). *Barbara Ann Mikulski (1936–)*. Retrieved from http://msa.maryland.gov/megafile/msa/speccol/sc3500/sc3520/002000/002094/html/2094extbio.html.

Philip Bump. (2016, January 19). Why #Millennials don't matter much in American politics. *The Washington Post*.

Davidson, S. (1994). *A heart in politics: Jeannette Rankin and Patsy T. Mink (women who dared)*. Seattle, WA: Seal Press.

Davis, A. F. (1964a). Settlement workers in politics, 1890–1914. *Review of Politics, 26*(4), 505–517.

Davis, A. F. (1964b). The social workers and the progressive party, 1912–1916. *American Historical Review, 69*(3), 671–688.

Dellums, R. V., & Halterman, H. L. (2000). *Lying down with the lions: A public life from the streets of Oakland to the halls of power*. Boston, MA: Beacon Press.

Dempsey, D. (1999). *NASW's electoral political program*. Retrieved October 14, 2007, from https://www.socialworkers.org/archives/advocacy/electoral/default.asp?back=yes.

Dempsey, D. (2003). *Electoral politics (revised statement)*. Washington, DC: National Association of Social Workers.

M. Fisher and Jenna Johnson. (2015, March 2). Mikulski, a role model for generations of women in politics, to retire in 2016. *The Washington Post*.

Fisher, R. (1995). Political social work. *Journal of Social Work Education, 31*(2), 194–203.

Joey Guerra. (2015, March 24). As a training director at First Person, Melanie Pang focuses on changing the way nonprofits operate. *Houston Chronicle*.

Huff, D. (n.d.). *Progress and reform: A cyberhistory of social work's formative years*. Retrieved from http://www.boisestate.edu/socwork/dhuff/history/central/tc.html.

Josephson, H. (1974). *First lady in Congress: Jeannette Rankin*. Indianapolis, IN: Bobbs-Merrill.

Kittilson, M. C., & Tate, K. (2005). Political parties, minorities, and elected office. In R. Hero & C. Wolbrecht (Eds.), *The politics of democratic inclusion* (pp. 163–185). Philadelphia, PA: Temple University Press.

Lane, S. R., & Humphreys, N. A. (2011). Social workers in politics: A national survey of social work candidates and elected officials. *Journal of Policy Practice, 10*, 225–244.

Leighninger, L. (1999). Social workers and the social order. *Journal of Progressive Human Services, 10*(2), 73–80.

Leighninger, L. (2004). Jane Addams and the campaign of Theodore Roosevelt. *Journal of Progessive Human Services, 15*(2), 57–60.

Levy, D., Tien, C., & Aved, R. (2001). Do differences matter? Women members of Congress and the Hyde Amendment. *Women & Politics, 23*(1–2), 105–127.

Lewis, C. E. (2015). Social workers to launch voter empowerment campaign. *Social Justice Solutions.* www.socialjusticesolutions.org/2015/09/21/social-workers-launch-voter-empowerment-campaign

Mahaffey, M. (1987). Political action in social work. In A. Minahan (Ed.), *Encyclopedia of social work* (Vol. Vol. 2, 18th ed., pp. 283–294). Silver Spring, MD: NASW Press.

Mahaffey, M., & Hanks, J. W. (1982). *Practical politics: Social work and political responsibility.* Silver Spring, MD: National Association of Social Workers.

Mathews, G. (1983). Social work PACs and state social work associations' purpose, history, and action strategies. *Journal of Sociology and Social Welfare, 10*(2), 347–354.

Mikulski, B., Hutchison, K. B., Feinstein, D., Boxer, B., Murray, P., Snowe, O., et al. (2000). *Nine and counting: The women of the senate.* New York, NY: HarperCollins Publishers.

National Association of Social Workers (2003). *Dr. Nancy Humphreys receives NASW Lifetime Achievement Award.* Washington, DC: National Association of Social Workers.

National Association of Social Workers. (2011). *NASW Mourns the loss of social work leader Gabe Zimmerman.* Washington, DC: National Association of Social Workers.

National Association of Social Workers. (2017). *Code of Ethics of the National Association of Social Workers.* Washington, DC: National Association of Social Workers.

National Association of Social Workers (n.d.). *History of the NASW Code of Ethics.* Retrieved from https://www.socialworkers.org/nasw/ethics/ethicshistory.asp.

Ostrander, J., Lane, S. R., McClendon, J., Hayes, C., & Rhodes Smith, T. (2017). Collective power to create political change: Increasing the political efficacy and engagement of social workers. *Journal of Policy Practice, 16*, 261–275.

Park, Y. (2008). Facilitating injustice: Tracing the role of social workers in the World War II internment of Japanese Americans. *Social Service Review, 82*(3), 447–483.

Piven, F. F., & Minnite, L. C. (2013). Voter education. In *Encyclopedia of Social Work.* Oxford: Oxford University Press.

Reisch, M. (2000). Social workers and politics in the new century. *Social Work, 45*(4), 293–297.

Rome, S. H., & Hoechstetter, S. (2010). Social work and civic engagement: The political participation of professional social workers. *Journal of Sociology and Social Welfare, 37*, 107–129.

Rose, S. J. (1999). Social workers as municipal legislators: Potholes, garbage and social activism. *Journal of Community Practice, 6*(4), 1–15.

Scanlon, E., Hartnett, H., & Harding, S. (2006). An analysis of the political activities of NASW state chapters. *Journal of Policy Practice, 5*(4), 41–54. https://doi.org/10.1300/J508v05n04_04.

Shamai, M., & Boehm, A. (2001). Politically oriented social work intervention. *International Social Work, 44*(3), 343–360.

Simon, B. L. (2002). Women of conscience: Jeannette Rankin and Barbara Lee. *Affilia, 17*(3), 384–388.

Smith, A. R. (2013). *The election, incorporation, and policy impact of women in city government.* Dissertation, Emory University.

Thomas, S. (1994). *How women legislate.* New York: Oxford University Press.

Weigel, D. (2013, March 20). Barb wire. *Slate.*

Contexts for Political Social Work Practice

2

© Springer International Publishing AG 2018
S.R. Lane, S. Pritzker, *Political Social Work*,
https://doi.org/10.1007/978-3-319-68588-5_2

Section 1: Overview

Political social workers practice in many contexts. They use their social work skills, values, and knowledge of the political context to navigate power dynamics. This process allows them to influence policy and the political process on behalf of clients, communities, organizations, and the social work profession. This chapter provides an in-depth discussion of professional political social work roles to guide readers in thinking about contexts in which you might incorporate political social work into your social work practice. These contexts include practice at the micro, mezzo, and macro levels. While there are many ways to engage in political social work practice, this chapter highlights practice in the five different domains introduced in Chap. 1: (1) expanding the political power of underrepresented clients and constituencies; (2) influencing the policy agendas and decision-making of candidates and policymakers; (3) holding professional and political staff appointments; (4) engaging with campaigns on behalf of, or in opposition to, candidates, ballot initiatives or referenda; and (5) seeking and holding elected office. Throughout this chapter, you will engage in interactive, reflective activities about the various political contexts within which you may practice.

Developing Social Work Competency
The Council on Social Work Education establishes educational standards for all social work programs in the USA. Content in this chapter supports building competency in the following areas that are considered core to the practice of social work:
COMPETENCY 1: Demonstrate Ethical and Professional Behavior
COMPETENCY 5: Engage in Policy Practice

Domains of Political Social Work	
1. Engaging individuals and communities in political processes	◄
2. Influencing policy agendas and decision-making	◄
3. Holding professional and political positions	◄
4. Engaging with electoral campaigns	◄
5. Seeking and holding elected office	◄

Section 2: Political Social Work Settings

All social workers, in both macro and direct practice positions, can use political knowledge and skills to address the Code of Ethics' charge to conduct social and political action to achieve social justice. **Macro practice** positions include "work in communities through public and private organizations that is designed to promote progressive social change contributing to the growth and empowerment of individuals, agencies, and communities. Macro responsibilities include, but are not limited to, program planning and management, administration, human resources, volunteer management, marketing, training and development, grant writing, community development, advocacy and policy practice, and research and evaluation" (Pritzker and Applewhite 2015). Titles identified in a survey of macro practitioners included CEO, executive director, chief program officer, director of development, director of public policy, program manager, research coordinator, community outreach liaison, legislative director, consultant, or grant writer (Pritzker and Applewhite 2015). These positions may not have the term "social worker" in the title and many will not be posted on social work websites or listings. The level of the position can range from entry level to senior. While some jobs may prefer those with direct practice experience, most expect potential employees to possess specific macro skills.

Political knowledge and skills are useful for executive directors, board members, and other leaders of nonprofit organizations in advocating on behalf of their agency or its mission. Social workers work directly with communities as community organizers or in community outreach roles where they help constituent groups achieve their political goals. Social workers may be policy practitioners who help draft, analyze, research, or evaluate policies implemented through the political system. This work takes place within advocacy organizations, government agencies, or in elected or political staff positions at all levels of government.

Social workers in **direct practice** work with individuals, families, and groups at both micro and mezzo levels of practice (Walsh 2016). Social workers in direct practice use their political knowledge and skills to assist individual clients, groups of clients, or vulnerable communities in their own political empowerment. They use their knowledge to help access resources for the agencies or communities in which they work (Saez 2017). Social workers in direct practice testify to legislators about the experience of their clients or communities (Marloff 2017). They speak on behalf of groups who may not be able to speak for themselves safely, such as undocumented immigrants or LGBT older adults (Koseff 2017).

Social workers also may engage in political social work outside of their professional positions. They engage in volunteer work, support campaigns, and participate in advocacy coalitions. They may be members or leaders of a local volunteer political group or caucus—this could be a local Democratic or Republican Party group, or an interest group that regularly endorses and supports candidates. Social workers also volunteer to support elections, for example as a **poll watcher**, who monitors polling sites to observe the voting process at a local voting precinct (Vladeck 2016), or as part of an nonpartisan organization like the League of Women Voters that seeks to expand voter participation.

In the sections below, we elaborate on each of the five domains of political social work practice introduced in Chap. 1, and discuss what political social work practice looks like in each domain.

Section 3: Engaging Individuals and Communities in Political Processes (Domain 1)

Strategies:

- Performing outreach to increase voting on the part of underrepresented groups
- Educating underrepresented groups to increase political awareness and engagement

- Registering eligible members of client systems to vote
- Advocating for expanded political power to underrepresented groups, including increased voting rights and more just and responsive electoral processes

Engaging voters and advocating for equal access to political power builds directly from the call for promoting meaningful participation of vulnerable populations in our profession's Code of Ethics (National Association of Social Workers 2017). Work under this domain may be partisan or nonpartisan. It often involves direct grassroots involvement within communities in order to build relationships and connect communities to political resources. Engaging voters can be frustrating as you encounter barriers to increased political access and watch vulnerable populations experience these barriers time and time again. Yet, it also can be incredibly meaningful as you see individuals gain access to the political process, often for the first time.

Voter Engagement and Social Work

In 2016, there were roughly 250 million people of voting age in the USA, approximately 230 million of whom were eligible to vote. Approximately 60% of voters, 139 million people, voted in that year's Presidential election (McDonald 2017). Participation rates vary widely from state to state, however. For example, only 42% of eligible voters in Hawaii and 50% of eligible West Virginians cast a vote for president, while 71% of those eligible to vote in New Hampshire and 74% of eligible Minnesotans did the same.

Social workers tackle such gaps in voter participation—particularly, the lack of voting among vulnerable populations—through **voter engagement**. The process of voter engagement is divided into three stages, voter registration, voter education, and voter outreach, which we explore in depth later in this book. In the wake of the National Voter Registration Act and the Help America Vote Act of 2002, which set standards for voter registration and voting across the country (U.S. Election Assistance Commission 2017), opportunities for engaging clients and communities have increased through the public, nonprofit, and for-profit sectors. Some social work groups such as the Humphreys Institute for Political Social Work at the University of Connecticut and the National Voter Empowerment Campaign (see Resources) argue that the Code of Ethics bounds all social workers to empower clients through voter engagement.

Social Workers Advocating for Expanded Political Power

Above, we described the US population that is eligible to vote. However, the USA has a long history of excluding various groups of citizens from the right to vote, based on race, income, and gender. Since the nation's early days, when the right to vote was generally limited to white male property owners, constitutional amendments have been ratified to expand the right to vote. Despite these changes to the US Constitution, discrimination and voter suppression continued, in forms such as voting taxes and literacy tests. In 1965, Congress passed the Voting Rights Act, banning such mechanisms and enforcing efforts against voting discrimination in areas of the country believed most likely to discriminate. Voting rights advocates argue, however, that more recent laws related to voting and voter registration—such as those that limit voter registration dates and access to early voting, those that require photo IDs to vote, and those that require periodic purges of voter rolls—continue to discriminate against low-income and racial minority voters (Brandeisky et al. 2014).

Within this broader context, many US residents today are not eligible to vote, whether because they are not citizens, have a felony conviction status (which varies by state), or have been determined ineligible to vote based on mental incapacitation. For some of these individuals, there is no realistic path to voting in the near term. However, even when there is a path to participation for some currently ineligible voters, it may be long and challenging. For example, in nine states, individuals convicted of felonies may have their voting rights restored only by applying to the state's Governor or through the judicial system (National Conference of State Legislatures 2016). Even where restoration of voting rights is automatic, ex-offenders may not know they are eligible, or often face a challenging process in re-registering to vote. This may involve substantial paperwork and documentation, interfacing with multiple state agencies, and application backlogs (National Conference of State Legislatures 2016).

Throughout our history, social workers have engaged in political justice efforts to expand suffrage. They work within advocacy and legal organizations to expand voting rights and create more just electoral processes. They monitor voting restrictions and challenge them when they are discriminatory. For example, during the 2013 Supreme Court deliberations which ruled that some portions of the Voting Rights Act are no longer needed, NASW's Legal Defense Fund filed an amicus brief with the Court on behalf of the Act (Pace 2013). After the 2013 Supreme Court ruling, NASW issued a statement in favor of an amended Voting Rights Act, stating that

"Discrimination in voting is real and it is not a thing of the past—it is still happening and we need tools to redress such injustices… NASW has always taken the position that voting discrimination can pose an existential threat to our democracy" (National Association of Social Workers 2014, p. 5–6).

Social workers also work with populations that have been deemed ineligible, helping them access voting rights. For example, social workers who reintegrate ex-offenders are well situated to help them navigate the challenging processes of voting rights restoration. Social workers also participate in advocacy efforts to challenge state laws and processes. The executive director of the Sentencing Project, a leading advocacy organization focused on criminal justice issues including felon disenfranchisement, is a social worker (The Sentencing Project 2017).

BUILD YOUR KNOWLEDGE: Voting in Your State

Read https://www.nytimes.com/2015/07/29/magazine/voting-rights-act-dream-undone.html and then find the voting laws in your state here or through your state's official election website (often the Secretary of State's website): http://www.nonprofitvote.org/voting-in-your-state/ (or go to http://www.nonprofit-vote.org/ and under the "Popular" tab, click "Voting In Your State").

Find the statistics for voter turnout in your state in the most recent federal election: http://www.electproject.org. How do you think your state's voting laws help or hinder turnout? What might you recommend to amend your state's voting laws?

Section 4: Influencing Policy Agendas and Decision-Making (Domain 2)

Strategies:

- Influencing the policy agendas of candidates
- Influencing policy agendas and policy decision-making by elected officials
- Influencing policy agendas and policy decision-making by government agencies

This domain emphasizes the work political social workers do to influence the political process from the outside. Political social workers influence candidates, policy agendas, and the policy process in a variety of settings. This work may be done by full-time political social workers. It is also done by those working in direct service or community work who find that they need to engage with the political process to make change for their clients or communities. Political social workers who engage with this domain work for elected officials, community-based organizations, or in private practice. This work takes place within grassroots community organizations, political parties or political action committees, for advocacy organizations or lobbying firms, or even on your own.

Social Workers Influencing Policy Agendas

A critical part of political social work involves influencing the policy agendas of candidates, elected officials, and government agencies. Forging relationships with candidates early on through endorsements, donations, and volunteer support can lay the groundwork for long-standing policy support as candidates become lawmakers. Organizations that endorse candidates often use forums and discussions with candidates before the endorsement to promote their policy agenda and to ask for candidates' commitments to this agenda. Haynes and Mickelson (2010) remind us that "a candidate remembers those who helped create the momentum of the campaign. Early money, volunteers, and other support may deter competition, create a 'winning attitude' for the chosen candidate, or both" (p. 153). Furthermore, "volunteers who join campaigns early have far greater opportunities to affect policy issues and play key campaign roles" (p. 154); this observation underscores the importance of time, relationship building, and commitment to a candidate for social workers seeking to influence a candidate's policy agenda.

Social Workers Influencing Decision-Making

As politicians are elected and reelected to office, social workers hold elected officials to the agendas they ran on and influence their continued policy decision-making. Politicians heavily rely on lobbyists and advocates who help them become aware of policy problems and the pros and cons of various policy solutions. As elected officials consider possible policy alternatives, social workers bring important perspectives to elected officials. In particular, social workers introduce the voices and perspectives of vulnerable populations who otherwise may not be heard in policy decision-making.

Social workers influence policy through **advocacy campaigns**, which target elected officials or others with decision-making power in order to secure their support or opposition to a policy issue. These efforts focus on elected officials in the executive or legislative branches, or on appointed or civil service employees (described in Section 5, below) who have influence over the policy development and implementation that takes place in government agencies. Social workers lead these efforts as professional advocates, as part of advocacy coalitions with other direct service professionals, or as agency leaders or board members. Social workers also hold professional positions as lobbyists. **Lobbying** efforts similarly target decision-makers to secure their support or opposition for a specific piece of legislation. Both advocacy and lobbying entail purposeful efforts to change policies.

Social workers who advocate or lobby for policy change use tactics such as meeting directly with policymakers by phone or in person, writing letters or sending postcards to policymakers, testifying at public hearings, and inviting policymakers to visit their agencies or communities to see first-hand the critical impact of policy decisions. Social media increasingly offers a critical path for influencing policymakers through eliciting a public audience for advocacy efforts (Edwards and Hoefer 2010; Guo and Saxton 2012). Influencing public decision-making also may involve suggesting that a policymaker's continued nonresponsiveness will result in endorsing or donating funds to a competitor in a future election. We examine practice in this domain in-depth throughout this book.

Section 5: Holding Professional and Political Staff Positions (Domain 3)

Strategies:

- Working on policy through civil service or other professional positions
- Serving as political appointees in a range of government offices
- Working in the offices of elected officials

As of March 2012, federal, state, and local governments employed 22 million people. Of these, 14.4 million full-time and 4.9 million part-time employees work for state and local governments across the USA (Jessie and Tarleton 2014). The Census Bureau defines a **government** as "an organized entity, which in addition to having governmental character, has sufficient discretion in the management of its own affairs to distinguish it as separate from the administrative structure of any other governmental unit" (Hogue 2013). This includes entities such as counties, municipalities, and townships, mosquito abatement districts, utility districts, water and sewer districts, and transit authorities. These governments perform functions that include financial administration, police protection, highway administration, hospitals, utilities, etc. Across these entities, social workers hold positions in both professional and political staff positions.

Civil Service and Social Work

The majority of government positions, especially at the federal level, are considered **civil service positions** (Krause et al. 2016). These positions require new hires to be vetted through standardized merit-based procedures designed to be separate from the political system. Civil service positions cover a wide range of opportunities, at all levels of government (Peterson's Staff 2013). Civil service positions may incorporate a significant amount of political or policy content, or none at all. Civil service positions with "social work" in the title likely involve direct service and include similar tasks as other direct service positions. Front-line workers who work directly with clients to administer various social welfare programs—such as Social Security, Temporary Assistance to Needy Families, and Supplemental Security Income—are civil servants. Macro civil service positions include such terms as "coordinator," "supervisor," or "analyst" in the title, and incorporate macro tasks and responsibilities such as management, administration, outreach, and budget or policy analysis.

Civil service positions are less prone to turnover than political appointments, often coming with some degree of job security. They typically show consistency around policy objectives (Krause et al. 2016), providing opportunities for steady, incremental progress when civil servants have policy expertise, objectively quantifiable knowledge, skills, and abilities, and long-term relationships with internal stakeholders across agencies. In a best-case situation, civil service positions increase agency morale and promote institutional memory. However, civil service positions—and bureaucracy in general—are often the source of much derision from political candidates or other political commentators, and even the occasional satirical book (see one example in the Resource section). Critiques of civil service include isolation from outside policy information and expertise, an institutional lack of responsiveness to changing environments, and an inability to remove individuals who are not performing at needed levels. These factors pose a risk of having government systems that enforce dysfunctional agency norms or foster inertia.

BUILD YOUR KNOWLEDGE: Government Employees

USAFacts, an independent organization created in 2017, is a nonpartisan, private organization. It has developed an extensive website collecting and organizing government data about the US society and its governments: http://usafacts.org. USAFacts presents year-by-year data about the distribution of employees across levels of government in the USA. Go to https://usafacts.org/government-finances/ and choose the tab for "Employment." Do these data match your own perceptions of who is employed by governments in the USA and what these employees do? What, if anything, do you find surprising in these data?

Political Appointments and Social Work

Political appointees are appointed to government positions through "at-will" systems that allow individuals to be hired and fired without going through the bureaucratic process. Political appointments cover a wide range of public-sector jobs, including more than 8000 federal jobs and many more at the state and local level. In addition to these full-time employee positions, political appointees may serve on boards, commissions, or advisory committees.

While some full-time positions are directly in elected officials' offices, political appointments are found in agencies throughout government. In fact, an early postgraduate position held by one of the book's authors was an appointed position as "Policy Advisor and Special Assistant for Community Relations," reporting to another political appointee within the office of the Virginia Secretary of Education. Some political appointee positions, like cabinet-level secretaries and deputies at the federal level, are subject to review by the legislative branch; many others are not.

The most recent list of federal political appointments can be found in the publication *United States Government Policy and Supporting Positions*, commonly referred to as the "Plum Book" (United States Senate 2016), published every 4 years, following the presidential election. Each state has its own system for publicizing these positions. The state of California lists all state-wide appointed positions on its website, including over 450 full-time and part-time jobs and unpaid volunteer opportunities (State of California 2017). In 2017, California's list included many positions that might be of interest to social workers. These include the state Director of Developmental Services, the Director of Social Services, and membership on the advisory committee of the No Place Like Home Program, which provides permanent supportive housing for Californians at the junction of critical mental health issues and homelessness.

Advocacy and trade organizations have sought to create "talent banks" of qualified individuals who are available to fill these positions, with the goal of increasing the diversity and range of perspectives of those considered. Talent banks exist on the federal, state, and local levels. An early talent bank used by the Nixon administration was created by the National Federation of Business and Professional Women's

Clubs (Encyclopedia of Women in American Politics 1999; Friends of the Iowa Commission on the Status of Women 2015). More recently, talent banks have been developed by the Gay and Lesbian Victory Institute's Presidential Appointment Initiative (Victory Institute 2017), Black Women's Roundtable (NCBCP 2017), and the National Hispanic Leadership Agenda's Latino Appointments Program (NHLA 2017).

In contrast to civil service positions, political appointments are designed to provide "responsive competence" (Krause et al. 2016). This is achieved by hiring individuals who reflect the ideas of the politicians who appoint them, and in theory, also the ideas of the voters who elected those politicians. Political appointments can counteract the inertia of a bureaucratic system, ensure that constituencies are represented, and bring in new ideas, ways of action, and risk-taking that may be difficult to find in civil service systems. Disadvantages to political appointee positions include lack of longevity, as political appointees may have their terms cut short by political changes or moves to other agencies, and political appointees' need for responding to political environments. There is often a perception that political appointee positions are forms of patronage, nepotism, or even corruption (Mannino 1989). Tensions can arise between political appointees and civil servants when perceived political imperatives conflict with long-standing agency goals and work. News coverage in the early months of President Trump's administration, identified heightened tensions, as new political appointees explicitly sought to undo some of the work that civil servants had long been engaged in (Davenport 2017).

Working Directly for Elected Officials

One subset of political appointees are those that work directly for elected officials. This can take place in the executive branch, in the offices of a president, vice-president, governor, lieutenant governor, or mayor. It also can take place in legislative offices at the local, state, or federal level. These positions are contingent not only on the will of the elected official, but also on whether the elected official continues to be reelected.

These jobs may take a different form than other political appointee positions, because staffers are in direct contact with the elected official on a very regular (often daily) basis. These appointees tend to have a dual responsibility—to look out for the elected official's constituency, but also to protect the best interests of the elected official. Staff for an elected official may be asked to represent the elected official to the community. This often involves speaking at community meetings on behalf of a City Council member, answering constituents' letters and phone calls, meeting with constituents, advocates, and lobbyists in the district office, and speaking to the media on behalf of a representative. Staffers are expected to keep up with issues and dynamics within the district the official represents and to prepare reports, speeches, drafts of legislation, etc. on a wide range of issues for their elected officials. Staff conduct much of the behind-the-scenes policy work within an elected official's office.

We outline some of the common positions you may find in offices of elected officials. Not all of these positions will be present in an office, depending on the office's size and its level of government. Some legislative offices in part-time legislatures have as few as one or two full-time staffers who fill many roles at once. U.S. Senators may have dozens of full-time staffers. Any of these positions have been held by social workers across the nation.

Common Roles in the Office of an Elected Official
• Chief of staff
• Policy or legislative director
• District or state director (for legislative officials where the capitol is far from the district)
• Scheduler
• Communications director/press secretary
• Office manager/administrative director
• Research director
• Legislative aide/assistant
• Legislative correspondent
• Social media manager
• Staff assistant
• Constituent services staffer/caseworker
• Outreach staffer
• Committee clerk
• Intern

Note: In smaller offices, one person may wear many hats

Section 6: Engaging with Electoral Campaigns (Domain 4)

Strategies:

- Working on campaigns as volunteers or paid staff
- Seeking passage or defeat of ballot initiatives or referenda
- Educating voters about policy issues that are part of candidate or issue campaigns
- Influencing which candidates run for elected office

Electoral campaigns focus on convincing voters to cast their ballot for or against a candidate or issue on a ballot. These can include partisan candidate races, nonpartisan candidate races, and issue campaigns, such as initiatives and referenda (Shaw 2014). Political social workers influence who runs for office and who is ultimately elected. Working with electoral campaigns can be exhilarating, exhausting, empowering, and demoralizing, often all within the same day. Campaigns are fast-moving and can take up much more of your time than planned. Engaging with campaigns offer a great opportunity to get to know a candidate, a political context, and a community, while also impacting the direction of, and leadership for, policy development in your community. Working, interning, or volunteering on a campaign can also offer excellent openings for future jobs, regardless of whether the candidate you are working for wins.

Candidate Emergence

While some individuals just decide one day to run for office, and have a clear path to do so, in many cases, candidates emerge through a process of recruitment and selection. Prospective candidates, even ones with an interest in running for office, often need to be recruited to consider a specific run. Once candidates declare an interest in running for office, training opportunities can help them become effective candidates. Organizational endorsements play a role in impacting a candidate's chance for success. At each of these points, recruitment, training, and endorsement, social workers can influence the process of candidate emergence.

Recruitment involves asking people to consider running for specific elective offices, helping them to consider potential support for their candidacies should they choose to run, and connecting them with resources to make an informed decision about their potential candidacy. Any individual can participate in candidate recruitment. Recruiting specific candidates can be a mechanism for you or the organizations with which you are affiliated to further policy issues of interest to you (Western Organization of Resource Councils 2011). In recruiting candidates, you are seeking candidates willing to strongly support your policy priorities. Other important considerations include whether the potential candidate is eligible (or able to become eligible) to run in the district on which you are focused, whether the candidate is active in the community, has a strong, positive social network, and would be willing to prioritize the race (Western Organization of Resource Councils 2011).

Research finds that potential female candidates are less likely to see themselves as qualified for office and are less likely to have been encouraged to run for office at any level of government (Lawless and Fox 2012). Given the preponderance of female social workers, we encourage you to keep these barriers in mind as you move forward in your social work career. When you encounter social work friends and colleagues who you think might make strong candidates, remember your own capacity to recruit, reach out to them and encourage them to seriously consider a run.

Candidate training involves preparing candidates with the skills necessary to run effectively. A range of national organizations train potential candidates. These include, but are not limited to, the following organizations (see links in Resources); many of whom also engage in candidate recruitment:

- *EMILY's List*: trains pro-choice women
- *Emerge America*: offers a 7-month training for Democratic women in various states
- *The Gay and Lesbian Victory Institute*: trains LGBT candidates
- *Higher Heights*: encourages local salons and other programming for Black women to explore their potential for political leadership

- *IGNITE*: teaches high school and college-aged girls and women to see their political power and consider future runs for office
- *Maggie's List*: trains conservative women for Congressional runs
- *The New American Leaders Project*: trains first and second generation immigrants to run for office and staff electoral campaigns
- *Veterans Campaign*: trains veterans and other members of the military community to run for office
- *Wellstone Action*: trains progressive candidates, organizers, and campaign staff

Social workers participate in these candidate trainings, but also design and offer trainings. Within social work, the Nancy A. Humphreys Institute for Political Social Work plays a leading role in preparing prospective social work candidates in advance of their runs through its Campaign School.

Finally, to influence candidate selection, social workers support potential candidates through endorsements, donations, volunteerism, and other work on behalf of their candidacies. **Endorsement** involves giving public support to a specific candidate. Political action committees like NASW PACE endorse and donate to candidates. In Houston, Texas, for example, state and local candidates regularly make the rounds of local organizations—the Houston GLBT Political Caucus, local unions, local political party groups, the Houston Area Realtors, the Northeast Ministerial Alliance, the Filipino American Caucus for Empowerment, etc.—seeking their endorsement and often, as a result, additional donations, volunteers, and word-of-mouth attention. Social workers screen candidates for such organizations; for example, social workers serve as members and former officers of Houston's GLBT Political Caucus.

Social Workers in Electoral Campaigns

Roles for social workers in electoral campaigns vary widely depending on the level of the campaign and its funding. Every candidate and issue campaign has a paid or unpaid campaign manager, who attends to tasks in the areas of finance, scheduling, fieldwork, research, communications, and/or manages staff or volunteers in each of those areas. Typically, a campaign manager engages in a combination of administrative tasks, management tasks, communication, and fundraising, and also often serves as a source of emotional support for the candidate.

Campaign staff positions can range in level from entry to senior, are often temporary, and may be paid or unpaid. Many Congressional campaigns may have one permanent staff member; in other campaigns, a staffer may be hired for just a few months or for the year preceding the election. Races at the state level are likely to have few paid staffers, and local races may be run solely by volunteers, especially in smaller towns and cities. Many who work full-time in electoral politics work as consultants for multiple campaigns at once. Working on a campaign, either in a paid or unpaid capacity, is a good way for social workers to break into political social work. In fact, the authors of this book have commonly seen students graduate their social work programs in May and start working as staff on state or local campaigns between May and November. This enables new graduates to build on-the-job skills and networks as they seek to secure a full-time, paid position.

Common campaign roles are listed in this section. While some of these roles may seem new to you, all of these positions depend on core social work skills, including verbal and written communication skills, establishing rapport, and active listening. As Haynes and Mickelson (2010) point out, "social workers are trained to meet people, listen to their problems, and help them find solutions. They know how to manage hostility, how to reach out to shy and quiet people, and how to deal with groups as well as individuals" (p. 169).

Common Roles in a Campaign

- Campaign manager
- Treasurer
- Field organizer
- Volunteer coordinator
- Scheduler
- Finance director
- Press secretary/communications director/spokesperson
- Speechwriter
- Field director
- Field organizer/regional field organizer/deputy field director
- Paid canvass director
- Political director/organizer
- Technology director/social media manager
- Research director
- Legal counsel

Note: These may be paid or volunteer; in smaller campaigns, one person may wear many hats

---

POLITICAL SOCIAL WORKER PROFILE: Kara Hahn, MSW
Majority Leader, Suffolk County Legislature, New York (Fig. 2.1).

Fig. 2.1 Kara Hahn, MSW

(continued)

When Kara Hahn chose to study social work at the University of Pennsylvania in 1995, running for elected office was the furthest thing from her mind. She wanted to serve people in the most effective way possible through social work's mission to improve outcomes and quality of life for vulnerable populations. After working in the nonprofit and corporate sectors, Kara joined the staff of the presiding officer of the Suffolk County (Long Island, New York) legislature; where she recognized the opportunity to harness public office to effect broad-scale change on behalf of the county's 1.4 million constituents, larger than 11 US states. In 2011, she was elected to represent the fifth district of Suffolk County. As an elected official, Kara's social work education and experience form the foundation of her policy perspective. During her 5 years in the Legislature, Kara's goal has been to make government more open and responsive, passing legislation to strengthen the County's central mission of protecting health and safety. In 2015, her colleagues elected her as Majority Leader, a leadership role with County-wide reach and influence.

Kara's social work background and understanding of systems and their impacts on individuals have shaped the significant legislation she has passed during her 5 years in office. Her priorities include addressing substance use disorders, supplying opioid antidotes to first responders training to lay persons to use the antidote, and follow-up treatment for addicts. She has also worked on issues around gun safety, domestic violence, and protection of children. Environmentally, she has focused on issues such as groundwater contamination, the sale of products containing microbeads that endanger ecosystems, preservation of open space and agricultural land, and improvement of parks.

"Much of the country is focused on what happens in Washington D.C.," Kara says. "Of course, that's important, yet, so much can be done at the local level to strengthen a community, protect the most vulnerable among us and help improve the quality of our lives. It's my privilege to serve the community where I was born and raised and am raising my own family."

Section 7: Seeking and Holding Elected Office (Domain 5)

Strategies:

- Running for elected office
- Serving in elected office

The fifth domain of political social work involves seeking or serving in elected office yourself. There are more than 500,000 elected officials in the USA (Nir 2015). Elected officials historically have been most likely to come from the fields of politics, law, and business, but the 115th Congress includes nine social workers. Social workers have served in Congress on and off since 1916 (Smith 2002), and research has identified close to 500 social workers that have served in state and local elected offices (Lane and Humphreys 2011). While this is a good start, the approximately 650,000 people in the USA with social work degrees (NASW n.d.) suggests that there is much room for social workers' presence in elected office to grow. We encourage all social workers to consider practice in this domain. Seeking elected office relies heavily on social work's professional competencies (Scott and Scott 2011). As former campaign manager and mayor of an Oregon city Catherine Shaw (2014) says of running for local office, "When it's all over, win or lose, you will be a different person, with a different outlook on our political process and a new respect for those who run and serve" (p. xi).

Running for elected office can be a full-time commitment at the federal, state, or even, in some large cities, at the local level. By some accounts, Congressional candidates are expected to spend 30 hours per week in fundraising calls alone (Master 2016). These fundraising obligations continue once in office, as long as the elected official plans to run for reelection. Former Senate Majority Leader Tom Daschle says that in the 2 years leading up to reelection, U.S. Senators spend as much as 2/3 of their time raising money (Goldmacher 2014).

Holding elected office at the federal level is generally a full-time commitment. However, time commitments—and the corresponding compensation—for state legislative offices vary substantially across states. Ten states have **full-time legislatures**; this includes states such as New York and Massachusetts that are in session all but 1 week each year. These legislators estimate that they spend 80% or more of their time in legislative and committee work, constituent services, running for office, and other responsibilities, with an average pay around $81,000 (State Scape 2017). Roughly half of the states have what is referred to as a **hybrid legislature**. California is an example of such a state, meeting every year from December through September. In hybrid states, legislators estimate that their position requires roughly 70% of the time of an equivalent full-time job, with average compensation around $43,000.

The final 16 states have **part-time legislatures**, with a lot of variation in how they are structured. Nevada meets every other year (in odd-numbered years) for 4 months, while Texas meets every other year for 5 months. Utah meets every year for 6 weeks, while Florida meets every year for 2 months. On average, these positions require about half of the time of a typical full-time job, according to legislators, with compensation at around $19,000 per year on average (State Scape 2017).

Elected officials in the more than 14,000 municipal bodies across the USA (O'Connor et al. 2016) may be volunteer, part-time, or full-time, ranging from city council members in Del Mar, Colorado, making $300 per year to full-time city council members of Los Angeles, making $178,789 per year in 2011 (Philadelphia Research Initiative 2011; Tierney 2016). County commissioners in Suffolk County, New York, are mostly full-time (Suffolk County Legislature n.d.) and make close to $100,000 (Brand 2014). The trend seems to be toward increases in local officials' pay. San Antonio, Texas, raised city council salaries from $1500 per year to $45,722 per year (Ballotpedia 2005), and in Nassau County, New York, county commissioner salaries increased from $40,000 to $70,000 (LaRocco 2015). Leaders of towns and cities (variously referred to as mayors, town council chairs, selectmen, or municipal executives) can make between 0 to $175,000 annually (Dunn n.d.).

BUILD YOUR KNOWLEDGE: Your Elected Officials

What government bodies and people represent you? Make a list of the legislative bodies that represent you (may include federal, state, county, and city levels). Include a list of at least five of your elected officials, their positions, and their salaries. What do they do professionally (if anything) other than holding their legislative seat? These resources may get you started:

- https://www.usa.gov/elected-officials (or go to https://www.usa.gov/ and under the "Government Agencies and Elected Officials" tab click the "Contact Elected Officials" link)
- http://www.npr.org/2017/01/09/508237086/low-pay-in-state-legislatures-means-some-cant-afford-the-job

Section 8: Moving Forward

Throughout this book, we discuss different ways political social workers practice in each of the five domains. You may already have an idea of how you would like to utilize your social work skills in the political arena, or you may still be thinking about what this might look like for you. As you read this book, we encourage you to think about the relevance not just of the political skills we outline in this book, but also of the broader set of social work skills you are developing. We particularly encourage those of you with micro skills and experience to think about the many ways that these can be an asset for you in the political arena, helping to amplify the voices of your clients, communities, and fellow social workers in the political arena.

Review of Key Terms and Concepts

Advocacy campaign: targeting elected officials or other people with power and asking them to support or oppose an issue.

Candidate training: preparing candidates with the skills necessary to run effectively.

Civil service position: a government position which requires new hires to be vetted through merit-based procedures designed to be separate from the political system.

Direct practice: includes practice with individuals, families, and groups, comprising both micro and mezzo levels of practice. Social workers in direct practice may use their political knowledge to assist individual clients or groups of clients in their own empowerment.

Electoral campaign: a campaign which works to convince voters to cast their ballot for or against a particular candidate or proposal.

Endorsement: giving public support to a specific candidate.

Full-time legislature: state legislatures which are estimated to take up 80% or more of the work time of members.

Government: any organized body of individuals that has discrete political management, operating separately from any other government structure, such as town districts, townships, municipalities, counties, states, and countries.

Hybrid legislature: state legislature which requires roughly 70% of the work time of a full-time job.

Macro practice: employment positions that are aimed at promoting social justice and change through their work of empowering individuals and groups within communities and organizations. Macro functions may include securing funding, developing programs, management and administration, community organizing, political advocacy, and research.

Part-time legislature: state legislatures which require roughly 50% of the work time of a full-time job.

Political appointees: those holding appointment in a wide range of "at-will" systems that allow individuals to be hired and fired without going through the bureaucratic process.

Poll watcher: person who monitors polling sites to observe the voting process at a local voting precinct.

Recruitment: asking people to consider running for specific elective offices, helping them to consider the potential support for their candidacies should they choose to run, and connecting them with resources to make an informed decision about their potential candidacy.

Resources

App

The Plum Book app: m.gpo.gov/plumbook

Book

Satirical book about civil service and accompanying website:
Geraghty, J. (2017). The Weed Agency: A comic tale of federal bureaucracy without limits. Retrieved from http://theweedagency.com.

Election Group Resources

Emily's List: https://www.emilyslist.org
Emerge America: http://www.emergeamerica.org/training
Higher Heights for America: http://www.higherheightsforamerica.org/
Ignite National: http://www.ignitenational.org
Maggie's List: http://maggieslist.org
New American Leaders: http://newamericanleaders.org

University of Connecticut School of Social Work Campaign School for Social Workers: http:// ssw.uconn.edu/our-community/centers-institutes-projects/nancy-a-humphreys-institute-for-political-social-work/annual-campaign-school/ or go to http://politicalinstitute.uconn.edu and click "Campaign School."

Veterans Campaign: http://www.veteranscampaign.org/workshops/

Victory Institute: https://victoryinstitute.org/trainings/candidate-campaign-trainings/ or go to https://victoryinstitute.org and in the menu under the "Trainings" tab click "Candidate & Campaign Trainings."

Wellstone Action: http://www.wellstone.org/focus-areas/camp-wellstone or go to http://www. wellstone.org and in the menu under the "Impact" tab click on "Camp Wellstone."

Talent Banks

The Connecticut General Assembly: https://www.cga.ct.gov/lprac/pages/talent.html or go to https://www.cga.ct.gov/ceo/, scroll down to the "Reference Websites" section and click on the "Latino and Puerto Rican Affairs Commission." In the menu on the left side of the Latino and Puerto Rican Affairs Commission landing page click "Talent Bank."

Friends of Iowa Commission on the Status of Women: http://friendsoficsw.org/TalentBank/ ViewtheTalentBank.aspx or go to http://friendsoficsw.org and in the menu under the "Talent Bank" tab, click "View the Talent Bank."

The National Hispanic Leadership Agenda: https://nationalhispanicleadership.org/steps-to-apply or go to https://nationalhispanicleadership.org and in the menu under "Programs" click "NHLA Latino Appointments Program," then scroll down to the Program Menu on the right of the page and click "Steps to Apply."

The Victory Institute: https://victoryinstitute.org/programs/presidential-appointments-initiative/ presidential-appointment-initiative-faq/ or go to https://victoryinstitute.org and in the menu under programs click "Presidential Appointments Initiative" and then scroll down to click the green "Frequently Asked Questions" button.

Examples of Municipal Talent Banks

The Apache Junction City Website: https://www.ajcity.net/Search/Results?searchPhrase= talent%20bank or go to https://www.ajcity.net and in the search bar type "Talent Bank." Click search and a list of resources will be displayed in the results.

The Greenville, North Carolina Government Website: http://www.greenvillenc.gov/government/ city-council/boards-and-commissions or go to http://www.greenvillenc.gov and in the menu under "Government" select "City Council."

City of Muskegon Government Website: http://www.muskegon-mi.gov/departments/city-clerk/serving-on-a-board/ or go to http://www.muskegon-mi.gov and in the menu under "Departments" click "City Clerk." On the landing page you arrive at scroll down to click the option "Serving on a Board, Commission or Committee."

References

Ballotpedia (2005, May). City of San Antonio Council and Mayor Salaries, Amendment 2. Retrieved April 20, 2017, from https://ballotpedia.org/City_of_San_ Antonio_Council_and_Mayor_Salaries,_Amendment_2_(May_2015).

Brand, R. (2014, March 8). Suffolk County lawmakers on the verge of $100G salary. *Newsday*.

Brandeisky, K., Chen, H., & Tigas, M. (2014, November 4). Everything that's happened since Supreme Court ruled on Voting Rights Act. *ProPublica*.

Melanie L. Campbell. (2017). The National Coalition on Black Civic Participation. Bios. Retrieved from http://www.ncbcp.org/who/bios/mcampbell/.

Davenport, C. (2017, February 16). E.P.A. workers try to block Pruitt in show of defiance. *The New York Times*.

Dunn, K. P. (n.d.). The salary of a mayor. *Chron.com*.

Edwards, H. R., & Hoefer, R. (2010). Are social work advocacy groups using Web 2.0 effectively? *Journal of Policy Practice, 9*, 220–239.

Encyclopedia of women in American politics. (1999). In J. D. Schultz & L. A. Van Assendelft (Eds.), *The American political landscape series*. Phoenix, AZ: The Oryx Press.

Friends of the Iowa Commission on the Status of Women (2015). Talent Bank Database. Retrieved from http://friendsoficsw.org/TalentBank/ViewtheTalentBank.aspx.

Shane Goldmacher. (2014). Former Senate leader says Senators spent two-thirds of time asking for money. *National Journal*.

Guo, C., & Saxton, G. D. (2012). Tweeting social change: How social media are changing non-profit advocacy. *Nonprofit and Voluntary Sector Quarterly*.

Haynes, K. S., & Mickelson, J. S. (2010). *Affecting change: Social workers in the political arena,* Boston, MA: Allyn & Bacon.

Hogue, C. (2013). Government organization summary report: 2012 (U.S. Department of Commerce: Economics and Statistics Administration, Trans.). Census of Governments.

Jessie, L., & Tarleton, M. (2014). 2012 Census of Governments: Employment summary report (U.S. Department of Education: National Center for Education Statistics, Trans.). Census of Governments.

Koseff, A. (2017, March 13). "Sanctuary state" bill amended to require reporting immigrants with violent felonies. *The Sacramento Bee*.

Krause, G. A., Lewis, D. E., & Douglas, J. W. (2016). Political appointments, civil service systems, and bureaucratic competence: Organizational balancing and executive branch revenue forecasts in the American states. *American Journal of Political Science, 50*(3), 770–787.

Lane, S. R., & Humphreys, N. A. (2011). Social workers in politics: A national survey of social work candidates and elected officials. *Journal of Policy Practice, 10*, 225–244.

LaRocco, P. (2015, December 21). Nassau legislators increase own pay from $39,500 to $75,000. *Newsday*.

Lawless, J. L., & Fox, R. L. (2012). *Men rule: The continued under-representation of women in U.S. Politics*. Washington, DC: Women & Politics Institute, American University School of Public Affairs.

M. Mannino. (1989, January 20. Mayor's talent bank doesn't represent political corruption; hard work and exams. *New York Times*.

Marloff, S. (2017, March 8). Bathroom bill flushed to Senate. *The Austin Chronicle*.

Master, C. (2016). *"60 Minutes": Fundraising demands turning lawmakers into telemarketers.* Retrieved from http://thehill.com/blogs/blog-briefing-room/news/277462-60-minutes-fundraising-demands-turning-lawmakers-into.

McDonald, M. (2017). 2016 November general election turnout rates. Retrieved from http://www.electproject.org/2016g.

National Association of Social Workers. (2014). *NASW statement on Senate consideration of Voting Rights Amendment Act*. Washington, DC: National Association of Social Workers.

National Association of Social Workers. (2017). *Code of Ethics of the National Association of Social Workers*. Washington, DC: National Association of Social Workers.

National Association of Social Workers. (n.d.). Social work profession. Retrieved from https://www.socialworkers.org/pressroom/features/general/profession.asp.

National Conference of State Legislatures. (2016). Felon voting rights. Retrieved from http://www.ncsl.org/research/elections-and-campaigns/felon-voting-rights.aspx.

National Hispanic Leadership Agenda. (2017). Steps to aply for NHLA's Appointments Program. Retrieved from https://nationalhispanicleadership.org/steps-to-apply.

Nir, D. (2015). *Just how many elected officials are there in the United States? The answer is mind-blowing.* Retrieved from http://www.dailykos.com/story/2015/3/29/137225/-Just-how-many-elected-officials-are-there-in-the-United-States-The-answer-is-mind-blowing.

O'Connor, R., Swift, N., & White, J. (2016). US local government and mayors of largest cities. Retrieved from http://www.citymayors.com/mayors/us-mayors.html.

Pace, P. (2013). NASW, social work students rally for Voting Rights Act outside the Supreme Court. *Social Work Blog* (Vol. 2017). Washington, DC: National Association of Social Workers.

Peterson's Staff. (2013). Career planning: Qualifications and requirements for civil service jobs. Retrieved from https://www.petersons.com/college-search/career-planning-service-civil. aspx - /sweeps-modal.

Philadelphia Research Initiative. (2011). City councils in Philadelphia and other major cities. The PEW Charitable Trusts.

Pritzker, S., & Applewhite, S. (2015). Going 'macro': Exploring the careers of macro practitioners. *Social Work, 60*(3), 191–199.

Saez X. (2017, February 23). Letter: Waltham schools need a more diverse staff. *Wicked Local Waltham.*

Scott, D., & Scott, R. (2011). Social worker as political candidate: Seeking a seat at the table. *Arete, 32*(2), 87–104.

Shaw, C. (2014). *The campaign manager: Running and winning local elections.* Boulder, CO: Westview Press.

Smith, N. (2002). *Jeannette Rankin, America's conscience.* Helena, MT: Montana Historical Society Press.

State of California. (2017). Appointments. Retrieved from https://www.gov.ca.gov/m_appointments.php.

State Scape. (2017). Session schedules. Retrieved from http://www.statescape.com/resources/legislative/session-schedules.aspx.

Suffolk County Legislature. (n.d.). Suffolk County Legislature's home on the web. Retrieved from http://legis.suffolkcountyny.gov.

The Sentencing Project. (2017). The Sentencing Project staff and board. Retrieved from http://www.sentencingproject.org/staff/.

Tierney, G. (2016, December 8). City council punts on pay raise. *Coronado Times.*

U.S. Election Assistance Commission. (2017). Help America Vote Act. Retrieved from https://www.eac.gov/about/help-america-vote-act/.

United States Senate. (2016). United States government policy and supporting positions (Plum book). Committee on Homeland Security and Governmental Affairs. Washington, DC: United States Government.

Victory Institute. (2017). Presidential appointment initiative FAQ. Retrieved from https://victoryinstitute.org/programs/presidential-appointments-initiative/presidential-appointment-initiative-faq/.

S Vladeck. (2016, October 29). What are poll watchers and what are they allowed to do? *CNN Politics.*

Walsh, J. (2016). Direct social work practice. In *Encyclopedia of social work.* Washington, DC: NASW Press and Oxford University Press.

Western Organization of Resource Councils. (2011). *How to recruit candidates to run for office.* Retrieved from http://www.worc.org/media/Recruit_Candidates_to_Run_for_Office.pdf.

"Promoting the General Welfare of Society": The Political Activity of Social Workers and Human Service Organizations

3

© Springer International Publishing AG 2018
S.R. Lane, S. Pritzker, *Political Social Work*,
https://doi.org/10.1007/978-3-319-68588-5_3

Section 1: Overview

Social workers are politically active both as individuals and as part of larger groups and organizations. This chapter provides an overview of social workers' current and past political activity, as well as factors that encourage or limit social workers, our profession, and our employers from engaging in the political process. We consider relevant legal issues that guide organizations' political activities and learn about rules that may apply to individual field placements or employers. Relevant theories and models are used to create a picture of social workers' political involvement, both individually and collectively. Political knowledge, skills, interest, efficacy, and mobilization and their influences on social workers' political activity are discussed, as readers are asked to reflect on political activities in which they have participated and on their potential future political activity. Activities include a political knowledge quiz and a survey that allows readers to compare their political efficacy with other social workers and the American public.

Developing Social Work Competency
The Council on Social Work Education establishes educational standards for all social work programs in the USA. Content in this chapter supports building competency in the following areas that are considered core to the practice of social work:
COMPETENCY 1: Demonstrate Ethical and Professional Behavior
COMPETENCY 2: Engage Diversity and Difference in Practice
COMPETENCY 3: Advance Human Rights and Social, Economic, and Environmental Justice
COMPETENCY 4: Engage in Practice-Informed Research and Research-Informed Practice
COMPETENCY 5: Engage in Policy Practice

Domains of Political Social Work	
1. Engaging individuals and communities in political processes	◄
2. Influencing policy agendas and decision-making	◄
3. Holding professional and political positions	◄
4. Engaging with electoral campaigns	◄
5. Seeking and holding elected office	◄

Section 2: What Is Political Activity?

As social workers, the NASW (2017) Code of Ethics calls on us to engage in social and political action to influence policy and promote social justice (6.04). It also requires that we "facilitate informed participation by the public in shaping social policies and institutions" (NASW 2017, 6.02). These critical expectations to engage politically and to help others to do so require knowledge about the various ways in which social workers and the public influence policy. This section outlines key concepts essential for understanding how social workers and the broader public engage in social and political action.

Civic Engagement

Civic engagement is a term commonly used to refer to involvement in social or political actions that help further a common good. Civic engagement entails both participation in the public arena and an emphasis on action that seeks to positively impact others or public decision-making (McBride 2008). Civic engagement is collective in nature and reflects a sense of societal belonging. Through civic engagement, we act as part of a society, with a concern for mutual responsibility for each other and for the common good (Hylton 2015).

Essential to understanding civic engagement is that it incorporates participation in two spheres: social and political (McBride et al. 2006). Within the **social sphere** of civic engagement, people seek to help their communities through such activities as volunteering; donating financial, time, or in-kind resources to individuals, groups, or organizations, or engaging in community problem-solving. In the **political sphere**, people seek to contribute to their communities by influencing political decision-making.

Political Activity

Civic engagement in the political sphere is most commonly thought of in terms of **political activity** or **political participation**. The first image that often comes to mind when people think of political activity is *voting*. It is the most common political activity in the USA (Patterson 2013), and the one through which we most immediately see results. Voting, especially as relates to Presidential elections, is the focus of months (if not years) of nearly nonstop media coverage in the USA. It is a critical way in which adult citizens influence *who* is responsible for making policy decisions—and, therefore, the content of those policies.

Nonetheless, political activity in actuality encompasses a much broader range of ways through which people communicate their policy preferences in order to influence who makes policy decisions, how they make decisions, and the content of those decisions. Political activity is, at its essence, a form of intervention to influence society. As Meyer (2013) notes, it is "individual or collective action intended to influence public discourse, the structure and policies of government, and ultimately the distribution of rights and resources in a society" (p. 66). Actions to influence elections and public officials' decision-making often take place on a continuum from cooperation to confrontation. Political activity can influence *existing* policy-makers through advocacy, lobbying, campaigning, or demonstrations. It also can try to *change* policy-makers or even the system through altering who holds positions of power or the rules of the system. Illustrating this broad range of political activity, research increasingly finds a shift in how people in the USA, particularly young people, seek to influence political decision-making in the early twenty-first century. Growing globalization and social media innovations seem to play a role, resulting in individuals seeking more expressive and potentially more meaningful avenues to political participation (Bennett et al. 2009; Zukin et al. 2006; Dalton 2008; Eagan et al. 2015).

Political Activity and Vulnerable Populations

Applying a broader lens to thinking about political activity is particularly critical for social workers who work with vulnerable populations. In the USA, groups such as children and youth, undocumented immigrants, immigrants who are not yet naturalized, and individuals with a prior felony conviction often lack the right to vote, but still possess an inherent human right to voice regarding policies that affect them. For example, the United Nations Convention on the Rights of the Child (CRC) speaks to the human rights that children, despite being too young to vote, have to express views regarding decision-making affecting their lives (United Nations General Assembly 1989). The CRC, ratified by 196 United Nations member countries (all except the USA), explicitly describes a child's right to expression, both as an individual and in assembly with others.

United National Convention on the Rights of the Child
Article 12.1: "States Parties shall assure to the child who is capable of forming his or her own views the right to express those views freely in all matters affecting the child, the views of the child being given due weight in accordance with the age and maturity of the child."
Article 13.1: "The child shall have the right to freedom of expression; this right shall include freedom to seek, receive and impart information and ideas of all kinds, regardless of frontiers, either orally, in writing or in print, in the form of art, or through any other media of the child's choice."
Article 15.1: "States Parties recognize the rights of the child to freedom of association and to freedom of peaceful assembly."

Individuals and groups who find themselves marginalized from political processes or policy-making may opt instead to seek out political strategies that incorporate activism and/or confrontation (Piven and Cloward 1977; Alinksy 1971). Such strategies offer people a way to essentially force their voices to be heard by policy-makers. Protests, rallies, boycotts, sit-ins, and demonstrations are some examples of tactics that are used. In the early twenty-first century, we see many examples of the power of activist tactics in impacting policy outcomes. Protests as part of the Black Lives Matter movement have led to policy changes such as requiring police to wear body cameras (Dunham and Peterson 2017). Undocumented immigrant youth led protests that resulted in former President Barack Obama's issuance of the Deferred Action for Childhood Arrivals (DACA) program. This program offered a legal way for some undocumented youth who arrived in the USA as children to stay in the country (Huber et al. 2014). Native American tribes and allies in North Dakota held protests that led the Obama administration to temporarily halt construction on an oil pipeline traversing native lands (Sisk 2016). The Women's Marches across the globe immediately following the election of President Donald Trump are another example of large-scale activism designed to get the attention of policy-makers. At the time of this writing, it remains to be seen whether policy outcomes will emerge from this effort.

POLITICAL SOCIAL WORKER PROFILE: Katie Richards-Schuster, MSW, PhD
Assistant Professor, School of Social Work, University of Michigan (Fig. 3.1).

Fig. 3.1 Katie Richards-Schuster, MSW, PhD

My research and teaching focus on youth participation in community change, youth civic engagement, and fostering civic activism in undergraduate students. I've always been involved in political work—as a youth, I was active in political campaigns. I attended my first national rally in high school (in support of affordable housing) and have been active in both political work and policy work ever since.

I first became interested in social work as a vehicle to create participatory policy structures—helping people have a voice in the policies that impact their communities. As an MSW student, I worked in a community center organizing neighborhood residents to have a voice in policies around housing and health (vouchers and lead paint policies, in particular) and then organized teachers around education policies.

Over the last 15 years, I've engaged young people to be heard in policy and community change initiatives in their schools and communities. They research

(continued)

issues and develop policy recommendations for changing institutions that impact their lives, as well as speaking out to policy makers about their lives through town halls, forums, and other advocacy outlets.

In working alongside youth and community partners, I've been a part of young people's efforts to change education policies; diversify their schools and their curriculums; advocate for funding for youth programming at the local, regional, and state levels; create policy statements about youth rights for state officials; create healthier schools and community programs; challenge school-to-prison pipelines; and organize for youth voice in city and state governments.

For me, youth participation in policy and politics is central to social work. It is about voice, empowerment, and power—who better to be engaged in developing and advocating around policies about their lives than young people? My role as a social worker is to help build the capacity of young people to engage in the issues that they care about; to develop the skills and tools they need to create change; and to empower them to see their own expertise, leadership, and voice as an essential tool for change.

Political social work is about changing power—whose voices are heard, whose voices shape how we come to know about issues, and whose voices help shape solutions. As social workers, we are called to help challenge the status quo and to help open spaces and opportunities for new voices to be engaged and heard.

FURTHER REFLECTION: Measure Your Own Political Activity
The Center for Information & Research on Civic Learning & Engagement, a leading research center on civic engagement, has developed and administered a national civic engagement survey. This survey is available online at the following link: http://www.civicyouth.org/PopUps/Final_Civic_Inds_Quiz_ 2006.pdf or go to http://civicyouth.org/tools-for-practice/ and click on "A short paper quiz using the core indicators."

Complete this survey, and evaluate how your civic engagement stacks up against the national survey results listed in that document and the data provided in this chapter. How does it compare to what you would like your civic engagement to be?

Section 3: Social Workers and Political Activity

In this section, we explore how political activity is viewed within the social work profession and how individual social workers engage in political activity. As you read this section, we encourage you to think about your own activity relative to that of other social workers.

Should Social Workers Participate Politically?

The National Association of Social Workers, social work's primary professional association in the USA, calls for social workers to engage in social and political action in pursuit of social justice. As discussed in Chap. 1, since 1996, the Code has obligated social workers "to engage in social and political action" (NASW n.d.). In recent years, the NASW has been vocal about social workers' role in impacting political systems. For example, in late 2016, following the election of President Donald Trump, NASW Chief Executive Officer Angelo McClain called on social workers to "stand up" and to "organize, oppose, resist, and educate" in support of the profession's mission (NASW 2016, n.p.).

The profession's call for social workers to be politically active explicitly involves social workers across methods, from micro to macro. Yet, as we have discussed, some have expressed concerns throughout the profession's history about social workers becoming involved in political activity. Such concerns have focused on maintaining social workers' professional status, not wanting to appear partial to certain groups, the potential harm to clients, and the legality of engaging in political activity as a government or nonprofit employee (explored further in Section 4 of this chapter) (Fisher 1995; Rocha et al. 2010).

While such concerns exist, scholars such as Rose (1990) and Davis (2010) argue that political activity is a critical social work tool for empowering vulnerable populations. Working with individuals with psychiatric disabilities, Davis (2010) suggests that connecting clients with opportunities to vote is essential for expanding clients' community integration and empowerment. Writing in the opinion pages of the *New York Times*, social worker Richard Brouillette (2016) similarly suggests that acknowledging social injustice and political context in the therapy session potentially may have positive, empowering impacts. "By focusing on fairness and justice, a patient may have a chance to find what has so frequently been lost: an ability to care for and stand up for herself" (Brouillette 2016, n.p.).

On the micro end of the continuum, scholars like Swenson (1998) contend that the profession's core value of social justice requires clinical social work practitioners to actively strive to strengthen clients' power and to advocate for services that increase clients' well-being. However, recent research on clinical social workers' political activity finds that political participation varies widely (Ostrander 2016). Gender is an important variable in clinician's political activity: With a small sample, Ostrander found evidence that female clinicians report less confidence in the political arena compared to their male counterparts. While acknowledging that policies significantly impact their clients, communities, and themselves, the clinical social workers Ostrander (2016) studied were split as to whether they perceived political action in their social work practice as ethical. In a similar vein, while social work educators and field instructors are highly involved politically, a 2001 study found that one-third did not see a role for social work in political contexts (Mary 2001).

How Active Are Social Workers?

Social workers at all points along the micro/macro continuum, from clinicians to full-time policy specialists, have engaged in political activities throughout the profession's history. These activities reflect each of the five domains of political social work. Furthermore, social workers have voted in presidential elections at consistently higher rates than the US general public for decades (e.g., Wolk 1981; Ezell 1993; Ritter 2007; Rome and Hoechstetter 2010). All recent studies of social workers, whether surveying students, educators, field instructors, or NASW members, have consistently found that each group is more likely to vote in presidential elections than their non-social work peers (Pritzker and Burwell 2016; Swank 2012; Mary 2001; Felderhoff et al. 2015; Pritzker and Garza 2017). Social workers and social work students continue to vote at higher rates than the general public in **downballot** or **downticket** races, offices below the top race on the ballot; however social workers vote in elections for these offices at much lower rates than for president (e.g., Pritzker and Burwell 2016). (In a Presidential election year, downballot refers to everything below president. In other elections, downballot also could refer to the races on a ballot below a governor or mayor.)

Some studies of social workers have sought to examine the broader range of political activities. Domanski (1998) studied ten distinct prototypes of political activity. Almost all of the medical social workers she studied engaged in at least one of these activity forms. The most common prototypes among the social workers she studied were communicators, who regularly discuss political and policy issues; advocates, who work for change on behalf of agencies, clients, or communities; and voters. Least common were activists, who engage in policy demonstrations; witnesses, who participate and testify at hearings on policy issues; and campaigners, who work or volunteer on behalf of political candidates.

Domanski's (1998) findings suggest that social workers commonly vote and pay attention to political news, but participate far less in many of the other political activities described in this chapter. More recent research finds that social workers engage in political activities requiring minimal effort or commitment (Ritter 2007). However, they are much less likely to participate in political activity requiring sustained or intensive commitment (such as volunteering for a candidate, contributing to a candidate, attending events in support of a candidate, or joining advocacy-based community groups) or engaging directly with power and conflict (such as protests or rallies) (Rome and Hoechstetter 2010; Pritzker and Burwell 2016; Hylton 2015).

Social workers' political activity seems to rise and fall depending on the political environment. In the 1980s and early 1990s, two studies found that the majority of social workers were either active or very active politically (Wolk 1981; Ezell 1993). Studies in the early twenty-first century, however, found this level of activity among fewer than half of social workers (Ritter 2007; Rome and Hoechstetter 2010). It is important to note that within the social work profession, research has consistently found that African-Americans, macro practitioners, NASW members, and social workers with higher degrees participate more actively than other social workers (Rome and Hoechstetter 2010). Social workers who are agency directors also exhibit extensive political involvement (Pawlak and Flynn 1990).

A subset of social workers choose not just to influence politics from the outside, but to run for elected office themselves, as with social workers Jeanette Rankin, Barbara Mikulski, and Kara Hahn discussed in earlier chapters. Over the last half-century, the profession's presence in elected office appears to have increased.

Section 4: Social Workers' Political Activity in Organizations

Much of social workers' professional lives are spent as part of organizations. As Mosley (2013b) points out, "in practice, because most social workers are based in organizations, advocacy almost always happens in an organizational context" (p. 233). At the same time, organizations often limit social workers' efforts to influence policy. This is attributable in part to misconceptions about legal constraints on the political activities of social work employees and the organizations in which they work (Rocha et al. 2010). These constraints and their impact on the practice of political social work within organizations are outlined here and discussed in more depth in the context of political spending in Chap. 12. In some cases, these constraints may affect what social workers are permitted to do on their own time.

Most social workers are employed by or affiliated with organizations that fit into one of the three types: for profit, public, or nonprofit, each covered by different rules and regulations regarding their political activity. **Public organizations** or **government agencies** are part of local, state, or federal governments. **For profit organizations** are owned by a single owner or shareholders, who are allowed to collect profit from their activities. **Nonprofit organizations**, also frequently referred to as non-governmental organizations (NGOs), voluntary organizations, or community-based organizations (CBOs), are organizations that have received one of a number of types of **tax-exempt** classifications from the federal Internal Revenue Service (IRS). A tax-exempt classification allows nonprofits to avoid paying taxes on certain purchases, in return for abiding by rules regarding activities and revenue. Essentially, the more freedom an organization has from tax payments, the more restrictions it faces.

Definitions and Restrictions for Nonprofit Organizations

Advocacy is frequently confused with lobbying. Advocacy encompasses pleading for or against causes, as well as supporting or recommending positions. The National Council of Nonprofits (2000) recommends "think[ing] of 'advocacy' as a giant tool box containing various tools that can be used to influence public policy. One tool can be used with administrative agencies. Another tool can be used in the courts. And the 'lobbying' tool is used when attempting to influence legislation." **Lobbying** (the legal definitions are described below) is a subset of advocacy, but much of the work involved in advocacy is not lobbying. Advocacy includes educating members on issues or the political process, gathering information from individuals or communities about how policies are affecting them, and asking legislators for help with specific problems that clients are encountering. As the Board Advocacy Project and others say, "All lobbying is advocacy, but not all advocacy is lobbying (National Community Land Trust Network n.d.)!"

Federal Guidelines

As social workers and the organizations we work with consider their options for engaging in political advocacy, understanding how the federal government characterizes political activities is key. IRS regulations define lobbying much more narrowly than commonly perceived, such that only a small portion of agencies' policy efforts actually constitute lobbying (Rocha et al. 2010; Internal Revenue Service 2017). The IRS has identified and defined two specific types of lobbying: direct lobbying and grassroots lobbying. Only activities that meet these specific definitions are considered lobbying under federal tax law.

Direct lobbying is explicitly defined by the federal government as *communicating* with a *legislator* to express a view on a *specific piece of legislation*. These three italicized terms—in combination with each other—are critical in determining what constitutes direct lobbying. **Communication** in this context includes both verbal and nonverbal communication of any sort; the only exception to this definition is testimony that has been specifically invited by a legislative body. A **legislator** refers only to an elected member of a state or federal legislative body (e.g., Congress, a state's elected legislature), staff that work directly for these legislators, and high-level executive branch officials (i.e., presidential and gubernatorial officials, and leaders of executive branch agencies). Federal law conceives of direct lobbying in terms of **specific pieces of legislation**, referring to specific bills introduced in a legislature or under consideration by an executive.

To constitute direct lobbying, all three of the above criteria must be met. For example, if an agency communicates with a legislator about the need for change in a particular area of policy, but does not reference a specific piece of legislation, this is not considered direct lobbying. As a result, the definition of direct lobbying does not include nonpartisan analyses, responses to officials' requests for technical assistance, nor an agency's or employee's examination or discussion of broad policy issues (Internal Revenue Service 2017). Each of these activities is not considered direct lobbying and is allowable at any time in any agency—nonprofit or for profit.

Grassroots lobbying is explicitly defined as *communicating* with *the public* to express a view on a *specific piece of legislation,* with a *call to action.* The definitions of communication and a specific piece of legislation are the same as above. **The public** can include any individuals or groups involved in the communication or action. A **call to action** involves asking members of an organization or any other groups of the public to contact legislators on behalf of a specific piece of legislation. This typically involves providing legislators' names and contact information to the public. Here, all four of these criteria must be met to constitute lobbying.

A nonprofit's specific tax status will determine how much time it and its members can spend on direct or grassroots lobbying. While many nonprofit organizations are limited to spending under 5% of their annual expenditures (including staff time) on lobbying, other IRS nonprofit classifications allow unlimited lobbying expenditures. Some nonprofits with significant federal funding will also fall under the Hatch Act (see below).

State Guidelines

States may have additional restrictions on lobbying. These will differ from state to state. For example, Connecticut defines a lobbyist as any person who:

- Expends (or agrees to expend) or receives (or agrees to receive) $2000 or more in a calendar year
- With that $2000 or more, communicates directly or solicits others to communicate with any public official or their staff in the legislative or executive branch, or in a quasi-public agency
- Uses that communication in an effort to influence legislative or administrative action (State of Connecticut Office of State Ethics 2012)

Connecticut also differentiates between a client lobbyist (an organization that pays more than $2000 per year to influence legislation) and a communicator lobbyist (someone who receives payment and lobbies, communicates, or solicits others to communicate). Anyone who meets these definitions in Connecticut must register with the state and is subject to state ethics requirements (State of Connecticut Office of State Ethics n.d.).

Organizational Characteristics

Beyond IRS or state designations, other characteristics within the organizational context of nonprofits facilitate or constrain political activities. For example, as Mosley (2013b) notes, when state or local governments face budget crises, non-profit agencies may be more likely to be sought out by government agencies for expertise and assistance. However, nonprofits' increasing reliance on government funding can lead them to focus advocacy resources toward seeking greater funding for agency goals rather than on behalf of substantive policy changes (Mosley 2013b).

Organization leaders impact how their organization approaches policy influence. As a current or future leader, you may be in the position to shape how an organization and its employees approach advocacy and political activity. How leaders are prepared for their positions and how motivated they are to influence governmental policy shape how an agency approaches advocacy. Jennifer Mosley (2013a), a leading scholar in this area, has found that organizational leaders who received macro-oriented academic training (whether in social work or in another profession) are more likely than leaders trained in direct service to see advocacy as important. Therefore, they are more likely to infuse advocacy into their organizational cultures. In contrast, leaders who received direct service-oriented training tend to see advocacy as an organizational luxury that can be avoided. Agency leaders who bring an interest in influencing governmental policy to the position find ways to promote organizational involvement in policy activities, even when they face institutional barriers to doing so (Mosley 2013a).

Definitions and Restrictions for Public Agencies

Employees of governmental agencies—whether local, state, or federal—also have specific legal guidelines on their political activities. Federal employees are governed by the federal Hatch Political Activity Act of 1939 (Hatch Act) and the Anti-Lobbying Act, while state agency employees are governed by what are commonly known as "Little Hatch Acts" or "Baby Hatch Acts" within state laws.

Federal Government Employees

Under the Hatch Act (U.S. Office of Special Counsel n.d.b), most federal government employees (see exceptions below) are specifically prohibited from some political activities in both their professional and personal lives (Thompson 1994). The majority of federal employees, particularly those in civil service positions, are referred to as "less restricted" employees. This subset of employees are prohibited specifically from activities that are **partisan** in nature (activity in support for or in opposition to a political party or candidate associated with a political party). Specifically, they *cannot*:

- Be a candidate in a partisan election
- Use official authority to influence election results
- Directly solicit or receive monetary contributions for a partisan political candidate or coerce contributions from subordinates on behalf of a candidate
- Express partisan opinions or engage in partisan activity on behalf of or in opposition to a partisan candidate while in a professional capacity, e.g., while on duty, in a government vehicle, or while wearing an official uniform

Under the Hatch Act, these "less restricted" federal employees *can* still participate in many of the kinds of political activities we discuss in this book. They can be candidates in nonpartisan elections, express opinions about or campaign for candidates when off-duty, contribute funds to political organizations and candidates, and attend political rallies or fundraisers. They can vote, help with nonpartisan voter registration drives, and actively participate in campaigns around constitutional amendments, referenda, or local ordinances. They also can express personal opinions about current events or policy issues in the workplace.

A separate subset of federal employees, typically those who work for intelligence and law enforcement agencies, are considered "further restricted" and face additional restrictions (U.S. Office of Special Counsel n.d.b). Unlike "less restricted" employees, these "further restricted" employees cannot be actively involved in managing partisan campaigns or associated activities such as political rallies and cannot help with partisan voter registration drives.

Some federal government employees are not covered by the Hatch Act. This includes a category of federal employee referred to as "special government employees," as well as uniformed services members, employees holding office in the city government of Washington, DC, and unpaid interns. "Special government employees" include certain part-time and temporary employees, for whom the Hatch Act only applies while they are directly engaged in government work (U.S. Federal

Labor Relations Authority n.d.). Given the range in how the Hatch Act applies to different subsets of federal employees, make sure to check with your employer or potential employer to determine which specific rules apply to your position.

Federal government employees' engagement in lobbying activity is governed by the Anti-Lobbying Act. This law prohibits federal employees from engaging in certain lobbying activities in their *professional* capacities. Refer back to the federal definitions of lobbying presented above. Prohibited activities include:

- Substantial grassroots lobbying
- Direct appeals to the public to contact elected officials regarding legislation
- Administrative support to assist private organizations with lobbying activities
- Preparing policy-related communications that do not clearly disclose the government's role in developing the documents

Federal employees are permitted to communicate with the public and elected officials in support of administration positions on policy and nominations (NIH 2013). There are no legal restrictions on federal employees engaging in lobbying or advocacy in a *personal* capacity. As the U.S Office of Special Counsel (n.d.b) specifies, "employees are free to express their views and take action as individual citizens on such questions as referendum matters, changes in municipal ordinances, constitutional amendments, pending legislation or other matters of public interest, like issues involving highways, schools, housing, and taxes" (n.p.).

POLITICAL SOCIAL WORKER PROFILE: Torey Ian Powell, MSW
Partnership and Outreach Coordinator, Center for Faith-Based and Neighborhood Partnerships, US Department of Agriculture (Fig. 3.2).

Fig. 3.2 Torey Ian Powell, MSW

As a veteran, Torey began his professional journey intending to give back to the military community by becoming a clinical social worker. "During my

(continued)

deployment to Afghanistan, I saw so many of my friends struggling to return back to normal life," he says. After taking several macro-oriented courses as an MSW student, Torey quickly learned that the change that he wanted to make was only possible at the macro level. He pivoted to policy work through a legislative internship during his MSW program. Torey observes, "I felt I could help more people by working through the policy world, and after the legislative internship program, there was no turning back."

After graduation, Torey was selected for the prestigious federal Presidential Management Fellowship (PMF) program and was immediately chosen for a position in Anchorage, Alaska, with the US Forest Service. Here, Torey discovered a passion for the intersection of social and environmental justice. The PMF program focuses on leadership development and creating a "cadre" of government leaders. It requires fellows to rotate to various government offices that expose them to the wide range of government offices and programs that often go unnoticed. Torey found a 4-month-old posting for a rotation that seemed "too good to pass up." He explains, "I knew it was a longshot, but figured I'd give it a try. After a nice long conversation with my potential boss, I was informed that the position was no longer available but they'd be willing to give me a shot. The stars aligned, and through a 4 month old Facebook post, I ended up with a highly rewarding job." While Torey's interviewer didn't quite understand the social work aspect of his background, the office appreciated his viewpoints and his already rigorous experiences in policy work.

Torey is responsible for a wide range of activities from "coordinating inter-agency responses to a White House Executive Order around faith-based engagement" to engaging youth with environmental justice issues. Torey works extensively on policy development, analysis, community outreach, and community engagement, relying heavily on his social work background in all of this work. No matter the task, Torey works to ensure that "everything I am working on has an equitable lens attached to it," and that a diverse group of voices are represented at the table in every important discussion.

The hardest part of Torey's job is recognizing "you can't solve every injustice." He has learned to pick "which are the most important battles to fight," which fights to put the most energy into, and where to hold back. He says, "It's a fine balance between fighting to address injustice and knowing that trying to fight every injustice diminishes your ability to effect change."

Torey's experience finding this balance came from being in the minority in many different arenas in his career, including during his legislative internship. "If you are operating in the majority party, you can push [policy] through without any other support ... but if you are in the minority party or have the minority view in an organization, you are forced to focus more on collaboration" with those who do not hold the same view as you. Torey's best learning comes from putting "yourself in the room with someone who has the farthest viewpoint from your own as much as you can." If you can come to an understanding with this person, then it will be much easier to do so with people who share viewpoints closer to your own.

State and Local Government Employees

Some Hatch Act restrictions are not limited to employees who work directly within the federal government. Aspects of the Hatch Act also apply to certain state and local government employees in positions supported by federal funds. As with most federal government employees, these state and local government employees may not use their position to impact an election; however, unless such employees' positions are completely federally funded, they may run for partisan political office (U.S. Office of Special Counsel n.d.a). Some Hatch Act limitations also apply to employees of state, local, or nonprofit agencies associated with work funded at least in part by federal funds (U.S. Office of Special Counsel n.d.b). Employees of federally funded programs should inquire with their supervisors to determine to what extent, if any, the Hatch Act applies to their activities.

State-level policies regarding government employees' political activity are generally somewhat less restrictive than the federal Hatch Act (with some exceptions) (Rocha et al. 2010). These "Baby Hatch Acts" or "Little Hatch Acts" similarly limit employees' participation in *partisan* activities. In Texas, for example, state employees are prohibited from these partisan activities related to a state legislative, executive, or judicial or federal campaigns (Political Activities by Certain Public Entities and Individuals n.d.):

- Engaging in partisan activity while in a state-owned vehicle
- Allowing a state program to affect which partisan candidate is nominated or elected
- Coercing or restricting a political contribution
- Using state funds to influence passage or defeat of legislation

While state employees typically are forbidden to use state funds to influence legislation, they are generally permitted to use state funds to provide information about policy issues to the public or to respond to information requests from policy-makers. What employees of local governments can do as far as engaging in political activity varies across states (National Conference of State Legislators 2015).

> **BUILD YOUR KNOWLEDGE: State Employee Political Activity**
> Find the website of your state's Ethics Commission or comparable office. Look up the laws governing employees' political activity in your state. What political activities are restricted? What does this mean for the political activities in which state employees can legally participate?

Encouragement for Organizations to Engage: Motor Voter

Both human service nonprofit agencies and government agencies engage in political activity through nonpartisan voter registration. Social worker Richard Cloward, along with Francis Fox Piven (profiled in Chap. 8), led a national effort to expand voter registration through Human SERVE (Service Employees Registration and Voter Education). In the 1980s, this national coalition began advocating for state and federal policies to facilitate more widespread voter registration (Piven and Minnite 2013). Ultimately, this work contributed to Congress' enactment of the National Voter Registration Act (NVRA or the "Motor Voter Act"). Section 7 of the Motor Voter Act requires all state-funded nonprofits and state government agencies that provide public assistance or services to persons with disabilities to provide voter registration forms and assistance in completing and submitting these forms to recipients of their services (U.S. Department of Justice 2015; LeRoux 2014). This law currently applies in 44 states. The District of Columbia, Idaho, Minnesota, New Hampshire, North Dakota, Wisconsin, and Wyoming are exempt from the law because their registration processes differ. At the law's last review in 1994, North Dakota had no voter registration and the remaining five states offered Election Day registration (United States Department of Justice 2016). While the NVRA does not cover agencies in the US territories (Puerto Rico, Guam, Virgin Islands, and American Samoa), armed forces recruitment offices are included in this requirement (United States Department of Justice 2016).

This law places human service agencies and employees in a unique position to help expand voter registration, especially among the vulnerable populations that they typically serve (LeRoux 2014). Nonprofit organizations are legally permitted not only to register voters, but also to provide nonpartisan voter education. Such education may include voter registration deadlines, nonpartisan candidate information (e.g., written information on candidate positions, voting records, candidate forums, and debates), nonpartisan information on ballot measures, polling locations, and nonpartisan guidance on completing a sample ballot (LeRoux 2014). Yet, fewer than one-third of US human service nonprofits participate in legally permitted activities to mobilize voters (LeRoux 2011).

APPLY YOUR SKILLS: Applying the Rules
Choose an organization you are affiliated with (your university, field placement, employer, or an organization that you volunteer with, are a member of, or believe in their goals) and discuss the following questions:

1. What is the type and legal structure of the organization?
2. What political activity can this organization do legally?
3. What political activity can members and/or employees do legally?
4. What political activity, if any, is prohibited for this organization and/or members/employees?

Section 5: Models of Political Activity

This section discusses three models of political activity that help explain individuals' political activity. The Civic Voluntarism Model provides a theoretical frame for understanding civic and political engagement broadly. While this model is widely used in both political science and social work literature, as we discuss below, some of the processes it describes may differ for individuals based on their identity. Therefore, we present two additional models that help us to understand how individuals act politically, especially how they consider runs for office. The candidate emergence model, deriving from the theory of gender and political ambition, addresses gender-based differences in participation. It focuses specifically on the processes by which individuals choose to run for elected office and the effect of gender and related topics. Much research suggests that race also impacts potential candidates' decisions and opportunities to run. The supply-side theory of minority representation provides insight into factors that affect this process, particularly for potential African-American candidates.

Together, these three models may help explain the experiences of politically active social workers, although they do not seek to explain how all groups enter into political activity or how multiple identities intersect to impact political participation. For an excellent discussion of the experiences of black women who have served as mayors of large cities, see the work by Constance Brooks (profiled in Chap. 6) in the resource section. Substantial work also has examined the experience of Latinx politicians (Casellas 2011). Researchers are beginning to examine the experiences of and attitudes toward politicians who identify as gay, lesbian, or transgender (Haider-Markel et al. 2017; Doan and Haider-Markel 2010; Riggle and Tadlock 1999).

Civic Voluntarism Model

The **Civic Voluntarism Model** (CVM) emerges from political science research to identify core factors that predict whether an individual will choose to participate in political activities (Verba et al. 1995). This model posits that three key factors influence individuals' political participation: access to resources to engage in political activity, psychological engagement, and being recruited. **Resources** refer specifically to individual assets that can facilitate participation—time to participate in political activities, money necessary to enable participation in political activities, and civic and political skills that enable individuals to know how to navigate political processes. **Psychological engagement** refers to an individual's orientation to politics (e.g., interest in politics generally or in specific political issues), **political efficacy** (the belief that one is capable of political participation), family influences that encourage involvement in political activities, and identification with a political party. Recruitment refers to whether people are asked to participate; most commonly, this takes place through membership in social networks or groups that encourage members to get involved politically.

Over the decades since the model was proposed, CVM has been empirically tested with large US samples. It also has guided substantial research on social workers' political participation (e.g., Ritter 2007; Lane and Humphreys 2011; Swank 2012; Hamilton and Fauri 2001). Social work research generally finds support for most aspects of this model. Social workers who exhibit political interest, efficacy, and political knowledge are more likely to be politically involved (Ritter 2008). Social work students who are directly asked through their interpersonal relationships to participate politically are more likely to do so; essentially, when students' networks foster participation, they participate (Swank 2012).

However, a few important questions have emerged from CVM research specific to social workers' political participation. In her research comparing social workers to the general public, Ritter (2006) found three important differences. First, in contrast to the general public who were less politically involved when they had less available time and money, resources did not impact social workers' political participation. Second, while partisanship predicted the general public's political activity, it did not do so for social workers. Lastly, while a majority of social work respondents belonged to a nonpolitical voluntary organization, such networks recruited very few of the social workers into political activity. In contrast, other research indicates that NASW membership is an important vehicle for social workers' political involvement (Rome and Hoechstetter 2010).

> **FURTHER REFLECTION: Why Would the CVM Show Differences Between Social Workers and the General Public?**
> Review the three differences that Ritter found between social workers and the general public in the previous paragraph. What do you think might explain why social workers differ from the general public in these three areas?

Candidate Emergence

Political science literature also informs our understanding of why social workers do (or do not) decide to run for elected office. The literature on social workers' political candidacies (Lane and Humphreys 2011) is heavily informed by work from Jennifer Lawless, which looks at candidate emergence and gender gap in **political ambition**, or the ability to view oneself as a candidate. Lawless critiques the long-standing **rational choice paradigm** (c.f., Black 1972). As described by Lawless, this paradigm suggests that a person's decisions to become a candidate and the office they target are based on political and structural circumstances such as the "number of open seats, term limits, levels of legislative professionalization, and party congruence with constituents" (2015). This approach, while useful in explaining some of the when, where, and how of candidates' decisions, has a blind spot in treating characteristics of a candidate, including gender, as irrelevant.

The cultural, social, and political context of women's lives, including traditional patterns of gender socialization, may result in what is commonly perceived as a "lack of ambition" among US women. As Lawless (2015) writes, "if the notion of a candidacy never crosses an individual's mind, then he/she will never face a political opportunity structure" (p. 353). Factors that affect gendered differences in exploring a run for political office include the continuing gender imbalance in care for children and housework, workplace structures that favor men's advancement, and socialized disapproval of ambition, confidence, and self-promotion by women. Women are also less likely to see themselves as potential candidates.

The Candidate Emergence Model provides useful information for understanding when, how, and where social workers see themselves as potential candidates. First, there is a heavy representation of females in the social work profession; 79% of social workers are female (NASW 2003). Additionally, social work is often viewed as a helping profession, which is constructed by society as "female work"—regardless of the gender of the person doing the work. The Candidate Emergence Model suggests that decisions to run for office happen in two stages:

- Stage one: Beginning to conceptualize oneself as a potential candidate. Many factors impact whether an individual runs for office; these include education, income, political knowledge, political interest, and previous political participation. Even with all of these factors being equal, women are 15% less likely to consider running for office than are men (Lawless 2015).
- Stage two: An individual's movement from thinking about running to making the decision to run for a specific office. Males, as well as those with higher levels of political interest and previous political participation, are more likely to decide to run for office (Lawless and Fox 2005). When women decide to run for office, they are more likely to seek local offices, while men are more likely to seek higher, state-level offices.

Gender-based dynamics not only impact one's own decision to run for office, but they also affect who is recruited to run (Moncreif et al. 2001; Lawless and Fox 2005). Candidates are commonly recruited by party leaders or local experts who persuade them of the potential success of their candidacy (Lawless and Fox 2005). Patterns of recruitment into a potential political run—also identified as a critical concept in the Civic Voluntarism Model—differ between men and women. Women regularly face both overt and subtle barriers from these electoral gatekeepers who make decisions about potential candidates.

Consistently, men are recruited to run for office at higher rates than women (Lawless and Fox 2005). This pattern also exists among those social workers who have been candidates or elected officials, although with a smaller (but statistically significant) gap between men and women. Based on a 2008 survey, male social workers who had run for office reported recruitment from an average of 3.69 out of 9 possible sources, while women were recruited from an average of 2.98 sources (Lane and Humphreys 2015). Although this difference may seem small, it is exacerbated due to the profession's gender dynamics. Although 79% of social workers identify as female, only 61% of the elected officials who participated in this study were female. This suggests that even within the profession of social work, there may be a gap in political ambition.

The Supply-Side Theory of Minority Representation

Elected officials across the country have begun to diversify over the past few decades, with 13% of state legislators now identifying as nonwhite. Mayors of US cities now include more than 500 black and 300 Latinx mayors. However, nonwhite groups are still significantly underrepresented in appointed and elected political positions. Shah (2014) posits a two-stage model for black representation similar to the Lawless model discussed above, where the process of choosing to run for office (emergence) is a distinct consideration from a candidate's chance of winning.

- Stage one: Running for office. Shah's examinations of African-American candidates in Louisiana suggest that a number of factors increase the likelihood of a black candidate running for office. These include the percentage of a district's electorate who are highly educated and identify as black and whether a black candidate has previously run. Black candidates are more likely to run in open seats than against incumbents, to run for legislative offices rather than executive or judicial seats, and to run at lower levels of government.
- Stage two: Winning election. When black candidates run, they have a higher than 50% success rate (Shah 2014). Black candidates are more likely to win if a black candidate has previously held the seat and if more than one black candidate is running. Black candidates are less likely to win executive seats than legislative or judicial.

Overall, research by Shah and others has found that the size and concentration of the black population, its education and employment, the size of a legislative body, the presence of white voters who are willing to vote for nonwhite candidates, or coalitions of nonwhite groups such as Latinx residents who will vote for black candidates each affect the likelihood of success for a black candidate. In the USA, "the majority of local jurisdictions continue to have no black representation at all" (Marschall et al. 2010).

APPLY YOUR SKILLS: Using Theories to Create Interventions
Figure 3.3 displays a political participation template developed by Dr. Katharine Hill, a social worker and professor in Minnesota. This template was designed to help motivate social workers and others to increase their political participation. Using the theories and models described above, what kinds of strategies might you implement to increase your social work peers' political participation? In what ways do these theories suggest other activities that could be added to this template?

RIGHT NOW!	For days when you have 1 minute or less	Still pretty darn easy	A little more complex, but worth the effort	OMG, I have to leave my house?!	Takes more time. Consider it anyway.

• Register to vote
• Who represents you?
  • Federal
  • State
  • Local
• Program their contact information into your phone
	• Sign an online petition
	• Retweet/like a tweet
	• Like, re-post, share on Facebook
	• Sign a pre-written email
	• Subscribe to a legitimate media source
	• Talk to a friend about how you are feeling about current events
		• Write an email on your own
		• Send a postcard or letter
		• Write your own tweet, FB post
		• Make a scripted phone call
		• Talk to 2 or more people about how you are feeling about current events
			• Make a telephone call where you speak your mind
			• Talk to 2 other people and ask them to take action too!
			• Follow (and read what they send you) your elected officials on FB, Twitter, email lists etc.
			• Identify groups that are doing work that you care about. Connect with them online. Support them financially if you can.
			• Donate money to a candidate that you support
				• Attend public meetings held by your elected officials. Ask them your questions face to face.
				• Go to your elected officials' offices. Either make an appointment or stop by. Tell them what matters to you and why.
				• Attend and participate in public protests.
				• Volunteer for a candidate that supports your views (including municipal, state, primary, and Congressional elections, not just Presidential)
					• Connect with media sources. Write letters to the editor and op-eds. Call reporters and newspapers and ask why they are or are not covering certain topics.
					• Sign up to give testimony before a legislative or decision-making body
					• Invite elected officials into your community. Create opportunities for them to get to know you and what you care about.
					• Think about running for office yourself. Who knows more about your community than you do?

Fig. 3.3 Political participation template (Source: Katherine Hill)

Section 6: Preparing for Political Participation: Assessing Yourself

The Civic Voluntarism Model described above outlines three critical factors that precede political participation. This section discusses these factors in more detail and enables you to explore your own preparation for engaging in political action. We encourage you to view this as an opportunity to gather a baseline self-assessment and to help you identify opportunities to continue to examine and strengthen your own orientation toward political participation. When you complete this book, we encourage you to reassess yourself to see if you have changed over the course of reading the book and if so, in what ways.

Civic Knowledge and Skills

Knowledge about the US political system and its historical context is believed to be necessary for successful participation in political action. Commonly referred to as **political knowledge** or **civic literacy**, this entails "a basic understanding of the structure and functioning of government as well as the political process through which decisions are shaped" (Hylton 2015). Essentially, political activity increases when we understand political structures and key current events, as well as the processes through which we can bring about political change.

Despite the critical nature of political knowledge for participation, Americans generally show low rates of political knowledge, with substantial disparities across income, race, and ethnicity (c.f. National Center for Education Statistics 2014). Like other Americans, social workers do not show high rates of civic literacy (Hylton 2015). Over the last decade, some public and private efforts have focused on expanding civic education in the USA, with the goal of expanding political knowledge. In 2015 and the first half of 2016 alone, 12 states passed a Civics Education Initiative, requiring increased accountability for civic education (Railey and Brennan 2016). In many of these states, legislation requires high school students to take the US Citizenship Civics Test prior to graduation. The US Citizenship Civics Test consists of 100 questions. Those applying to be naturalized citizens must answer a set of ten questions from this list before becoming citizens. Below is an opportunity for you to take sample questions from the US Citizenship Civics Test.

SELF-ASSESSMENT: Test Your Political Knowledge
Take some sample questions from the US Citizenship Civics Test: http://civicseducationinitiative.org/take-the-test/ or go to http://civicseducationinitiative.org and click "take the test." How does your civic knowledge match up against these questions that immigrants must answer in order to become US citizens?

Political skill refers to one's ability to navigate various strategies involved in political participation. This could range from knowing how to use a voting machine at the Election Day polling site to being competent at reaching out to donors for your own or another's campaign. Political skill can be understood more broadly to refer to "the types of strategies and tactics people employ in efforts to behave politically" (Ferris et al. 2005).

> **SELF-ASSESSMENT: Test your Political Skills**
> Take the following Political Skills Inventory, developed by Ferris et al. (2005)
> This book is designed to help you develop political skills for engaging in political action. Below is an opportunity for you to assess a set of general political skills that can help you navigate political situations. These skills are useful both in governmental settings and in navigating power in your field practica, places of employment, or even within your social work program!

Instructions: Using the following scale, please place a number in the blank next to each item that best describes how much you agree with each statement about yourself:

1 = Strongly disagree
2 = Disagree
3 = Slightly disagree
4 = Neutral
5 = Slightly agree
6 = Agree
7 = Strongly agree

1. _____I spend a lot of time and effort at work networking with others. (NA)
2. _____ I am able to make most people feel comfortable and at ease around me. (II)
3. _____ I am able to communicate easily and effectively with others. (II)
4. _____ It is easy for me to develop good rapport with most people. (II)
5. _____ I understand people very well. (SA)
6. _____ I am good at building relationships with influential people at work. (NA)
7. _____ I am particularly good at sensing the motivations and hidden agendas of others. (SA)
8. _____ When communicating with others, I try to be genuine in what I say and do. (AS)
9. _____ I have developed a large network of colleagues and associates at work who I can call on for support when I really need to get things done. (NA)
10. _____ At work, I know a lot of important people and am well connected. (NA)
11. _____ I spend a lot of time and effort at work developing connections with others. (NA)
12. _____ I am good at getting people to like me. (II)

13. _____ It is important that people believe I am sincere in what I say and do. (AS)

14. _____ I try to show a genuine interest in other people. (AS)

15. _____ I am good at using my connections and network to make things happen at work. (NA)

16. _____ I have good intuition or "savvy" about how to present myself to others. (SA)

17. _____ I always seem to instinctively know the right things to say or do to influence others. (SA)

18. _____ I pay close attention to peoples' facial expressions. (SA)

> How does your mean score (average of your item scores) measure up with what you would expect? How did you do on each of the subscales: networking ability (NA), interpersonal influence (II), social astuteness (SA), and apparent sincerity (AS)? What connections do you see between these political skills and core social work skills?

Psychological Engagement

Psychological engagement in the political realm incorporates both political attitudes and political ideology. These attitudes include interest in politics and government, trust in government, and political efficacy. Political science distinguishes between two types of political efficacy: **internal efficacy**, which refers to an individual's belief in one's own capability to impact government decisions, and **external efficacy**, which refers to an individual's belief that government can be responsive to one's concerns.

While research is consistent in finding that political attitudes are linked to political participation, it is mixed as to the specific ways in which such political attitudes shape political participation. As Pritzker (2012) notes in her review of the literature, while higher levels of political trust are commonly linked with higher levels of political participation, some scholars find that *mis*trust in government may in fact increase political participation for some groups. For example, Kahne and Westheimer (2006) found a contrast in how external efficacy impacts the political participation of white youth as compared to youth of color. While positive views of government may lead to higher levels of participation for some youth, for youth of color, negative views of government's responsiveness may instead spur participation.

Political ideology refers to the set of beliefs that an individual holds about how society should function. These beliefs, in turn, shape how we believe policy should be designed to support our vision of society. For example, ideological perspectives have been linked with public perception of presidential candidates and key issue stances (Jacoby 2009). Within the USA, ideology is commonly conceived of in a left/right spectrum—from conservative to liberal—although Pew Research Center (2014) and others argue that, in reality, political ideologies are much more complex than this.

Social workers are often linked with liberal ideologies. Data consistently show that a plurality—and, more recently, a majority—of social workers identify as liberals. In a 2006 study, Rosenwald (2006) found that 41% of elected social workers identified as liberal, while 34% identified as moderate and 10% as conservative. Among social workers who have run for office, 60% identified as liberal, 38% as moderate, and 2% as conservative (Lane and Humphreys 2011). National surveys of social work students concurrent with the 2012 and 2016 elections confirm that over 60% of social work students self-identify with liberal ideologies (Pritzker and Burwell 2016; Pritzker and Garza 2017). In both 2012 and 2016, fewer than 10% of social work students identified as conservative.

Hodge (2004) argues that the profession's ideological makeup can leave social work students and professors who hold more conservative ideologies feeling discouraged in addressing their viewpoints. He argues that educational content in social work may frame liberal ideology more favorably, impeding political engagement on the part of students who do not share this ideology (Hodge 2004).

SELF-ASSESSMENT: Explore Your Own Political Ideology
Take the Pew Research Center's Political Typology Quiz: http://www.people-press.org/quiz/political-typology/. How does the typology that was produced compare with what you expected? What other groups do you think might describe you?

Our ideologies often are linked closely with **party identification**, an important part of how we behave within a political environment (see more explanation of this in the Pew report in the resource section). Party identification refers specifically to the attachment an individual feels toward a political party (Rockaway 2011). As we discuss throughout this book, party identification is an important part of how individuals and groups behave within a political environment. Critical links exist between our ideologies and how we affiliate with a political party (Pew Research Center 2015). Table 3.1 highlights the ideological categories of the Pew quiz and the likely alignment of individuals in each category with one of the two major political parties, Republican and Democratic.

Party identification often explains *how* we vote better than specific policy ideas (Houghton 2011). As of May 2017, 29% of Americans identified with the Republican party and 28% with the Democratic party. Forty percent of the remainder identified as Independent. **Independents** generally do not formally affiliate with one of the two major political parties; however, this group splits almost evenly between leaning toward the Republican (45%) or Democratic (44%) party. A small minority identify with a **third party**, a term used for any nonmajor political party in the USA.

FURTHER REFLECTION: Your Political Identification
Based on the Pew typology survey, does your party identification match that predicted by the chart in Table 3.1? If not, explain how the party you have chosen (or your decision not to choose a party) is in alignment with your beliefs.

Table 3.1 Ideology and political party

Pew ideological category	Likely alignment (with the two major parties)
Steadfast conservative	Republican (strong)
Business conservative	Republican (strong)
Young outsiders	Republican (not strong)
Hard-pressed skeptics	Democratic (not strong)
Next generation left	Democratic (not strong)
Faith and family left	Democratic (not strong)
Solid liberal	Democratic (strong)
Bystanders	Neither

Political Recruitment

When asked by someone we know personally to participate in political action, we are more likely to do so (Verba et al. 1995). Participation in voluntary organizations often serves as a route to recruitment, as both personal "asks" and organizational opportunities to participate may emerge. Social work research consistently finds that social workers involved in professional organizations like NASW are more likely to participate politically (Hamilton and Fauri 2001; Ritter 2008).

Pritzker et al. (2015) found that college students were more likely to engage in an array of political behaviors when contacted by someone they personally know to work for or contribute to a political party or candidate. Similarly, Swank (2012) found that social work students who received personal requests from friends to engage in political causes were more likely to participate politically. However, research on social work education finds that one-fourth of BSW and MSW programs do not offer any structured opportunities, such as voter registration drives or invited panels of elected officials, to communicate to students that electoral involvement is important or to recruit them into action (Pritzker and Burwell 2016).

> **SELF-ASSESSMENT: Explore Your Experience with Political Recruitment**
> Have you ever been contacted by someone that you know personally to work for or contribute money to a candidate, party, or any other organization that supports candidates? Have you ever been contacted by someone that you know personally to vote? Has someone you know personally ever suggested that you consider running for office? Have you ever asked someone else to participate in a political activity? Based on these questions, reflect on your own experience with being recruited—or recruiting others—to political action.

Review of Key Terms and Concepts

Advocacy: activities which encompass pleading for or against causes, as well as supporting or recommending positions.

Call to action (in regard to "grassroots lobbying"): the act of asking members of an organization or any other public groups to contact legislators on behalf of a specific piece of legislation. This typically involves providing legislators' names and contact information to the public.

Civic engagement: a term commonly used to refer to involvement in social or political actions that help further a common good. Civic engagement entails both participation in the public arena and an emphasis on action in order to positively impact others or to impact public decision-making.

Civic literacy: please refer to "political knowledge" (below).

Civic Voluntarism Model: a model that identifies core factors that predict whether an individual will choose to participate in political activities. The model posits that three key factors influence political participation: resources to engage in political activity, psychological engagement, and recruitment. (Please refer to "political activity," "psychological engagement," and "recruitment" for more information.)

Communication (in regard to "direct lobbying" and "grassroots lobbying"): both verbal and nonverbal interactions of any sort, unless the organization or employee has been specifically invited by a legislative body to provide testimony.

Direct lobbying: defined by federal law as the act of communicating with a legislator to express a view on a specific piece of legislation. (Please refer to "communication," "legislator," and "specific piece of legislation" for more information.)

Downballot (or **downticket**): offices below the top race on an electoral ticket or ballot. In a Presidential election year, this refers to everything below President. This could also refer to the other candidates on a ballot below a governor or mayor.

External efficacy: an individual's belief that the government can be responsive to one's concerns.

For-profit organization: company owned by a single owner or shareholder; the owner or shareholders are allowed to collect profit from their activities.

Government agency: please refer to "public organizations."

Grassroots lobbying: defined by federal law as the act of communicating with the public to express a view on a specific piece of legislation with a specific call to action. (Please refer to "communication," "public," "specific piece of legislation," and "call to action" for more information.)

Independents: individuals who generally are not formally affiliated with any political party.

Internal efficacy: an individual's belief in one's own capability to impact government decisions.

Legislator (in regard to "direct lobbying"): an elected member of a state or federal legislative body.

Lobbying: a subset of advocacy, communicating with legislators or the public about specific pieces of legislation. (Please refer to "direct lobbying" and "grassroots lobbying" for more information.)

Nonprofit organization: agency that has asked the federal Internal Revenue Service (IRS) for a tax-exempt classification. (Please refer to "tax-exempt" below for more information.)

Partisan: activity that is in support of or in opposition to a political party or a candidate associated with a political party.

Party identification: the attachment an individual feels toward a political party.

Political ambition: the aspiration to be a candidate for political office.

Political efficacy: the belief that one is capable of political participation in a responsive system.

Political ideology: the set of beliefs that an individual holds about how society should function. These beliefs, in turn, shape how we believe policy should be designed to support our vision of society.

Political knowledge (or **civic literacy**): an understanding of a country's political system and history.

Political participation (or **political activity**): civic engagement in the political arena, which encompasses a range of ways through which people can communicate their policy preferences in order to influence who makes policy decisions, how they make decisions, and the content of those decisions.

Political skill: one's ability to navigate the various strategies involved in political participation.

Political sphere: the context in which people contribute to their communities by seeking to influence political decision-making.

Psychological engagement: an individual's orientation to politics (e.g., interest in politics generally or in specific political issues, political efficacy, family influences to get involved in political activities, and identification with a political party).

Public (in regard to "grassroots lobbying"): individuals or groups who are involved in grassroots communication or action.

Public organizations (or **government agencies**): agencies that are part of local, state, or federal governments.

Rational choice paradigm: an approach that suggests that decisions such as choosing to become a candidate and which office one chooses as their target are based on political and structural circumstances.

Resources: assets that can facilitate participation (e.g., time to participate in political activities, the money necessary to enable participation in political activities, and civic and political skills that enable individuals to know how to navigate political processes).

Social sphere: the context in which people help their communities through activities such as volunteering; donating financial, time, or in-kind resources to individuals, groups, or organizations; or engaging in community problem-solving.

Specific piece of legislation (in regard to "direct lobbying" and "grassroots lobbying"): a potential bill that has been introduced by a legislature or is under consideration by an executive.

Tax-exempt: a classification that allows nonprofits to avoid paying taxes on certain purchases, in return for abiding by rules regarding activities and revenue.

Third parties: smaller parties than the two major US political parties that hold the majority of power and positions in the political realm (currently the Republican and the Democratic parties). Examples of third parties include the Green, Libertarian, and Independent parties.

Resources

Dissertation

Brooks, C. J. (2012). *Identity and intersectionality for big city mayors: A phenomenological analysis of black women* (Order No. 3554809). Available from ProQuest Dissertations & Theses Global. (1317627218).

Websites

The Hatch Act: https://osc.gov/Pages/HatchAct.aspx
IRS Section 527—Political Organizations: https://www.irs.gov/pub/irs-drop/rr-04-6.pdf
Political Party Identification Data from the Pew Research Center: http://www.pewresearch.org/data-trend/political-attitudes/party-identification/ or go to http://www.pewresearch.org and in the menu under "Home", click the "Data" tab, then scroll down to the "Political Attitudes" section and click "Party Identification".
Presidential Management Fellowship: https://www.pmf.gov

References

Alinksy, S. (1971). *Rules for radicals*. New York, NY: Vintage Books.
Bennett, W. L., Wells, C., & Rank, A. (2009). Young citizens and civic learning: Two paradigms of citizenship in the digital age. *Citizenship Studies, 13*(2), 105–120. https://doi.org/10.1080/13621020902731116.
Black, G. S. (1972). A theory of political ambition: Career choices and the role of structural incentives. *American Political Science Review, 66*(1), 144–159.
Brouillette, R. (2016, March 15). Why therapists should talk politics. *New York Times*.
Casellas, J. P. (2011). Latinas in legislatures. *Aztlán: A Journal of Chicano Studies, 36*(1), 171–189.
Dalton, R. (2008). Citizenship norms and the expansion of political participation. *Political Studies, 56*, 76–98.
Davis, J. K. (2010). Voting as empowerment practice. *American Journal of Psychiatric Rehabilitation, 13*, 243–257.
Doan, A. E., & Haider-Markel, D. P. (2010). The role of intersectional stereotypes on evaluations of gay and lesbian political candidates. *Politics & Gender, 6*(1), 63–91.
Domanski, M. D. (1998). Prototypes of social work political participation: An empirical model. *Social Work, 43*(2), 156–167.
Dunham, R. G., & Peterson, N. (2017). Making black lives matter. *Criminology & Public Policy, 16*(1), 341–348.

Eagan, K., Stolzenberg, E., Bates, A., Aragon, M., Suchard, M., & Rios-Aguilar, C. (2015). *The American freshman: national norms fall 2015.* Los Angeles, CA: Higher Education Research Institute, University of California, Los Angeles.

Ezell, M. (1993). The political activity of social workers: A post-Reagan update. *Journal of Sociology and Social Welfare, 20*(4), 81–97.

Felderhoff, B. J., Hoefer, R., & Watson, L. D. (2015). Living up to the Code's exhortations? Social workers' political knowledge sources, expectations, and behaviors. *Social Work.* https://doi.org/10.1093/sw/swv053.

Ferris, G. R., Treadway, D. C., Kolodinsky, R. W., Hochwarter, W. A., Kacmar, C. J., Douglas, C., et al. (2005). Development and validation of the Political Skill Inventory. *Journal of Management, 31*(1), 126–152.

Fisher, R. (1995). Political social work. *Journal of Social Work Education, 31*(2), 194–203.

Haider-Markel, D. P., Miller, P., Flores, A., Lewis, D. C., Tadlock, B. L., & Taylor, J. (2017). Bringing "T" to the table: Understanding individual support of transgender candidates for public office. *Politics, Groups, and Identities, 5,* 1–19.

Hamilton, D., & Fauri, D. (2001). Social workers' political participation: Strengthening the political confidence of social work students. *Journal of Social Work Education, 37*(2), 321–332.

Hodge, D. R. (2004). Who we are, where we come from, and some of our perceptions: Comparison of social workers and the general population. *Social Work, 42*(9), 261–268.

Houghton, D. (2011). Political psychology. In T. Ishiyama & M. Breuning (Eds.), *21st century political science: A reference handbook* (pp. 51–59). Thousand Oaks, CA: Sage.

Huber, L. P., Villanueva, B. P., Guarneros, N., Vélez, V. N., & Solórzano, D. G. (2014). DACAmented in California: The impact of the Deferred Action for Childhood Arrivals program on Latina/os. In C. A. Noriega (Ed.), *CSRC.* Los Angeles, CA: UCLA.

Hylton, M. (2015). Civic engagement and civic literacy among social work students: Where do we stand? *Journal of Policy Practice, 14*(3/4), 292–307. https://doi.org/10.1080/15588742.2015.1004396.

Internal Revenue Service. (2017). *"Direct" and "grass roots" lobbying defined.* Retrieved from https://www.irs.gov/charities-non-profits/direct-and-grass-roots-lobbying-defined.

Jacoby, W. G. (2009). Ideology and vote choice in the 2004 election. *Electoral Studies, 28,* 584–594.

Kahne, J., & Westheimer, J. (2006). The limits of political efficacy: Educating citizens for a democratic society. *PS: Political Science and Politics, 39*(2), 289–296.

Lane, S. R., & Humphreys, N. A. (2011). Social workers in politics: A national survey of social work candidates and elected officials. *Journal of Policy Practice, 10,* 225–244.

Lane, S. R., & Humphreys, N. A. (2015). Gender and social workers' political activity. *Affilia: Journal of Women & Social Work, 30*(2), 232–245.

Lawless, J. L., (2015). Female candidates and legislators. *Annual Review of Political Science, 18,* 349–366.

Lawless, J. L., & Fox, R. L. (2005). *It takes a candidate: Why women don't run for office.* New York, NY: Cambridge University Press.

LeRoux, K. (2011). Examining implementation of the National Voter Registration Act by nonprofit organizations: An institutional explanation. *The Policy Studies Journal, 39*(4), 565–589.

LeRoux, K. (2014). Social justice and the role of nonprofit human service organizations in amplifying client voice. In M. J. Austin (Ed.), *Social justice and social work: Rediscovering a core value of the profession* (pp. 325–338). Thousand Oaks, CA: Sage.

Marschall, M., Ruhil, A. V., & Shah, P. (2010). The new racial calculus: Electoral institutions and black representation in local legislatures. *American Journal of Political Science, 54*(1), 107–124.

Mary, N. L. (2001). Political activism of social work educators. *Journal of Community Practice, 9*(4), 1–20.

McBride, A. M. (2008). Civic engagement. In *Encyclopedia of social work* (20th ed.). New York, NY: Oxford University Press.

McBride, A. M., Sherraden, M., & Pritzker, S. (2006). Civic engagement among low-income and low-wealth families: In their words. *Family Relations, 55,* 152–162.

Meyer, M. (2013). Political interventions. In *Encyclopedia of social work*. New York: Oxford University Press.

Moncreif, G. F., Squire, P., & Jewell, M. E. (2001). *Who runs for the legislature?* Upper Saddle River, NJ: Prentice Hall.

Mosley, J. E. (2013a). The beliefs of homeless service managers about policy advocacy: Definitions, legal understanding and motivations to participate. *Administration in Social Work, 37*, 73–89.

Mosley, J. E. (2013b). Recognizing new opportunities: Conceptualizing policy advocacy in everyday organizational practice. *Social Work, 58*(3), 231–239.

National Association of Social Workers. (2003). *Demographics: Practice research network*. Washington, DC: NASW.

National Association of Social Workers. (2016). *NASW CEO McClain sends holiday message, response to Trump presidency*. Retrieved from https://www.youtube.com/watch?v=cRnlvEP2QAU.

National Association of Social Workers. (2017). *Code of Ethics of the National Association of Social Workers*. Washington, DC: National Association of Social Workers.

National Association of Social Workers. (n.d.). *History of the NASW Code of Ethics*. Retrieved from https://www.socialworkers.org/nasw/ethics/ethicshistory.asp.

National Center for Education Statistics. (2014). *The nation's report card: 2014 civics assessment*. Retrieved February 16, 2017, from https://nationsreportcard.gov/hgc_2014/ -civics

National Community Land Trust Network. (n.d.). *Advocacy vs. lobbying*. Retrieved from http://cltnetwork.org/wp-content/uploads/2014/01/Advocacy-vs-Lobbying-1-28-14-final.pdf.

National Conference of State Legislators. (2015). *Staff and political activity—statutes*. Retrieved May 2, 2017, from http://www.ncsl.org/research/ethics/50statetablestaffandpoliticalactivitysta tutes.aspx.

National Council of Nonprofits. (2000). *Words matter; The power of language; Government" words*. Retrieved from https://www.councilofnonprofits.org/words-matter - sthash.98OnUnYi.dpuf.

National Institutes of Health. NIH Ethics Program. (2013). *Lobbying activities*. Retrieved from February 15, 2017, from https://ethics.od.nih.gov/topics/lobbying.htm

Ostrander, J. A. (2016). *To participate or not to participate, that is the question: A critical phenomenological study of clinical social workers and their political participation*. Doctoral dissertations, University of Connecticut, 1296.

Patterson, T. (2013). *The American democracy* (11th ed.). New York, NY: McGraw-Hill.

Pawlak, E. J., & Flynn, J. P. (1990). Executive directors' political activities. *Social Work, 35*(4), 307–312.

Pew Research Center. (2014). *Beyond red vs. blue: The political typology*. Retrieved February 15, 2017, from http://www.people-press.org/2014/06/26/the-political-typology-beyond-red-vs-blue/.

Pew Research Center. (2015). *A deep dive into party affiliation*. Retrieved from http://www.people-press.org/2015/04/07/a-deep-dive-into-party-affiliation/.

Piven, F. F., & Cloward, R. A. (1977). *Poor people's movements: Why they succeed, how they fail*. New York, NY: Vintage Books.

Piven, F. F., & Minnite, L. C. (2013). Voter education. In *Encyclopedia of Social Work*: New York, NY: Oxford University Press.

Political activities by certain public entities and individuals. (n.d.). *Texas Government Code*.

Pritzker, S. (2012). Pathways to adolescent political participation across race and ethnicity. *Journal of Human Behavior in the Social Environment, 22*(7), 801–821.

Pritzker, S., & Burwell, C. (2016). Promoting election-related policy practice among social work students. *Journal of Social Work Education, 52*(4), 434–447.

Pritzker, S., & Garza, G. (2017). *Sanders, Clinton, Trump: Social work students' political engagement in 2016*. Paper presented at the Policy Conference 2.0, St. Louis, MO.

Pritzker, S., Springer, M., & McBride, A. M. (2015). Learning to vote: Influencing political participation among college students. *Journal of Community Engagement and Scholarship, 8*(1), 69–79.

Railey, H., & Brennan, J. (2016). *The Civics Education Initiative 2015–2016*. Denver, CO: Education Commission of the States.

Riggle, E. D., & Tadlock, B. L. (1999). *Gays and lesbians in the democratic process: Public policy, public opinion, and political representation*, New York, NY, Columbia University Press.

Ritter, J. (2006). *An empirical study evaluating the political participation of licensed social workers in the United States: A multi-state study*. Dissertation, University of Texas at Austin, Austin.

Ritter, J. (2007). Evaluating the political participation of licensed social workers in the new millenium. *Journal of Policy Practice, 6*(4), 61–78.

Ritter, J. (2008). A national study predicting licensed social workers levels of political participation: The role of resources, psychological engagement, and recruitment networks. *Social Work, 53*(4), 347–357. https://doi.org/10.1093/sw/53.4.347.

Rocha, C., Poe, B., & Thomas, V. (2010). Political activities of social workers: Addressing perceived barriers to political participation. *Social Work, 55*(4), 317–325. https://doi.org/10.1093/sw/55.4.317.

Rockaway, C. (2011). Campaigns. In J. T. Ishiyama & M. Breuning (Eds.), *21st century political science: A reference handbook* (pp. 796–804). Thousand Oaks, CA: Sage.

Rome, S. H., & Hoechstetter, S. (2010). Social work and civic engagement: The political participation of professional social workers. *Journal of Sociology & Social Welfare, 37*, 107–129.

Rose, S. M. (1990). Advocacy/empowerment: An approach to clinical practice for social work. *Journal of Sociology and Social Welfare, 17*(2), 41–51.

Rosenwald, M. (2006). Exploring the political ideologies of licensed social workers. *Social Work Research, 30*(2), 121–126.

Shah, P. (2014). It takes a black candidate: A supply-side theory of minority representation. *Political Research Quarterly, 67*(2), 266–279.

Sisk, A. (2016, September 10). In victory for protesters, Obama administration halts North Dakota pipeline. *National Public Radio*.

State of Connecticut Office of State Ethics. (2012). *Client lobbyist guide to the Code of Ethics*. Retrieved from http://www.ct.gov/ethics/lib/ethics/guid.

State of Connecticut Office of State Ethics. (n.d.). *Researching lobbyists registered in Connecticut*. Retrieved from https://www.cga.ct.gov/lib/documents/Researching%20lobbyists%20registered%20in%20Connecticut.pdf

Swank, E. W. (2012). Predictors of political activism among social work students. *Journal of Social Work Education, 48*(2), 245–266. https://doi.org/10.5175/jswe.2012.200900111.

Swenson, C. R. (1998). Clinical social work's contribution to a social justice perspective. *Social Work, 43*(6), 527–537.

Thompson, J. J. (1994). Social workers and politics: Beyond the Hatch Act. *Social Work, 39*(4), 457–465.

U.S. Department of Justice. (2015). *About the National Voter Registration Act*. Retrieved February 15, 2017, from https://www.justice.gov/crt/about-national-voter-registration-act.

U.S. Federal Labor Relations Authority. (n.d.). *Ethics rules for special government employees (SGEs)*. Retrieved May 2, 2017, from https://www.flra.gov/Ethics_Rules_for_SGE

U.S. Office of Special Counsel. (n.d.a). *Congress allows most state and local public employees to run for partisan office*. Retrieved May 2, 2017, from https://osc.gov/Resources/Hatch%20Act%20Modernization%20Act%20Guidance%20for%20State%20and%20Local%20Employees.pdf

U.S. Office of Special Counsel. (n.d.b. *How does the Hatch Act affect me*. Retrieved February 15, 2017, from https://osc.gov/pages/hatchact-affectsme.aspx.

United Nations General Assembly. (1989). *Convention on the rights of the child*. Retrieved from http://www.ohchr.org/english/law/pdf/crc.pdf.

United States Department of Justice. (2016). The *National Voter Registration Act of 1993 (NVRA)*. Retieved from https://www.justice.gov/crt/national-voter-registration-act-1993-nvra.

Verba, S., Schlozman, K. L., & Brady, H. E. (1995). *Voice and equality: Civic voluntarism in American politics*. Cambridge, MA: Harvard University Press.

Wolk, J. L. (1981). Are social workers politically active? *Social Work, 26*(4), 283–288.

Zukin, C., Keeter, S., Andolina, M., Jenkins, K., & Delli Carpini, M. (2006). *A new engagement? Political participation, civic life, and the changing American citizen*. Oxford: Oxford University Press.

Power, Empowerment, and Conflict: Engaging Effectively with Power in Political Settings

4

© Springer International Publishing AG 2018
S.R. Lane, S. Pritzker, *Political Social Work*,
https://doi.org/10.1007/978-3-319-68588-5_4

Section 1: Overview

How can political social workers constructively engage with power and conflict in order to promote social change? Although a commonly used word, *power* has a variety of uses, definitions, and connotations that are explored in this chapter. Is power something held by individuals or given through a web of structures and institutions? Is power negative or positive? Is there a finite ("zero-sum") amount of power so that in order for one person or group to gain power, another must give up or have power taken away—resulting in conflict and power struggles? Or is power something that can be shared, grown, and created? Specific tools that political social workers can use to assess power dynamics in political contexts are presented.

Developing Social Work Competency
The Council on Social Work Education establishes educational standards for all social work programs in the USA. Content in this chapter supports building competency in the following areas that are considered core to the practice of social work:
COMPETENCY 2: Engage Diversity and Difference in Practice
COMPETENCY 3: Advance Human Rights and Social, Economic, and Environmental Justice
COMPETENCY 5: Engage in Policy Practice
COMPETENCY 6: Engage with Individuals, Families, Groups, Organizations, and Communities
COMPETENCY 7: Assess Individuals, Families, Groups, Organizations, and Communities

Domains of Political Social Work	
1. Engaging individuals and communities in political processes	◄
2. Influencing policy agendas and decision-making	◄
3. Holding professional and political positions	◄
4. Engaging with electoral campaigns	◄
5. Seeking and holding elected office	◄

Section 2: Understanding Power

Power is key to social change in every society around the world. It is a central factor of human social life (1990). Eyben et al. (2006) advise that

> … *global economic and political factors are entrenching poverty and inequality and reducing the agency of citizens to influence the processes that affect their lives… [P]eople living in poverty are cut off from real avenues of power… [T]he realisation of people's rights will depend in part on forging links of solidarity between people and organisations at different*

levels so that they can better understand the dynamics of power between citizens and government, and within global and national institutions—with a view to changing them. (p. 1)

As social workers, we spend a significant amount of time learning and thinking about oppression, diversity, human rights, and privilege. Power is an important part of each of these concepts and is especially crucial for political social work. Work in the political arena involves understanding power around you, your own power, and the ability to navigate power effectively.

The assignment of power within a society—as well as an individual, group, family, or community's ability to access power—is heavily influenced by characteristics such as race, ethnicity, gender, socioeconomic class, educational level, and access to resources. Societal structures such as the way the legal system is set up, the media's role, and the role religious institutions hold also influence the distribution of power within a society.

FURTHER REFLECTION: Social Work Code of Ethics
Read the following statement from the NASW Code of Ethics (2017). Choose at least one of the personal characteristics discussed in that statement. While power will be defined and discussed in much more detail in the subsequent sections, what are your initial thoughts about how power is distributed in the US society in terms of this characteristic?

Social workers should act to prevent and eliminate domination of, exploitation of, and discrimination against any person, group, or class on the basis of race, ethnicity, national origin, color, sex, sexual orientation, gender identity or expression, age, marital status, political belief, religion, immigration status, or mental or physical disability.

Defining Power

Definitions of power are extensive and multifaceted. Take a few minutes to consider your own experiences and definitions of power. Reflecting on this construct may help you think about how you will use power within the political arena.

SELF-ASSESSMENT: Your Own Definition of Power
Which of these ideas of power, adapted from the Institute for Development Studies (2011) comes the closest to your definition of power? (You may choose multiple responses.):

- Something held by individuals; some people are powerful, some people are powerless
- There is only a finite amount of power available, so it is a "zero-sum game"; for one person to get more power, they have to take it from another

- Power is a negative concept that is used to control others
- Power is structural and built into the systems that oversee important functions
- Power is pervasive and embodied in all relationships and discourses
- Power is fluid and it is possible for one person or group to gain power without taking it from others
- Power is a positive concept, necessary for agency and positive action
- Power is connected to your identity and the groups you belong to
- Power is connected to your relationships with others

Why do you define power in this way?

Social worker Mark Homan (2016) defines power as "the capacity to move people in a desired direction to accomplish some desired end" (p. 52). As he points out, power is essential to accomplishing any goals and, therefore, is critical to the work we do as political social workers. Other commonly used definitions of power include "the capacity to bring about significant effects: to effect changes or prevent them" (Lukes 2005, n.p.) and "the ability of people to achieve the change they want" (Hunjan and Pettit 2011). Power can also be seen as "the degree of control over material, human, intellectual and financial resources exercised by different sections" of a society or community (Batliwala 1993, as quoted in VeneKlasen and Miller 2007). In each of these definitions, power is used to influence the actions of others in some way.

Power can be exercised both individually and collectively in many ways. Some ways that you might see power exercised in political contexts include:

1. Depriving the opposition of something they want, such as votes or the ability to do business as usual
2. Giving the opposition something they want, such as votes, endorsement, or an audience for their message
3. Electing someone who supports your issues (Bobo et al. 2010)

Characteristics of Power

Power runs the gamut from expressions that we might see as negative (e.g., domination) to those that are strength based and positive (e.g., collaboration and transformation), to those that can be seen as either. For example, resistance may have either a positive or a negative connotation, depending on the context. It is common to think of power in a negative sense; for instance, keeping people from doing something they want to do or making them do something they do not want to do. However, we also can use power positively—to create new ways to enable people to do what they want.

Power is relative, not absolute. Someone who has a great deal of power in one situation (e.g., a social worker who has the power to decide whether a client receives services from an agency) may have little power in other situations (e.g., that same social worker may not have a say in agency policies). This distinction underscores that power is not a fixed characteristic of a person or community and is instead variable. Even in the same setting, an individual's power may vary. An elected social worker in the legislature might go from possessing a large amount of power to a small amount, if their party loses control of the majority or if they are removed from a key committee.

Power can be thought of as relational or non-relational—"power to" versus "power over" something or someone (Wartenberg 1990). Consider the following four types of power:

- **Power "over"**—the ability of the powerful to affect the actions and thoughts of those who are powerless
- **Power "to"**—the capacity to act; capability
- **Power "with"**—collective action, social mobilization, and alliance building
- **Power "within"**—a sense of dignity and self-worth at the individual or collective level (Institute for Development Studies 2011)

You might find the first type of power uncomfortable, and you might instead feel more comfortable and compatible with social work's emphasis on values such as empowerment and self-determination. Yet, as social workers we may find ourselves with power over others in a variety of ways. In fact, Piven and Cloward (1971) argued that over the profession's history, social work has moved away from mobilizing our communities (power with) and toward exerting social control (power over). We can find ourselves in this role even when it is not a conscious choice on our part. For example, social workers who work on the front lines with clients helping them navigate public assistance programs may find themselves in a position where they are charged with requiring applicants to behave in ways that conform to the program's rules. This is an illustration of power "over." In contrast, we may prefer to be in a role where we can work "with" our clients to consider ways in which such rules might disadvantage the people in the community and might need to be changed.

Power can be formal, imbued due to one's specific role or position (e.g., president, governor, executive director, CEO/chief executive), or informal. While we commonly associate power with individuals, groups, families, communities, or societies who have money or status, Homan (2016) and others describe a number of other characteristics often associated with those who hold power (similar to the "power over" discussed above). These include:

- The ability to use connections to mobilize resources
- Access to information, or the ability to control whether and how information flows to others
- Knowledge of local history and traditions (you may have worked with someone who jumps in to tell everyone else the way the organization has always done things in the past)

- The authority to make or interpret laws or rules
- Access to large constituencies who depend on you in some way
- A charismatic or an intimidating personality
- Being willing to flaunt the law in a way that challenges other power sources (e.g., terrorists, criminals in some cases)

While our societal impression of power is often an individual who takes control using fear (Hunjan and Pettit 2011), Keltner (2016) argues that altruism and social intelligence are important components in helping an individual *keep* power.

Dimensions of Power

Power is stronger when it is less visible. Lukes (2005) defines three dimensions of power, each increasingly less visible than the previous dimension. As John Gaventa summarizes, distinctions between these dimensions can be described as follows:

> *Power can be the ability to act visibly in ways that affect others, but it is also the power to act behind closed doors through more hidden and invisible means. Power can be about what is on the agenda, but also what is kept off; about who speaks, but also who does not; about whose voices count, as well as whose voices go unheard. As such, power is about what we see easily and experience directly, as well as what we do not see.* (Hunjan and Pettit 2011)

Each of Lukes' (2005) three dimensions of power are outlined below:

Dimension 1: Power exercised by one group over another when conflict exists between the interests of the two groups: The winning side might use the "rules of the game," threats, or the offer of rewards to win.

We often see this power dimension in the political arena when a political party wins an election. In the middle of a fight with Congressional Republicans over the threat of a government shutdown in 2013, then-President Barack Obama exercised this dimension when he emphasized the power he gained by winning his Presidential reelection: "You don't like a particular policy or a particular president? Then argue for your position. Go out there and win an election. Push to change it. But don't break it" (Cillizza 2013).

Dimension 2: Power used to decide which issues are placed on the agenda to be debated and discussed: This power is wielded when the group setting the agenda prioritizes its interests and/or excludes the interests of a group with less power. This happens intentionally, by denying one group the opportunity to have their grievances heard by the larger group, through censorship, or by manipulating the rules of the game to ensure that some voices are not heard. It also happens directly, but unintentionally, when a group focused on emphasizing their own interests unconsciously denies the interests of another group in order to do so.

This second dimension of power is common in the political arena. Some ways in which it is exercised in political settings (Jansson 2017) include the following:

- **Reward power**: Those with power promise incentives to others to support a political move. For example, as part of an attempt in 2017 to repeal and replace President Obama's Affordable Care Act, Senate Republicans added the "Kodiak Kickback" to one version of the repeal bill. This provision was specifically designed to provide benefits for Alaskans, in an effort to convince Alaska Senator Lisa Murkowski to vote for this bill (Stein 2017). Ultimately, this effort was unsuccessful in securing her vote.
- **Substantive power**: Those with power propose a strategic compromise that pairs a change that is unpopular with one that is popular. This is done with to elicit support from people who would otherwise disagree with the unpopular change.
- **Procedural power**: Those with power use built-in institutional procedures to support or block a policy proposal. One common way this happens is when the Speaker of the House of Representatives bypasses the committee to which a bill might normally be assigned, and instead assigns the bill to a committee that is likely to kill it. Another example of a political actor with substantial procedural power is the parliamentarian of the US Senate. This individual has the authority to review all bills before the Senate and to determine which aspects of the bill need just a simple majority of votes to pass and which should be subject to a higher standard.
- **Process power**: Those with power use processes that exist within the political system to influence others. They may intentionally increase or decrease conflict, control how much time exists for deliberations, or limit the scope of discussion allowed. When politicians term the end of an opposing party's term as a "lame-duck session," they are using process power to frame this time period as one in which no substantive policy work should happen. In contrast, when a governor terms a bill "emergency legislation," she is using process power to prioritize this bill over all other bills under consideration.

Dimension 3: Power that shapes the preferences and perceptions of those without power through framing issues and shaping public beliefs. This results in those without power actively engaging or complying with situations that might actually be against their own interests.

Lukes' first and second dimensions may feel especially familiar and obvious. You may readily be able to come up with examples of each from your own observations. In contrast, this third dimension may be less apparent, with critical implications for the suppression of conflict. Mechanisms that exercise this third dimension of power include mass media, news media, or "cultural transmission" (Lukes 2005). These subtly create norms around fashion and body image, gender roles, age, or ideologies in ways that the public may not realize.

Lukes (2005) provides a striking description of this third dimension of power:

> *Identity-related or what we can call recognitional domination can take more complex forms still where the dominant group or nation, in control of the means of interpretation and communication, project their own experience and culture as the norm, rendering invisible the*

perspective of those they dominate, while simultaneously stereotyping them and marking them out as 'other.' In doing so, they employ a range of power mechanisms, as the black poet Aimé Césaire observed when he wrote, 'I am talking of millions of men who have been skill-fully injected with fear, inferiority complexes, trepidation, servility, despair, abasement.' These words are quoted by Frantz Fanon at the very beginning of his first book, Black Skin, White Masks. In this and other books, Fanon explored the psychological, social, and politi-cal dimensions of this form of domination and the intimate relations between language, personality, sexual relations, and political experience in the context of the struggle for independence and the post-colonial experience in Algeria and elsewhere in Africa. Yet it is important, finally, to note that the injection will only be partially effective: that the domi-nated will never fully internalize ways of interpreting the world that devalue and stereotype them but rather experience what the black American political thinker W.E.B. Du Bois called a kind of 'double consciousness,' namely: "this sense of always looking at one's self through the eyes of others, of measuring one's soul by the tape of a world that looks on in amused contempt and pity. (p. 120)

The writer Chimamanda Ngozi Adichie described in her TED talk (2009) the "single story," a story that shows "a people as one thing, as only one thing, over and over again, and that is what they become." Her example further illustrates this third dimension:

It is impossible to talk about the single story without talking about power. There is a word, an Igbo word, that I think about whenever I think about the power structures of the world, and it is "nkali." It's a noun that loosely translates to "to be greater than another." Like our economic and political worlds, stories too are defined by the principle of nkali: How they are told, who tells them, when they're told, how many stories are told, are really dependent on power. Power is the ability not just to tell the story of another person, but to make it the definitive story of that person. The Palestinian poet Mourid Barghouti writes that if you want to dispossess a people, the simplest way to do it is to tell their story and to start with, "secondly." Start the story with the arrows of the Native Americans, and not with the arrival of the British, and you have an entirely different story. Start the story with the failure of the African state, and not with the colonial creation of the African state, and you have an entirely different story.

The process by which this third dimension of power is created and sustained is outside the scope of this book, but we recommend Bobbie Harro's (1982) cycle of socialization as one avenue to understand how this third dimension of power operates.

APPLY YOUR SKILLS: Exploring Dimensions of Power
Choose a successful advocacy effort for a cause you believe in. This may be an effort you were a part of, or one that has captured your interest. Describe specific ways that each of these three dimensions of power were utilized by the advocates or in response to the advocates.

Oppression

Political social workers need to be aware of how power plays out through **oppression** and prejudice in both the political processes within which we work and the policies that result from those processes. Oppression can be defined as "the domination of a powerful group—politically, economically, socially, culturally—over subordinate groups" or "an institutionalized, unequal power relationship" that combines prejudice with power (Van Soest 2008, n.p.). Oppression exists when some groups are granted power and opportunities at the expense of others, frequently in a way that sets up the dominant group as "normal" or "right" and people outside of that group as "the other." Oppression is not just a matter of individual attitudes toward those who are different. Rather, it is institutionalized into the systems within which we live, including political systems. It is perpetuated particularly through the third dimension of power, as a society creates implicit norms and traditions. "All oppressed people suffer some inhibition of their ability to develop and exercise their capacities and express their needs, thoughts, and feelings," but their experiences are not identical (Young 1990).

Young (1990) defines five categories or "faces" of oppression:

1. **Exploitation**: Seriously unequal distribution of wealth, income, and other resources, based on structure and group identity
2. **Marginalization**: Deliberate exclusion of some people from opportunities such as work and other participation in social life
3. **Powerlessness**: Lack of opportunity to develop opportunities, lack of autonomy (particularly in the workplace), disrespectful treatment due to lack of status
4. **Cultural imperialism**: Establishing the dominant group's culture as the "norm" and other cultures as deviant or inferior; makes developing stereotypes easier
5. **Violence**: Unprovoked attacks designed to harm, humiliate, or destroy someone because of membership in a marginalized group, often tolerated by dominant systems

The existence and extent of oppression, as well as perceptions about which groups are oppressed, are a source of controversy in US society. Social workers in the USA—as well as globally—have been raised in systems that create and replicate oppression. As social workers, we abide by the National Association of Social Workers (2017) Code of Ethics, which states "Social workers are sensitive to cultural and ethnic diversity and strive to end discrimination, oppression, poverty, and other forms of social injustice." The Educational Policy and Accreditation Standards of the Council on Social Work Education (2015), which accredits all US social work programs, explicitly mentions oppression in describing two core educational competencies: Competency 2 (engaging diversity and difference in practice) and Competency 3 (advancing human rights and social, economic, and environmental justice). We recommend the NASW Standards for Cultural Competence in Social Work Practice (in Resource section) for more information. Despite this significant attention to oppression and cultural competence within the profession, it would be naïve to suggest that all social workers are comfortable with discussing or addressing oppression and privilege, or that there is consensus among social workers as to their meaning and solutions. We encourage you to spend some time understanding the structural roots and history of these issues, even if it is a challenging journey.

The skills described throughout this book can be used to disrupt oppression in a variety of ways—from ensuring that candidates are elected who will work toward more equitable and just policies to organizing communities around the disruption of inequitable and unjust systems. Political social workers, as is the case for individual social workers in every setting, must continuously assess the options available to them to fight for social justice within and outside of systems and determine what methods they can most effectively use to challenge oppression.

Privilege

In order for oppression to exist, some groups must have **privilege** while other groups lack privilege. This means that power and opportunity are distributed inequitably. Privilege is a process in which power is transferred from one person or group to another. However, it is not just power that is transferred. As Franks and Riedel (2008, para 1) state, privilege

> … is the invisible advantage and resultant unearned benefits afforded to dominant groups of people because of a variety of sociodemographic traits. Privilege provides economic and social boosts to dominant groups while supporting the structural barriers to other groups imposed by prejudice.

In the US context, privilege is often linked with the above characteristics listed in the NASW Code of Ethics. These significant areas of inequity in our society include race, gender, sexual orientation, sexual identity, disability status, class, age, nationality, and religion. Privilege may also emerge in less obvious ways; for example, living in urban areas may confer privileges unavailable to those in rural areas. For many of us, the areas in which we have privilege are invisible to us. We are more aware of the areas in which we lack privilege. It may be easier for the authors as white women to see the ways in which gender decreases our privilege than it is to see the ways in which race increases our privilege. This is because the privilege that comes with race is simply our lived experience. Without attention to our privilege, we might assume unconsciously that this is everyone's experience.

Oppression may be magnified by membership in multiple groups that lack status. Similarly, privilege may be magnified by membership in groups with high status. Scholars of **intersectionality** note that "both oppression and privilege occur at multiple levels and sites and are experienced relationally and dynamically between and among individuals, identities, and groups" (Hillock 2012, p. 39). Intersectionality is defined as the ways in which our various social identities and the related systems of oppression, domination, discrimination, and disadvantage apply to an individual or group. This perspective highlights ways in which the location of an individual at the "intersection" of multiple identities (for example race and gender, immigration status and sexual orientation, or all of the above) makes their actual experience of a phenomenon different from those who are not at that same intersection (Crenshaw 1991).

The topic of privilege is a challenging one for social work. It did not warrant an entry in the *Encyclopedia of Social Work* until 1995. It is mentioned only once (in the discussion of Competency 2, engaging diversity and difference in practice) in the Council on Social Work Education (2015) Educational Policy and Accreditation Standards. The concept does not appear in the National Association of Social Workers (2017) Code of Ethics. In fact, the word "privilege" is used only to describe privileged, or private, communications. Yet, social workers often enter into our work with communities from a position of privilege. We may bring privilege in through one or more of our identities, such as race, gender, class, or sexual orientation. Certainly, most social workers have privilege through education at the B.S.W., M.S.W., or Ph.D./D.S.W. levels. We carry privilege with us through our paid employment with agencies that provide funding or oversight of significant community efforts. We may have privilege through positions as elected officials or political staffers, or through the authority to make decisions about what others are permitted to do. These areas of privilege may interact with constraints that exist or are perceived by the communities with which we work.

Section 3: Engaging Power and Empowerment as a Political Social Worker

Oppression and Privilege in Political Social Work Practice

While some individual social workers may fear threatening their employment or livelihood by acting in ways that downplay their own privilege or that help groups they work with to increase their power, this work is a crucial part of social work practice. It requires continued reflection and improvement. On a macro level, the social work literature offers models for challenging oppression embedded in existing power structures not just in political social work, but also in organizational change (Latting and Ramsey 2009; Blitz and Kohl 2012), group work (Berg and Simon 2013), community-based research (Chavez et al. 2008), and community organizing (Mizrahi and Morrison 1993). Despite these models' existence, research finds that social work students may graduate without sufficient knowledge to begin addressing issues of privilege and oppression (Shine 2011). The process of unpacking privilege and oppression—undoing lessons about the supremacy of some groups and the perceived shortcomings of others that we have been taught throughout our lives—is an ongoing, difficult process. We hope that some of the resources in this chapter and in this book can be helpful to you in doing so.

Political social workers often have to make hard decisions in practice that center around oppression and privilege. Some of these questions include the following: Do we work within mezzo and macro systems that consistently advantage some groups while marginalizing others? Do we fight from the outside to change these mezzo and macro systems, even though that type of change can take a long time and can be a painful process? Every social worker who wishes to make change on the macro level has to consider whether to do so within or outside of existing power structures.

Such questions seem increasingly prevalent in the early twenty-first century, as we see an increasing public willingness to question long-standing societal institutions. An important perspective worth considering comes from the legendary and controversial organizer Saul Alinksy (1971):

> *As an organizer, I start from where the world is, not as I would like it to be. That we accept the world as it is does not in any sense weaken our desire to change it into what we believe it should be—it is necessary to begin where the world is if we are going to change it into what we think it should be. That means working in the system.* (p. xix)

As they work to challenge oppression, political social workers also face questions such as the following: If we are in a situation where we have power and privilege, do we use our own privilege as a tool to share power with others? And, how do we organize in ways that enable community members' voices to come through, even if they are not saying what is popular or "right" to those in power?

When engaging with communities that have been disadvantaged by current systems, political social workers also consider: Does one need to be a member of the community they seek to organize or support? The reality is that in order to create change as a political social worker, you will likely find yourself working in a variety of communities in which you may not be a member. For example, in an electoral campaign, political social workers frequently find themselves working outside of their own local geographic community. In an advocacy campaign, if there are not enough members of your own community or group to create change, you may need to join with other groups in order to make change happen. At the same time, many argue for the importance of community membership, because a community member is better equipped to understand the community's culture and brings "a personal understanding of the political oppression experienced in marginalized communities" (Hardina 2004, n.p.). This perspective suggests that social workers should be of the same racial or ethnic background or share other identity characteristics with those in the community they are organizing. Others argue that social workers who, in the spirit of Paulo Freire (2000), emphasize partnership, dialogue, and mutual learning can organize outside of their own community successfully. Conversely, organizing within one's own community risks problematic conflicts of interests, leading social workers to have difficulty remaining neutral in discussions of strategies and tactics (Hardina 2004).

Whether as an insider or outsider to the community for which you work, social workers need to possess the self-awareness to place themselves in relation to the community, to understand the oppression experienced by that community, and to be able to recognize the effects that their own identity may have on their work with the community. Social workers working within marginalized communities also must recognize that such communities may not have favorable opinions of the social work profession because of historically negative interactions with social workers. If you find communities resistant to social workers, consider the history of social work within that community. (See, for example, Sheryl Grossman's profile in Chap. 13, and her discussion of how social workers have been viewed in some disability communities.) As social workers who bring our own identities and privileges into a situation, we must be careful of our potential positionality "as an oppressor, as an unfairly advantaged person, or as a participant in a damaged culture" (McIntosh 2007 as cited in Hillock 2012).

POLITICAL SOCIAL WORKER PROFILE: Ana Rodriguez, MSW
Immigrant Justice Organizer with the Colorado People's Alliance (Fig. 4.1).

Fig. 4.1 Ana Rodriguez, MSW

Ana began her journey to political social work at a young age, when she felt politicized due to her undocumented legal status. As a political science undergraduate, she felt that she needed to find a path into working on the ground for people like her. She enrolled in the MSW program at the University of Houston to pursue a political social work degree and internship opportunities in the Texas Legislature. Ana says that working with Texas legislators felt like the right "next step in the trajectory that [she] really wanted to embark on."

Ana worked on a Notario Bill in the Texas Legislature to punish notary publics who claimed to be attorneys by deceiving the immigrant community into paying them for legal services that they are not licensed to perform. "This was legislation that seemed good, seemed necessary … there was political will to work on it, political will to have it pass." While the legislation passed, Ana realized that it was not a policy that the community was actively advocating for, making implementation challenging. Legislators could have spent that time working on "legislation that was more difficult to pass" that the community really prioritized. While Ana had amazing experiences working for a progressive legislator at the Texas Legislature who centered his work on people of color and immigrants, she found herself realizing the "limits of working within the existing political system."

(continued)

Ana felt that if she "truly wanted to live the values of a social worker and implement the changes that were needed in the community … working within the [established] political system wasn't enough." She needed to work in an organization that holds politicians and those in power accountable. She now "build[s] campaigns for immigrant justice that are led by membership" of the Colorado People's Alliance. She works closely with community members to develop organizing strategies and push for changes in legislation. Because the organization is "member-led, members get to decide what strategies are the best, what strategies stay." The organization is guided by what "members of the community have capacity for." For example, staff proposed creating a traffic blockade to protest the lack of accessibility of Colorado's immigrant driver's license program, a program they felt unfairly excluded certain immigrants from obtaining a license. However, "because membership is largely immigrant and largely undocumented and given the political climate, they don't have the flexibility or ability to take those kinds of risks or engage in those kinds of actions." The organization listened to the voices and expressed needs of the community, and adjusted to political plans that did not endanger community members.

Empowerment

Just as understanding and using power is a crucial part of being a social worker, engaging in practices that build power among, or **empower**, marginalized, vulnerable, and oppressed populations is also critical to the profession. The first sentence of our Code of Ethics underscores this, saying that "the primary mission of the social work profession is to enhance human well-being and help meet the basic human needs of all people, with particular attention to the needs and empowerment of people who are vulnerable, oppressed, and living in poverty" (National Association of Social Workers 2017). Empowerment refers to enhancing power on a personal, interpersonal, and/or political level (Gutiérrez 1990). It can be a process, an outcome, or a social work intervention, focused on "not coping or adaptation, but an increase in the actual power of the client or community so that action can be taken to change and prevent the problems clients are facing" (Gutierrez et al. 1995).

In political social work practice, we focus especially on **political empowerment**, that is, helping to reduce powerlessness and strengthening the political power individuals and groups hold. A focus on political empowerment is strongly grounded in conflict theory (Gutiérrez 1990), with its focus on altering levels of power held by different groups in society.

A psychological process of change is generally part of the empowerment process, involving an increased awareness of power that already "exists within any individual, family, group, or community" (Gutierrez et al. 1995). Through this process, social workers support individuals, groups, and communities in developing awareness of their own power. Katie Richards-Schuster's profile in Chap. 3 provides an illustration of this, as she discusses supporting children and youth to discover their own power to impact policy. Leonardsen (2007) suggests that social workers should focus both on individual empowerment and empowerment in relation to others; otherwise, he argues, they risk becoming moralizing agents rather than facilitators of empowerment.

Social work practice focused on political empowerment emphasizes promoting meaningful participation among vulnerable populations (Richards-Schuster et al. in press). It is important to differentiate **participation** from **meaningful participation**. Many programs and structures provide opportunities for public participation. Rarely, though, do these opportunities enable the public to meaningfully impact decisions—decisions that often directly impact their lives and well-being. An important guide to thinking about this distinction between participation and meaningful participation is the seminal *Ladder of Participation* developed by Arnstein (1969). This ladder illustrated and "modeled ways in which citizens were being engaged in community-based policy programs in the 1960s and 1970s" (Richards-Schuster et al. in press).

The rungs of Arnstein's *Ladder* are listed in this section. As you read this, visualize a ladder with eight rungs. The lowest level of participation is listed at rung 1, at the bottom of the figure. The highest level of participation is listed at rung 8, at the top of the figure. As you go up the ladder's rungs, from 1 to 8, participation by vulnerable individuals and communities becomes increasingly meaningful. As participation expands and becomes more meaningful along the rungs of this ladder, we also see increasing amounts of people power. As Arnstein (1969) notes:

> *Citizen participation is a categorical term for citizen power. It is the redistribution of power that enables the have-not citizens, presently excluded from the political and economic process, to be deliberately included in the future.* (p. 216)

Arnstein's (1969) Ladder of Participation (from the highest rung to the lowest)

Citizen power

8. Individuals or groups hold decision-making power through **citizen control** of specific programs, institutions, or communities.

7. Power-holders **delegate** or assign decision-making regarding specific issues, boards, or neighborhoods to individuals or groups in the community.

6. Individuals and power-holders **partner** to share in planning and decision-making, sometimes referred to as "power-sharing."

Tokenism

5. Individuals are **placated**, as power-holders hand-pick representatives to serve on decision-making bodies (e.g., boards, commissions, advisory groups), but in such a way that these representatives can easily be outnumbered.

4. Individuals are **consulted** for their input and perspectives; however, there is no mechanism to take these perspectives into account.

3. Participation focuses on a **one-way information flow**, where information is given to individuals, with no real opportunity for feedback.

Non-participation

2. Individuals are engaged in what Arnstein (1969) sees as group therapy—masked as participation, people are incorporated into participation specifically with the goal of changing their individual attitudes or behavior.

1. Individuals are **manipulated** by power-holders; they are merely involved as rubber stamps, rather than educating them to make informed decisions.

APPLY YOUR SKILLS: Applying the Ladder of Participation
Reflecting on your own life experiences, identify a situation for each of the following:

1. Where your input was, in actuality, non-participation
2. Where your participation was tokenistic
3. Where you experienced real voice and decision-making influence

In political social work, empowering vulnerable—and commonly oppressed—populations in meaningful ways can be particularly challenging. How do social workers convince those who have power because of the existing system to change that system in a way that might reduce their power? Choosing to relinquish some element of power in order to *partner*, *delegate*, or *enable citizen control* over decision-making requires a major shift. Such a shift can be very difficult for many people in power. In our own efforts, how do we ensure that engagement is truly participation—that it is not tokenistic, and that it is meaningful—reflecting true empowerment? Furthermore, how do we engage communities or populations who have been denied power by larger systems in social change efforts, when these efforts have proven unsuccessful or even damaging to them in the past?

APPLY YOUR SKILLS: Empowerment Assessment and Planning
Thinking about your current or most recent field placement or place of employment, identify one method the agency uses to solicit feedback from clients or community members. Describe this process and where it falls on Arnstein's Ladder of Participation. How much power do clients or community members have relative to the agency's participation processes? Identify a plan to move participation up at least one rung. What might that participation look like?

For Further Reflection
What are some specific steps you could take to move participation to a higher rung? Who would be allies in that effort? Who would be opposed? What barriers do you see in seeking to do this in this setting?

Engaging with Your Own Power as a Political Social Worker

Hasenfeld (1987) argues that the social work profession makes a critical mistake in not giving enough attention to the concept of power. Power can take many forms in social work practice, requiring thoughtful attention to engaging with power in a meaningful—and influential—way. The kinds of political change we discuss in this book typically involve altering the dynamics of power at a community or societal level. Bobo et al. (2010) argue that the three main ways to alter the dynamics of power, or **power relations**, are:

- To build strong, lasting organizations
- To change the laws and regulations that affect power
- To change the people who are elected to office so that elected offices are held by those who believe in shared values and causes

They suggest that changing power relations involves a long-term investment in system-level changes.

Often, however, social workers express discomfort with power. Furthermore, compared to men, women express less interest and less comfort engaging with power (Hays 2013). While power can be exercised individually or collectively, in general, many social workers feel most comfortable engaging with collective power exercised by a group, community, or population to achieve shared goals. We also might be more comfortable with power that is considered positive or beneficent—used to serve the interest of others.

While feeling uncomfortable with power or with using power is understandable, it does not reflect the reality of social work practice. As a social worker at any level and in any field, an important part of your ability to do your job is being able to assess who holds power in a given situation, and choosing whether or not to use the power that you bring into that situation. Power is part of every professional interaction you have as a social worker. It is particularly so in the case of political social work. For example, among social workers who have run for office, both men and women express overwhelmingly consistent and positive perceptions about using power in their political position (Lane and Humphreys 2015). If the idea of wielding power makes you uncomfortable, consider how you can hold yourself accountable for your use of power. Ask others to hold you accountable as well, and continually reflect on opportunities to transfer your power to those who do not have access to power.

FURTHER REFLECTION and SELF-ASSESSMENT: Power Self-Reflection
This exercise (based on ideas in Hunjan and Pettit 2011) involves three steps.

1) Make a list of 5–10 categories of social identity that you think are most relevant in your geographic community or another community to which you feel connected. You may wish to include some from the list in the NASW Code of Ethics: *race, ethnicity, national origin, color, sex, sexual orientation, gender identity or expression, age, marital status, political belief, religion, immigration status, and mental or physical disability.*

2) For each of these categories of social identity, write down your own identity. For example, if you chose national origin, you might put born in the U.S., immigrant, member of sovereign tribe, etc.

3) Think of the majority of people who hold formal or informal power in your community. Does their identity match yours in these areas? Put a + next to the categories where you have the same identity as those in power, and a − next to those where you do not.

When you have finished, reflect on what this exercise reveals about the ways in which you might have access to power and the ways in which you might be blocked from access to power in your community.

To build comfort with power and to become effective empowerment agents, Leonardsen (2007) argues that social workers need opportunities and structures to practice their own empowerment during their social work education. Leonardsen distinguishes between indoctrination and a politicization of empowerment. In indoctrination, students are taught to view and adapt to situations through the same lens as their educators. Through politicization of empowerment, students themselves are empowered through their education to engage in processes of dialogue and reflection as they develop their own competence in approaching systemic challenges. By becoming empowered through their own education, Leonardsen (2007) argues that social workers will be better prepared to support their clients in building their own competence and confidence to engage in action.

Working in the political realm is a way for individual social workers to access their own power, and to help share that sense of power with others. If you see power as something oppressive and impenetrable, you may be wary of learning about it and using it. But we encourage you to, instead, think of yourself as a firefighter with a fire hose. You may be afraid of the power of that fire hose, but at some point the valve is going to open up and send highly pressurized water through it. If you are not prepared for the force of the water coming through the hose, you may end up drowning someone rather than putting out the fire. Power is like any other tool that you can harness as part of the social work process. Used poorly or with ill intent, it can increase injustice, harm lives, and cause more harm than good. Ignored, it can lead to the failure of the best intended social change processes. Used well, it can create opportunities for structural change and build the capacity of communities.

Engaging in Collective Power

As we engage in political social work practice, we may frequently (but not always!) find ourselves being outspent by those on the other side of the issue from us. In these situations, it is important to consider ways groups with limited resources harness collective power to counter those with significant resources. We often access power in six general areas (adapted from Samuel, as described in VeneKlasen and Miller 2007).

1. *The power of the people*: Social workers create social change gain power from large groups of citizens coming together to rally, contact elected officials, or vote. Even if those who participate have a small amount of power as individuals, collective action creates the opportunity for their power to be accessed and used.
2. *The power of knowledge*: Social workers harness knowledge of the electoral process, policy-making process, information about key issues to be discussed, and understanding of how policies affect disadvantaged individuals and communities to bring these sources of power to the change process.
3. *The power of constitutional guarantees*: Social workers in the USA have power through the right to free speech and other protections of the Bill of Rights that are not accessible to many change agents throughout the world.

4. *The power of networks*: Social workers are part of networks of professionals, clients, advocates, and other change agents, which offer critical knowledge, resources, and abilities.
5. *The power of solidarity*: Social workers harness power from engaging in change activities with groups of like-minded allies. **Solidarity** refers to the "union or fellowship arising from common responsibilities and interests, as between members of a group or between classes, peoples, etc.; community of feelings, purposes, etc.; communities of responsibilities and interests" (Solidarity 2016).
6. *The power of passion for a cause*: Social workers gain power through working on behalf of causes that they believe in, rather than ones that benefit the individual advocate. Social workers who advocate or lobby for underdog, underfunded groups without voice in political processes might refer to themselves as **white-hat lobbyists** (not a reference to *Scandal!*) (Vance 2008).

While challenging the power of opponents with substantial financial resources might sound challenging, social workers and allied groups frequently find success using these areas of collective power, particularly the passion and interest of committed people.

APPLY YOUR SKILLS: Accessing Power
Earlier in this chapter, you selected an example of a successful advocacy effort for a cause you believe in. Describe and discuss with friends or classmates whether, and how, each of the above areas of collective power came into play in the advocacy effort. Do you think that the advocacy effort would have benefited from more attention to one or more of these areas of power?

CASE STUDY: Immigrant Rights Advocacy
The following case study is based on the reflections of social worker Berenice Hernandez Becerra, an active participant in immigrant rights advocacy. Many of the experiences described here came from her undergraduate days at Texas A&M University, where she was an officer of the Minority Council for Student Affairs, an affiliate organization of United We Dream. United We Dream is a national organization completely led by immigrant youth and is the largest of its kind in the nation (United We Dream n.d.).

As of 2012, an estimated 1.8 million people in the USA were unauthorized youth who came to the country as children (American Immigration Council 2012). To address the issues faced by this population, the Development, Relief and Education of Alien Minors Act (DREAM) Act was introduced in Congress in 2001, and continued to be reintroduced throughout the subsequent decade. The proposed DREAM Act included a pathway to citizenship for those who

(continued)

had immigrated to the USA as children (often referred to as "DREAMers"), and provided a way for eligible individuals to attain permanent legal status. The DREAM Act ultimately passed the US House of Representatives in 2010, but did not pass the Senate.

Throughout this time, DREAMers consistently engaged in political actions to push for policy change utilizing strategies that best fit their collaborative approach. In 2011, after the DREAM Act had failed in Congress, and there was no immediate prospect for its passage, the organization shifted its strategy to emphasize the immigrant youth community who were DREAMers sharing their stories. The motivation behind sharing their stories was to educate and bring awareness to the greater public about who the DREAMers were. As there was no national policy offering protections to this population at the time, collaborating and bringing understanding to the community were especially vital. Through their stories, DREAMers presented themselves to the public as educated individuals who had no choice in coming to the USA, since they came as children, and as individuals who give back to their communities.

Painting this image for the public contributed to new outside community collaborations—and ultimately to the implementation of the Deferred Action for Childhood Arrivals (DACA) program (U.S. Citizenship and Immigration Services 2016). In place of the DREAM Act, President Barack Obama implemented DACA to create an avenue for approved applicants to temporarily avoid deportation and attain a permit to work in the USA (Svajlenka and Singer 2013). However, unlike the DREAM Act, DACA did not include a pathway to citizenship and therefore offered no opportunities for applicants to gain permanent legal status. In August 2012, DACA began accepting applications for undocumented individuals who came to the USA as children (Svajlenka and Singer 2013). Approximately 800,000 people were affected by DACA as of 2017 (Shear and Yee 2017).

While emphasizing positive images of DREAMers contributed to the development of DACA, Berenice, a DACA recipient, explains that it ultimately left behind many parents and family members that did not fit this specific image, and was perceived as blaming the parents who made the choice to come to the USA. To combat this skewed perception, a new focus on sharing the stories of youth and parents alike began. A diverse population of immigrants who were undocumented strategized together as to how to best share their stories in a manner that helped cultivate empathy and understanding among those that could have a say in politics through their vote.

One particular event that illustrated this shift was a 2013 event focused on gaining more support for the DREAM Act at Texas A & M University. Berenice and other members of the Minority Council for Student Affairs held a rally to bring awareness to Comprehensive Immigration Reform. The group deliberately sought to engage the surrounding community and to educate

(continued)

them about who immigrants were: that they were neighbors, friends, and individuals who were not merely "other," but who shared the human experience, with hopes, dreams, and struggles. Mothers and families who were undocumented shared their stories for the first time, and in doing so empowered the immigrant community to stand in solidarity. Simultaneously, this event involved the outside community by providing an honest glimpse into the realities of undocumented people living in the USA.

Berenice expresses the significance of sharing these stories: "In being quiet, it wasn't letting yourself be free… In trying to protect myself, I was doing the opposite." In this way, sharing their stories created a ripple effect of boldness among the undocumented population and allowed for a greater political movement to push forward. Because these activists understood that progress could not be made as efficiently if the community was not involved, the outside community was seen as a needed ally in creating effective and sustainable political change. Through raising awareness, educating, networking, collaborative efforts, community engagement, and creating alliances with members of the community that held political clout, the voice of a population often ignored in political discourse was able to be amplified.

FURTHER REFLECTION: Power and Empowerment in Immigrant Rights Advocacy
Respond to the following questions:

1. What concepts of power from this chapter do you see reflected in this case study?
2. The activists in this case study found themselves caught between (1) achieving policy change while silencing some voices in their community and (2) amplifying these voices, risking a longer path to further policy change. How would you approach this tension? Why? Does the Code of Ethics provide you any guidance?
3. In this case study, Berenice Hernandez Becerra says, "In being quiet, it wasn't letting yourself be free … In trying to protect myself, I was doing the opposite." What does this quote mean to you?

Section 4: Assessing Power Dynamics in the Political Context

Assessment in social work practice (Badger 2014) is both an outcome (I completed a biopsychosocial *assessment* of a client) and a process (I *assessed* the community resources for those in poverty). Assessment is key to social work practice regardless of the social worker's role, practice setting, client population, or level of practice. Assessment can be used (a) at the beginning of engagement to understand presenting problems and the context for the work, (b) during the process of work to evaluate progress and outcomes and determine whether the actions being used are effective or to adapt to changing circumstances, and (c) at the termination of work to assess whether the work was successful and what follow-up plans should be made.

In political social work, assessment skills are critical for assessing both the political context within which we are trying to influence change *and* for assessing power dynamics among individuals and communities. Political social workers regularly engage in assessment to determine who holds power over their policy goal(s) and how best to influence and reach them. In this section, we provide an overview of three methods commonly used to assess power dynamics in political settings: power analysis, power mapping, and decision-maker analysis.

Power Analysis

Power analysis is a method to assess the many power dynamics that exist within the broad context in which we plan our change effort. A power analysis requires gathering information on key players and structures involved in policy change. A variety of approaches to power analysis exist.

One rigorous approach to power analysis, implemented over the course of several months, is a tool developed by the Swedish International Development Cooperation Agency (SIDA). This tool assesses both formal and informal power relations and the power embedded in various macro-level structures. The SIDA power analysis can be used to assess political contexts—often within an entire country—to create meaningful strategies for change, and to help us better understand why previous change efforts worked or failed. According to the World Bank (2007), the goal is to discover "how power is distributed geographically, institutionally, and socially. It might also point to what kind of power is exercised and how, as well as how this power is perceived, and by whom" (p. 116). This power analysis approach begins with an in-depth review of existing documents and interviews with key informants. The data collected through this review are then used to create a narrative describing the power players, structures, and relationships. This tool may take up to 6 months due to its qualitative methods, grounded in the experiences of those who live in a political environment and know it well. If you have the time to take a careful, rigorous approach to power analysis, SIDA provides an excellent tool and process.

Another tool for analyzing power dynamics has been developed by Donna Hardina (2002) for guiding community organizers. This tool can be implemented in a shorter period of time. Below, we present a slightly modified version of the questions Hardina (2002) poses to guide you in conducting a power analysis surrounding your political change effort:

- Identify the policy or political change that you are seeking.
- Identify the decision-makers and interest groups likely to influence whether this change will happen.
- For each decision-maker and interest group you identify, assess the person's or group's:
  - Likely position on your proposed change
  - Source of decision-making power
  - Vested interests or motivations
- Identify potential contextual influences (e.g., social, political, economic, cultural, environmental, or media).
- Identify any alliances or coalitions among the decision-makers and interest groups.
- Describe the strategies that the decision-makers and interest groups are likely to use in support or opposition of your proposed change.

Power Mapping

Power mapping applies concepts of power to assess the power individuals and organizations hold around a desired policy change. Policy mapping helps us assess whether our desired policy change is viable given where the power centers are. It also helps us determine on whom we need to focus our efforts to strengthen the possibility of achieving this policy change.

One example of a power mapping tool is the Power Map created by Advocates for Youth, which political social workers can use to assess the power, support, and opposition for a desired policy change among key individuals and organizations (Reticker-Flynn 2013). Figure 4.2 presents a sample of a Power Map completed by Reticker-Flynn (2013). This Power Map tool can help you think about which individuals or organizations hold the most sway regarding your proposed policy change. It can inform an advocacy campaign, or it can be used to map out key players relative to an electoral campaign. You also can use this tool to identify allies who might be good partners in either type of campaign.

Figure 4.3 presents a blank Power Map that you can fill in with power players in your own campaigns, advocacy efforts, or organizational change work. On this map, plot each key individual and organization in your political context relevant to your desired policy change. Plot each individual and organization along the horizontal x-axis based on their level of support for your proposed solution (from "die hard ally" to "die hard opponent"). Plot each individual and organization along the vertical y-axis based on your assessment of their decision-making power relative to your desired policy change.

Once your map is complete, use it to help you to figure out where to focus your campaign's efforts. As Reticker-Flynn (2013) notes, "on the power map you want to shift people towards agreeing to your demands (left) and build your power (top)" (p. 12).

Electoral campaigns can use a variation on the Power Map to assess potential voters. Rather than measuring power, the vertical y-axis can instead be used to assess likelihood of voting in the upcoming election, and the x-axis to assess the level of support for your candidate. To measure likelihood of voting (the y-axis),

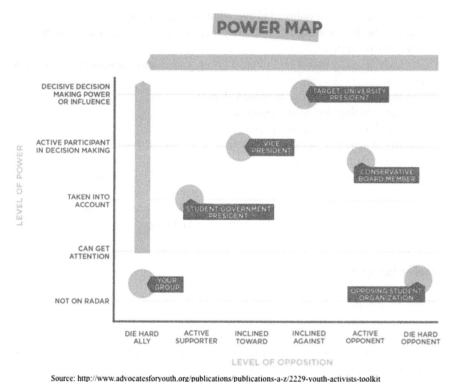

Source: http://www.advocatesforyouth.org/publications/publications-a-z/2229-youth-activists-toolkit

Fig. 4.2 Completed power map (Reticker-Flynn 2013)

campaigns rank voters from very likely to vote (those who have voted in two out of the last three elections, or those who have voted in similar elections) to very unlikely to vote (those who are not registered to vote or who have not voted in long periods of time). To measure the level of support (the x-axis), campaigns identify or "ID" voters, asking them directly to support the candidate. They then rate the person based on their response, from someone who is a strong supporter to someone who strongly supports the opponent. The most commonly used scale has five points:

1 = Strongly support your candidate
2 = Leaning toward your candidate
3 = Undecided ("there's an election?")
4 = Leaning toward your opponent
5 = Strongly support your opponent

Decision-Maker Analysis

Another method to analyze power held by specific individuals involved in policy decision-making is **decision-maker analysis**—that is, evaluating where specific

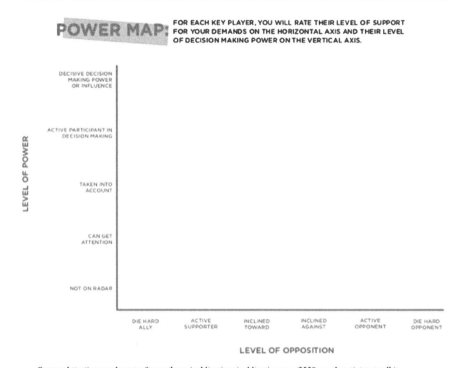

Source: http://www.advocatesforyouth.org/publications/publications-a-z/2229-youth-activists-toolkit

Fig. 4.3 Uncompleted power map (Reticker-Flynn 2013)

decision-makers stand regarding a desired policy change or other action. This method guides us in collecting and organizing information about individual decision-makers. We can use it to assess whether and how we might be able to influence them to act in the desired way.

One example of a decision-maker analysis is the Decision Maker Matrix developed by the Center for Tobacco Policy & Organizing and American Lung Association in California (n.d.). A modified version of the Decision Maker Matrix is presented in Fig. 4.4. This matrix requires identifying each individual person who has the power to make a decision regarding our desired policy change.

First, list each individual's name on a separate row under the first column. Then, under the second column, indicate whether each individual supports, opposes, or is undecided about the proposed policy change. Under the fourth and fifth columns, list all the information that you can collect about each decision-maker that may be relevant to understanding either where the decision-maker stands on the proposed policy change or factors that might help convince the individual decision-maker to support the change. Under the final column, focus on any relevant allies of the decision-maker. This information can help to think about ways that their relationships might offer an opportunity for us to try to influence the decision-maker.

Decision Maker Matrix
(adapted from The Center for Tobacco Policy & Organizing)

Decision maker	Supports your policy change?	Relevant vote record; term end date	Any prior relationship with you or your organization	Other information relevant to their stance on your proposed policy change	Relevant allies of the decision maker
List each individual who has the power to make a decision about your proposed policy change	Yes/ no/ undecided			Family, profession, ideology	Individuals and groups with whom the decision maker is affiliated

Fig. 4.4 Adapted decision-maker matrix (modified from the Center for Tobacco Policy & Organizing and American Lung Association in California n.d.)

While this matrix was initially designed for advocacy campaigns, it can be a useful tool for electoral campaigns as well. For example, you can use it to help you assess potential endorsements from influential community members, interest groups, donors, or other key figures.

APPLY YOUR SKILLS: Assessing Power Dynamics
Based on the same successful advocacy effort you have previously identified in this chapter, conduct an analysis of the power dynamics that were involved in the effort. Use any one of the three methods of assessing power dynamics described above. What does this process tell you about the situation that you did not know before the analysis?

Section 5: Managing and Resolving Conflict in Political Social Work

Discussions of power, using power, and attempts to shift the balance of power are all likely to result in some degree of conflict. In fact, Christopher Moore (2014) argues that **conflict** is a part of all relationships, whether between individuals, communities, organizations, nations, or between people and their government. Therefore, he argues, conflict should be viewed as a fact of life rather than something bad, dysfunctional, or abnormal. Conflicts can include behavioral, emotional, and cognitive aspects, and can have roots in a variety of issues, from survival to identities (Mayer 2008).

In the political arena, issues of power, resources, and status typically trigger conflicts. While conflict that is acknowledged and dealt with can be productive and lead to growth, unmanaged conflict has the potential to be damaging and destructive. This suggests that political social workers should develop competencies in managing and resolving conflict.

Moore (2014) divides conflicts between those that are genuine: "real, tangible, and objective differences between parties" (p. 114), and those that are unnecessary: those that occur because of a subjective view that there is a dispute, but lack objective causes. He suggests that assessing conflict is a necessary step before managing and resolving it. This assessment needs to include review of the major issues, needs, and interests of the parties involved. Moore (2014) also advises assessing:

> ... the identities of the people or parties involved; their histories, relationships, and interactions; their emotions; their communications; the information available or not available to them that is relevant for resolving differences; the available procedures used by the parties to try to resolve the dispute; the parties' possession and use of power and influence to influence outcomes; a range of structural factors that create limits or parameters in which a dispute may or can be resolved; and beliefs, values, and attitudes. (p. 116)

Although conflict appears in all areas of social work, we often are not aware of our innate reactions to conflict, nor our own abilities to manage conflict. The

Thomas-Kilmann Conflict Mode Instrument (TKI) is one tool to classify how individuals handle interpersonal conflict (CPP: The Meyers Briggs Company n.d.). This tool identifies five distinct categories of conflict management, depending on whether the individual tries to satisfy his or her own concerns (which the authors call *assertiveness*) or those of others (which the authors call *cooperativeness*).

These five categories of handling interpersonal conflict are competing, collaborating, compromising, accommodating, and avoiding (CPP: The Meyers Briggs Company n.d.). Someone who responds to conflict by **competing** will be determined to win the conflict, regardless of the consequences for others; self-interest takes over. A **collaborator**'s response might be to ensure that everyone gets what they want, even at the expense of a decision being made. The response of a **compromiser** is somewhere in the middle of these five categories. Someone who is **accommodating** allows others to get what they want, even if it doesn't meet his or her own needs. Someone who is **avoiding** conflict does not deal with it at all.

Some conflicts do not require resolution. Avoidance or simple problem-solving may be the appropriate response. In other cases, if those involved in the conflict cannot resolve it through one of these approaches, it may ultimately be resolved through an outside party's authority and/or nonviolent action. In some cases, a negotiation process can be used to solve conflicts. In other cases, conflicts between groups that involve significant injustice may require resolution on a legal or legislative level.

To be clear, however, mechanisms for managing and resolving conflict will be affected by the autonomy and power of those involved. Where possible, political social workers should strive to approach conflict with clear communication and should resist the urge to use coercive tactics (Mayer 2008).

SELF-ASSESSMENT: Assessing Your Conflict Response

Think about the most recent time you experienced conflict in a professional setting and reflect on the following questions:

1. What was the situation? Who were the parties involved? Describe the interaction as you might in a process recording or other reflection on a practice interaction.
2. Was this response typical of how you respond to conflict? Why or why not?
3. Based on this reflection, which of the five categories discussed above (competing, collaborating, compromising, accommodating, and avoiding) do you think accurately reflects your conflict response strategy?
4. How might your approach to conflict play into your practice as a political social worker?

Review of Key Terms and Concepts

Accommodation: a response to interpersonal conflict which allows others to get what they want, even if it doesn't meet the wants or needs of the conceding party.

Assessment: both an outcome and a process in social work practice that can be used in the beginning, middle, and termination phases of work.

Avoidance: a response to interpersonal conflict in which the conflict is not addressed.

Citizen control: individuals or groups who hold decision-making power in specific programs, institutions, or communities.

Collaboration: a response to interpersonal conflict which seeks to ensure that all parties involved receive what they are requesting, even at the expense of a decision being made.

Competition: a response to interpersonal conflict in which an individual is determined to win the conflict, regardless of the consequences for others.

Compromise: a response to interpersonal conflict in which the parties involved make concessions in order to reach an agreement.

Conflict: a typical part of all relationships. Includes behavioral, emotional, and cognitive aspects, and is frequently triggered by issues of power, resources, and status in the political arena.

Consultation: a type of participation in which individuals are asked to provide their input and perspectives.

Decision-maker analysis: evaluating where specific decision-makers stand regarding a desired policy change or other action. This method guides the collection and organization of information about individual decision-makers and can be used to assess whether and how to influence them to act in the desired way.

Delegate: assign decision-making regarding specific issues, boards, or neighborhoods to individuals or groups in the community.

Empowerment: a process, an outcome, or a social work intervention, focused on increasing the actual power of the client or community so that action can be taken to create social change.

Intersectionality: the ways in which our various social identities and the related systems of oppression, domination, discrimination, or disadvantage apply to an individual or a group.

Manipulation: a process in which individuals are influenced by power holders rather than educated to make informed decisions.

Meaningful participation: the utilization of an opportunity for the public to significantly impact decisions that often directly impact their lives and well-being.

One-way information flow: a process by which information is given to individuals without providing opportunity for feedback.

Oppression: the domination of a powerful group over subordinate groups in multiple domains, including politics, economy, social structure, and culture.

Participation: the opportunity for public involvement in decision-making, which may or may not be meaningful.

Partnering: a process in which individuals and power holders share in planning and decision-making, sometimes referred to as "power-sharing."

Placation: a process in which power holders hand-pick representatives to serve on decision-making bodies (e.g., boards, commissions, advisory groups), but in such a way that the representatives can easily be outnumbered.

Political empowerment: helping to reduce powerlessness and strengthening the political power held by individuals and groups.

Power analysis: a method that aids in the assessment of the many power dynamics that may exist within the broad context in which a change effort is planned. It involves gathering information on key players and structures involved in policy change.

Power mapping: a method that enables the application of concepts of power in order to assess the power that individuals and organizations hold around a desired policy change, determine whether the desired policy change is viable, and establish appropriate targets.

Power relations: the ways in which groups interact with, control, and are controlled by other groups.

Power "over": the ability of the powerful to affect the actions and thoughts of the powerless.

Power "to": the capacity to act; capability.

Power "with": collective action, social mobilization, and alliance building.

Power "within": a sense of dignity and self-worth at the individual or collective level.

Privilege: the invisible advantage and resultant unearned economic and social benefits afforded to dominant groups of people because of a variety of sociodemographic traits.

Procedural power: the exercise of power in which those with power use built-in institutional policies to support or block a policy proposal.

Process power: the exercise of power in which those with power use political activities to influence others.

Reward power: the exercise of power in which those with power promise incentives to others to support a political move.

Solidarity: common experience arising from common responsibilities and interests.

Substantive power: the exercise of power in which those with power propose a strategic compromise that pairs an unpopular change with a popular change, in order to elicit support from people who might otherwise disagree.

White-hat lobbyist: those who advocate or lobby for underdog, underfunded groups who often do not have a voice in political processes.

Resources

Book Chapter

The Five Faces of Oppression: http://www.sunypress.edu/pdf/62970.pdf

Books

Getting to Yes: Negotiating Agreement without Giving In, by Roger Fisher, William L. Ury, Bruce Patton: http://www.hmhco.com/shop/books/Getting-to-Yes/9780395631249

Power—A Practical Guide for Facilitating Social Change, by Raji Hunjan and Jethro Pettit: http://www.carnegieuktrust.org.uk/publications/power-a-practical-guide-for-facilitating-social-change/

Power Analysis: a Practical Guide, by Jethro Pettit: http://www.sida.se/contentassets/83f0232c54 04440082c9762ba3107d55/power-analysis-a-practical-guide_3704.pdf

Promoting Community Change: Making It Happen in the Real World, by Mark S. Homan: https://www.cengage.com/c/promoting-community-change-making-it-happen-in-the-real-world-6e-homan

The Action Guide for Advocacy and Citizen Participation, Chap. 3: Power and empowerment, by Lisa VeneKlasen and Valerie Miller: http://www.justassociates.org/sites/justassociates.org/files/new-weave-eng-ch3-power-empowerment.pdf

The Power Paradox: How We Gain and Lose Influence, by Dacher Keltner: https://www.penguinrandomhouse.com/books/312367/the-power-paradox-by-dacher-keltner/9780143110293/

Podcast

NPR's The Perils of Power: http://www.npr.org/2016/09/06/492305430/the-perils-of-power

Every Little Thing episode on the Senate Parliamentarian: https://gimletmedia.com/episode/the-senate-whisperer/

TED Talk

Kimberle Crenshaw on the Urgency of Intersectionality: https://www.ted.com/talks/kimberle_crenshaw_the_urgency_of_intersectionality

Websites

Powercube: https://www.powercube.net/resources/ or go to https://www.powercube.net/ and on the bottom left of the page click "Resources".

Standards and Indicators for Cultural Competence in Social Work Practice: https://www.socialworkers.org/practice/standards/NASWCulturalStandards.pdf

References

Adichie, C. N. (2009). *The danger of a single story*. Retrieved from https://www.ted.com/talks/chimamanda_adichie_the_danger_of_a_single_story?language=en - t-594757.

Alinksy, S. (1971). *Rules for radicals*. New York, NY: Vintage Books.

American Immigration Council. (2012). *Who and where the DREAMers are, revised estimates*. Washington, DC: American Immigration Council.

Arnstein, S. R. (1969). A ladder of citizen participation. *Journal of the American Institute of Planners, 8*(3), 216–224.

Badger, K. (2014). Assessment. In *Oxford bibliographies online*. http://www.oxfordbibliographies.com/view/document/obo-9780195389678/obo-9780195389678-0152.xml.

Berg, K. K., & Simon, S. (2013). Developing a white anti-racism identity: A psycho-educational group model. *Groupwork, 23*(1), 7–33. https://doi.org/10.1921/1401230102.

Blitz, L. V., & Kohl, B. G. (2012). Addressing racism in the organization: The role of white racial affinity groups in creating change. *Administration in Social Work, 36*(5), 479–498. https://doi.org/10.1080/03643107.2011.624261.

Bobo, K., Kendall, J., & Max, S. (2010). *Organizing for social change* (4th ed.). Santa Ana, CA: Forum Press.

Chavez, V., Duran, B., Baker, Q. E., & Wallerstein, N. (2008). The dance of race and privilege in CBPR. In M. Minkler & N. Wallerstein (Eds.), *Community-based participatory research for health: From process to outcomes* (2nd ed.). San Francisco, CA: Jossey-Bass.

C. Cillizza. (2013, October 17). President Obama to Republicans: I won. Deal with it. *The Washington Post.*

Council on Social Work Education. (2015). Educational Policy and Accreditation Standards. https://www.cswe.org/getattachment/Accreditation/Accreditation-Process/2015-EPAS/2015EPAS_Web_FINAL.pdf.aspx.

CPP: The Meyers Briggs Company. (n.d.). *Thomas-Kilmann Conflict Mode Instrument (TKI®).* Retrieved from https://www.cpp.com/products/tki/index.aspx.

Crenshaw, K. (1991). Mapping the margins: Intersectionality, identity politics, and violence against women of color. *Stanford Law Review, 43*, 1241–1299.

Eyben, R., Harris, C., & Pettit, J. (2006). Introduction: Exploring power for change. *IDS Bulletin, 37*(6), 1–10.

Franks, C. L., & Riedel, M. (2008). Privilege. In *Encyclopedia of Social Work*. New York, NY: Oxford University Press.

Freire, P. (2000). *Pedagogy of the Oppressed* (3rd ed.). New York, NY: Continuum.

Gutierrez, L., Maye, L. G., & De Lois, K. (1995). The organizational context of empowerment practice: Implications for social work administration. *Social Work, 40*(2), 249–258.

Gutiérrez, L. M. (1990). Working with women of color: An empowerment perspective. *Social Work, 35*(2), 149.

Hardina, D. (2002). *Analytical skills for community organization practice*. New York, NY: Columbia University Press.

Hardina, D. (2004). Guidelines for ethical practice in community organization. *Social Work, 49*(4), 595–604.

Harro, B. (1982). *The cycle of socialization*. Retrieved from https://sc.edu/eop/trainings/Cycle_ofSocializationHandout.pdf.

Hasenfeld, Y. (1987). Power in social work practice. *Social Service Review, 61*(3), 469–483.

Hays, N. A. (2013). Fear and loving in social hierarchy: Sex differences in preferences for power versus status. *Journal of Experimental Social Psychology, 49*(6), 1130–1136. https://doi.org/10.1016/j.jesp.2013.08.007.

Hillock, S. (2012). Conceptualizations and experiences of oppression: Gender differences. *Affilia, 27*(1), 38–50.

Homan, M. (2016). *Promoting community change: Making it happen in the real world* (6th ed). Boston, MA: Cengage Learning.

Hunjan, R., & Pettit, J. (2011). *Power: A practical guide for facilitating social change*. Carnegie UH Trust and Joseph Rowntree Foundation (Ed.). Dunfermline: Carnegie United Kingdom Trust.

Institute for Development Studies, University of Sussex. (2011). *Power pack: Understanding power for social change*. Retrieved from https://www.powercube.net/resources/.

Jansson, B. S. (2017). *Becoming an effective policy advocate*. Belmont, CA: Cengage Learning.

Keltner, D. (2016). *The power paradox: How we gain and lose influence*. New York, NY: Penguin Books.

Lane, S. R., & Humphreys, N. A. (2015). Gender and social workers' political activity. *Affilia: Journal of Women & Social Work, 30*(2), 232–245.

Latting, J., & Ramsey, V. J. (2009). *Reframing change: How to deal with workplace dynamics, influence others, and bring people together to initiate positive change*. Santa Barbara, CA: ABC-CLIO, LLC.

Leonardsen, D. (2007). Empowerment in social work: An individual vs. a relational perspective. *International Journal of Social Welfare, 16*(1), 3–11.

Lukes, S. (2005). *Power: A radical view*. London: Palgrave.

Mayer, B. (2008). Conflict resolution. In *Encyclopedia of Social Work*. Washington, DC: NASW Press

Mizrahi, T., & Morrison, J. D. (1993). *Community organization and social administration: Advanced trends and emerging principles*. London: Routledge.

Moore, C. W. (2014). *The mediation process: Practical strategies for resolving conflict* (4th ed.). Somerset: San Francisco, CA.

National Association of Social Workers. (2017). *Code of Ethics of the National Association of Social Workers*. Washington, DC: National Association of Social Workers.

Piven, F. F., & Cloward, R. A. (1971). *Regulating the poor: The functions of public welfare*. London: Latimer Trend and Co..

Reticker-Flynn, J. (2013). Youth activist's toolkit. In *Advocates for Youth* (Ed.). Washington, DC. http://www.advocatesforyouth.org/storage/advfy/documents/Activist_Toolkit/activisttoolkit. pdf

Richards-Schuster, K., Pritzker, S., & Rodriguez-Newhall, A. (in press). Youth empowerment. *Encyclopedia of Social Work*. C. Franklin (Ed.), Washington, DC and New York, NY: NASW Press and Oxford University Press.

Michael D. Shear, & Vivian Yee. (2017, June 16). 'Dreamers' to stay in U.S. for now, but long-term fate is unclear. *The New York Times*.

Shine, P. (2011). White professors taking responsibility for teaching White students about race, racism, and privilege. *Journal of Progressive Human Services, 22*(1), 50–67.

Solidarity. (2016). Retrieved from http://www.dictionary.com/browse/solidarity.

Stein, J. (2017, July 15). *The Kodian Kickback: The quiet payoff for an Alaska senator in the Senate health bill*. Retrieved from Vox.com.

Svajlenka, N. P., & Singer, A. (2013). Immigration facts: Deferred action for childhood arrivals (DACA). https://www.brookings.edu/research/immigration-facts-deferred-action-for-child-hood-arrivals-daca/

The Center for Tobacco Policy & Organizing, & American Lung Association in California. (n.d.). *Decision maker matrix*. Retrieved April 2, 2017, from http://center4tobaccopolicy.org/wp-content/uploads/2017/03/Decision-Maker-Matrix-The-Center-FEB-2017.pdf.

U.S. Citizenship and Immigration Services. (2016). *Consideration of Deferred Action for Childhood Arrivals (DACA)*. Retrieved from https://www.uscis.gov/humanitarian/consideration-deferred-action-childhood-arrivals-daca.

United We Dream. (n.d.). *Home page*. Retrieved from https://unitedwedream.org/.

Van Soest, D. (2008). Oppression. In C. Franklin (Ed.), *Encyclopedia of Social Work*. New York, NY: Oxford University Press.

Vance, S. (2008). *White hats vs. black hats in lobbying*. Retrieved from http://advocacyassociates. blogspot.com/2008/06/white-hats-vs-black-hats-in-lobbying.html.

VeneKlasen, L., & Miller, V. (2007). The basics of planning for citizen-centered advocacy. *A new weave of power, people, & politics: the action guide for advocacy and citizen participation*. Washington, DC: Just Associates.

Wartenberg, T. (1990). *The forms of power: From domination to transformation*. Philadelphia, PA: Temple University Press.

World Bank. (2007). *Tools for institutional, political, and social analysis of policy reform: A sourcebook for development practitioners*. Washington, DC: World Bank. Retrieved from http://siteresources.worldbank.org/EXTTOPPSISOU/Resources/1424002-1185304794278/TIPs_Sourcebook_English.pdf.

Young, I. M. (1990). Five faces of oppression. In *Justice and the politics of difference*. Princeton, NJ: Princeton University Press.

Part II

Assessing and Planning Effective Political Social Work Strategies

"[S]omebody must be able to sit in on the strategy conferences and plot a course. There must be strategies...to carry out the program. That's our role."

Whitney M. Young, Jr., MSW

Getting on the Agenda: Assessing the Political Context and Developing Political Strategy

5

© Springer International Publishing AG 2018
S.R. Lane, S. Pritzker, *Political Social Work*,
https://doi.org/10.1007/978-3-319-68588-5_5

Section 1: Overview

Political social work is most effective when it has a clear vision, goals, and strategy. Strategic planning must be a thoughtful process that takes into account an assessment of the context in which you are working. This chapter introduces and explains five steps of political strategy development, including:

1. Determining the specific purpose of the political change effort; that is, what specifically you are trying to change
2. Assessing the internal (organizational) and external (environmental) context
3. Identifying the change effort's goals
4. Selecting the specific targets of the political change effort
5. Identifying and selecting of tactics that are likely to influence the target or targets.

Activities throughout the chapter allow opportunities to practice skills in each of these areas.

Developing Social Work Competency
The Council on Social Work Education establishes educational standards for all social work programs in the USA. Content in this chapter supports building competency in the following areas that are considered core to the practice of social work:
COMPETENCY 3: Advance Human Rights and Social, Economic, and Environmental Justice
COMPETENCY 5: Engage in Policy Practice
COMPETENCY 7: Assess Individuals, Families, Groups, Organizations, and Communities
COMPETENCY 8: Intervene with Individuals, Families, Groups, Organizations, and Communities

Domains of Political Social Work	
1. Engaging individuals and communities in political processes	◄
2. Influencing policy agendas and decision-making	◄
3. Holding professional and political positions	◄
4. Engaging with electoral campaigns	◄
5. Seeking and holding elected office	◄

Section 2: The Importance of Political Strategy

Clear, calculated **strategy** is critical to effective political social work. While anyone can—and many people do—get frustrated about governmental policies and decide to engage in efforts to try to create change, what increases the likelihood of these efforts being *effective* is an intentional and deliberative focus on strategy.

Marshall Ganz (2005), a leading scholar and practitioner on social movements and organizing, explains that strategy is "how we turn what we have into what we need to get what we want" (p. 214). Essentially, this means that before starting a political change effort, we must make sure that we have a clear sense of what we want to accomplish. Why are we engaging in this effort? What, specifically, do we seek to achieve? In addition, we also need to assess what resources are available to help achieve our goals, and to think carefully and purposefully about what steps we plan to take to achieve these goals.

As social workers, our professional reality may include limited resources or time to achieve policy change or electoral goals. The nonprofit organizations that employ many social workers have limited money and staff time to devote to advocacy. The "usual suspects" who help facilitate newcomers into potential runs for office may be less open to us because of our gender, race, profession, or another outsider status. Particularly in the nonprofit and public worlds, we are also increasingly accountable to funders and other constituencies that require us to show that we are using our resources wisely in a relatively short time period.

Limited access to time, money, and other resources does not rule out success. These factors do, however, make it critical that we effectively and efficiently utilize our resources in a way best designed to achieve our intended results. For example, we need to carefully consider questions such as: Should our campaign spend limited volunteer time and money knocking on doors for the candidate on a street where very few residents have historically voted for our candidate's political party? Or, instead, should we focus our campaign resources on voter outreach efforts in a neighborhood with 100 individuals who have previously voted for candidates with similar policy platforms? Alternatively, should we spend our organization's limited time targeting a generally supportive legislator by organizing a grassroots letter campaign about a specific bill; or should we instead focus that time on building a relationship with a legislator who is on the fence about the bill and sits on the committee to which it was assigned? These—and much more complex versions of these questions—are common kinds of choices that we need to carefully consider as we plan political change efforts.

Ganz (2005) further explains the intersection of strategy and resources, as he states that strategy is "how we transform our resources into the power to achieve our purposes" (p. 214). Ganz's comments emphasize that strategy is not only about how we effectively use resources, but it is also a critical mechanism through which we address power imbalances. In Chap. 4's section *Engaging with your own power as a political social worker*, we identified six areas of power that social workers can use to counter opponents with greater financial resources. Each of these is an

FURTHER REFLECTION: Effects of Major Events

Listen to the story of US policy shifts in the wake of the September 11 terrorist attacks as described in the Radiolab podcast *60 words:* http://www.radiolab.org/story/60-words/.

How did these attacks shift policy-making, in social worker and Rep. Barbara Lee's (D-CA) eyes? Can you identify another example of where events or situations quickly shift the policy context?

example of a way, through careful attention to strategy, to convert our resources into power.

Of course, even the best-laid strategy must be adaptable, given the constantly changing nature of politics. In our current fast-paced social context, with new events quickly changing policy and political norms, we can become easily distracted. A false accusation is made about your candidate. A politician tweets something that quickly shifts the public's mood about a bill you oppose. A new amendment is proposed that undermines a bill for which you have been advocating, on the day it is being considered. A major news event happens and completely changes the priorities of the public, the legislature, or other decision-makers. Events like these can quickly throw us off of our focus, and require that we be able to determine whether and how our strategy should adjust to the changed political context within which we are working.

Clear strategic planning done in advance of your advocacy effort, legislative session, or political campaign can help keep the team rooted in their purpose. This guides political social workers in adapting to new circumstances and changing contexts smoothly and effectively, while keeping focused on overall vision and goals. Planning can help identify challenges and avoid potential surprises (Breitrose 2011) and can guide us in preparing contingency plans and fallback positions (Richan 2006). In advocating for the importance of careful political strategizing, Ganz (2005) points out that successful change efforts also must involve creative thinking in order to adapt strategy to new challenges that arise.

In this book, we apply a five-stage approach to designing intentional and thoughtful strategy for political change, including both advocacy and electoral efforts. These five stages are as follows:

1. Determine the specific purpose of the political change effort.
2. Assess the internal (organizational) and external (environmental) context for the political change effort.
3. Identify the long-term, intermediate, and short-term goals of the political change effort.
4. Select specific targets for the political change effort.
5. Identify and select the tactics that will be used in the political change effort.

The subsequent sections of this chapter introduce you to each of these stages. Then, in the next two chapters, you will apply each of these stages more specifically to planning an advocacy campaign (Chap. 6) and an electoral campaign (Chap. 7).

Section 3: What Are You Trying to Change Through Your Political Change Effort? (Stage 1)

Without clarity of focus, it is hard to pursue an effective political change strategy. Therefore, the first stage in identifying a strategy is to determine the specific purpose of the political change effort; that is, what, specifically, are you trying to change?

- Is there an incumbent in the state legislature who routinely works against your values, and an opponent (maybe you!) who would vote more in line with your beliefs?
- Is there an upcoming policy issue before your local school board that could be decided by one vote, and an open seat in the upcoming election?
- Is there a specific social problem in your community that could be solved or improved through a policy change?
- Is there a current policy that is causing harm to vulnerable populations whose voices are not being heard by those in power?
- Is there a group of people in your community, maybe including clients of your workplace or internship, who have not been heard in the political process?

> **APPLY YOUR SKILLS: Identify a Political Change**
> Take a few minutes and reflect on a political change you would like to see in your local community. If you were to successfully achieve this change, what do you expect would look different in your community as a result?

In thinking about *what* you want to work to change, it is important to also think about *why* you want to see this change. Ganz (2005) argues that having clear *motivations*—deriving meaning from your work—is critical to engaging in successful policy change efforts. He illustrates this argument using the Biblical story of David standing up to Goliath, suggesting that David was ultimately successful against his stronger foe because he "knew why he had to do it before he knew how he could do it" (p. 217). We encourage you to reflect on your motivations as you begin to consider your political change strategy. Why do you want to make sure a new elected official is elected? Why are you choosing to run for office? Why is it important to you that a specific policy be changed?

SELF-ASSESSMENT/FURTHER REFLECTION: What Motivates You?

Simon Sinek, a leadership expert and author of the book, *Start with Why: How Great Leaders Inspire Everyone to Take Action*, reminds leaders to focus on their motivations; that is, the emotional core of why they do what they do (Sinek 2011). Visit the TED website (www.ted.com) and watch his talk, "How great leaders inspire action" by typing the title into the search bar.

As you watch this brief video, take some time to reflect and write notes about your personal "why." What motivates you to engage in political action? With a friend or classmate, reflect on your "why" and how this might guide you in pursuing political social work practice.

Stopping to consider our motivations is a step that we too often overlook. Instead, we find ourselves subsumed by the effort itself and lose sight of why we are engaging in it. Unfortunately, this can lead us to become distracted from our goals, or perhaps even face burnout. Clarity about your motivations—and reminding yourself about these motivations as you move forward—can keep you focused on your goals. This also can be a good source of self-care in the face of challenges you may face in pursuit of these goals.

As you examine your motivations for engaging in a political change effort, continue to revisit and refine your thoughts about what specifically it is that you are trying to change, and *why*.

Section 4: Assessing the Internal and External Context (Stage 2)

The second stage in planning an effective political change strategy is to assess the internal (organizational) and external (environmental) context in which we will act. The internal context refers to the assets and deficits you and your organization possess as you prepare to embark on your policy change effort. External opportunities and constraints exist within the broad context in which you are working: the specific social, economic, and political climate in which you seek policy change.

In our assessments, we need to clearly examine what resources are available to us, as well as the opportunities *and* challenges that we will face both internally and within the larger external context. As VeneKlasen and Miller (2007) state, "Being strategic means making careful choices about how to use and leverage scarce resources… Being strategic demands a careful analysis of external opportunities and constraints and internal organizational resources for addressing a problem" (p. 100). In this section, we present specific questions to guide your assessments. One tool that you may find helpful to use in conjunction with these questions is **SWOT analysis**, which stands for strengths, weaknesses, opportunities, and threats. SWOT analysis is a process of looking internally at an organization's strengths and weaknesses, and externally at its environmental opportunities and threats. You may have used SWOT analysis in other settings—it is very common in nonprofit strategic planning. See the Resource list to further explore ways that this tool might help you in assessing your effort's internal and external contexts.

Assessing Your Individual and Organizational Context

Before you move forward with any political strategy, take a serious and realistic look at both the resources you have available to expend on the policy change effort and any challenges you face. If you are working on your change effort as part of a larger group, campaign slate, coalition, human services agency, etc., these questions are best discussed and reflected upon as a group. Five core internal assessment questions are important to consider at this stage:

1. Are you and your allies fully prepared to embark on this effort?
2. What time, money, and people resources do you and your allies have to support these political change efforts?
3. What prior experience and expertise do you and your allies bring to support this political change effort?
4. What sources of political power do you and your allies possess relevant to this political change effort?
5. What challenges do you and your allies face as you enter into this political change effort?

Your answers to these questions influence subsequent decisions throughout the strategic planning process. Because answers to these questions will inevitably differ by individual and organization, your strategic plan may look different from that of another organization seeking the same policy change, or from another candidate seeking the same position.

Be self-reflective and honest about your individual and organizational capacity as you conduct this internal assessment. This is not the time to inflate your resources—for example, if a political campaign designs its strategy under the assumption that it can fundraise $1 million, then it will find itself in a world of trouble when it realizes 1 month before the election that it would have been much more appropriate to estimate that the campaign could raise $250,000.

APPLY YOUR SKILLS/SELF-ASSESSMENT: Assessing the Internal Context
Based on the political change you identified in Stage 1, briefly answer each of the five questions posed here about the internal environment. As you answer these questions, assume you are acting alone in your political change effort, not as part of an organization. Based on this assessment, what are the two biggest strengths you bring to this political change effort, and what are the two biggest challenges you might face?

Assessing the Social, Economic, and Political Environment

Your political strategy benefits from establishing a full understanding of the social, economic, and political environment surrounding the proposed policy change. Accessing as many sources of data as possible will provide the most complete picture of the environment and players. In this assessment process, seek to identify the critical contextual issues that will likely influence how key players and the public view your proposal.

Three sets of core questions should guide your assessment:

- What is the current **social climate** on the municipal, state, or federal level at which your change is focused? Social climate includes the social context and psychological climate in a given community or group. It is rooted in perception, not necessarily data or an objective fact (Bennett 2010). How might the social climate impact openness and/or resistance to your proposed change?
- What is the current **economic climate** on the municipal, state, or federal level at which your change is focused? This evaluates perception of economic issues, and may differ from what one might expect looking at numerical economic indicators. How might the economic climate impact openness and/or resistance to your proposed change?
- What is the current **political climate** on the municipal, state, or federal level at which your change is focused? What are people's opinions or attitudes toward the political system in their area? Is there likely to be a sufficient constituency open or resistant to your change? Is there realistic potential for this political climate to shift in the near future?

The two subsections below provide further information to help you conduct this external assessment. First, we discuss the relevant levels of government in which you might be working. Secondly, we overview helpful sources of information to gather information to answer these three sets of questions.

Levels of Government

To assess the external climate, you must first identify the level of government at which your change should be focused. To do this, we need to understand the differences in levels of government (municipal, state, federal) and the different responsibilities of each level. While the content below may be a review for some readers, it is important context to help ensure that you are focusing your energies effectively. It may be useful to review it with a specific social change in mind, to think about what aspect of the change is relevant to each aspect of government. Below, we distinguish between each of these core levels of US government and outline the key institutions involved in government policy-making at each level.

As you proceed in identifying the level of government at which you will focus your change effort, make sure to also consider which specific country, state, or municipality needs your attention. Consider that the geographic area in which you need to focus your change strategy is not always the area in which you are geographically located. The policy change you seek may need to be put into place by a government to which you are not a constituent. For example, if you are working in a city center, but live in an adjoining town, key players in that city may be more relevant in creating policy change that affects your constituency.

Federal Government

The **federal government** is the level of government responsible for providing policy governance and oversight of the entire USA. The U.S. Constitution specifically delineates the areas of policy over which the federal government has authority (Constitution of the United States of America: Analysis and Interpretation 2016). These include issues related to national border security (defense, immigration), issues that cross state lines (transportation, drug enforcement), and providing for "the general Welfare of the United States," a clause that has been interpreted in a variety of ways and has been the focus of much disagreement throughout the nation's history.

The structure of the US federal government, as defined by the Constitution, is organized into three branches: legislative, executive, and judicial. The **bicameral legislature**, broken into two houses—the U.S. House of Representatives (where you are most directly represented by your district representative) and the U.S. Senate (where two senators represent your state)—*makes laws*. The **executive** branch, consisting of the president, vice president, and the executive branch agencies, *carries out the laws*. The **judicial** branch, which includes the U.S. Supreme Court and federal district and appeals courts, *evaluates laws* to clarify their meaning, decides how laws apply in specific cases, and determines whether laws meet the requirements of the Constitution. Some version of this three-branch structure is replicated at the state level and in many local governments across the country.

> **BUILD YOUR KNOWLEDGE: The Legislative Process—From Theory to Practice**
> Watch everyone's favorite video about government, "I'm Just a Bill" from Schoolhouse Rock: https://www.youtube.com/watch?v=tyeJ55o3El0. Now watch this video providing an example of the Georgia state legislative process regarding the backlog of untested rape kits in that state: https://www.youtube.com/watch?v=UrxTrR5_8Zo.
>
> As you watch these two videos, what similarities do you see between the process in theory (Schoolhouse Rock) and in practice (Georgia's process)? What differences do you see?

By design, the U.S. Constitution places these three branches in conflict with each other through a system of "checks and balances." At the federal level, this means that each of the three branches of government has the power to provide input into the work of the other branches. As a result, this can slow or even stop the work of another branch. In early 2017, this dynamic was illustrated by federal courts halting the Trump administration's Executive Order banning visas to travelers to the USA from certain countries (Gerstein 2017). In practice, checks and balances work as follows:

- *Congress* is checked by the *President,* who can either sign or veto legislation passed by Congress, and by the *Supreme Court* (and other federal courts), who can declare passed legislation unconstitutional.
- The *president* is checked by *Congress,* who must approve his or her appointments and budget and who can impeach him or her in certain situations, and by the *Supreme Court,* who can declare the president's orders unconstitutional.
- The *Supreme Court* is checked by the *president,* who nominates judges that serve on it and other federal courts, and by *Congress,* who approves the nomination of these judges via the Senate and who can impeach judges in certain situations.

This process of checks and balances can be frustrating at times, especially when we watch one branch of the government stop a policy we like that originated in another branch. However, this framework was very intentionally designed by our nation's founders, to prevent any one branch from becoming too powerful. (If you've ever heard the song "Nonstop" from the musical *Hamilton*, you've listened to the process of designing these checks and balances (Miranda 2015).)

You may have heard the media referred to as the "fourth branch of government," the fourth estate, or the fourth power. While the media is not included in our Constitutional system of checks and balances, this term illuminates the role the media plays in providing informal crucial checks and balances to these three formal branches of government (Luberda 2014).

While the three-branch structure—and the accompanying checks and balance system—captures the broad essence of US policy-making, the reality of federal governmental policy-making is frequently more complex. In some cases at the executive branch level, for example, the president can use **executive orders** to make laws. Executive orders were designed to allow the president to directly manage executive branch operations (National Archives and Records Administration n.d.). In application, their uses seem to expand beyond this. While political rhetoric often treats the use of executive orders as a modern problem involving recent presidents, executive order usage stretches back to George Washington's administration (Zavis 2017). For example, the World War II-era Japanese internment camps discussed in Chap. 1 came about through an executive order, demonstrating that sweeping or controversial executive orders are not a new phenomenon. You can see the range of what executive orders may entail by looking at the Federal Register's compilation of executive orders from the last four presidencies (see a link to these downloadable, searchable spreadsheets in the Resources section). There are limits on the ability of a president to legislate via executive order. However, the practice of using these orders and the pushback from Congress and the judicial system has varied substantially over the years. Phillip Cooper's book (in the Resource section) provides an overview of this process up through the Obama administration.

The Schoolhouse Rock version of the law-making process requires that the legislative branch pass legislation and send it to the president for his or her signature.

However, to add another wrinkle to federal policy-making, legislation that Congress passes often includes just a broad overview of the law that Congress has in mind. Once a bill is passed and signed into law, the specific federal agency (or agencies) responsible for implementing the new law is required to further develop the law's details. These include determining who is responsible for implementing the law, how it will be implemented, and specific details of what the program or policy (including eligibility guidelines) will look like. Even after a law is implemented, the president can request that an agency modify the way it implements current legislation.

Executive branch agencies use a process known as the **regulatory process** to determine how laws will be implemented. Through the regulatory process, an executive branch agency puts forth or "promulgates" **regulations** specifying its proposed implementation details. These are disseminated through a document called the *Federal Register*, available both in hard copy and online. By law, once published in the *Federal Register*, proposed regulations are open for public comment for a specified time period; individuals, advocates, lobbyists, businesses, and the general public may provide public comment during this time period. The agency reviews public comments prior to issuing its "final rule"—these regulations then carry the force of law.

Regulations often directly address policy content related to issues of access, eligibility, and types of social welfare services, thus impacting the vulnerable populations that social workers serve. For example, agencies within the U.S. Department of Health and Human Services, as well as agencies such as the U.S. Department of Labor, have issued large numbers of federal regulations related to health care. To get a sense of what federal regulations related to health care reform look like, see the Federal Register link provided in the Resource section.

APPLY YOUR SKILLS: Commenting on Federal Regulations
Go to https://www.regulations.gov/ and find a proposed regulation relevant to your community, employment, field placement, or interest that is currently open for comments. Submit a comment on this regulation.

All of the following resources discuss the process of submitting comments and/or best practices for doing it well. Pick at least one of these to read as you prepare your public comment:

https://www.regulations.gov/docs/Tips_For_Submitting_Effective_Comments.pdf

https://www.regulations.gov/faqs

https://www.reginfo.gov/public/jsp/Utilities/faq.jsp

http://www.foreffectivegov.org/node/4059

http://eli-ocean.org/wp-content/blogs.dir/2/files/Written-Commenting.pdf

There is often confusion—and sometimes partisan debate—around whether a law (either legislation or regulation) is being implemented as intended or whether it applies in specific situations. In such cases, the law can be challenged through the courts of the judicial branch—potentially all the way up to the Supreme Court. Depending on the context of the challenge, the judiciary branch can rule on: (1) whether Congress correctly passed the law under the Constitution, (2) whether in implementing the law, the executive branch is correctly applying **legislative intent** (what Congress had in mind in passing the law), and (3) whether implementation of the law is consistent with the Constitution. Federal courts can uphold the entire law or declare the entire law unconstitutional. (While this isn't a history book, the process by which this choice developed is fascinating—see the Resources section of this chapter for more information.) However, federal courts often choose to find a middle ground, resulting in striking changes in the way a law may ultimately be implemented. One example of a middle ground ruling with far-reaching implications was the 2012 Supreme Court ruling in *National Federation of Independent Business v. Sebelius*. This ruling determined the Affordable Care Act's constitutionality, but struck down its requirement that all 50 states must expand Medicaid to low-income adults (The Henry J. Kaiser Family Foundation 2012).

State Government

The US government is a **federalist system** (Ishiyama and Breuning 2010), in which power is shared between state governments and a central government in one political system. In crafting this system, the U.S. Constitution very specifically and deliberately states, "The powers not delegated to the United States by the Constitution, nor prohibited by it to the States, are reserved to the States respectively, or to the people" (Constitution of the United States of America: Analysis and Interpretation 2016). This is a critical point in understanding the unique system of government in the USA—*all* governmental powers (though exactly what this means is subject to interpretation) that are not explicitly granted to the federal government within the Constitution belong to the 50 states (or the people) (The White House n.d.). Therefore, while the federal government has a great deal of power, there are many issues for which it is necessary or more effective to influence policy through **state governments**.

The role of state governments in policy-making saw an expansion during the latter half of the twentieth century and in the early part of the twenty-first century, through mechanisms such as **block grants**. Prior to the emergence of block grants, states were often required to implement certain federal programs (e.g., Aid to Families with Dependent Children) as designed by the federal government. In contrast, block grants give states a specific amount of federal money. The federal government broadly defines how the states are expected to use this money, but states have substantial authority to determine their own processes for eligibility, benefits, and other aspects of policy implementation (What Is a Block Grant? 2016). Block grants provide more discretion and flexibility for states than a typical federal program administered by the states. However, it is important to note that block grants are often instituted in order to place limits on federal expenditures; this then reduces the availability of funding to meet increases in need.

Block grants are used for programs as diverse as community development and income support (social welfare) and, at the time of this writing, have been proposed for Medicaid (Luthra 2017).

All 50 states are governed by their own legislature, executive branch (led by the governor), and judicial branch, with the three branches in each state performing the same basic functions as those described above. State structures may differ slightly, as defined by each state's Constitution. For example, unlike Congress and 49 other states, Nebraska's legislature is a **unicameral legislature**, meaning that there is only one house in its legislative body (Nebraska Legislature n.d.).

Each state also has a regulatory process similar to that of the federal government, through which state agencies develop regulations to implement state laws (see an example from Washington State in the Resource section). State-level regulatory processes may be of particular interest for political social workers interested in policy issues such as child welfare, mental health care provision, nursing home guidelines, social work licensing, etc., which are guided heavily by regulations by state government regulations.

Municipal Government

Within the USA, each of us lives within at least one local municipality: a town, village, city, parish, and/or county. **Municipal governments** manage issues at the local level. The names for municipal government structures vary. In Louisiana, your Parish Police Jury serves the same role as a Township Committee might in New Jersey or a City Council in Michigan. In Virginia, a Board of County Supervisors might govern your county, whereas in Texas, your county is governed by a Commissioners Court. Municipalities provide many services that touch our everyday lives. States often set parameters for how much power municipalities may have. This differs by state, but in some cases, may also differ by type or size of municipality within a state. In one example, the Georgia Constitution prescribes 16 different services that a municipality may provide (Chambers 2016):

- Police and fire protection
- Garbage and solid-waste collection and disposal
- Public health facilities and services
- Street and road construction and maintenance
- Parks, recreational areas, programs, and facilities
- Storm-water and sewage collection and disposal systems
- Water development, storage, treatment, purification, and distribution
- Public housing
- Public transportation
- Libraries, archives, and arts and sciences programs and facilities
- Terminal and dock facilities and parking facilities
- Codes, including building, housing, plumbing, and electrical
- Air-quality control
- Creation, modification, and maintenance of retirement or pension systems for local-government employees

- Planning, zoning, and community redevelopment

Some social workers may question whether many of these issues are relevant to social work; however, we encourage you to think and reflect on the ramifications each of these types of services may have for the well-being of vulnerable communities and for issues of social or environmental justice. Consider one initiative of cities across the country: to "respond to racial tensions in their communities and address the historical, systemic and structural barriers that further inequity and racism in our nation's cities" (National League of Cities 2016b). In a jarring example, an in-depth 2017 article in *The Atlantic* (see the full article in the Resource section) explores the decades-long persistence of lead poisoning among children living in New Orleans public housing developments (Newkirk 2017). Lead poisoning is known to have negative physical and behavioral impacts on children, along with lowered IQ scores. Despite consistent cases of children testing positive for high levels of lead, the city resisted efforts to abate lead in its public housing units or remediate lead present in city public parks.

A municipal charter generally defines the structure of a municipal government. A charter defines the organization, powers, functions, and essential procedures of the municipal government, although some structure also might come from the state constitution and laws (National League of Cities 2016a). Municipalities are most likely to use one of five major forms of organization: council-manager, mayor-council, commission, town meeting, or representative town meeting. Nearly 90% of US municipalities use either the council-manager system (where an elected city council oversees policy and budget and hires a nonelected professional administrator to oversee the day-to-day operations of the town) or the mayor-council system (where an elected council has legislative power, but a separately elected mayor has significant administrative and budgetary power).

District of Columbia and Puerto Rico

The District of Columbia (D.C.) and Puerto Rico deserve a special note here because their government does not fit the "level of government" model discussed above, and often leaves them with less representation and power than other US citizens (Duany 2017; Raven-Hansen 1974–1975). D.C. is a federal district, overseen by Congress, with the city of Washington inside it. The legislative body of the district is the Council of the District of Columbia, with 13 members including the chairman (often called the mayor). Every law passed by the Council is subject to congressional review (Council of the District of Columbia 2017). Puerto Rico is a commonwealth or unincorporated organized territory, with its own constitution, where the U.S. Constitution only partially applies. The legislative body is the Legislative Assembly of Puerto Rico, with a 27-seat Senate and a 51-seat House of Representatives (Ballotpedia n.d.).

Sources of Information for Your External Assessment

Now that you have the information necessary to determine which level of government is your focus, you are ready to gather indicator data to answer the three external assessment questions (social, economic, and political contexts) outlined at the beginning of this section. A good place to begin is to access and review reputable online sources, including government data, think tank reports, and reports issued by various research centers (see Resource section for a guide to assessing online resources).

Media sources that regularly cover the specific environment with which you are concerned are key sources of information. If you are trying to understand the political context within which policy decisions are being made at a federal level, *The Washington Post* is generally a must-read. If, for example, you are trying to assess the external context for a policy change at the state level in Texas, the media source that you would likely find most helpful is *The Texas Tribune*, as it regularly provides in-depth coverage of both politics and policy issues within the Texas legislature. There may be a newspaper or blog in your local municipality that covers the critical behind-the-scene dynamics of your local government, like the *Valley Independent Sentinel*, which covers several small towns in Connecticut.

While much of the information you need to answer the three external assessment questions is available online and through media sources, no amount of research on your computer can take the place of going out into the community and talking with people individually to get their perspectives of the social, economic, and political situation. This first-hand gathering of information is critical in political social work, especially because how people *feel* about their environment (and therefore potentially how they vote) sometimes differs substantially from the *reality* shown by data. For example, Pew Research Center finds that while national crime statistics showed a double-digit drop in crime rates between 2008 and 2015, the majority of 2016 voters believed that crime rates instead increased during that time period (Gramlich 2016).

The key to gathering information from people and groups in your political context is to engage your core social work practice skills, such as active listening (Cournoyer 2008b). As you meet with people to learn about the political context, listen more than you talk. Stay present, take notes, and reflect back what you hear to be sure you have understood them correctly. Also keep in mind that you will get different (sometimes wildly different) impressions of the same political situation from different stakeholders, just as you would if you were gathering information from different members of a family that you might work with in a clinical setting. Be thoughtful about the information you share from one interview to the next, and be respectful of the privacy of those who tell you their experiences. Consider a variety of ways of interacting with people. Regularly attending community events will give you a long-term sense of community issues and perspectives, while interviews or focus groups will give you a snapshot.

Where possible, supplement individual and group perspectives with resources such as polling data, letters to the editor in the community's newspapers, or engaging with people through online groups. Economic data can be located through local chambers of commerce, regional economic development councils or statewide departments of labor or economic development commissions. A community's perceptions of the economic climate might be understood through polls on economic anxiety or consumer confidence (Marketplace 2015). Those who live in different types of communities or who have different identities perceive these economic data in significantly different ways (American Psychological Association 2017). Combining bigger data with individual interactions can help you see a more nuanced picture.

APPLY YOUR SKILLS: Assessing the External Environment
Using the political change you identified in Stages 1 and 2 of this chapter, identify the appropriate level of government on which to focus. Briefly conduct an assessment in response to each of the three external environment questions (social, economic, and political contexts) posed in this section. What are your core findings? What are some ways in which these findings might impact the viability of your political change at this time?

A Special Note: Helping Clients and Client Systems Assess Their Political Context

Before we move on to the next section of this chapter, take a moment to consider how you can use the information you've learned so far in this chapter as an empowerment tool for the clients or communities with whom you work. What information about their political context is available and easily accessible to those in the community or local agencies? All social workers can incorporate this political information and assessment into practice with clients, whether or not your primary professional focus is political social work.

Whether we are educating clients about the voting process, providing resources that make it possible for community members to engage with their elected officials, or working with communities to create political power through voting or advocating, *all* social workers have the opportunity to increase the political empowerment of their clients. Social workers who work with clients who are unable to vote, perhaps because of their age, immigration status, or due to a felony conviction can help their clients find other ways to have their voices heard. Note: As we will discuss elsewhere in this book, in some states, ex-felons face substantial barriers to regaining the right to vote after completing their sentence (National Conference of State Legislatures 2016). Without asking, you may not know if your clients are interested in the political process. Leaving political power out of our assessment and work with clients and communities is disempowering, and antithetical to the values of the social work profession.

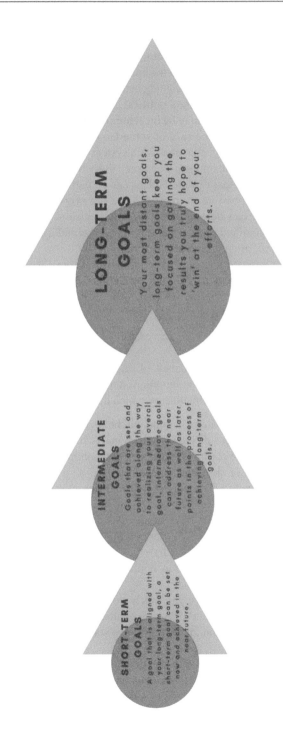

Fig. 5.1 Relationships between advocacy goals

Section 5: Identifying Political Social Work Goals (Stage 3)

In other parts of your social work program, you have likely learned a great deal about setting goals with your clients or other constituencies. In political social work, you also need to set goals as part of designing and implementing well-planned strategy. Thus, the third stage of planning a political change strategy is to identify the change effort's goals. These goals may be **incremental** and move you in small steps toward your overall goal or, in the case of some large-scale advocacy campaigns, focused on **fundamental** change that changes a system or a policy at its roots.

Goals guide our strategic planning and can keep us focused as we begin to engage with the real-life messiness that is politics. This can be particularly helpful at times when it no longer seems possible for us to achieve our original goal(s). Clarity in what we are aiming for can help us make difficult decisions such as whether to move from our ideal goal and instead put our energy behind a possible **fall-back position**, an alternative, often less-than-ideal goal.

A helpful tool for approaching strategizing in political social work practice is to apply the SMART Goal mnemonic (Cournoyer 2008a). As you develop goals for your political social work efforts, specify goals that meet the following criteria:

Specific—are very clear
Measurable—you know if you are successfully making progress toward your goals
Achievable—can practically be attained, given the external environment
Realistic—are based on realistic assumptions about your internal context
Time-bound—have a specific timeline by which they need to be achieved

Keeping the SMART Goal criteria in mind will help you craft goals that can meet your needs as well as the needs of the organizational and political contexts within which you are working. Goal clarity also can help you continually evaluate progress throughout your advocacy or electoral campaign.

In setting goals, we need to distinguish between different types of change goals, split up by time-frame (Breitrose 2011):

Short-term goals: These are typically achievable within a short timeframe, providing your effort with proximal benchmarks to meet. They move you closer to achieving one or more of your intermediate goals. Achieving short-term policy-focused goals often provides celebration opportunities as you continue to work toward your long-term goals.

Intermediate goals: These move you much closer to your overall goals. They serve as building blocks toward your long-term goal(s). Like short-term goals, these can provide celebration opportunities that motivate staff or volunteers involved in the change effort.

Long-term goals: These focus on the specific policy or political outcomes you want to have achieved at the end of your change effort. Long-term goals often require more time and effort, and build upon achieving your short-term and intermediate goals (Fig. 5.1).

In setting these goals, think carefully about the kinds of change you want to achieve through your political efforts. Goals for any *particular* effort may not necessarily be the same as the policy change we are *ultimately* working to achieve. Why? Because often in politics and policy, we do not achieve our preferred policy change on our first try. While we certainly aim high and hope that we achieve our preferred change quickly, it is also the reality of politics that it typically takes many years for legislation to move from the idea stage to being enacted into law. So, while we may have a long-term goal of getting House Bill 235 passed by our state legislature, our short-term goal for this legislative session may more realistically be for the bill to have a committee hearing. In terms of electoral campaigns, it is not uncommon for candidates to lose races before winning election to their desired office. Even strong campaigners such as Bill Clinton, George W. Bush, and Barack Obama lost their first Congressional races, before later being elected president of the USA.

The contextual assessments we conducted in Section 4 can help us identify appropriate goals for our specific effort. In a political environment where our bill is not favored by the political party in power, our advocacy campaign's short-term and intermediate goals may need to look different than they would with a different political make-up of the legislature. (This may even mean that we will also want to consider an electoral strategy, to change the makeup of the legislature.) Similarly, short-term and intermediate goals for an electoral campaign might differ based on the nature of the current political climate. For example, is this likely to be a "**wave election**," an election where one political party is expected to make substantial gains in the number of seats it holds, shifting the political status quo? Is this wave expected to be in our candidate's direction or away from it, and if so, how might that impact the numbers of voters we need to get to the polls?

Section 6: Identifying and Selecting Targets (Stage 4)

Once your goals are clearly defined, the fourth stage of a political strategy is to select the *specific* **targets** of your political change effort. That is, you need to determine who will be the focus of your efforts to bring about your goals. We start this target selection process by assessing key players with the power to influence whether or not your specified goals can be achieved.

Key Players in a Political Context

Often social workers and others assume that only legislators or the executive (mayor, governor, president) can make policy change. In reality, there are a significant number of other individuals who can play key determinative roles in making policy change. Such individuals may include those responsible for policy changes within executive branch agencies, those who can control access to other key players, and those who can assert influence from outside of government. In the authors' social work careers, we have served as staff members in legislative offices, worked for executive agencies, and conducted research that influenced policy, all roles in which we had the opportunity to create change as well as to influence other key decision-makers. Below, we outline how to identify and assess key players and the power they have to influence policy changes.

As you meet with individuals who are politically involved within your context, ask them questions such as: *Who else should I get to know? Who really understands this process/issue/problem?* You will find that from answers to these questions as well as from discussions with your contacts, you will be able to create a list of the key players in your area. Make this a living document—one that you constantly update as key players are elected, retire, move, or gain prominence. (Keep this document safe and backed up in multiple locations. Use a password-protected flash drive <u>and</u> cloud storage!)

Key Players in Government

At all levels of government, there are potential key players who have the power to make decisions around the policy issues in which you are interested. Some of these key players are obvious and in very visible positions—e.g., the president and members of Congress, the governor and members of the state legislature, or the elected leaders of your municipality. Others are less obvious and, therefore, may need to be sought out.

Executive Branch Players

As described earlier in this chapter, a tremendous amount of policy-making happens within executive branch agencies at all levels of government. Therefore, one set of key governmental players are those in the executive branch with the direct ability to influence policy through the regulatory, budgetary, and implementation processes (Hoefer 2016). These include presidents, governors, and mayors, as well as leaders of executive branch agencies (e.g., the Secretary of Education and her deputy and assistant secretaries). Political social workers also work with career and appointed (political) staffers within executive branch agencies who write regulations. They work with municipal, state, and federal government agency staffers charged with implementing legislation and those involved in writing draft versions of municipal, state, and federal government **budgets**. Budgets are documents that lay out a government's proposed spending and revenue and are a critical way to communicate and reinforce policy priorities.

Legislative Branch Players

Legislative bodies provide a window into many ways in which someone may be considered a key player or decision-maker. All US citizens have elected officials in their municipal, state, and federal legislatures who specifically represent their home and the district in which they live. Even if you are not a US citizen, these elected officials have responsibility for the well-being of your neighborhood and community. As a constituent of these elected officials, your direct representatives are the ones most likely to be responsive to your efforts to influence them. They are, essentially, your employees—which makes you their boss.

As you identify a legislative target(s), it is helpful to understand the approximate number of constituents each legislator serves. The 400 members of New Hampshire's State House of Representatives represent about 3300 New Hampshirites each. In contrast, the most populous state, California, has only 80 members of the lower house (the California State Assembly), so each member represents about 475,000 Californians. Accordingly, in designing an advocacy strategy, it is important to know that it will be easier to gain the attention of a New Hampshire representative by rallying her constituents than doing so to try to get the attention of a California state assembly member.

In addition to your direct representative, other members of these legislative bodies have power to influence your policy issues. In particular, this includes those who serve on legislative committees that oversee policy in your area, hold official or unofficial leadership positions, or can participate in floor votes related to your policy area of interest. If you are working within the Nebraska Unicameral Legislature, with only 49 total legislators or in Alaska with 60 legislators, it is important to realize that each one of these members has a significant amount of comparative power. If you are working in New Hampshire, with 424 senators and representatives in its General Court (that is not a typo; the next biggest legislature is Pennsylvania's with 253), each member has proportionally less power (National Conference of State Legislators 2013a). You would need to build relationships with a larger percentage of these members.

The National Conference of each state legislature's keeps track of state legislatures' leadership. View your legislature's leaders on the list in the Resource section (National Conference of State Legislators 2017). This list can help you find out how many members hold leadership positions, although some titles may not clearly tell you what the leader does. For example, one common leadership position is a **whip**, generally responsible for "counting votes." This person is responsible for knowing how many members are planning to vote for their party's proposals (National Conference of State Legislatures 2013b). Of Connecticut's 36 state senators, 25 hold leadership positions; 18 of Hawaii's 51 state representatives are leaders.

Formal leadership positions do not necessarily tell you much about how power is actually held in a legislature, or who possesses influential informal power. Legislative bodies commonly have distinct power dynamics that influence policy outcomes. These dynamics differentially determine individual members' ability to influence final results. Some dynamics are related to the political party distribution within a legislative body. Other dynamics have to do with the personalities and leadership approaches of those elected to legislative leadership positions. For example, New York's state government's leadership style is often described as "three men in a room," meaning that the governor, majority leader of the State Senate, and speaker of the State Assembly "work in secret and without accountability to decide most vital issues" (Santora 2015). Worth noting: In recent years, the men holding two of the three of those offices have been convicted of corruption—one more reason that more social workers can and should be elected officials (Clark 2016).

Many legislators at all levels of government have long-standing interpersonal and professional relationships among themselves that influence whether they entertain different pieces of legislation. Leaders of opposing parties may have a positive relationship in which they communicate regularly with each other, as was the case between former Senators Tom Daschle (D-SD) and Trent Lott (R-MS) when they were the U.S. Senate majority and minority leaders. Their friendship remained strong long after, including authoring a book together (Lott et al. 2016). In other cases, leaders of different parties may refuse to be in the same room together, as reported about Illinois state leaders in 2015 (Kadner 2015).

Other interpersonal dynamics also shape the informal power structure within legislatures. For example, it is not uncommon for legislative leadership to "punish" a member who acts in a way that they do not approve of. This might involve assigning the member to less influential committees or even burying all legislation that the member proposes. Such dynamics are important to learn as you prepare to pursue any political endeavor. For example, if you are planning a run for office, are there elected officials, who, if they were to endorse your campaign, would result in other officials refusing to support the campaign? Would work with members on the "other side of the aisle" or for an unpopular executive mean that members of the party you identify with would essentially disown you?

To effectively influence policy, political social workers need to learn about legislative power dynamics. Start by creating relationships with those who work regularly in the legislature. Refer to websites such as Vote Smart that can provide you with basic information about your elected officials, including those in the state and federal legislatures and executive offices. You also can find useful information about key players from the editorial and opinion pages of your local newspaper, popular accounts on social media, and websites and meetings of legislative bodies and your local political parties.

While not always feasible, the best way to assess legislative power dynamics is by immersing yourself in the political contexts you seek to influence. Former social work student Chenelle's reflection on her experiences interning in a state legislature demonstrates the depth of learning about informal politics that one can gain through immersion.

A REFLECTION ON POLITICAL DYNAMICS AND POWER IN A STATE LEGISLATURE: The Grey Area in Politics
By Chenelle Hammonds, University of Houston Graduate College of Social Work Austin Legislative Internship Program intern

My time serving as an intern during the Texas 85th Legislature was extremely informative. Perhaps one of the biggest lessons I learned during my time here is that politics is not black and white; voting decisions and political stances are not always as simple as a vote with Republicans or a vote with Democrats, at least in Texas anyway. Before arriving, I previously thought that Republicans and Democrats, for the most part, voted a certain way and

(continued)

seldom agreed with one another. However, after being here I've learned that various other "factions" exist beyond political affiliation. In Texas there seem to be "coalitions" formed along geographical lines, and between rural and urban elected officials. Often times there would be debates between rural members on issues specific to their districts like water access and the abatement of feral hogs, which would then turn into pretty contentious debates against members representing more urban districts. Sometimes there would even be division between urban districts as well, with members from large-city districts forming their own coalitions to advocate for issues unique to their cities (i.e., Houston delegation, Dallas delegation, Austin delegation, etc.). Some of the more prominent issues that created a division between large cities were property tax relief reform, pensions for local firefighters, and state-wide regulations for ridesharing applications like Uber and Lyft. To see Democrats and Republicans come together as members of rural districts, or come together as members of the Houston Delegation was something that I had not anticipated prior to my experience in the legislature. While it was pleasing to witness bipartisanship across party lines, it was also a bit concerning seeing bickering *within* the two political parties.

In the Texas Legislature you have intraparty divisions, most notably between "Conservative Democrats," "Moderate Republicans," and "Freedom Caucus Republicans." Similarly, it was not uncommon to see Conservative or Southern-border Democrats supporting pro-life legislation or voting for measures that reinforce traditional gender definitions. Interestingly enough, I would witness moderate Republicans like Representative Sarah Davis standing up for gay rights and a woman's right to choose. I was moved to see Republicans like Representative Byron Cook stand up against the "Show Me Your Papers" amendment to Senate Bill 4 and tell his Republican colleagues to follow suit. Although he authored a bill requiring burials for aborted fetal remains, interestingly enough, he also carried HB 3771 which removed ectopic pregnancy surgery from the State definition of abortion and withheld various overreaching pro-life bills (like women being charged with murder for abortions). He also kept bills like the bathroom bill (the "Texas Right to Privacy Act") and ending in-state tuition for DREAMers from passing out of committee as Chairman of the House State Affairs Committee. Others like Republican Representative John Zerwas came out publicly against school choice vouchers and the "bathroom bill."

Representative J.D. Sheffield, another moderate Republican and a physician, stood with Democrats this session against anti-vaccine measures and attempted to pass bills aimed at educating parents about the life-saving benefits of vaccinations. He also was the lone member of the House Republican caucus last session who voted against campus carry. Hence, the lines between "Republican" and "Democrat" in the Texas legislature can sometimes be blurred. This gave me a bit of hope, seeing that even in such a hostile political

(continued)

climate as we are living in today, there are still elected officials who believe in voting their conscience, voting for what's right, and not merely "cosigning" on whatever positions their colleagues have taken.

Moreover, one might find it strange to know that even the most hard-line Conservatives in the Texas legislature, known as the "Texas Freedom Caucus," actually worked alongside Democrats on a few issues. Most notably, the Freedom Caucus and House Democrats joined forces on two key pieces of legislation relating to criminal justice reform authored by Representative Harold Dutton: HB 122 which proposed raising the age of criminal responsibility to 18, and HB 152 which would have allowed offenders to make an appeal to restore their constitutional rights if previously convicted in Texas. To my surprise, coming to the defense of Representative Dutton's proposed justice reforms were Tea Party members like Representative Matt Schaefer and Representative Jonathan Stickland urging other Republicans to vote with them in support of these bills. Even more shocking was hearing one of the most Conservative members in the Texas House and Tea Party member Representative Kyle Biedermann admit that he had been staunchly against raising the criminal age of responsibility to 18, but after hearing countless testimonies arguing about the positive impact this law would have on Texas, he shifted to support of this law. Although both of these criminal justice bills ended up dying eventually, it was astounding to see the same Republicans who caught heat this session for killing hundreds of good bills and tacking on controversial amendments to others be amenable to siding with the Dems on a few important issues. (The "strengths-based perspective" is coming in handy right now!)

So why is this information important to know for social workers? As social workers, we are likely to encounter other professionals in the workplace who have different values, perspectives, and ethics from us. We may not always agree with a colleague's value system or their perspective on what is the best way to handle social issues that harm our clients or even the logistics behind a not-for-profit startup; however, we must still work together. What my time in the Texas Legislature has taught me the most is that common ground can be found even among the unlikeliest of sources. Dismissing others whom you seemingly disagree with "on paper" only takes away opportunities for teamwork, coalition building, and community advancement for the greater common good. Although we all have our own set of beliefs, whether they be informed by our life experiences, our careers, our political identification, etc., we all can stand to put personal differences aside and focus on what we *can* agree on. Due to the complexities of social work practice, which is inundated with several "grey areas," I encourage all of us to dig a little deeper for that common ground each time we find ourselves conflicted by personal disagreements both in and outside of the workplace.

Previously posted online at the blog of the University of Houston Graduate College of Social Work's Austin Legislative Internship Program: https://gcsw-legislativeinterns.wordpress.com.

Judicial Branch Players

Political social workers also work with judiciary branch clerks and other judicial staff in order to create policy change. While judges make the ultimate rulings in the judiciary branch and cannot be directly lobbied outside of the courtroom, relationships with clerks and judicial staff can be a helpful source of information. One common way for social workers to work through the judiciary branch is through submitting **amicus curiae**, or "friend of the court" briefs that offer information relevant to the case under consideration. (A great resource for social work in the judicial policy realm is *Social Work and Law: Judicial Policy and Forensic Practice* by Sunny Harris Rome (2012)).

Key Interest Group Players

Interest groups are often referred to as special interest groups (SIGs), advocacy groups, lobbying groups, pressure groups, or special interests (Hoefer 2016). Members and leaders of these groups are key players in the political process. These include interest groups that share a concern with you, as well as lobbyists and advocates working for these interest groups who have a thorough understanding of legislative or regulatory processes. In some cases, they already work on your issues or in support of your campaigns. In other cases, you will want to develop a relationship with these players.

Significant interest group players may have power via a key endorsement that helps a candidate stand out in a crowded field. They may be able to access donors who can contribute to an advocacy or electoral campaign. They may help you establish relationships with legislators who will be willing to take a meeting with you if the right person recommends it. They also can be great sources of information about what they have learned through successes and failures in past legislative sessions or election cycles.

Key Players in Media

As discussed above, the media play a key role in the political context in the USA. A 2013 survey of social workers in Texas (Felderhoff et al. 2015) found that respondents got their political news most frequently from Internet-based news services (69%), public radio (49%), conversations with friends and family (58%), television news (53%), newspapers (51%), social media (43%), public television (42%), email newsletters (42%), and television news stations (30%). Those who control the way news about the political world is reported and shaped in these circles are key players in the political process.

Both traditional and social media influence what information about the political realm gets to voters, policy-makers, and other stakeholders. Social media plays a key role in today's politics—or, if you ask some people, is ruining it (Carr 2015). Two-thirds of Americans use Facebook, and half of them get their news from that site, totaling 30% of the US population (Anderson and Caumont 2014). If you add in YouTube, Twitter, and Reddit, the social media landscape's influence on how the public views elections and policy becomes even more significant. In 2013, the national periodical *Campaigns and Elections* named 50 of the most influential people in national politics; of these, 13 had connections to digital and social media (Campaigns & Elections Staff 2013). The methods and strategies used by politicians and the media to communicate with the public have changed significantly in the last 20 years, and continue to change rapidly. The rise of partisan cable news and the methods used to gain audience by those networks (Sobieraj and Berry 2011), as well as the extensive use of Twitter by President Donald Trump to communicate his message directly to the public, highlight a remarkably different environment in political news.

While alternative media sources have increased their influence, those who investigate and report the news in traditional media sources (including newspapers, television, and radio) still wield considerable influence in shaping public opinion and in publicizing candidates or issues. Later in this book, we provide an in-depth discussion of how to identify the specific reporters (targets) who are most likely to influence media coverage on your specific policy issue.

Other Key Policy Players in the Community

As discussed previously, many sources of power accrue to specific individuals and groups within our local, state, or national communities. These sources of power (money, information, status, etc.) can result in key players who are able to influence policy, even without specific positions in government, interest groups, or media. For example, numerous articles and interviews appeared after the inauguration of President Donald Trump, writing about the persistent influence of the billionaire Mercer family on Trump's campaign and policy decisions (Fresh Air 2017). Similar stories have been written about the influence of George Soros on Democratic campaigns and elected officials (Vogel 2016).

Coalitions are another type of community player with the capacity to influence policy. A coalition is a collection of organizations that comes together for a common goal (Bobo et al. 2010). They are commonly used as part of political change efforts, with many advantages for social change. (A variety of coalitions are listed in the Resources section as examples.) Coalitions may be defined by an issue (e.g., Religious Coalition for Reproductive Choice), geographic area (e.g., Midwest Coalition for Human Rights), constituency (e.g., African-American Health Coalition), and often by a combination of those. They may work on one issue or on a range of issues, or even in support of an electoral campaign. Coalitions frequently bring in several types of collective power: the power of the people, the power of knowledge (when they include groups of experts), the power of networks, the power of solidarity, and the power of passion for a cause.

Some coalitions are temporary, coming together for a short period of time (e.g., one legislative session) to work together on a single policy change strategy. Others are permanent, working together year after year on issues of interest to the coalition's member organizations. For example, CAC2 (the Coalition Against Childhood

Cancer; a link is provided in the Resources section) has dozens of member organizations and has worked since 2011 to unify organizations working on solutions to childhood cancer. They coordinate their actions, leverage the strength of their community, and work to minimize duplication of effort by multiple organizations.

Before embarking on a political change strategy, identify whether there are any coalitions already working on your policy issue and which individuals and organizations are part of this coalition. As some coalitions are stronger and more effective than others, assess the power and influence that this coalition has previously had on relevant policy decision-makers. As part of your strategy, you may want to consider joining up with a larger coalition or creating your own.

BUILD YOUR KNOWLEDGE and APPLY YOUR SKILLS: Finding Key Players
Create a map of the key players in your state or municipal political context. Include key players in government, interest groups, media, and/or communities. Start by following a key player in government or media on their column, blog, Twitter, or Facebook. Add to your map other key players who are mentioned, retweeted, followed, or connected. How are they connected? Use the layout of your map to show which players have higher numbers of connections. Do those with more connections seem to be more influential?

Selecting Targets

As you identify the specific key players who can most help bring your proposed policy change to fruition, you are developing a list of individuals who both have power over your specific area of policy interest and are located in your specific geographic area of interest. This forms the basis for "targeting" in political social work. In examining the various key players that you have identified, now it is time to determine who, specifically, is your target(s); that is, who has the direct power to make possible the particular policy goals you seek.

Understanding Your Target

Once you identify your target(s), it is critical that you seek to understand as much as you can about what factors influence them. This is where a tool like the Decision-Maker Matrix can come in handy, as it provides you with a clear framework for identifying potential contextual and personal factors that affect your target's decision-making process.

POLITICAL SOCIAL WORKER PROFILE: Sally Tamarkin, MSW
Senior Editor, Buzzfeed Health (Fig. 5.2).

Fig. 5.2 Sally Tamarkin, MSW

Sally grew up and attended public school in New Haven, CT. "I grew up going to schools that were racially and economically diverse... and I had a seed planted in me at a very young age about equality and justice." Identifying as both a queer person and a person with privilege, Sally feels that she was able to recognize the marginalization of people around her. In Sally's early work for Leadership, Education & Athletics in Partnership (LEAP), she was introduced to the community development aspect of social work. She realized that the social work lens to community organizing "gelled with my interests and also my approach to making change."

With an MSW focused on community organizing, her career path included work at Planned Parenthood of Southern New England, "training college students around the state on how to do organizing and political advocacy around reproductive justice" and then as an organizer for ctEQUALITY, formerly known as the Anti-Discrimination Coalition. The main focus of the Coalition at the time was to "get a bill passed that would add gender identity and gender expression to Connecticut state non-discrimination law." Prior efforts on this bill had not made it out of committee in multiple legislative sessions. Sally was hired to try to bring the whole coalition together as one cohesive unit. "My job was to take the infrastructure that was already there, and strengthen it" by building a bigger base, reaching more people around the state, and working more with lobbyists to connect to representatives. A lot of Sally's work involved empowering people from all backgrounds to become involved in the political process. She held trainings where lobbyists explained to community members how to become citizen activists.

The coalition "was trying to get queer identified people to stand up for rights that didn't have to do with same sex marriage, which was a very big deal at the time." In order to get new people involved in the fight, Sally made education and awareness-raising an important part of her organizing

(continued)

activities. The goal was for more people to see and understand the extent to which transgender people in Connecticut were being denied basic civil and human rights. It was difficult to get people to rally around trans rights in 2010, so a lot of the organizing work centered around educating the community on what trans folks needed and where their rights were being limited. When the citizens of CT became empowered, they were better equipped to make their representatives feel that they were demanding equality in their state. This, along with the tireless work of a lobbyist and coalition volunteers and the allyship of the governor and several outspoken legislators helped pass the bill.

Currently, Sally is a senior editor for Buzzfeed Health. Even though Sally is not practicing social work in a traditional setting, her social work background is integrated into her outlook and informs her work. She feels that social work values and the Code of Ethics influence everything she does in her current position. "I believe that the Code of Ethics set social work aside from any other 'helping' profession," Sally says. She presents stories that counter the "mainstream narratives around health and our bodies, particularly the bodies of women and queer people," which present bodies as only a means for consumption. Sally cites her social work education as the reason she feels empowered to bring these stories to light with "compassion, generosity, humility, and an open mind."

Section 7: Selecting Tactics for Political Intervention (Stage 5)

The fifth and final stage of the political strategy planning process is selecting tactics that are likely to influence your target. To carry out a political strategy, you need to identify specific activity steps, also known as **tactics**, which will help you move forward toward achieving your goals. Tactics are "short-term activities undertaken as part of a change-oriented strategy" (Hardina 2002). Think of them as the actions that will make your change happen.

Too often, we let our preferred tactics lead our political change efforts. For example, we may think protests are a great way to get our voice heard, so we plan a protest before strategically thinking through whether a protest is actually the most effective tactic for our priority goals and our intended targets. Bobo et al. (2001) underscore this point in their handbook for community organizers and advocates for social change, stating, "The worst mistake an organizer can make is to act tactically instead of strategically" (p. 49). Hardina (2002) notes that rather than selecting tactics on the basis of the specific political situation or one's resources, tactic selection is too often guided by personal values or one's comfort level with tactics.

Instead, selected tactics should be carefully chosen as part of your strategic planning process. They should be chosen on the basis of what will best support your full strategy. That is, what tactics will help you build the leverage necessary to persuade your target(s) to advance the policy goal(s) you have identified? In this tactic selection process, decisions are made such as: whether an advocacy organization will hold a protest at the City Council steps or, instead, recruit community members to provide testimony at the next City Council meeting. Similarly, tactic selection is involved when deciding whether a political campaign will seek to shape perceptions of its opponent via a commercial on local TV or through a Facebook ad.

Careful and intentional selection of tactics is crucial to effective political strategy. Selection of tactics needs to be logical and systematic, but also creative and flexible. Key considerations in selecting tactics (Bobo et al. 2001) include:

- *Which tactics are most likely to help you achieve your goals?* Tactics should be linked <u>directly</u> to the types of goals you are seeking. If you are raising money for your campaign, do so in direct service of your campaign goals. For example, if your electoral campaign decides to hold a press event, it should be for the purpose of making the message of your campaign clear. Getting press for the sake of garnering attention will not further your goal.
- *Which tactics are most likely to influence your target?* Tactics should be selected based on your knowledge about your target(s), contextual influences on your target, and your relationship with the target. A classic episode of the TV show, *The West Wing* (although not strictly procedurally accurate) highlights the way that a politician's identification as a grandfather might influence others who are also grandfathers to behave in a certain way (Sorkin 2001).
- *What is your individual and organizational capacity?* Here, we apply our earlier assessments to determine which tactics you and/or your organization are able to carry out effectively (i.e., you wouldn't want to design a strategy that relies on heavy use of TV commercials for your candidate if you do not have a large enough campaign budget to afford this). Avoid spreading yourself or your organization too thinly by taking on too many tactics, leaving none of them to ultimately be effective. Also consider your own power and credibility. Are there tactics that might be perceived as controversial when you use them, even if they would not be perceived that way when used by another actor?
- *What is your organizational style?* Are there certain tactics that are strengths of your organization or campaign? Do you or your organization's leadership have certain preferences in terms of how you approach relationships with decision-makers? For example, during the fight for women's suffrage in the USA, the National American Women's Suffrage Association worked state by state through the conventional legislative process, while the National Women's Party (headed by social worker Alice Paul) instead followed its organizational style, garnering national attention and support through large, attention-grabbing events such as protests that led to arrests (National Park Service n.d.).
- *Do you need to build public sympathy, and are certain tactics worth the risk to public support?* Sometimes tactics might move us closer to persuading our target in the short-term, but might risk harming public support for our goals in the long-term. Weigh the benefits and risks as you select tactics. For example, if large numbers of teachers in a school district call in absent to testify at the state capitol, forcing school to close for the day, is the controversy this may cause among

parents forced to scramble for child care worth the potential benefits from the testimony?

- *Could the tactics you are considering put clients or constituent groups at personal risk?* As social workers, it is important that we engage and empower our constituents to be active and meaningful participants in political change efforts. At times, however, some of the tactics we might consider could have negative repercussions for our constituents. Informed consent and self-determination on the part of our constituencies are important in such situations, as is thoughtful consideration beforehand of potential risks. For example, what are the risks of publicizing a rally on the steps of the capitol featuring speakers who are undocumented at a time when the federal government is engaged in high-profile immigrant raids (de Vogue et al. 2017)? If we think civil disobedience is necessary to further our goals, have we thought through how the risk of being arrested may differentially impact our constituencies based on differences in race, socioeconomic status, immigration status, or sexual orientation?

- *Are the tactics you are considering consistent with the profession's Code of Ethics?*

  The NASW (2017) Code of Ethics clearly identifies a set of six core values of our profession: Social justice, social justice, dignity and worth of the person, importance of human relationships, integrity, and competence. As you evaluate possible tactics, consider whether they support these values. It is not uncommon, however, in selecting tactics to find that these values may be in tension with each other. These considerations are explored in depth in Chap. 13, including sample scenarios related to ethical dilemmas in tactic selection.

It is also important to recognize that tactics that might be effective in one situation might not necessarily work in another similar situation. Teles and Schmitt (2011) point out that over time, political tactics may have declining returns. For example, the tenth time an advocacy organization boycotts a retailer, it may be less effective at changing company policy than the first several times it did so.

As you assess the possible impacts from the tactics you select, keep in mind that tactic selection should be both well-thought-out *and* flexible. Political social workers need to be alert and prepared to course-correct in innovative ways as the political reality moves forward (Teles and Schmitt 2011). Politics around both advocacy and campaigns can shift rapidly, requiring different tactics, even as political social workers must remain focused on their desired goals. Take, for example, the 2016 presidential election. As Michael Barone (2016) argued immediately after that election in the conservative National Review magazine:

> Over the 40-some years that I have been working or closely observing the political-campaign business, the rules of the game haven't changed much. Technology has changed the business somewhat, but the people who ran campaigns in the 1970s could have (and in some cases actually have) run them decades later. But suddenly this year, the rules seemed to change.

Barone (2016) outlines six key changes that he saw during the 2016 presidential election, with potential ramifications for how both advocacy and electoral campaigns select tactics moving forward:

1. Financial expenditures seem less relevant, as the winning presidential campaign spent just more than half as much money as the losing presidential campaign, opting to rely instead on media coverage.
2. Campaign ads on television were less influential than in prior elections, with social media (e.g., tweets and videos) garnering more attention and influence.
3. Celebrity support did not seem to carry as much weight as in prior elections.
4. Voters seeking change were not dissuaded by a candidate's "outrageous statements," when such statements had been disqualifying in prior elections.
5. Campaigns with better "big data" (extensive data on individual voters) had been more successful in recent years. However, in 2016, data seemed less successful if the data were not paired with increasing attention to sensitivity in data interpretation.
6. Campaigns need to increasingly understand how the opposition is thinking, especially when the opposing campaign is choosing not to follow "the old rules."

These changes illustrate the importance of individuals and organizations strategically planning their political tactics, but also underscore two key points we have emphasized in this chapter: (1) being attuned to the changing political context, and (2) remaining flexible enough to adapt your tactics mid-campaign as needed.

APPLY YOUR SKILLS: Tactic Selection
Identify a recent advocacy campaign that you have participated in or one that you learned about through media sources—perhaps the one you used in Stages 1 and 2. What tactics did the advocacy campaign use to try to influence decision-makers? How did decision-makers, supporters, and opponents respond to these tactics?

Review of Key Terms and Concepts

Amicus curia: "friend of the court" briefs that offer information relevant to the case under consideration by a court (plural is amicus curiae).

Bicameral legislature: a law-making body consisting of two chambers. In the USA, this form is used by Congress (the two chambers are the House of Representatives and the Senate) and 49 state legislatures.

Block grant: a set of aid monies awarded to states. States are granted substantial flexibility to implement broadly defined functions such as social welfare programs or health services, while facing fewer requirements than with other types of federal funding.

Budget: document which lays out proposed spending and revenue for a government.

Coalition: a collection of organizations that converge for a common goal. These are commonly used as part of political change efforts, with many advantages for social change.

Economic climate: the perceived atmosphere of an economy, reflecting the status of major markets, the availability of jobs, credit, and other economic issues apparent to the public.

Executive branch: the branch of government responsible for executing laws. On the federal level in the USA, this refers to the president, vice president, cabinet members, and numerous executive branch agencies. At the state level, this generally consists of the governor, statewide elected officials, and other state-level agencies.

Executive order: an order issued by the president, holding the force of law, to another executive branch member or agency, through which the president manages operations of the executive branch of government.

Fall-back position: an alternative goal employed when achieving an original goal no longer seems possible.

Federal government: the level of government responsible for providing policy governance and oversight of the entire USA.

Federalist system: a form of government, used in the USA, in which power between state governments and a central government is shared in one political system.

Fundamental change: change that modifies a system or a policy at its roots.

Incremental change: change executed in small steps to gradually reach an outcome.

Intermediate goals: goals that serve as building blocks toward long-term goals.

Judicial branch: the branch of government that evaluates laws to clarify their meaning, decides how laws apply in specific cases, and (at the federal and state level) determines whether laws meet the requirements of the Constitution.

Long-term goals: goals that focus on the specific desired policy outcomes an advocate seeks to achieve as a result of a change effort.

Municipal governments: governmental bodies responsible for managing policy issues at the local level. May refer to a town, village, city, parish, or county government.

Political climate: a population's perception of the atmosphere of the political realm in a society.

Regulations: rules made and maintained by an executive branch authority, with the force of policy. These often specify implementation details for policies adopted by the legislature.

Regulatory process: a process through which the executive branch agency puts forth, or "promulgates" regulations.

Short-term goals: goals that are typically achievable within an immediate timeframe.

Social climate: the perceived social and psychological context in a given community or group.

State government: the level of government that makes and enforces laws for a state or equivalent subdivision within a country.

Strategy: the art of planning actions directed toward fulfilling the achievement of a goal(s).

SWOT analysis: a strategic review process that entails looking internally at an organization's strengths and weaknesses, and externally at the opportunities and threats in its environment.

Tactics: specific, short-term activity steps which help move change efforts forward toward goal achievement.

Target: the individual(s) with the decision-making power to bring a policy goal into fruition; typically the focus of advocacy efforts.

Unicameral legislature: a law-making body composed of one chamber, such as Nebraska.

Wave election: an election where one political party is expected to make substantial gains in the number of seats it holds, shifting the political status quo.

Whip: a leadership position encompassing the responsibility for counting votes, meaning this person should know how many people are planning to vote for their party's proposals.

Resources

Assessment

University of Kansas Community Tool Box, "SWOT Analysis: Strengths, Weaknesses, Opportunities, and Threats:" http://ctb.ku.edu/en/table-of-contents/assessment/assessing-community-needs-and-resources/swot-analysis/main

Books

Cooper, P. J. (2014). *By order of the President: The use and abuse of executive direct action.* Lawrence, Kansas: University Press of Kansas

Lott, T., Daschle, T., & Sternfeld, J. (2016). *Crisis point: Why we must and how we can overcome our broken politics in Washington and across America.* New York, NY: Bloomsbury Publishing.

Federal Register

In-depth discussion of the regulatory/rulemaking process: https://www.federalregister.gov/uploads/2011/01/the_rulemaking_process.pdf

Main page: https://www.federalregister.gov/

Spreadsheet of executive orders: https://www.federalregister.gov/executive-orders

Coalitions

African American Health Coalition: http://www.flhsa.org/issues/african-american-coalition or go
to http://www.flhsa.org and in the menu under the "Issues" tab click "Health Disparities", then
scroll down to click "African American Health Coaltion" on the right of the page.

Coalition Against Childhood Cancer: www.cac2.org

Midwest Coalition for Human Rights: http://hrlibrary.umn.edu/MCHR.html

Religious Coalition for Reproductive Choice: http://rcrc.org/

Websites

Assessing online sources: http://libguides.adelphi.edu/fake_news

The Atlantic on lead poisoning in New Orleans: "The Poisoned Generation": https://www.theatlantic.
com/politics/archive/2017/05/the-poisoned-generation/527229/

Crisis Point interview: https://dianerehm.org/shows/2016-01-19/former-senators-trent-lott-and-
tom-daschle-crisis-point.

Example of state regulatory process: http://leg.wa.gov/CodeReviser/Documents/registerflowchart.
pdf

Federal Rulemaking Process: An Overview: https://www.fas.org/sgp/crs/misc/RL32240.pdf

Marbury v. Madison (1803): http://www.ourdocuments.gov/doc.php?flash=true&doc=19 or go to
https://www.ourdocuments.gov/ and in the menu on the right hand side of the home page click
"100 milestone documents", then scroll down to click on "Marbury v. Madison (1803)".

National Conference of State Legislators' list of state leaders: http://www.ncsl.org/legislators-staff/
legislators/legislative-leaders/2017-state-legislative-leaders.aspx#tableRegulations related to
health care reform: https://www.federalregister.gov/health-care-reform

Vote Smart to learn about your elected officials: http://votesmart.org/

References

American Psychological Association. (2017). *Stress in America: Coping with change.* Washington,
DC: American Psychological Association. https://www.apa.org/news/press/releases/
stress/2016/coping-with-change.PDF

Anderson, M., & Caumont, A. (2014). *How social media is reshaping news.* http://www.pewre-
search.org/fact-tank/2014/09/24/how-social-media-is-reshaping-news/

Ballotpedia. (n.d.). *Puerto Rico Legislative Assembly.* Retrieved from https://ballotpedia.org/
Puerto_Rico_Legislative_Assembly

Barone, M. 2016, December 18. How the political rules changed in 2016. *National Review.*

Bennett, J. B. (2010). Social climate research. In Corsini (Ed.), *Encyclopedia of psychology.*
Washington, D.C: American Psychological Association.

Bobo, K., Kendall, J., & Max, S. (2001). Developing a strategy. In *Organizing for social change*
(3rd ed., pp. 34–35). Santa Ana, CA: Seven Locks Press.

Bobo, K., Kendall, J., & Max, S. (2010). *Organizing for social change* (4th ed.). Santa Ana, CA:
The Forum Press.

Breitrose, P. (2011). Developing a plan for advocacy. In University of Kansas Work Group for
Community Health and Development (Ed.), *Community tool box.* Lawrence, KS: University
of Kansas.

Campaigns & Elections Staff. (2013, November 17). The influencers 50: Activists. *Campaigns &
Elections.*

Carr, N. (2015, September 2) How social media is ruining politics. *Politico Magazine.*

Chambers, R. L. (2016). *Municipal services*. Retrieved from http://www.georgiaencyclopedia.org/articles/government-politics/municipal-services.

Clark, D. (2016, September 19). Yes, New York has more corrupt officials than any other state. *Politifact New York/The Buffalo News*.

Constitution of the United States of America: Analysis and Interpretation. (2016). Retrieved from https://www.congress.gov/constitution-annotated.

Council of the District of Columbia. (2017). *About us*. Retrieved from http://dccouncil.us/.

Cournoyer, B. (2008a). Contracting. In *The social work skills workbook* (5th ed., pp. 411–442). Belmont, CA: Thomson Higher Education.

Cournoyer, B. (2008b). Talking and listening: The basic interpersonal skills. In *The social work skills workbook* (5th ed., pp. 127–154). Belmont, CA: Thomson Higher Education.

Duany, J. (2017). *Puerto Rico: What everyone needs to know*. Oxford: Oxford University Press.

Felderhoff, B. J., Hoefer, R., & Watson, L. D. (2015). Living up to the Code's exhortations? Social workers' political knowledge sources, expectations, and behaviors. *Social Work*. https://doi.org/10.1093/sw/swv053.

Fresh Air. (2017). *Inside the wealthy family that has been funding Steve Bannon's plan for years*. Retrieved from http://www.npr.org/2017/03/22/521083950/inside-the-wealthy-family-that-has-been-funding-steve-bannon-s-plan-for-years.

Ganz, M. (2005). Why David sometimes wins: Strategic capacity in social movements. In D. Messick & R. Kramer (Eds.), *The psychology of leadership: New perspectives and research* (pp. 209–231). Mahwah, NJ: Lawrence Erlbaum Associates.

Gerstein, J. (2017, June 1). Trump administration asks Supreme Court to reinstate travel ban. *Politico*.

Gramlich, J. (2016). Voter' perceptions of crime continue to conflict with reality. Factank: *News in the numbers* Pew Research Center. http://www.pewresearch.org/fact-tank/2016/11/16/voters-perceptions-of-crime-continue-to-conflict-with-reality/

Hardina, D. (2002). *Analytical skills for community organization practice*. New York, NY: Columbia University Press.

Hoefer, R. (2016). *Advocacy practice for social justice* (3rd ed.). Chicago, IL: Lyceum Books.

Ishiyama, J. T., & Breuning, M. (2010). *21st century political science: A reference handbook*.

Kadner, P. (2015, October 28). Begging elected leaders to act 'like adults'. *Chicago Tribune*.

Lott, T., Daschle, T., & Sternfeld, J. (2016). *Crisis point: Why we must—And how we can—Overcome our broken politics in Washington and across America*. New York, NY: Bloomsbury Press.

Luberda, R. (2014). The fourth branch of the government: Evaluation the media's role in overseeing the independent judiciary. *Notre Dame Journal of Law, Ethics, & Public Policy, 22*(2), 507–532.

Luthra, S. (2017). *Repeal and replace watch: Everything you need to know about block grants-the heart of GOP's Medicaid plan*. Retrieved from http://khn.org/news/block-grants-medicaid-faq/.

Marketplace. (2015, October 26). The Economic Anxiety Index, explained.

Miranda, L.-M. (2015). Non-stop. *Hamilton*.

National Archives and Records Administration, Office of the Federal Register. (n.d.). *Executive orders*. Retrieved from https://www.federalregister.gov/executive-orders

National Association of Social Workers. (2017). *Code of Ethics of the National Association of Social Workers*. Washington, DC: National Association of Social Workers.

National Conference of State Legislators. (2013a). *Number of legislators and lengths of terms in years*. Retrieved from http://www.ncsl.org/research/about-state-legislatures/number-of-legislators-and-length-of-terms.aspx.

National Conference of State Legislatures. (2013b). *Roles and responsibilities of selected leadership positions*. Retrieved from http://www.ncsl.org/legislators-staff/legislators/legislative-leaders/roles-and-responsibilities-of-selected-leadership-positions.aspx - 508.

National Conference of State Legislatures. (2016). *Felon voting rights*. Retrieved April 2, 2017, from http://www.ncsl.org/research/elections-and-campaigns/felon-voting-rights.aspx.

National Conference of State Legislators. (2017). *2017 state legislative leaders*. Retrieved from http://www.ncsl.org/legislators-staff/legislators/legislative-leaders/2017-state-legislative-leaders.aspx - table.

National League of Cities. (2016a). *Forms of municipal government*. Retrieved from http://www.nlc.org/build-skills-and-networks/resources/cities-101/city-structures/forms-of-municipal-government.

National League of Cities. (2016b). *Race, equity, and leadership (REAL)*. Retrieved from http://www.nlc.org/REAL.

National Park Service. (n.d.). *Setting the stage*. Retrieved from https://www.nps.gov/nr/twhp/wwwlps/lessons/148sewallbelmont/148setting.htm.

Nebraska Legislature. (n.d.). *Nebraska legislature: The official site of the Nebraska Unicameral Legislature*. Retrieved from http://nebraskalegislature.gov/.

Newkirk, V. R.. (2017, May 21). The poisoned generation. *The Atlantic*.

Raven-Hansen, P. (1974–1975). Congressional representation for the District of Columbia: A constitutional analysis. *Harvard Journal of Legislation, 12*, 275–296.

Richan, W. (2006). Setting an action agenda. In *Lobbying for social change* (3rd ed., pp. 37–57). New York, NY: Routledge

Rome, S. H. (2012). *Social work and law: Judicial policy and forensic practice*. Boston, MA: Pearson.

Santora, M. (2015, January 23). U.S. Attorney criticizes Albany's 'Three Men in a Room' culture. *The New York Times*.

Sinek, S. (2011). *Start with why: How great leaders inspire everyone to take action*. New York, NY: Penguin Group.

Sobieraj, S., & Berry, J. M. (2011). From incivility to outrage: Political discourse in blogs, talk radio, and cable news. *Political Communication, 28*(1), 19–41.

Sorkin, A. (2001). The Stackhouse filibuster *The West Wing*.

Teles, S., & Schmitt, M. (2011). The elusive craft of evaluating advocacy. *Stanford Social Innovation Review*.

The Henry J. Kaiser Family Foundation. (2012). *Focus on health reform: A guide to the Supreme Court's Affordable Care Act decision*. Washington, DC: The Henry J. Kaiser Family Foundation.

The White House. (n.d.). *State & local government*. Retrieved from https://www.whitehouse.gov/1600/state-and-local-government.

VeneKlasen, L., & Miller, V. (2007). The basics of planning for citizen-centered advocacy. *A new weave of power, people, & politics: The action guide for advocacy and citizen participation*. Washington, DC: Just Associates.

Vogel, K.P. (2016, July 27. George Soros rises again. *Politico*.

Ariane de Vogue, Jamiel Lynch, & Nick Valencia. (2017, March 7). Detained DREAMer files petition to go free. Retrieved from CNN.com.

What Is a Block Grant? (2016). https://blog.grants.gov/2016/06/15/what-is-a-block-grant/

Zavis, A. (2017, February 3). Presidents since George Washington have been signing executive orders. How do Trump's stack up? *Los Angeles Times*.

Planning the Political Intervention: Advocacy Campaigns

6

© Springer International Publishing AG 2018
S.R. Lane, S. Pritzker, *Political Social Work*,
https://doi.org/10.1007/978-3-319-68588-5_6

Section 1: Overview

This chapter builds from the five-stage process for developing political strategy introduced in Chap. 5, and adapts it specifically to the process of planning an advocacy campaign. An advocacy campaign is a political change effort focused on bringing about a specific policy change or changes. This process is most relevant to domains 1 and 2, specifically to strategies involving advocating for expanded political power, and for influencing policy agendas and policy decision-making.

In this chapter, you will select a specific policy problem and then use this five-stage process to design a campaign to advocate for a policy change that resolves this problem, using all that you have learned so far in this book. Each of the planning elements described in this chapter can be applied to either a campaign you carry out individually or one you carry out as part of an organization. As a quick review, the five stages are as follows:

1. Determining the specific purpose of the advocacy campaign
2. Assessing the internal (organizational) and external (environmental) context for the advocacy campaign
3. Identifying the campaign's long-term, intermediate, and short-term goals
4. Selecting specific targets for the advocacy campaign
5. Identifying and selecting the advocacy tactics the campaign will use

Developing Social Work Competency
The Council on Social Work Education establishes educational standards for all social work programs in the USA. Content in this chapter supports building competency in the following areas that are considered core to the practice of social work:
COMPETENCY 3: Advance Human Rights and Social, Economic, and Environmental Justice
COMPETENCY 4: Engage in Practice-Informed Research and Research-Informed Practice
COMPETENCY 5: Engage in Policy Practice
COMPETENCY 7: Assess Individuals, Families, Groups, Organizations, and Communities
COMPETENCY 8: Intervene with Individuals, Families, Groups, Organizations, and Communities

Domains of Political Social Work	
1. Engaging individuals and communities in political processes	◄
2. Influencing policy agendas and decision-making	◄
3. Holding professional and political positions	
4. Engaging with electoral campaigns	
5. Seeking and holding elected office	

Section 2: What Are You Trying to Achieve Through Your Advocacy Campaign? (Stage 1)

In this section, we focus on the first stage of planning an advocacy strategy: determining the specific purpose of the advocacy campaign.

Identify the Policy Problem You Want to Change

Before you can start planning the details of your advocacy campaign, you need to know what you are seeking to change. This is a good place to apply policy analysis skills in order to identify a specific problem that needs to be addressed through policy. In identifying this problem, some questions to consider include the following:

1. *Does a specific aspect of a policy (or lack of policy) consistently impede your clients' success?* For example, in your work with victims of intimate partner violence, do you consistently see similar problems when clients seek to secure a protective order against their abuser? One of the authors worked on legislation that began when intimate partner violence survivors discussed the financial difficulties of leaving an abuser with the advocates with whom they worked. The financial cost of breaking a lease was so much that survivors felt they had no choice but to stay in an apartment with their abusive partner, or to be homeless. Advocates worked to pass legislation that would allow survivors to break their leases without forfeiting their security deposits, if the correct steps were taken. This policy change derived from a challenge faced by clients and sought to lessen the financial costs of leaving an abusive situation and increase survivors' options to leave.

2. *Is a current policy oppressive to a population with whom you work?* For example, in their work with individuals convicted of a felony who have completed their sentences, some social workers have noticed that their states make it difficult to restore clients' voting rights. Governor McAuliffe in Virginia sought to resolve this problem when he used an executive order to restore the rights of Virginians who had served their sentences but, by state law, were barred from voting for life. (Only four states permanently disenfranchise those who have been convicted of felonies—in addition to Virginia, they are Florida, Iowa, and Kentucky; Alabama and Delaware also permanently disenfranchise some voters.) Following a court process that rejected his executive order, the Governor found

a way under existing law to restore voting rights to more than 140,000 people. This sparked conversations in the state legislature about changing the state's law (Brennan Center for Justice 2017).

3. *Does your client population lack specific rights, protections, or services they need?* The work of two University of Houston Graduate College of Social Work students illustrates how this question can guide policy change efforts. Through their work with youth in the foster care system, they learned that these youth are disproportionately likely to end up as victims of human trafficking. Subsequently, they learned that despite a large human trafficking presence in Texas, the state did not offer trafficking awareness training to foster care caseworkers. This led them to implement an advocacy campaign to include a statewide human trafficking awareness curriculum in training requirements for all Texas Department of Family and Protective Services caseworkers (Cooper and Hairston 2014).

4. *Have you seen a policy in another city, county, or state that better addresses a gap in how the needs of a vulnerable population are addressed?* A social worker concerned with how her state's child welfare system addresses the needs of children might discover that in her state, child welfare caseworkers are not required to have earned a 4-year bachelor's degree (Associated Press 2016). Through her research, she finds that another state, with more positive outcomes for children, requires caseworkers to have both a bachelor's degree and at least 2 years of social work experience. The other state's policy may form the basis for a policy change effort in her state.

These four questions, along with any needed policy research and analysis, prepare you for the first step of planning your advocacy strategy: identifying a specific policy problem that <u>should</u> be changed <u>and</u> can be changed (Hoefer 2006).

APPLY YOUR SKILLS: Identify the Policy Problem Your Advocacy Campaign Will Seek to Address

Identify a specific policy problem that you think should be changed <u>and</u> that you think can be changed through implementing a strategic advocacy plan. Find one advocacy organization or group that is currently working to change policy in this area. What type of policy problem are they seeking to address?

Assess the State of Current Policy Surrounding Your Policy Problem

Once you have a clear sense of the policy problem you are seeking to address, you will need to *very specifically* identify a policy change proposal that will be the focus of your advocacy campaign. Before advocates can do this, they examine where policy in this area currently stands and which policy changes may be possible given the reality of the current context. This involves making sure that you understand the *current state of policy* surrounding your problem in *your current geographic context*. If you have taken prior social work policy courses, this step will draw on the policy analysis skills you have learned in those classes.

Questions that you need to consider—and research—include the following: What policies currently address your policy problem? What do they do well, and what is missing? Which level(s) of government are currently addressing your policy problem? Is the problem you identify the responsibility of a specific level of government? For example, a social worker might be concerned that her clients consistently face barriers to accessing protective orders that would protect them from their abusers. Before advocating for change to address this problem, determine whether the barrier that clients face is something that is typically the responsibility of your state government or whether each county in your state separately governs protective orders.

Your proposed policy change also will be stronger if you assess what other changes have recently been proposed in response to your policy problem. Is there a bill, ordinance, or regulation currently under consideration that seeks to resolve the problem? If so, does it seek to resolve the problem in an appealing way? If there is already an appropriate proposal under consideration, by whom is it under consideration, and at what stage of the process? For example, if a bill moving through the legislative process incorporates a realistic and appropriate solution to your problem, you may not need to come up with your own bill idea. Instead, your desired policy change can be to see this bill passed. Maybe there is no appropriate bill under consideration, but your state's **bill filing deadline**, a date after which no further bills may be proposed during that legislative session, has passed. Instead, the best way to move a proposed policy change forward in the short term might be through an amendment to a bill already likely to pass the legislature.

While the general steps for how a bill becomes a law are similar across states, intricacies of the legislative process differ. As you move forward with engaging in advocacy campaigns, you will want to become familiar with the various stages bills must go through before becoming law in your specific geographic context. This is also critical for following legislation at the federal and municipal level. Figure 6.1 depicts how a bill becomes a law in Texas—specifically, a bill that originates in the state's House of Representatives. In Texas, as with most other states, bills also can originate in the state's Senate. Those bills essentially move in the opposite direction of what is shown in here.

BUILD YOUR KNOWLEDGE: Identify the Legislative Process in Your State
Search the legislative website for your state legislature (see guidance for doing this below). Find a description or diagram of the process by which a bill becomes a law in your state. What stands out to you about this process, as you look at the various stages involved?

As advocates look at bills, ordinances, or regulations currently under consideration, we need to both identify proposed policies that would help resolve the problem *and* examine whether any proposals currently under consideration would worsen the problem. The reality is that addressing your problem at certain moments might necessitate focusing your attention on "killing" a harmful bill or ordinance winding its way through the legislature or City Council.

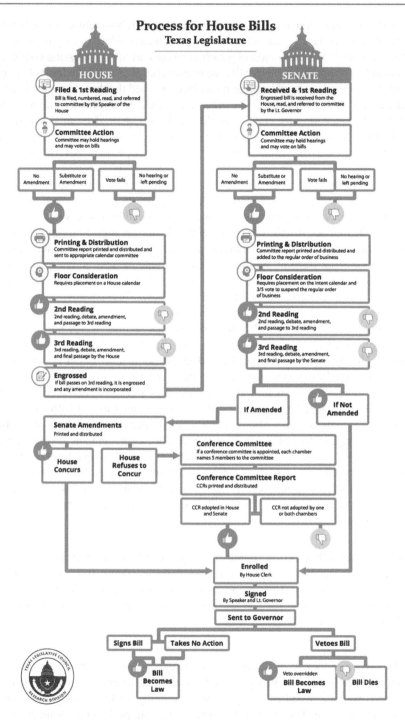

Fig. 6.1 Diagram of House Bill Legislative process in Texas (Texas Legislative Council Research Division n.d.)

Some of the issues we raise may seem daunting now, but you will find that much of this information becomes part of your everyday practice knowledge as you develop experience as a political social worker. Below, we describe some important resources advocates use regularly to examine the current state of policy: legislative websites, local government websites, government agency websites, interest groups, and media.

Legislative websites: These websites enable you to learn about bills that have been proposed and to track them as they move through legislative processes. These websites also offer tools that enable you to look up current **statutes**, all of the written (and previously passed) laws that govern your state or the country. The entire body of statutes for a specific government may be referred to as a **code**. For example, the full set of statutes that govern the USA are referred to as the "United States Code" (see link in Resources). Statutes are organized differently within each state, but are often organized by subject area. In some states, separate "chapters" or "titles" contain all of the laws addressing a specific subject area. This is how the laws are organized in Nebraska, for example, where laws dealing with primary and secondary education are located in Chap. 79, and all laws related to public colleges, universities, and other postsecondary educational institutions are located in Chap. 85 (Nebraska Legislature n.d.). In other states, laws are broken into separate named codes organized by subject. For example, laws in California related to primary, secondary, and higher education are spelled out in the "Education Code," while laws related to criminal justice fall within the "Penal Code" (California Legislative Information n.d.).

The best source for finding information about Congressional bills and federal statutes is http://www.congress.gov. Basic information about your state government can be found by selecting your state from this list: https://www.usa.gov/states-and-territories. The National Conference of State Legislatures (http://www.ncsl.org) is a great resource for information about legislatures across the country, including how they are organized and when they meet.

When you are looking for specific state-level bills and statutes, go directly to your state's legislative information website. Each state has its own, as shown in Figs. 6.2 and 6.3.

Several key commonalities exist between these sites. All include a tool for searching bills currently under consideration and a link to state statutes. As you can see in Figs. 6.2 and 6.3, these sites also provide links to pages for each individual member of the state legislature, to legislative committee information, to daily legislative calendars, and even to mechanisms for watching legislative proceedings from your own computer, phone, or tablet. Many states also have legislative reference libraries (e.g., the Legislative Reference Library of Texas and the Wisconsin Legislative Reference Bureau) from which you can access historical information about specific policies and policy discussions. A great tool on many state legislative websites (see the Tennessee State Legislature's "My Bills" service in Fig. 6.4) is the ability to set up an account and create searches with alerts. This enables you to be notified about new bills relating to your interest as they are introduced and as they wind through the legislative process.

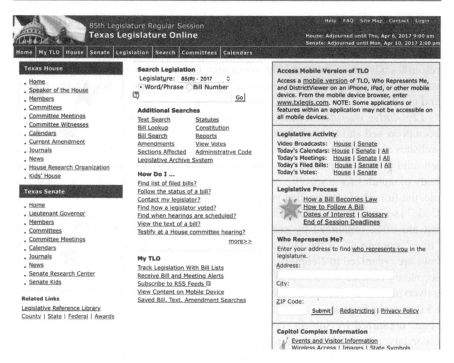

Fig. 6.2 Texas Legislature Online (http://www.capitol.state.tx.us)

Local government websites: Unlike state information websites, which provide fairly consistent types of information across states, the quality and thoroughness of local government websites vary widely. On many municipalities' websites, a good place to start is on the segment of the website devoted specifically to governance. This page typically lists the names and contact information for members of the City Council, the Board of Supervisors, or your Town Council. It also is likely to provide links to information that it is required to release to the public, such as meeting agendas and minutes. Some municipal websites may list current or proposed ordinances/policies and even meeting videos. (These websites are not always maintained as well as we might like. One of our students went to her town's website and found that many of the links were broken. She called the town to let them know; they asked her to send a list of broken links. They were fixed that week, and the town employees were very appreciative that she had let them know.)

Other Web-based information sources about your local government's policies may include the local library's website as well as the National League of Cities (see Resources). Your state may have a portal that collects information about local governments, which can be very useful if you work in a region with multiple towns or cities. For example, the Arkansas Municipal League offers multiple ways to search for Arkansas towns, including cities, zip codes, and counties.

As Fig. 6.5 shows, this site includes information about more than 500 municipalities in Arkansas, from Little Rock (population 193,524) to Valley Springs

Fig. 6.3 Wisconsin State Legislature (https://legis.wisconsin.gov)

Fig. 6.4 Tennessee State Legislature (http://wapp.capitol.tn.gov/Apps/MyBills)

Fig. 6.5 Arkansas Municipal League (http://local.arkansas.gov/)

(population 183). While not every town has a website, those that do are listed on this site, along with their local elected officials, e-mail addresses, regularly scheduled board or commission meetings, and school districts. Realistically, however, finding up-to-date information about local policies under consideration, particularly in smaller municipalities, may require contacting key local decision-makers.

APPLY YOUR SKILLS: Finding Information About Municipal-Level Policy
Take a few minutes to search around your local government (e.g., city, county, town, parish) website. Are you able to find what policy proposals are currently under consideration by your municipality's elected leadership? If so, what are some of the major issues they are currently considering? Are you able to find what laws currently exist for your locality? If you cannot find this information on this website, is there somewhere else that you can go to find it instead?

Government agency websites: Executive agency websites at the federal, state, or local levels can be good sources of policy information. Federal agency websites, such as the website for the US Department of Health and Human Services (see Resources), include public information about both the various programs the agency operates and major federal policies impacting the agency's work. State agency websites, such as the Utah Department of Child and Family Services, similarly provide both general information and services and information about legislative policies governing the agency's work. As the "Policy" link at the top of Fig. 6.6 demonstrates, state agency websites often provide information about administrative regulations and agency policies that guide the agency's interactions with the public.

Interest groups: **Interest groups** refer to groups who seek to influence policy based on members' common interests and concerns. These include **trade**

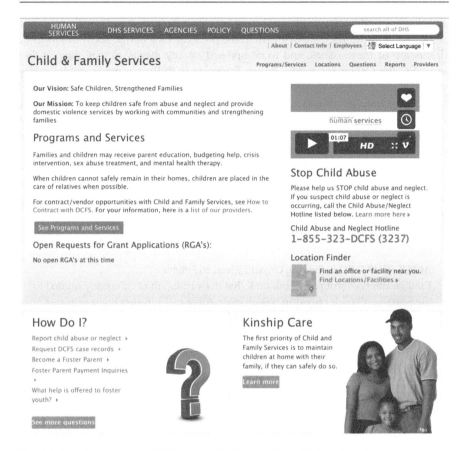

Fig. 6.6 Utah Department of Child and Family Services (https://dcfs.utah.gov/)

associations, where members share some sort of business or trade interest, and **professional organizations** such as NASW where members share a professional interest. Some of these have their own distinctions under tax law. **Think tanks**, also known as public policy organizations, and policy research institutes conduct research on policy issues and disseminate this research to impact policy. These groups often employ or work with **lobbyists**, who seek to influence legislation on their behalf. These groups represent diverse political perspectives and can be good sources of in-depth information about your area of policy. However, each of these is likely to bring a particular bias into their work depending on their membership, funding, and perspective. If using resources from a group unfamiliar to you, read through their "about us" section, pull up the IRS 990 form that discusses their funding, and/or read their publications with a critical eye until you are more confident of the quality of their work.

Many of these organizations publish legislative updates, and some also publish analyses of legislation. Look for the websites of organizations that are major players in your area of policy, and sign up for their legislative lists, mailing lists, or e-mailed newsletters. Follow the organizations and their staffers on social media to gain a sense of the issues they are discussing, the political factors that seem to influence discussion of these issues, and to be updated on key events as they happen. For example, the Center for Public Policy Priorities (CPPP) is a major public policy organization in Texas that produces data and in-depth policy analyses on a variety of social welfare issues and is heavily engaged in state-level policy advocacy. One of the authors of this textbook follows CPPP (@CPPP_TX) on Twitter, as well as the organization's executive director and several staffers, in order to keep abreast of political discussion in Texas surrounding these issues.

A more active yet effective approach to learning from these organizations is to reach out directly to the key players involved in these organizations. Engage your social work practice skills to ask them about the current state of policy in your area and to listen reflectively to their responses.

APPLY YOUR SKILLS: Finding Organizations to Follow

Find an interest group or think tank that does research or advocacy related to the issue you've identified in this chapter. Answer the following questions:

1. What is the organization's name and website?
2. What is their mission?
3. Who funds them? (You may need to go to guidestar.com and look up the organization's tax form, called a 990, to answer this question.)
4. Who are the senior staff members at this organization and/or the staffers who do the work most relevant to your policy issue?
5. Do you feel this organization is credible? What else would you need to know in order to answer this question?
6. If you believe they are credible, and you use social media, follow the organization and at least one staff member on Twitter, Facebook, or other social media as a way to stay up to date on your issue.

Media: Both traditional and social media can be important sources of information for learning about current policies and the political context surrounding these policies. Read newspapers that regularly cover policy at the appropriate local, state, or federal level of government. Watch policy-oriented television news shows. Use social media to help you identify *reputable* articles that discuss key policy and describe legislative processes and internal government politics. For a guide to assessing which media resources are reputable, see the Resource section.

Many states have a blog(s) devoted to the behind-the-scenes politics of state government, like New York State's "Capitol Confidential." Podcasts like *Left, Right, and Center*, NPR's *Up First*, or the New York Times' *The Daily* are great modes of catching up on current policy while you commute, work out, or do chores. Some political podcasts have "cult followings": fans of the liberal *Pod Save America* number in the hundreds of thousands. Many follow the hosts on Twitter and discuss episodes at length on Slack channels (Nazaryan 2017).

BUILD YOUR KNOWLEDGE: Assess the State of Current Policy
Go back to the questions listed at the beginning of this section and the policy problem you identified. Using the resources described in this chapter, examine the current state of policy surrounding the specific policy problem you have identified. What policies currently address your policy problem? Is there a specific level of government at which your proposed change should be focused? Are there any relevant policy proposals currently under consideration?

Identify the Policy Change You Think Is Necessary to Address This Problem

Now that you have a good sense of the current state of policy addressing your policy problem, you are ready to identify a specific policy change. The proposed change that you identify needs to directly seek to resolve at least a part of the policy problem. One way to think about conceptualizing this proposed policy change is to fill in the blanks in the following sentence:

I/we want _____[who]_____to do_____[what]_____by _____[when]_____.

Sometimes the proposed change you identify will be immediately clear, with consensus among all involved parties (e.g., we want to stop Senate Bill 6 that is currently up for a vote in the state legislature by the end of the legislative session). At other times, identifying a single proposed change can be quite challenging, especially when advocates work within a large organization or in coalition with other organizations. Critical to this process is making sure that we and our coworkers or allies have consensus on a clear set of policy priorities (Richan 2006).

Hoefer (2006) suggests that we begin the process of identifying a specific policy proposal by first identifying a range of possible policy changes that would resolve our policy problem. He offers a helpful guide to identifying a range of policy changes through creative thinking: "Although the phrase *think outside the box* has become so overused that it may be considered trite, solutions should be developed that are not bound by currently perceived boundaries or structures" (Hoefer 2006). He suggests a variety of tools to use in trying to identify creative policy solutions, including brainstorming, considering the "opposite" approach to what has typically been done, and a "win-win" approach in which a social work advocate takes a broad-sighted approach to consider what solutions could exist if we prioritized advancing equity and efficiency (Hoefer 2006). Using such tools can give you a broad area of policy solutions to consider.

Once you decide upon a proposed policy change, make sure that the change is very clear to you, your organization, and any other allies on this advocacy campaign. Ask yourself what do you (and your colleagues) expect to see if your policy change is adopted? Consider whether you and your colleagues can clearly articulate the answer to this question. Effective advocacy depends on everyone associated with your advocacy campaign working toward the same end. If you cannot clearly and consistently articulate an answer to this question, you'll need to continue to discuss, reflect, and refine your proposed policy change until you can.

APPLY YOUR SKILLS: Identify the Policy Change Your Advocacy Campaign Will Seek to Achieve
Identify a specific policy change that addresses the policy problem that you previously identified. Use the following formulation: I/we want _____[who]_____ to do _____[what]_____ by _____[when]_____.

POLITICAL SOCIAL WORKER PROFILE: Nancy Amidei, MSW
Senior Lecturer Emeritus, University of Washington School of Social Work (Fig. 6.7).

Fig. 6.7 Nancy Amidei, MSW

Advocacy and strategic policy change may seem like an enormous task. Where to begin when the issues social work seeks to mediate seem levels deep and centuries old? Nancy Amidei does not answer this question with a slew of complex suggestions. Instead, she describes straightforward tools that she has used throughout her career. Her wisdom, gathered over the years, includes incredibly effective, simple, and cost-efficient strategies such as the following:

- Read the biographies of policy-makers/elected officials before you ever meet with them to find out what is important to them.
- Bring along a board member from an organization that deals with your advocacy issue when you meet with elected officials, as many elected officials are community board members themselves and "people relate more readily to those they regard as their peers."
- Invite a targeted legislator to moderate a panel of hand-chosen experts and service recipients, so that the legislator need not make a speech, but instead is given the opportunity to listen and become informed on an advocacy issue by those who know it best.

(continued)

For Amidei, data and statistics do not speak to people unfamiliar with the issue like a story does. She sees stories as essential to advocacy because they "grab your heart" and beg the question "what are we going to do now … together?" Stories lead to a powerful call to action and leave people wanting more than to merely stand by and wait for something to be done.

Amidei's own story is a call to action for social workers. She began her career through a chance opportunity to intern in Washington, DC under the US Department of Health, Education, and Welfare while at the University of Michigan School of Social Work. This opportunity came about as a result of a common interest she shared with a professor as they had both spent time in Nigeria (Amidei as a member of the Peace Corps). As she sat in the professor's office, a phone call came in that would change the trajectory of her life. That call was from a political appointee who was considering accepting social work students as interns, and called to ask the professor what type of student he was thinking of sending. As Amidei sat in front of him, he asked her if she would like to go to Washington. She agreed, the professor described her, and the appointee accepted her on the spot.

In D.C., Amidei pursued this internship followed by a variety of professional positions, including as Deputy Assistant Secretary for Legislation in the Department of Health, Education, and Welfare; staff director of the US Senate Select Committee on Nutrition and Human Needs; and executive director of the Food Research and Action Center. She later served as senior lecturer in the School of Social Work and project director of the Civic Engagement Project at the University of Washington; and she has authored numerous op-eds and resource guides for advocates. Throughout her career, Amidei has fought tirelessly for vulnerable populations and their rights. In doing so, she has left her mark, and leaves us with the question, "What are we going to do now … together?"

Section 3: Assessing the Context for Advocacy: Determining the Opportunities and Constraints Your Campaign May Face (Stage 2)

Our first instinct in planning an advocacy campaign is often to jump right in to try to secure our desired policy change. However, before we move forward, consider the opportunities and constraints that exist within our organization/coalitions and within the current social, economic, and political contexts. This will enable us to adapt our plan accordingly. In this section, we focus on the second stage of planning an advocacy strategy: assessing the internal (organizational) and external (environmental) context for the advocacy campaign. While a range of approaches can be used to conduct this analysis, a SWOT analysis is a common tool for examining your campaign's internal and external context.

Assessing the Individual and Organizational Context

Social workers' advocacy work often takes place within the scope of our professional or volunteer work with human service nonprofits. As you prepare to plan and participate in advocacy campaigns within these organizations, assess your organizational context to determine what you have the capacity to do. This assessment should start with the questions outlined in Chap. 5 under "Assessing your individual and organizational context." Pay particular attention to opportunities and constraints in the following areas:

- Readiness to embark on this advocacy campaign (Bobo et al. 2010), including whether this specific policy change proposal fits within your organization's purpose and mission and whether it aligns with the ethics and values of the social work profession
- Staff, volunteer, and financial resources to dedicate to this specific advocacy campaign
- Prior experiences, areas of expertise, and relationships with decision-makers and allies relevant to this specific advocacy campaign.

Assessing the Social, Economic, and Political Contexts

Earlier in this chapter, you learned about the importance of evaluating where policy in your area currently stands as you identify the proposed policy change for which you will advocate. Now that you have identified that change, this stage requires you to assess the opportunities and challenges to moving forward within the current social, economic, and political climate. Refer to the assessment questions introduced in Chap. 5 in the section "Assessing the social, economic, and political environment." Pay particular attention to the following considerations as you conduct this external assessment:

- Whether this specific policy change seems achievable in the current social, economic, and political context
- Whether there is likely to be substantial support or opposition, and, if so, from what sources
- Whether the current context is conducive to large-scale change in response to your policy problem, or if incremental change—or even laying the groundwork for future change—is more realistic at this point in time (Richan 2006).

APPLY YOUR SKILLS: Exploring the Context for Your Advocacy Campaign
Conduct a brief assessment of the context for your advocacy campaign. Using the specific considerations described above, create a list of each of the following:

- Relevant internal strengths of your advocacy campaign
- Relevant internal weaknesses of your advocacy campaign
- Relevant external opportunities for your advocacy campaign
- Relevant external threats to your advocacy campaign

Reflect on your assessment: How do these factors influence how you think you might approach your advocacy campaign moving forward?

Section 4: Defining Advocacy Goals: How to Determine What Will Constitute a Policy "Victory" (Stage 3)

The next stage of planning your campaign is to identify the specific milestones that need to be achieved to move the proposed policy change forward. In this section, we focus on the third stage of planning an advocacy strategy: identifying the campaign's long-term, intermediate, and short-term goals.

In the context of an advocacy campaign, goals reflect the "victories" we will need to achieve from someone else. Perhaps different from other strategic planning you have previously engaged in, advocacy goals are result oriented. They are not measures of what we will *do*, but rather of what we will *achieve* through our efforts. reaching these goals should show us <u>not</u> that we are *doing work*, but, rather, that *we are achieving policy progress*.

For the remainder of this advocacy planning process, we will be using a modified version (see Fig. 6.8) of a strategic planning chart developed by Midwest Academy (Bobo et al. 2010). At this stage, we are concerned with the first three columns of this chart: the long-term, intermediate, and short-term goals for our advocacy campaign.

Long-term goals are our most distant goals—the advocacy results we truly hope to "win" at the end of our advocacy campaign. Short-term and intermediate goals are more immediate goals that we are able to achieve along the way as we work toward our long-term goals. As illustrated in Fig. 6.9, each of these goals are progressive—achieving short-term goals facilitates our achievement of intermediate goals; and achieving intermediate goals facilitates our achievement of long-term goals. In essence, our short-term and intermediate goals move us closer to "winning" our long-term goals.

Applying the S.M.A.R.T. Goal criteria shown in Fig. 6.9, example advocacy goal statements might look like the following:

Problem: _____
Solution: _____

Long-term goals	Intermediate goals	Short-term goals	Primary targets	Secondary targets	Tactics

Fig. 6.8 Advocacy campaign planning chart

Your Advocacy Goal: _____

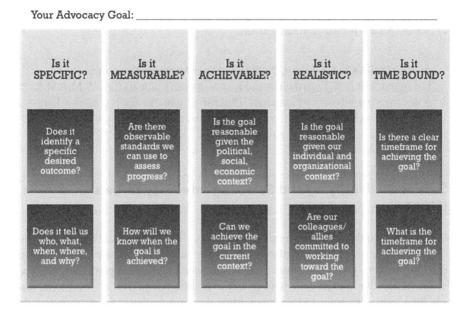

Fig. 6.9 Identifying S.M.A.R.T. advocacy goals (Vance 2011)

- *Long-term goal*: The House and Senate of our state will vote to pass a bill that provides an explicit set of protections for children in the foster care system during the 2019 legislative session.
- *Intermediate goal:* With the support of the Health and Human Services Committee Chair, a bill will be introduced in the House at the start of the 2019 legislative session, with a companion Senate bill, focusing on providing an explicit set of protections for children in the foster care system.
- *Intermediate goal:* The House Human Services Committee will require the study commission to complete a report prior to December 2018 on the prevalence of, and factors contributing to, deaths in the state foster care system.
- *Intermediate goal:* The House Human Services Committee will vote by June 2017 to create a study commission to examine the prevalence of, and factors contributing to, deaths in the state foster care system.
- *Short-term goal:* The House Human Services Committee will schedule a hearing during the 2017 legislative session on House Bill 3259, which calls for reform of the state foster care system.

Note that each of these goal statements focuses on step-by-step policy victories. The short-term goal reflects a first round of policy achievements that enable the intermediate policy achievements to happen. The intermediate goals reflect achievements necessary for the final goal to be achieved. Each goal marks a step closer to success for the advocacy effort.

> **APPLY YOUR SKILLS: Defining the Goals of Your Advocacy Campaign**
> Using the S.M.A.R.T. goal chart in Fig. 6.9, identify at least three S.M.A.R.T. goals for your advocacy campaign. Determine whether each goal is a long-term, intermediate, or short-term goal; then place each goal in the appropriate spot on your Advocacy Campaign Planning Chart provided in Fig. 6.8.

Section 5: Identifying and Selecting Advocacy Targets (Stage 4)

On whom should we focus our advocacy efforts? This is a critical question as we develop a strategic advocacy plan. Our answer lies in identifying the individual decision-maker(s) with the power to make our specific goals happen. There may be different decision-makers who have power over different goals (i.e., short term versus long term). We refer to these individual decision-maker(s) as our target(s). In this section, we focus on the fourth stage of planning an advocacy strategy: selecting specific target(s) for the advocacy campaign.

A critical part of target identification in advocacy campaign planning is to "**personalize the target**," meaning that we need to select specific individual(s), not entities, to target (Bobo et al. 2010). For example, if we are trying to get a bill passed by the House Human Services Committee, we would not want to define our advocacy target as the whole Human Services Committee (although the committee as a whole may ultimately vote on our bill). Instead, we focus on the individual committee members who are essential to achieving our advocacy goals. We might select as a target Rep. Jane Doe, who is typically the swing vote on the committee on issues like the one on which our bill focuses. Personalizing the target is essential because institutions (e.g., a city council, a legislature, Congress, a committee) are comprised of individual people who each may be influenced in different ways. "Each person has different attitudes, constituencies, and interests that we need to take into account" in designing an effective advocacy campaign (Sen 2003). While we may have multiple targets within a committee, we will likely approach these different individuals in somewhat different ways.

Primary and Secondary Targets

Individual advocacy targets generally fall into two different categories:

Primary targets: The primary target refers to the specific person or persons with the real power to give you what you want, i.e., make your goals happen. This might be the person who has the deciding vote on a bill, or the individual who controls the budget that could fund your initiative.

Secondary targets: A secondary target is an individual who has more power over your primary target than you do. Typically, the secondary target has a direct link to the primary target, but is also someone who is more likely to be able to be influenced by you.

All advocacy efforts have at least one primary target. Even when you or your organization has a close relationship with the primary target, it is good practice to have at least one secondary target. Identifying a clear secondary target is particularly helpful when an individual or organizational advocate does not have a close relationship—or even direct access to—the primary target. A secondary target must be someone with whom we have more direct access than our primary target <u>and</u> must be someone to whom the primary target feels some formal or informal accountability. This may include people who are **gatekeepers** and control access to policymakers, or those who have high credibility and will be able to present information in a way that the target will take seriously. This might include legislative or campaign staff, well-known experts in your field, or people who have known and worked with the primary targets for many years. It also could include spouses or family members, influential constituents, campaign contributors, or leaders in the local community who have worked closely with the primary target.

Both for primary and secondary targets, it is important to use our core social work skills focused on relationship building. We need to get to know our targets. This is one benefit to political social workers' involvement in electoral work and larger advocacy efforts; these efforts provide opportunities to build relationships with those who may be in a decision-making position in the future. For example, when social workers volunteer as a group to support a candidate, candidates notice and may be more responsive to social workers once elected. In reverse, if social workers do not show up to support a candidate, they may not have the influence later.

Identifying and Selecting Specific Individual Targets

The analyses of power dynamics and of key players that you learned about in previous chapters are good starting points for identifying the primary targets who are truly the pivotal players with the power to make your goals happen. By assessing where power and support for your desired policy goals intersect, you can identify which individual(s) is both (a) most capable of making the goals you seek happen and (b) most likely to be responsive to your advocacy efforts.

Haynes and Mickelson (2010) caution that "many lobbyists focus their efforts on legislators who share values and goals similar to their own," rather than on the undecided decision-makers—those in the middle—who often can make or break the success of your desired policy change (p. 109). While it is important to continue to cultivate the support of targets who are like-minded (through appreciative messages, brief office visits and phone calls, etc.), these are rarely the individuals who will make the difference in whether your desired policy change comes to fruition. Political social workers need to differentiate between decision-makers who are clearly supportive, clearly opposed, and those who are undecided. Especially when your decision-makers are members of a policy-making group (a council, a legislature, or a commission), it is the undecided or "swing" members who often need to be the focus of your advocacy effort. In some cases, those who are already convinced have the types of relationships that enable them to persuade others. They then may be effective secondary targets. In general, however, the majority of your time should focus on the targets whose new support is essential for making your change happen.

There are various sources of data we can use to identify the most appropriate individual target(s) for an advocacy campaign. Two key sources are outlined below.

Voting Records

Elected members of local, state, and federal policy-making bodies have typically engaged in a range of votes during their time in office. If you are unfamiliar with the stances of a specific policy-maker, voting records can help you assess the likelihood of receiving support for your desired policy change from this policy-maker. Current and past voting records of federal elected officials can be found through websites maintained by the Library of Congress (in Resources).

The bipartisan Vote Smart organization (see Resources) maintains a website that tracks selected votes of Members of Congress and legislators in all 50 states. Figure 6.10 shows an example of the information maintained by Vote Smart on the voting record of social worker and Illinois State Senator Christine Radogno (Vote Smart 2017). Municipal voting records are generally harder to locate. In some cases, historical voting records may be found through municipal websites, local library materials, or through newspaper archives.

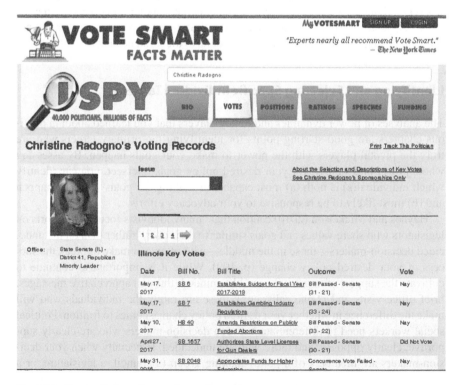

Fig. 6.10 Senator Radogno's record on vote smart

Interest Group Report Cards

Various interest groups, political action committees, and other organizations across the political spectrum maintain records of politician's votes on particular issues. These organizations select bills that support their mission and goals and then track politician's vote records to determine whether their votes are in line with the organization's preferred stance (Haynes and Mickelson 2010). Organizations may tally these votes on report cards publicly distributed to allies and supporters of the organization, with the intent of influencing politicians' behavior and how the public views these politicians. Figs. 6.11 and 6.12 show two examples of report cards focused on US Senators' votes. The first is from the League of Conservation Voters and focuses on environmental protection. The second is from the conservative Freedom Works organization and focuses on economic freedom.

SENATE VOTES

KEY
✓ = Pro-environment action
✗ = Anti-environment action
① = Ineligible to vote
? = Absence (counts as negative)

LCV SCORES

	Party	% 2016	% 114th Congress	% Lifetime	Extreme Attack on Clean Water Protections (CRA)	Clean Energy Funding	National Monuments	Energy Efficiency	Fast Tracking Natural Gas Pipelines	Limiting Public Safeguards	Taxpayer Handouts for Fossil Fuel Companies	Genetically Modified Food Labeling	Encouraging Energy-Efficient Homes	Land and Water Conservation Fund (LWCF)	Wind Energy Transmission Line	Victory Bonds for Clean Energy	Attack on the Clean Water Rule	Attack on Advanced Vehicles	Water Conservation Program	Mitigating Impacts on Fish & Wildlife	Revenue Sharing for Offshore Drilling
HAWAII																					
Hirono	D	100	100	94	✓	✓	✓	✓	✓	✓	✓	✓	✓	✓	✓	✓	✓	✓	✓	✓	✓
Schatz	D	100	98	95	✓	✓	✓	✓	✓	✓	✓	✓	✓	✓	✓	✓	✓	✓	✓	✓	✓
IDAHO																					
Crapo	R	12	5	7	✗	✓	✗	✗	✗	✗	✗	✗	✗	✓	✗	✗	✗	✗	✗	✗	✗
Risch	R	12	5	9	✗	✓	✗	✗	✗	✗	✗	✗	✗	✓	✗	✗	✗	✗	✗	✗	✗
ILLINOIS																					
Durbin	D	100	100	87	✓	✓	✓	✓	✓	✓	✓	✓	✓	✓	✓	✓	✓	✓	✓	✓	✓
Kirk	R	35	38	55	✗	✗	✓	✗	✗	✗	✗	✗	✓	✓	✓	✓	✗	✗	✓	✗	✗
INDIANA																					
Coats	R	0	0	22	✗	✗	✗	✗	✗	✗	✗	✗	✗	✗	✗	✗	✗	✗	✗	✗	✗
Donnelly	D	76	71	58	✗	✓	✓	✓	✓	✓	✗	✗	✓	✓	✓	✓	✗	✓	✓	✓	✓
IOWA																					
Ernst	R	0	0	0	✗	✗	✗	✗	✗	✗	✗	✗	✗	✗	✗	✗	✗	✗	✗	✗	✗
Grassley	R	6	5	19	✗	✗	✗	✗	✗	✗	✗	✗	✗	✗	✗	✗	✗	✗	✗	✓	✗
KANSAS																					
Moran	R	0	0	8	✗	✗	✗	✗	✗	✗	✗	✗	✗	✗	✗	✗	✗	✗	✗	✗	✗
Roberts	R	0	0	9	✗	✗	✗	✗	✗	✗	✗	✗	✗	✗	✗	✗	✗	✗	✗	✗	✗
KENTUCKY																					
McConnell	R	12	5	7	✗	✗	✗	✗	✗	✗	✗	✓	✗	✗	✗	✗	✗	✗	✓	✗	✗
Paul	R	12	10	9	✗	?	✗	✗	✗	✗	✗	✓	✗	✗	✗	✗	✗	✗	✗	✗	✓
LOUISIANA																					
Cassidy	R	18	7	8	✗	✗	✗	✗	✗	✗	✗	✗	✓	✗	✗	✗	✗	✓	✓	✗	✗

2. SENATE SCORES

Fig. 6.11 League of Conservation Voters scorecard (http://scorecard.lcv.org/scorecard)

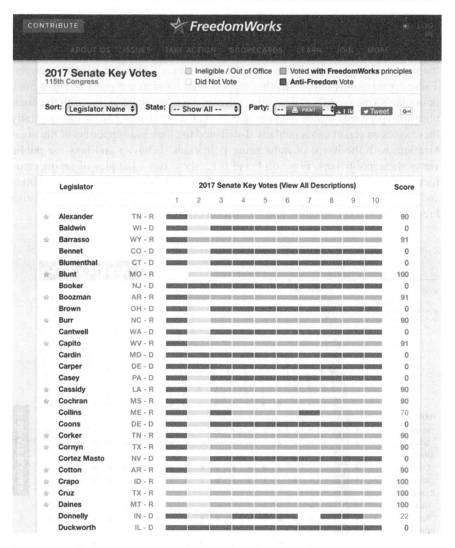

Fig. 6.12 Freedom Works report card (http://congress.freedomworks.org/)

APPLY YOUR SKILLS: Identifying Swing Voters
Follow this link to look more closely at the League of Conservation Voters' (LCV) Scorecard: http://scorecard.lcv.org/scorecard. This scorecard gets updated annually, and therefore may look different than Fig. 6.11 when you go directly to the site. Download the full Scorecard, and identify which Senators are likely to be the swing voters who LCV targets for the next environment-related bill considered by the US Senate.

APPLY YOUR SKILLS: Selecting Appropriate Advocacy Targets
For the three S.M.A.R.T. goals you identified earlier in this chapter, identify primary and secondary targets for your campaign. Use voting records or interest group report cards as appropriate. Remember to personalize your targets by identifying specific individuals who can make your goals happen. Then place each target in the appropriate spot on your Advocacy Campaign Planning Chart provided in Fig. 6.8.

POLITICAL SOCIAL WORKER PROFILE: Constance J. Brooks, BSW, MSW, PhD
Vice Chancellor for Government and Community Affairs, Nevada System of Higher Education (NSHE) (Fig. 6.13).

Fig. 6.13 Constance J. Brooks, BSW, MSW, PhD

Practicing social work as a lobbyist for over 10 years is exactly the type of advocacy I feel I was born to do. This aspect of political social work provides me the opportunity to serve as a champion and change agent for Nevada's 106,000 university and community college students—20,000 faculty and staff in 8 institutions—with an annual budget of over $500 million. I am an integral member of the NSHE Chancellor's Cabinet and leadership team, serving as the chief advisor for government affairs, policies, and analytics, working collaboratively to develop system-wide initiatives, targeted messaging, and communication strategies. I am also the spokesperson and liaison for the NSHE Board of Regents regarding legislative, community, and diversity initiatives.

Representing NSHE within local government, the Nevada State Legislature and the legislative branch of the US Government is no small feat. The 2015 Nevada Legislative Session brought about significant state-funded need-based financial aid through the Silver State Opportunity Grant, providing funding to

(continued)

low-income, full-time students to assist them in completing a degree program. In addition to marshaling NSHE's budget request through the legislative process and tracking over 200 bills, I was responsible for advocating for this grant and seeing its passage through the Nevada Legislature. This is one of the proudest moments of my career.

The primary strategy employed was old-fashioned campaign coordination and coalition building; that is, engaging nontraditional groups such as the Chamber of Commerce, local governments, and student organizations. While in the political realm, this approach is called campaigning or coalition building, it is akin to the systems theory in social work practice. The interconnection of individual or group needs and expectations within a complex system requires the direct involvement of diverse groups, communities, and individuals to effectuate change. This was a successful approach, as the pressing need resonated with legislators, and $5 million in funding was made available to assist over 1000 low-income, hard-working students.

The need for advocacy within the political arena remains constant. Assisting lawmakers in making public policy decisions will always be necessary. Advocating for vulnerable populations will forever be critical to the advancement of our country, our state, our communities, and our neighborhoods. The foundation of social work is arguably the best at preparing individuals to advocate at the macro level. The understanding of how systems operate; the interplay of federal, state, and local budget processes; and coalition-building, facilitation, and negotiation are fundamental in lobbying—all of which I honed in my bachelors and master's-level social work programs.

Section 6: Identifying and Selecting Advocacy Tactics (Stage 5)

In this section, we focus on the fifth stage of planning an advocacy strategy: identifying and selecting the advocacy tactics the campaign will use.

A wide range of tactics are available to advocacy campaigns. It is important to be aware of this range of tactics, particularly as different targets may find different tactics more or less persuasive. Just as the political context is ever changing, and technology continues to open up new advocacy avenues, new tactics are likely to continue to be introduced into common use in advocacy campaigns.

The range of available tactics can be thought of in multiple ways. Mosley (2011) distinguishes between two categories of advocacy tactics commonly used by human service nonprofits: insider tactics and indirect tactics. Insider tactics refer to tactics in which organizations work directly with decision-makers, inside of political processes. These include providing testimony, serving on government commissions, and other forms of advocating directly to decision-makers. Indirect tactics are more likely to take place outside of political institutions and focus on raising public concern about policy problems and awareness of policy solutions. These include being part of advocacy coalitions, providing public education, and communicating via media. Mosley (2011) finds that more institutionalized human service nonprofits are more likely to use insider tactics.

Community organizing offers another way to categorize tactics, along a continuum ranging from collaborative tactics to those that are more confrontational (Reticker-Flynn 2013). Advocates tend to select tactics that build upon each other, or "escalate," increasing pressure on the target over time as needed. In general, we aim to start with collegial tactics, only using confrontational tactics when the gentler tactics seem to have no impact. Often these more confrontational tactics are sought out by groups that find themselves marginalized from political processes and seek a way to ensure that their voices are heard by policy-makers (Piven and Cloward 1977; Alinksy 1971).

Advocacy campaigns use an array of tactics, which can be grouped into several categories. Below, we present these categories along a loosely organized continuum, acknowledging that this continuum may look different depending on the targets and contexts involved:

- **Collaborative tactics:** Used when advocates are trying to work together with their target to achieve their advocacy goals by identifying common interests, sharing resources, and acting collaboratively.
- **Public education tactics:** Used to elicit public concern and support for a policy change.
- **Grassroots tactics:** Used to grow support from key constituents who may then directly seek to influence the target.
- **Persuasive tactics:** Used to resolve differences between advocates and their targets, to bring them into agreement.
- **Electoral tactics:** Taking a long-range approach to changing who has decision-making power around your problem/change; used when persuasive tactics consistently have no impact on your target.
- **Litigation tactics:** Commonly used where other tactics have not successfully prevented constitutional concerns.
- **Demonstrative tactics:** Used to show intensity of public concern regarding your advocacy goals.
- **Contest/confrontational tactics**: Used when there are significant differences between advocates and their targets and little hope of coming to an agreement; often used to try to force a concession. At times, these tactics may even be illegal.

Our list of sample advocacy activities identifies many of the tactics within each category commonly used by advocacy campaigns. Please note that this is not intended to be a comprehensive list of tactics.

Sample advocacy tactics	
Collaborative tactics	• Invite the target to join a coalition focused on the identified policy problem • Invite the target to visit your social work agency • One-on-one meetings with the target • Ongoing relationship-building with the target • Serve on government boards or commissions
Public education tactics	• Paid media spots, on television, radio, social media outlets, in newspapers • Free media, e.g., public service announcements on television or radio • Media event • Educate the public via social network postings • Educate community leaders • Letters to the editor, op-eds • Work with reporters and bloggers to communicate the message • Distribute fact sheets
Grassroots tactics	• Door-to-door canvassing • Rallies • Postcard campaigns • Distribute action alerts to individuals who may become mobilized • Train clients to share their stories with legislators or media audiences
Persuasive tactics	• One-on-one meetings with the target • Send a letter to the target • Call the target • Direct lobbying • Lobby days • Attend and ask questions at town halls/public hearings/accountability sessions, where the target has to respond to constituents • Distribute fact sheets/policy briefs to the target • Develop draft legislation • Provide feedback on developing/revising regulations • Poll/communicate polling showing where the public stands • Provide testimony • Invite clients to share their stories with the target
Electoral tactics	• Register new voters • Educate voters about candidate stances relative to the advocacy goals • Get out the vote efforts • Endorse candidates who support the advocacy goals • Educate candidates about the proposed change and advocacy goals • Campaign on behalf of supportive candidates • Fundraise on behalf of supportive candidates, or in opposition to incumbents who do not support the advocacy goals
Litigation tactics	• File lawsuits to seek enforcement of existing policy/law • File lawsuits to challenge existing policy/law • Identify test cases to challenge an existing policy/law—this can be an important role for social workers who often work closely with individuals whose rights may be violated by existing policy

Sample advocacy tactics	
Demonstrative tactics	• Marches/rallies • Demonstrations • Thunderclaps (your audience sharing the same message simultaneously on social media)
Contest/ confrontational tactics	• Strikes/picketing • Sit-ins • Boycotts • Civil disobedience

FURTHER REFLECTION: Thinking About Advocacy Tactics
Review the identified list of sample advocacy tactics. What tactics have you seen in advocacy campaigns that seem to be missing here? List as many additional tactics as you can and organize them along this continuum.

Organizations may find different categories of tactics to be more or less comfortable. Many social workers tend to start with collaborative tactics, seeking to build coalitions with allies and with targets. The advantages of working in coalitions are fairly obvious: they involve a collegial approach to advocacy while increasing the amount of resources, people, and energy that can be applied to a political effort (Bobo et al. 2010). However, the disadvantages of coalitions are also significant: think of every group project you have been a part of. Coalition work requires the need for compromise, so that all participants might get some of what they want, but it is difficult for everyone to get everything they want. Coalitions may require extensive time to coordinate and communicate, and risk enabling more power on the part of bigger, louder coalition members.

In selecting tactics and in considering your role in any specific tactic selected by your organization, how these intersect with your own identity and personal characteristics is an important consideration. Likewise, it is also important to consider how your clients and constituencies may experience these tactics. Consider whether your tactics are accessible to individuals with disabilities. If you are engaging single parents who work long hours, they may be unable to attend a Lobby Day that requires unpaid time off of work. Trans individuals who do not publically identify as trans because of safety concerns may not feel they can safely advocate for LGBTQ+ rights in public. Individuals who have previously been convicted of a crime or those who are undocumented may find the risk of participating in a sit-in or civil disobedience too high.

Some organizations may feel more comfortable with tactics that are less aggressive, finding contest/confrontational tactics to be problematic (Hardina 2002). In fact, there is some dispute among social workers as to whether some of the more aggressive tactics are consistent with the National Association of Social Workers (2017) Code of Ethics. This builds on a history of debate, both within and outside of social work, between the "means" that we use and the social justice "ends" we may achieve. Essentially, at issue is whether it is appropriate to use any tactic—no matter how problematic—if it is likely to lead to more socially just policy, or whether certain tactics cross an ethical line, regardless of their potential outcomes. In the well-known book on challenging power structures, *Rules for Radicals*, Saul Alinksy (1971) argues for the former stance, that "ends justify the means," meaning that any tactic is acceptable if it helps to bring about success in fighting for social justice. As an advocate, this is an important question to ask yourself and to reflect upon with your colleagues and allies. Later in this book, we explore these and other ethical considerations in much more depth, including examples of scenarios you might encounter in your advocacy campaigns.

FURTHER REFLECTION: Do the Ends Justify the Means?
Before you continue reading, take a few minutes and reflect on this debate between ends and means. Do you believe that any tactic can be justifiable if it moves the needle toward social justice in an advocacy campaign? Why or why not? Are there any tactics that you would find problematic in an advocacy campaign regardless of the ends they achieve? Which ones, and why? What does the Code of Ethics have to say on this topic?

At the same time, tactics should be chosen strategically, based on what is most likely to move your target, given the specific political context at hand. In selecting your tactics, it is important to keep in mind that there should be a clear, logical link between all of the different aspects of your strategic advocacy plan. Make sure to ask yourself whether the tactics you have selected are the most appropriate for your identified targets, your goals, and your overall strategy. Reflect on why you think that the specific tactics you select will help you change your target's mind.

APPLY YOUR SKILLS: Selecting Appropriate Advocacy Tactics
Reflecting on the goals and targets you have developed, identify at least three tactics for your advocacy campaign. Place each tactic in the appropriate spot on your Advocacy Campaign Planning Chart provided in Fig. 6.8.

Review of Key Terms and Concepts

Bill filing deadline: a date after which no further bills may be proposed during that legislative session.

Code: the entire body of statutes for a specific government.

Collaborative tactics: strategies typically used when you are trying to work together with your target to achieve your advocacy goals.

Contest/confrontational tactics: strategies used when there are significant differences between you and your target and little hope of coming to an agreement; often used to try to force a concession. At times, these tactics may even be illegal.

Demonstrative tactics: strategies typically used to show intensity of public concern regarding your advocacy goals.

Electoral tactics: strategies involving taking a long-range approach to changing who has decision-making power around your problem/change. These are often used when persuasive tactics consistently have no impact on your target.

Gatekeeper: individuals who control access to policy-makers, or those who have high credibility and will be able to present information that the target will take seriously.

Grassroots tactics: strategies typically used to grow support from key constituents who may then directly seek to influence your target.

Interest group: groups who seek to influence policy based on members' common interests and concerns.

Interest group report cards: records of voting behaviors of politicians on specific issues, tracked by various interest groups, political action committees, and other organizations. (Please refer to "Voting Records" for more information.)

Litigation tactics: strategies commonly used in cases where other tactics have not successfully prevented constitutional concerns.

Personalize the target: a type of target identification in advocacy campaign planning that focuses on specific individual(s), not entities.

Persuasive tactics: strategies typically used to resolve differences between you and your target, to bring them into agreement with you.

Primary target: the specific person or persons with the real power to give you what you want, i.e., make your goals happen. For example, this may be the person who has the deciding vote on a bill, or the person who has control over the budget that is needed to fund an initiative.

Professional organizations: type of nonprofit in which the members share a common professional interest.

Public education tactics: strategies typically used to elicit public concern and support for your policy change.

Secondary target: an individual who has more power over your primary target than you do. Typically, the secondary target has a direct link to the primary target, but is also someone who is more likely to be able to be influenced by you.

Statutes: written laws that govern a state or country.

Think tank: organization which conducts research on policy issues and disseminates this research to impact policy.

Trade association: members share a common business or trade interest.

Voting records: records of the voting behaviors of elected officials.

Resources

Bipartisan Vote Tracking Resources

Examples of vote tracking resources at the state level:
Kentucky Votes: http://www.kentuckyvotes.org
Michigan Votes: http://www.michiganvotes.org
Vote Smart: http://www.votesmart.org

Websites

Assessing whether online sources are reputable: http://libguides.adelphi.edu/fake_news

Bolder Advocacy: http://www.bolderadvocacy.org/tools-for-effective-advocacy/evaluating-advocacy/advocacy-capacity-tool or go to https://www.bolderadvocacy.org/ and in the menu under "Tools for Effective Advocacy" click "Evaluating Advocacy", then under the "Resources" heading click "Advocacy Capacity Tool".

Center for Public Policy Priorities (CPPP): http://forabettertexas.org/home.html

Choosing Strategies to Promote Community Health and Development: http://ctb.ku.edu/en/table-of-contents-community-assessment/choosing-strategies-to-promote-community-health-and-development

Getting Issues on the Agenda: http://ctb.ku.edu/en/table-of-contents/assessment/getting-issues-on-the-public-agenda

Legislative Reference Library of Texas: http://www.lrl.state.tx.us

Library of Congress websites for voting records:
https://www.congress.gov/roll-call-votes

Michigan State University Advocacy Scholars Program:

Assessing Community Needs and Resources: http://ctb.ku.edu/en/assessing-community-needs-and-resources

National League of Cities: www.nlc.org

New York State's "Capitol Confidential": http://blog.timesunion.com/capitol/

United States Code: http://uscode.house.gov/

U.S. Department of Health and Human Services: https://www.hhs.gov

U.S. House of Representatives roll call votes: http://clerk.house.gov/legislative/legvotes.aspx

U.S. Senate roll call votes: https://www.senate.gov/reference/Index/Votes.htm or go to https://www.senate.gov and in the menu under "Reference" click the "Statistics and Lists" tab, then click "Votes" on the right hand side of the landing page. Or go to https://www.senate.gov/pagelayout/legislative/a_three_sections_with_teasers/votes.htm

Utah Department of Child and Family Services: https://dcfs.utah.gov

Wisconsin Legislative Reference Bureau: https://legis.wisconsin.gov/lrb

---

References

Alinksy, S. (1971). *Rules for Radicals: A Practical Primer for Realistic Radicals*. New York, NY: Vintage Books.

Associated Press. (2016, May 19). Texas lowering education requirements for CPS caseworkers. *The Washington Times*.

Bobo, K., Kendall, J., & Max, S. (2010). *Organizing for social change* (4th ed.). Santa Ana, CA: The Forum Press.

Brennan Center for Justice. (2017). *Voting rights restoration efforts in Virginia*. Retrieved from https://www.brennancenter.org/analysis/voting-rights-restoration-efforts-virginia.

California Legislative Information. (n.d.). *California Law Code search*. Retrieved from http://leginfo.legislature.ca.gov/faces/codes.xhtml.

Cooper, J., & Hairston, D. (2014). *Leveraging MSW coursework to set and implement a policy agenda*. Policy conference 2.0, Austin, TX.

Hardina, D. (2002). *Analytical skills for community organization practice*. New York, NY: Columbia University Press.

Haynes, K. S., & Mickelson, J. S. (2010). *Affecting change: Social workers in the political arena* (6th ed.). Boston, MA: Allyn & Bacon.

Hoefer, R. (2006). Understanding the issue. In *Advocacy practice for social justice* (3rd ed., pp. 52–74). Oxford: Oxford University Press.

Mosley, J. E. (2011). Institutionalization, privatization, and political opportunity: What tactical choices reveal about the policy advocacy of human service nonprofits. *Nonprofit and Voluntary Sector Quarterly, 403*(3), 435–457.

National Association of Social Workers. (2017). *Code of Ethics of the National Association of Social Workers*. Washington, DC: National Association of Social Workers.

Nazaryan, A. (2017, Crooked media fights Trump with 'Pod Save America'. *Newsweek*.

Nebraska Legislature. (n.d.). *Search laws*. Retrieved from http://www.nebraskalegislature.gov/laws/laws.php.

Piven, F. F., & Cloward, R. A. (1977). *Poor people's movements: Why they succeed, how they fail*. New York, NY: Vintage Books.

Reticker-Flynn, J. (2013). Youth activist's toolkit. In Advocates for Youth (Ed.). Washington, DC. http://www.advocatesforyouth.org/storage/advfy/documents/Activist_Toolkit/activisttoolkit.pdf.

Richan, W. (2006). Setting an action agenda. In *Lobbying for social change* (3rd ed., pp. 37–57). Routledge: New York.

Sen, R. (2003). Stir it up: Lessons in community organizing and advocacy. Jossey-Bass: San Francisco, CA.

Texas Legislative Council Research Division. (n.d.). *Process for House Bills: Texas Legislature*. Retrieved from http://www.tlc.texas.gov/docs/billprocess/BillProcessHouse_Final.pdf.

Vance, S. (2011). *The advocacy handbook: A practitioner's guide to achieving policy goals through organization networks*. Bethesda, MA: Columbia Books Inc.

Vote Smart. (2017). *Christine Radogno's voting records*. Retrieved from http://votesmart.org/candidate/key-votes/9515/christine-radogno - WRSJhmn1DIU.

Planning the Political Intervention: Electoral Campaigns

7

Table of Contents

© Springer International Publishing AG 2018
S.R. Lane, S. Pritzker, *Political Social Work*,
https://doi.org/10.1007/978-3-319-68588-5_7

Section 1: Overview

In this chapter, we build from the five-stage process for developing political strategy introduced in Chap. 5, and adapt it to take you through the process of planning an electoral campaign. Electoral campaigns are those that focus on convincing voters to cast their ballot for or against a particular candidate or issue. They "represent the core of representative democracy" (Rackaway 2011). In fact, "the quality of a democratic society can be easily linked to the quality of its election campaigns" (para 1).

The five-stage process outlined in this chapter is most relevant to domains 1, 4, and 5, specifically to strategies involving increasing voter registration, working on campaigns or running for office, seeking passage or defeat of ballot initiatives or referenda, and educating voters and underrepresented groups about policy issues that are part of electoral campaigns. As a quick review, these five stages are as follows:

1. Determining the specific purpose of the electoral campaign.
2. Assessing the internal (organizational) and external (environmental) context for the electoral campaign.
3. Identifying the campaign's long-term, intermediate, and short-term goals.
4. Selecting specific targets for the electoral campaign.
5. Identifying and selecting the tactics the campaign will use.

Developing Social Work Competency
The Council on Social Work Education establishes educational standards for all social work programs in the USA. Content in this chapter supports building competency in the following areas that are considered core to the practice of social work:
COMPETENCY 3: Advance Human Rights and Social, Economic, and Environmental Justice
COMPETENCY 4: Engage in Practice-Informed Research and Research-Informed Practice
COMPETENCY 5: Engage in Policy Practice
COMPETENCY 7: Assess Individuals, Families, Groups, Organizations, and Communities
COMPETENCY 8: Intervene with Individuals, Families, Groups, Organizations, and Communities

Domains of Political Social Work	
1. Engaging individuals and communities in political processes	◄
2. Influencing policy agendas and decision-making	
3. Holding professional and political positions	
4. Engaging with electoral campaigns	◄
5. Seeking and holding elected office	◄

Section 2: Determining the Specific Purpose of the Electoral Campaign (Stage 1)

A campaign plan is one of the earliest products of your campaign effort. It includes the blueprint of all of the activities you will do throughout the course of the campaign, starting at day 1 (including the primary election if there is one) and ending on the days after Election Day (Shaw 2014). A campaign plan is an internal document but might be shared with others, such as potential donors or staff members, to demonstrate the viability of your campaign. We have provided a link to a sample campaign plan from Wellstone Action in the Resources section at the end of this chapter to illustrate what a full plan for an electoral campaign might look like.

A good campaign plan includes each of the following elements:

- An overview of the campaign's strategy
- Voter targeting
- Field and voter contact plans
- Outreach plans
- The campaign timeline
- The campaign's overall message
- Campaign staff and volunteer roles and responsibilities
- Plans for raising and spending money

In this chapter, we focus on the first five elements. Subsequent chapters of this book examine messaging, staffing, and financial issues in more depth.

As we begin the process of developing a campaign plan, we start by identifying the specific purpose of the electoral campaign. Of course, the primary purpose of any electoral campaign is to win! It is important, however, to be even clearer and more specific in defining your campaign's purpose. In this section, we explore critical concepts to keep in mind as we do this. In advancing a cause through the electoral process, we will choose from two types of electoral campaigns: (1) a candidate campaign, where we are seeking votes for a specific individual to hold elected office, or (2) an issue campaign, where we are seeking votes for or against a specific issue. Within these types of campaigns, your purpose may differ based on the details described below.

Candidate Elections

First, in a **candidate election**, designed to elect a person or slate of people to office, determine the kind of election in which you are participating, and what this means for what the campaign is seeking to accomplish. Is it seeking to defeat one candidate or multiple candidates; to win a majority or plurality of votes; to situate the candidate for a run in a subsequent election; or perhaps to push back on an attempt to get your candidate out of office?

A key factor to consider in identifying the purpose of your campaign is whether the election in which your candidate will be running is partisan or nonpartisan. A **partisan race** is one in which each candidate is nominated by a political party. This could happen as part of a primary election or caucus or as part of a **nominating** process by the official members of that party. Either selection process gives the candidate the right to use the label of that political party during the corresponding general election and to access that party's resources, including money, volunteers, and reputation. A **nonpartisan race** is one in which candidates run without any party affiliation in a general election. In the USA, nonpartisan elections are most common for judicial elections, but are also seen in municipal elections, including Los Angeles, Portland, Chicago, and Phoenix (National League of Cities 2016), and in village and school board elections in New York state.

Candidate elections can generally be divided into one of four categories that impact the dynamics of your specific electoral campaign: primary elections, general elections, special elections, and recall elections (Ishiyama and Breuning 2010).

Partisan Elections: Primaries, Caucuses, and Conventions
In the USA, the process by which political parties choose the candidates who will represent them in the general election are, in the words of the National Conference of State Legislators (2016b), "complex and nuanced, to say the least" and "a cause of confusion among voters and election administrators alike" (para 1). **Primary elections** are almost always partisan, and are one way to winnow down a large field of candidates into a smaller list. They allow members of a political party to decide who will represent them in a future general or regular election. When planning for a primary campaign, your campaign's purpose is to get your candidate to the general election.

Primary elections may be held for federal, state, and municipal elections. Primaries for federal and state offices are typically conducted by state governments.

U.S. States by Primary Election Type

Fig. 7.1 U.S. States by Presidential primary election type. Created by Dr. Thomas Felke, Florida Gulf Coast University Department of Social Work, from data provided by the National Conference of State Legislators (2016b)

Members of political parties, whether Democratic, Republican, Green, Libertarian, or another party, work within existing state laws to choose candidates. Primaries, as practiced in the USA, generally reinforce our **two-party system**, where the two major political parties hold the majority of the power and positions in the political realm. **Third parties** or smaller parties hold few seats. Fewer still are held by those who are **unaffiliated**, officially connected with no political party (Ishiyama and Breuning 2010; Snyder and Ting 2002).

 Primaries or **primary elections** can be divided into six categories from most restrictive to least restrictive (NCSL 2016b). Figure 7.1 illustrates this diversity in types of Presidential primaries in the USA, as of 2018:

1. Nine states with **closed primaries** require voters to be registered with a specific party in order to participate in the primary. Voters cannot participate in a primary for a party for which they are not registered, leaving independent or unaffiliated voters with no opportunity to vote in the state's primaries.
2. Seven states with **partially closed primaries** give political parties the opportunity to choose whether unaffiliated voters can participate in that party's primary, but do not allow those registered with a different party to participate. This allows more flexibility from year to year, but may lead to confusion about who can vote. (One author has lived in two of these states and had no idea that either had this system, and despite active political involvement, had no idea.)

3. Six states with **partially open primaries** let voters cross party lines but they have to publically declare their ballot choice. Voting in a party's primary may be considered registering for that party.
4. In nine states with **primaries open to unaffiliated voters** you must choose the ballot of the party you are registered with, but if you are unaffiliated, you can choose any party's ballot. Some states may require you to affiliate with a party if you choose this option.
5. Fifteen states with **open primaries** do not require voters to declare a party on their voter registration form. This system provides maximum flexibility and privacy, but may make it harder for parties to nominate candidates who represent that party's interests.
6. The final category, "**top-two**" **primaries**, includes four states that list all candidates on one ballot. Some, but not all of these list party affiliation or party preference next to each candidate's name. The top two candidates go on to the general election, so you may end up with two candidates from the same party in that election.

States are not required to apply the same rules both to presidential and state-level primary elections. While some do, California uses the top-two primary system for state level races, but holds separate party primaries for president (NCSL 2016b). In many states, state-level and presidential primaries are held on the same day (the least costly way of doing it), while in others, they are held on different days. Instead of primaries, 12 states (most famously Iowa) use **caucuses** to select presidential candidates. Caucuses can be thought of as more like a neighborhood meeting rather than a standard voting booth-type election (Montanaro 2016). There is no one standard way to hold a caucus. As a result, in Iowa, Democrats and Republicans use different processes, with Democrats gathering in public groups to support their candidate and Republicans voting informally via secret ballot. The Iowa Democratic caucus process is fairly complicated. To help you understand it, we provide a link to a fun video, in the Resources section, of the Lego people explaining the Iowa caucus.

For presidential elections, delegates are awarded according to party rules, based on the results of voting at the state level or other party guidelines, and those delegates determine which candidates are officially nominated at national nominating **conventions**. Many state parties also hold statewide conventions to select state party leaders and adopt party platforms. A few states use these conventions as part of their process for determining which candidates will represent the party in statewide elections (Sabato et al. 2013).

General Elections
General elections or **regular elections** are the binding elections that decide who will hold a given elected position (Lipset 2000; Schmitter and Karl 1991). In a general election campaign, the purpose of your campaign is to help your candidate to win, and therefore gain the desired elected office.

In general elections in most of the USA, the winner is the person who gets the most votes. This is usually the case, even if there are multiple candidates and the winner only receives a **plurality** (the most votes) but not a **majority** (more than

50%) of the votes. In a few places, the winner must receive at least 50% of the vote to win, and if no candidate gets at least 50% of the vote, a runoff election will be held. Runoff election systems in some states, like many voting systems, have a deep history linked with efforts to keep power away from African-Americans. For further discussion of this history, see Wilson (2014).

When general elections are held depends on the level of government involved in the election. By federal statute (3 USC Ch. 1, § 1), the Presidential Election Day is defined as follows (U.S. National Archives and Records Administration n.d.):

> § 1. The electors of President and Vice President shall be appointed, in each State, on the Tuesday next after the first Monday in November, in every fourth year succeeding every election of a President and Vice President.

This date was set in 1845 (The Twenty-Eighth Congress of the United States n.d.), as shown in Fig. 7.2.

Elections for members of the U.S. House of Representatives, who serve 2-year terms, always fall on the presidential Election Day (e.g., 2020, 2024) and on the Tuesday after the first Monday in November every even year in between the

ACTS OF THE TWENTY-EIGHTH CONGRESS

OF THE

UNITED STATES,

Passed at the second session, which was begun and held at the City of Washington, in the district of Columbia, on Monday, the 2d day of December, 1844, and ended the 3d day of March, 1845.

JOHN TYLER, President of the United States. WILLIE P. MANGUM, President of the Senate, pro tempore. JOHN W. JONES, Speaker of the House of Representatives.

STATUTE II.

CHAP. I.—*An Act to establish a uniform time for holding elections for electors of President and Vice President in all the States of the Union.*(a)   Jan. 23, 1845.

Be it enacted by the Senate and House of Representatives of the United States of America in Congress assembled, That the electors of President and Vice President shall be appointed in each State on the Tuesday next after the first Monday in the month of November of the year in which they are to be appointed: *Provided,* That each State may by law provide for the filling of any vacancy or vacancies which may occur in its college of electors when such college meets to give its electoral vote: *And provided, also,* when any State shall have held an election for the purpose of choosing electors, and shall fail to make a choice on the day aforesaid, then the electors may be appointed on a subsequent day in such manner as the State shall by law provide.   Election day fixed. / Vacancies. / In case of no election.

APPROVED, January 23, 1845.

Fig. 7.2 Establishment of Election Day

Presidential Election years (e.g., 2018, 2022, 2026). These latter, in-between year elections are referred to as **midterm elections**. Elections for U.S. Senators, who serve staggered 6-year terms may take place either on the presidential Election Day or on the November midterm election day. Generally, many fewer people vote in midterm elections than in Presidential elections.

State law governs when state and local offices are on the ballot, thus these election days vary widely across the country. While many states hold elections for state and local seats on the November Election Day, in order to increase turnout and save the expense of running a separate election, this is up to the discretion of the state. This results in individual states holding elections on their own calendars. For example, in Connecticut, all municipal elections are held in the odd-numbered years (also called "off" years, when there are no Congressional elections). In some towns in Connecticut, those elections are held on the second Tuesday in November. In others, the elections are held on the first Monday in May. Other states that hold at least some regular or general municipal elections outside of November include Massachusetts and Wisconsin. Virginia and New Jersey hold gubernatorial elections in November of the odd year immediately following a presidential election (e.g., 2017, 2021, 2025), which means that these two states' elections often garner national attention as signals of how voters are feeling about the president's administration after almost a year in office (Malone 2013).

Special Elections

Special elections are held when there is a vacancy in an elected position outside of the usual election timeframe. Vacancies commonly emerge when an executive appoints an elected official to a high-ranking government position, when elected officials resign, or upon an official's serious illness or death. The process for filling vacancies differs from state to state, but if the state's statute calls for it, a special election can be held quickly to fill the seat. In 2017, resignations resulted in two vacancies in the Connecticut State Senate on the day the State Senate convened, triggering special elections by Connecticut statute. The winner of one of those elections was a sitting member of the Connecticut General Assembly (the lower house of Connecticut state government). In a domino effect, his win required that another special election be held for his General Assembly seat (Pazniokas 2017). In special elections, your campaign's purpose is to get your candidate elected to the vacant position, often in a tighter time frame than your campaign would have in a typical general election. When the special election is set for an irregular voting day, this election is likely to receive lower turnout than if it would have taken place on a regular Election Day.

BUILD YOUR KNOWLEDGE: Revisiting Election Day
Why do we vote on Tuesdays? Visit the TedEd website (https://ed.ted.com/) and search for the video *Why do Americans vote on Tuesdays?* After you watch this video, devise an alternative to our current Election Day. Reflect on why your alternative might be an improvement on the current system. What are the pros and cons of your alternative?

Recall Elections

A **recall** is the opposite of a typical election. It is the process by which a local or state official can be removed from office through a vote before his or her term has ended. The majority of states allow for the recall of local and/or state officials (NCSL 2016a), although the process and grounds for said recall vary wildly. In Montana, for example, grounds for a recall include "physical or mental lack of fitness, incompetence, violation of oath of office, official misconduct, or conviction of a felony offense" (NCSL 2017c). Recall elections may occur outside of the regular general election timeframe. In a recall election, your campaign's purpose depends on which side of the recall you are working. If you are part of the recall campaign, your purpose is to succeed in getting the targeted official removed from office. If you are part of the official's campaign, your purpose is to push back on the recall effort and keep the official in office.

In one example earning national attention, in 2011 and 2012, petitions circulated with enough signatures in Wisconsin to have Governor Scott Walker, the Lieutenant Governor, and a total of 13 out of 33 members of the Wisconsin State Senate stand for recall elections. Three of the state senators were recalled (NCSL 2016a), one additional state senator resigned, and by 2012, the control of the State Senate had shifted from Republican to Democrat, while the governor and lieutenant governor prevailed in their elections. In a controversial 2012 decision that took place during this recall effort, the Wisconsin Government Accountability Board voted to make signatures on recall petitions more easily available to the public via a searchable form on the web (Associated Press 2012). Unlike an individual's vote, recall petitions, including signatures, are public documents.

Issue Campaigns

In an issue campaign, you similarly need to determine the kind of election in which you are participating, and what it means for what your campaign is seeking to accomplish. For example, are you seeking to compel a legislative body to consider an issue, trying to force repeal of a bill or ordinance that has passed in your state or municipality, or seeking to change the state's constitution?

Above, we focused on electoral campaigns that allow for **representative democracy**, democracy in which citizens elect individuals who govern on their behalf. In some cases, in a practice of **direct democracy,** state laws allow citizens to vote directly on specific state or municipal issues. **Issue campaigns**, often in the form of **ballot initiatives** and **referendum campaigns**, ask voters to decide about anything from the school budget to, in most states, a state constitutional amendment. (Note that while processes for amending state constitutions vary widely, Delaware is the only state in the USA in which some form of voter ratification is *not* necessary to amend the state's constitution (Erickson and Barilla 2002).) In issue campaigns, specific ideas are on the ballot rather than people.

On the state level, direct democracy can take one of two forms. An **initiative** is a "process that enables citizens to bypass their state legislature by placing proposed statutes and, in some states, constitutional amendments on the ballot" (NCSL 2012, para 1). Twenty-four states have provisions in their state Constitutions for an initiative process, first adopted by South Dakota in 1898. Mississippi was the most recent state to add an initiative process, in 1992. An issue campaign interested in placing an initiative on the ballot for public vote will generally need to collect enough signatures to prove its issue is valid. Initiative language and petition signatures are subject to review by state officials to ensure that they are valid and in compliance with existing laws. The validity of signatures may be challenged by the opposing campaign. Once determined valid, in some states, the initiative is then placed directly on the ballot. In others, the legislature first has the opportunity to act on the initiative or even to simultaneously propose its own competing ballot measure.

A **referendum** is similar in many ways to an initiative. It also appears on the ballot for direct voter decision-making. It can be in the form of a **legislative referendum**, where the state legislature refers a measure to the public for a vote after it has been approved by that body, or a **citizen referendum**, which comes directly from the public. Referenda can be used either to support or repeal a bill passed by a legislative body. For example, in Nevada, the legislature can refer a piece of legislation directly to the public in the form of a legislative referendum. This is most often used in the state for a particularly controversial bill (Kant 2005). If the public wants to nullify a policy passed by the state legislature, Nevada grants public authority to gather signatures to put a policy on the ballot (Kant 2005). If the public votes against the law, it becomes void.

Issue campaigns may take somewhat differing forms at the municipal level, though in many ways they mirror the state processes described above. In some municipalities, citizens can propose legislation through direct initiative. For example, in specific large cities in Texas that have special state-granted "home rule" status, voters can petition for a public vote on behalf a new ordinance (an initiative) or to repeal an existing ordinance (a referendum). These enable the public to bypass a city council that they believe is not appropriately acting on the ordinance (Texas Municipal League 2015).

In contrast, issue campaigns in approximately 1000 towns, including those in six New England states (Connecticut, Maine, Massachusetts, New Hampshire, Rhode Island, and Vermont) and some Minnesota townships (Minnesota Association of Townships 2017), focus on influencing citizens' participation in **town meetings**. In town meetings, decisions about the municipality are made directly by town residents who choose (and are able) to show up (Zimmerman 1999). In Vermont, 230+ towns hold meetings annually, generally the first Tuesday after the first Monday in March (Bryan 2003). We refer here specifically to the type of town meetings that allow citizens to vote directly on issues. Towns also may hold town meetings where there are discussions but not votes. Elected officials may also hold town meetings as opportunities for residents of their districts to voice their opinions.

APPLY YOUR SKILLS: Your State's Options for Direct Democracy
Visit the National Conference of State Legislatures resource page on elections and campaigns (http://www.ncsl.org/research/elections-and-campaigns). Follow the link to "Initiative and Referendum," and find your state's rules on initiatives and referenda. Does your state allow initiatives or referenda? If so, find out the latest initiative or referendum that came to a public vote in your state. What was it, and did it succeed or fail?

CASE STUDY: An Initiative Process

In 2015, the Center for Public Integrity awarded South Dakota a grade of "F" in state integrity. Concerns about integrity and transparency in South Dakota's state government have crystallized in recent years after several high-profile news stories about corruption. One such story included an apparent suicide by a high-level political appointee. After his suicide, the public learned that he had been accused of felony theft from state and federal funds. A long investigation followed, ensnaring other South Dakota politicians, including the former Governor—now U.S. Senator Mike Rounds. Ultimately, a legislative committee conducted hearings and determined that only the initial employee was responsible for any problematic or unethical activity (Tupper 2015).

Following this, South Dakotan voters brought forth a public initiative on the 2016 ballot. Initiated Measure 22, "an Act to revise certain provisions concerning campaign finance and lobbying, to create a democracy credit program, to establish an ethics commission, and to make an appropriation therefor," also referred to as the "South Dakota Government Accountability and Anti-Corruption Act" (South Dakota Secretary of State 2017), was one of ten ballot measures up for direct public vote that year (Fig. 7.3).

The initiative passed on November 8, 2016, with 51.62% of the popular vote in favor of the measure and 48.38% opposed (South Dakota Secretary of State 2017). However, success for the initiative's supporters was short-lived. A few months later, the state legislature in South Dakota used "emergency rules" to

INITIATIVE PETITION

WE, THE UNDERSIGNED qualified voters of the state of South Dakota, petition that the following proposed law be submitted to the voters of the state of South Dakota at the general election on November 8, 2016 for their approval or rejection pursuant to the Constitution of the State of South Dakota.

Title: An initiated measure to revise State campaign finance and lobbying laws, create a publicly funded campaign finance program, create an ethics commission, and appropriate funds

Attorney General's Explanation: This measure extensively revises State campaign finance laws. It requires additional disclosures and increased reporting. It lowers contribution amounts to political action committees; political parties; and candidates for statewide, legislative, or county office. It also imposes limits on contributions from candidate campaign committees, political action committees, and political parties.

The measure creates a publicly funded campaign finance program for statewide and legislative candidates who choose to participate and agree to limits on campaign contributions and expenditures. Under the program, two "credits" are issued to each registered voter, who assigns them to participating candidates. The credits are redeemed from the program, which is funded by an annual State general-fund appropriation of $9 per registered voter. The program fund may not exceed $12 million at any time.

The measure creates an appointed ethics commission to administer the credit program and to enforce campaign finance and lobbying laws.

The measure prohibits certain State officials and high-level employees from lobbying until two years after leaving State government. It also places limitations on lobbyists' gifts to certain state officials and staff members.

If approved, the measure may be challenged in court on constitutional grounds. **RECEIVED**

The text of the proposed law is as follows: 2:53 am   NOV 06 2015

Fig. 7.3 Initiative petition for ethics reform in South Dakota, 2015

(continued)

overturn the public's decision. This was achieved through a 54-13 vote in the South Dakota House, a 270-8 vote in the South Dakota Senate, and a signature by the Governor (Krieg 2017).

While the state legislature overturned the specific initiative voted on by the public, it passed several pieces of legislation with the stated goal of addressing the same ethical issues as the repealed initiative (Albers 2017). These were signed by Governor Daugaard on March 10, 2017.

Proponents and opponents of Initiated Measure 22 disagree about whether the new legislation will achieve the same goals as the repealed initiative. However, it is worth noting that without the initiative, it is unlikely that the legislature would have considered any bills seeking ethics reform.

The future ramifications of this process remain to be seen. As all South Dakotan legislators serve 2-year terms, all members of the South Dakota House of Representatives and Senate will be on the ballot again in 2018, as will the state's Governor. In addition, the South Dakota legislature is considering changing the process to make initiated measures and other ballot initiatives more difficult to enact (Mercer 2017). Want to watch the Initiative Referendum Task Force debating this? We provide a link in Resources.

FURTHER REFLECTION: Initiative Case Study Reflection
Discussion question #1: This case study offers an interesting juxtaposition of direct democracy (South Dakotans' support for a popular initiative) and representative democracy (South Dakotan legislators' opposition to this initiative, while supporting other reforms). What are your thoughts about the comparative importance of direct and representative democracy?

Discussion question #2: In this case study, advocates pursued an electoral strategy in South Dakota, although the South Dakota Government Accountability and Anti-Corruption Act was not implemented. In your opinion, were they successful in moving the conversation on ethics forward?

Section 3: Assessing the Internal (Organizational) and External (Environmental) Context for the Electoral Campaign (Stage 2)

In an electoral campaign, as with other social work efforts, conducting a thorough assessment of both the internal and external context is critical. For an electoral campaign, preliminary assessments often start long before we actually take the plunge into running for office or working on a campaign. Then, once your campaign is active and starting to think about strategy, it is time to engage your leadership team in a full and honest assessment of the internal and external context for your campaign. Careful assessment of the internal and external strengths and limitations of your campaign helps you both identify the assets upon which you can build as you design your strategy, and anticipate where the campaign may be vulnerable.

At the same time you are conducting your assessment, others will be conducting their own assessment. A number of groups recruit and train candidates for electoral office. Political parties, especially the two main US political parties, serve as informal gatekeepers as they actively recruit candidates. On the federal level, the Democratic Congressional Campaign Committee (DCCC) and the National Republican Congressional Committee (NRCC) seek out and support specific candidates that they see as most likely to be successful at garnering both the funds and votes necessary for a successful race for Congress. This party recruitment can start very early in the campaign cycle. For example, 1 day before Inauguration Day in January 2017, the NRCC head of candidate recruitment announced that her top priorities for the 2018 Congressional elections included recruiting female Republican candidates (Marcos 2017). Three months later, DCCC leaders reported that they had already met with over 250 possible candidates in 64 Congressional districts in advance of the 2018 elections (Dovere 2017). Your assessment needs to be thoughtful and well-done; however, if your assessment takes too long, you might already be playing catch up!

APPLY YOUR SKILLS: Potential Electoral Campaign Scenarios
Read each of the following scenarios and discuss the corresponding question(s).

Scenario 1: You hear rumors that your local member of Congress is considering retiring in the next few years. He has held the seat for 20 years, so this is an exciting opportunity for your district and for individuals who have contemplated a run for higher office. You have been active in local politics for many years, and have held a seat on your school board. Because of your involvement, you have been asked to sit on the committee formed by your local political party that will decide which candidate(s) they will endorse.

Discussion question #1: What benefit would there be to having a social worker serve on this committee?

Discussion question #2: Should you agree to serve on the committee, consider running for this position, or both? Why?

Scenario 2: You have been the campaign manager for your hometown's state representative in three separate elections. Your candidate was successful in the first campaign, and became a state representative. Two years later, you ran her campaign when she won again. Last year, she ran for reelection, but this time, she lost. The candidate has decided she needs a break from politics and will not run in next year's election. Several people in the community who are in your political party have expressed potential interest in running, but no one has formally **declared** (said they were running).

(continued)

Discussion question #1: Should you consider running for this position? Why or why not?

Discussion question #1: What benefit would there be to having a social worker run for this position?

Scenario 3: You are the executive director of a statewide nonprofit organization and have been very active in state and local politics. Your lease is up and you and your family are ready to decide where to live for at least the next few years. You have always wanted to run for office, but your political views are a minority in your current town, so you never considered a campaign possible.

Discussion question #1: Should you consider your political goals when moving?

Discussion question #2: If so, what factors should you consider when looking to move to a new town?

Assessing Your Individual and Organizational Context

Before we begin discussion of how to assess your campaign's internal context, we encourage you to complete the activity apply your skills: potential electoral campaign scenarios.

The considerations raised in these scenarios are critical to the kinds of self-focused internal assessment that is necessary before embarking on an electoral campaign, regardless of the role you will ultimately play. As a social worker who may be considering running for office or who is looking for a political campaign that you can contribute to, we encourage you to reflect on the types of issues raised by these scenarios. Do you already have a candidate in mind to support (yourself, for example)? Is there a particular race in which you are interested: for example, are you particularly bothered by the way that your district's incumbent state representative has been voting, and are committed to seeing this representative replaced? What kind of role are you seeking? Are you interested in running yourself, or in developing experience and connections for a future run?

Consider your own values as you embark on an electoral campaign. Given that no candidate is ever going to align perfectly with your values, political beliefs, and issue positions (unless you run yourself!), you need to know your "deal breakers." On which issues are you willing or unwilling to compromise? Think very carefully before considering working for a candidate who does not align with values and priorities that are important to you. If the best candidate in the race aligns with some of your values, but not others, are you comfortable working for that candidate? There is no one right answer to this question, but it is a common question that those of us who work in the political arena face. As with choosing which candidate to vote for in an election, each one of us makes this calculation based on our professional social work values, as well as our own personal values and priorities.

Whether you are considering running for office yourself or are considering whether to work for a candidate, consider whether the candidate is able to do the internal work necessary to win an election. That is, does the candidate have the capacity and desire to create an organization that can win? The internal assessment questions raised in Chap. 5 are particularly helpful with this evaluation. These include questions assessing the time, money, and people resources the campaign will have access to, its access to expertise, its sources of power, and—of critical importance— whether the candidate is fully prepared to embark on all that a run for office entails.

Once you are on board with a campaign and ready to begin strategic planning, internal assessment must involve a comprehensive assessment of your candidate's strengths *and* weaknesses relative to the specific **district** in which you are situated. A district is a political subdivision that is grouped together to elect a specific representative(s) to a government body. Just as we look for a match between the person and environment in direct practice (Gitterman and Germain 2008), we look for a match between the candidate and the specific district and race in political practice. This focused assessment will help us to determine whether the candidate is a good match for the district. This assessment also will be very useful in subsequent stages for helping the campaign communicate to voters why the candidate should be elected to represent the district.

POLITICAL SOCIAL WORKER PROFILE: Jessica J. Mitchell, MSW
Democratic Political Consultant (Fig. 7.4).

Fig. 7.4 Jessica
J. Mitchell, MSW

Usually, I work on the finance side of campaigns, so I spend a lot of time coaching a candidate to help them raise money, and doing related paperwork. While I've always had an interest in politics, attending my MSW program finally pushed me to pursue politics as a full time career. The importance of having progressive, open minded, elected officials was made all the more clear to me while studying and working with the most vulnerable among us. Without progressive elected officials, I became concerned that our government would continue to ignore the plight of those most in need of services.

It is so hard to describe life on a campaign, because no <u>one</u> story can give someone a better understanding what working on a campaign is like. Campaigns (like so many other social work jobs) can't be summed up in one simple story or explanation. Some days are normal campaign days, but for the most part every day is different, starting with a plan that is off track by 9:05 a.m.

(continued)

There are definitely days where unexpected things happen. For example, during the weekend before Election Day, everyone is up for 18–20 hours a day. We are out at 1 a.m. putting out the last of our yard signs. Nothing is more depressing then finishing a campaign (especially if you lose) with leftover signs. Last year I worked on a congressional campaign for a woman who was a sitting town council person. In New York, elected officials are empowered to perform marriages, and she had one scheduled on her lunch break. Out of the blue, she texted me to meet her at a nearby park. It turned out that the couple did not know they needed witnesses for their marriage certificate, so I spent my lunch break as a witness at a wedding of two people I had never met.

Every skill you are taught in social work school is essential to campaign life, no matter what job you hold on a campaign. Most of a campaign is a long stretch of building relationships—with donors, volunteers, local political types and elected officials—and a few weeks of asking them to do stuff that needs to get done. These skills also apply to working with candidates, who I've grown to think of as my clients over the years.

The most important thing to remember, in any job, is to stay true to yourself. This is no different in politics. Many people in my life—family and friends and other social workers that I meet—are surprised (and sometimes horrified) to find out that I work in politics; others don't understand how, or why, a social worker ended up working in politics. However, every time I am working with or for a candidate, I am thinking about the next time that a bill will come up to increase funding for education, food stamps, student loan forgiveness or so many other important issues. I know that the candidate I am supporting will be voting in favor. Most everything that social workers do after graduation is authorized and funded by a government agency, one of many reasons it is so important for social workers to become actively aware and actively involved in the political process. Without a voice at the table, our interests and those of our clients will not be served.

Assessing the Social, Economic, and Political Context

Assessing the external environment for your campaign is relevant at two stages: (1) as you consider whether to jump into a particular election or race, whether as a potential candidate, staff, or volunteer and (2) as you begin the strategic planning process. In considering whether to become involved in a specific race, assess whether it is possible, or likely, for you or your candidate to win it. This process is important to your considerations about whether a candidate is a good match for the particular campaign. If your candidate does not seem likely to win the race, consider whether the context suggests some other benefit to you in running in or working on this race. For example, there are large numbers of **uncontested** races in the USA, where only one candidate from one party runs in the election. While there is much disagreement on this point, some argue that parties should not leave a district uncontested, because it communicates to voters that the party not running is disinterested in their issues, and therefore may have ripple effects for other elections on the ballot (Braden 2017). External considerations also help you to think through the various challenges present in the context that your campaign will want to address in order to be successful.

Can I (or My Candidate) Win?

It is not an exact science to determine whether a particular candidate can win a race. Otherwise we would just do the analysis and never hold actual elections. In fact, candidates do win even when conventional wisdom says they have no chance. However, an external assessment of the likelihood of your campaign winning, given the resources and context available, remains a critical step before the campaign begins. It gives your campaign important insight into your strengths and weaknesses, and will inform your campaign strategy.

This assessment can be conducted informally or formally, and it can be done well in advance of a campaign. You could conduct this assessment when choosing whether to run for office, or in choosing a place to live when you know you are interested in a future run. The data you gather at this stage will also help you estimate your win number, which is the actual number of voters you need to win, and the number of voters you need to contact to get to that number.

The first step of this assessment is perhaps the most important factor in determining whether you can win. Find out the status of the office. Does it have an **incumbent**, a person who is currently holding the office with no plans to leave? Is it an **open seat**, meaning there is no incumbent holding the seat? In the USA, incumbents have a sizeable advantage over their challengers. Incumbents in the U.S. Congress tend to win more than 85% of the time (The Center for Responsive Politics n.d.). At the state legislative level, incumbents win more than 90% of the time (Casey 2016). The common wisdom is that it is often not a good use of time to challenge an incumbent, and many incumbents are not challenged at all (Rogers 2014). In general, incumbents are more likely to be challenged in poor economic times, or as members of an unpopular leader's party. An exception is a **vulnerable** incumbent, one who is facing their first reelection, won last time by a small margin, is touched by scandal, or has other weaknesses (Biersack et al. 1993).

APPLY YOUR SKILLS: Find a Race

Find a potential electoral candidate campaign in your area—local, state, or federal—that you would like to more know about. You will refer back to this race in exercises throughout this chapter. Here, briefly describe the core characteristics of the campaign. What office is the candidate seeking, for what level of government? Who currently holds this office, and which party does this incumbent represent? As far as you can tell, is the incumbent planning to run for the office again in the next election?

Dist	Clinton	Trump	Clint%	Trump%	Obama	Romney	Obama%	Romney%
134	50,043	35,983	54.7%	39.3%	34,731	46,926	41.7%	56.4%
102	30,291	24,768	52.3%	42.7%	24,958	29,198	45.3%	53.0%
114	35,259	29,221	52.1%	43.2%	28,182	35,795	43.5%	55.2%
105	25,087	20,979	52.1%	43.6%	20,710	23,228	46.5%	52.1%
115	30,897	26,158	51.5%	43.6%	23,353	29,861	43.2%	55.3%
108	39,584	34,622	50.3%	44.0%	27,031	40,564	39.3%	59.0%
113	27,532	26,468	49.1%	47.2%	23,893	27,098	46.3%	52.5%
112	26,735	26,081	48.3%	47.1%	22,308	28,221	43.5%	55.0%
138	24,706	24,670	47.6%	47.5%	18,256	27,489	39.3%	59.2%
136	37,324	35,348	46.7%	44.2%	26,423	35,296	41.2%	55.1%

Fig. 7.5 Texas House district breakdown by presidential vote, 2016 and 2012 (Reproduced from Kuffner 2017)

Dist	Burns	Keasler	Burns%	Keasl%	Hampton	Keller	Hampt%	Keller%
105	23,012	21,842	49.0%	46.5%	19,580	21,745	45.8%	50.8%
113	25,411	26,940	46.4%	49.2%	22,651	25,693	45.6%	51.7%
115	26,876	28,999	45.8%	49.4%	21,431	28,402	41.5%	55.0%
134	39,985	44,560	45.4%	50.6%	33,000	42,538	42.3%	54.5%
102	26,096	28,210	45.3%	49.1%	23,232	27,295	44.3%	52.1%
043	21,812	25,213	44.3%	51.2%	21,565	22,434	47.5%	49.4%
112	23,798	27,901	43.9%	51.4%	20,942	26,810	42.4%	54.3%
135	25,998	31,365	43.7%	52.8%	20,745	30,922	39.2%	58.4%
138	22,119	26,669	43.6%	52.6%	17,470	26,224	38.9%	58.4%
114	28,774	35,129	43.3%	52.8%	26,441	33,128	43.1%	53.9%
136	32,436	37,883	42.7%	49.9%	23,925	32,484	39.3%	53.3%
132	29,179	36,667	42.7%	53.6%	20,237	30,515	38.9%	58.6%
065	26,010	32,772	42.4%	53.4%	20,732	30,377	39.1%	57.3%
052	28,698	34,976	42.2%	51.4%	21,947	28,562	40.8%	53.1%
054	22,114	27,979	42.0%	53.1%	20,110	24,571	43.5%	53.2%
045	31,530	39,309	41.7%	52.0%	24,897	32,734	40.6%	53.3%

Fig. 7.6 Texas House district breakdown by Court of Criminal Appeals vote, 2016 and 2012 (Reproduced from Kuffner 2017)

The second step of this process is to assess the district and the precincts that make up that district. At the district level, find out the typical voter turnout, the typical **party affiliation** of voters (with which party are they registered), and how the district typically votes by party.

In Figs. 7.5 and 7.6, we provide some examples from a newspaper-affiliated blog that broke down legislative districts in Texas by their voting numbers and percentages for both presidential and local races (Kuffner 2017). We encourage you to read the full post, linked in the Resources section. Figure 7.5 highlights an analysis of key Texas legislative districts by the candidates for which voters voted in the 2016 and 2012 presidential races. The first column is the state House district, followed by four columns showing the number and percentage of votes for each major party Presidential candidate in that district in 2016. The subsequent columns show the number and percentage of votes for each major party Presidential candidate in that district in 2012.

Figure 7.6 includes many of the same legislative districts in the same years, but instead reflects the votes for a statewide position, a seat on the state's Court of Criminal Appeals. (Judges are not elected in all states, nor are judicial elections partisan in all states, but in Texas, this is a partisan seat.) The first column once again is the state legislative district. The next four columns show the number and percentage of votes for two major party judge candidates in 2016. Burns was the Democrat, and Keasler was the Republican. The final four columns show the number and percentage of votes for the two major party candidates in 2012. Hampton was the Democrat, and Keller was the Republican candidate.

APPLY YOUR SKILLS: Analyze District Data

Find a district represented in both of the charts above. (The full charts can be found at http://blog.chron.com/kuffsworld/2017/03/precinct-analysis-the-targets-for-2018/.) Look at the vote in that district in 2012 for both president and Court of Criminal Appeals. Were the percentages of voters supporting Democratic and Republican candidates similar in the two races? Repeat the exercise for 2016 for both president and court of criminal appeals. Then compare within the district—what changes happened between 2012 and 2016?

APPLY YOUR SKILLS: Find Data About a Chosen Race

For the campaign you described earlier in this chapter, what data can you find about voting in that district? Using local news reports or election offices, can you determine what the voter turnout was in the district in the last three elections for that office? Which candidates ran in those races, and how many votes did they each get? Based on these data, what do you think are some key considerations for a potential candidate in the next election?

Although district-level analyses are critical, in an electoral campaign, you will need to focus most of your attention on the precinct level. A **precinct** is a subset of a district, the smallest subdivision within a state, and is a small geographic area in which voters are provided ballots for a particular office. Precincts are also sometimes referred to as electoral districts, voting districts, boxes, beats, or wards (U.S. Election Assistance Commission 2015). There are approximately 175,000 precincts in the USA. The number of voters in each precinct varies substantially depending on state law. For more information about the way that elections are administered in states across the country, we recommend the U.S. Election Assistance Commission report in the Resource section.

In a **precinct analysis**, you look at publically available records in your community to find out what the voting trends are and what candidates or methods have been successful in reaching voters in the past. During this process, data is collected on each precinct within the boundaries of the district. There are several main sources for gathering precinct analysis data, typically available for free or at a low cost (Shaw 2014):

- Local elections offices (available to everyone, may cost money)
- Local political parties (see more about this below)
- Local advocacy groups (if you have a relationship with them)
- The U.S. Census (free and publically available but can be difficult to navigate)

Precinct analysis can be conducted well in advance of a campaign. Completing the analysis prior to the campaign allows it to inform all of your strategic planning. Shaw's excellent description of precinct analysis includes the following considerations:

1. Consider the type of election. For a partisan primary election, gather information only about those who can vote in that party's primary. In a nonpartisan primary or general election, gather information for all eligible voters. Compare apples to apples: if it is a special election, compare to other special elections.
2. Reach out to your local election office. Do they have the data available on their website? Can they email you the data or provide it on a CD? Data that is already in Excel or can be converted from a PDF is ideal, but we work with what we get.
3. If a political party has endorsed the campaign, ask the party for any analyses they have already completed of your district.

Once you have access to the data, Shaw's (2014) book for campaign managers (see Resources) includes a sample template for an Excel spreadsheet that you can use for each of the comparable elections you are looking at. (This is a great task for a campaign volunteer or a friend who is good with data entry.) Once you have created the spreadsheets, use these numbers to help you and your team understand both the total numbers of voters per precinct and the overall turnout percentages. These spreadsheets may look similar to in format to the district spreadsheets in Figs. 7.5 and 7.6.

The final step of the precinct analysis is a review for trends and patterns, as the Carolina Public Press does in the link provided in the Resource section. This review helps you understand which candidates, from which parties, have the most realistic chance of winning in the chosen district. Depending on the time you have available, the size of the district, and your needs, this process can allow for very specific analysis of this data (Shaw 2014).

BUILD YOUR KNOWLEDGE: Find a Precinct
Enter your street address into the interactive map at the bottom of this page: https://decisiondeskhq.com/data-dives/creating-a-national-precinct-map/. What is your precinct name, the total number of votes in your precinct at the last election, and the percentage of votes won by each candidate in your precinct? Did you find any surprises?

Role of Parties and Partisanship in Your Campaign

Your external assessment should examine how political parties are viewed in your district and the extent to which voters in your district align themselves with these parties. This assessment will help your campaign make decisions about the role of political parties in your campaign, and about how you want to situate your candidate relative to a party.

The following assessment process will help you answer two questions: (1) Do you want to affiliate with a political party? (2) If so, what role do you want that party to play in your election? While we reference political parties specifically, the same process can help you determine whether to affiliate with other outside organizations; for example, should you pursue the endorsement of the National Association of Social Workers, a local union, or the American Conservative Union?

Questions to consider:

1. What is the candidate's personal political identification? Does the candidate's ideology and value system suggest that affiliation with a political party is an ethical, appropriate choice?
2. What does partisan identification look like with in your district? Is party affiliation a key aspect of winning in your area? Consider your precinct analysis and the history of races in your area. If the majority of registered voters in your area belong to a major party, the battle for a third party or unaffiliated candidate can be substantially harder.
3. What resources does the party have to offer? Would it be in the campaign's best interest to be connected with the party because of the name recognition, money, or volunteers they could contribute?
4. What do you know about the party leaders and activists in your area (see the discussion of key leaders below)? Are they people that are likely to provide support to your campaign? What will they think about working with your candidate?

Party affiliation is not required to run for office, but as discussed earlier in this chapter, it can be a requirement for voting in a primary election. Independent or third party candidates hold offices around the country, while many municipal and judicial offices are nonpartisan. The major national third parties as of this writing are the Libertarian and Green parties, with some presence in all or nearly all states. Other significant third parties include the Constitution party, Working Families party, and Reform party. Links to all of these party websites are in the Resources section. As of 2017, two U.S. Senators identify as Independents: Bernie Sanders and Angus King. Both caucus with (or affiliate with) the Democrats in the Senate. As a result, both vote for the Democratic leader to be the leader of the Senate, and receive committee assignments from the Democrats (O'Keefe 2014). These affiliations are not necessarily exclusive; for example, Senator King has expressed a willingness to caucus with Senate Republicans if he sees it to be in the best interests of his state of Maine.

Determining how involved the campaign wants the political party to be is an important decision. Political parties can play an important role in partisan campaigns, and it is important for each campaign to consider this. Kraus (2011) outlines several roles that political parties may play in US campaigns:

- Serving as symbols for partisan identification for voters, providing voters with motivation and a framework for participation.
- Taking on much of the responsibility of socializing and educating voters on important issues, as well as encouraging participation in the process. Some argue, however, that this plays a role in channeling social conflict away from systemic issues and into reinforcement of the existing system.
- Recruiting and nominating or sponsoring political candidates. This process generally involves significant amount of power given to party insiders and leaders, particularly at the national level.
- Mobilizing voters to support candidates who have been nominated. Parties spend a significant amount of resources communicating with voters during campaigns about all aspects of the candidates and voting process.
- After the election has concluded, facilitating cooperation between members of the party who have been elected, including between those in different branches and different levels of government.

BUILD YOUR KNOWLEDGE: Role of Parties in Your Area
Look into the political parties in your area and/or in the district you chose in the "find a race" activity above. How do the two major parties compare in terms of voter registration? Are there any viable third parties in your area? In recent years, have any candidates who were not affiliated with one of the two major parties or were not endorsed by one of the two major parties been successful?

External Strengths and Weaknesses Assessment

A meaningful electoral campaign assessment absolutely must include a full analysis of the strengths and weaknesses of your candidate, described above as part of your internal assessment. In addition, a careful assessment of the strengths and weaknesses of your opponent(s) or expected opponent and of the political climate external to the campaign is essential. Review news articles, word-of-mouth reputation, voting histories, even **opposition research**, information that may be used to weaken your opponent. This process allows you to conduct a complete assessment of the strengths and weaknesses relative to your specific district of the candidate(s) you are running against. This will help you determine how strong the opposition is likely to be, as well as your opponent's potential points of vulnerability. Your assessment also should incorporate analysis of the strengths and weaknesses of the political environment. The SWOT analysis framework discussed previously can be a helpful tool to assist you with this process. In a page or two outline these factors; and, based on these, identify what you see as your campaign's keys to winning.

Section 4: Identifying the Campaign's Long-Term, Intermediate, and Short-Term Goals (Stage 3)

The goals of an electoral campaign are generally organized around three categories:

- Short term: getting the candidate or issue on the ballot
- Intermediate: achieving benchmarks in the campaign plan
- Long term: achieving enough votes for victory on Election Day

Short-Term Goal: Getting on the Ballot

Your first goal in an electoral campaign is to get your candidate or issue on the ballot. To specify what this goal entails, determine the steps necessary to accomplish this in your particular geographic context and the deadline by which this goal must be completed. In the case of ballot initiatives, recall elections, and many candidate elections, gaining voter support via petition signatures is essential. Third party candidates may face stiff burdens to get on the ballot as compared to major party candidates.

To get your candidate or issue on the ballot, you must know the specific state and local rules that apply to your campaign. The best place to start is your state or territory's election office website. You can find a link to the appropriate site by looking online for the election office by name. This office is most commonly located within a state's office of the Secretary of State (or Secretary of the Commonwealth in some states), but also may be called the Election Office or Office of Elections, Election Commission, Board of Elections, Lieutenant Governor, Election System, Division of Elections, Government Accountability Board, or Department of Elections.

These websites post state-specific rules related to getting an issue or candidate on the ballot, as well as a calendar of dates for all election-related activities that apply to your individual campaign, to political parties, and to election officials. These include deadlines for **candidate filing** (completing the necessary paperwork to declare an intent to be on the ballot) or for collecting and submitting petition signatures to place your issue on a ballot. Other relevant deadlines on the election calendar include those for voter registration, absentee ballot applications, and when primaries can be held, as well as deadlines for when election officials must mail absentee ballots or certify candidates and issues. These websites generally also include additional information relevant to your campaign, including:

- Results of the most recent election.
- Members of the elections commission/board, method of their selection, how often they meet, and agendas and minutes of their meetings.
- Resources individual voters can use to register to vote, check their voter registration, move their registration to a new address, and more.
- Special information for those without ID, those with disabilities, or other special circumstances.
- Often, assistance for finding your polling place. Some might even allow you to apply for an absentee ballot or to be an elections official online.

Hawaii's state website offers an example of how information about getting on the ballot can be organized in a helpful manner (State of Hawaii Office of Elections 2017). In a separate section for candidates, the website outlines the time period in which you can file and weekly updates of those who have filed. The website also includes a 75-page manual that walks candidates through running for office, including understanding the electoral process and getting on the ballot.

Some municipalities or counties may have their own elections agencies separate from the state agencies. These agencies may provide useful information, as well as any municipal-specific guidelines for getting on the ballot. For example, New York City has its own board of elections, although many services are split up by the borough or county in which residents live. Information is presented in five languages on its website, along with a mobile app that helps you find your polling place (Board of Elections in the City of New York 2014).

In working toward your campaign's goal of getting on the ballot, make sure that you know specific federal rules applicable to your race. A great place to start in identifying this information is https://www.usa.gov/voting. This website contains resources about federal election laws and their histories, as well as about the presidential election process. It also provides useful campaign resources that clarify information about voter registration requirements, deadlines, and processes.

In addition to official government websites, some nonprofit organizations provide very useful sites to guide your campaign through getting a candidate or issue on the ballot. The National Conference of State Legislatures (NCSL), a bipartisan organization that helps state legislators and legislatures, has a wealth of online resources on initiatives and referenda, campaign finance, election laws, technology and procedures, and election results and analysis (NCSL 2011, 2017a). Similar resources exist on the state and local levels.

However, even the best website can only tell you so much. Make contact with those in your area to learn more about the process beyond the rules on paper. Visit your local voter registrar, county clerk, election office, or city recorder (positions vary by municipality) to understand how the laws apply on the local level. These are the experts who can give you their interpretation of local and state election laws (Shaw 2014).

Accomplishing the short-term goal of getting an issue on the ballot typically includes the following steps outlined by the NCSL (2017b); however, the specifics vary from state to state:

1. Preliminary filing of a proposed petition with a designated state official.
2. Reviewing the petition for confirmity with statutory requirements and, in several states, reviewing the proposal's language by state officials.
3. Preparing a ballot title and summary.
4. Circulating the petition to obtain the required number of registered voters' signatures, usually a percentage of the votes cast for a statewide office in the preceding general election.
5. Submitting the petitions to the state elections official, who must verify the number of signatures.

If enough valid signatures are obtained, the question goes on the ballot or, in states with an indirect process, is sent to the legislature.

The process of getting on the ballot in a candidate election also varies from state to state. The six factors that are generally considered in this process (NCSL 2011) are:

1. What are the **filing fees** (the charge that must be paid to the elections officials in order to get on the ballot)?
2. What are the **filing dates** (the deadlines by which candidates must officially file for an election; after this date, candidates would likely have to run as a write-in candidate)?
3. How many signatures do you need to get on the ballot, and who is eligible to sign?
4. Who is legally allowed to collect signatures: Do they have to be registered voters, residents of the area, members of the party they are collecting for, be a Notary Publics, etc.?
5. What are the rules for getting on the ballot as a nominee of a party (if desired, as discussed above)?
6. What are the rules about **fusion**, being listed on the ballot as a nominee of two different parties? Fusion voting used to be much more common, but as of this writing is only allowed in eight states, Connecticut, Delaware, Idaho, Mississippi, New York, Oregon, South Carolina and Vermont (The Daily Rundown 2014).

APPLY YOUR SKILLS: How Would You Get Your Name on the Ballot?
Looking at the elected position you selected earlier in this chapter, describe the process, start to finish, that you would need to go through in order to become an official candidate for that office. Does the process seem hard? Straightforward? Accessible to all?

Intermediate Goal: Achieving Benchmarks in the Campaign Plan

While the short-term and long-term goals are fairly standard across electoral campaigns, the intermediate goals are not. Intermediate goals focus on the specific areas in which your campaign needs to move forward once it is on the ballot, and the measurable ways that the campaign will know it is successfully reaching voters. Your campaign sets these specific goals, and tracks whether they are achieved in each area of your campaign. These goals may center on such factors as:

- Whether and how the campaign's **message** will be received by voters
- How many campaign donations will be solicited and how much will be donated to the campaign
- How many likely voters will express support for your candidate
- How many new donors or volunteers commit to the campaign
- Whether and how media will cover the campaign

Goals focus on the desired results of your campaign's efforts: what voters, volunteers, donors, or media are doing. Your campaign's actions (through targeting and tactics described below) are what will help make these goals happen. Effective campaigns constantly evaluate whether they are successfully making progress on these goals using qualitative and quantitative data measures. The frequency with which the campaign tracks these goals may change as it moves forward.

Long-Term Goal: Achieving Enough Votes for Victory on Election Day

In setting this long-term goal, a campaign must lay out the number of votes that it needs to win, within the specific characteristics of the district and the race. We outline the process for determining your WIN Number in Chap. 13, or you can see the process laid out on websites such as Wellstone Action's "WIN Number Calculator," provided in the Resource section. The district and precinct assessments discussed above help you pull together all of the data needed to make this determination.

Section 5: Selecting Specific Targets for the Electoral Campaign (Stage 4)

The decision-makers capable of bringing your candidate to victory in the US electoral system are the voters. In an electoral campaign, your efforts focus on targeting and outreach to those voters who are "gettable"; that is, who are potential voters for your candidate. Focused, strategic attention to targeting voters helps you maximize the number of persuadable voters the campaign encounters, in light of the time, people, and money available to your campaign.

Within an electoral campaign, the plan for targeting voters is referred to as a **field plan**. The field plan involves setting benchmarks for the campaign. These are based on the total number of votes needed to win, as well as the amount of time the candidate, staff, and/or volunteers will need to accomplish voter contact. The plan specifically addresses outreach to these targeted voters, and identifies community groups and community leaders who are likely to need concerted attention from the campaign. For example, if the candidate is a social worker, the campaign plan might involve coordinating with the local NASW chapter. The plan might specify intended asks for endorsements from local individuals who have credibility in the community.

Voters

In a perfect world, we would reach out to every potential voter in a district, hear their concerns, encourage them to vote, educate them on the candidates and the voting process, and help them get to the polls on Election Day. The problem with this: no campaign has unlimited time, money, and people, which are necessary to make that happen. Every campaign has to make decisions about how to prioritize the voters they can reach within their available, and often finite, resources. Once you know how much money is likely to be available to your campaign, you will be able to estimate how many voters you will realistically be able to reach.

Given that a campaign cannot reach all potential voters directly, a campaign must determine the subset of voters it will seek to reach. If your district has 20,000 eligible voters and you only have the money to call and knock on the doors of 7000, how do you choose which voters you will try to reach through your targeting efforts?

As a campaign looks at the district in which the candidate is running, it assesses each potential voter target as belonging to one of three groups (personal communication, Jessica J. Mitchell, July 9, 2017):

1. Is the person likely to vote and likely to vote for your candidate? They are in your **base** group.
2. Is the person likely to vote and you don't know if they will vote for you? They are in your **persuasion** group.
3. Is the person likely to vote for you but you don't know if they will vote? They are in your **turnout** group.

Political professionals typically use tried and true methods from the past to identify the voters who are likely to vote for the candidate and thus who to target. Each of these groups requires a different set of tactics (discussed further in Section 6).

Campaigns with limited resources might utilize publically available data to do this targeting. With more resources, you might use polls or focus groups. Professionals also utilize knowledge grounded in theories about why and how people vote, including the influences of social capital, psychology, rational decision making, mass media, and social conditions. We recommend Williams' excellent review of the knowledge in this area (see Resources).

In national campaigns or state-level campaigns with significant resources, campaigns increasingly use technology-based techniques such as micro targeting to pinpoint specific voters who will be receptive to their messages (TargetPoint n.d.). These techniques are impressive (and perhaps disconcerting), but they are expensive. We note, however, that in the 2016 Presidential election, Donald Trump's campaign may have benefited from moving away from these common methods of voter identification. Instead, the Trump campaign took a more experimental approach with voter targeting, using social media to identify potential voters that previous campaigns may not have identified as persuadable, and to reach out to them through mass social media messaging (Fischer and Hart 2017).

Who Is Likely To Vote

It is not good use of a campaign's time to persuade someone of the merits of your candidate if they are unable or unwilling to vote. Therefore, campaigns start by identifying **likely voters,** those who are probably going to vote in the election in which your candidate is running. There are a number of different ways in which campaigns might define likely voters, e.g., as those who generally vote (for example, have voted in two of the last three elections), those who are members of groups who generally vote (e.g., older Americans, union members, or social workers), or simply those who say they are going to vote. National polls that seek to capture the views of likely voters generally use one or more of these methods. Whether as a citizen or as a member of a campaign staff, it is a good idea when you read polls to make sure you look at the methods to see how the polling company is defining likely voters (Newport 2000). In the Resources section, we have included an interesting discussion of why it is important to understand how a poll defines likely voters written by Nate Silver, a well-known polling analyst.

A good illustration comes from Grassroots Initiative's (n.d.) work with underrepresented communities in New York City politics. In their work, they outline a hypothetical district with 165,000 people, of whom approximately 80,000 are eligible to vote. Based on partisan identification, about 60,000 of those individuals would be eligible to vote in a Democratic primary. Based on past similar elections, Grassroots Initiative estimates that just 20% (approximately 12,000) of these Democrats will actually vote in the primary. While the campaign might want to see all the district's residents engaged in politics, they determine that their limited resources would be better spent targeting the 12,000 voters likely to show up on Election Day. But how do we know who those specific 12,000 likely voters are?

Get a list of voters in your district. Your prize asset will be an accurate voter list that you get from the board of elections or an official party or party software vendor. You can purchase it for a small fee from your elections authorities. For more money, you can buy it from well-respected database companies. (Stick with database companies that have a good reputation in your community and within your party, if you are affiliated). If your party endorses you, they may share their list for free. The voter list should include at a minimum the voter's name, address, gender, age, and phone numbers. The more expensive versions, through your party, may allow you to create lists of voters based on certain criteria. You can add to this with information you gather through your campaign. Buying lists from any other source could mean the list is inaccurate or that it has been taken from another campaign—it is not worth the risk.

Sometimes, lists already have been **cleaned**, meaning someone has gone through the list and removed duplicates, mistakes, and names of voters who are deceased or have moved. These practices vary significantly based on the jurisdiction. A cleaned list can save your campaign a lot of time and increase the likelihood that you are reaching the voters you intend to reach. Both authors have participated in campaign phone banking in which we found ourselves spending a lot of time calling pages and pages of individuals whose information was no longer correct. Recent technology (similar to that used by telemarketers) allows campaigns to use automatic call software that saves some of that work. Essentially, the phone numbers on a list are auto-dialed, and when a number goes through, the volunteer gets the chance to speak to the voter.

Examine voting history. **Voting history**, which prior elections voters have voted in, is a key aspect of a voter list, and critical to identifying likely voters. While the specific candidate for whom you vote is secret, the fact that you voted is considered public information. If you are preparing for a primary campaign, you will look to individuals' primary voting history to identify likely voters. If you are preparing for a general election campaign in a non-presidential year, you will look to individuals' voting history in similar elections. Knowing in which elections individuals have voted in the past is critical for determining likely voters. Many people vote only in presidential years, and some never vote in primaries or special elections. You also may find it helpful to look at when individuals on your list registered to vote. For example, a recently registered individual might well be a likely voter. Perhaps the individual has not had had the opportunity to vote in prior elections (i.e., a new citizen or a young voter), or has some reason to specifically register to vote in an upcoming election.

Campaigns often categorize voters based on their voting history. For example, we might categorize people who always vote as "Prime," people who voted in the last two elections as "Double Prime," and in the last three elections as "Triple Prime." It is up to your campaign how you want to prioritize voters. For example, if you are planning for a municipal election, you might target those who have voted in two out of the last three municipal elections, or in a primary, focus on those who previously voted in primaries.

As you look more carefully at your list of likely voters, you may find that they seem different from your district as whole, particularly in terms of demographics like age, gender, ethnicity, etc. In addition to voting history and absentee voting status or voting by mail if available, research finds that voter characteristics like education, income, and age (over 65) are consistently linked with higher rates of voting (Shaw 2014).

These demographics underscore a thought you may be having, that big groups of people are missing from your list of likely voters. What about people who are not registered to vote? What does targeting only individuals with substantial voting histories communicate about people who are registered but do not vote regularly? Might they become more regular voters if campaigns reached out to them in targeting, especially given the importance of campaign mobilization as a factor contributing to political participation (Verba et al. 1995)? These are all important questions to ask, and consistent with values in the NASW (2017) Code of Ethics. As social workers, our values lead us to want to reach out to everyone, particularly those who have felt like they have not had a voice in the past. Electoral campaigns rarely reach out to these individuals, because their concern is securing votes for their candidate in an efficient manner. The best predictor of whether someone will vote in the future is whether they voted in the past. You will have to make hard decisions about how to spend limited resources. Nonprofit organizations are more likely to engage in the necessary work to expand the electorate.

Who Is Likely To Vote for You

Analyze demographics. Once you have identified likely voters in your district, it is time to determine which ones are likely to vote for you. Start by taking a more careful look at your list of likely voters. In general, demographics and partisan election behavior are highly correlated, so there may be some assumptions you can make based on demographics either on the individual or neighborhood level. For example, young people, those who identify as Asian, Latinx, or black, and unmarried white women tend to vote Democratic, while older Americans, white men, and married white women tend to vote Republican (Shaw 2009). Of course, demographic assumptions are not determinative. There are many older Americans who do not vote, Millennials who do, and people who identify as African-American who vote (or run for office) as Republicans. Furthermore, these general trends may be less true depending on the specific candidate or context (e.g., larger percentages of Latinos vote for Republicans in Texas than in many other states), but they can help inform your voter targeting.

Listening and observing. You may already have a sense of which groups will respond best to your candidate and the campaign message. The campaign's initial experiences in the district either in this campaign or in any prior campaigns also can provide you with important information about this. Listening tours, focus groups, and conversations with both leaders in your community and with individual voters can help a campaign understand which voters are motivated by its message. Use your core social work skills that focus on attending to what individual voters are saying, active listening, and reflecting back what you hear. Keep track of your campaign's contacts with individual voters and what they tell you about their support for the candidate. Make sure to add those records into the overall file so they can be used to refine your campaign's targeting. You might use the voter categorization system identified in Chap. 4:

1 = strongly support your candidate
2 = leaning toward your candidate
3 = undecided ("there's an election?")
4 = leaning toward your opponent
5 = strongly support your opponent

Identifying the "1s" (strong supporters) and "2s" (people leaning toward your candidate), helps your campaign have a sense of whether you have enough supporters to win. If not, you will need to think carefully about what tactics might help expand your supporters.

Key Influencers

In addition to outreach directly to targeted voters, a field plan should incorporate attention to certain key influencers in the community who can support these outreach efforts. These key influencers can help control access to voters and the way in which voters hear your message. These key influencers may be formal leaders within political systems or informal leaders who influence systems from the outside, including policy-makers, significant interest group leaders, media influencers, members of coalitions, and those in the community with money and power. Depending on the context of the district and the candidates' connections, key influencers in a specific district might include:

- Current and former elected officials whose views align with the candidate
- Former colleagues or others who can speak to the candidates' strengths (e.g., in the sample Wellstone Action campaign plan linked to in the Resource section, the candidate who is a long-time teacher identified former students as key influencers in the community)
- Other people in the candidate's professional community (in the above example, these included teachers and parents)
- Union leaders who can help access endorsements, volunteers, and potential fundraising
- Leaders of community, business, and neighborhood associations

Your plan should include a list of specific key influencers (by name) to which your campaign will reach out, in an effort to get them on board with your campaign. Wellstone Action (link provided in the Resource section) advises compiling a list of "100 influential individuals" in the community. These should be individuals who, if specifically targeted, might be willing to endorse the candidate, donate money, write letters to the editor on the candidate's behalf, or host a house party or fundraiser to connect the campaign to their networks of voters, volunteers, and/or donors.

APPLY YOUR SKILLS: Finding Key Influencers
If you were going to run for office tomorrow, who are ten key influencers in your community you would want to have on your side? These might be current or former elected officials, respected leaders of local religious groups or congregations, political party leaders or activists, well-known community leaders, etc.

Section 6: Identifying and Selecting the Tactics the Campaign Will Use (Stage 5)

Tactics in an electoral campaign center around the steps you will take to persuade your identified likely voters to vote for your candidate or issue. In general, with limited resources, you want to focus on tactics that are as **targeted** as possible—tactics that will reach the specific voters you are looking for and not cast a wide net. Many of these tactics take place as part of a campaign's **field operation**, the group of staff and volunteers who coordinate direct contact with voters.

Targeted tactics include those that involve one-on-one contact with voters: direct mail to specific homes, knocking on doors, phone calls, and emails to specific lists. Each of these one-on-one tactics may be used as part of voter registration, absentee ballot or early vote efforts, and Get Out the Vote (GOTV) efforts. **House parties**, small gatherings hosted by a supporter and attended by those in the supporter's personal network, are also excellent targeted tactics. They allow the campaign to reach out to a supporter's network, and the supporter is likely to invite those who are most receptive to the campaign's message. A newer form of targeted advertisement is digital advertisement, reaching people on their computer, phone, or tablet (Tamrakar 2016). Social media outreach and advertising also has the potential to be targeted, depending on how it is implemented (Meyer 2016).

Non-targeted tactics are those tactics that will reach a wider set of potential voters. These may include press releases, most television and radio advertising, and letters to the editor. We share a selection of tactics frequently used in electoral campaigns, organized by the categories introduced in Chap. 6. You will see a significant amount of overlap in the tactics used by both advocacy and electoral campaigns.

Sample electoral campaign tactics	
Collaborative tactics	• One-on-one meetings with key leaders • Ongoing relationship-building with key leaders
Public education tactics	• Paid media spots, on television, radio, social media outlets, in newspapers, or in digital advertising • Free media, e.g., public service announcements on television or radio • Media event • Educate voters via social network postings • Educate community leaders • Letters to the editor, op-eds • Work with reporters and bloggers to communicate the message • Distributing campaign literature to key leaders and voters
Grassroots tactics	• Door-to-door canvassing of voters • Rallies • Postcard campaigns to voters • House parties
Persuasive tactics	• One-on-one meetings with key leaders or voters • Send letters to key leaders or voters • Call key leaders or voters • Direct lobbying • Distribute campaign literature to key leaders or voters • Poll/communicate polling

(continued)

Sample electoral campaign tactics	
Electoral tactics	• Register new voters • Educate voters about candidate stances • Get out the vote efforts • Endorse candidates with similar values • Campaign on behalf of candidates with similar values • Fundraise on behalf of candidates with similar values, or in opposition to incumbents who do not hold similar values
Litigation tactics	• Educate key leaders and voters about voting law and procedures • Work with legal experts to defend the rights of voters who may have their rights violated
Demonstrative tactics	• Marches/rallies
Contest/ confrontational tactics	• Share opposition research with key media allies • Negative attacks on the opponent via traditional or social media

FURTHER REFLECTION: Thinking About Campaign Tactics
Review the identified list of Sample Electoral Campaign Tactics. What tactics have you seen in electoral campaigns that seem to be missing here? List as many additional tactics as you can and organize them along this continuum.

In selecting tactics for your electoral campaign, make sure that your tactics are chosen strategically, based on what is most likely to move likely voters toward your candidate. Using the categories of voters identified in Section 5, start early with your persuasion and turnout **universes** (groups of voters) to be sure they get the information needed to convince them to vote, and that they are convinced the election is important (and know it is happening). As your campaign progresses, combine those who have been persuaded from these two with your base universe who are your most reliable voters. Then focus your specific GOTV tactics on this new group when they need to vote. As you consider and implement specific tactics, continually reflect on why the specific tactics you select will help increase your votes and move you toward your win number.

APPLY YOUR SKILLS: Selecting Appropriate Campaign Tactics
Reflecting on the race you chose above, identify at least three tactics you think would be effective in your electoral campaign. Which category(ies) of voters do these tactics target? Why do you think they will be effective for this category(ies)?

Section 7: Campaign Timeline

Given the time-limited nature of an electoral campaign, a campaign timeline is an essential component of your campaign plan. The timeline should be developed at the outset of your campaign, but it is important to acknowledge that this is work in progress that changes as the campaign goes on. The overall campaign timeline should highlight the significant actions of each part of the campaign and when each will take place. It helps clarify how the different parts of the campaign can work together (for an example of this, see the National Democratic Institute for International Affairs political campaign planning manual in the Resource section). For example, the candidate cannot knock on doors until target lists are created and the campaign literature is ordered. The literature cannot be ordered until enough funds have been raised to do so. Funds cannot be raised until the candidate has officially filed paperwork saying he/she is running. Additionally, your timeline might include a list of key events and dates around which the campaign might want to arrange press events or tailor message "themes" (e.g., highlighting the candidate's educational stances during the week of local school graduations, policies related to veterans during the week of July 4).

Depending on your candidate's needs, this timeline may in fact include several different timelines, including weekly calendars for the candidate and other key individuals (the campaign manager, family members, etc.). These separate individual calendars help the campaign consider when the candidate will be able to do the most important activities of the campaign: contact with voters and raising money. This is also a good way to find out if there are going to be significant time conflicts that the campaign must plan around. For example, a candidate who works evenings in a residential program is going to be hard-pressed to be able to knock on doors or call voters during the few hours voters are reachable at home. Developing a timeline for the candidate helps key campaign staff process this challenge, so a plan can be made. It is also an opportunity to protect time for the candidate to spend with family or take a break from the campaign. This self-care time is important, and should be prioritized in the candidate's calendar.

Review of Key Terms and Concepts

Ballot initiatives (or **referendum campaigns**): those in which voters are asked to decide about anything from the school budget to a constitutional amendment—ideas are on the ballot rather than people

Base voters: voters in your district who are likely to vote and are likely to vote for you.

Candidate elections: designed to elect a person or slate of people to office. They can generally be divided into one of three categories: general elections, primary elections, and special elections.

Candidate filing: completing the necessary paperwork to declare an intent to be on the ballot.

Caucus: a primary process (see entry on "primary elections") where party members gather together to select their party's candidate rather than a traditional election format.

Citizen referendum: a referendum which comes directly from the people, not the legislature. (Please refer to "referendum" for more information.)

Cleaned voter list: a list of voters in which the duplicates, mistakes, and names of voters who are deceased or have moved have been removed.

Closed primaries: states' primary elections that require voters to be registered with a specific party in order to vote in the primary. Voters cannot vote in a closed primary for which they are not registered, leaving independent or unaffiliated voters no opportunity to vote in the state's primary.

Convention: national, state, or local meetings held by political parties to officially nominate party leaders and adopt party platforms.

Direct democracy: a practice in which state law allows citizens to vote directly on issues they care about.

District: a political subdivision that is grouped together to elect a specific representative(s) to a government body.

Field operation: the group of staff and volunteers on a campaign who coordinate direct contact with voters through methods such as knocking on doors and phone calls. Field efforts might include voter registration, absentee ballot or early vote efforts, and GOTV efforts.

Field plan: plan for targeting the voters you want to reach.

General election (or **regular election**): the binding election that decides who will hold a given electoral political position, including legislative, executive, and judicial, where applicable.

House parties: small gatherings hosted by a supporter and attended by those in the supporter's personal network.

Ideology: the set of ethics, ideals, and principles that describe how we believe the world works or should work.

Incumbent: a person who is currently holding office.

Initiative: an organized process in which citizens are able to place items (statues or constitutional amendments) on the ballet without needing to go through their state's legislature.

Legislative referendum: a measure that appears on the ballot, referred by the state legislature after approval by that body, which is for direct voter decision.

Likely voters: those who are probably going to vote in the election.

Message: A short, concise statement to be used during one's campaign, aimed at a specific audience, that captures what a specific group should know about the candidate.

Midterm elections: federal general elections that are held in between presidential elections (2 years after a presidential election). They include races for Congress and one-third of the Senate but not for President.

Nominate: the act of a political party endorsing political candidates.

Nonpartisan races: those in which candidates run without any party affiliation in a general election, and generally the winner takes all. In the USA, nonpartisan elections are most common for judicial elections.

Open primaries: states' primary elections that do not require voters to declare a party on their voter registration form. This system provides maximum flexibility and privacy, but minimal ability for parties to nominate candidates that represent the party's platform.

Open seat: there is no incumbent running for office at the time of the election.

Partially closed primaries: states' primary elections that give political parties the opportunity to choose whether unaffiliated voters can vote in that party's primary, but do not allow those registered with a different party to vote. This allows more flexibility from year to year, but may lead to confusion about who can vote.

Partisan races: those in which each candidate is given or wins the nomination of a political party. This could happen as part of a primary election or caucus, or as part of a nominating process by the official members of that party. Either of these gives the candidate the right to use the label of that political party during the general elections.

Party affiliation: the party that a voter is registered with.

Persuasion voters: voters in your district who are likely to vote and but have not yet decided to vote for you.

Precinct: the division of a geographic area in which voters are provided ballots for a particular office. They also may be referred to as election districts, electoral districts, voting districts, boxes, beats, or wards.

Precinct analysis: the process of collecting publically available records in order to determine what voting trends are in a precinct and what candidates or methods have been successful in reaching voters in the past.

Primaries open to unaffiliated voters: states' primary elections where voters must choose the ballot of the party they are registered with, but if they are unaffiliated, they can choose any party's ballot. Like the partially open primaries, some states may require voters to affiliate with a party if they choose this option.

Primary elections (or **primaries**): those that allow members of a political party to decide who will represent them in a future general or regular election (although there are other ways for this process to happen). Primaries can be divided into six categories from most restrictive to least restrictive. They are one way to winnow down a large field of candidates into a smaller list, and as practiced in the USA, generally reinforce our two-party system.

Recall: the process by which a local or state official can be removed from office through a vote before his or her term has ended. The majority of states allow for the recall of local and/or state officials, although the process and grounds for said recall vary wildly.

Referendum: a measure that appears on the ballot for direct voter decision, often similar to an initiative. There are two types of referendums: legislative and citizen.

Referendum campaigns: please refer to "ballot initiative."

Regular elections: please refer to "general elections."

Representative democracy: a political system in which citizens elect individuals to govern on their own behalf.

Special elections: held when a vacancy exists in an elected position and it needs to be filled outside of the usual election timeframe.

Targeted tactics: campaign tactics that will reach the specific voters you are looking for (versus casting a wide net). Targeted tactics include those that involve one-on-one contact with voters: direct mail to specific homes, knocking on doors, phone calls, emails to specific lists, and house parties.

Third parties: smaller parties than the two major political parties (in the USA, the Republican and the Democratic parties) holding the majority of power and positions in the political realm. Examples of third parties include the Green, Libertarian, and Independent parties.

Top-two primaries: states' primary elections that represent all candidates on one ballot, and may list party affiliation or party preference next to them. The top two candidates go on to the general election, which may result in two candidates from the same party in that election.

Town meetings: public meetings held by cities or towns where decisions are made directly by the residents of the town who are present at the meetings.

Turnout voters: voters in your district who may not vote, but are likely to vote for you if they do vote.

Two-party system: as in the US government, this is a system in which the two major political parties hold the majority of the power and positions in the political realm, and few seats are held by third parties, or smaller parties, and fewer still by those who are unaffiliated.

Unaffiliated: not officially connected with any political party.

Uncontested: only one candidate from one party runs in the general election, or one member of a party "runs" in a primary election.

Universe: group of voters.

Voting history: a record of the elections in which a voter has cast a ballot.

Vulnerable incumbent: one who is facing their first reelection, won by a small margin, is touched by scandal, or has other weaknesses.

Resources

Books and book chapters

Bryan, F. M. (n.d.) *Real democracy*. Retrieved from http://www.press.uchicago.edu/ucp/books/book/chicago/R/bo3641466.html.

Shaw, C. (2014). *The campaign manager: Running and winning local elections*. Boulder, CO: Westview Press.

Kraus, J. (2011). American political parties. In J. T. Ishiyama, & M. Breuning (Eds.), *21st century political science: A reference handbook* (pp. 769–778). Thousand Oaks, CA: Sage Publications Ltd. doi: https://doi.org/10.4135/9781412979351.n89.

Rackaway, C. (2011). Campaigns. In J. T. Ishiyama, & M. Breuning (Eds.), *21st century political science: A reference handbook* (pp. 796–804). Thousand Oaks, CA: Sage Publications Ltd. doi: https://doi.org/10.4135/9781412979351.n92.

Williams, C. (2011). Voting behavior. In J. T. Ishiyama & M. Breuning (Eds.), *21st century political science: A reference handbook* (pp. 813–821). Thousand Oaks, CA: Sage Publications Ltd. doi: https://doi.org/10.4135/9781412979351.n94.

Websites

Carolina Public Press precinct trend analysis: http://carolinapublicpress.org/26190/breaking-down-mountains-precinct-level-analysis-wncs-vote/

Fresh Air interview about primaries: http://www.npr.org/2016/03/23/471563611/the-mind-boggling-story-of-our-arcane-and-convoluted-primary-politics

Grassroots Initiative
    Homepage: http://gograssroots.org/
    How to Identify and Analyze Likely Voters: http://gograssroots.org/files/analyzevoters.pdf

Houston Chronicle's precinct analysis: http://blog.chron.com/kuffsworld/2017/03/precinct-analysis-the-targets-for-2018/

Lego people explain the Iowa Democratic caucus: https://youtu.be/SJqv--jyXPg

Municipal Research and Services Center: http://mrsc.org/Home.aspx

Nate Silver discussion of likely voters in polls: https://fivethirtyeight.com/features/likely-voters-and-unlikely-scenarios/

National Conference of State Legislatures
    Elections and Campaigns: http://www.ncsl.org/research/elections-and-campaigns.aspx
    State Primary Election Systems: http://www.ncsl.org/documents/Elections/Primary_Types_Table_2016.pdf

National Democratic Institute
    Campaign Planning Manual:
    https://www.ndi.org/files/Political_Campaign_Planning_Manual_Malaysia.pdf

Campaign Schools Handbook: https://www.ndi.org/files/Campaign%20Skills%20Handbook_EN.pdf

Political Parties:
    Democratic Party: https://www.democrats.org/
    Green Party: http://www.gp.org/
    Libertarian Party: https://www.lp.org/
    Reform Party: http://www.reformparty.org/
    Republican Party: https://www.gop.com/
    Working Families Party: http://workingfamilies.org/

South Dakota Initiative Referendum Task Force meetings: http://www.sd.net/blogs/archive/.

State election website examples:
    Colorado: http://www.sos.state.co.us/pubs/elections/vote/VoterHome.html?menuheaders=5 or go to https://www.sos.state.co.us/ and in the menu click on "Elections" then click "Voters."
    Hawaii: http://elections.hawaii.gov/
    Idaho: http://www.sos.idaho.gov/elect/2016Calendar.html
    Tennessee: http://sos.tn.gov/products/elections/state-election-commission-meetings or go to http://sos.tn.gov/ and in the menu under "Elections" select "State Election Commission," then select "State Election Commission Meetings" on the landing page.
    Wisconsin: http://www.gab.wi.gov/elections-voting/results or go to http://elections.wi.gov/ and in the menu under "Elections" select "Election Results."

U.S. Election Assistance Commission 2014 report on election administration: https://www.eac.gov/assets/1/1/2014_EAC_EAVS_Comprehensive_Report_508_Compliant.pdf

Wellstone Action
    Main website: http://www.wellstone.org

Campaign Plan: http://www.wellstone.org/resources/sample-campaign-plan or go to http://www.wellstone.org and click on "Tools" then scroll down to click on "Sample Campaign Plan."

WIN Number Calculator: http://www.wellstone.org/resources/win-number-calculator or go to http://www.wellstone.org and click on "Tools" then scroll down to click on "WIN Number Calculator."

References

Albers, M. (2017, March 10). Governor signs new laws to replace Initiated Measure 22. *KDLT News*.

Associated Press. (2012, April 2). Wisconsin elections board offers searchable database of recall petition signers. *Twin Cities Pioneer Press*.

Biersack, R., Herrnson, P. S., & Wilcox, C. (1993). Seeds for success: Early money in congressional elections. *Legislative Studies Quarterly, 18*(4), 535–551.

Board of Elections in the City of New York. (2014). *Home*. Retrieved from http://vote.nyc.ny.us/html/home/home.shtml

Braden, D. (2017). Running in "Red America"—District 65 Virginia House of Delegates needs a Democratic contender! *The Full Slate Project*.

Bryan, F. M. (2003). *The New England town meeting and how it works*. Chicago, IL: The University of Chicago Press.

Casey, L. (2016). 2013 and 2014: Money and Incumbency in State Legislative Races. https://www.followthemoney.org/research/institute-reports/2013-and-2014-money-and-incumbency-in-state-legislative-races/

Dovere, E.-I. (2017, April 4. Democrats recruit veterans early for 2018 battle. *Politico*.

Erickson, B., & Barilla, J. (2002). Legislative powers to amend a state constitution. *Journal of the American Society of Legislative Clerks and Secretaries*, 1–6. sdlegislature.gov/docs/interim/2017/documents/DIRT06212017-H.pdf

Fischer, S., & Hart, K. (2017) How Trump's data operation helped him win. *Axios*.

Gitterman, A., & Germain, C. B. (2008). *The life model of social work practice: Advances in theory and practice* (3ed.). New York, NY: Columbia University Press.

Grassroots Initiatve's. (n.d.). *How to identify and analyze likely voters*. Retrieved from http://gograssroots.org/files/analyzevoters.pdf

Ishiyama, J. T., & Breuning, M. (2010). *21st century political science: A reference handbook*. Thousand Oaks, CA: Sage

Kant, C. (2005). Summary of the Nevada State Constitution. sites.csn.edu/wdavis/nvconstitution-summary.pdf

Krieg, G. (2017). South Dakota GOP uses 'emergency' rules to repeal anti-corruption. *CNN*.

Kuffner, C. (2017). Precinct analysis: The targets for 2018. Kuff's World, *Houston Chronicle*.

Lipset, S. M. (2000). The indispensability of political parties. *Journal of Democracy, 11*(1), 48–55.

Malone S. (2013, November 6). Christie wins big in New Jersey, Democrat takes Virginia in governors' races. *Chicago Tribune*.

Marcos, C. (2017, January 19). GOP recruitment goal: More women on ticket. *The Hill*.

Mercer, B. (2017, June 21). Task force on ballot measures takes testimony for three hours. *Capital Journal*.

Meyer, R. (2016, April 18). How Facebook could tilt the 2016 election. *The Atlantic*.

Minnesota Association of Townships. (2017). *Town meetings*. Retrieved from http://www.mntownships.org/index.asp?SEC=856B0344-2511-44B9-A677-6420F89F1790&Type=B_BASIC.

Montanaro, D. (2016, January 30). How exactly do the Iowa caususes work? *National Public Radio*.

National Association of Social Workers. (2017). *Code of Ethics of the National Association of social workers*. Washington, DC: National Association of Social Workers.

National Conference of State Legislatures. (2011). *Getting on the ballot: What it takes*. Retrieved from http://www.ncsl.org/documents/legismgt/elect/Canvass_Feb_2012_No_27.pdf.

National Conference of State Legislators. (2012). *Initiative, referendum and recall*. Retrieved from http://www.ncsl.org/research/elections-and-campaigns/initiative-referendum-and-recall-overview.aspx.

National Conference of State Legislators. (2016a). *Recall of state officials*. Retrieved from http://www.ncsl.org/research/elections-and-campaigns/recall-of-state-officials.aspx.

National Conference of State Legislators. (2016b). State primary election systems. www.ncsl.org/documents/Elections/Primary_Types_Table_2017.pdf

National Conference of State Legislators. (2017a). *Elections and campaigns*. Retrieved from http://www.ncsl.org/research/elections-and-campaigns.aspx

National Conference of State Legislators. (2017b). *Initiative process 101*. Retrieved from http://www.ncsl.org/research/elections-and-campaigns/initiative-process-101.aspx

National Conference of State Legislators. (2017c). *Recall of local officials*. Retrieved from http://www.ncsl.org/research/elections-and-campaigns/recall-of-local-officials.aspx.

National League of Cities. (2016). *Partisan vs. nonpartisan elections*. Retrieved from http://www.nlc.org/partisan-vs-nonpartisan-elections.

Newport, F. (2000). *How do you define "likely voters"?* Retrieved from http://www.gallup.com/poll/4636/how-define-likely-voters.aspx

O'Keefe, E. (2014, April 10). Angus King suggests he may caucus with GOP if it retakes Senate. *Washington Post*.

Pazniokas, M. (2017, February 28). Democrats win 2 of 3, keep control of General Assembly. *The CT Mirror*.

Rackaway, C. (2011). Campaigns. In J. T. Ishiyama & M. Breuning (Eds.), *21st century political science: A reference handbook* (pp. 796–804). Thousand Oaks, CA: Sage.

Rogers, S. (2014). Strategic challenger entry in a federal system: The role of economic and political conditions in state legislative competition. *Legislative Studies Quarterly, 40*(4), 539–570.

Sabato, L. J., Kondik, K., & Skelley, G. (2013). *So what just happened in Virginia? A brief history of Old Dominion nomination battles*. Retrieved from http://www.centerforpolitics.org/crystalball/articles/are-primaries-or-conventions-more-successful-for-a-party/.

Schmitter, P. C., & Karl, T. L. (1991). What democracy is...and is not. *Journal of Democracy, 2*(3), 75–88.

Shaw, C. (2014). *The campaign manager: Running and winning local elections*. Boulder, CO: Westview Press.

Snyder, J. M., & Ting, M. M. (2002). An informational rationale for political parties. *American Journal of Political Science, 46*, 90–110.

South Dakota Secretary of State. (2017). *Statewide ballot questions*. Retrieved from http://electionresults.sd.gov/resultsSW.aspx?type=BQ&map=CTY.

State of Hawaii Office of Elections. (2017). *Candidate filing*. Retrieved from http://elections.hawaii.gov/candidates/candidate-filing/

Tamrakar, A. (2016). Political advertising on digital: 15 must-know stats. *Social Code*.

TargetPoint. (n.d.). Microtargeting: knowing the voter intimately. *Winning Campaigns Magazine, 4*(1).

Texas Municipal League. (2015). Chapter one: Local government in Texas. In *Handbook for mayors and councilmembers* (pp. 9–15). Austin, TX: Texas Municipal League.

The Center for Responsive Politics. (n.d.). *Reelection rates over the years*. Retrieved from https://www.opensecrets.org/overview/reelect.php

The Daily Rundown. (2014). *How fusion voting played a role in American politics*. Retrieved from http://www.msnbc.com/the-daily-rundown/fusion-votings-role-american-politics

The Twenty-Eighth Congress of the United States. (n.d.). Election Day.

Tupper, S. (2015, November 9). South Dakota gets F grade in 2015 State Integrity Investigation. *The Center for Public Integrity*.

U.S. Election Assistance Commission. (2015, June 30). The 2014 EAC Election Administration and Voting Survey Comprehensive Report: A Report to the 114th Congress. https://www.eac. gov/.../2014_EAC_EAVS_Comprehensive_Report_508_Compliant.pdf

U.S. National Archives and Records Administration. (n.d.). *Presidential election laws*. Retrieved from https://www.archives.gov/federal-register/electoral-college/provisions.html.

Verba, S., Schlozman, K. L., & Brady, H. (1995). *Voice and equality: Civic voluntarism in American politics*. Cambridge, MA: Harvard University Press.

Wilson, R. (2014, June 4). Runoff elections a relic of the Democratic South. *The Washington Post*.

Zimmerman, J. F. (1999). *The New England town meeting: Democracy in action*. Westport, CT: Praeger Publishers.

Planning the Political Intervention: Voter Engagement

8

© Springer International Publishing AG 2018
S.R. Lane, S. Pritzker, *Political Social Work*,
https://doi.org/10.1007/978-3-319-68588-5_8

Section 1: Overview

Community members engage in advocacy and electoral efforts in a number of ways. This chapter focuses on ways in which individuals and communities express their power through voting, and ways that social workers can use voter engagement, including voter registration, education, and mobilization, as a tool in our work. This chapter looks at the values and meanings assigned to the act of voting, the history of voting and the right to vote in the USA, and current knowledge about voter participation and key issues. We acknowledge at the outset that laws and policies that relate to voting are constantly changing, and vary significantly from state to state. It is generally a good idea to check with the local election authority in your area to confirm the current laws before moving forward on projects related to voting.

Developing Social Work Competency
The Council on Social Work Education establishes educational standards for all social work programs in the USA. Content in this chapter supports building competency in the following areas that are considered core to the practice of social work:
COMPETENCY 2: Engage Diversity and Difference in Practice
COMPETENCY 3: Advance Human Rights and Social, Economic, and Environmental Justice
COMPETENCY 5: Engage in Policy Practice
COMPETENCY 6: Engage with Individuals, Families, Groups, Organizations, and Communities
COMPETENCY 8: Intervene with Individuals, Families, Groups, Organizations, and Communities

Domains of Political Social Work	
1. Engaging individuals and communities in political processes	◄
2. Influencing policy agendas and decision-making	◄
3. Holding professional and political positions	◄
4. Engaging with electoral campaigns	◄
5. Seeking and holding elected office	◄

Section 2: Voting and Social Work

The right to vote is the core symbol of democratic politics...the feature of the democratic polity that makes all other rights significant.—Frances Fox Piven and Richard Cloward, MSW.

While some social workers have a history of engaging clients by registering them to vote, not all social workers see this as part of their mission. Many agencies and social workers, in fact, are often reluctant to be seen as "political" and therefore avoid voter engagement work.

Yet, nonpartisan voter engagement is legal for nearly all agencies that employ social workers, including government and nonprofit agencies. It is important for social workers to clearly differentiate between nonpartisan and partisan voter engagement activities. **Nonpartisan** activities are those that engage voters without supporting or opposing any particular candidate or political party, as compared with **partisan** activities that advance a specific candidate or party. To be clear, voter engagement activities can take place in either a nonpartisan or partisan manner. Based on information compiled by Nonprofit VOTE (2017b), Table 8.1 compares nonpartisan and partisan voter engagement activities and the types of organizations in which they are allowed.

The 1993 National Voter Registration Act (NVRA) actually *requires* most state agencies that provide public assistance to offer voter registration forms and assistance in completing these forms to service recipients (LeRoux 2014). The passage of this law was influenced heavily by social worker Richard Cloward, along with his colleague Francis Fox Piven. As part of their efforts to expand voter engagement among vulnerable populations, they also founded Human SERVE (Service Employees Registration and Voter Education) in the 1980s, a program that sought to register voters through NASW and schools of social work. Due to the efforts of these social workers and their coalition, seven million new voters were registered to vote (Piven and Cloward 2000).

Nonpartisan voter registration is also legal within nonprofits. In fact, when nonprofits promote nonpartisan registration and voting, they significantly impact voter participation, particularly among underrepresented groups such as persons of color, those who are younger, and those with lower incomes (Nonprofit VOTE 2017a). A great resource for how social workers and other professionals can engage in nonpartisan voter registration within nonprofit agencies is **Nonprofit VOTE**, founded in 2005 by a consortium of state nonprofit associations and national nonprofit networks (See Resources at the end of the chapter). Nonprofit VOTE is the largest

Table 8.1 Voter engagement activities

Voter engagement activities	Nonpartisan	Partisan
Allowable in what types of organizations?	Most public, private, and nonprofit organizations	Some nonprofit organizations and most private organizations
Which voters can be registered, and on whose behalf?	*Any* person or group, regardless of the party with which they choose to affiliate	Any person or group, typically on behalf of a *specific* candidate or party
Educates others about the voter registration process?	Yes	Yes
Educates voters about the dates and times of elections or early voting?	Yes	Yes
Educates voters about the mechanisms of voting?	Yes; for example, through a mock election or sample ballot	Yes
Educates voters about the issues on the ballot?	Through a nonpartisan guide, not endorsing any particular issues.	By endorsing the issue stances of a specific candidate or party, through a variety of educational techniques
Encourages others to vote?	Regardless of candidate or party	For a specific candidate or party
Endorsement of ballot initiatives?	Yes, can take a position on a ballot initiative	Endorsing one side of a ballot initiative
Invites candidate in an election to address voters?	All candidates are invited	Typically invites one candidate or party's candidates to address voters
Offers assistance to voters (i.e., a ride to the polls)?	Yes, regardless of candidate or party preference	Only to those who have committed to vote for a specific candidate or party
Aims to inform all voters about voting rights?	Yes	Possibly—not as a primary goal

provider of resources and trainings to the nonprofit sector on integrating nonpartisan voter participation and election activities into ongoing activities and services. It is a great resource for guiding nonprofits to integrate voter engagement into ongoing activities and services, and can be helpful to you throughout your career as a political social worker—in fact, the authors both refer to this resource regularly.

Within and outside of these organizations, social workers participate in voter engagement in a variety of ways. The voter engagement ladder in Fig. 8.1 offers one framework for thinking about what voter engagement can look like, along a continuum, from minimal commitment to larger commitment. The three primary areas in which social workers are commonly involved in voter engagement are: voter registration, voter education, and voter outreach.

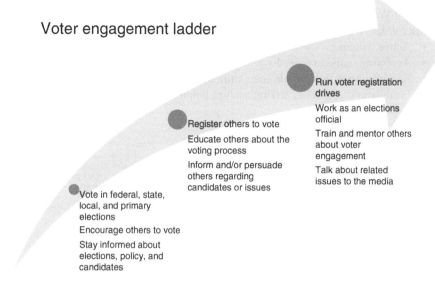

Fig. 8.1 Voter engagement ladder

Little is known currently about the extent to which social workers participate in voter engagement efforts. What little we do know focuses on social work education. Over 30% of accredited BSW and MSW programs in the USA offer no voter registration opportunities to their students. Approximately half of programs expose fewer than half of their students to voter registration efforts (Pritzker 2017). In 2015, the social work *Voter Empowerment Campaign* was launched. This collaboration among social work organizations and educational programs seeks to embed voter engagement into social work education and practice through its website votingissocialwork.org, work with individual schools, and trainings across the country.

As we discuss in more depth throughout this chapter, social work skills are a critical asset to voter engagement work. They can be used in a variety of ways to empower individuals, community groups, and agencies around voting. Some of the social work skills that you might draw on as part of voter engagement (drawn from many sources including Austin et al. 2005) include:

Social Work Skills Used in Voter Engagement

Micro/Mezzo Skills

- Active listening
- Assessing individual needs
- Engaging with individuals and communities
- Establishing empathic, strength-based helping relationships with a diversity of people
- Facilitating groups
- Matching needs with interventions
- Monitoring and evaluating the helping process
- Negotiation
- Persuasion
- Purposeful self-disclosure
- Reflection
- Reframing
- Self-awareness
- Understanding basic psychological processes
- Understanding empowerment
- Understanding the importance of culture

Macro Skills

- Assessing community needs
- Assessing group and community needs and goals
- Assessing the environment
- Build trust with diverse community members
- Building coalitions
- Communicating with policymakers
- Engaging with communities
- Evaluation of effectiveness of interventions or policies
- Framing and reframing issues
- Managing conflict
- Monitoring and evaluating the change process
- Organizing
- Planning
- Research
- Understanding empowerment
- Understanding relevant policies and rules
- Understanding the importance of culture

APPLY YOUR SKILLS: Social Work Skills and Voter Engagement

Watch this video of voter engagement in Reno, Nevada. While the individuals in this video are not social workers, they use some key skills we develop as social workers. Which of the social work skills listed above do you see used in this video? https://youtu.be/Paa8goiOW3s?list=UUHEP8VISy0wCuPrH Myk1o2w

POLITICAL SOCIAL WORKER PROFILE: Richard Cloward, MSW and Francis Fox Piven
Groundbreaking professors, authors, and activists

Treating the client as expert, practicing empowerment, and engaging in collaborative efforts are all critical aspects of political social work. Dr. Richard Cloward, a social worker and sociologist, and Dr. Frances Fox Piven, a sociologist and political scientist, lived those ethics. In 1965, they collaborated on a paper called *Mobilizing the poor: How it can be done*. Together, they mobilized theory and activism to found the National Welfare Rights Organization (NWRO), the first in a series of efforts to disrupt the status quo treatment of people who were poor. Cloward and Piven wrote *Regulating the poor: The functions of public welfare* which remains a classic study of welfare policies in the USA.

In 1988, Cloward and Piven (who eventually married) turned their attention to increasing political power by people who had been silenced, writing *Why people don't vote: And why politicians want it that way*. This book argued that the USA is an outlier in Western democracies for requiring individuals to seek out voter registration. Cloward captured their view that existing political parties have an interest in creating barriers to voting, stating, "Politicians don't want new voters, they just want the ones who elected them" (Woo 2001).

They co-founded the Human Service Employees Registration and Voter Education Fund (Human SERVE), a national voter registration reform group active from 1982 to 2000. This group played a leading role in winning congressional approval of the National Voter Registration Act of 1993, commonly known as the Motor Voter Act. This act allows people to register to vote in motor vehicle offices and at other government agencies, including libraries and welfare offices.

Cloward and Piven's work, collaboratively and separately, brought together academics and activism to try to understand the root causes of issues and to find practical ways to address them. They held to their beliefs that the poor deserve a radical shift in the structure of the US welfare system and the rights they are afforded. They demanded respect and dignity for the poor, even if it involved stepping on middle class toes, or was perceived as divisive or radical (Flanders 2001).

Cloward passed away in 2001 after more than 55 years at the Columbia School of Social Work. Piven continues her teaching, scholarship, and activism at the Graduate Center, City University of New York.

Self-Determination, Power, and Voting

Before we explore voter engagement in more depth, a few words about self-determination and voting. As you talk with potential voters throughout the process of voter engagement, always keep your power and your role in mind, as well as the rights of individuals to choose not to participate in the political process. Many US communities have been treated poorly by the political process and do not believe that they want to be a part of this process. Furthermore, some individuals with whom you engage may be ineligible to vote because of felony convictions or citizenship status and may feel uncomfortable sharing that information with you, due to stigma or safety concerns. Whether you are participating in voter engagement as part of an agency where you work, as part of a campaign, or in your individual or volunteer work, be mindful of designing your voter engagement efforts to maximize individual self-determination and to minimize your power over those you are engaging. Whatever your role in this process, your social work values and ethics should guide you in your work and interactions with others.

Section 3: Voter Participation

As we examine communities' political participation, voting is a key aspect of that participation. This section examines what we know about voter participation in the USA today, including ways in which voting is framed and a central modern political debate surrounding voting.

The Importance of Voting

As we discussed earlier in this book, US elections are generally marked by lower participation than in other countries. Voter turnout is generally about 60% in Presidential elections, and lower for elections at all other levels of government. In comparison, turnout is approximately 87% in Belgium, and 82% in Sweden. Even within the USA, the voting rate ranges, from 42% of eligible voters in Hawaii to 74% of Minnesotans, tending higher in states with less restrictive laws or in states hotly contested in significant elections (DeSilver 2017; United States Election Project 2017).

It is not uncommon to hear the refrain, "I don't vote, because my vote doesn't matter." The reality, however, is that elections can be decided by a small number of votes. Slight increases in the low rates of voter participation could make a crucial impact on election results. In 2015, for example, Republican Mark Tullos and Democrat Blaine "Bo" Eaton were tied on election night in their race for a seat in the Mississippi state legislature (District 79), with 4589 votes each. Per Mississippi state law, the race was decided by drawing straws, and Eaton believed he had won because he pulled the long straw. However, the Republican state legislature disqualified five provisional ballots for Eaton, and voted to give the seat to Tullos. A group of voters brought a lawsuit contesting the results under the federal guarantee for equal protection (Wagster Pettus 2016). As of Spring 2017, 16 months after the election, and 1 year into Tullos' 4-year term, the case is still ongoing (Summers 2017).

Low participation can translate into close elections at the federal level as well. We see examples of this in contests for the U.S. House of Representatives. In 2006, Democrat Joe Courtney became a member of Congress from Connecticut's Second District, winning by 83 votes out of 242,413 cast, a difference of less than four hundredths of one percent (Connecticut Secretary of State 2006). The same district had earlier been decided by just four votes out of 186,000 (a margin of 0.0002%) in 1994, when Democrat Sam Gejdenson kept his seat over Republican Edward Munster. Similar close races have emerged in U.S. Senate elections. In 2002, Democrat Tim Johnson retained his U.S. Senate seat in South Dakota with a margin of 524 votes out of 337,508 cast (two tenths of one percent) over John Thune, who went on to win the other South Dakota Senate seat in 2004 (S.D. candidates may face recount 2004).

We even see extremely close races at the Presidential level. In 2000, the race for U.S. President came down to which candidate would win Florida's electoral votes (State Elections Offices 2001). The official vote count in Florida was 2,912,790 votes for George W. Bush and 2,912,253 for Al Gore, with just 537 out of a total 5,861,785 votes, a difference of 0.00009%, separating the two candidates in the state (see Resources).

Certainly not all election races are close, and many people understandably choose not to vote because they believe their vote does not count. Given this, what are some reasons, other than the possibility of determining an election, for which social workers might want to encourage community members, clients, and other social workers to vote? We argue that voting has benefits for individuals, representation at the polls has benefits for communities, and increasing the diversity of those who participate in the political process has impacts on policy outcomes. While individual voting may not rationally lead to a hoped-for outcome at all times, voting as part of a collective bloc does. In essence, it is the practical act that represents the idea that individuals can make a difference through "tiny contribution to a collective activity…added to many similar contributions that will together produce a highly desirable outcome" (Maskivker 2016).

Individuals who vote tend to have higher levels of civic participation and stronger community connections. Voting has been linked with positive outcomes in health, social connections, mental health, and overall well-being. Links between increased levels of voting and positive markers of community health have been found in the USA (Purtle 2013) and internationally (Kim et al. 2015), and through both systematic reviews and meta-analyses (Gilbert et al. 2013). Individuals may benefit from reframing their personal problems as systemic problems, and coming together as a community to take action (Nickerson 2008).

Groups who feel powerless or disengaged from societal systems, including young people, racial and ethnic minorities, and low-income populations, tend to be underrepresented at the polls (Henderson 2011). While understandable, the consequences to giving up this political power are great. Elected officials pay attention to voters, and evidence suggests that policies don't reflect the interests of those who stay home. For example, states with the highest rates of voting among lower socioeconomic groups are less likely than states with lower voting rates to enact punitive work requirements, time limits or family caps as part of welfare policy implementation. They also make fewer cuts in welfare spending (Hill et al. 1995).

As this body of research shows, engaging our client populations in voting can impact both election outcomes and the policies that result. Political power is one of the clearest and most direct ways for individuals to influence society, particularly if they are able to come together as a voting bloc to use the power of the vote (Piven and Cloward 2000).

> **FURTHER REFLECTION: Imagine 100% Voter Turnout**
> A thought exercise: Imagine for a moment that 100% of the people in your city or state of voting age were active voters. How might the balance of power look different? How might your community look different? Why?

Values and Voting

In the past few decades, much of the debate about voting in the USA has centered on the question of whether voting should be framed as a right, a privilege, a responsibility, or some combination of the three (Searcy 2011). Essentially, these are three different value perspectives on how voting interrelates with citizenship in the USA. The perspectives that you hold toward voting affect how you view debates regarding voting and voting rights, as well as proposed legislation and procedures.

If you believe that voting is a **right**, guaranteed to all who qualify (generally, those who are citizens and meet the legal requirements), then you might support proposals that make it as easy as possible for individuals to vote. These include automatic voter registration, elimination of complex processes of voter registration, access to voting through mail-in, early voting, or online voting. President Lyndon Johnson (1965) encapsulated this value perspective when he stated, "This right to vote is the basic right without which all others are meaningless. It gives people, people as individuals, control over their own destinies."

If, on the other hand, you may believe that voting is a **privilege** that only should be available to those who have earned it, and withheld from those who have not. If so, you might support laws that create or strengthen requirements for voter identification, or those that prohibit an individual convicted of a felony from voting. Iowa Governor Terry Branstad captured this perspective in stating, "Voting is a privilege that has been given to us as citizens by hundreds of thousands of men and women who have fought and died for our representative democracy" (Obradovich 2016).

If you conceive of voting as a **responsibility** or a duty for all, you might instead support a compulsory voting system that requires everyone to vote and imposes a penalty on those who do not vote. Jeffrey Howard and Ben Saunders state, "The job of the citizen, I believe, places moral demands on those who hold it. Voting is one of those demands. Citizens have obligations to make their societies more just and, as others have argued, to refrain from being an accomplice—however minor—to injustice" (The Conversation 2015).

EXPLORE YOUR VALUES: Social Work Values and Voting
Read the National Association of Social Workers' policy statement on voter participation (found at https://www.socialworkers.org/assets/secured/documents/da/da2010/referred/Voter%20Participation.pdf or in the most recent version of *Social Work Speaks*). As you read this statement, which of the three values discussed above (voting as a right, privilege, and/or responsibility) do you feel is most reflected in the statement? How does NASW's stance align with how you personally conceptualize voting?

A Central Debate Surrounding Voting in the USA

One central way that these different values around voting play out is in the modern debate over voting restrictions. Specifically at issue is whether certain restrictions are needed in order to protect the **franchise**, or right to vote. Those who view voting as a privilege often express concerns about what they perceive as **voter fraud**. Specifically, they fear that those who are not eligible to vote are abusing the electoral process, and that people are taking advantage of the system by voting multiple times. Such concerns have been highlighted by the Presidential Commission on Electoral Integrity established by President Donald Trump (The White House Office of the Press Secretary 2017). They also have been emphasized by the Heritage Foundation and the Public Interest Legal Foundation, who produced the report pictured in Fig. 8.2. These advocates propose tighter restrictions to reduce the possibility of fraud, including measures requiring identification to vote and limited early voting windows.

Others argue that such restrictions are not necessary. They argue that fraud is minimal, and instead perceive restrictions as facilitating **voter suppression**, disrupting the ability of eligible voters to cast their ballots through mechanisms that are discriminatory, intimidating, or otherwise create barriers. Advocates concerned about voter suppression argue that laws designed to stop voter fraud prevent eligible voters from participating in the political process. They further argue that the words used to describe voter fraud trigger biases against those who are "other," particularly non-whites, reinforcing the legitimacy of these biases (Denise Lieberman, personal communication, June 2, 2017). Groups widely known for their efforts to challenge voter suppression include the Advancement Project, the American Civil Liberties Union, and the Brennan Center for Justice.

APPLY YOUR SKILLS: Debate on Voter Fraud Versus Voter Suppression
Engage in a debate with classmates or friends around this central debate. If you are in a classroom setting, separate into two groups. One group will argue that voter fraud is the more significant concern, and the other will argue that voter suppression is most significant. Or, on your own, choose the side of the

(continued)

debate that seems most distant from your own view, and make the case for that point of view for yourself. Ground your debate in data and analysis, not opinion. You may find the following resources to be good places to start researching voter fraud and voter suppression and personal stories of individuals affected by each.

Resources:

Advancement Project: http://www.advancementproject.org/
American Civil Liberties Union: https://www.aclu.org/issues/voting-rights
Brennan Center for Justice: https://www.brennancenter.org/issues/voting-rights-elections
Heritage Foundation http://www.heritage.org/election-integrity
Public Interest Legal Foundation: https://publicinterestlegal.org/reports/
US Election Assistance Commission: https://www.eac.gov/voters/national-voter-registration-act-studies/
Profiles of plaintiffs in related lawsuits:
Bettye   Jones: http://www.politico.com/story/2013/12/one-mothers-struggle-for-voting-rights-100842
Rosanell Eaton: https://www.thenation.com/article/the-92-year-old-civil-rights-pioneer-who-is-now-challenging-north-carolinas-voter-id-law/

Fig. 8.2 Alien Invasion in Virginia, published by the Public Interest Legal Foundation (2017)

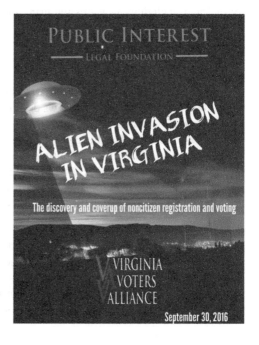

Section 4: History of Voting in the USA

While much of the content of this book deals directly with issues of social justice and with navigating political processes, we have not yet directly engaged with the concept of **political justice**. Political justice refers to the equitable distribution of political rights. Specifically, it is concerned with issues such as access to voting rights and political representation. The USA has had—and continues to have—a challenging history as relates to political justice. As we embark on voter engagement, it is important for social workers to have a sense of how this history has developed.

While the Constitution enumerates a series of rights for US citizens, the original Bill of Rights did not specifically identify voting as a right. Yet, from the earliest days of the USA, voting has been part of citizenship for at least some citizens. White male owners of significant property were allowed to vote. What percentage of the population this constituted is a subject of debate, but has been reported to be as low as 5–6% or as high as 10–20% of the population (Ratcliffe 2013; Lepore 2008; Constitutional Rights Foundation 1991). The lack of voting as an explicit Constitutional right is directly related to the history of race and slavery in our country (Denise Lieberman, personal communication, June 2, 2017). This was not accidental. As John Adams (1776) commented:

> Depend upon it, sir, it is dangerous to open So fruitfull a Source of Controversy and Altercation, as would be opened by attempting to alter the Qualifications of Voters. There will be no End of it. New Claims will arise. Women will demand a Vote. Lads from 12 to 21 will think their Rights not enough attended to, and every Man, who has not a Farthing, will demand an equal Voice with any other in all Acts of State. It tends to confound and destroy all Distinctions, and prostrate all Ranks, to one common Levell.

In the history of voting in the USA, every step forward in increasing access to voting for more Americans is followed shortly by attempts to reduce the impact of those changes. The franchise was expanded by 1850 to include almost all adult males, but was soon followed in 1855 by the first literacy test (Thornton n.d.). This was created by the state of Connecticut to keep Irish Catholics from voting. Literacy tests continued to be used for more than a century after that to restrict voting by African-Americans, Latinos, and immigrant groups. Literacy tests for federal elections were declared unconstitutional in 1915, but literacy tests remained for nonfederal elections in some states. In Connecticut, for example, literacy tests remained until 1970.

The Jim Crow Era

The 15th amendment to the Constitution was passed in 1870, widely perceived as giving former slaves the right to vote. However, many, like Dr. Darryl Paulson (2013), note that:

> Despite common perception, the 15th Amendment did not guarantee blacks the right to vote. Rather, it is a negative statement. It says the right to vote cannot be denied because of race. The distinction is critical. It allowed the South to develop barriers to voting that would eliminate blacks' votes without coming into conflict with the 15th Amendment (para. 3).

Shortly thereafter (1889), Florida and ten other Southern states instituted a poll tax (Heritage Foundation 2017). Other vote-limiting strategies were introduced to turn African-American voters away from the polls or discount their votes (Paulson 2013; Behring Center n.d.). Literacy tests were instituted, with grandfather clauses for poor whites who couldn't read. Other strategies included elaborate registration systems, whites-only party primaries (not struck down by the Supreme Court until 1944), violence, and threats of violence. In one example, the literacy test in Dallas County, Alabama (home of Selma), required that potential black voters name all 67 county judges in the state (Berman 2015).

During this time, states also enacted laws that prohibited those with criminal records from voting. However, these laws did not apply to all crimes equally; instead, crimes most often committed by African-Americans were the ones that resulted in **disenfranchisement**, having the right to vote taken away. In Mississippi, for example, an individual lost the right to vote for arson, but not for committing murder. In Alabama, wife-beating resulted in disenfranchisement, but wife murder did not (Sentencing Project 2017). To this day, disenfranchisement due to felony convictions persists in many states, with disproportionate impacts on African-American males. See "Section 5" below for more discussion of this.

These Jim Crow laws and related actions throughout the south contributed to substantial disenfranchisement of African-American men, at a time when women were not yet eligible to vote. As the Smithsonian National Museum of American History (n.d.) notes,

> The laws proved very effective. In Mississippi, fewer than 9,000 of the 147,000 voting-age African Americans were registered after 1890. In Louisiana, where more than 130,000 black voters had been registered in 1896, the number had plummeted to 1,342 by 1904 (para. 4).

Likewise, after Alabama passed a new constitution in 1901 that included significant voting restrictions, the number of black registered voters dropped from 182,000 to 4000 (Berman 2015).

Ultimately, these laws were effective in blunting the power of the African-American vote. Soon after the enactment of the 15th amendment, 16 African Americans served in Congress. One hundred years later (before passage of the Civil Rights Act), there were just three (Denise Lieberman, personal communication, June 2, 2017).

FURTHER REFLECTION: Lived Experience of Jim Crow Laws
Listen to one of the following stories of individuals describing their experiences under Jim Crow laws:
  https://storycorps.org/animation/a-more-perfect-union/
  http://www.npr.org/2017/01/13/509495656/what-one-family-sacrificed-to-help-black-people-vote-in-1966
Spend some time thinking about your reactions to these stories. How do you feel when you hear the details of these individual's experiences? Why?

Twentieth Century Expansion of Voting Rights

In the early part of the twentieth century, several shifts expanded voting access to some US populations. Prior to 1913, members of the U.S. Senate had been selected by state legislatures. In 1913, however, the 17th Amendment to the U.S. Constitution was ratified, giving the power of electing members of the U.S. Senate directly to the people (Bomboy 2016). In 1920, the 19th Amendment was ratified, giving women the right to vote. A wide array of women's suffrage groups were involved in this effort, including many early social workers. One social worker who played a substantial role in these efforts was Alice Paul, who, alongside other women, engaged in decades of activism and protests to obtain this right (Reiter 2017). Even within the women's suffrage movement, however, there were deep divides over whether to promote expansion of the franchise solely to women or to also support the right to vote for black men. One women's suffrage group, the National Women's Suffrage Association, opposed the ratification of the 15th Amendment, which prohibited denying the right to vote based on race (National Park Service n.d.). In 1924, Native Americans were granted US citizenship, theoretically including the right to vote, although some individual states kept Native Americans from voting until passage of the Civil Rights Act in 1957 (Rios 2016).

The passage of the Civil Rights Act marked the "first occasion since Reconstruction that the federal government undertook significant legislative action to protect civil rights" (Civil Rights Digital Library 2017, para 1). Among other components of the law, it "established the Civil Rights Division in the Justice Department, and empowered federal officials to prosecute individuals that conspired to deny or abridge another citizen's right to vote. Moreover, it also created a six-member U.S. Civil Rights Commission charged with investigating allegations of voter infringement" (Civil Rights Digital Library 2017, para 1).

A further step in increasing suffrage came in 1961. The 23rd Amendment was ratified, granting voters in the District of Columbia (D.C.), primarily identifying as African American, the right to participate in presidential elections. However, even today, D.C. voters lack the right to elect voting members to the U.S. House of Representatives or Senate, a point illustrated by the slogan "taxation without representation" that appears on D.C. license plates (Leadership Conference 2017).

The most significant voting legislation of the twentieth century was the **Voting Rights Act** (VRA) in 1965, a law that was intended to end Jim Crow laws and to ensure that voting rights of all eligible voters were protected. The VRA outlawed discriminatory practices such as literacy tests. It required jurisdictions shown to be discriminating to get **preclearance** from the Department of Justice. Preclearance meant that these jurisdictions' laws had to be reviewed by the Justice Department before they could go into effect (Legal Information Institute n.d.). In the short term, the VRA allowed the Justice Department to send examiners to areas where black voter registration was below 50% of the voting age population. Within 10 years, states that were the focus of the law increased their percentages of black voters substantially, and the number of black elected officials representing those areas at the state and local levels increased from 72 to 1000 (Cobb 2015).

Later revisions of the law and a number of Supreme Court decisions in the 1960s and 1970s further removed voting restrictions, although some efforts to reduce voting remained. The 1993 National Voter Registration Act (NVRA), also called the Motor Voter Act, further addressed voting barriers, requiring that voter registration opportunities be available at all agencies that administer public assistance programs (including, at a minimum, Medicaid, Food Stamps, TANF, and/or WIC), as well as programs serving people with disabilities (Piven and Cloward 2000).

Following the turbulent 2000 election, the Help America Vote Act (HAVA) passed in 2002. This law encouraged states to update voting machines and systems and to computerize voting lists (yes, in 2002 this was not always the case!). It increased voter identification requirements, and mandated systems for poll worker trainings, addressing complaints, and **provisional ballots** (Williams 2004). Provisional ballots, also referred to as challenge ballots or affidavit ballots, are cast by voters if there is some question about their identification or identity. These ballots are held separately until after the election, when election officials see if the issue can be resolved. If it is resolved favorably, the vote is counted (NCSL 2015).

A Modern Backlash?

After over 50 years of expanding voting rights and increasing access to voter registration, evidence suggests that the tide is shifting. From 2011 to 2015, 395 new restrictions on voting were introduced in 29 states (Berman 2015). The most significant recent change occurred in 2013, when the U.S. Supreme Court ruled in *Shelby County [Ala.] v. Holder* that the Voting Rights Act had accomplished its goal in the 48 years since its passage. Accordingly, the Supreme Court ruled that portions of the VRA, specifically Sect. 5 which governed preclearance, were no longer needed (Cobb 2015). Essentially, this reduced Justice Department oversight of jurisdictions that have had a history of enacting barriers to voting for African-American or other citizens. Most recently, President Donald Trump has created a Presidential Commission on Electoral Integrity, led in part by individuals with a long history of introducing strict voting restrictions (Wise and Lowry 2017). At the time of this writing, advocates for voting rights are concerned that efforts to weaken or challenge the Motor Voter Act also are under consideration at the highest levels of government (Fessler 2017).

As discussed in Sect. 3 proponents of these restrictions believe that they are essential to preventing voter fraud and protecting the franchise. Voting rights advocates, on the other hand, argue these efforts to restrict voting and reduce VRA oversight are part of a historical trend of taking steps backward each time the franchise has increased. In one expert's view, the backlash is increasing because voters of color are fast becoming the new majority in the USA (personal communication, Denise Lieberman, June 2, 2017).

> **BUILD YOUR KNOWLEDGE: Research Proposals About Voting Laws**
> The National Council on State Legislatures has a webpage dedicated to state election laws and procedures: (http://www.ncsl.org/research/elections-and-campaigns/election-laws-and-procedures-overview.aspx). Visit this page, and choose one of the areas listed. Read the resources provided under your selected area. Have there been any recent proposals in this area in your state? Do the proposals in this area reflect voting as a right, privilege, or responsibility?

Section 5: Social Workers and Voter Registration

For social workers who want to engage potential voters, the first step is to help them gain access through **voter registration**. Voter registration is the process by which voters in 49 states and the District of Columbia add themselves to the voting rolls in advance of an election (Nonprofit VOTE 2017c). Only North Dakota does not have voter registration. Specific laws regarding voter registration differ substantially from state to state. Some states offer ways for voters to register online or on Election Day. Others have in place much more stringent registration requirements, such as completing voter registration on a printed form, witnessed by a deputized registrar, no less than 1 month prior to an election (NCSL 2016). Some states allow 16- or 17-year-olds to "pre-register" before they turn 18; others do not have provisions for registration prior to turning 18. Since 2015, seven states have begun to automatically register voters when they get their driver's license (NCSL 2017b). Significant changes have been made in recent years. In 2016 alone, 422 bills were introduced in 41 states to enhance access to registration and/or voting, and 77 bills were introduced in 28 states to restrict such access (Brennan Center for Justice 2016).

Social workers may get involved with voter registration as part of an electoral campaign, an advocacy campaign, community empowerment work, or regular agency practice. The Voter Empowerment Campaign argues that all social workers should participate in nonpartisan voter engagement, beginning with voter registration. To get you started in this work, we encourage you to watch the Buzzfeed video in the Resources section that offers a humorous look at voter registration.

Some ways that social workers can effectively incorporate voter registration into social work practice (Nancy A. Humphreys Institute for Political Social Work 2016) include:

- Providing registration forms and information in the waiting room of an agency or near a check-in location;
- Including registration forms with other intake or renewal forms;
- Providing tables with information and forms at special events;

Fig. 8.3 Google search
for voter registration in
California

- Using social media, posters, and word-of-mouth networking; and
- Offering to check voter registration information for individuals, to see if it is up
  to date and lists the correct information.

The Voter Registration Process

In order to register others to vote, you need to know the rules in your state, as there
are substantial differences between states. Start by typing "voter registration" or
"how to vote" and your state's name into your Internet search. Google has introduced a tool that enables people to use their phones to easily search for state-specific voter registration information (Schonberg 2016). For example, if you conduct
this search in California, you will see the information shown in Fig. 8.3. Here you
can see the information you need to have in order to register and your different
options for doing so.

Of course it is not always this simple. When you are working with potential voters, you will want to help them figure out whether they are eligible to vote, and if
they are, whether they have already registered. If they are not eligible to vote, this is
the end of the voter registration process (but not the end of the advocacy process).
If they are eligible and unregistered, you can help them register to vote using one of
the options of methods your state offers.

If the potential voters you are working with think they are registered, it is still
helpful to check and make sure that their registration is still active and connected to

Fig. 8.4 Chicago Board of Elections website

their current address. People who move frequently or who do not vote regularly may find themselves taken off of the voting rolls or registered at the wrong address. These challenges are more common for populations who move frequently or live in low-income areas (Bergin et al. 2016). Often, checking the accuracy of an existing registration can be as important as a first-time registration. Every state and many municipalities have websites that allow individuals to access their status online. For example, the website in Fig. 8.4 from the Chicago Board of Elections allows potential voters to check whether they are registered to vote.

Using a website to confirm registration status also can help identify whether potential voting challenges exist. You can confirm if a potential voter has affiliated with a specific party. This impacts whether a voter may participate in various primary or caucus elections. You also can determine where a voter's polling place is. Using the Chicago site, one of this book's authors entered the last name and address of a family member in Chicago. After discovering that she was registered to vote, with an active registration, the author discovered that her polling place was not accessible for people with disabilities, which could be a problem for someone with a mobility impairment.

TurboVote (see Resources) is a great new resource for tracking voter registrations. This website, part of a project by Democracy Works to make the process of

- A 3PVRO must promptly deliver applications to the Division of Elections or the Supervisor of Elections—no later than 10 days from date of collection or the deadline for registration for an upcoming election, whichever is sooner.
- The date the applicant signed the voter registration application is presumed to be the date the 3PVRO received or collected the application. The 3PVRO must print the date the applicant completed the application in a conspicuous space on the bottom portion of the back side of the application in a way that does not obscure any other entry.
- The 3PVRO itself is liable for the following fines for untimely delivery or failure to deliver:

Activity	Fine per Application	Willful Act per Application
✓Application not received until more than 10 days from date of collection ✓Application postmarked more than 10 days from date of collection (If the Division of Elections or the Supervisor of Elections' Office is closed at the 10-day deadline, the deadline is extended to the next business day)	$50	$250
✓Application collected *before* book closing for any given election for federal or state office but received *after* the book closing deadline.	$100	$500
✓Application never submitted	$500	$1000
Maximum aggregate fine that can be assessed against a 3PVRO, including affiliate organizations, for violations committed in a calendar year is $1,000.		

Fig. 8.5 Penalties for a 3PVRO not promptly delivering voter registration applications

voting easier, helps voters register to vote, check whether their voter registration is active, change their address, ask for an absentee ballot, and get updates about upcoming elections. Voters also can use this site to request absentee ballots. Another excellent site that helps people check and clarify their voter registration is Vote411 from the League of Women Voters (see Resources).

To register voters, you also need to understand what rules exist regarding registering others to vote. While in some states, any person (registered or not) can register voters (Kasdan 2012), other states have very restrictive rules about who can do this and the processes they can use. In Florida, for example, as shown in Fig. 8.5, groups that wish to register voters must first register with the state as a Third Party Voter Registration Organization (3PVRO). They face significant fines if they do not submit voter registration forms within a specified time or if they break other rules related to registration, as the image below indicates (Florida Division of Elections n.d.):

The Brennan Center for Justice maintains a list of restrictions states place on registering voters as of 2012 (some may have changed since). Please see the Resource section for a link to this list.

FURTHER REFLECTION: Your Voter Registration

Based on the information above, determine whether you are eligible to vote. If so, either register to vote, or check your existing voter registration to verify that it is active and accurate. How difficult was this process for you? Do you feel confident that you could explain it to others?

Voter Registration in Primary Elections

States organize their primary or caucus elections in varied ways. How these are organized have differing implications for voter registration in each state. Registration deadlines and rules for registering with parties can affect individuals' ability to vote during these important elections.

APPLY YOUR SKILLS: Voter Registration and Primaries
Using your state's election-related website, or contact with election officials, create a fact sheet or infographic that describes the process of registering for a caucus or primary in your state's next election. It should be targeted to voters and should include the following information:

1. What type of primary or caucus is used (closed, partially closed, partially open, open to unaffiliated, open, top-two, or something else)? What does that mean for voters?
2. What is the deadline to register and/or change parties before a primary?
3. When is the next primary election?
4. Where can a voter go to get more information or check their registration status?

Special Considerations in Registering Voters

It is important to keep in mind that not all people that we work with as social workers are eligible to register to vote. If individuals are not eligible to vote, there may be other ways to engage them with civic and political processes. Even among those who are eligible to vote, specific populations that we work with as social workers may face unique circumstances surrounding their access to the vote. These often ultimately keep them from voting. For example, you may find that some individuals who identify as transgender are reluctant to vote, either because they don't feel safe or because their identification doesn't match the gender they identify with. Helping them access absentee voting or supporting them to vote together in groups may be helpful.

In general, social workers work from an assumption that people should have the opportunity to maximize their voting rights, even if that requires special assistance, such as absentee ballots for people with disabilities or the aging population who have difficulty leaving their homes, or translated materials for those who speak languages other than English. Your social work skills can help you engage with individuals around their specific barriers to voting.

Here, we highlight five specific populations that social workers may engage with that face challenges surrounding their access to vote. We identify specific resources to support voter registration with each group. For each population, we also encourage you to educate yourselves on the related policies of your specific state. Talk with your local elections officials, or reach out to the Humphreys Institute for Political Social Work if you have questions about working with specific populations.

Individuals with Felony Convictions

Approximately 5.85 million Americans are prevented from voting due to felony (and in some states misdemeanor) convictions (American Civil Liberties Union 2017). State laws vary widely, with four states (Iowa, Florida, Kentucky, and Virginia) permanently disenfranchising those who have been convicted of felonies. In contrast, Maine and Vermont do not take away voting rights at any point during the legal process. In some states, the right to vote is denied only while individuals are in prison. In other states, it is denied during prison and parole or during prison, parole, and probation. Because people of color are disproportionately incarcerated, these policies have disproportionately disenfranchised African-American men. Approximately 1 in 40 US adults and 1 in 13 African-American adults are disenfranchised due to their convictions (Uggen et al. 2016); in Iowa and Florida, this is one in four African American men (Turner-Lee 2017).

APPLY YOUR SKILLS/EXPLORE YOUR VALUES: Felony Disenfranchisement
Read more about voting and felony convictions at https://www.aclu.org/issues/voting-rights/criminal-re-enfranchisement or another resource of your choice. Use your state's election-related website, or reach out to election officials to identify the rules about felon disenfranchisement in your state. Do you feel that those rules reflect social work values? Why or why not?

Survivors of Domestic Violence

Maintaining the privacy of voters is a significant issue for many groups, including those who work in law enforcement, survivors of crime, or those who work for the courts. Here, we specifically highlight the barriers that this poses to survivors of domestic violence. Survivors may be hesitant to vote because of the public nature of voting, including the need to go to the polls in person and the public availability of information about individuals who are registered to vote. Voter registration may involve individuals being asked their date of birth, home address, phone number, or social security or driver's license numbers (California Voter Foundation 2012). It is not always clear to potential voters which information is required and what will be publicly available.

To address these privacy concerns, 40 states have established some sort of address or voter confidentiality program to protect the privacy of survivors of domestic violence. Rules vary from state to state about who is included and what the procedures are for qualifying, enrolling, and participating. The other ten states, as well as the District of Columbia, Puerto Rico, and the Virgin Islands, have no such program in statute.

> **APPLY YOUR SKILLS/EXPLORE YOUR VALUES: Survivors of Domestic Violence and Voting**
> Read more about voter registration for survivors of domestic violence at http://nnedv.org/ by searching "Survivor Privacy," or using another resource of your choice. Use your state's election-related website, or reach out to election officials to identify the rules about privacy for survivors of domestic violence in your state. Do you feel that those rules reflect social work values? Why or why not?

Individuals Who Are Homeless

Being homeless does not automatically disqualify someone from voting, but many individuals who are homeless face significant barriers when attempting to vote. Homeless individuals may find that their lack of permanent residency, not having proof of identification, limited access to resources to educate themselves about election-related issues, and limited ability to access transportation to polls prevents them from voting. Efforts to improve access to voting for those who are homeless have been ongoing. In 2016, a group of national homelessness advocacy organizations created a nationwide campaign called "You don't need a home to vote," designed to help homeless and low-income individuals participate in the political process.

> **APPLY YOUR SKILLS/EXPLORE YOUR VALUES: Homelessness and Voting**
> Read more about voter registration for people who are homeless at the toolkit at http://nationalhomeless.org/campaigns/voting/ or another resource of your choice. Use your state's election-related website, or reach out to election officials to identify the rules for homeless individuals in your state who wish to vote. Do you feel that those rules reflect social work values? Why or why not?

Individuals with Differing Abilities

People who have physical, cognitive, or other disabilities often vote at significantly lower rates than other Americans. Some may assume that a disability disqualifies them from voting. Others may be socially isolated, which can result in not receiving communications from candidates, parties, or community groups. The process of voting itself can include many barriers that leave some individuals with disabilities unable to participate. Individuals with disabilities make up approximately 17% of voters overall, and have voting rates nearly 6% lower than those without disabilities, a difference of approximately three million voters. Nearly one-third of voters with disabilities reported experiencing problems with voting, compared to approximately 8% of those without disabilities (American Association of People with Disabilities 2016).

Some state laws address the voting rights of people with cognitive disabilities or mental illness in a negative manner, including states that deny the right to vote to "idiots or insane persons" (e.g., Kentucky, Mississippi, New Mexico, and Ohio), those of "unsound mind" (e.g., Alaska, Montana, and West Virginia), or guardianship (Tennessee) (Disability Justice 2017). In contrast, other states have affirmative language that states that all people should be given the right to vote whenever possible. For example, Rhode Island specifically states that "Patients admitted to a facility [for treatment of mental illness] shall not be deprived of the right to vote and participate in political activity" and that a "[c]ommunity residence resident will not be deprived of right to vote just because of admission and has right to reasonable assistance in registration and voting if desired" (Bazelon Center for Mental Health Law n.d.).

APPLY YOUR SKILLS/EXPLORE YOUR VALUES: Voting with Differing Abilities
Read more about voting with disabilities at http://disabilityjustice.org/right-to-vote/, http://www.aapd.com/our-focus/voting/, or http://www.yourvotey-ourvoicemn.org/present/communities/people-disabilities-present, or another resource of your choice. Use your state's election-related website, or reach out to election officials to identify the rules about disability voting in your state. Do you feel that those rules reflect social work values? Why or why not?

Military and Overseas Voters

Citizens who live away from the USA or who serve on active duty in the military retain their right to vote in US elections. These rights are protected by the Uniformed and Overseas Citizens Absentee Voting Act (UOCAVA) of 1986 and were expanded significantly by the 2009 Military and Overseas Voter Empowerment Act (called the MOVE Act). Unlike many of the populations described above, federal law specifically protects voting by these two groups; therefore, requirements are not dependent on the laws of individual states. Among other things, these laws require that states send absentee ballots to these qualified voters upon request at least 45 days before an election (U.S. Department of Justice 2010). The Federal Voting Assistance Program, which ensures that the requirements of the law are met, is run through the Department of Defense.

APPLY YOUR SKILLS/EXPLORE YOUR VALUES: Voting While Living or Stationed Overseas
Read more about voting while overseas or in the military at https://www.fvap.gov/ or another resource of your choice. Do you feel that those rules reflect social work values? Why or why not? What are your thoughts about why laws for these groups are handled through a federal program, rather than on a state-by-state level like the other types of laws discussed above?

Section 6: Social Workers and Voter Education

Registering voters is only the first step in voter engagement. The next step in engaging voters is **voter education**. Voter education teaches voters the mechanics of voting (where to vote, what the deadlines are, the process of voting), information about the issues that are on the ballot or are being considered by candidates, and why their vote matters (Nonprofit VOTE 2017b). Voter education can be conducted in a non-partisan manner if you are affiliated with a nonprofit or public agency, or in a partisan manner if you are affiliated with a campaign or political party.

Voter education can be thought of in two main categories: education about the voting process and education about candidates. Education about the voting process includes:

- Providing days, times, and locations of upcoming elections;
- Sharing information about options for early or absentee voting;
- Showing voters a sample ballot;
- Walking them through the process of using the voting equipment in their area; and/or
- Putting together a document with frequently asked questions about voting.

Education about the voting process also includes reminding people that there is an election! In years where there is a big campaign underway, this might not seem necessary. It is, however. Even when people are aware of the contests on the top of the ticket, like Presidential races, people may not know about, or do not see the importance of, other races on the ballot. Local elections, in particular, have a huge influence on town services, local school districts, and many decisions that affect people intimately. Yet these elections tend to have extremely low participation. In Longmeadow, Massachusetts, for example, the June 2016 election included candidates for Select Board (similar to a town council), School Committee (school board), Planning Board, and Housing Authority. A total of 551 people voted, just 4.87% of the registered voters in town (Ingram 2016). And to his surprise, although he had not campaigned or expressed interest in the post, a resident named Phil Hallahan found after the election that he had won a seat on the Housing Authority with just nine votes as a write-in candidate (Goudreau 2016).

In a nonpartisan organization, it is important to avoid endorsing a specific candidate or party, to be neutral when discussing candidates, and to not share your personal opinion (Humphreys Institute 2016). This does not prevent social workers from encouraging voting and providing thoughtful, nonpartisan information. Sources like TurboVote and the League of Women Voters mentioned earlier in this chapter, as well as Ballot Ready (see Resources), can help in this work. Education about candidates includes:

- Creating and distributing questionnaires to candidates, allowing all candidates the opportunity to answer questions, and then sharing the results.
- Passing out sample ballots and voter guides produced by your organization or other organizations.

- Explaining the responsibilities of offices at issue in the election, e.g., What does a Board of Finance member do? What is the difference between the duties of the City Council and the County Commission? What does the Board of Zoning Appeals do? What does the State Board of Education handle as opposed to the town's Board of Education?
- Describing the kinds of issues that are handled at each level of government, to help voters understand the issues likely to arise at the local, state, and federal level.

If you are engaging in voter education as part of a partisan effort, through a campaign or party, you are allowed to educate voters about the ways in which your candidate or party best serves their needs or aligns with their values. Generally done in conjunction with other electoral activities, this type of voter education is usually referred to as **Voter Identification (ID) or Persuasion**. This involves reaching out to potential voters to assess whether they currently support your candidate or party (Wellstone Action n.d.). Current supporters are included in a list of people to follow up with through the voter outreach process (described in the section below). If they are unsure of their support, take the opportunity to try to persuade them that your candidate or party is the right choice for them. If they are not supporters, thank them for their time and move on; these individuals are not included in voter outreach. An example is provided for a sample Voter ID script from a social worker's campaign for State Representative in Connecticut.

Sample Voter ID Script

HQ phone number/for rides: XXX-XXX-XXXX

Hello, I'm a volunteer with the Laura Bartok for State Representative campaign. May I speak with _____?

There is a Democratic primary on Tuesday, August 9th and we're letting people know about why Laura is the best candidate to represent this district. With ten years of experience working at the state capitol and with nonprofits, she knows how to get the job done on day one. She is also the endorsed Democrat in the race.

Can we count on your support for Laura Bartok in the upcoming primary on Tuesday, August 9th?

YES:

Okay, thank you!

1. Will you need an absentee ballot?
2. Would you like a lawn sign?

Then: Thank you for the time. Have a nice day.

UNDECIDED: If you want more information, you can call XXX-XXX-XXXX or visit LauraBartok.com to learn more about her and why she's running.

NO: Alright, well thank you for your time. Have a nice day.

POLITICAL SOCIAL WORKER PROFILE: Tanya Rhodes Smith, MSW
Director, Nancy A. Humphreys Institute for Political Social Work, University of Connecticut School of Social Work (Fig. 8.6).

Fig. 8.6 Tanya Rhodes Smith, MSW

At the Humphreys Institute, we work to increase the political participation of social workers and the communities they serve. While we want all social workers to be more politically active, not all political action is equal. True political power comes from voting, so we believe that every social worker should help the people and communities they serve to vote. We have been training students and social workers for the past several years on why voting matters to social work's mission and impact, and I have been stunned by the energy and enthusiasm for this work. Voting is about relationships, and there is real power in asking someone to vote.

Nonvoters are generally ignored by candidates and political parties. As a BSW student at the University of Nevada-Reno described after participating in a voter engagement project:

> Another resident was blind in one eye and explained that he couldn't see the paperwork so there was no sense in voting. I told him that I could be his eyes, and that he had a right like everyone else to participate. By the end of our discussion, he had tears in his eyes, and said 'Thank you for making me matter.'

This experience isn't uncommon. We often see it with individuals with a felony record. There are 20 million people with a felony record in our country, 6 million of whom can't vote. Perhaps the other 14 million will one day choose to speak together as a powerful voting bloc! Because states determine who can vote with a felony conviction, however, there is misinformation leading most people (including social workers) to assume that people with a felony conviction can't vote.

(continued)

Recently, the Humphreys Institute launched a campaign in a local city to create a new culture of voting. Voting is about relationships, so we are training social service providers why voting matters to their mission and impact and how to integrate nonpartisan voter registration, education and outreach into their service delivery. We also have a task force in the city addressing the barriers to voting, including those that could be fixed easily with better policy and election management by registrars of voters.

After learning that felons could vote after their parole ends, one of our volunteers went to a local career fair for formerly incarcerated people in order to register voters. She quickly connected with five men who had no idea they could vote. They walked together next door to City Hall and each one registered. The woman said that each man left that building "a foot taller." No one had ever asked them to vote.

Section 7: Social Workers and Voter Outreach/GOTV

Registering voters and providing them with election-related information is important, but it often is not enough. Being asked to vote is an incredibly powerful motivator—consistent with the Civic Voluntarism Model, mobilization, or asking someone to vote, is a critical predictor of political participation (Verba et al. 1995; Bedolla and Michelson 2012). While we talk in this section specifically about outreach to those who have already expressed an interest in voting, asking for participation from those who rarely or never vote is also an important role that social workers can, and should, play. **Voter outreach** or **"Get Out The Vote (GOTV)"** activities are a crucial step in voter engagement, specifically reaching out to community members and asking them to vote. In these outreach efforts, potential voters are reminded about upcoming elections and directly encouraged to vote, excitement is created about these elections, and potential voters are helped to break through barriers to casting their ballots and having their voices heard.

Social workers who focus on voter registration drives may miss this step if they do not reach back out to registered individuals to help them get to the polls. Parties, campaigns, community groups, and schools of social work are all potential venues for voter outreach activities. GOTV can be done via phone calls, mailings, or in-person (Humphreys Institute 2016).

Engaging in GOTV Efforts

While the GOTV schedule may vary from state to state, in general, the last 2 weeks before an election are the best time to get people energized and planning to vote on Election Day. This time is used in different ways depending on the election. If you are engaging voters around a primary, special election, or municipal election, potential voters may not know an election is coming, or why it is important. GOTV efforts can be used to make sure they are aware and ready for the election. In big elections, where there has been a lot of press about a particular office or issue, we don't have to worry that people will forget to vote. However, we may have to worry that they are so turned off by TV ads or negative campaigning that they will choose not to vote. The first electoral campaign for one of this book's authors was a hotly contested U.S. Senate campaign in South Dakota, where media is very cheap to buy, so every TV and radio advertising break was completely filled with political ads. By Election Day, voters were so sick of the election that they were choosing not to vote out of frustration. While a fairly rare occurrence, this is something to think about if a campaign has been particularly negative, or if a lot of campaign money has been spent in your area.

GOTV also may focus on making sure that people not only go to the polls, but that they know that they can vote for races other than the top of the ticket races. We have discussed previously that downballot or downticket races generally get fewer votes than the top of the ticket races. We call this **dropoff**, when voters come to the polls and vote for a few races but stop voting as they move down the ballot. Voter outreach can encourage voters to vote for candidates or races that they might otherwise skip. For example, while most of the public's attention during the 2016 election focused on the presidential race between Donald Trump and Hillary Clinton, one of this book's authors helped make GOTV calls that focused voters' attention on the many close races for elected offices in metropolitan Harris County, Texas.

Critical to voter outreach/GOTV efforts is identifying barriers to voting for potential supporters of your campaign, and identifying solutions to address these barriers. It is not enough to remind people of an election if they don't have a car, cannot get off work to vote, or are not registered to vote. Common barriers and voter outreach solutions are listed in Table 8.2. In a nonpartisan voter outreach effort, be sure that your solutions don't include endorsement of any specific candidate or party.

Table 8.2 Voter outreach barriers and solutions

Barrier	Solution
I forgot about the election	Provide education about the election
I don't have a car or a way to get to the polls	Offer them a ride or connect them with a service that provides rides
I have to work or I won't be in town on Election Day	Let them know what protections are in state law for employees to vote (if any), offer them options such as early voting (if applicable), absentee ballots, or mail in ballots (if applicable)
I don't know enough about the candidates, or they are all alike	Provide education about the candidates
I'm not registered to vote	Explain Election Day Registration (if applicable) or the process for registering for the next election
This election doesn't affect me	Provide education about the candidates
I have a disability and can't access the polls	Provide assistance in accessing services to allow them to vote or absentee ballots

APPLY YOUR SKILLS: Voter Outreach Practice

Role play a voter outreach call with a friend or classmate. Each of you should take a turn being the voter and the caller. The voter should provide at least one reason they are not going to vote, and the caller should be prepared to respond.

Campaigns typically use a standard script for GOTV phone calls, incorporating the concepts identified here. We provide one example of a GOTV script, used by the same social worker as in the campaign discussed in the previous section.

Behavioral psychology research suggests a few ways to increase the effectiveness of GOTV calls and visits to people's doors. Dr. Todd Rogers (2012; see his video in the resource section) suggests several ways to do this work well, including asking potential voters about making a plan for voting. Questions might include: What time are you planning to vote? How will you get to the polls? Where will you be coming from? These types of questions may be useful in helping someone planning to vote realize barriers that might keep them from voting on Election Day. Identifying and working through such barriers in advance helps to increase individuals' likelihood of voting.

Rogers (2012) also suggests increasing people's personal accountability, perhaps by indicating that voting records are public (not who you voted for, but whether you vote) or that the caller might follow up after the election. This increases voting for most people—and, in fact, is one reason that pledge cards can be very effective (Humphreys Institute 2016). It is important though to be aware that some people may react negatively to efforts to increase accountability. Rogers (2012) argues that when some campaigns engage in voter outreach by telling people that voter turnout

Sample GOTV Script

Hello, I'm a volunteer with the Laura Bartok for State Representative campaign. May I speak with _____?

The Democratic Primary is on Tuesday, August 9th and we're asking people to come out and support Laura. She is the best candidate to represent this district and has lived here all her life. Laura has a BSW and a MSW (Master of Social Work) in policy with a focus on aging. She has the right budget priorities and will fight for families and business.

Can we count on you to vote in the Democratic Primary on Tuesday, August 9th and will you support for Laura Bartok?

YES:

Okay, thank you!

Will you need a ride to the poll?

YES: Note it.

Then: Thank you for the time. Have a nice day.

UNDECIDED: If you want more information, I can have Laura contact you. (If yes: when is a good time to call?)

NO: All right, well thank you for your time. Have a nice day.

HQ phone number/for rides: XXX-XXX-XXXX

will be low, this is not effective, because people like to do what others do. Highlighting low turnout may make people feel like they do not need to participate in this election. Instead, Rogers suggests emphasizing that the person to whom you are speaking is "the kind of person who votes" or "a voter." This simple framing change can help to make voting part of a person's identity.

Early Voting

Traditionally in the USA, we think of voter outreach as helping people get to the polls on Election Day. However, depending on the rules in your state, you may need to engage in voter outreach during earlier time periods. How do you know if you should be encouraging voters to vote on Election Day or earlier? How do you know if GOTV efforts are needed earlier in the election season?

Voting before Election Day typically comes in one of three forms: early voting, absentee voting, and mail voting. **Early voting** means that voters can show up at a designated site (such as the local town hall) in advance of an election and vote early, with no reason or justification needed. Early voting laws are designed to ensure that people have access to voting if their situation does not allow them to come to the polls during the designated time on Election Day. Currently, 37 states and the District of Columbia offer some form of early voting. The early voting time window varies from state to state and in some states have been decreased or eliminated in recent years. It is important to be up-to-date on what is available in your state during each election.

Early voting has both benefits and drawbacks. It can facilitate voting by those who are not able to vote in person on Election Day because of work or other commitments. It has the potential to reduce the wait time for voting and thereby increase accessibility, since the same number of people are voting over a longer period of time. However, in states with a significant amount of early voting, voters may not be able to respond to events that happen right before Election Day if they have already cast their ballot. For example, a well-publicized altercation took place between a Congressional candidate in Montana and a reporter days before a special election in 2017. Individuals who might have chosen to change their vote because of that altercation (either toward or away from that candidate) were unable to do so if they were part of the more than 60% of voters who had already voted through early voting (Enten 2017).

In states with early voting, GOTV efforts are targeted at a variety of dates, not just Election Day. For example, in many states, "Souls to the Polls" campaigns bring voters directly from Sunday church services to polling stations open on Sundays (Reid 2016).

In **absentee voting**, a voter can request that elections officials mail a ballot to them prior to Election Day. The ballot has to be mailed back or returned in person by the time the polls close. All states have this as an option. In 20 states, you have to provide a justification for why you need to vote absentee. In 27 states and the District of Columbia, you just need to ask for the ballot—you don't need to have a reason. In eight states (Arizona, California, Hawaii, Minnesota, Montana, New Jersey, Utah) and the District of Columbia, voters may ask to be on a permanent absentee ballot list, and can receive an absentee ballot for every election after they sign up.

As with early voting, absentee voting has the potential to provide voters increased access to voting. However, it generally requires voters to either present themselves to an elections official during business hours or locate an absentee ballot form, fill it out, sign it, send it in, and then fill out and sign a ballot when it comes. Any time multiple steps are introduced into the voting process, there is the potential for people to not complete them. Absentee voting can have the same drawbacks as early voting, in that people who have already voted may be unable to react to changes in campaigns that happen on or near Election Day.

In contrast to these other models, in three states—Colorado, Oregon, and Washington—a ballot is automatically mailed to every eligible voter (NCSL 2017a). This is known as **mail voting**. Some in-person options are available for those who prefer it or require special services. Other states may offer some mail-in election options. In states that utilize mail voting, voter outreach efforts are centered on making sure people fill out and mail the ballot back, and that can happen over a longer period of time.

Know the early voting rules in your state and consider how they should affect your voter outreach efforts. For example, Massachusetts has early voting only during even-year November elections. Elections at other times and in odd years, including primaries, municipal elections, and special elections, do not provide voters an early voting option. As a political social worker, knowing the rules is key to being able to provide correct information to potential voters and giving them the best chance of participating in elections.

BUILD YOUR KNOWLEDGE: Voting Options in Your State
Go to http://www.canivote.org/ or http://www.ncsl.org/research/elections-and-campaigns/absentee-and-early-voting.aspx or your local elections website to find out the voting rules for your state. What are the rules for early voting, absentee voting, and/or mail voting in your state?

Review of Key Terms and Concepts

Absentee voting: a method of voting in which a voter can request that the elections officials mail them a ballot prior to Election Day. The ballot has to be mailed back or returned in person by the time the polls closed. All states have this as an option.

Disenfranchisement: having the right to vote taken away.

Dropoff: when voters come to the polls and vote for a few races but stop voting as they move down the ballot.

Early voting: a method of voting in which voters show up at a designated site (such as their local town hall) in advance of the election and vote early. No reason or justification is needed.

Franchise: the right to vote.

Get Out The Vote (GOTV): please refer to "voter outreach."

Mail voting: a method of voting in Colorado, Oregon, and Washington, in which a ballot is automatically mailed to every eligible voter.

Nonpartisan voter engagement: activities that are not biased toward a particular candidate or political party and do not support or oppose any particular candidate or party. This may include voter education, voter outreach, and voter registration.

Nonprofit VOTE: the largest provider of nonpartisan resources and trainings to the nonprofit sector on integrating nonpartisan voter participation and election activities into ongoing activities and services. www.nonprofitvote.org

Partisan voter engagement: activities that advance a specific candidate or political party when assisting citizens with voter registration and voting. May include voter education, voter outreach, and voter registration.

Political justice: refers to the equitable distribution of political rights. Specifically, it is concerned with issues such as access to voting rights and political representation.

Preclearance: seeking approval from the Department of Justice for voting-related changes.

Privilege: in the context of political justice, a right earned by or granted to a specific person or group of people.

Provisional ballots: ballots cast by voters if there is some question about their identification or identity, and held separately until after the election to see if the issue is resolved. If resolved favorably, the vote is counted. Provisional ballots also may be called challenge ballots or affidavit ballots.

Responsibility: a duty for all.

Right: an entitlement guaranteed to all who qualify.

Voter education: teaches voters the mechanics of voting (where to vote, what the deadlines are, and the process of voting) and information about the issues on the ballot or considered by candidates.

Voter fraud: abuse of the electoral process by those who are not eligible to vote, or by those who are eligible to vote who use the system to vote multiple times.

Voter Identification (ID) or Persuasion: reaching out to potential voters to assess whether they are current supporters of your candidate or party.

Voter outreach or **"Get out the Vote (GOTV)"**: activities that remind people about the election, create excitement about elections, encourage people to vote, and help them get to the polls.

Voter registration: the process by which voters in 49 states and the District of Columbia add themselves to the voting rolls in advance of an election. North Dakota does not have voter registration. Laws regarding voter registration differ drastically from state to state.

Voter suppression: the disruption of the ability of eligible voters to cast their ballots through mechanisms that are discriminatory, intimidating, or otherwise create barriers to the act of voting.

Voting Rights Act: passed in 1965, the most significant voting legislation of the twentieth century. Intended to put an end to Jim Crow laws.

Resources

Books:

Abigail Thernstrom: *Whose votes count?* (conservative counterpoint to the voting rights argument) http://www.hup.harvard.edu/catalog.php?isbn=9780674951969

Ari Berman: *Give us the ballot: The modern struggle for voting rights in America* https://www.amazon.com/Give-Us-Ballot-Struggle-America/dp/1250094720

Richard Cloward and Frances Fox Piven:

https://www.amazon.com/Frances-Fox-Piven/e/B001ITTHW4/ref=dp_byline_cont_book_1

Mobilizing the poor: How it can be done.

Regulating the poor: The functions of public welfare.

Why people don't vote: And why politicians want it that way.

Podcasts & Videos:

Adam Ruins Everything—an excellent resource on voting: http://www.trutv.com/full-episodes/adam-ruins-everything/2065341/index.html. You may need a login from your cable company for the full episode, but clips are available on You Tube.

Freakonomics podcast which includes a section on the value of an individual vote: http://freakonomics.com/podcast/freakonomics-radio-your-freak-quently-asked-questions-answered/ and the related New York Times magazine article: http://www.nytimes.com/2005/11/06/magazine/why-vote.html

Interview about voter fraud: http://www.cc.com/video-clips/37udj7/the-daily-show-with-trevor-noah-jesse-williams---stepping-into-the-spotlight-on--grey-s-anatomy----extended-interview

On Point podcast on Voter ID laws: http://www.wbur.org/onpoint/2016/08/03/voting-rights-voter-id-ballot-access

Rock the Vote video about history of voting: https://www.youtube.com/watch?v=ar7r5aG_B0Y

Stanford professor Todd Rogers discusses research about ways to make GOTV more effective: https://www.youtube.com/watch?time_continue=1&v=TkWQSsw93CU

Story Corps animation about Jim Crow and voting (3 min): https://www.youtube.com/watch?v=AA87JWa0bEw

TED Talks:

E-voting: http://www.ted.com/talks/david_bismark_e_voting_without_fraud

Getting young people to vote: https://www.youtube.com/watch?v=nlYpMGI6iNQ

Research on racism and voting: https://www.ted.com/talks/nate_silver_on_race_and_politics

Voter engagement: https://www.youtube.com/watch?v=kYIpDmuMFpw

Websites—Organizations:

Advancement Project: http://www.advancementproject.org/

Alliance for Justice: https://www.afj.org/

American Civil Liberties Union: https://www.aclu.org/issues/voting-rights

Ballot Ready https://www.ballotready.org/

Brennan Center for Justice: https://www.brennancenter.org/

https://www.brennancenter.org/issues/voting-rights-elections

https://www.brennancenter.org/publication/state-restrictions-voter-registration-drives

Election Project: http://www.electproject.org/

Fair Vote: http://www.fairvote.org/.

Nancy A. Humphreys Institute for Political Social Work: http://politicalinstitute.uconn.edu

National Coalition for the Homeless: https://www.nationalhomeless.org/

National Law Center on Homelessness & Poverty: https://www.nlchp.org/

Nonprofit VOTE: http://www.nonprofitvote.org

http://www.nonprofitvote.org/voting-in-your-state/

http://www.nonprofitvote.org/resource-library/voting-in-your-state-2/

Project Vote: http://www.projectvote.org

Public Interest Legal Foundation: https://publicinterestlegal.org/reports/

Sentencing Project: http://sentencingproject.org/.

TurboVote: http://democracy.works/turbovote/

U.S. Election Assistance Commission: https://www.eac.gov/voters/national-voter-registration-act-studies/

Vote411 from the League of Women Voters: http://www.vote411.org/.

Vote Smart: http://votesmart.org/.

Voting is Social Work: http://www.votingissocialwork.org

Websites—Resources:

Absentee & Early Voting:

http://www.ncsl.org/research/elections-and-campaigns/absentee-and-early-voting.aspx

Buzzfeed humorous video on voter registration:

https://www.buzzfeed.com/briggles/registering-to-vote-with-president-obama

Introduction to Federal Voting Rights Laws: https://www.justice.gov/crt/introduction-federal-voting-rights-laws-0 or go to https://www.justice.gov/ and in the menu under "Agencies" click "Alphabetical Listing," then on the landing page click "Civil Rights Division." In the sidebar on the left hand side of the page under "Voting" click "History of Voting Rights Laws" then on the landing page click "Introduction to Federal Voting Rights Laws" at the top.

Profiles of plaintiffs in voting rights lawsuits:

https://www.thenation.com/article/the-92-year-old-civil-rights-pioneer-who-is-now-challenging-north-carolinas-voter-id-law/

http://www.politico.com/story/2013/12/one-mothers-struggle-for-voting-rights-100842

Tips for Effective Voter Contact Scripts: http://www.wellstone.org/sites/default/files/attachments/Effective-Phone-and-Door-Scripts_0.pdf

Voter Privacy: http://www.calvoter.org/issues/votprivacy/index.html or go to http://www.calvoter.org/ and in the sidebar menu under "Issues & Publications" click "Voter Privacy".

Voting Rights: http://www.civilrights.org/votingrights

References

Adams, J. (1776). *Letter to James Sullivan.*

American Association of People with Disabilities. (2016). *Statistics & data.* Retrieved from http://www.aapd.com/our-focus/voting/statistics/

American Civil Liberties Union. (2017). *State criminal re-enfranchisement laws.* Retrieved from https://www.aclu.org/map/state-criminal-re-enfranchisement-laws-map

Austin, M. J., Coombs, M., & Barr, B. (2005). Community-centered clinical practice: Is the integration of micro and macro social work practice possible? *Journal of Community Practice, 4,* 9–30.

Bazelon Center for Mental Health Law. (n.d.). *State laws affecting the voting rights of people with mental disabilities.* Retrieved from https://www.866ourvote.org/newsroom/publications/body/0049.pdf

Bedolla, L. G., & Michelson, M. R. (2012). *Mobilizing inclusion: Transforming the electorate through get-out-the-vote campaigns.* New Haven, CT: Yale University Press.

Bergin, B., Keefe, J., & Ye, J. (2016, June 21). Brooklyn voter purge hit Hispanics hardest. *WNYC.*

Bomboy, S. (2016). *What would the Senate look like in 2016 without the 17th Amendment?* Constitution Daily National Constitution Center.

Berman, A. (2015). *Give us the ballot: The modern struggle for voting rights in America.* New York, NY: Macmillan Publishers.

Brennan Center for Justice. (2016). *Voting laws roundup 2016.* Retrieved from http://www.brennancenter.org/analysis/voting-laws-roundup-2016

California Voter Foundation. (2012). *Voter privacy in the digital age: Key findings and recommendations.* Retrieved from http://www.calvoter.org/issues/votprivacy/pub/voterprivacy/keyfindings.html

Civil Rights Digital Library. (2017). *Civil Rights Act of 1957.* Retrieved from http://crdl.usg.edu/events/civil_rights_act_1957/?Welcome

Cobb, J. C. (2015, August 6). The Voting Rights Act at 50: How it changed the world. *Time.*

Connecticut Secretary of State. (2006). *Election results for Representative in Congress.* Retrieved from http://www.sots.ct.gov/sots/cwp/view.asp?a=3188&q=392572-Second

Constitutional Rights Foundation. (1991). *Who voted in early America?* Retrieved from http://www.crf-usa.org/bill-of-rights-in-action/bria-8-1-b-who-voted-in-early-america

DeSilver, D. (2017). *U.S. trails most developed countries in voter turnout.* Pew Research Center.

Disability Justice. (2017). *The right to vote: Interplay of federal and state law on voting rights.* Retrieved from http://disabilityjustice.org/right-to-vote/

Enten, H. (2017, May 25). *Montana's special election could give the GOP another reason to fret.* Retrieved from Fivethirtyeight.com

Fessler, P. (2017). *Advocates worry Trump administration wants to revamp motor voter law.* Retrieved from NPR.com

Flanders, S. (2001). Richard Cloward, Welfare rights activist dies at 74. *New York Times.*

Florida Division of Elections. (n.d.). *Third party voter registration organizations.* Retrieved from http://dos.myflorida.com/elections/for-voters/voter-registration/third-party-voter-registration-organizations/

Gilbert, K. L., Quinn, S. C., Goodman, R. M., Butler, J., & Wallace, J. (2013). A meta-analysis of social capital and health: A case for needed research. *Journal of Health Psychology, 18*(11), 1385–1399. https://doi.org/10.1177/1359105311435983.

Goudreau, C. (2016, June 23). Hallahan accepts Longmeadow housing authority position. *The Reminder*.

Henderson, W. (2011). Civic engagement among registered citizens and non-registered eligible citizens. In *The Center for Information and Research on Civic Learning and Engagement*. CIRCLE Blog.

Heritage Foundation. (2017). *Poll taxes*. Retrieved from http://www.heritage.org/constitution/-!/amendments/24/essays/186/poll-taxes

Hill, K. Q., Leighley, J., & Hinton-Anderson, A. (1995). Lower-class mobilization and policy linkage in the United States. *American Journal of Political Science, 39*(1), 75–86.

Ingram, K. T. (2016). *Town of Longmeadow annual election minutes*. http://www.longmeadow.org/Archive.aspx?ADID=579

Johnson, L. (1965). *Remarks on the signing of the Voting Rights Act*. UVA Miller Center.

Kasdan, D. (2012). *State restrictions on voter registration drives*. https://www.brennancenter.org/page/-/publications/state%20restrictions%20on%20voter%20registration%20drives.pdf

Kim, S., Kim, C., & You, M. S. (2015). Civic participation and self-rated health: A cross-national multi-level analysis using the world value survey. *Journal of Preventive Medicine and Public Health, 48*(1), 18–27. https://doi.org/10.3961/jpmph.14.031.

Leadership Conference. (2017). *Why DC voting rights matter*. Retrieved from http://www.civilrights.org/voting-rights/dc-voting-rights/why-dc-voting-rights.html

Legal Information Institute. (n.d.). *Preclearance and bail-out*. Retrieved from https://www.law.cornell.edu/wex/voting_rights_act-Preclearance

Lepore, J. (2008. Rock, paper, scissors: How we used to vote. *The New Yorker*.

LeRoux, K. (2014). Social justice and the role of nonprofit human service organizations in amplifying client voice. In M. J. Austin (Ed.), *Social justice and social work: Rediscovering a core value of the profession* (pp. 325–338). Thousand Oaks, CA: SAGE Publications.

Maskivker, J. (2016, November 2). It's your moral duty to vote. Here are 3 reasons. *Washington Post*.

Nancy A. Humphreys Institute for Political Social Work. (2016). *Voting is social work: Training social workers on nonpartisan voter registration, education and outreach*. Retrieved from http://votingissocialwork.org/wp-content/uploads/2016/06/How-to-do-Nonpartisan-Voter-Engagement-Any-State.pdf

National Conference of State Legislators. (2016). *Voter registration*. Retrieved from http://www.ncsl.org/research/elections-and-campaigns/voter-registration.aspx

National Conference of State Legislators. (2017a). *Absentee and early voting*. Retrieved from http://www.ncsl.org/research/elections-and-campaigns/absentee-and-early-voting.aspx

National Conference of State Legislators. (2017b). *Automatic voter registration*. Retrieved from http://www.ncsl.org/research/elections-and-campaigns/automatic-voter-registration.aspx

National Conference of State Legislatures. (2015). *Provisional ballots*. Retrieved from http://www.ncsl.org/research/elections-and-campaigns/provisional-ballots.aspx

National Park Service. (n.d.). *Virginia Minor and women's right to vote*. Retrieved from https://www.nps.gov/jeff/learn/historyculture/the-virginia-minor-case.htm

Nickerson, D. W. (2008). Is voting contagious? Evidence from two field experiments. *The American Political Science Association, 102*(1), 49–57.

Nonprofit VOTE. (2017a). *2012 evaluation: Nonprofits increase voting*. Retrieved from http://www.nonprofitvote.org/2012-evaluation-nonprofits-increase-voting/

Nonprofit VOTE. (2017b). *Voter education*. Retrieved from http://www.nonprofitvote.org/nonprofits-voting-elections-online/voter-education/

Nonprofit VOTE. (2017c). *Voting in your state*. Retrieved from http://www.nonprofitvote.org/voting-in-your-state/

Obradovich, K. (2016, July 11). Branstad: Voting is a privilege, not a right. *The Des Moines Register*.

Paulson, D. (2013, October 10). *Florida's history of suppressing blacks' votes*. St. Petersburg: Tampa Bay Times.

Piven, F. F., & Cloward, R. A. (2000). *Why Americans still don't vote*. Boston, MA: Beacon Press.

Pritzker, S. (2017). *A baseline assessment of policy education in social work*. Council on Social Work Education.

Public Interest Legal Foundation. (2017). *Alien Invasion II: The sequel to the discovery and cover-up of non-citizen registration and voting in Virginia*. Retrieved from https://publicinterestlegal. org/blog/alien-invasion-ii-sequel-discovery-cover-non-citizen-registration-voting-virginia/

Purtle, J. (2013). Felon disenfranchisement in the United States: A health equity perspective. *American Journal of Public Health, 103*(4), 632–637. https://doi.org/10.2105/ AJPH.2012.300933.

Ratcliffe, D. (2013). The right to vote and the rise of democracy, 1787–1828. *Journal of the Early Republic, 33*, 219–254.

Reid, J. (2016). *Souls to the polls & the power of early voting*. http://www.msnbc.com/am-joy/ watch/souls-to-the-polls-the-power-of-early-voting-802252868000

Reiter, A. (2017). *Fearless radicalism: Alice Paul and her fight for women's suffrage*. Retrieved from https://www.armstrong.edu/history-journal/ history-journal-fearless-radicalism-alice-paul-and-her-fight-for-womens-suf

Rios, E. (2016, March 25). Native Americans are taking the fight for voting rights to court. *Mother Jones*.

Rogers, T. (2012). *Getting out the vote*. https://www.youtube.com/watch?time_continue=1&v= TkWQSsw93CU

S.D. candidates may face recount. (2004). Retrieved from http://www.foxnews.com/ story/2004/11/01/sd-candidates-may-face-recount.print.html

Schonberg, J. (2016). *A voice for everyone in 2016*. Retrieved from https://www.blog.google/ topics/politics-elections/a-voice-for-everyone-in-2016/

Searcy, D. (2011). Voting: A right, a privilege, or a responsibility? *Right to Vote Blog*.

Sentencing Project. (2017). *Felony disenfranchisement: A primer [Policy Brief]*.

Smithsonian National Museum of History: Behring Center. (n.d.). *White only: Jim Crow in America*. Retrieved from http://americanhistory.si.edu/brown/history/1-segregated/white-only-1.html

State Elections Offices. (2001). *2000 Official presidential general elections results*. Retrieved from http://www.fec.gov/pubrec/2000presgeresults.htm

Summers, T. (2017, January 27). *Court denies attempts to dismiss election complaint for "straw contest"*. Jackson: Jackson Free Press.

The Conversation. (2015). *Debate: do citizens have a moral duty to vote?* Retrieved from http:// theconversation.com/debate-do-citizens-have-a-moral-duty-to-vote-37880

Thornton, S. (n.d.). *Literacy tests and the right to vote*. Retrieved from http://connecticuthistory. org/literacy-tests-and-the-right-to-vote/

Turner-Lee, N. (2017). *Trump's election integrity commission needs to redress voter suppression, not fraud*. FixGov: Brookings.

U.S. Department of Justice. (2010). *Fact sheet: MOVE Act*. Retrieved from https://www.justice. gov/opa/pr/fact-sheet-move-act

Uggen, C., Larson, R., & Shannon, S. (2016). 6 million lost voters: State-level estimates of felony disenfranchisement, 2016. In *Research and advocacy for reform*. Washington, DC: The Sentencing Project.

United States Election Project. (2017). *2016 November general election turnout rates*. Retrieved January 22, 2017 from http://www.electproject.org/2016g

Verba, S., Schlozman, K. L., & Brady, H. (1995). *Voice and equality: Civic voluntarism in American politics*. Cambridge, MA: Harvard University Press.

Wagster Pettus, E. (2016) U.S. Judge hears arguments in Mississippi House election spat. *WJTV*.

Wellstone Action. (n.d.). *Tips for effective voter contact scripts (door and phone)*. Retrieved from http://www.wellstone.org/sites/default/files/attachments/Effective-Phone-and-Door-Scripts_0.pdf

White House Office of the Press Secretary. (2017). *President announces formation of bipartisan Presidential Commission on Election Integrity*. Retrieved from https://www.whitehouse.gov/the-press-office/2017/05/11/president-announces-formation-bipartisan-presidential-commission

Williams, K. (2004). *Key provisions of the Help America Vote Act*. Retrieved from https://www.brennancenter.org/analysis/key-provisions-help-america-vote-act; https://www.eac.gov/about/help-america-vote-act/

Wise, L., & Lowry, B. (2017, May 11). *Civil rights groups fume about Trump's choice of Kris Kobach for voter fraud panel*. Kansas: The Kansas City Star.

Woo, E. (2001). Richard A. Cloward; Sociologist Fought for Welfare, Voter Rights. *Los Angeles Times*.

Part III

Engaging and Intervening with Effective Political Social Work Strategies

"I want to be remembered as someone who used herself and anything she could touch to work for justice and freedom, I want to be remembered as one who tried."

–Dr. Dorothy Irene Height, MSW

Persuasive Political Communication

9

© Springer International Publishing AG 2018
S.R. Lane, S. Pritzker, *Political Social Work*,
https://doi.org/10.1007/978-3-319-68588-5_9

Section 1: Overview

Being able to communicate your message is key in political social work. Here we focus on best practices of persuasive political communication, including tailoring messages and communications to your audience. This chapter includes overall communication skills, such as framing, strategic use of language, and importance of being clear about your "ask"—what you want your target to do, support, or learn. Traditional media topics include definitions and benefits of various types of media, news hooks, selecting faces and visuals for a campaign, creating soundbites, and key terms such as on the record, off the record, and on background. Social media topics include the variety of available social media platforms and audiences, benefits, drawbacks, and communication strategies for each, as well as ways to keep abreast of emerging social media platforms and abilities. Interpersonal communication topics include public speaking, effective writing, and legislative testimony. Readers will develop a message, create media messaging, and practice "staying on message" as a candidate.

Developing Social Work Competency
The Council on Social Work Education establishes educational standards for all social work programs in the USA. Content in this chapter supports building competency in the following areas that are considered core to the practice of social work:
COMPETENCY 1: Demonstrate Ethical and Professional Behavior
COMPETENCY 5: Engage in Policy Practice
COMPETENCY 6: Engage with Individuals, Families, Groups, Organizations, and Communities
COMPETENCY 7: Assess Individuals, Families, Groups, Organizations, and Communities
COMPETENCY 8: Intervene with Individuals, Families, Groups, Organizations, and Communities

Domains of Political Social Work	
1. Engaging individuals and communities in political processes	◄
2. Influencing policy agendas and decision-making	◄
3. Holding professional and political positions	◄
4. Engaging with electoral campaigns	◄
5. Seeking and holding elected office	◄

Section 2: Communication

Effective and strategic use of communication is essential to political social work practice. Each of the tactics you identify as part of your strategic planning requires clear communication with your target and/or the public about your goals. If we do not communicate clearly, we run the risk that targets will find themselves frustrated and will lose interest in what we are saying. Our arguments, when not communicated clearly, may hinder our ability to persuade our targets to support our campaign goals. Worse, our targets (the individuals whose support we are seeking) will misunderstand what we are asking for. The last thing we want is to put our heart, soul, and resources into a political strategy, and then to not achieve our goals because of poor communication. To avoid this, and to strengthen your ability to effectively communicate, this chapter begins by walking you through five essential components for crafting any political communication: professional use of self, assessing your target, framing and messaging, use of language, and clarity.

Professional Use of Self

In social work practice, we often talk about **professional use of self**—the idea that we, as individual social workers, are an essential component of our practice interventions with clients. This is an important part of both direct practice and political social work practice. The effectiveness of your social work intervention (whether via an advocacy campaign, an electoral campaign, or a voter engagement effort) is impacted substantially by your own use of self.

As a political candidate or an elected official, you are the face of your campaign or office. As a campaign staffer or as a political staffer, how you communicate and present yourself is perceived as a reflection of the candidate or elected official for whom you work. As an advocate, your communications often are interpreted to reflect positively or negatively on the broader issue for which you are advocating.

This may seem like a lot of pressure on you—and it certainly can be—but it also provides a great opportunity to apply the social work skills that you have learned elsewhere in your social work program to your political social work practice. Some crucial skills are active listening, engaging diversity, deliberate attention to verbal and nonverbal communications, and self-awareness (Cournoyer 2008). Ability to understand and work within ethical values such as integrity and competence is also key (National Association of Social Workers 2017). Some critical considerations to keep in mind as you prepare your political communications are outlined below.

Know your personal comfort level, style, and strengths: Reflect upon and self-assess your communication strengths and weaknesses. For example, if writing is not your strong suit, have you identified a colleague who can review your written communications before you send them out to your target(s)? If public speaking makes you nervous, have you built in time to practice your testimony or to sign up for a program to help you strengthen your public speaking, like Toastmasters? If humor has always been an effective tool for you, have you thought about an appropriate way to incorporate it into your verbal communications?

Know your assumptions: We each bring assumptions to the various policy issues with which we work. Being able to differentiate between our personal opinions and assumptions and objective fact can be difficult. However, knowing this distinction can help us more effectively communicate with targets who do not share the same assumptions as we do (Lavine 2002). We have previously discussed the power of bias and stereotypes. Be aware of your own biases and actively resist the use of stereotypes. Often, we seek to persuade policy decision-makers or constituents who do not share our core assumptions and values. Being able to acknowledge what specific differences exist can help us to more effectively craft communications that reach out to these targets.

Establish credibility: **Credibility**, being considered worthy of trust, is critical in political settings where many motivations guide players' actions. Your targets need to know why to listen to your arguments. They want to have confidence in the information you provide, as well as your ability to back up your words with action (Center for Community Change 1997). In local and state political settings, especially, where elected officials tend to have limited staff resources, they depend heavily on the work of lobbyists, advocates, and other allies, but don't want to be caught in a position where they have trusted the wrong information sources. Credibility comes from professional or personal experience, expertise, and from being someone who consistently provides reliable information when asked.

Be authentic: Just as authenticity is important to direct social work practice with clients, it is important in a political setting. While the public often perceives politicians to be less than sincere, sincerity is a political asset. For candidates, voters, volunteers, and donors like to feel that they can trust what they hear you say. For advocates and staffers, being trustworthy—closely tied to our core social work value of integrity—helps you to be taken more seriously.

Be prepared: In political social work practice, we regularly make claims about a wide range of policy issues. Make sure that you have done your research, as you are responsible for all of the claims you make and the data you provide. For example, do your research so that you can avoid over-generalizations about populations. To say "everyone" will lose benefits under this bill is to open the door to an opponent bringing forward someone who will not, thus undercutting the credibility of your argument. When you are unable to be fully prepared, bring together your credibility and authenticity. As with many social work situations, if you do not know the answer to a question, avoid making up an answer. Instead, be honest and say, "I don't know the answer, but I will find out and get back to you" (and then do so).

Engage thoughtfully with political diversity and difference: The social work profession has been criticized for how well it prepares students to engage with diverse political viewpoints (Hodge 2004). Yet achieving our political social work goals often requires us to engage with, and perhaps partner with, those who differ with us significantly in political ideology. As you work with targets, coalition members, or community members who have strong opposing views from you, think about:

- How can you approach difference with empathy?
- Where can you find common ground with those who are different?
- If someone expresses anger toward you during a political discussion, is that aimed at you, or might there be other context for this emotion?

- Can you and those whose beliefs differ from yours move beyond hyperbole to authentically discuss concerns, fears, and goals?

Often, maintaining a respectful demeanor toward your targets, even when you disagree with their ideology or viewpoints, can help you effectively communicate your argument to decision-makers and constituents. The common phrase "politics makes strange bedfellows" truly is an accurate description of the dynamics you will encounter in your political work. As has been discussed, the individual you are working against today may be your ally on a different policy issue tomorrow. However they get to the same place as you, engaging and building relationships with those holding diverse ideologies, when it is safe for you, will often be key to working together toward your long-term goals.

We want to underscore that this does not mean that you are required to be respectful to people who direct hate toward you or your community. It is not realistic to expect you to be respectful toward people who are actively objectionable toward you, or even to engage with them at all.

Assessing Your Target

Effective political communications rely on assessing your target; that is, having a strong sense of who your target(s) is and the types of factors that shape the decisions your target(s) makes. We have discussed previously how to identify and get to know what factors impact your target(s). Here we focus on how we can use this information to help communicate with targets.

As Lavine (2002) points out in his "Cardinal Rule 1" of advocacy, a primary consideration is whether our argument is tailored to our specific target(s). Go back to the strategic plan you have developed. The target(s) you have identified in that plan should be the person/people to whom your argument is tailored. For example, if you are trying to persuade Rep. Juliana Jones, a staunch supporter of tight fiscal spending caps, that she should support a bill to increase state spending on mental health services, then your testimony/letter/phone call should steer away from arguments about why it is socially just to expand mental health funding. Instead, a fiscally based argument showing how increasing spending on mental health services in other states led to a reduction in other costs to those states might be more effective.

One of the authors' favorite quotes from marketing is the following: "If you want to sell to fish, don't use skywriting." At its essence, this quote means that it does not matter how good your argument may be; if it is made to a target that will not find this argument persuasive, it is ineffective. If fish cannot see the beautiful argument you have written in the air, the skywriting argument will not work. This is part of why it is so important to personalize your target(s) in advocacy campaigns. Because of their personal orientations, each target may require somewhat different arguments and communication techniques.

Using your assessment of your target, try to put yourself in their shoes and understand what factors affect your target's decision-making. Some specific factors to consider before developing your communications include the following:

- *What sways your target*: Political affiliation and allegiances? Religious affiliation? Specific values? How peers view the target? How the public views your target?
- *Why might your target hold specific attitudes toward your proposed policy solution or your candidacy*: Personal history and experiences? Professional experiences? Values or ideological beliefs? Personality?
- *Are there constraints through which your target views policy choices or candidacies*: Do they perceive an environment conducive to change, do they feel more comfortable with the status quo, or are they most comfortable just making things a little less bad? Do the elected officials you are targeting perceive a climate with limited resources, where their choice is between funding your solution or another, not both?
- *Are there larger news issues, trends, and public concerns that are likely to impact how your target hears your arguments?* Has there been a recent tragedy or episode of violence in your community? Has a natural disaster in your community or elsewhere made news and impacted people's perceptions? Have there been recent public debates, arguments, or protests about related policy issues that may impact your target's perceptions of the issue?

Once you have fully assessed the factors that affect your target's decision-making, you will find yourself more equipped to tailor your argument to the target. An important starting point in communicating with your target is to seek to establish common ground with them, even when it feels like you are coming from very different ideological and value bases (Lens 2005). You can do this by identifying areas of agreement, however small, and addressing these up front before you move to making your case for your candidate or policy proposal. Is there some value that you share that is relevant to this issue? Might this solution offer a way to bridge your ideological divide? For example, "I know we both care deeply about the well-being of children in this state ...."

Your assessment of your target also should guide you in determining the kinds of evidence that are best suited both to your goals and that your target will most likely find persuasive (Lens 2005). Does your target respond best to financial data? To empirical data? To vivid first-person examples? To anecdotes that show impact on populations near and dear to the target's heart?

Use of Language

In political communications, "knowing how to say something can be as important as the content" (Lens 2005). The language that we use can vastly impact the reception our messages get and, therefore, our ability to elicit policy change.

Professionalism is essential in how we use language in political communications. As Cournoyer (2008) describes in discussing essential communication skills for all social workers:

> In written communications, adopt a professional attitude consistent with the qualities and characteristics of professionalism …. Badly written, poorly formatted documents that contain spelling and grammatical errors, logical fallacies, and fail to reflect critical thought, a scholarly perspective, or the universal intellectual standards are likely to be dismissed by recipients.

These same concepts apply to political communications. Spelling and grammatical errors and poorly articulated or disorganized arguments can make it difficult for your target(s) to take your argument seriously, no matter how valid it may be.

Our verbal and written political communications should use widely **accessible language**, appropriate to our target's vocabulary and experiences. Jargon, acronyms, and terms used by insiders should be avoided. Sometimes we are so familiar with our areas of practice and expertise that we do not realize the extent to which we use jargon in our communications. However, to persuade someone who is not as familiar with this language, we need to use language that they will understand. This also applies to presenting data. Where possible, use simple charts and graphs to present numbers and statistics.

Avoid **universal claims** in your language. As discussed previously, there is always an exception that can make your argument vulnerable. For example, instead of "all" or "everyone," consider using less assailable words like "most," "many," or "some," or, where possible, use specific numbers or percentages.

Be succinct and brief with your communications. Targets of political communication are often bombarded with messages from a variety of sources, and have limited time to hear, read, and process these communications. Spend substantial time reviewing your verbal and written communications to make them as succinct and brief as possible. Lens (2005) cites the famous writer George Orwell to advise social work advocates, "If it is possible to cut a word out, always cut it out" (p. 236). This is relevant for any public communications, but particularly so for those that involve the media. Developing and stating quotable **soundbites**, a short, self-contained version of your message, is critical for garnering media coverage that promotes your message.

Pay careful attention to word choice. Sometimes, we jump quickly into the words that we use, without attention to how those words may be interpreted by others. In political communications, however, how others may interpret our words is of utmost importance. As Lens (2005) notes, a small wording change can lead to vastly different perceptions of the issue. For example, if we call the tax that some individuals' descendants pay on their property an "estate tax," the public visualizes wealthy families passing on an estate to their families, garnering public support for the tax. On the other hand, if we call the same tax a "death tax," the public visualizes people being taxed upon their family member's death, leading to public opposition for the tax. Same tax, different public reactions. Another very public example is the use of the term "Obamacare" rather than the "Affordable Care Act" to refer to the healthcare reform instituted under President Obama. Polls as of 2017 consistently showed broad support for the Affordable Care Act and substantial opposition to Obamacare, despite the fact that these two terms refer to exactly the same thing (Dropp and Nyhan 2017)!

A final consideration in using language in political communications is *awareness of the tone that you use*. The **tone**, including the sound, pitch, and speed of one's voice, that a speaker uses can communicate its own set of messages. Where possible, be attuned to the tone that you are using. Try to stay positive and avoid argumentation. Focus on where you may be coming across arrogantly and try to avoid this. Passion is often appropriate, but where possible, try to adopt a tone that may appear reasonable and nonthreatening. Often, you may not be aware of how your tone comes across. Watching videos of your verbal communications and identifying colleagues who will give you honest feedback can help you to become more aware of your tone and to moderate it as needed.

Issues of power and privilege are relevant to this discussion. As we talk about messaging, it is critical that we acknowledge that culture, race, gender, political ideology, and other aspects of identity—yours and that of your audience—impact how your tone and message are received. A common theme that emerges in blog posts written by social work students interning at the Texas Legislature is that messages with similar tones are received differently in that environment, depending on who is communicating the message (University of Houston Graduate College of Social Work n.d.). For example, one student described how emotionally laden speeches by female, Democratic members of the House of Representatives were received more negatively than a similarly emotional speech by a white male Republican member. Self-reflection on the extent to which you are personally comfortable working within the framework of implicit, and sometimes explicit, biases in the political arena is part of your own development as a political social worker. When you are the one in a position of power, be mindful of the stereotypes that you hold and how they affect your responses to others. Just as you would in direct practice, acknowledge your own implicit bias and do the work to treat others fairly.

Clarity

As you craft political communications, make sure not to lose sight of your purpose, and make sure that anyone who reads, sees, or hears your communications will know exactly what the purpose is. In all of your communications, it is essential that your target(s) knows exactly why you are communicating with them, and exactly what you want them to do as a result of the communication. Often it takes many exposures to your message before it registers with your target, which explains why you hear the same message from political campaigns over and over (and over and over).

Do not overload your communications. Limit them to two or three main points, so that your message remains clear. A common structure for political communications, regardless of format, is a clear beginning that summarizes your argument; a middle that builds the case for your solution and where possible heads off major objections; and an end that summarizes your argument and explicitly states what you want your target to do (**your "ask"**). This will be described in more detail and applied to various forms of political communications in Sect. 4.

Framing and Messaging

Framing is a common term in political communications, referring to how we present an issue to our audience and how it is portrayed (Wallack et al. 1999). Candidates, elected officials and their staff, advocates and lobbyists, and the media use framing to shape how audiences think about an issue.

In our own political framing—whether of our advocacy solution or our candidate—we are trying to control messaging and lay the groundwork for successfully achieving our goals. Framing starts with identifying a very clear **message**—what is the important point or theme that we want to communicate about our advocacy solution or our candidate? Once we identify this message, we need to test with colleagues, allies, or constituents whether this message is truly clear, understandable, and relevant to the general public.

APPLY YOUR SKILLS: Developing a Message

In Chap. 6, you developed an advocacy campaign around a specific policy change. Who is the target of this campaign? What do you want to communicate to that target?

Imagine you have 30 seconds in an elevator with that person (say, at a visit to the state capitol or a chance encounter at a professional meeting). What would you say in that 30 seconds? Be as specific and clear as possible. Test this message out with a colleague or friend. What resonates with your friend, what does not? What might you change to strengthen your message?

Crafting a Candidate Message: A Message Box Exercise

In an electoral campaign, the campaign message is as important for what it is not as what it is. It is not the candidate's biography, all of the things they will do when elected, or the details of all the issues they care about. It is a short concise statement, aimed at a specific audience that captures what you want those who will vote to know about you.

A tool commonly used in developing electoral campaign messages is the **message box exercise** (personal communication, Kate Coyne-McCoy, March 3, 2017). It requires your campaign to seriously and honestly reflect upon and outline four distinct categories of information:

1. "Us on Us": the positive things you will say about your candidate
2. "Them on Them": the positive things your opponent will say about himself/herself

3. "Us on Them": the negative things you *might* be able to say about your opponent
   (even if you will not necessarily say them directly)
4. "Them on Us": the negative things they *might* say about your candidate

Much of the information necessary to complete this exercise builds off the
assessments of the candidate and opponent's strengths and weaknesses. This exercise could also be adapted for an issue campaign or an advocacy campaign.

Below, we provide an example of what a message box exercise might look like
for a hypothetical election race between early social workers Jane Addams and
Mary Richmond. The sample message box is what one might look like if developed
by the Addams campaign (information from Franklin 1986).

Us on Us:	Them on Them:
What Jane Addams says about herself	*What Mary Richmond says about herself*
• Founder of successful Settlement House	• Leader of successful Charity Organization
• Reformer	Society
• Listens to the community	• Innovator
• Focuses on people's experiences	• Scientific
• Intellectual	• Efficient
• Skilled writer	• Professional
• Work informed by theories	• Worked her way up from entry level with
• First woman president of National Conference	only a high school diploma through hard
of Charities & Corrections	work
• First woman to receive an honorary degree	• Practical
from Yale University	• Work is natural and effective
• Nationally visible	• Headed the Russell Sage Foundation,
• Supported women's right to vote, workers'	which gave nearly $5.8 million in grants
rights, child labor laws, and laws to improve	over 24 years
housing conditions	• Supported services to soldiers, sailors, and
• Seconded Theodore Roosevelt's presidential	their families
nomination for the Progressive Party	• Supports the development of evidence-
• Leader in anti-war efforts; won a Nobel Peace	based techniques for work with individuals
Prize for her efforts	• Wrote the first social work textbook
Us on Them:	Them on Us:
What Jane Addams says about Mary Richmond	*What Mary Richmond says about Jane*
• Ignores context	*Addams*
• Too hard on the poor	• Too soft on the poor
• Cold and indifferent	• Old fashioned
• Doesn't understand social sciences	• Doing more harm than good by telling
• Lacks education	people that the system is the problem
• Opposes minimum wage, workers' rights,	• Doesn't understand "real" science
labor laws, and worker safety	• Grew up with a silver spoon in her mouth
• Pro-war	• Environmental reform work is a distraction
• Doesn't believe in client confidentiality	from the "real" work of social work
• Doesn't use theory	(casework)
• No experience in politics	• Too partisan
• Blames the poor for their problems	• Opposes social work becoming more
• Not known outside of social work	professional
	• Never received an honorary degree from a
	school of social work

APPLY YOUR SKILLS: Create a Campaign Message

Based on the message box above, create a campaign message for either Jane Addams or Mary Richmond in a fictional campaign for presidency of the National Council of Charities and Corrections (now the National Association of Social Workers). Share your message with colleagues, friends, or other social workers. What was effective?

For candidates, two common challenges emerge in creating your own message. First, being authentically yourself can be a challenge when creating a message that is also trying to accomplish a specific goal. Take a moment to watch the campaign ads of politicians you think of as being authentic. What about their message feels authentic to you?

Second, for candidates who differ from the "typical politician," implicit bias that others might hold can impact how your message is heard. For example, a social worker working in a political field was once told that "all social workers are socialists." If you have young children, particularly if you are a woman, people may question why you are campaigning instead of parenting your children. If you are a person of color, people might implicitly question whether you have the authority needed to hold office. It is challenging—but important, nonetheless—to consider whether and how your message should address or seek to diffuse these perceptions. The issues of power and privilege discussed earlier are especially relevant here.

APPLY YOUR SKILLS: Create a Campaign Message for Yourself

Using this message box, create a campaign message for your own campaign for an office of your choice (maybe President of NASW, President of the USA, or President of the Student Association) against an imaginary opponent. Share your messages with colleagues, friends, or other social workers. What was effective?

Us on Us:	Them on Them:
What you say about yourself	*What your opponent says about themselves*
Us on Them:	**Them on Us:**
What you say about your opponent	*What your opponent says about you*

Staying on Message

Once our message is established, we **stay on message**, repeatedly emphasizing this message in our communications. We want to see consistent messaging by our whole team, whether the staff of an organization, a coalition, or a political campaign. Create boiler-plate language that enables your message to be repeated clearly, consistently, and frequently. Work together to develop buy-in among anyone who might be called on as a spokesperson.

Framing is often helped by compelling visuals, symbols, and even social media memes, used to reinforce the message (Wallack et al. 1999). For example, METUP, a group that advocates for research to save the lives of the 522,000 people who die of metastatic breast cancer every year conducts "die-ins" where the visual is 113 people lying on the ground, to represent the 113 people who die per day from this disease (Schattner 2015). Another way to frame an issue is to personalize it, by selecting a person to be the "**face**" of the policy problem. In an electoral campaign, the "face" is typically the candidate. In an advocacy campaign, however, the "face" is carefully selected to paint a clear picture of the impacts of your policy problem or proposed policy change. Much care must go into picking the face for your message. In an interview with Claudette Colvin, included in the Resource section, she discusses why Rosa Parks was chosen to be the face of the Montgomery Bus Boycott in 1955, even though Claudette Colvin herself had been arrested for refusing to move off the bus 9 months before Rosa Parks.

It is common practice to pick and train (e.g., through role plays) the person who will represent your message so that they do not steer your message off-track. Some excellent examples of this are in the radio episode *Imperfect Plaintiffs* linked in the Resource section. Where possible, an authentic, unshakeable "face" of the message, who can speak genuinely, from direct experience with the problem, can evoke an emotional connection from your audience. At the same time, as social workers, we need to seriously consider our profession's ethical standards in making this decision (National Association of Social Workers 2017). For example, is the individual fully aware of the risks and benefits of being a public representative of your policy problem/solution (informed consent)? Has this individual truly made their own decision to serve in this role (self-determination)?

APPLY YOUR SKILLS: Selecting Faces

Identify a recent advocacy campaign that you have observed, either in your local community or covered in the media. Consider the following questions on your own or with a friend: Was there a "face" of this message? Who was the "face" of this message? How well did this "face" communicate the message? What challenges, if any, did this "face" seem to experience as part of the advocacy campaign?

POLITICAL SOCIAL WORKER PROFILE: Stephanie Mace, MSW, MPP
Senior Director of Public Policy, United Way of Metropolitan Dallas (Fig. 9.1).

Fig. 9.1 Stephanie Mace,
MSW, MPP

On the first day of my MSW internship at the Texas Capitol, my new boss walked me and my new colleagues around the Capitol to give us the history of the building and an overview of the legislative process. The elevator stopped and a gentleman got on. He was maybe in his 50s, wearing jeans and a white polo with a beer logo on it. When the gentleman got off, my boss whispered, "That man is a legislator … Representative" so-and-so. That brief encounter debunked my preconceived notion that elected officials were superior to me. It made me realize that they are regular, normal people too. Also, it taught me to never gossip at the Capitol because you never know who's around.

You use the same principles for making a case to an elected official as you would to a parent, professor, spouse, or boss. Be honest with the elected official, and make sure to say why there would be opposition to your issue. Provide reasonable remedies or policy solutions to your problem. Also, putting a face to an issue by sharing a client's story is powerful.

In advance of a meeting with an elected official, determine what would make it a successful meeting and then develop your talking points. Make sure that everyone in the meeting has the opportunity to speak and provides a different perspective on the issue. Do not inundate the legislator with information—either orally or in your handouts. A one-pager (front and back) on the issue is an ideal amount. Remember that changing a policy usually takes multiple years, so building a working relationship is more important than one vote. Take time to build rapport with the official and their staff, thank them for their hard work, and try to have fun.

Section 3: Working with Traditional and Social Media

While many political communications are focused directly on your target(s), relying on media platforms to garner public support is a critical part of political strategy. A guest speaker in one of the authors' courses once described the media both as a campaign's "best friend and worst enemy." This quote underscores the challenges that political social workers can face when seeking attention through traditional and/or social media.

In an electoral campaign, media coverage can help a candidate get on the map and build name recognition. In an advocacy campaign, media coverage can help advocates gain public support for their policy goals. It can create the impression of widespread public support for these goals, and/or show decision-makers that they will be able to get media attention for their efforts if they choose to engage with the advocates. At the same time, negative media attention can harm our campaigns. Media often will cover a negative story about a candidate or about someone affiliated with an advocacy campaign. If you publicize that 500 people will show up for a rally in front of your Congressional representative's office, and instead 50 show up, you might pick up your phone only to find a mocking Tweet, accompanied by a picture of your sparse attendance. If your candidate loses his or her cool during a campaign event, a video of this slip-up may be shared widely on social media, ultimately becoming front-page news.

An early example of how the twenty-first-century media climate caught a candidate in its crosshairs involved former Virginia Governor and then-Senator George Allen. In the middle of a 2006 campaign event, Allen pointed to a young volunteer videographer in the crowd of Indian descent, who was working for his opponent, and said, "This fellow here, over here with the yellow shirt, Macaca, or whatever his name is. He's with my opponent. He's following us around here. And it's just great" (Craig and Shear 2006). Video of this incident and commentary about his use of what was widely seen as a derogatory term spread quickly through traditional media and across political blogs. Three months later, the incumbent Allen lost his reelection race.

In this section, we discuss how political social workers can work with traditional and social media outlets to increase the likelihood of positive coverage for your campaigns.

Types of Traditional Media

Traditional media primarily refers primarily to print (newspapers and newsmagazines) and broadcast media (radio and television). While print journalism may not have the same influence that it once had, print and broadcast media and the journalists who investigate and report news through these outlets retain substantial political influence.

Traditional media maintains an extensive footprint. In the Houston, Texas, area, for example, as of 2011, there was one major nationally known daily English-language newspaper. In addition, there were 114 other daily, weekly, and monthly newspapers and 106 magazines, often targeted to various economic, ethnic, racial, or religious subgroups. The metropolitan area also was home to 19 television stations and 58 radio stations. Figure 9.2 displays some of the diversity you might find within traditional media sources.

A wide variety of traditional media outlets offer political social workers many choices for communicating their political messages. To determine where to go to try to gain media coverage, start with identifying the media outlets in your town, city,

Fig. 9.2 Example of the diversity of traditional media outlets in Houston, Texas

county, or state. Where possible, seek out access to a local media distribution list. Start to develop a list of media contacts, with media outlets, reporters who cover politics and your substantive policy area, and contact information.

Types of Social Media

Social media has arisen in the twenty-first century as both a major media force and a major political force. **Social media** refers to websites and applications ("apps") that allow users to share content and interact without meeting in person. It includes platforms such as Facebook, Twitter, Instagram, YouTube, Reddit, and Snapchat, as well as blogs and listservs. While these platforms are all open to the broad general public, like traditional media outlets, they tend to reach different populations. In 2016, 68% of US adults used Facebook, as opposed to the 28% of US adults who used Instagram and the 21% who used Twitter (Greenwood et al. 2016). Some platforms are better than others at reaching various population subgroups. Facebook is popular among adults of all ages, all educational backgrounds, all geographic areas, and all income levels. In contrast, Instagram is most commonly used by Millennials, while Pinterest is most popular among women (Greenwood et al. 2016).

Many traditional media journalists extensively use and share their journalism through social media, opening up access to news stories to readers who might not otherwise subscribe to their newspapers or watch their news shows and blurring the distinction between the two types of media. At the same time, social media also provides a fairly inexpensive, decentralized space for any individual or group to carefully craft and share political messages without the filter of traditional media. "For advocacy nonprofits in particular, social media sites provide a way to expand advocacy efforts by reaching new networks of community actors and by mobilizing those networks to take action" (Guo and Saxton 2012).

Social media offers an opportunity for "two-way communication (advocate to public and public to advocate)" (Hoefer 2016); the same applies for campaigns. This two-way communication offers a great opportunity for you to engage and mobilize supporters around your campaign, but it also offers challenges. As Scott and Maryman (2016) note, "quality campaigns require concerted time and thoughtful consideration" (p. 12). Quality use of social media as part of a political communication strategy requires resources to maintain a regular flow of posts. Comments, replies, retweets, etc. need to be monitored to ensure that what started out as a positive message for your campaign does not turn into a negative message as a public conversation ensues. Recently, social media sites have become a hub for "fake news," material reported in a news outlet that is false. This requires electoral and advocacy campaigns to monitor social media to ensure that they do not become a target for incorrect stories, and to integrate a rapid response system allowing a campaign to respond quickly to problematic postings.

Resource considerations have been identified as barriers for social work organizations to engage in Web-based advocacy. However, recent tools make it easier to facilitate and monitor crucial engagement with the public around this work (Edwards and Hoefer 2010).

Media Strategy

Planning a media strategy begins by assessing whether and how your campaign or area of policy is currently being covered. Questions to explore include the following:

1. Is the campaign or policy issue currently being covered in traditional or social media? If so, by which outlets? Do you want to see a shift in which outlets are covering it?
2. How is it being covered? Do you want to see a shift in the framing or direction of the coverage?
3. Who are the journalists reporting on this issue?
4. Who are presented as key spokespeople in relation to the campaign or policy issue? Do they reflect your candidate or proposed policy solution?
5. Are there facts or perspectives missing from current coverage that would strengthen support for your candidate or stance?

As you prepare to engage with traditional media journalists, make sure that you are familiar with rules and expectations that govern interactions with journalists. Your advocacy or electoral campaign should have a spokesperson(s) specifically designated to speak on its behalf to the media. The spokesperson should be someone who speaks articulately and carefully, can think on their feet, is able to establish positive relationships with journalists, and is fully knowledgeable about your campaign (Whitman 2011).

Before social workers engage with journalists, it is critical to understand the categories of information a source can provide to a reporter. Below are the specific definitions used by the Associated Press (n.d.) to describe how a journalist is expected to handle information and materials provided by a source:

On the record	The information can be used with no caveats, quoting the source by name.
Off the record	The information cannot be used for publication.
Background	The information can be published but only under conditions negotiated with the source. Generally, the sources do not want their names published but will agree to a description of their position.
Deep background	The information can be used but without attribution. The source does not want to be identified in any way, even on condition of anonymity.

To protect yourself and your organization, do not agree to make an "off-the-record" statement to a journalist. While using this designation may keep your statement from being directly quoted on air or in a publication, it does not forbid journalists from using this information to try to gather information from another source. Moreover, as Whitman (2011) advises,

> Assume that anything you say will turn up in a media report, probably with your name attached to it. Don't say anything to the media unless you're willing to see it made public. All politicians know this, and you should, too.

In summary, whether on or off the record, be careful only to tell journalists information you are comfortable having widely known in the public sphere.

In engaging with journalists, know that laws vary by state as to whether journalists (or you) can record phone calls without the other party's consent. In 38 states and the District of Columbia, journalists and other individuals can record conversations of which they are part, without the consent of any other party (Reporters Committee for Freedom of the Press 2012). In 12 states, all parties to the conversation must consent to recording. Look into the laws in your state before speaking with journalists, and be prepared with an answer if you are asked for recording permission.

As you develop your media strategy, consider how frequently you will seek coverage. Traditional media coverage rarely results from a single effort to gain media attention. Relying on a single media event or press release can be risky, as the story might not get covered, or might be upstaged by some other event that happens that day. While some campaigns and advocates opt to try to gain a single big media splash, many prefer to try to seek continuous coverage.

Relationship Building

Forming personal working relationships with reporters, bloggers, and others who have access to power in media coverage is an important part of a media strategy (Whitman 2011). Social work's emphasis on the value of human relationships can help us to develop relationships with reporters who trust and respect us, and who therefore seek us out for information and comments. Strong working relationships with reporters also enable us to have contacts who are likely to be interested when we pitch them a story.

The local media distribution list described earlier in this chapter is an important starting point for identifying with which individual reporters or bloggers to connect. Select media outlets or blogs that reach out to the segment of the public that you are targeting, and then begin to monitor which reporters typically cover political campaigns in this area or the area of policy on which you are focusing. Read and/or watch these media outlets regularly. If your advocacy campaign centers around education policy, for example, who are the reporter(s) who are assigned to the education beat? Are there other reporters at these media outlets who cover related stories in a way that you like, even if they are not assigned to the specific beat?

Once you have identified these reporters, the media spokesperson should reach out to establish personal contact (Whitman 2011). Do not limit this to a quick e-mail or text—this is a good time to have a conversation by phone or even over coffee. This relationship should be nurtured, even when you do not have an immediately newsworthy story to share. There are some good ways to nurture relationships with reporters. For one, share stories that you think the reporter might be interested in related to your issue, even if the stories are not directly related to your advocacy proposal or campaign.

Interpersonal skills are critical in nurturing and maintaining relationships with reporters. Seek to establish a reputation as a go-to person for reporters by being responsive, helpful, trustworthy, and respectful. Make your contact information easily available to interested reporters, and return all contacts quickly, within their deadline. Both print and broadcast media are shaped by deadlines—a missed return contact can mean that a reporter lacks necessary information for a story, or that your perspective is excluded.

Be helpful by answering reporters' questions, verifying their facts, and clarifying your positions as needed. Be honest in your responses; lying to a reporter is a fast way to sever your relationship. Do not promise an answer if you cannot give one, and do not make up responses if you do not know the answer to a reporter's question. Instead, try a response like, "I don't know, but I will find out the answer to that question for you. How quickly do you need an answer?" and then get the answer to the reporter within that time frame. Also be sure to thank reporters when they cover your campaign or advocacy issue positively, rather than limiting your feedback to criticism of negative stories.

As you enter into a media strategy, you are likely thinking about how you can impact media coverage. Reporters, on the other hand, have different motivations that are important to understand as you build relationships with them. Reporters typically serve in a watchdog role, seeking to report important information that impacts the public, but also are motivated by identifying stories that will garner readers and/or viewers (Whitman 2011). When a reporter reaches out to you, ask them questions to assess how they are thinking about the story, e.g., why they called you, where they got your name, and who else have they talked to. This information can help you get a sense of how the story is being shaped, guiding how you respond and who else you encourage them to contact.

BUILD YOUR SKILLS: Answering Reporters' Questions
Strategic communication with reporters around your electoral or advocacy campaign involves predicting and preparing for the challenging questions reporters might ask you. On your own or with a friend, brainstorm three questions a reporter might ask about one of the campaigns you developed earlier in this book. After identifying these three questions, develop a response to each question.

News Hooks

Pitching a story to reporters can be challenging, as they have many competing stories that they can be covering. It is essential, then, to pitch stories in such a way that make them appear compelling and significant. A common way to make stories appear newsworthy and capture reporters' attention is via "**news hooks**" (SPIN Project 2003).

Common news hooks include the following:

- Using *dramatic visuals* that support the campaign's message: Television and social media, in particular, are attracted to captivating visuals. For example, in opposition to Don't Ask, Don't Tell policy regarding sexual orientation policies in the U.S. military, Lt. Dan Choi captured media attention by chaining himself to the fence surrounding the White House (Dan Choi handcuffs himself to White House in Don't Ask, Don't Tell protest 2010).
- Demonstration of *broad, passionate support*: For example, highlighting the 1000 people who came to the steps of City Council to rally in support of your campaign is likely to attract attention.
- Providing a *local angle to a national story* involves tying your electoral platform or advocacy goals to a story that is current garnering national media attention.
- Bringing a *human interest angle* to the story personalizes how real people are impacted by a policy issue. These last two tactics may be combined. For example, after a federal budget proposed cutting 20% of the National Institutes of Health budget, a cancer research center in Seattle held a press conference featuring Beth Caldwell, a 38-year-old Seattle resident with Stage IV cancer who had been treated at that center, putting a very human, local, relatable face on the issue of federal funding for cancer research (video link in Resources).
- A *calendar hook*, in which the story is tied to some sort of anniversary (e.g., 1 year since the campaign kicked off, a decade since the current policy was passed) or time of the year (a relevant holiday, the season, etc.)
- Highlighting *celebrities*, powerful, popular people, who are supporting the campaign: For example, few Americans knew much about the Armenian genocide until Kim Kardashian visited Armenia in 2015 (Puente 2015). You may not have access to a Kardashian, but who are your local celebrities? On campus, they might be alumni who are well known, athletes, and coaches, or those who are known for their performing arts work or roles in student government; in your

town they might include everyone's favorite librarian or a retired teacher who has a lot of influence.

- Highlighting *conflict or controversy* often engages the public, and may be particularly helpful if the campaign is framed as an underdog.
- *Responding to your opposition*, especially when the opposition's actions or statements have received media attention.

In seeking to gain traditional media coverage using your news hooks, strategic attention to timing is necessary. All traditional media sources have **media deadlines**, which they must accommodate, i.e., times when articles must be completed to go to press and deadlines for various television and radio news programs. Highlighting news hooks earlier in the day increases the likelihood that a story might be covered in the evening news or appear in the next day's newspaper. With traditional media, there are also common "news holes," where major news stories are less frequent. "News holes," such as over holidays and on Monday mornings, offer opportunities for advocates to garner coverage for their campaigns. In contrast, political campaigns sometimes use Friday evening "news dumps" as a way to release information that they would prefer get little media or public attention. When working with a media source, your first question should always be "what is your deadline?"

While news hooks are commonly associated with gaining traditional media attention, many of these news hooks also are helpful in garnering attention on social media. Just as with traditional media, relevant and compelling content is more likely to gain attention. News hooks such as dramatic visuals, visual demonstrations of broad passionate support, calendar hooks, and highlighting celebrity support also can help to make your stories compelling in a social media environment.

Social Media Strategies

Ray (2011) recommends starting with a centralized social media strategy. This involves choosing a primary social media platform that will serve as the hub for your political efforts. In selecting this initial platform, think strategically about which platform is most likely to reach your target audience(s) (Hoefer 2016). This may be one of the platforms identified in the section "Types of Social Media" above, or a platform that has newly emerged since publication of this book. Once you or your organization is comfortable with this platform, then you might add other social media platforms to your strategy, but take care to target your use of each social media platform to the audience and communication style of that platform.

APPLY YOUR SKILLS: Selecting a Social Media Platform
With a partner, discuss the primary audience for your campaign strategy. What might be the most appropriate social media platform to use to reach this audience? Why did you choose this platform? You might find it helpful to look through organizations that are known for their advocacy work to see how they handle social media.

Each platform has different customs and rules. Make sure that you fully understand these before actively engaging with the platform as part of your campaign. In communicating across different platforms, some common themes exist, including the following:

- Be authentic, genuine, and relatable in postings.
- Limit postings that appear solely promotional. Some sources suggest that "your ratio of non-self-interested material to self-interested material should be roughly three to one" (Ray 2011).
- Strive for a combination of information-sharing (more likely to be re-shared, therefore increasing awareness of your campaign), engaging in conversations and dialogue with supporters (which builds relationships and increases collaboration), and calls to action (mobilizing supporters) (Scott and Maryman 2016).
- Communicate messages in an interesting and compelling way; visuals or engaging memes can help with this.
- Share relevant and meaningful postings from allies.
- Use hashtags where appropriate to help support message framing and connect with others who share similar interests.
- On platforms like Twitter where information moves rapidly, repost critical content multiple times to increase the likelihood it reaches a broader audience. Others will understand when you say "ICYMI" (in case you missed it) when sharing information multiple times.
- Credit information that is repeated or shared from other sources. It is the right thing to do, and increases the likelihood that others will share your information as well.

Social media platforms provide campaigns with opportunities to recruit supporters and to build their awareness of the campaign and its goals. However, political social workers "must strive to convert this awareness into actions that support the cause," moving supporters from clicks and shares to political action that supports the campaign's goals (Scott and Maryman 2016). Political social workers using social media communications as part of their electoral or advocacy campaign should be intentional in frequently including public calls to action to further the campaign's goals and to mobilize supporters (Hoefer 2016; Scott and Maryman 2016).

Once you are familiar with your social media platform(s), think strategically about developing a social media plan, including what you will post, how and where you will post it, and a calendar of when you will post (keeping in mind the calendar hooks described previously). For electoral campaigns especially, a rapid response strategy should be incorporated into any media plan, so that you are prepared to quickly respond to your opponent as needed.

Monitor your social media sites using apps that allow you to manage and track multiple accounts, hashtags, and keywords. As of 2017, the most commonly used resources for this are Hootsuite to manage postings and Google Alerts and Klout to track output metrics and monitor the reach of your postings. As social media plat-forms and apps change on such a rapid basis, your social media plan must be flexi-ble enough to enable you to adapt your techniques to new technologies that emerge (Ray 2011). As McNutt and Menon (2008) point out, rapid changes in the technol-ogy being used for advocacy and activism will continue to open up opportunities for new political change tactics.

Section 4: Strategic Communications

The extensive data and information that you have collected on your candidate or policy solution, along with your core message, serve as the basis for your cam-paign's strategic political communications. Within a single campaign, you utilize the same information, but the message and evidence are reframed to different audi-ences, using different formats. In order to make final choices about your choice of tactics and to begin to develop these communications, you will first need to answer three key questions:

1. Who is the audience for the communication?
2. To which communication formats is your specific audience most likely to respond (e.g., one-on-one meetings, policy briefs, action alerts, letters to the edi-tor, testimony, campaign mailings, press releases, media messaging)?
3. Which arguments and evidence will your specific audience find most salient?

Your answers to these questions will help you clarify your audience for each communication and strategically prepare it for that audience. In the section below, we summarize the intended audience, purpose, format, and content of seven com-monly used political tactics.

One-on-One Meeting

Audience: In advocacy campaigns, the audience of a one-on-one meeting is typi-cally a policy decision-maker, commonly an elected official or a member of the official's staff. In electoral campaigns, the audience of a one-on-meeting is com-monly a donor, a voter, or someone with clout in the community. Given the time constraints of electoral campaigns, one-on-one meetings are limited for candidates but may be held by staff members or other surrogates or proxies.

Purpose: A one-on-one meeting typically seeks to influence a policy decision-maker to help advance your policy goals, or to influence a donor, voter, or powerful individual to support your candidate with money, a vote, or a public statement of support.

Format: In an advocacy campaign you will ideally work with target's scheduler to schedule a substantial amount of time to sit down with your target. Even if your meeting is scheduled ahead of time, be understanding if the target is late, and do not be surprised if you are interrupted during your meeting. Sometimes, one-on-one meetings happen on the fly or in more informal settings—e.g., an interaction in the elevator, in a restaurant or bar near the Capitol, or at a coffee shop. Prepare ahead of time to make the most of the limited time you are likely to have. Know what your specific ask is before the meeting starts.

During this meeting, be prepared to defend your stance, but avoid directly attacking your target for disagreeing with you. As we've discussed previously, relationships are critical currency in political work—the target you attack today could be the potential ally you need tomorrow. Note also that sometimes targets express disagreement because they, in fact, disagree with you. At other times, targets express a skeptical stance in order to test how strong your argument is, and perhaps to ultimately adopt your argument for their own use in later supporting your stance.

In an electoral campaign, one-on-one meetings often take place when you knock on a potential voter's door. You can prepare to talk about yourself, or your candidate, but you won't know much about the target other than their name, age, and political party. Active listening skills are key here, as your job is to listen and find out how to communicate your message in such a way that it connects with the voter.

Content: One-on-one meetings can be both informative and persuasive. Prepare talking points ahead of time, so that you can keep on point. Start by establishing your credibility up front: As an advocate: who are you, who do you represent, are you a constituent? As a candidate/campaigner: who are you, who is the candidate? Build rapport by thanking your target for meeting with you. Then, simply and directly describe your message or stance and why you hold this stance, providing personal anecdotes and case examples to support your stance where possible. Present a clear, specific request of what you want from your target, and reiterate this at the end of your meeting. "I am asking you to vote to move this bill out of committee" or "I am asking for your vote on November 8" are better than "I hope you will support this cause" or "Maybe you could think about voting for me."

Always leave brief, easily reviewable written materials behind after your meeting. Brief fact sheets, letters from constituents or a newspaper article or editorial supporting your stance are all appropriate materials for an advocacy meeting. A small piece of campaign literature or one-page summary is appropriate for a campaign interaction. Follow up an advocacy meeting or a meeting with a donor with a thank-you note. Include any information you agreed to provide, and a brief summary of the position your target took at this meeting.

Policy Brief

Audience: **Policy briefs** are aimed at policy decision-makers, often elected officials who may have the opportunity to vote on policy recommendations, but may not have time to fully research the policy. On an electoral campaign, policy briefs might be used to help the candidate understand an issue before they attend an event, interview, or debate, or to help others understand the candidate's policy stances or proposals.

Purpose: Policy briefs are concise written analyses of a policy or policy problem. They are designed to provide an in-depth, but concise, summary of policy research, in order to influence policy decision-makers regarding specific policy change recommendations or inform others about the candidate's stance.

Format: A policy brief is usually a multipage document, concise and designed to be quickly read by policy-makers. It typically includes, at a minimum, an engaging title; research-based analysis of a policy problem; and, emerging from the analysis, concrete policy recommendations to address the policy problem. Policy briefs often use headings, brief sections, and tables, graphs, or charts. The language and layout will depend on the audience and their background in the issue.

Content: Policy briefs are both informative and persuasive, grounded in evidence. Effective policy briefs include a clear take-home message and specific and detailed policy change recommendations or policy summaries.

Action Alert

Audience: Action alerts are aimed at a community or action network that a campaign seeks to mobilize. This might include current or potential grassroots activists or volunteers, voters, or donors.

Purpose: **Action alerts** are used in both electoral and advocacy campaigns in order to inform supporters in a network about a policy solution or candidate and inspire them to action on its behalf. They might provide a quick update or a recent development and ask people to take related action.

Format: An action alert typically takes the form of a one-page document or is incorporated into a brief e-mail. It also can be posted to a website and linked to a social media post. It is concise and designed to be quickly readable by people who are supporters, but who may not act on behalf of the campaign if information about how to do so is not easily accessible. Action alerts present any relevant facts and data necessary to inform the reader about the policy problem or candidate and the action steps that the reader should take to act on this information. Action alerts are designed to instill a sense of urgency to act and to provide clear action steps to readers. Commonly, the action steps are incorporated directly into the alert (click here to donate, call this number to be connected to your representative, etc.).

Content: Action alerts are both informative and persuasive. Effective action alerts include relevant facts and statistics that readers can understand and easily repeat, along with presenting a clear action(s) for readers to take.

POLITICAL SOCIAL WORKER PROFILE: Melanie Pang, MSW
Qualitative Research and Evaluation Manager, The Salvation Army (Fig. 9.3).

Fig. 9.3 Melanie Pang,
MSW, by Eric Edward
Schell of Pride Portraits

When I graduated with my MSW in 2012, I had no plan, but I did give myself two biased and embarrassing, criteria: (1) Do not work for a faith-based organization because they might fire you for being gay, and (2) do not work with kids because it sounds really difficult and kids do not like you. Thirty job applications, five phone interviews, two in-person interviews, and only one job offer later, my first and only opportunity to use my degree came in the form of a case management position at a Catholic organization working with refugee children in foster care. Not only was this job offer the one I thought I shouldn't take, it actually became the job that helped me the most in growing my understanding of how many systems can touch a single person's life. Humbled, I took the job and found ways to advocate within it.

After this case management experience, I got my first glimpse into working on an issue campaign when the Houston Equal Rights Ordinance (HERO) was proposed before the Houston, Texas, City Council in 2014. The ordinance would have banned discrimination on the basis of sexual orientation, gender identity, sex, race, color, ethnicity, national origin, age, religion, disability, pregnancy, genetic information, family, marital, and military status. A lack of understanding of the ordinance's protections, combined with a lack of empathy for the LGBTQ community, specifically the transgender community, among the general population resulted in a crushing loss of the ordinance by referendum, with 60.97% voting against it. I still remember the butterflies in my stomach each time I stepped up to the microphone to speak to City Council, and how I had to shorten my testimony to 1 minute due to the hundreds of speakers who filled City Hall, waiting for their turn to speak truth to power late into the night.

In 2017, I felt the familiar nerves return when I, along with thousands of others, arrived at the Texas Capitol the morning of March 7 at 7:30 a.m. to provide my testimony against Senate Bill 6, a bill that would require transgender people to use bathrooms in public schools, government buildings, and

(continued)

public universities based on "biological sex." Once the testimonies began, it was clear that there was a large divide between the people testifying and the people elected to represent them. I felt the weight of each story as if it were being told in an intimate space, as if their trauma was being shared for healing beyond advocacy, not being recorded and livestreamed for the world to see (even though it was). Unfortunately, many of the senators on the State Affairs Committee had already made up their minds about the bill, and the only comfort available to us was each other. Watching the gestures of support between those testifying kept me alert for hours.

I testified a little after midnight, and I was only halfway through the list of names signed up to testify. I had rewritten my testimony multiple times throughout the day as I saw committee members unmoved by emotional testimony. I realized that instead, I needed to speak to all of Texas. Deviating from my usual approach of "catching more flies with honey," my testimony wasn't persuasive; it was closer to accusatory. It ended with pointed questions like "Why is this cis-gender person's comfort worth more than a trans person's life? And how much business will you have to lose before a trans person's life matters to you?" Despite overwhelming opposition to the bill by those testifying, the bill passed. While those final policies are important, the discourse, the struggle, matters just as much. The contentious discourse in Texas around transgender people's right to exist in public has created a wave of anti-trans sentiment.

It can feel like our wins are few and far between, but they are always worth fighting for and inspiration is never scarce. Being a queer, Asian-American woman in Texas, I've stopped relying on hope as a sole source of motivation, and instead focus on love. Hope makes the work sustainable; love keeps the work a priority. I am privileged enough and have been lucky enough to work for organizations and social justice-minded leaders who support me and believe in the things I advocate for: equity, lived equality, and treating people with dignity.

Testimony to a Legislative Committee, Board, or Agency

Audience: Unlike the communications described thus far, the audience for your testimony (like the testimony Melanie describes) often includes multiple decision-makers (such as an entire legislative committee, county commission, or local school board membership). Testimony is more public than the other communications we have discussed, meaning that you need to also be aware of the possible presence of media and the broader general public who may be in attendance or have access to the testimony via media.

Purpose: **Testimony** is often used as a part of advocacy campaigns, and is designed to persuade policy decision-makers to help advance your policy goals. Testimony also is often designed to influence the larger narrative around your advocacy issue through media coverage. It is important to note that providing testimony—whether in oral or written format—explicitly puts your stance in the public record. You may also incorporate testimony into other communications to show your campaign's stance on an issue or as an example of your ongoing work.

Format: When we think of providing testimony, we typically think of oral testimony, in which an advocate or community member stands up and speaks before a committee or board. However, we strongly encourage you to prepare and submit written testimony alongside your oral testimony. Among the reasons for this: Sometimes local or state committees have hundreds of people signed up to provide testimony on a particular issue and do not have time to hear everyone. Having written testimony available ensures that you will have the opportunity to get your stance on the record. Above, Melanie describes her experiences when the Texas Senate considered a bill that would require individuals to use the bathroom that matched their birth gender. Over 400 individuals signed up to provide oral testimony on this bill—9 hours in, just 200 of these individuals had spoken (Ura 2017). Preparing written testimony provides a way for those who are unable to testify orally to have their voices heard. It also serves another benefit. It allows you to point legislators to more detailed information while summarizing only your most significant points in your time-limited oral testimony.

Before you testify, it is helpful to reach out to the staffer assigned in charge of the hearing process—this staffer is often called the "clerk" or "secretary." Ask ahead of time how much time you will have for your testimony, and whether and how you sign up to testify. Time allotted for testimony often varies across federal, state, and local legislative committees. Congressional testimony is typically invited and may be extensive, at the discretion of a Congressional committee. In contrast, state and local governments typically incorporate time-limited opportunities for voluntary, brief public testimony. Invited Congressional testimony is typically limited to 5 minutes. Advocates wanting to speak before a legislative committee in Texas and Connecticut typically are limited to no more than 3 minutes. These time allotments may be further reduced based on the number of people present to provide testimony on a given day, so be prepared to speed up if requested to do so.

Also determine registration processes before the committee hearing begins, as these also differ by state and municipality. In Texas, for example, an advocate wanting to provide oral testimony before a House committee must register to testify in-person using a paperless system on the day of the committee hearing, while an advocate wanting to testify before a Senate committee must do so using a paper card. In Connecticut, the rules vary from one committee to another. In West Virginia, those who testify must be under oath when they testify. In Colorado, the legislature offers remote locations for testimony.

Content: Begin by introducing yourself and briefly establishing your credibility to speak to this issue. Build rapport by thanking the committee and chair for taking the time to hear you. Begin with a clear statement of your stance (i.e., for or against a bill, a budget item, or an amendment) and a clear and succinct message about why you hold this stance. Limit your testimony to no more than 2–3 main points. Use the body of your testimony to sincerely justify your stance and/or counter opposing proposals with data, anecdotes, or a vivid case example. Make sure that you are prepared with a strong finish—a solid closing paragraph that you can jump to if your time is cut. This closing statement should reiterate your main points and express your willingness to provide more information and to answer any questions the committee has.

Be attuned to your style of conversation, making sure that your testimony is clear, to the point, and brief, and that you avoid jargon the community members may not understand. Be prepared for questions; these commonly focus on issues of feasibility, costs, benefits, or impacts of your recommendations. Respond directly and honestly to your questioner, using their name and title if possible, and avoid getting into a public debate with a legislator. Instead, remain poised by acknowledging disagreement and, if appropriate, restating your position. If you do not know an answer to a question, offer to get that information and then do not forget to provide it to the committee after your testimony. Where possible, make yourself available after testimony so that legislators or their staff can follow up on your comments. One of the authors once testified on a bill relating to social work licensure in Connecticut. Many students were there to testify, and she stayed until the end of the hearing to support them. Afterwards, a woman in the audience introduced herself. She was the Commissioner of a major state Department who asked a few questions about licensure and was willing to use her influence with the legislators to help move the bill forward.

APPLY YOUR SKILLS: Prepare for, Write, and Deliver Legislative Testimony
Find a committee of your state legislature that considers issues that are of concern to you. Research the process of testimony in front of that committee. How do you sign up to testify? What are the constraints placed on public testimony? Write and practice delivering a 3-minutes testimony related to a goal of your advocacy strategy.

Direct Campaign Mailing

Audience: Campaign mailings are often aimed at a targeted subset of constituents that an electoral campaign seeks to mobilize to vote.

Purpose: Campaign mailings are used in electoral campaigns as part of a direct mail strategy, in order to reinforce your campaign message, to educate voters, and to remind and encourage supporters to go to the polls to vote for your candidate. Early in the campaign, your campaign plan should include the development of a mail strategy that coordinates with the election calendar and major events, and communicates your campaign message coherently.

Format: Your campaign mailing should be easy to read, with visuals, and creatively designed. Mailings designed to educate or encourage voters should assume that recipients will take no more than 3–4 seconds to look at this mailing, so you want to communicate your message clearly and quickly, and in an attractive way, with professional-quality photographs (Wellstone Action n.d.). Photographs should show your candidate interacting with the public in a genuine way, not canned shots. Pictures of people from the community who support the candidate or issue are also excellent additions. A small number of short headlines are essential for grabbing readers' attention. Keep your mailing easy to read by limiting text, busy graphics, and variations in font size.

Content: Determine ahead of time what you are seeking to accomplish in this mailing: e.g., to introduce your candidate to potential voters, to contrast your candidate with an opponent(s), to deliver a negative message about an opponent, or to encourage the recipient to vote. Even within these different purposes, your campaign may have different messages for different targeted audiences. Clarity of purpose is essential before designing your mailing, so that you can make sure that it communicates a specific and clear message about your candidate to its audience.

Make sure that there is a clear call to action—whether to vote, volunteer, talk to a neighbor, or contribute to the campaign. Make sure also that details about the candidate, the candidates' desired office, what you want the reader to do, when to do it, and contact information for the campaign are clear. Disclaimers required by state and federal election law about who funded and who authorized the mailing must be included to meet all relevant legal mandates.

Press Release

Audience: The audience for a **press release** is typically journalists who are associated with a traditional media source: newspaper or newsmagazine reporters, broadcast journalists or radio and television news producers. Of course, a secondary audience is the public who you hope will ultimately read or view the story you are pushing.

Purpose: Press releases are typically used to persuade media audiences that a particular upcoming event is worthy of their coverage. They also can be used to persuade media that a particular policy issue or candidate is important to cover. Your advocacy or electoral campaign might use a press release to issue a statement or take a stand on an issue appearing in the news, or to provide information to supplement a current story in the news.

In particular, a campaign might use a press release when it has scheduled a newsworthy event to bring attention to the candidate or to the desired policy change. A campaign also might use a press release when it can link the candidate or policy issue to a newsworthy event, like a report being released and an endorsement by a well-respected and well-known community member.

Sample press release format

Date   Contact
<u>FOR IMMEDIATE RELEASE</u>   Title
                                                            Organizational Affiliation
                                                            Phone Number

TITLE INTENDED TO CATCH THE READER'S EYE

LOCATION [CALLED THE DATELINE] – First sentence sums up the story concisely: who/what/where/when.

In the second paragraph, indicate why this issue or candidate event is significant and newsworthy. Include a quote from an expert, the candidate, or a respected community member emphasizing its significance, with the person's full name and title. Put the most important information at the beginning of the press release; less important information towards the end. This allows a newspaper to print the press release directly in the paper, but shorten it to meet space requirements.

Include basic details toward the end of the press release that will allow the story to be covered, even if a reporter is unable to attend the event or contact additional sources. An additional quote or two from other respected figure(s) is acceptable.

# # # #

If an organization is issuing the press release, provide a brief description of the organization here, including its name and purpose.

Format: For a press release, the ideal length is no more than one page. Press releases are typically single spaced, and use short 2–3-sentence paragraphs. Your formatting should look professional. Make sure that all of the information in your press release can be verified. A common press release format is presented here.

Content: Press releases focused on the work of advocacy campaigns must have a news hook that give journalists a reason to cover your issue at this time. Press releases may be run in full as an article by a paper—particularly in the case of local news sources—so make sure to write your press release in a typical news article style: address the who, what, where, when, why, and how of the issue around which you want coverage. Including a quote from the candidate or a person affected by the issue also increases the likelihood of the content being used. (Make sure to get the person's approval for the quote before you send it out.)

It is important to understand that reporters get many press releases, and cannot follow up on all of them. You want yours to be the one they follow up on. After you send your press release to a news outlet, make sure to follow up directly with a phone call to key reporters.

Media Messaging: For Traditional and Social Media

Audience: With media messaging, the audience is typically multifaceted. The intended audience for media messages in advocacy often includes policy decision-makers, the media who you want to cover your issue or candidate, and subsets of the public who you want to inform and mobilize. In electoral campaigns, potential voters are the audience for these messages.

Purpose: The purpose of your media message is to influence public perception, and in the case of an advocacy campaign, ultimately, your advocacy target(s), via traditional and/or social media coverage.

Format: Traditional media coverage is often very brief; very little of what you say is likely to make it into the final print or broadcast piece. Similarly, social media platforms allow for very limited space for communications, e.g., Twitter's 280-character limit. We provide some examples of media messages and their format.

Example Media Messages
(Identified by Wallack et al. 1999 and Dorfman and Krasnow 2014)

"It took vision to save Yosemite, dig the Panama Canal, build the Golden Gate Bridge, or go to the moon, but we did it. Some believe universal preschool is the next big idea. Count me in as one of those who believes."

"It is easy to think of smoking as an adult problem. It is adults who die from tobacco-related diseases. [But]… nicotine addiction begins when most tobacco users are teenagers, so let's call this what it really is: a pediatric disease."

"Toys are subjected to strict safety measures … and yet in the gun industry, there is absolutely no regulation or standards of manufacture."

What this means is that having and communicating a clear and succinct message is essential for communications using all forms of media. Even when your issue is complex, media messages need to be very, very concise and very clear (Wallack et al. 1999)—typically limited to 15 seconds for broadcast media, 280 characters on Twitter, or a single picture or meme that can be viewed and shared on platforms like Instagram, Snapchat, Facebook, or Twitter. Media messages should briefly communicate a take-home message about your issue or candidate in a way that will stick with the reader or viewer.

While a journalist may interview you for much longer than 15 seconds, continue to bring your points back to your core media message. Think about many of the politicians you have seen being interviewed on television—for the most part, they pivot their responses to almost any question back to the same message repeatedly. As frustrating as it can be to watch this, it also does the job—we tend to remember the message these politicians want us to remember, and we often see this message repeated via other media outlets.

Content: Media messages are intended to be persuasive, communicating your stance clearly. Verbal media messages use accessible language designed to evoke a visual that helps guide how readers/viewers think about an issue or a candidate, while visual media messages directly incorporate the visual. Media messages often seek to speak to common values shared by the public, tying your candidate or issue to these common values. They paint a picture of what supporting your campaign's goals will mean to people (e.g., who is affected, and how, by the issue) (Wallack et al. 1999).

APPLY YOUR SKILLS: Media Messages

Develop a media message for your advocacy or electoral campaign. If you are using this book in a class or group setting, work with a partner to practice and refine it. Your message should include:

- A verbal media message that could be used in a one-on-one meeting or an interview
- A picture or meme that could be used on Instagram or Pinterest (many free meme generators can be found in a quick Web search)
- A Tweet

What is your "hook"?

Review of Key Terms and Concepts

Accessible language: language that is appropriate to the target's vocabulary and experiences, and does not include jargon, acronyms, and terms used by insiders.

Action alert: a communication used in both electoral and advocacy campaigns to inform supporters in a network about a policy solution or candidate and inspire them to act on its behalf.

Ask: an explicit statement of what you want your target to do.

Background: information that can be published, but only under conditions negotiated with the source. Generally, sources do not want their names published but will agree to a description of their position.

Credibility: being considered worthy of trust.

Deep background: information that can be used but without attribution. The source does not want to be identified in any way, even on condition of anonymity.

Face: a person utilized as a representative of an idea, i.e., a policy problem or message.

Framing: how an issue is presented to an audience and how it is portrayed.

Media deadline: the time when articles must be completed to go to press or to meet deadlines for various television and radio news programs.

Message: the important point or theme that we want to communicate.

Message box exercise: a common way to develop message, which requires you to outline the positive things you say about yourself/your candidate, the positive things your opponent will say about himself/herself, the negative things you might say about them, and the negative things they might say about you/your candidate.

News hook: information included in a press release which catches readers' attention and assists in the development of a deeper interest of the topic presented within the reader.

Off the record: information that cannot be used for publication.

On the record: information that can be used with no caveats, quoting the source by name.

Policy brief: policy summary aimed at decision-makers, often elected officials who may have the opportunity to vote on policy recommendations, but may not have time to fully research the policy.

Press release: communication used to persuade media audiences to cover an event, an issue, or a candidate.

Professional use of self: the idea that we, as individual social workers, are an essential component of our interventions.

Professionalism: adhering to standards of behavior which reflect positive work ethic, responsibility, and credibility. Important in interpersonal relationships and in written and oral communications.

Social media: websites and applications ("apps") that allow users to share content and interact without meeting in person.

Soundbite: a short, self-contained version of your message.

Stay on message: consistently emphasizing the same message in communications.

Testimony: a statement often used as a part of advocacy campaigns, designed to persuade policy decision-makers to help advance your policy goals and influence the narrative around your advocacy issue.

Tone: the sound, pitch, and speed of one's voice that a speaker uses.

Traditional media: refers to print (newspapers and newsmagazines) and broadcast media (radio and television).

Universal claim: a claim that something is true of every single member of a group or class, without exception.

Resources

Podcasts and Videos

Beth Caldwell press conference (Beth's statement starts around 5 minutes in): http://www.fred-hutch.org/en/news/fred-hutch-statement-regarding-proposed-budget-cuts.html

Claudette Colvin interview: http://www.npr.org/2009/03/15/101719889/before-rosa-parks-there-was-claudette-colvin and book: https://www.amazon.com/Claudette-Colvin-Twice-Toward-Justice/dp/0312661053

More Perfect radio episode: http://www.wnyc.org/story/imperfect-plaintiff

Podcast on politics and family:
http://www.npr.org/2016/09/13/493615864/when-it-comes-to-our-politics-family-matters

Podcast about social workers and the media: http://socialworkpodcast.blogspot.com/2013/02/social-workers-and-media-interview-with.html

Other Resources

Communications to Promote Interest:
http://ctb.ku.edu/en/table-of-contents/participation/promoting-interest

Wellstone resource on direct mail and campaign literature: http://www.wellstone.org/resources/ tips-direct-mail-and-campaign-literature or go to http://www.wellstone.org/ and click on "Tools" in the menu bar. On the landing page click "By Keyword" in the search bar and type in "Direct Mail". Press "enter" and in the results, click "Direct Mail and Campaign Literature".

References

Associated Press. (n.d.). *News values and principles.* Retrieved from https://www.ap.org/about/ our-story/news-values

Center for Community Change. (1997). *How to tell and sell your story: A guide to developing effective messages and good stories about your work.* Washington, DC: Center for Community Change.

Cournoyer, B. (2008). Talking and listening: The basic interpersonal skills. In *The social work skills workbook* (5th ed., pp. 127–154). Belmont, CA: Thomson Higher Education.

Craig, T., & Shear, M. D. (2006, August 15). Allen quip provokes outrage, apology. *The Washington Post.*

Dan Choi handcuffs himself to White House in Don't Ask, Don't Tell protest. (2010, May 28). *Huffington Post.* Retrieved from https://www.huffingtonpost.com/2010/03/18/dan-choi-hand-cuffs-himsel_n_504439.html.

Dorfman, L., & Krasnow, I. D. (2014). Public health and media advocacy. *Annual Review of Public Health, 35,* 293–306.

Dropp, K., & Nyhan, B. (2017). *One-third don't know Obamacare and the Affordable Care Act are the same.* The Upshot: The New York Times.

Edwards, H. R., & Hoefer, R. (2010). Are social work advocacy groups using web 2.0 effectively? *Journal of Policy Practice, 9,* 220–239.

Franklin, D. (1986). Mary Richmond and Jane Addams: From moral certainty to rational inquiry in social work practice. *Social Service Review, 60*(4), 504–525.

Greenwood, S., Perrin, A., & Duggan, M. (2016). *Social media update 2016.* Pew Research Center.

Guo, C., & Saxton, G. D. (2012). Tweeting social change: How social media are changing non-profit advocacy. *Nonprofit and Voluntary Sector Quarterly.*

Hodge, D. R. (2004). Who we are, where we come from, and some of our perceptions: Comparison of social workers and the general population. *Social Work, 42*(9), 261–268.

Hoefer, R. (2016). *Advocacy practice for social justice* (3rd ed.). Chicago, IL: Lyceum Books.

Lavine, D. S. (2002). The necessity of properly identifying your audience and tailoring your arguments to its needs. In *Cardinal rules of advocacy: Understanding and mastering fundamental principles of persuasion* (pp. 5–30). Cleveland, OH: NITA.

Lens, V. (2005). Advocacy and argumentation in the public arena: A guide for social workers. *Social Work, 50*(3), 231–283.

McNutt, J. G., & Menon, G. (2008). The rise of cyberactivism: Implications for the future of advocacy in the human services. *Families in Society: The Journal of Contemporary Human Services, 89*(1), 33–38.

National Association of Social Workers. (2017). *Code of Ethics of the National Association of Social Workers.* Washington, DC: National Association of Social Workers.

Puente, M. (2015, April 8). Why is Kim Kardashian in Armenia? *Huffington Post.*

Ray, H. B. (2011). Using social media for digital advocacy. In *University of Kansas Work Group for community health and development, community tool box.* Kansas: University of Kansas. Retrieved from http://ctb.ku.edu/en/table-of-contents/advocacy/direct-action/ electronic-advocacy/main.

Reporters Committee for Freedom of the Press. (2012). *Reporter's recording guide.* Arlington, VA: Reporters Committee for Freedom of the Press.

Schattner, E. (2015, October 30). Notes from the die-in, a demonstration for metastatic breast cancer. *Forbes.com.*

Scott, J. T., & Maryman, J. (2016). Using social media as a tool to complement advocacy efforts. *Global Journal of Community Psychology Practice, 7*(1S), 1–22.

SPIN Project. (2003). *Winning wages: A media kit for successful living wage strategies.*

University of Houston Graduate College of Social Work. (n.d.). *Austin Legislative Internship Program.*

Ura, A. (2017, March 7). "Bathroom bill" testimony runs late into Tuesday evening. *Texas Tribune.*

Wallack, L., Woodruff, K., Dorfman, L., & Diaz, I. (1999). Thinking like an advocate. In *News for a change: An Advocate's guide to working with the media Thousand Oaks*, CA : Sage Publications (pp. 53–69).

Wellstone Action. (n.d.). *Tips for direct mail and campaign literature.* Retrieved from http://www. wellstone.org/resources/tips-direct-mail-and-campaign-literature

Whitman, A. (2011). Working with the media. In *University of Kansas Work Group for community health and development, community tool box.* Kansas: University of Kansas. Retrieved from http://ctb.ku.edu/en/table-of-contents/advocacy/media-advocacy/working-with-media/main.

Volunteer and Staff Management

10

© Springer International Publishing AG 2018
S.R. Lane, S. Pritzker, *Political Social Work*,
https://doi.org/10.1007/978-3-319-68588-5_10

Section 1: Overview:

Electoral and advocacy campaigns, as well as voter engagement, depend on human capital, access to individuals who are willing to work or volunteer their time in order to support the political effort. This chapter breaks down various categories of staff and volunteer positions in political settings. The typical duties and time commitment of each are discussed, including tasks accomplished by electoral campaign workers, interns, nonprofit board members, and more. Strategies and processes for interviewing potential volunteers and staff members, assigning tasks, managing, and helping volunteers and staff advance in their careers are discussed in the pages that follow.

Developing Social Work Competency
The Council on Social Work Education establishes educational standards for all social work programs in the USA. Content in this chapter supports building competency in the following areas that are considered core to the practice of social work:
COMPETENCY 5: Engage in policy practice
COMPETENCY 6: Engage with individuals, families, groups, organizations, and communities
COMPETENCY 8: Intervene with individuals, families, groups, organizations, and communities

Domains of Political Social Work	
1. Engaging individuals and communities in political processes	◄
2. Influencing policy agendas and decision-making	◄
3. Holding professional and political positions	◄
4. Engaging with electoral campaigns	◄
5. Seeking and holding elected office	◄

Section 2: Management in Political Settings

Managers in many social work settings face a challenging environment that increasingly expects more results with fewer resources (Hopkins et al. 2014; McBeath 2016). To function successfully in this environment, good management of staff and volunteers is necessary. However, good management is time intensive and can be particularly challenging in environments that are marked by intense activity, high turnover, and stressful deadlines. Developing and practicing management competencies are therefore crucial for political social workers who hire and supervise interns and staff. Among the areas to consider are the need for understanding general hiring practices and laws, best practices to promote empowerment, and staff development.

General Hiring Practices

Before you begin recruiting or hiring for a position, be thoughtful about both what you need and expect from your staff or volunteers. The nonprofit management literature suggests a **job analysis** (Kettner 2013), which asks questions like:

- What does the person in the job need to do?
- How will they do those tasks?
- What are the expected results if the job is done correctly?
- What are the essential functions of the job?
- What characteristics will a successful person have?
- What is the context of the work (based on an assessment of the organization/ setting)?
- What education and experience are required?
- What knowledge and skills are required?

To thoroughly answer these questions, Kettner (2013) advises an organization take a series of internal steps. We encourage you to refer to this resource for more detailed guidance on analyzing the context of a potential position.

While you may not be able to conduct a full job analysis when faced with limited time constraints, it is critical, even in fast-paced political settings, for your organization to take time to consider your requirements and expectations. Are the expectations realistic given the skills, education, and experience of the available staff/volunteers/interns? It can be tempting in political settings, particularly with limited budgets, to rely heavily on volunteers and interns to avoid the costs of hiring staff. This is frequently seen in legislative settings, particularly during state legislative sessions or the summer months of Congress. However, while unpaid assistance may reduce some costs—and, in fact, may be essential in political settings—volunteers and interns who are untrained or unsupervised have limited effectiveness. Political social workers must consider whether necessary tasks can be sufficiently completed by people without specialized training, or by people who might only show up once or twice. Any tasks for which the answer to this question is "no" should be completed only by paid staff or long-term volunteers.

Plan accordingly for the time needed to recruit, hire, and supervise staff, interns, or volunteers. Before you start your recruitment process, assess what resources are available in your agency. Many, but not all, campaigns and nonprofits have staff members who dedicate all or a significant portion of their time to volunteer management or staff recruitment. The title of this position depends on the context, e.g., volunteer coordinator, office manager, and field organizer. Some agencies have dedicated human resources staff or centralized internship programs, particularly public agencies or larger nonprofits. Smaller nonprofit organizations, campaigns, or offices of state or local elected officials will likely not have these resources.

There also may be specific laws that impact hiring practices in your setting. To find out about these laws, we recommend that you connect with a national or state-wide assistance organization that focuses on your setting, such as the National Council of Nonprofits or the National Conference of State Legislatures.

FURTHER REFLECTION: Your Work Experiences
Think about an agency or campaign where you have volunteered, interned, or worked (this does not have to be a political organization). What resources were available in the organization for finding and hiring volunteers, interns, or staff members? Which volunteer or staff hiring systems did you think were helpful to the organization or worked well? What did you like about those systems?

Empowerment and Diversity

Social work literature consistently argues that organizations that foster the voices of those who work for them are more likely to also create empowering situations for clients and communities. In contrast, organizations that disempower staff may not support the development of voice and power among the clients or communities with whom they work. This is an important reminder that how political social workers interact with our staff matters for multiple reasons. The social work value of dignity and worth of the person calls on us to respect our colleagues and coworkers; by doing so, we also create an environment that fosters respect for the dignity and worth of those on whose behalf we work.

Hardina's (2005) conceptualization of "empowerment-oriented organizations" offers a model for management in political social work settings. Empowerment-oriented organizations are those that promote broad participation in organizational decision-making, leading to positive outcomes for individuals, the organization, communities, and social change. Hardina (2005) identifies a series of strategies for creating organizations that value empowerment of staff, clients, and communities. While these strategies were based on service-delivery organizations, they are applicable to creating campaigns, offices, and organizations that reflect diverse viewpoints, empower employees, volunteers, and communities, and are able to responsively recognize and address bias.

Adapting Hardina's framework, we outline below several management approaches for political social workers who hire and supervise interns, volunteers, and staff to consider. Please see the Resource section for information about Hardina's article, if you are interested in a more expansive discussion of what these approaches might look like in practice.

1. Intentionally create office structures that support *meaningful* participation by diverse stakeholders. These structures should include a variety of perspectives among those who volunteer and work for the organization.
2. Develop organizational policies and procedures that can be used to bridge cultural, ethnic, gender, and other demographic barriers between individuals and groups. Include policies that promote hiring of people from diverse groups *and* ensure these hires are active participants in decision-making.

3. Develop organizational decision-making practices that minimize power differentials among staff members, but also between staff and community stakeholders.
4. Promote team building and collaboration among staff and with community members and stakeholders.
5. Implement strategies that consciously seek to increase the psychological empowerment of staff as well as community members and stakeholders.
6. Intentionally seek to increase job satisfaction among both employees and volunteers.
7. Encourage staff to advocate for improvements to organizational policies and procedures, and provide space for them to do so.
8. Seek to increase your organization's political power, as well as to increase the political influence of community members and stakeholders. This one might be comparatively easy in political settings, as this is often reflected in these organizations' goals.
9. Hire leaders who are fully committed to empowering staff *and* who are committed to empowering community members and stakeholders.
10. Engage directly and create *true* partnerships with the communities and constituencies who are the desired beneficiaries of the organization's actions. As a common statement in the disability rights activism says, "Nothing about us, without us" (Charlton 2000).

Staff Development

Staff development is a process by which employers intentionally create learning experiences that are designed to enhance employee's long-term personal and professional growth. These experiences are separate from **employee training**, which helps individuals develop the skills or knowledge needed specifically for the job at hand. Through staff development, employees prepare for future opportunities either within the organization or in their future careers (Kettner 2013). We recommend Kettner's *Excellence in human service organization management* for more detail on this topic. While prioritizing the growth of staff is an important management goal, it is especially challenging in intensive political settings like campaigns or in small, resource-limited nonprofit environments. In Section 4 we discuss ways political social workers might approach fostering professional growth among volunteers.

POLITICAL SOCIAL WORKER PROFILE: Joanne Cannon, MSW
Deputy State Director, Office of U.S. Senator Chris Murphy (D-CT).

Joanne developed an interest in politics from watching her father serve on the Board of Education, but spent the first half of her professional career in the world of finance. Once at the University of Connecticut School of Social Work, Joanne enrolled in a course on political social work and found her new passion.

Joanne began her journey working with then—State Senator Chris Murphy as a social work intern on his underdog Congressional campaign. She "worked

(continued)

several hours there more than required because I liked it so much" and was happy to be asked to stay with the campaign once her internship came to a close. Joanne remained on staff with now-Senator Murphy through his 6 years as a U.S. Representative and election to the U.S. Senate.

As deputy state director, Joanne is second in command for managing the office. Her main responsibility is managing office personnel (including three other social workers), using a lot of her social work skills. It requires "listening to what people want," but also "helping people grow, learn, and be challenged every day." Joanne prioritizes making sure that everyone in the office feels that they are on a team together. As she says, "everyone has a very important role" in the office, and it is important for the staff and interns to feel that they are contributing. Of course, Joanne also has to make sure that the actual work of the Senator's office is getting done.

In this work, Joanne has also "held on to what my passion is, which is case-work." She manages all of the office's "casework," or constituent service, opera-tions. She and her colleagues act as a "conduit between the constituent and the federal agency to try to get assistance for these folks." Joanne practices her active listening skills that she learned as a social work student when working with these constituents. "Listening is probably the most crucial skill in political social work. People want to be heard, and to be heard, someone has to be listening." She leads the office in "actively, constantly, analytically thinking of how to solve this per-son's problem" because not every issue can be solved with a simple phone call.

Joanne's advice to social workers entering a political staff management position is to remember to be understanding. "Everybody has demands on their life outside of the office, and sometimes those demands creep into office life," she says. Even though the office still needs to accomplish its work, there are things in the personal lives of staff members that are bigger, and it is important to be understanding of how those issues affect them. "It can be a balance and a juggling act," Joanne says, but it is important to remember and be understand-ing of the issues we all have outside of work that demand our time.

Section 3: Types of Volunteers

Very few political social work tasks can be done without the help of volunteers. From campaign volunteers who hold signs at the polling place on Election Day to the board members of nonprofit organizations who invest time and energy in an organization for years and are legally responsible for its workings, volunteers come in all types and are frequently the lifeblood of political social workers' efforts. Volunteering is a huge asset to political work, and also brings significant, nonmon-etary rewards to those who volunteer (Kenny et al. 2008). Individuals can volunteer in countless ways. In this section, we break down the types of volunteers most com-mon in political social work contexts. These include interns from within and outside of social work, advocacy and electoral campaign volunteers, and three types of political volunteers with significant responsibility: members of a "kitchen cabinet," campaign treasurers, and nonprofit board members.

Interns—Nonsocial Work

Internships are very common in political settings. Interns regularly come to campaigns or political offices from fields or programs both inside and outside of social work, including, but not limited to, political science, public policy, public administration, and law. Depending on the program or the context of the internship (e.g., some students are interning for the experience, not for course credit in a program), the requirements, hours, and flexibility may differ substantially. Here, we show a flyer seeking interns to support a campaign for a state legislature seat. This listing is somewhat unusual, in that it specifically reaches out to social work majors. We cannot be any clearer about this—whether or not an announcement for a volunteer or internship opportunity with a campaign or in a legislative office lists social work, *consider yourself qualified to apply*. At the end of this book, we offer tips on highlighting your social work background as an asset to political employers who may not be familiar with the assets we bring.

Sample Campaign Internship Opportunity

This competitive race for State Representative seeks students from a variety of backgrounds to get involved in our campaign. No political experience is necessary! We are looking for hard workers who are dedicated to the community and looking to learn.

Internship responsibilities may include:
- Contacting voters
- Coordinating events with volunteers, media, and other organizations
- Volunteer recruitment, training, and management

Internships may be offered for course credit or community service hours. All majors are welcome, including English or communications, psychology or social work, political science, business, and law.

For More Information, Contact Our Field Organizer Today!
campaign@campaign.org; ###-###-####

As a political social worker working with interns, here are some important factors to consider:

1. What work does the campaign or office need to have done? Is the work appropriate for the educational level, experience, and academic field of the student? Competencies and learning needs may be different for interns at different educational levels and coming from different fields.
2. What are the requirements of the intern's educational program? Fields and programs each have their own requirements for supervision, tasks, and evaluation. Before an intern and campaign have committed to each other, be sure that the requirements can be met in the particular setting.
3. In general, interns who are working for credit have a set number of hours they should be fulfilling in their internship. Does the campaign or office have enough hours for them to work? If there is more work needed than the set hour requirement, what are the expectations of the campaign or office and the student? If the student is enrolled in coursework during the internship, are expectations clear

about how the student is prioritizing attending classes and completing work? These expectations should be clear and communicated in advance by both parties. It is very easy to end up in a situation where the campaign or office has needs that extend beyond the student's committed time. Tension or conflict can ensue without clear communication.

4. Is the internship paid or unpaid? Whether interns can or should be paid depends on a number of variables. The U.S. Department of Labor (2010) outlines standards to determine whether interns are entitled to payment of at least minimum wage. Considerations include whether the internship is similar to educational training, whether it benefits the intern, whether regular employees are displaced, whether the employer benefits from the interns or occasionally finds activities impeded, whether a job is automatically offered the intern at the end, and whether both parties understand that the intern is not working for wages. It is very important to understand how these rules apply in your setting to be sure you are in compliance with applicable regulations (Minton and Young Entrepreneur Council 2013; National Council of Nonprofits n.d.). In general, these rules allow for educational internships in political settings to be unpaid, but expert advice is recommended in setting up these internships to be sure you are in line with these standards.

Interns—Social Work

Social work students bring specific requirements for supervision, tasks, and evaluation to their internships in political settings. Typically, social work interns must complete a specific clock-hour requirement and must receive direct supervision. Qualified supervisors are generally expected to have 2 years of practice experience after their social work degree *or* a program may identify an alternative way of ensuring that students receive a social work perspective on their fieldwork (Council on Social Work Education 2015). States may impose their own additional requirements; for example, New York requires supervisors of MSW interns to hold an LMSW license (NASW New York City Chapter 2013). Social work interns also must engage in tasks that support a specified set of educational competencies, and their learning must be evaluated.

Despite these common requirements, it is important to recognize that social work internships in electoral and advocacy campaigns or in the offices of elected officials may differ significantly from "typical" social work internships. An internship in a political setting—whether with an advocacy or electoral campaign or in the office of an elected official—offers students a tremendous opportunity to apply social work skills in a macro setting, to network with decision-makers and potential employers, and to develop practical skills to influence policy. Research finds that students interning in legislative settings may gain a wide range of practical knowledge and skills—each of which are critical for effectively influencing policy throughout a political social work career. These include real-life knowledge of how policy-making works from the inside, strategic knowledge of what works to influence policy, and stronger personal (self-awareness, confidence, resilience) and interpersonal (networking) skills (Pritzker and Barros Lane in press).

Despite the learning benefits that accrue from these placements, political internships are an underutilized aspect of social work education. In a survey of field directors across the country, 59% of BSW programs place some students in field placements where they interact with professional policy advocates, and 54% of programs have at least some students who are exposed to advocacy or lobbying, but just 15% of BSW programs place students with elected officials and only 9% provide any students access to electoral politics (Pritzker and Lane 2014). At the MSW level, generalist students have similar opportunities to work with professional advocates (59%) and advocacy/lobbying (56%), while fewer than one-fourth of programs place students with elected officials (22%) or expose them to electoral politics (12%). At these generalist program levels, many field directors express concerns that they cannot locate internships that include both political and direct practice content. Specifically, they fear that political content comes at the expense of other needed content, particularly clinical content. As you move forward in your professional career, *you* can contribute to the education of further social work students by volunteering to supervise social work interns. Consider creating and emphasizing the availability of internship opportunities that expose students both to policy work *and* to working in a direct and interpersonal manner with clients, constituents, or community members. While people unfamiliar with internships in political settings may consider these to be solely macro settings where interns deal only with policy, we hope that this book illustrates how central micro social work skills are to political settings.

Policy or political responsibilities in field are most prevalent at the specialized MSW level (Pritzker and Lane 2014). In 62% of MSW programs, some specialized students interact with professional policy advocates, and 64% offer some placements with advocacy/lobbying content. Among specialized programs, 28% offer some opportunities to work with elected officials, and 20% offer some opportunities related to electoral politics. Yet, these placements too face barriers. These include finding adequate supervision, what field directors perceive as a lack of interest or preparation by students for policy placements, and distance from places where directors think of policy being made, such as Washington, DC, or the state capitol.

FURTHER REFLECTION: Advice to a Social Work Supervisor in a Political Setting
Picture yourself 5–10 years from now as a supervisor of social work interns in a political setting. The setting could be an advocacy or electoral campaign, the office of an elected official, or some other political context. Based on your recent experiences as a social work student and intern, write a brief letter to this "future you." What advice do you have for "future you" in supervising social work interns in a political setting?

Advocacy and Electoral Campaign Volunteers

Volunteer tasks for advocacy and electoral campaign volunteers range widely: from a volunteer who shows up to one or two events to hold a sign or knock on a few doors, to someone who helps create relationships with their elected officials to promote advocacy work, to someone who works many hours per week for the duration of a campaign. In a small campaign, all roles, from campaign manager down, are likely filled by volunteers. In a larger campaign, significant roles are filled by paid staff, and, particularly at the federal level, even some canvassers who knock on doors may be paid. Often, volunteers begin by making phone calls to voters or elected officials, attending rallies, or knocking on doors, and then gradually take on more responsibility in a campaign. The "ladder" by which someone moves from a casual volunteer to a volunteer with more responsibility is discussed below.

Electoral campaigns in the USA spend a huge portion of their time, energy, and resources deploying volunteers to call and knock on the doors of potential voters. In just one illustration of this, the two major party's presidential candidates in 2012 reported millions of volunteers contacting potential voters (Enos and Hersh 2015). The Obama campaign recruited 2.3 million volunteers, and on Election Day alone (November 6, 2012), reported that 100,000 volunteers and paid campaign staffers knocked on 7 million doors around the country. The Romney campaign reported 225 million voter contacts by volunteers and paid staff throughout the election (Enos and Hersh 2015). These numbers only include the presidential race—volunteers also performed voter contact in Congressional, state, and local elections throughout the country.

This **direct voter contact**, often called "canvassing," "ground game," or "field work," leans heavily on volunteers for its success. This outreach is used to reach voters individually, and ideally, to contact them through members of their own community who support the candidate. Increasingly, this work may be done remotely, with volunteers making phone calls from their homes, sometimes through internet apps. These remote efforts have the potential to engage more volunteers, but come with their own specific challenges (Moon and Sproull 2008). Volunteers who operate away from paid staff may not be as well-trained as those who work in person. Accordingly, this increases the risk that their contact with potential voters includes inaccurate information or does more harm than good.

"Kitchen Cabinet"

The phrase **kitchen cabinet** was coined during Andrew Jackson's presidency by his opponents to describe a group of informal advisors who served him. He instituted this after his dysfunctional official cabinet stopped meeting (Blair House 2014). In modern times, this phrase is used in political circles to describe the volunteer advisors who surround a candidate or officeholder and provide informal advice and counsel. These are the advisors you (or your candidate) trust the most. As a group, they may be more influential than those who hold formal leadership positions. The kitchen cabinet might include the candidate's family members, close friends, and political mentors. Picture candidate Donald Trump being advised closely by a kitchen cabinet including Jared Kushner and Ivanka Trump, who remained close advisors as he moved into his presidency. In a higher-profile race, the kitchen cabinet also might include representatives of a variety of interest and/or identity groups.

Campaign Treasurer

The **treasurer** is a key position on an electoral campaign. Because in many states, the campaign treasurer's name appears on all campaign materials, the reputation of the campaign's treasurer in your local geographic area is key. This is a critical early selection in a campaign, and needs to be someone the candidate fully trusts. A good treasurer is very detail oriented, honest, dependable, well known in the area, fully committed to the campaign, with good people skills (Shaw 2014). In smaller campaigns, treasurers are generally volunteers. They may be paid in larger elections.

Depending on their areas of expertise, the treasurer may take on a number of responsibilities during the campaign. These range from filling out reporting paperwork to depositing checks, developing a budget, and communicating with fundraising staff. The candidate, the campaign manager, and the treasurer all should know the campaign finance rules of your state. Training classes are often available both in-person and online through the state office which enforces campaign finance rules (see example in Resources).

Most importantly, the campaign treasurer is legally responsible for ensuring that the campaign honors legal and financial rules. For this reason, many campaigns use a financial professional, campaign professional, or accountant to support the treasurer's work and ensure that all relevant rules, filing deadlines, and paperwork are completed (Shaw 2014). This individual is often a volunteer. While this professional works closely with the treasurer to ensure the campaign is completely operating within relevant rules, the buck stops at the treasurer or the candidate. The old phrase "there is no such thing as bad publicity" (sometimes credited to showman and nineteenth century Connecticut state legislator PT Barnum) was not referring to publicity around campaign finance violations!

Nonprofit Board Members

Nonprofit board members, like campaign treasurers, have more responsibilities and legal liabilities than other kinds of volunteers. In any nonprofit, the range of board member responsibilities may include determining an organization's mission; choosing, hiring, and supervising the nonprofit's chief executive; strategic planning; and/or fiscal oversight and management. In a nonprofit conducting political work, board members may be responsible for participating in the advocacy work and leveraging their own connections with policy-makers to create opportunities for the organization's advocacy to be successful.

While there are many excellent resources for board members or those considering board membership, the legal duties of a board of directors are particularly critical for political social workers to understand. Board members' legal duties can be divided into three categories (BoardSource 2011).

1. **Duty of care**: the responsibility to participate actively in the work of the board and use their expertise to benefit the organization. In a nonprofit organization, this carries significant weight within the organization's operations (Takagi 2006).
2. **Duty of loyalty**: the responsibility to put the needs of the organization above the board member's own personal or professional interests.
3. **Duty of obedience**: the responsibility to ensure that the board is working in accordance with its mission and in compliance with all relevant state and federal laws, such as tax laws.

Because of the significance of the board member role in terms of time, responsibility, and legal duties, board recruitment should be conducted in a thoughtful, thorough manner. For a nonprofit conducting political work, it is important to make sure that potential board members understand what political involvement is expected of them. Board members should be clearly informed of their responsibilities in advance of their acceptance of the role and should serve limited terms that are renewed thoughtfully and carefully.

Section 4: Hiring and Managing Volunteers

The processes of finding, hiring, and maintaining volunteers vary depending on the position, setting, and length of any relationships between the campaign or office and the volunteer. It can include a formal process of recruiting, hiring, and supervision or may be done much more informally through networking or word of mouth.

Recruiting and Finding Volunteers

Put yourself in the shoes of a political candidate, campaign manager, advocacy campaign coordinator, or chief of staff. Where do you find volunteers? Some ideas are below. These are often the same groups of people who might donate money to a campaign.

1. You! As the candidate, elected official or a campaign staffer, others will not be willing to give of their time unless they see that you are committed to it as well. If a campaign wants people to volunteer their time to help a cause, those volunteers will be more likely to come back if they see the candidate or advocacy leadership also working long hours and doing the grunt work. One author interned for a U.S. Senator who seemed to never sleep. He came into work every morning with a stack of new ideas for work he could do to help his constituents.

That kind of dedication is not a great example of work-life balance, but feels inspiring to those asked to give of their time.

2. People who love you. Family and close friends of the candidate and staff are a great place to start. Ask them to give of their time in support of you. As a bonus, you know them well, so you know their strengths and skills. Stuffing envelopes for a Congressional campaign letter late at night, alongside the candidate's partner and family, encourages volunteers to feel they are part of the family.

3. Allies. This group includes people who believe in similar things to you. Giving of their time is another good way for them to advance that cause. Keep track of others who are in coalitions with you or working toward similar goals. Expect to donate time to their efforts, and ask them to support yours.

4. People seeking power. These are people who might not believe in the same things as you, but they benefit from you winning. Ask them to give their time to support you. In a recent campaign at the local level, an author met a number of people who are planning to run for governor in 2 years. These people want to support local candidates in order to inspire local activists to support them in the future.

5. Enemy of your enemy. These people really don't care about you but they *really* don't like your opponent or those who are working on the other side. Ask them to commit time in order to keep the other side from winning.

Students, particularly those interested in possibly getting into political work professionally themselves one day, are excellent potential political volunteers. They may be interested in interning or volunteering for the office of an elected official to get their foot in the door and build skills and contacts, or they may be interested in volunteering for an electoral campaign to build skills while supporting a candidate or issue they care about. While some of the other groups mentioned in this section include individuals with a great deal of political volunteer experience, students may be new to political volunteering. Some may be interested in volunteering for your office or campaign, but may not reach out because they do not know where to start. Reaching out to like-minded high school or college student organizations could be a good place to start in recruiting student volunteers.

Seeking groups of volunteers (within the restrictions in your area about coordinating with outside groups) may be most efficient. Sources of potential volunteers include groups that already have members organized. For example, many state chapters of the National Association of Social Workers organize social workers to volunteer for candidates who have been endorsed by PACE (Political Action for Candidate Election). This is also true of other groups, such as labor unions, interest groups, service groups, religious groups, school associations, and groups who have worked on other campaigns (Shaw 2014). You also might recruit volunteers through groups motivated by specific issues aligned with your electoral or advocacy campaign, such as veterans, those who identify as pro-life or pro-choice, environmentalists, hunters, seniors, or union members (Shaw 2014). Asking groups of allies to dedicate their time together makes it more likely that they will show up, because it is more comfortable to do new things with other people you know. It also allows the members of that group to share a common goal and bond with each other.

Electoral and advocacy campaigns should look for volunteers wherever they go. Campaign staffers and volunteers should take volunteer sign-up sheets with them to meetings, community events, fundraisers, etc. (Shaw 2014). Websites of campaign and advocacy organizations should include a bright button that says "get involved," "volunteer," or "join the movement" and connects people directly with the volunteer coordinator or other appropriate members of the team. If you include this button, make sure that your campaign follows up with people who sign up to volunteer. Students have repeatedly shared with one of the book's authors their frustrations when, for the first time in their life, they sign up on a candidate's website to volunteer, and then the campaign never reaches out to them.

Publicizing marches, rallies, fundraisers, and other one-time events where people can come and show support for a candidate or cause creates situations where attendees might then be interested in getting more involved. Political social workers should keep an eye on people we meet who might be interested in increasing involvement. One way to highlight the social work value of empowerment and increase representation of community voices is to specifically reach out for volunteers in communities that are directly affected by the candidate election or issues involved in the advocacy campaign.

As political social workers collect the names of potential volunteers, it is important to gather contact information, connect with them about their availability, track their skills and experience, know who has volunteered, thank them, and ask them to volunteer again.

Interviewing and Hiring

The processes of interviewing and hiring for formal staff positions are covered at length in other resources, particularly Kettner (2013) and the Community Tool Box, and are discussed briefly in Section 5. These processes may differ significantly for volunteers, especially in campaigns moving at a very fast pace. If you have prepared a job analysis prior to the busy times of the advocacy or electoral campaigns, legislative session, etc., you will have a good sense of the requirements that must be accomplished by volunteers and the skills for which you are looking.

While the "hiring" process for volunteers doesn't always resemble a formal hiring process, it should involve some sort of initial discussion and assessment, even if done very informally. Skipping this step can have negative consequences. An electoral campaign volunteer who is knocking on doors may be the only person from the campaign that the voter ever meets. In general, since volunteers identify themselves as such, voters will not expect them to be experts. At the same time, if they make a strong negative impression, it could certainly be held against the candidate. In an advocacy campaign, a volunteer who alienates a crucial member of the legislature can set back the whole campaign. In an elected official's office, interns are often viewed as a direct extension of the elected official, with negative behavior tending to reflect poorly on the official.

This initial discussion and assessment can be formal, including written or verbal questions as with a traditional interview, or it can be done casually through a getting-to-know-you conversation. Some things to consider in this discussion are:

- Has the person ever volunteered in a political setting before? If not, can they be assigned a task with a partner or mentor, or one that does not require full autonomy, while they get to know the work and the setting?
- What is the volunteer's knowledge of the issues and/or candidate? If limited, are you able to provide them with resources to help them learn essential points?
- Is the volunteer from the community in which they will be working? If not, is the volunteer likely to be able to connect with community members? Research suggests that those who volunteer for campaigns may be more ideologically extreme than voters, and may not be from the geographic area in which they are volunteering (Enos and Hersh 2015). While the common wisdom is that you do not ever want to turn volunteers away, think about whether constituents are going to welcome an "outsider" coming in to tell them how to vote. Similarly, callers to an elected official's office may be frustrated if the person they talk with does not know basic geography or context of the district or mispronounces the name of key cities. Consider whether there are ways to utilize the volunteer that will not create a potential problem for the campaign or office.
- What particular skills does the volunteer bring to the table? See the examples of possible volunteer skills listed here. How can these skills be utilized to best support the strategic needs of the campaign or office?
- Does the volunteer have connections that may be beneficial to the campaign? For example, does the volunteer have:
  - Connections to other groups or individuals that might also volunteer,
  - Connections with people or companies who could be potential donors,
  - Connections with decision-makers or others with power, or
  - Connections with the media?

Samples of Useful Political Volunteer Skills
• Computer expertise
• Social media
• Graphic design
• Fundraising
• Written communication
• Oral communication
• Attention to detail
• Language proficiency (for example, if Spanish is spoken as the primary language by a significant number of voters or constituents in your district, volunteers who speak Spanish are crucial to success.)

Assigning Volunteer Tasks

Task assignments should be based on the skills identified during an interview or an initial **on-boarding**. On-boarding refers to the process of bringing a new volunteer or employee into your organization and training them on any systems or processes that they will need for their work.

Volunteers can be assigned to a variety of tasks to support the work of your campaign or office. Each of these requires varying amounts of time—therefore, a volunteer's time availability is an important consideration in assigning volunteer tasks. Table 10.1 provides some examples from Shaw (2014) of types of volunteer tasks and the amount of work that volunteers can be expected to complete for each task. Her estimates were for electoral campaigns; however, below we also included comparisons with advocacy campaigns and offices of elected officials. Note that these time estimates do not include the time involved with preparation work, such as preparing scripts and lists, training, or gathering materials for volunteers.

With first-time volunteers, begin by giving them discrete task(s). It is preferable to start with one task in order to allow the volunteer to focus and be successful in one area. A good discrete task is one with a short time-frame and a clear definition of what "successful" completion means. For example, electoral campaign volunteers often start out phone banking or door knocking, and advocacy campaign volunteers often start by making phone calls or sending emails. These tasks are straightforward and enable volunteers to be paired with a more experienced person on their first try.

Train volunteers for the tasks they will be completing. For example, for phone banking or door knocking, volunteers should be given a script and an opportunity to practice. They should know that saying, "I don't know but I'll find out," is an acceptable answer—and that it is much better for a volunteer to plead ignorance and have a staffer or someone with more experience get back to the voter than to give out incorrect information. While this is an important skill for volunteers, staff, and supervisors alike to learn, it is particularly important for campaign volunteers. There are rarely opportunities for campaigns to know that incorrect information was given or to correct the misinformation.

One useful volunteer task that does not need to be centralized in a campaign office is writing a letter to the editor. This is a valuable way for community members to communicate with their neighbors and highlight their commitment to your candidate or support for your issue. Volunteers can write letters to the editor in a relatively short amount of time, from their homes. This makes them an attractive task for busy volunteers, especially if the volunteer is provided support. A campaign may want to show sample letters to the editor to volunteers and provide a list of topics (connected with your campaign calendar "theme" of the week, perhaps) to highlight in the letters. See our suggestions for some keys to a good letter to the editor. Note that a volunteer who has successfully written letters to the editor also may be a good person to ask to reach out to their networks to recruit other volunteers.

Table 10.1 Volunteer tasks

Phone banking	Making phone calls at a set time with a group of other people: 20–30 calls per hour in an electoral campaign.
	More calls may be able to be completed, depending on the amount of time needed for each call and the time of day at which the calls are being made. Automated software like predictive dialers that automatically make the calls and only connect the volunteer when there is a voter on the line can *significantly* increase this number. In advocacy campaigns, the number of calls that can be completed depends on the type of phone call. Calls to turn out volunteers at rallies, events, etc. may be as fast as electoral phone calls. Phone calls to policy-makers are generally more involved and take more time, depending on how complicated the script is and what you are asking of the policy-maker. In elected officials' offices, you may be tasked with calling around to other offices to get commitments on a bill, or to key stakeholders to ask them to lend support on an issue. These calls are more involved, and you should expect them to take longer. Cold calls to potential voters or grassroots activists are challenging, given that many people are hesitant to pick up a call from a strange number.
Door knocking	Knocking on the doors of potential voters, also referred to as **canvassing**: 10–15 doors per hour in both electoral and advocacy campaigns, however, there is a lot of variation.
	If your volunteers are knocking on doors in an urban area with many apartments (presuming they can get into the apartment buildings) or houses located close together, they can knock on doors more quickly. In a rural area where volunteers must drive from house to house, or in an area that requires walking up/down hills, speeds are slower. If your volunteers are only leaving information (a "literature drop" or "**lit drop**") and not seeking to talk to people, they will get to more houses. This is generally not a requirement of political social work jobs in elected officials' offices.
Mailings	Sending out mail as needed by the campaign or elected official: A group of volunteers can send out approximately 500 pieces of mail in 1 hour, including stuffing, stamping, sealing, and addressing envelopes.
	This should be similar for each political setting. In many campaigns, mailings are handled by consultants or outside firms rather than by volunteers, but in small advocacy and electoral campaigns, mailings may be a responsibility for volunteers. Mail that needs to be individualized, such as thank you letters, responses to requests for substantive information, etc. is much more time consuming and may be more appropriately done by long-term volunteers or staff.
Lawn signs	Setting up signs posted in yards or in certain public locations that express support for a candidate or issue: A two-person team can put out roughly 12 lawn signs an hour for an advocacy or electoral campaign.
	Rules as to where and for how long lawn signs may be legally posted typically differ by localities and can be a factor in the amount of time needed to complete this task. There may even be lawn sign rules associated with specific apartment complexes or neighborhood associations. For example, in an author's neighborhood in Texas, the local homeowners' association restricts each home to only one political lawn sign at a time. Depending on local rules, you also may need volunteers to take the lawn signs away within a certain amount of time after the election. For example, in Knox County, Tennessee, signs must be removed within 3 weeks of the election (Knox County Tennessee n.d.), while in Arizona, signs should be removed within 7 days (Hiland 2014). Those working for elected officials should not expect to manage lawn signs, as it is generally not allowed.

(continued)

Writing a Letter to the Editor Source: (Zero to Three 2017)
• Review the newspaper's guidelines. In general, letters to the editor are 250 words or less, and are more likely to be printed if they are from someone in the community.
• Connect to something relevant in the community the newspaper serves. The newspaper is unlikely to print a letter about a candidate on the other side of the state. The audience is unlikely to be interested in that as well.
• Make the point of your letter to the editor clear. If writing to support a candidate, the first sentence should reference the candidate and why you support them.
• As with other methods of communication, tone is important. If you make people angry, they might associate those negative emotions with your candidate, so choose your words and your strategy wisely.
• Generally, newspapers will require you to include your name, address, and phone number so that they can confirm you wrote it.

APPLY YOUR SKILLS: Write a Letter to the Editor
Choose a local newspaper, and research the guidelines for submitting a letter to the editor. What are the methods for submission, length restrictions, and any other requirements? Draft a letter in support of a candidate currently running for office in your area, or in relation to the advocacy issue you have been working on throughout the book. We encourage you to submit the letter!

Managing Volunteers

Managing volunteers in political settings can be difficult. Campaigns—and even the day-to-day work in offices of elected officials—often can be fast-paced environments, with little time available to conduct thorough assessments of volunteers' strengths and needs or to provide in-depth training or supervision. For example, some social work students interning in an intensive state legislative environment with tight deadlines and high stress report facing a lack of clear expectations for their work, a lack of clear accountability structures, and minimal constructive feedback on their work (Pritzker and Barros Lane in press). (To be clear, they found the work fulfilling, but had to adapt to receiving less supervision and mentorship than they were used to in other settings.)

Management of volunteers in electoral and advocacy campaigns is particularly challenging because volunteers tend to cycle through campaigns, meaning that a volunteer may come just once or sporadically. Because of their irregularity, these volunteers need to be trained again every time they come. Furthermore, volunteers are often members of the community, meaning that they may be voters, constituents, or other stakeholders of the work of the campaign. "Firing" a voter or stakeholder who is working for free can be problematic.

Recently, some national campaigns have shifted to "**neighbor to neighbor**" campaigning, popularized by the Obama campaign. Its key feature is asking voters to reach out directly to other voters without much supervision from the campaign.

For example, the Obama campaign used this technique to recruit volunteers to canvass their own neighborhoods and host neighborhood house parties in support of the candidate, so that voter outreach was conducted by friends and neighbors, rather than by staff or volunteers with limited personal connections to the community. While this technique allows for an increase in the number of people who can be contacted, it, or similar approaches, can make managing volunteers particularly challenging. In particular, it significantly decreases opportunities for the campaign to supervise and control what is happening during volunteer outreach, necessitating more attention to providing initial support and training to volunteers. Currently, this is a not a significant feature of most local campaigns, but this dynamic may shift in the future.

Given these challenges, but also the critical nature of volunteers to work in political settings, making sure that volunteers are effectively supervised is key. A voter or decision-maker will not make a distinction between a volunteer and a paid campaign staffer. As we discussed previously in this chapter, a negative impression of a volunteer may easily be generalized to the candidate or campaign in general. A particularly egregious example that illustrates this point—and one the campaign could not be expected to have been able to control—took place in the summer of 2017. An individual showed up at a baseball practice for members of Congress and staffers, and shot several people, including a Republican member of Congress. It turned out that this shooter had volunteered for the campaign of Bernie Sanders, a candidate in the 2016 Democratic presidential primary. News sources across the USA broadcast the shooter's links with Sanders' campaign and Sanders spoke on the floor of the Senate announcing that he "was sickened by this despicable act" (Watkins et al. 2017). Meanwhile, some critics took the opportunity to link the shooting directly to Sanders, suggesting that Sanders himself had encouraged violence (Shalby 2017).

Supervising volunteers includes matching volunteers to appropriate tasks, giving them the resources and training to do the task well, checking in with volunteers to be sure they are doing tasks correctly, and providing them with supportive assistance if they are not. It also involves **debriefing** with volunteers after they have completed the discrete task they are assigned; that is, provide a brief opportunity for the volunteer to report what happened, what went well, any problems, and anything that the person delegating to them needs to know about how the task went. On your end, this involves developing rapport with volunteers, and engaging active listening techniques to fully hear what your volunteers are telling you. This might only take a few minutes. This is especially important when individuals volunteer for the first time. During this debrief, make sure to thank volunteers for their work, ask how their experience was, and ask if anything came up they were uncertain about. At the end of this debrief, thank them again, and (assuming all went well), *ask them to volunteer again*. This ask to volunteer again should be specific and discrete.

Supervising volunteers also involves keeping records of which volunteers did which tasks so that you can use that information when they come back to volunteer again. See Catherine Shaw's excellent book (information provided in the Resources section) for specific examples of trainings, resources, and scheduling techniques for campaign volunteers.

Above all, make the most of a volunteer's time—remember, they are giving their valuable time to help your candidate, cause, or work. Critical to doing this are several key priorities:

1. Respect your volunteers' time—this is a precious resource. Being respectful of people's time encourages them to come back (and bring friends!). Be ready to begin at the time you ask people to arrive, and have all of the preparation for the volunteers to do their work complete (i.e., have routes or "**turf**" already planned or "cut," material to hand out or "**literature**" divided, phone lists ready).
2. Be smart in matching volunteers and tasks in ways that set people up for success, so that they continue to want to support your efforts.
3. Keep in mind that volunteers are often also stakeholders in other ways—they could be potential voters, donors, constituents, etc.
4. Communicate clearly. Set definite times and tasks. Ask people to do one thing at a time, be clear about what it will involve, how much time they will need, and what they need to do to prepare (should they wear comfortable shoes, bring a clipboard, pay for their own parking, wear a particular color, etc.). Provide written instructions whenever possible. When you can, call in advance to remind them of essential instructions, and listen actively to any concerns or challenges they share with you.
5. Through the above priorities, make them feel like a part of the bigger campaign effort. You can never thank volunteers enough. Make sure they hear their efforts contribute to the overall work of the campaign or office, how things are going, and what a difference they make.

FURTHER REFLECTION: Your Volunteer Activity
Think back to a recent time you were asked to volunteer for a cause or candidate. How were you asked? Did you participate? If yes, was it a good experience? If no, why not? What could the campaign or organization have done to make people more likely to participate, and to make it a better experience for those involved?

You could also ask these same questions about an event or effort for which you asked others to volunteer. How did you ask? Did people participate? What could you have done to make people more likely to participate, and to make it a better experience for those involved?

Developing Volunteers to Move Up the Volunteer Ladder

A critical part of effective volunteer management in political settings is volunteer development. Assuming that initial experiences with a volunteer go well, smart campaigns think about ways to develop a volunteer and then help volunteers to do so. **Volunteer development** involves recognizing the assets that your volunteers bring to their work, and encouraging them to build upon those assets in new ways to support your campaign. This can involve helping the volunteer grow into a long-term volunteer or supporting the volunteer in being able to take on more substantive responsibilities.

As you work with volunteers, keep records of the tasks they complete, their strengths, individual interests, availability, etc. This will help you develop volunteers into more committed volunteers or to assess the potential they may have for different volunteer positions or paid positions. For example, many internships have the potential to lead to paid work, but if you have not supervised your interns well or gathered information on their performance, you and your colleagues will not have the information needed to determine whether they are a good fit for a paid opening.

Think of volunteer development as a ladder with increasing responsibilities and time commitment that a volunteer may have. This image can guide you in thinking about ways to help connect volunteers with more committed or more long-term volunteer assignments. For example, if someone has attended a volunteer event, a campaign might ask whether the volunteer would be willing to organize a group to come volunteer together. If a volunteer has written an email for the campaign, perhaps the volunteer would next be willing to make a phone call or meet with a legislator. If someone has agreed to place a lawn sign at their house, a campaign might encourage the volunteer to consider putting up lawn signs in other places. If a volunteer has been active in your advocacy campaign for a long time, are they interested in joining the board of your organization?

While an image of a ladder can serve as a useful guide for developing volunteers, keep in mind that success at one volunteer task does not necessarily lead to success in other areas. If you have a volunteer who shows aptitude for making successful phone calls, that does not necessarily mean you should "promote" them to other tasks. If they are good at phone calls and like to do them, you may instead want to support and encourage them to become an expert in that area.

Section 5: Key Political Social Work Staff Positions

While volunteers are used extensively in political settings, the right team is critical to the success of your campaign or work in your political office. In many settings, that includes paid staff members. We have listed several key books, journals, and websites in the Resources of this chapter that you may find helpful if you are part of the hiring and management process.

Common roles in an advocacy or electoral campaign include the following. In some larger campaigns, each role is carried by a different individual(s). In smaller campaigns, individuals may take on multiple roles.

- Campaign manager
- Treasurer
- Field organizer
- Volunteer coordinator
- Scheduler
- Finance director

- Press secretary/communications director/spokesperson
- Speechwriter
- Field director
- Field organizer/regional field organizer/deputy field director
- Paid canvass director
- Political director/organizer
- Technology director/social media manager
- Research director
- Legal counsel

Key roles in the office of an elected official (which also may be combined in small offices) include the following.

- Chief of staff
- Policy or legislative director
- District or state director (for legislative officials, where the capitol is far from the district)
- Scheduler
- Communications director/press secretary
- Office manager/administrative director
- Research director
- Legislative aide/assistant
- Legislative correspondent
- Social media manager
- Staff assistant
- Constituent services staffer/caseworker
- Outreach staffer
- Committee clerk (along with other committee staff, may work for the chair/ranking member)
- Intern

POLITICAL SOCIAL WORKER PROFILE: Susan Collins, MSW
Chief of Staff, U.S. Representative Luis Gutierrez (D-IL) (Fig. 10.1).

Fig. 10.1 Susan Collins, MSW

(continued)

"Most of my work before coming to DC was working with immigrant populations," in Texas and as a volunteer in Nicaragua along the US-Mexico Border. This work inspired Susan to pursue an MSW degree with a specialization in political social work. After graduation, Susan continued to work with immigrant populations, specifically newly arrived families with children. Through this work, Susan came to understand that "a huge part of [immigrants'] ability, or lack of ability, to do the best they can and to raise their children the way they want comes down to their legal status," and that these barriers are further "complicated by issues of poverty and not speaking the language".

In 2001, Susan pursued a fellowship to work on immigration policy in Washington, D.C. She has not left D.C. since, and now works for U.S. Representative Luis Gutierrez (D-IL), "the national leader on immigration reform." She continues to focus on immigration every day, along with Rep. Gutierrez. Susan says, "As a Chief of Staff, it is really my job to make sure that everyone is working together as a team to make sure that the legislator meets his policy goals," as well as being the legislator's lead advisor on those goals.

At any given time, Susan manages 20 staff members in the office, which can include "mentoring, motivating the team, managing the budget... anything from the practical to the human aspects of running the office." Although these staff members hold a range of duties, Susan notes that "no one works in this office without doing some policy work." Susan has always felt that her social work training and experience has been beneficial to all her job duties. Social workers are trained to focus on "people's strengths, how to set goals, and how to reach them," and this translates directly to the mentoring work that Susan does with her staff.

Working in a "Congressional setting is very competitive." This can mean that conflicts that would seem extreme in a nonprofit setting are more common in getting political business done. Susan reports that she finds "my ability to work with all kinds of people" and to "remain calm and not take things personally" benefits her in this very competitive climate. She attributes these skills to her social work training.

Ultimately, Susan doesn't see a significant difference between managing and supporting staff or volunteers and many of the direct service positions she has held. She believes that "it's all about helping people reach their best potential." Most of her management work involves helping staff or volunteers "to identify [systematic] obstacles that are in their way, or figuring out ways for them to become better advocates for themselves."

Who Is in Charge?

The most senior position in a political setting is typically the campaign manager, executive director, chief of staff, or another position with a similarly senior title.

In electoral campaign efforts, your campaign manager is the most important hire. The campaign manager should have a solid understanding of campaign finance and election laws at the geographic location and level of the campaign. Generally, an electoral campaign manager focuses on a single campaign, although in smaller races, this position may focus on an entire slate. For federal, state-wide, state legislative races, and larger cities, this position is generally a paid staff member, while for down-ballot races, the campaign manager may be a key volunteer.

An advocacy campaign may be led by an executive director, campaign director, campaign chair, or lead organizer. They could be focused on a single electoral or advocacy campaign, or they could be running these efforts as part of a larger job. This key hire could be working on a volunteer basis or as a paid staffer; as with electoral campaigns, the size of the campaign often determines whether this person is paid.

In the office of an elected official, this key hire is typically the chief of staff, which is typically a paid position. Elected officials in small localities may have no staff members, while smaller state legislatures may share one staff member among several elected officials. If the "staff" of the elected official is only one person, that person might be called a legislative aide or clerk.

Regardless of the setting or title, essential attributes in the key political hire are excellent people skills, ability to communicate with media, good time management, and an ability to see the big picture and think beyond day-to-day situations and crises. This key hire will frequently be the face of the campaign or elected official, and often functions when necessary as a **surrogate**, a proxy for the candidate or elected official. As with the treasurer, the reputation of your key hire and their relationships with others in the community are essential, and reflect on your campaign.

It is critical that this key hire be able to communicate with the candidate, elected official, or board of directors and provide them with honest critical feedback as needed (Shaw 2014)—and it is critical that this hire is someone that the decision-maker trusts. For most candidates, elected officials, or board members to be confident leaving significant decisions in the hands of the key hire, they need to trust this person's judgment and competency. In order to be able to give the candidate or elected official honest feedback, the campaign manager should be someone who has some distance, so it is not generally seen as best practice for this hire to be a family member, and **nepotism laws** may make it illegal for elected officials to hire relatives.

The role of campaign manager in an electoral campaign is especially challenging as it is the candidate's own name and personal reputation that are under review by the public. Hiring and supervising an electoral campaign manager can be complicated if there are conflicting opinions about whether the campaign manager or candidate has final say in decisions. Haynes and Mickelson (2010) argue that the candidate's time is best served by talking to undecided voters, and the campaign manager should make all significant campaign decisions, albeit with input from the candidate. A similar dynamic takes place with chiefs of staff. Clarity of who is responsible for decision-making of various types in an elected official's office is essential.

The Hiring Process

At times, these key hires are found through a formal search process. Often, however, hiring in political settings is done through networking and recommendations of others. Challenging questions are tied up in the issue of how to approach hiring both key hires and other political staff. It is widely acknowledged in the political world that hiring staff members through word of mouth is a preferable approach. This approach leads to interviewing and hiring staff who have shown themselves to be successful in similar settings and who have built a positive reputation. At the same time, it is exactly this type of process—hiring through word of mouth—that historically has prevented women, people of color, and even social workers from entering into political settings. We encourage you to consider ways to balance both of these factors: take references and reputations seriously, but also be mindful of seeking out yet-undiscovered talent.

However you choose to approach the hiring process for key hires, asking for contact information for several references is critical. Where feasible, we suggest a similar process for all senior hires, including campaign consultants, fundraisers, and schedulers, as well as district directors and legislative directors. For campaign staff, ask for references not just from campaigns where the potential staffer's side was successful, but also from campaigns where they were not successful. You may be familiar with hiring situations in which reference contact information is collected, but references are never contacted. This could be because the employer gathers information about the candidate from other connections not on the reference list, or because the employer chooses not to reach out to references. In a political setting, we strongly encourage you to contact references. You want to be fully aware of any concerns about your potential hire. Questions to references should include would the reference work with this person again? What was their level of trust in the potential hire? Reputation is one's livelihood in the political world. Comparing your impressions of potential key hires with those of people who have worked directly with them in the trenches can give you a good picture of whether they would be good fits for your office, campaign, and candidate.

Especially when hiring for key roles in an advocacy campaign, ask potential hires (and references) to discuss the presence and quality of the relationships the potential hire has built with decision-makers and stakeholders. What existing relationships does the person have with community members, members of your board of directors, donors, staff, and activists? It is certainly possible for a key hire to build relationships from scratch (you may well choose to hire a well-regarded and highly successful advocate from Maryland to lead your advocacy campaign in Wisconsin), but it is important to be fully aware of whether your potential hire already has relationships that she can draw on. If the potential hire does not have relationships with stakeholders in your area, is there evidence that he has been able to build them in past campaigns? Relationships with decision-makers or their gatekeepers are important, but relationships with community stakeholders are also very important to successful political efforts. If you are hiring someone to lead an advocacy campaign on behalf of a community, are you hiring someone who is a member of that community? If not, then why not? What will you do then to ensure that the community voice is heard?

Similarly, for each of these settings, it is important to ask potential hires to discuss their familiarity with the specific legal and/or political processes that shape the work that your office or campaign does. While this knowledge, too, can be built from scratch, you need to be aware that a hire who does not have this knowledge is starting with this deficit. In Texas, for example, it is common for advocacy campaigns and offices of elected officials at the state level to limit their paid staff hires to individuals who have interned or worked in a prior legislative session (a great incentive to gain this experience as a social work intern!), and who therefore both bring existing relationships and knowledge of the intricacies of the legislative process to their work. Some legislators may even prefer to hire staff that also have electoral campaign experience. This enables staff to understand the processes involved in both arenas, making them well equipped to consider both the policy and political ramifications of potential decisions.

> **FURTHER REFLECTION: Your Kitchen Cabinet and Campaign Manager**
> Put yourself in the position of a first-time candidate for a local office. Who would be in your kitchen cabinet? What are the most important attributes in your campaign manager?

Review of Key Terms and Concepts

Debriefing: provides a brief opportunity for the volunteer to report what happened, what went well, any problems, and anything that the person delegating to them needs to know about how the task went.

Direct voter contact: often called "canvassing," "ground game," or "field work," this outreach is used to reach voters individually. It leans heavily on volunteers for its success.

Door knocking: knocking on the doors of potential voters, also referred to as canvassing.

Duty of care: the responsibility for board members to participate actively in the work of the board and use their expertise to benefit the organization.

Duty of loyalty: the responsibility for board members to put the needs of the organization above the board member's own personal or professional interests.

Duty of obedience: the responsibility for board members to ensure that the board is working in accordance with its mission and in compliance with all relevant state and federal laws.

Kitchen cabinet: volunteer advisors who provide informal advice and counsel to a candidate or officeholder.

Lawn signs: signs posted in yards or in certain public locations to express support for a candidate or issue.

Lit drop: the process of leaving campaign literature by volunteers who don't talk with the voters directly (also called a "literature drop").

Mailing: a set of mail sent out as needed by the campaign.

"Neighbor to neighbor": campaigning in which the key feature is asking voters to reach out directly to other voters without much supervision from the campaign.

Nonprofit board members: the group of volunteers who are legally responsible for the governance of a nonprofit organization.

On-boarding: the process of bringing a new volunteer or employee into an organization and training them on any systems or processes needed for their work.

Phone banking: making phone calls for a campaign at a set time with a group of other people.

Treasurer: the person legally responsible for ensuring that legal and financial rules are honored by the campaign.

Volunteer development: recognizing the assets that volunteers bring to their work, and encouraging them to build upon those assets in new ways to support a campaign.

Resources

Books:

Bobo, K. A., Kendall, J., & Max, S. (2010). *Organizing for social change: Midwest Academy manual for activists*. Santa Ana: CA The Forum Press.

Kettner, P.M. (2013). *Excellence in human service organization management*. (2nd ed.).Upper Saddle River, NJ: Pearson Education, Inc.

Latting, J., & Ramsey, V. J. (2009). *Reframing change: How to deal with workplace dynamics, influence others, and bring people together to initiate positive change*. Santa Barbara, CA: ABC-CLIO, LLC

Shaw, C. (2014). *The campaign manager: Running and winning local elections*. Boulder, CO: Westview Press.

Articles:

Hardina, D. (2005). Ten characteristics of empowerment-oriented social service   organizations. *Administration in Social Work, 29*(3), 23–42.

Levinson, N. (2007, Nov). Managing your volunteers: 19 ways to work wonders. *Nonprofit World, 25*, 24–25. Retrieved from http://search.proquest.com.libproxy.adelphi.edu:2048/do cview/22 1333757?accountid=8204

Journal:

Human Service Organizations: Leadership, Management and Governance Journal (formerly called *Administration in Social Work*): https://socialworkmanager.org/journal/

Websites:

Austin Legislative Internship Program Blog: https://gcswlegislativeinterns.wordpress.com/
Becoming an Effective Manager:
http://ctb.ku.edu/en/table-of-contents/leadership/effective-manager
Center for Nonprofit Leadership at Adelphi University: http://nonprofit.adelphi.edu/
Developing a Strategic Plan and Organizational Structure: http://ctb.ku.edu/en/developing-strategic
-plan-and-organizational-structure
Example of state campaign finance training from Colorado:
https://www.sos.state.co.us/pubs/elections/CampaignFinance/CPFtraining.html
National Conference of State Legislatures: http://www.ncsl.org/
National Council of Nonprofits.
    Main website: https://www.councilofnonprofits.org/
Resources for employees: https://www.councilofnonprofits.org/tools-resources-tags/employment
Resources for management: https://www.councilofnonprofits.org/tools-resources-tags/management
"Neighbor to Neighbor" campaigning from the Obama Campaign: https://my.barackobama.com/
    page/content/n2nhostguide
Network for Social Work Management: https://socialworkmanager.org/resources/downloadable-
    documents/ or go to https://socialworkmanager.org and in the menu under "Resources" click
    "Download Documents."

References

Blair House. (2014). *President Andrew Jackson and the "Kitchen Cabinet" (1829–1831)*. Retrieved from http://www.blairhouse.org/history/historical-events/jackson-and-the-kitchen-cabinet
BoardSource. (2011). *The nonprofit board answer book: A practical guide for board members and chief executives*. San Francisco, CA: Wiley.
Charlton, J. I. (2000). *Nothing about us without us: Disability oppression and empowerment*. Oakland, CA: University of California Press.
Council on Social Work Education. (2015). *Educational Policy and Accreditation Standards*. Retrieved from https://www.cswe.org/getattachment/Accreditation/Accreditation-Process/2015-EPAS/2015EPAS_Web_FINAL.pdf.aspx
Enos, R. D., & Hersh, E. D. (2015). Party activists as campaign advertisers: The ground campaign as a principal-agent problem. *The American Political Science Review, 109*(2), 252–278.
Hardina, D. (2005). Ten characteristics of empowerment-oriented social service organizations. *Administration in Social Work, 29*(3), 23–42.
Haynes, K. S., & Mickelson, J. S. (2010). *Affecting change: Social workers in the political arena*. Boston, MA: Allyn & Bacon.
Hiland, A. (2014, August 14). Asked: Rules for placing, removing campaign signs? *The Arizona Republic*. Retrieved from http://www.azcentral.com/story/news/local/asked-answered/2014/08/14/asked-answered-campaign-sign-rules/13201919/
Hopkins, K., Meyer, M., Shera, W., & Peters, S. C. (2014). Leadership challenges facing non-profit human service organizations in a post-recession era. *Human Service Organizations: Management, Leadership & Governance, 38*(5), 419–422.

Kenny, S., McNevin, A., & Hogan, L. (2008). Voluntary activity and local government: Managing volunteers or facilitating active citizenship? *Social Alternatives, 27*(2), 45–49.

Kettner, P. M. (2013). *Excellence in human service organization management* (2nd ed.). Upper Saddle River, NJ: Pearson Education.

Knox County Tennessee. (n.d.). *Signage code*. Retrieved from https://www.knoxcounty.org/election/signage_code.php

McBeath, B. (2016). Re-envisioning macro social work practice. *Families in Society: The Journal of Contemporary Social Services, 97*, 5–14.

Minton, P. I., & Young Entrepreneur Council. (2013, April 19). Legal requirements for unpaid internship programs. *Forbes.com*. Retrieved from https://www.forbes.com/sites/theyec/2013/04/19/6-legal-requirements-for-unpaid-internship-programs/

Moon, J. Y., & Sproull, L. S. (2008). The role of feedback in managing the internet-based volunteer work force. *Information Systems Research, 19*(4), 494–515. 517–518.

NASW New York City Chapter. (2013). *18 basic points about licensing in New York State*. Retrieved from http://www.naswnyc.org/?155

National Council of Nonprofits. (n.d.). *Interns: Employee or volunteer*. Retrieved from https://www.councilofnonprofits.org/tools-resources/interns-employee-or-volunteer

Pritzker, S., & Lane, S. R. (2014). Field Note—Integrating policy and political content in BSW and MSW field placements. *Journal of Social Work Education, 50*(4), 730–739. https://doi.org/10.1080/10437797.2014.947905.

Pritzker, S., & Barros Lane, L. (in press). Supporting field-based education in political settings. *Journal of Social Work Education*.

Shalby, C. (2017, June 14). How fake news starts: Trump supporters tie Bernie Sanders to Alexandria shooting using a fake quote. *Los Angeles Times*. Retrieved from http://www.latimes.com/politics/washington/la-na-essential-washington-updates-trump-supporter-links-congressional-1497472393-htmlstory.html

Shaw, C. (2014). *The campaign manager: Running and winning local elections*. Boulder, CO: Westview Press.

Takagi, G. (2006, May 14) *Duty of care*. Retrieved from www.nonprofitlawblog.com/duty_of_care

U.S. Department of Labor Wage and Hour Division. (2010). *Internship programs under the fair labor standards act (Fact Sheet #71)*. Retrieved from https://www.dol.gov/whd/regs/compliance/whdfs71.pdf

Watkins, E., Landers, E., & Zeleny, J. (2017, June 14). Sanders condemns shooter who 'apparently' volunteered on campaign. *CNN.com*. Retrieved from http://www.cnn.com/2017/06/14/politics/bernie-sanders-baseball-shooting/index.html

Zero to Three. (2017). *How to write a letter to the editor and an opinion editorial*. Retrieved from https://www.zerotothree.org/resources/480-how-to-write-a-letter-to-the-editor-and-an-opinion-editorial

Understanding and Raising Resources

11

Table of Contents

© Springer International Publishing AG 2018
S.R. Lane, S. Pritzker, *Political Social Work*,
https://doi.org/10.1007/978-3-319-68588-5_11

Section 1: Overview

The ability to understand, acquire, and manage financial resources is essential for electoral campaigns, advocacy efforts in nonprofit organizations, and work in the offices of elected officials or public agencies. This chapter and Chap. 12 serve as a pair to provide you the necessary information to begin raising and managing financial resources in political settings. Effective political strategies require political social workers to think carefully and strategically about money. As Mutch (2016) describes in regard to electoral campaigns:

> Money is necessary because campaigns are expensive, but money alone rarely wins elections. Think of running for elective office as like playing blackjack in Las Vegas. Having a lot of money is no guarantee that you will win, but without money you cannot even get into the game (p. 5).

To help you "get into the game," this chapter provides an overview of the rules related to fundraising in electoral campaigns and nonprofit organizations and to revenue in public agencies. We focus on key rules that guide practice in each of these settings, including campaign finance laws and Internal Revenue Service rules that govern raising money in nonprofit organizations. We also present resources that can guide you in researching the revenue rules in your own political context. However, when dealing with political finances, we encourage readers to *always consult experts who can help you be up to date in understanding and following all relevant laws.*

Developing Social Work Competency
The Council on Social Work Education establishes educational standards for all social work programs in the USA. Content in this chapter supports building competency in the following areas that are considered core to the practice of social work:
COMPETENCY 5: Engage in Policy Practice
COMPETENCY 6: Engage with Individuals, Families, Groups, Organizations, and Communities
COMPETENCY 7: Assess Individuals, Families, Groups, Organizations, and Communities

Domains of Political Social Work	
1. Engaging individuals and communities in political processes	
2. Influencing policy agendas and decision-making	◀
3. Holding professional and political positions	◀
4. Engaging with electoral campaigns	◀
5. Seeking and holding elected office	◀

Section 2: Campaign Finance History and Practice

Campaign finance refers specifically to the ways in which money is raised and spent in order to fund electoral campaigns (Mutch 2016). **Campaign finance laws** refer to the federal, state, and sometimes municipal laws, regulations, and legal decisions that define the parameters of campaign finance. These laws cover both raising and spending money. In this chapter, we discuss how these laws guide electoral fundraising. In Chap. 12, we discuss how these laws guide spending in and on behalf of electoral campaigns. These chapters will not make you an expert on campaign finance, but we hope that they will provide a starting point for your political social work practice. We highly recommend Robert Mutch's (2016) book *Campaign finance: What everyone needs to know*, as well as training resources offered in your state (discussed below) to help you learn more.

Federal electoral campaigns follow federal campaign finance laws and report their fundraising and spending to federal oversight. Candidates at the state level (either state-wide or state legislative races) must follow their state's laws and report to their state oversight agencies. Municipal candidates (county, city, town, etc.) may have requirements from the state level, the municipal level, or both to follow. The range of municipal options throughout the country is as varied as the municipalities that exist (Bjerg 2013), so this chapter focuses on the state and federal rules. However, we encourage you to reach out to your state and municipal election officials to be sure that you clearly understand and are in compliance with all relevant rules. In addition, you may wish to check out the Sunlight Foundation's resources on best practices in municipal campaign finance (see Resources).

Campaign Finance History

US campaign finance has had a long and tumultuous history. In Table 11.1, we outline a chronology of key federal campaign legislation (Mutch 2016). Examination of this history suggests that there is general agreement that bribing voters and corruption are bad. At the same time, there are very complicated opinions about the best ways to ensure that corruption is not taking place in electoral campaigns and the role of political spending in free speech.

Recent Developments in Campaign Finance: Citizens United

If you spend much time in the political world or reading coverage of political news, you may have heard people talking about *Citizens United v Federal Election Commission*, a 2010 Supreme Court ruling that created seismic changes in US campaign finance law (Citizens United v. Federal Election Commission n.d.). This lawsuit was a challenge to the McCain-Feingold Act/Bipartisan Campaign Reform Act's restrictions on certain "electioneering activities." McCain-Feingold prevented corporations and labor unions from using their general treasuries to fund election communications, meaning that money for these activities had to be specifically raised and set aside for elections. It also required public identification or **disclaimers**, of those who fund election communications. A "Stand by your Ad" provision required ads to end with a statement about whether the message had been authorized by the supported candidate. A video link to some examples from 2008 is provided in the Resources section.

Table 11.1 Key legislation in federal campaign finance history (Mutch 2016)

Year	Law	Description
1907	Tillman Act/Public Law 59–36	First federal campaign finance law. Prohibited corporations from contributing to elections.
1910/ 1911	Public Law 61–274 Public Law 62–32	Required campaigns to disclose from whom they got money and how they spent it. Changes in 1911 required disclosure before Election Day, expanded coverage to include primary and general elections, limited spending on congressional campaigns.
1918	Public Law 65–222	Prohibited bribing voters.
1925	Federal Corrupt Practices Act/Public Law 65–506	Further strengthened campaign disclosure laws by increasing non-election-year reporting requirements. Removed regulation of primary election spending disclosure
1939/ 1940	**Hatch Act**/Public Law 76–252 Hatch Act II/Public Law 76–753	Prohibited federal government employees from engaging in election campaigns, even if they are not "on duty." In 1940, expanded to include people who had state jobs funded at least partly from government funds. Also included a $5000 contribution limit and $3 million spending limit to federal campaigns.
1943	Smith–Connally Act/ Public Law 78–89/War Labor Disputes Act	Prevented labor unions from making political contributions. The first PAC was created by the Congress of Industrial Organizations (CIO) in response to this act.
1947	Taft-Hartley Act/Public Law 80–101/ Amendment to the National Labor Relations Act	Permanently banned union political contributions and political spending by unions and corporations. Several cases related to this law were subsequently filed by labor unions and their members, at least four of which made it all the way to the Supreme Court
1966	**Presidential Election Campaign Fund Act** of 1966/Public Law 89–809	This first presidential public funding law authorized placement of a checkoff box on the federal income tax return to create a fund to finance presidential campaigns. After it passed, opposition by both parties kept it from being implemented.
1971	**Federal Election Campaign Act** (FECA) of 1971/Public Law 92–225	Major update to campaign finance laws. Repealed contribution and overall spending limits while limiting the amount of money that could be spent on media. Legalized labor PACs. Specified oversight responsibility for presidential and congressional election compliance.
1971	Revenue Act of 1971/ Public Law 92–178	Provided tax incentives to those who made small campaign contributions. Implemented the **Presidential Election Campaign Fund**, the income tax checkoff authorized in 1966; first appeared on tax returns in 1973.

(continued)

Table 11.1 (continued)

Year	Law	Description
1974	Federal Election Campaign Act Amendments of 1974/ Public Law 93–443	Amendments in aftermath of the Watergate scandal imposed stricter restrictions on campaign contributions and campaign spending and firmly established the presidential public funding program. Created the **Federal Election Commission** (FEC) to enforce campaign compliance and oversee public election funding. In subsequent legal challenges, public funding and the FEC remained, but the Supreme Court struck down limits on campaign spending and regulation of political ads, arguing that political spending should have the same First Amendment protection as political speech.
1976	Federal Election Campaign Act Amendments of 1976/ Public Law 94–283	To comply with the Supreme Court rulings, repealed regulations on issue ads, campaign contribution limits (except when presidential candidates use public funding), added contribution limits for political parties and PACs, limited PAC contributions to parties, and revised rules about PACs.
1979	Federal Election Campaign Act Amendments of 1979/ Public Law 96–187	Decreased the restrictiveness of some disclosure regulations. Exempted some get-out-the-vote activities from the Act's limits
1986	Tax Reform Act of 1986/Public Law 99–514	Repealed a tax credit for individuals who contributed to political campaigns.
2002	**McCain-Feingold Act/ Bipartisan Campaign Reform Act of 2002** (BCRA)/Public Law 107–155	Prohibited national candidates and parties from raising and spending money on nonfederal elections (such as state or municipal elections). Also limited the ability of state and local parties to use their money to pay for party activities. Introduced new rules about **electioneering communications**: Any ad mentioning a federal candidate within 30 days of a primary or 60 days of a general election must be paid for with money regulated by the FEC, with the ad spending reported. Raised the individual contribution limit to $2000, allowing it to rise with inflation). Raised the amount that individuals and parties can give to congressional candidates who are **self-funded** (pay for their campaign with their own money). Several legal challenges have resulted in this law's weakening, including through the *Citizens United* decision discussed below.
2014	Gabriella Miller Kids First Research Act/ Public Law 113–94	Redirected money from the Presidential Election Campaign Fund to a pediatric research fund.
2016	Consolidated and Further Continuing Appropriations Act of 2015/Public Law 113–59	Increased by 800% (not a typo) the limits on donations to political parties.

Citizens United is a type of nonprofit called a 501(c)(4) social welfare organization that challenged this law. Citizens United (n.d.) describes its mission as:

> an organization dedicated to restoring our government to citizens' control. Through a combination of education, advocacy, and grass roots organization, Citizens United seeks to reassert the traditional American values of limited government, freedom of enterprise, strong families, and national sovereignty and security. Citizens United's goal is to restore the founding fathers' vision of a free nation, guided by the honesty, common sense, and good will of its citizens.

Citizens United asked to be exempted from the provisions of McCain-Feingold for producing and allowing free downloads of *Hillary: The Movie*. This movie "expressed opinions about whether Senator Hillary Rodham Clinton would make a good president" (Citizens United v. Federal Election Commission n.d.). (Spoiler alert: they did not think she would make a good president.) A link to the trailer of this highly controversial movie is listed in the Resources section at the end of this chapter. A District Court ruled against Citizens United's argument. Citizens United then appealed this ruling to the Supreme Court. The Supreme Court denied Citizens United's eligibility for an exemption. However, the Court took the opportunity to instead ask Citizens United to submit arguments as to the constitutionality of the relevant provisions of the law (Mutch 2016).

Ultimately, in a final 5–4 decision authored by Justice Anthony M. Kennedy, the Supreme Court ruled that the First Amendment protects independent political communications regarding candidate elections. Therefore, corporate funding of these communications could not be limited. Essentially, the Court upheld McCain-Feingold's disclosure requirements while ruling that political contributions are protected political speech. As a result of this decision and related decisions in *Speechnow.org v. FEC* a few months later, the Sunlight Foundation and other watchdog organizations expect that campaign spending will continue to grow. Much of these monies are expected to go to organizations that don't have to disclose the names of their donors (Watson 2016).

FURTHER REFLECTION: Political Donations and Free Speech

As the history above outlines, there are strong disagreements in the USA surrounding campaign finance. In 1975, Supreme Court Justice Potter Stewart summarized one side of this argument as "money is speech and speech is money," essentially that political donations are a form of constitutionally protected speech.

In his 2010 *Citizens United* dissent, Supreme Court Justice Paul Stevens stated an opposing argument: "The conceit that corporations must be treated identically to natural persons in the political sphere is not only inaccurate but also inadequate to justify the Court's disposition of this case." He argues that corporations do not have the same free speech constitutional protections as individuals.

Reflecting on these arguments, do you believe that political contributions from corporations should be treated as a form of constitutionally protected political speech? Why or why not?

Current Federal Campaign Finance Practices

In addition to specifying how money can be given and spent, campaign finance laws specify whether and how donations must be publicly disclosed. **Disclosure** refers to rules about which donation details must be shared, e.g., regarding who gave how much money and to whom. While the laws, court decisions, and subsequent regulations discussed above address these issues, much of how campaign finance is currently handled also reflects the evolution of practices over time. This combination of federal laws and practices is quite complex.

While federal campaign finance law specifies how these processes take place, it is campaign finance practice that has defined different "types" of political donations. Those who work in campaign finance currently divide donations to federal candidate campaigns or to organizations trying to affect federal campaigns into three different "types" depending on where the money came from and how it was disclosed (Mutch 2016). The most common terminology used refers to donations that are hard money, soft money, and dark money.

- **Hard money** is "difficult to raise and easy to spend" (Marcus 1997, n.p.). It refers to campaign contributions donated by individuals within the limits set by federal laws such as FECA. These contributions can be given to either a party or candidate and can be spent on almost anything related to a campaign. These donations must be disclosed.
- **Soft money** is the opposite: easy to raise, but difficult to spend. It includes contributions from corporations or from individuals who donate outside the FECA maximum for candidates. Candidates cannot directly raise soft money. When political parties raise soft money, it is only supposed to be used for general election-related activities like getting out the vote, or administrative expenses, not to support a particular candidate. These donations must be disclosed.
- **Dark money** refers to contributions that are not required by law to be disclosed, often because they were given to 501(c)(4) organizations that are not obligated to report their donors (Yeager 2015). Those who oppose campaign finance disclosure laws call this "anonymous speech" (Mutch 2016).

At the federal level, the Federal Election Commission (FEC) oversees disclosure. To meet disclosure requirements, over 100,000 reports are filed with the FEC from federal candidate campaigns, parties, and nonprofit organizations each election cycle, including the name, address, occupation, and employer of everyone who gives more than $200, and everything the campaign spends that exceeds $200 (Mutch 2016). The FEC is required to make the information public within 48 hours of the time it is received from the campaign (see Resources for a link to this information).

Restrictions on the size and source of campaign contributions (called **receipts** by the FEC) as well as on spending campaign funds depend on the type of donor and the type of organization that receives the donation. For example, as of 2017, the maximum an individual can donate per *federal* candidate per election is $2700. An individual also can donate up to $5000 a year to a federal PAC, $10,000 per year combined to FEC-specified state, district, and local party committees, $33,900 per year to a national party committee, and up to $101,700 to special national party accounts. Special party accounts must be specifically for any of the following: a headquarters building, a national party convention, and/or for election recounts or other legal procedures. If a national party has an account for each of these three special purposes, an individual can donate up to a maximum of $339,000 to that party in a year (Federal Election Commission n.d.).

State Campaign Finance Laws

Each state has its own sets of requirements regarding raising, spending, and reporting on political money. The requirements states set apply to state campaigns and typically to municipal campaigns. State requirements about how much individuals can contribute to *state* and *local* candidates and parties are widely divergent. For example, in Alaska, an individual can contribute no more than $500 to a gubernatorial campaign per year, while in Texas, individual contributions to a candidate for governor are unlimited (National Conference of State Legislators n.d.).

Including Texas, 12 states have no individual contribution limits to state and municipal candidates (National Conference of State Legislators n.d.). The majority of states allow corporations to donate to candidates, with no limits on corporate funding in four states (Missouri, Oregon, Utah, and Virginia). Nine states and some municipalities such as New York City offer limited public subsidies to candidates who meet specific rules, typically referred to as **public financing**. Arizona, Connecticut, Maine, and New Mexico offer "Clean Elections" funding. This refers to full public funding for candidates who are running for governor, lieutenant governor, and the state legislature if they raise a certain amount of funding in small donations from individuals within their districts and agree not to spend more than a state-specified amount (Miller 2014). Fourteen states require that large donations (typically more than $500) be reported within 48 hours.

Disclosure laws often require candidates to collect information about a donor, such as their occupation, employer, and the employer's location, in order to accept the money. If you are a candidate or raising funds for a candidate, it is critical that you learn these laws for your specific state. Figure 11.1 shows an example of a donation page, used by social worker Diego Hernandez (n.d.) in his successful 2016 race for State Representative in Oregon. You can see in the bottom section the information required to be collected from donors by Oregon law.

A **coordinated campaign** generally takes place when a political party works together with campaigns to get candidates elected (Garrett and Whitaker 2016). Typically, the party and the campaigns work together to do early identification of voters, messaging, or get out the vote for candidates (Federal Election Commission 2015). For example, a state political party might work to get out the vote for all candidates it endorses. If you are running any kind of federal-state coordinated campaign, federal candidates will need to be aware of both federal and state rules and

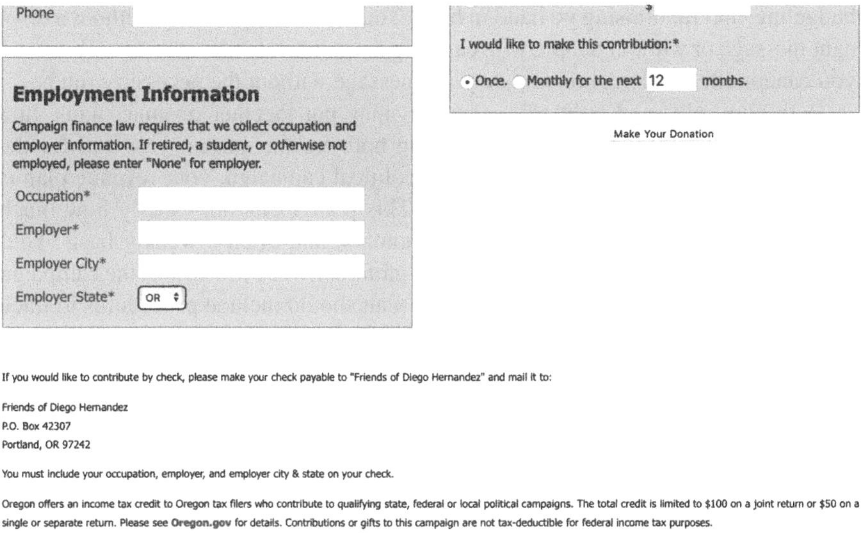

Phone

Employment Information

Campaign finance law requires that we collect occupation and employer information. If retired, a student, or otherwise not employed, please enter "None" for employer.

Occupation*

Employer*

Employer City*

Employer State* OR ▾

I would like to make this contribution:*

• Once. ◯ Monthly for the next 12 months.

Make Your Donation

If you would like to contribute by check, please make your check payable to "Friends of Diego Hernandez" and mail it to:

Friends of Diego Hernandez
P.O. Box 42307
Portland, OR 97242

You must include your occupation, employer, and employer city & state on your check.

Oregon offers an income tax credit to Oregon tax filers who contribute to qualifying state, federal or local political campaigns. The total credit is limited to $100 on a joint return or $50 on a single or separate return. Please see **Oregon.gov** for details. Contributions or gifts to this campaign are not tax-deductible for federal income tax purposes.

Fig. 11.1 Diego Hernandez campaign website donation page (http://www.diego4oregon.com)

their limitations. In general, a disbursement of funds that is coordinated with a candidate's campaign counts as a contribution to that campaign (Macleod-Ball 2014). As with contribution limits, state rules on coordinated campaigns vary significantly, impacting how campaigns coordinate in your state. The resource section of this chapter includes links to information about coordinated campaigns, and to the National Conference of State Legislatures (NCSL) and Follow the Money, both of whom track issues related to campaign finance at the state level.

Section 3: Planning to Raise Money

With this primer on campaign finance law, we now explore important considerations surrounding raising funds in political settings and in macro settings where political social work practice may take place. We specifically explore factors relevant in political campaigns, in nonprofits that may engage in advocacy, lobbying, or voter engagement work, and in public agencies where policy is made. These factors include the type of organization, the expected sources and amounts of revenue, the timeline within which revenue is likely to be raised, and the methods available to raise the specified amounts of money from those sources. The authors gratefully acknowledge Kate Coyne-McCoy for many of the fundraising insights discussed in this chapter.

Expected **revenues**, or income available to your organization, come from a variety of sources depending on the type of organization in question. Plans to raise donations or contributions should be connected to your strategic plan and to your budget. While we do not discuss budgeting until the next chapter, planning, budgeting, and fundraising go hand in hand. You cannot raise money without a resonant message or without people who can help communicate that message. However, you cannot effectively communicate your message without the necessary funds.

Both nonprofits and political campaigns may put together revenue plans. In a nonprofit, such plans may involve planning both for the current year and for the long-term health of the organization. In a political campaign, your revenue plan is commonly referred to as a **finance plan**. This plan spells out exactly how much money you seek to raise on a quarterly, monthly, and often a weekly basis. Your fundraising goals may differ from month to month or week to week as the campaign goes through different stages. Your finance plan should include procedures to track your revenues at each of these time periods, so that you know when you are behind, meeting, or exceeding your goals.

Sources and Amounts of Revenue

Electoral Campaigns

Candidate campaigns are funded primarily through individual donations. These typically come in two forms: **small-dollar donations**, sometimes as little as $3 or $5, and **major donor donations**. As allowed by federal and state laws, campaigns may receive in-kind donations and additional support from political parties. Other campaign types may have access to other sources of funding. For example, political parties are permitted to receive corporate donations.

Individual donations given in support of the two main 2016 presidential candidates amounted to nearly $2.4 billion (Narayanswamy et al. 2016). Of those donations, however, less than half were given directly to the candidate's campaigns. The majority of funds were given to organizations that were not technically affiliated with either candidate, but were instead organized to campaign on behalf of one or the other candidate. Of the money raised in support of Hillary Clinton, 45% was given directly to her campaign, 42% was given to Democratic Party committees, and 15% was given to Super PACs. Of the money raised in support of Donald Trump, 35% was given directly to his campaign, 57% was given to Republican Party committees, and 8% was given to Super PACs.

Keep in mind that these amounts discussed above only include hard and soft money, as dark money does not have to be disclosed. These amounts also do not include the $658 million raised by other Democratic presidential candidates and their supporters or the $740 million raised by other Republican presidential candidates and their supporters (Narayanswamy et al. 2016). These numbers highlight the huge amount of money spent on presidential politics. They also illustrate the complicated web of organizations involved in political fundraising and why concerns are consistently raised about the influence of money in politics.

In discussing electoral campaign fundraising, it is important to note that fundraising is not always directly linked with an election victory. It seems logical that the candidate with the most money is most likely to win the election. While this is true in many cases, it does not always explain the election outcome. Perhaps a candidate's win was not due to having more money, but rather, the candidate raised more money because people like to back the candidate they perceive as a winner. Also, the candidate who raises the most money does not always win. In the 2016 US presidential election, for example, Hillary Clinton lost, despite her campaign, party committees, and PACs outraising those of Donald Trump by more than $442 million (Narayanswamy et al. 2016).

Nonprofit Agencies

Political social work practice often takes place in **nonprofit organizations**, especially those that engage in advocacy, lobbying, and/or voter engagement. While we have discussed nonprofit organizations throughout this book, in this context, it is necessary to underscore the relationship between nonprofit organizations and their revenues. Nonprofits can use their revenues only to maintain the organization and to provide services. While nonprofits can bring in a "**profit**" by raising more money than they spend in a given year, this profit cannot be given to staff or board members. Instead, it must be invested in the organization's future. While we commonly think of some nonprofit organizations as providing social welfare services, in the political world, the term "social welfare organization" has a specific meaning, referring to a specific type of nonprofit, often formed to promote a specific ideological agenda.

The federal Internal Revenue Service and associated federal laws and regulations guide how nonprofits can raise and spend money and the political activities that they are permitted to carry out. Federal law identifies different types of nonprofits, each with different rules around how they manage and spend money. These rules are outlined in detail by type of nonprofit in Chap. 12.

Table 11.2 shows the variety of sources that typically fund US nonprofits (McKeever 2015). These sources are discussed in detail through the rest of this section. The largest overall source of nonprofit revenues comes from fees for services and goods that private sources pay. This is sometimes referred to as **earned income**. Most of this money comes into private universities and nonprofit hospitals, with fees for services and goods including such items as tuition payments, ticket sales, and hospital patient payments (not including Medicaid and Medicare). Fees for services and goods also may include **membership fees** (if your membership gets you admission to a museum, for example) or membership contributions (Tschirhart and

Table 11.2 Nonprofit revenue by source (McKeever 2015)

Source	Percent of revenue for all reporting charities (%)
Fees for services and goods (private sources)	47.5
Fees for services and goods (government contracts/Medicaid/Medicare)	24.5
Private contributions	13.3
Government grants	8
Investment income	4.7
Other income	1.9

Bielefeld 2012). Membership fees are distinct from "membership drives" like the kind you might hear about on public radio. Fees are essentially a price of admission, whereas contributions are not required to access a service. Fees for services and goods from government are those moneys that come from government contracts, Medicaid, and Medicare (McKeever 2015). Generally, to receive these fees, a nonprofit provides services that have been purchased by the government using a **government contract**. A government contract is a transaction agreement developed between the nonprofit and a government (Tschirhart and Bielefeld 2012).

Private contributions to nonprofits are often referred to as **philanthropy**. As defined by Robert Payton, philanthropy is "voluntary action for the public good" and is a subset of **charity**, gifts to those in need (Tschirhart and Bielefeld 2012; Lenkowsky 2011). These donations may come from individuals, organizations, or other nonprofits. **Foundations**, donor organizations that are set up to provide funding to other nonprofits, are one source of philanthropy. Of the private contributions made to nonprofits in 2016, 72% (almost $282 billion) was given by individuals, 15% ($59 billion) from foundations, and 5% ($18.5 billion) from corporations (Giving USA Foundation 2017). An additional 8% ($30 billion) came from bequests (McKeever 2015).

These philanthropic private contributions may be monetary or **in-kind**, referring to donations of a product or service rather than money. They may be given for a specific purpose, for example to a specific program or scholarship, or as **unrestricted** funds, meaning they can be used for anything the organization or campaign chooses. They may be given immediately or as a **pledge**, a promise of a future gift. They may be **solicited** through a specific appeal or request or **unsolicited**, given of the giver's own volition, without a specific ask. Contributions may be publically recognized or given anonymously, to the extent allowed by law (Tschirhart and Bielefeld 2012).

As with electoral campaigns, individual donations come as small-dollar donations and as major donor donations. The size of the nonprofit and its fundraising campaign typically determines what is considered a small-dollar amount or a major donor amount. For a grassroots nonprofit, anything over $100 might be considered a major donor, while a large nonprofit like a university might consider major donors as those whose giving is over $100,000. Individual donations are an important area of nonprofit fundraising. We provide guidance on making an ask below, but recommend the Tschirhart and Bielefeld (2012) book listed in the resource section if you are interested in learning more.

Revenue to nonprofits can also come from **government grants**, financial assistance to a grantee that must generally be used for a public purpose. While both grants and contracts are often competitive, government grants are significantly different from the government contracts discussed above. Generally, contracts require more reporting, are less flexible, and are governed by more regulations, with financial consequences if the goals of the contract are not met (University of Pittsburgh Office of Research 2017).

For small nonprofits, **investment income** may not be a significant source of income, but it can be substantial for many larger nonprofits. Investment income is

Table 11.3 Federal government revenue in 2015 (Center on Budget and Policy Priorities 2016)

Tax	Percent of total revenue in 2015 (%)	Progressive or regressive
Individual income tax	47	Progressive
Payroll tax	33	Regressive
Corporate income taxes	11	n/a
Excise, estate, and other taxes	9	Generally regressive

an optional revenue source for organizations that are able to set aside a significant amount of money for an **endowment**, a permanent fund that is invested. Income from that investment is then returned to the organization to be used to further the organization's goals. For example, Yale University's current endowment is $25.4 billion (Yale Investments Office 2016). Income from this endowment supports 34% of the university's operating expenses. Generally, nonprofits try to spend no more than 5% of their endowment each year (Tschirhart and Bielefeld 2012).

Public Agencies

Unlike political campaigns and nonprofits, governments do not rely heavily on voluntary individual donations. The federal government and therefore its agencies and programs are funded primarily by income, payroll, corporate, and other taxes. These taxes can be considered either progressive or regressive. A **progressive tax** is one in which higher income households pay a larger share of their income in tax than lower income households. A **regressive tax** is one in which lower income households pay a higher percentage of their income toward the tax than higher income households.

The largest source of revenue for the federal government in 2015 was income taxes paid by individuals, approximately 47% of total federal revenue that year (Center on Budget and Policy Priorities 2016), as shown in Table 11.3. Payroll taxes automatically come out of almost all workers' checks, with a share also paid by employers. These taxes, 33% of revenue, pay for Social Security and Medicare Hospital Insurance (FICA). (Unemployment insurance, a state-operated program, also comes out of payroll taxes.) The maximum amount of wages subject to the 6.2% Social Security tax is $127,200 as of 2017; any wages above that are not taxed (Schreiber 2016). For FICA, 1.45% is charged on all income, with no limit. Corporate income taxes made up 11% of federal revenue. Excise, estate, and other taxes make up the remaining 9% of federal revenue. **Excise taxes** are taxes for a specific good such as fuel, alcohol, or tobacco. **Estate taxes** are tax assets above a certain threshold ($5.49 million in 2016) owned by an individual upon their death (Center on Budget and Policy Priorities 2016; Internal Revenue Service 2016).

Taxes are the primary funding source for state government agencies as well, with revenue coming from property, sales, income, corporate, motor vehicle, and/or other taxes (U.S. Census Bureau n.d.; Malm and Kant 2013), as shown in Table 11.4. While property taxes comprise a small percentage of state tax revenues overall, there is a lot of variation among states in terms of property taxes. Fourteen states do not collect any state-level property tax, while property taxes comprise 34% of state

Table 11.4 Taxes collected by state governments, 2016 (U.S. Census Bureau n.d.; Malm and Kant 2013)

Category	Total amount collected	Percentage of overall taxes collected (%)
Sales/gross receipt taxes	$442,909,995	47.6
Income taxes	$392,286,910	42.2
License taxes	$ 52,164,396	5.6
Property taxes	$ 18,364,298	2.0
Other taxes	$ 24,538,146	2.6
Total	$930,263,745	100

tax revenue in Vermont (Tax Policy Center 2016a; U.S. Census Bureau n.d.). Local governments raise money from some of these same sources, especially property and sales taxes (Tax Policy Center 2016b, see Resources for more information about municipal revenue). In fact, property taxes comprise almost half (47%) of local government revenue and are particularly important for school districts (Tax Policy Center 2016a; U.S. Census Bureau n.d.). The connection between property taxes and schooling in the USA has been linked with issues of education inequality, providing a compelling example of how the process of funding government can relate to social justice outcomes (Ostrander 2015).

Taxes are not the only source of state revenue. In Connecticut, for example, while 84% of revenue comes from taxes, revenue also comes from federal grants, licenses, permits, fees, revenue from casinos run by the Mashantucket Pequot tribe, rents paid to the state, investment income, and sales of commodities and services (Connecticut Office of the State Comptroller 2016). State budgets also may include revenues from sources such as lottery tickets, services provided to residents, unclaimed property, or government-owned resources (for example, the Alaska Permanent Fund). State and local agency budgets also may include money transferred from the federal government through grants designated for specific purposes, such as education or transportation. For example, in 2018, states are expected to spend approximately $92 billion on Medicaid expansion, 90% of which is in transfers from federal funds (National Association of State Budget Officers 2017).

Revenue Timelines

In planning your organization's work, realistically estimate how much time it will take to raise funds from different sources. This will help you make decisions about what sources of revenue to seek. Consider the turnaround time between when you request money, when the donor pledges it (whether an individual donor, foundation, or grant), and when it will come into your bank account. When considering tax revenue, some types of taxes are paid annually, while some are paid twice per year or quarterly. These considerations are relevant for multiple reasons. First, they help you determine what funds will truly be available for the activities your organization intends to carry out. Second, they help you determine how to prioritize approaching various revenue sources so that you can raise money at the times you need.

There are often benefits to raising funds quickly in political social work practice. In electoral campaigns, raising money quickly is a way to prove your candidate's **viability**, meaning it is one sign that your campaign is capable of success. An early show of fundraising ability might convince another candidate to stay out of the race, because they worry they cannot keep up with you. It also might convince those who have the power to help you get on the ballot that you are committed to the campaign and have a good base of support. Raising early money also can help you access early media attention, attract experienced campaign staff, and help voters think of you first before other candidates. The classic example of this strategy is EMILY's List, one of the biggest PACs in the country. EMILY stands for Early Money is Like Yeast. The name is intended to paint a picture of the yeast that makes dough rise (Malcolm and Unger 2016). Early money makes it easier to raise money ("dough"). Research on congressional campaigns suggests that early money improves the ability to succeed with fundraising later in the election cycle particularly for first-time candidates (Biersack and Wilcox 1993).

It is important to note that fundraising may go through different phases. It may be easiest to raise money from personal contacts and strong supporters at the beginning of a campaign, while contributions from individual or organizational donors who will take more development (PACs, allies, external networks, etc.) may come later. Fundraising events that introduce the campaign or organization to potential new donors may be well situated at times where you anticipate a slower rate of individual contributions. In Section 4, we list individuals who will make up the core of your potential donors. We recommend in planning your revenue timeline that you start with asking those with the closest relationship to you and then move your way down the list.

Nonprofit and public agencies also may face situations where they need to have **seed money** on hand. Seed money refers to money designated to start a specific project. This money is referred to as seed money because it is intended to help you grow other money. It works in a similar way as early money in campaigns. Having seed money on hand shows that nonprofits or public agencies are committed to the project and will be ready to put money into action when they apply for grants from government or private sources.

As you consider *how* you will go about raising revenue for your political work, keep these timeline issues in mind. Do you have time before the funds are needed? Seek and apply for a grant or contract that connects with your mission. Do you need money quickly? Instead of planning a big dinner that takes 6 weeks to happen, pick up the phone and call some committed supporters or past donors. Are you cultivating a large donor who wants to first see that you have support from a lot of small-dollar donors? A direct e-mail solicitation that asks people to contribute $5 online to show that they support your mission, issue, or candidate might be just the thing. Develop a calendar as part of your strategic planning process that includes the specific dates by which you will need money. Work backwards from these dates to implement specific methods (described in the section below) that will ensure that your funds will be raised and in-hand by these dates.

Methods of Fundraising

While revenue may be raised from a number of sources as described above, this section focuses primarily on raising private contributions. This is a crucial skill for political social workers who practice in political settings, especially with electoral or advocacy campaigns or in nonprofit organizations. In Table 11.5, we outline common methods that are used in political fundraising, as well as relevant considerations in using each method. We include cost estimates for engaging in each of these methods; however, please note that the cost estimates are generalized over many different types and sizes of campaigns. They include assumptions that may not be true for your organization. The more experienced and efficient your organization's fundraising efforts are, with an eye toward ways to stretching your money, the lower these costs will be across the board (Affinity Resources n.d.).

Fundraising methods that involve direct personal contact with your own constituencies (whether voters in your district or people in the community your organization serves) are an important part of fundraising. They should remain a critical part of your revenue plans, even as online fundraising methods grow in usage. At the same time, we encourage you to be attuned to the growing use of digital fundraising, and the potential it provides for raising funds rapidly from both within and outside your community. At the time of this writing, knowledge about how to do this effectively is quite young. Tools and approaches are constantly being developed and tested, often in real time. One common approach is to include website and donation links in all videos related to your campaign or organization. In the Resource section, we include a 2017 campaign video from a Wisconsin Congressional candidate, engaged in a race to unseat the incumbent Speaker of the US House of Representatives, Paul Ryan. This engaging video illustrates the potential of digital fundraising. It went viral, capturing nearly half a million views in its first 2 weeks, and raising challenger Randy Bryce's campaign over $100,000 in 24 hours (Stafford 2017).

Electoral campaigns often have a **finance committee** that helps with fundraising. Members of the campaign or candidate finance committee are supporters who solicit contributions to the campaign and may make spending decisions in order to influence voters' actions in the specific election. Typically, the finance committee members solicit major donor donations. Your campaign also may seek out **bundlers**, individuals who solicit and collect contributions to the candidate from other individuals and deliver them to the candidate in a "bundle." This is a role that your major donors may play; consider asking them to solicit other donors to your candidate or cause. It must be done thoughtfully and with a clear understanding of relevant campaign finance law in order to be an effective tool, however (Davidson 2015).

Table 11.5 Methods of fundraising in settings where political social work practice takes place

Method	Types of settings	Description	Cost	Timeline
Board solicitation	Nonprofits	Nonprofit board members give money and/or solicit their networks. In many boards, this is a requirement for board service—in colloquial terms, this is often referred to as "**give/get**, or get off" the board.	Minimal	Can be scheduled throughout the year and used to create seed money for advocacy work. Direct donations from board members may come relative quickly; money from networks can take longer.
Call time (also called **dialing for dollars**)	Electoral and nonprofits	Electoral campaigns generally rely heavily on this method, literally calling potential donors individually one at a time to ask for money. Nonprofits also might use phone calls to raise money for the organization or advocacy campaign, but more likely as a follow-up to an event or mail solicitation.	Minimal, other than staff time	Requires substantial time. Funds generally come in immediately, especially if you ask for payment method while you have them on the phone
Capital campaign/ major gift efforts/ planned giving	Nonprofits	Large drive focused on major donors, often with a substantial, public fundraising goal. Asks are often made in small or one-on-one meetings with donors and staff, organizational leadership, and/or board members.	Staff or board leadership and time required. May cost $0.05–0.10 per dollar raised for capital or major gift campaigns, $0.25 per dollar raised for planned giving	Requires significant relationship-building with donors over the long term.

(continued)

Table 11.5 (continued)

Method	Types of settings	Description	Cost	Timeline
Digital	Electoral and nonprofits	Increasingly used, especially by electoral campaigns. Includes placing donation links on campaign videos and in social media shares so viewers can donate on the spot as well as online advertising, which can be specifically targeted.	Generally nothing or next to nothing. With videos, you are already spending this money anyway, capitalizes on interest in your candidate, even from outside of your district. Cost of online advertisement can vary depending on the number of ads you buy.	Funds come in immediately if you connect to an online donation site.
E-mail solicitations	Electoral and nonprofits	Easy to send out. Tend to have very low **open rates** (number of e-mails that actually get opened) and **click rates** (number of people who actually click on the link). Low response rates of people who actually give money.	Minimal	Funds come in immediately if you connect to an online donation site.
Events (other than house parties)	Electoral and nonprofits	Types of events vary widely. May range from an informal event where donations are suggested to a VIP event with private candidate face time for major donors.	Tend to be very staff intensive. May cost as much as $0.50 for every dollar you raise. Sufficient cash flow may be needed to pay for expenses before event.	Money tends to take a while to come in. You might put a substantial amount of money into paying event costs for weeks or months before you start to see a return. Money should come in immediately on the night of the event, either through checks, credit cards (use an app where they can swipe the card there), or people donating online at the party.

Grant writing	Nonprofits	Requires identifying potential government or foundation grant opportunities, writing grant applications. Some funders fund advocacy campaigns. Staff expertise a plus.	Mostly in staff time: May cost $0.20 per dollar received.	Money comes in over the long term, often with specific requirements attached.
House parties	Electoral and nonprofits	These are informal events, hosted by supporters, often in their own home. Hosts often invite their own networks to meet with the candidate.	Typically an in-kind donation from the event host.	Because these take less time to plan than other campaign events, the money comes in faster overall. Money should come in immediately on the night of the event, either through checks, credit cards (use an app where they can swipe a card on-site), or people donating online at the party.
Mail solicitations	Electoral and nonprofits	These can take up a significant amount of resources and time to send out. They have a lower response rate than more active methods (like call time), but a higher response rate than more passive methods (like emails) (Charity Science n.d.).	Anywhere from $0.20 if you are soliciting people who have given in the past to $1.25 if you are soliciting new donors, per $1.00 raised. The high cost is considered an investment in identifying new donors.	Long wait time for checks to come in. If you provide a website option, some people will donate there instead.

Before you begin your fundraising, set a goal for each method of fundraising, and know how much of your overall budget you plan to secure through each method. In an electoral campaign, try to identify how much was raised and spent in your specific race in the past (in the same way that you look at prior elections to assess prior to voter turnout). Sites like Open Secrets or reviewing FEC reports from prior elections in your district (see Resources) can help you estimate your budget.

An example finance plan for an electoral campaign (say a state legislative race) that needs approximately $100,000 is outlined in Table 11.6 (based loosely on the sample plan created by Wellstone Action (n.d.)). The finance plan describes how much money you will need to raise from each method you use. You can use a similar process for planning donations to nonprofits. How you calculate your plan varies depending on how much money you are allowed to get from each donor, rules in your state about donations, etc. Your plan should also outline the times in the campaign when you will conduct each type of solicitation. Also develop a plan for monitoring each method, determining what is successful, and making adjustments based on those outcomes.

Table 11.6 Sample finance plan (November general election, no primary)

Method	Goal	Percentage of total budget (%)	When to implement
Call time (20 hours per week)	$40,000	40	May–November
Donations from PACs	$20,000	20	August
Events/house parties	$25,000	25	House parties in May and August, events June–July
Digital fundraising	$10,000	10	May–November (emphasis right before major disclosure deadlines)
Direct mail	$ 5000	5	May, August

POLITICAL SOCIAL WORKER PROFILE: Steve Kornell, MSW
Member, St. Petersburg City Council (Fig. 11.2).

Fig. 11.2 Steve Kornell, MSW

(continued)

In 2008, I volunteered as the Deputy Campaign Manager for a State House race in my hometown of St. Petersburg, Florida. The candidate was a wonderful person with a strong message. Unfortunately he was outspent by a 5 to 1 margin and lost his bid for office by a wide margin. I learned that fundraising is an essential part of a winning campaign. Campaigns that do not raise enough funds to reach a threshold of viability are unsuccessful in placing their preferred candidate in elective office. Voter communication wins campaigns and that communication is not free.

Shortly after this experience I filed to run for an open seat on the St. Petersburg City Council. My earlier campaign experience left me determined to raise the necessary money to make my own campaign viable. This was not easy. I was tentative at first—asking friends and family for campaign donations was uncomfortable. My presumption had been that some people are natural born fundraisers, but by the end of my first campaign, I knew better. Fundraising is a learned skill, perfected through hours of practice. When I felt discouraged, I reflected on my experience from the earlier campaign, helping me summon the courage to make "the ask."

Over time, my small campaign developed a strong fundraising operation. I would sit in my campaign's donated office space, with my two paid campaign staffers by my side, calling potential donors. Doing this for hours at a time was not my favorite way to spend a day. However, the potential to lose my campaign due to being outspent by large donations from special interests pushed me to keep going.

In its entire 106-year history St. Petersburg had never elected an openly gay City Council member. Breaking that barrier strongly motivated me to raise the needed campaign funds. Homophobic attacks were a real possibility and countering potential attacks would take money.

I learned to not let negative people deter me from my goal. If people became upset that I was calling for donations, I was quick to explain why I was the better candidate. I pointed out the homophobic attacks that happened to previous candidates. I spent hundreds of hours on the phone persuading perfect strangers to donate money to help me run a vigorous campaign. Over time, I became more comfortable with the process.

One day, I was scheduled for a full day of fundraising calls at my campaign office. I tried every possible excuse to get out of it, but my campaign manager did not let me off the hook. The entire morning was a disaster. I was yelled at by several people. As lunchtime approached, I had not secured a single donation. Next door to the office was a restaurant with an outdoor patio. I noticed a friend having lunch. Needing a break from my frustrating morning, I walked over to say hello. As it turned out, my friend's lunch companion had a strong interest in local politics. After lunch he came to the campaign office and made a $500 donation to my campaign. Had I stayed in bed that morning, this would have never happened. The very next call you make could be the one that changes your day, or even the trajectory of your entire campaign.

(continued)

On January 2, 2010, I was sworn in as the first openly gay City Council member in St. Petersburg history. My winning campaign raised the most money ever in any City Council election up to that point, approximately $72,000. As a school social worker I did not have a large group of wealthy friends, so raising this money was not easy. If I can do it, you can too!

Section 4: Making a Fundraising "Ask"

Many of the methods listed above require that you ask individuals for money, whether in your role as a candidate or as a staff member. You may be asking individuals to contribute their own money or funds on behalf of their foundation or business. Particularly in an electoral campaign, whether you are running for president or governor, school board or dog catcher, if you want to raise money, you will need to ask for money from individuals (Mutch 2016). While some people contribute money without being solicited, the vast majority need to be asked to give (Tschirhart and Bielefeld 2012).

SELF-ASSESSMENT: Asking for Money
What is your initial reaction to the thought of raising money directly from individuals? Before you continue, write down the thoughts, feelings, and words that come to mind.

If you are like many people, you shy away from the idea. Asking for money might feel rude, intimidating, or scary. However, consider whether asking people to help support a campaign might promote the social work goal of *empowerment*. By asking individuals to contribute to your candidate or cause, you may be providing them an opportunity to contribute to a goal that is important to them, and one that presumably will help their community, family, or society. This may be a way that they can be part of an effort to make something good happen. One tenet of empowerment is to trust others to make the best decisions for themselves. When we ask people to participate in our campaigns and organizations, we are trusting them to make the decision about whether they are able to contribute.

Who Do We Ask For Money, And Why Do They Contribute?

When thinking of the people who might give money to your candidate, issue, or organization, reflect on the many reasons why people typically donate to individuals, causes, or organizations. Below we outline groups of people we might ask for money and why they might be motivated to donate. Social exchange theory suggests that many people donate because they perceive a benefit to themselves from doing so (Tschirhart and Bielefeld 2012). For each of these groups, we consider what their benefit might be.

1. ***You!*** If the candidate or staff and board members of a nonprofit give of their own resources, that shows they believe in the cause. Don't have much to give? That's ok, just the simple act of giving is important. Many nonprofits start a fundraising campaign by asking everyone on the board or everyone who works there to contribute as little as a dollar. Keep in mind that there can be ethical issues in asking staff members to donate. Is there a power differential between those asking and giving? Are people free to refuse if they are not able or prefer not to give? Do not ask people who are government employees of elected officials to donate to the campaign of their employer, as that violates many ethics rules.

2. ***People who love you.*** Family and close friends are an important audience for a fundraising ask. An urban legend which illustrates this point is the saying that the most consistent donors to many nonprofits are the parents of the executive director. The motivation for this group is that they care about you and want you to be happy and succeed. They may be your parents who just do not want you to have to move home and live in their basement. They also may share many of your ideals and values. People who care about you often see your involvement with an organization or a campaign as validation that it is worth their investment.

3. ***Allies.*** These are people who believe in the same things that the candidate or organization cares about. They are ideologically similar to you, and electing your candidate or getting your advocacy issue advanced is something they want to support. Your success moves their own goals forward.

4. ***Enemy of your enemy.*** These people do not have a particular interest in you, but they *really* do not like your opponent or those who are working on the other side. They know from experience that your opponent will not listen to them or be receptive to their views. They may support you just to ensure that the opposing side does not win.

5. ***Power.*** These are people who might not believe in the same things as you, but they think that supporting you will be helpful to them. They may benefit through a tax donation for a gift to an eligible nonprofit, a chance to help shape the outcomes of an issue or a candidate election, increasing their social or business standing, or through an eventual policy outcome. Maybe they are in your political party, and electing your party is good for them. While these individuals might be hesitant at the beginning, they may be more likely to give later in the campaign once you show that you are a force to be reckoned with. This way they can be sure that they are on your good side if and when you win. Often this group will only donate money once you have shown yourself to be an effective fundraiser.

Regardless of the other motivations they hold, it is important to keep in mind that individuals from each of these groups give because *they were asked*. You might hope that people will hear about your important campaign or read an article about you running for office and decide they just have to donate, but those individuals are few and far between. Even if someone wants to do this, what are the chances they will have the urge, remember, look you up, find your website, and type in their credit card number? A direct ask can make the difference between an interest and an actual contribution.

In an electoral campaign—this same approach can work in a nonprofit or other political setting—candidates are typically encouraged to set up a spreadsheet with all of their contacts. It is useful to start making this list before you even begin running for office—this can be a version of your holiday card list. As you develop this list, save a copy of it online, so you do not lose it if something happens to your computer. Plan to maintain and update it throughout your campaign using software specifically designed for campaign contact tracking. Good-quality contact tracking software will help you stay in compliance with campaign finance law, making it worth the investment.

In this spreadsheet, literally list everyone you know. Then, go back and expand this list even further, using the categories listed above. Are there old acquaintances, colleagues, and neighbors who would remember you and might be interested in seeing you in office? You might find it helpful to think about this as a somewhat similar process to the eco-map you may have developed as part of your social work education. An eco-map is a tool often used to help map out formal and informal supports and connections for an individual or a family. As you begin to develop your fundraising list, instead of focusing on a client's supports and connections, identify your own formal and informal connections. Once you have drafted your fundraising contact list, consider reviewing it with a few friends and family members who can help you think about whether your list is as complete as possible and who can help add to your map.

Once you feel like your list is complete, add two columns to it. The first (and most important) column is the amount that you will ask for from each person on the list, taking relevant campaign finance laws into consideration. The second column is the number that each person can raise for you if they go to their network to get money or hold a fundraiser for you. In asking for cash donations, people often struggle with knowing how much to ask for from each individual. This often feels awkward or intrusive. If you are not sure how much to ask for, consider these two options:

1. If the law has a limit, ask for the maximum the individual is allowed to give by law. Know this number before you get started.
2. **Rate** them. This means to use any information available to you about the potential donor to estimate how much the individual is able to give. Based on this analysis, estimate the best amount to ask for.

Once you have your list and your ask amount, start calling. Start with the easiest calls—your family and close friends—and move forward from there. Keep in mind when you select your ask amount that our tendency is to ask potential donors for too little. However, when we do this, we often end up going back to these donors again to ask for more later in the cycle. In addition, if we ask for too little, it might be seen as a sign of insecurity or lack of confidence. Also, do not assume that an individual will not be able to donate based on their background. Let individuals determine themselves whether they are able to donate. As you call, where possible, take the donation over the phone by credit card.

Once you have completed the easiest calls, continue to work your way down the list. You might go back to people at the beginning if they have not given the maximum (in an electoral campaign) or you have not asked in a while (an advocacy campaign). Remember that as you move forward in fundraising, the people who are most likely to give you money are the people who have already given you money. They have already invested in you, your campaign, or your cause!

As you reach out to potential donors, also, think of those who are connected to these people—members of their professional networks, personal networks, etc. How could the people on your list connect you with their networks to increase your list of potential donors? Political fundraising experts often recommend asking donors not only if they will donate, but also if they would help raise additional funds from their networks.

Also, as you begin to engage in fundraising, think of ways to make this often-challenging process personally meaningful to you, beyond the monetary donations. We know of a state legislator who makes her fundraising calls from the beach, a long-time elected official who makes all of his calls walking around to get exercise, and many who set fundraising milestones and celebrate each of them when they are achieved.

APPLY YOUR SKILLS: Creating a List of Potential Donors
Imagine that you have just been asked to run for local office in your town. You have finished this class and are excited at the opportunity to create social change in your community. In order to run for office, the local mentor who has encouraged you to run suggests that you create a list of potential campaign donors. These donors can be anyone—from the community or far away, voters or nonvoters, family, friends, important people in the community, former teachers or professors, classmates, or coworkers. The maximum amount of money any individual person can donate to the campaign is $200, and you need to raise at least $2000–$5000 to show that you are a viable candidate.

Go through your contact lists, and make a list of the people you would ask. Using the categories described above, review this initial list, and add more people to your list. Do not forget to think about the groups above and the networks to which they are connected. Then, go back through this list and write in a new column the amount you would ask each contact to give (up to the $200 limit).

How Do You Ask?

Whatever you are going to ask someone directly to donate, the most important thing to do is to ask. As shown in Table 11.5, this can be done by e-mail, mail, by phone, or in person, though the latter two options tend to be more effective. Although you may be nervous to ask by phone or in person, remember that even if you ask in an imperfect way, people will know that it is a difficult thing to do. They will forgive you any stumbles. This is a great opportunity to use your social work interpersonal engagement skills. When you are nervous and new to fundraising, it might feel like this is about you. Ultimately, the ask is really about them and why donating to your campaign or organization can meet their needs. From a self-care perspective, do what you can to refocus your attention away from making this about you. It is easier to ask for money when you focus on how it can help forward a mission.

Think about any times before when you have asked friends or family to donate to something important to you. Perhaps you asked them to contribute money to a charity fundraiser such as Relay for Life or a danceathon; purchase candles, chocolate bars, or wrapping paper to support a school activity; or purchase cookies to support your Girl Scout troop. Perhaps you asked them to supply in-kind materials like lumber, supplies, tools, food, or expertise to help support your Eagle Scout project. If you have done any of these things successfully, you have already used all of the skills you will need to ask for money for your political work:

1. You did not assume people knew you could use their help.
2. You thought specifically about what you needed, setting a goal for amount raised, or making a list of the in-kind donations you needed.
3. You created a list of people who might have the resources you needed.
4. You created a script or message to use when explaining to people what you were doing and what you wanted them to do to help.
5. You asked!

Think also about how you approached these efforts. What did you do when you asked people to support you?

1. You made small talk, asked how they were, reminded them of your connection, or otherwise engaged with them.
2. You asked, being specific about what you needed and why.
3. You then stayed silent, giving them the opportunity to answer your all-important question.
4. You used your active listening skills and gave them a chance to say how they could help.
5. If needed, you used your negotiation skills to get what you needed, and you remembered that sometimes "no" might just mean "not right now."

Include the specific amount you will ask for and any personalization relevant to the individual you are soliciting into a **script**. This plan for what you will say will help you not let your nerves get the better of you, so you do not forget to actually make the ask! We provide an outline of what a script might look like when you reach out to an individual contact to ask for a donation.

> **APPLY YOUR SKILLS: Make a Fundraising "Ask"**
> Based on the scenario in the last activity, craft a script to ask for money. Choose one of the people you listed in that activity, and role-play with a friend or classmate. Each of you should get a chance to ask for money, and each of you should get a chance to be asked. How did it go?

> **SELF-ASSESSMENT: Asking for Money**
> Now that you have learned some of the practices for asking for donations from an individual, what are your thoughts and feelings about doing this? Have they changed at all? If you are still uncomfortable, what would you need to do to become more comfortable?

Say Thank You!

Make saying thank you to your donors part of your fundraising plan. When donors give money to your campaign, cause, or organization, be sure to send a thank you in the mail. Nonprofit organizations are required to provide receipts to their donors for tax purposes, but make sure that these receipts are accompanied by a specific thank-you note. For electoral campaigns, a hard copy thank-you letter, in the mail, is still the norm. This is important for showing respect to your donors. It also helps you maintain positive relationships with your donors, which can increase the likelihood of your donors wanting to continue this relationship.

> **Catch up/small talk/engagement**
> Write down actual things you want to say, so you do not have to struggle to come up with this on the fly while you're nervous. Nothing fancy, just a few notes like:
> *Daughter just left for college; congratulate on award last month from Social Work Student Association; passed licensing exam, yay!; ask if they finished the book from book club.*
> These are all things that you would remember to talk about easily if you weren't nervous, but you don't want to forget.
> **Description**
> Describe the office you are running for/campaign you are working on/nonprofit you are working for, and how it connects directly to them and their needs:
> *Remember how we always said if we were in charge of the school budget, we would make sure that teachers got paid enough that they wouldn't have to take second jobs? Well, I've been asked to run for school board, and I think this is my chance to follow through on that! I know if I get elected, I could vote for education policies that will help our kids when they go through these schools someday.*

A specific ask

The limit for contributions for this race is $200, and I am hoping to raise as much as I can in a short time so I can spend all of my time knocking on doors and introducing myself to people in the district. Can I count on you to give $200?

Quiet time to let *them* think and respond

You may literally want to write a note to yourself to be quiet, take a drink of water, and let them talk. Remember that as social workers, we live with awkward silences in a lot of settings—we can survive awkward silence here if necessary. Let the other person think and fill the space.

Listen to what they have to say

Your response

Include a few different options in your script:

- If they say yes: *Great!* Can I take your credit card donation now (or pass you to my assistant now to make a credit card donation)? (It is important here to use your skills of being quiet, and not let your nerves take over before you actually take the donation.)
- If they don't say yes, but they don't say no, listen to the reason, and respond. If they say "wow that's a lot," keep practicing your quiet, and wait until they think through it.

  Do they need more information? Provide it.

  Do they need to check with a partner or wait for a paycheck? *When is a good time to call back?*

  Are they willing to donate, but less than the maximum? *Great!* Take this opportunity to make a second ask at a lower amount. Do not automatically ask for half of the amount you started with. While that may be your instinct, remember you asked for the original amount for a reason. Instead, ask for a number that is 75% or higher of original amount. Repeat as needed, until they identify a donation amount, and then go to the yes script. Make a note to call back in a month or so and ask for money again.
- If they flat out say no, don't take it personally! People do not donate for a lot of reasons, very few of which are about you. The person might change their mind about donating in the future, and your relationship with them is important to maintain.

Thank you

Whatever their answer, thank them for their time!

Review of Key Terms and Concepts

Bundler: individual who solicits and collects contributions to the candidate from other individuals and delivers them to the candidate in a "bundle."

Call time: a time during which candidates call potential donors individually, one at a time, to ask for money.

Campaign finance: the ways in which money is raised and spent in order to fund electoral campaigns.

Campaign finance laws: the federal, state, and sometimes municipal laws, regulations, and legal decisions that define the parameters of campaign finance.

Charity: Gifts to those in need.

Citizens United v Federal Election Commission: a 2010 US Supreme Court ruling challenging campaign finance restrictions on certain "electioneering activities," and requiring public identification of those who fund election communications.

Clean elections: full public funding offered in several states for candidates who are running for governor, lieutenant governor, and state legislature. To qualify for this funding, candidates must raise a certain amount of funding in small donations from individuals within their districts and agree not to spend more than a state-specified amount.

Click rates: the number of people who actually click on the link in solicitation e-mails to take action or donate money.

Coordinated campaign: joint efforts by different campaigns and party committees to get out the vote for their candidates.

Dark money: contributions that are not required by law to be disclosed, often given to 501(c)(4) organizations that are not obligated to report their donors.

Dialing for dollars: See "call time" above.

Disclaimer: A statement included on a communication from an electoral campaign, specifying who paid for and who authorized the communication.

Disclosure: Rules about which campaign donation or spending details must be shared publically, including who gave how much money and to whom.

Earned income: see "profit" below.

Electioneering communication: any ad mentioning a federal candidate within 30 days of a primary or 60 days of a general election, paid for with money regulated by the FEC. Disclosure is governed by federal law.

Endowment: a permanent fund that has been invested, bequeathed, or given to a nonprofit organization.

Estate tax: tax on assets above $5.49 million (in 2016) that are bequeathed to one's heirs from a person who has died.

Excise tax: taxes for a specific good such as fuel, alcohol, or tobacco.

Federal Election Campaign Act: also known as FECA, this act updated campaign finance laws and repealed contribution and overall spending limits while limiting the amount of money that could be spent on media. It legalized labor PACs, and specified oversight responsibility for presidential and congressional election compliance.

Federal Election Commission: otherwise known as the FEC, the commission which enforces campaign compliance and oversees public election funding.

Finance committee: the group who provides oversight of an electoral campaign's fundraising.

Finance plan: also referred to as a revenue plan, this plan spells out exactly how much money a campaign seeks to raise on a quarterly, monthly, and often a weekly basis, including procedures to track revenues.

Foundations: donor organizations that are set up to provide funding to other nonprofits as one source of philanthropy.

Give/get: board solicitation, in which nonprofit board members give money to the nonprofit and/or solicit their networks.

Government contract: a transaction agreement developed between the nonprofit and a government.

Government grant: a source of revenue for nonprofits, grants are a form of financial assistance to a grantee (or receiver of the grant) that must generally be used for a public purpose.

Hard money: campaign contributions donated by individuals within the limits set by federal laws such as FECA given to either a party or candidate; these must be disclosed.

Hatch Act: this federal law prohibits federal government employees from engaging in election campaigns, even if they are not "on duty."

In-kind: donations of a product or service rather than money.

Investment income: an optional revenue source for organizations that are able to set aside a significant amount of money for an endowment; these funds are returned to the organization to be used to further the organization's goals.

Major donor donation: donations from individuals considered a relatively large sum of money (the amount that makes something a major donation will vary depending on the circumstances).

McCain-Feingold Act/Bipartisan Campaign Reform Act of 2002: otherwise known as the BCRA, this act prohibited national candidates and parties from raising and spending money on nonfederal elections (such as state or municipal elections) and limited the ability of state and local parties to use their money to pay for party activities.

Membership fees: distinct from "membership drives," fees are essentially a price of admission to access goods or services.

Nonprofit organization: a business granted tax-exempt status by the IRS.

Open rate: the number of solicitation e-mails that actually get opened by recipients.

Philanthropy: private contributions to nonprofits; a subset of charity.

Pledge: A promise of a future donation.

Presidential Election Campaign Fund: an attempt to publically fund elections through utilizing public money to finance presidential primaries, general election campaigns, and national party conventions, authorized by the **Presidential Election Campaign Fund Act**.

Profit: money that can be raised by nonprofits that exceeds their spending in a given year. This money cannot be given to staff or members of the board and must be invested in the organization's future.

Progressive tax: a tax in which higher income households pay a larger share of their income in tax than lower income households.

Public financing: involves providing government funding to candidates running for office.

Rate: the act of using available information about a potential donor to estimate how much the individual is able to give.

Receipts: campaign contributions, as described in federal law.

Regressive tax: a tax in which lower income households pay a higher percentage of their income toward the tax than higher income households.

Revenue: income available to an organization.

Script: a plan for what to say when soliciting potential donors.

Seed money: money designated to start a specific project, intended to help grow other money.

Self-funded: political campaigns which use the candidate's money rather than asking others for donations.

Small-dollar donation: a source of campaign funding given by individuals, sometimes as little as $3 or $5.

Soft money: contributions from corporations or from individuals who donate outside the legal maximum for candidates.

Soliciting donations: the act of specifically requesting contributions for a campaign or an organization.

Unrestricted funds: money that can be used for anything the organization or campaign chooses.

Unsolicited donation: contributions given of the giver's own volition, without a specific ask.

Viability: the public perception of a campaign's capability of succeeding.

Resources

Citizens United Resources

Assessing Accountability in a Post-Citizens United Era:
http://themonkeycage.org/wp-content/uploads/2012/03/brooks_murov.pdf
Citizens United and the Illusion of Coherence: http://repository.law.umich.edu/cgi/viewcontent.cgi?article=1166&context=mlr
Citizens United v. Federal Election Commission:
http://www.scotusblog.com/case-files/cases/citizens-united-v-federal-election-commission/

Coordinated Campaigns

Coordinated Communications and Independent Expenditures: https://transition.fec.gov/pages/brochures/indexp.shtml
Coordinated Party Expenditures in Federal Elections: An Overview:
https://fas.org/sgp/crs/misc/RS22644.pdf
FEC's Coordination Definition Is a Big Hot Mess:
https://www.aclu.org/blog/fecs-coordination-definition-big-hot-mess

Municipal Revenue

National League of Cities, Local Revenue Structures: http://www.nlc.org/local-revenue-structures
The Sunlight Foundation: https://sunlightfoundation.com/policy/municipal_campaign_finance/ or
    go to https://sunlightfoundation.com and in the menu under "Policy" click "Local", then scroll
    down to "Campaign Finance" and click "Learn more…".

Campaign Fundraising

Customer Relationship Management (CRM) tools are used to collect donations. For an electoral
    campaign, use tools made for politics because they collect correct compliance information.
    One example is Nation Builder (a nonpartisan tool): http://nationbuilder.com
Digital fundraising, Randy Bryce video: https://www.youtube.com/watch?v=794-lwvdkhQ
Local Revenue Structures: http://www.nlc.org/local-revenue-structures
Follow the Money: https://www.followthemoney.org/.
CrowdPAC: an online conditional fundraising tool which allows you to start raising money before
    you file, to assess what you might be able to raise: https://www.crowdpac.com

Federal Campaign Finance Resources

FEC publicly available data: https://www.fec.gov/data/.

State Campaign Finance Resources

Campaign Finance:
http://www.ncsl.org/research/elections-and-campaigns/campaign-finance.aspx
Campaign Finance Webpages:
http://www.ncsl.org/research/elections-and-campaigns/ncsl-s-campaign-finance-webpages.aspx

Other Resources

Examples of "Stand by your Ad" candidate commercials from 2008: https://www.youtube.com/
    watch?v=yCBmBExZE90

References

Affinity Resources. (n.d.). *Home*. Retrieved from http://www.affinityresources.com/pgs/articles/
    fundriasing_costs.html
Biersack, R. S. H. P., & Wilcox, C. (1993). Seeds for success: Early money in congressional elec-
    tions. *Legislative Studies Quarterly, 18*(4), 535–551.
Bjerg, A. (2013). *The state of municipal campaign finance in California*. Ca FWD.
Center on Budget and Policy Priorities. (2016). *Policy basics: Where do federal tax revenues come
    from?*

Charity Science. (n.d.). *Shallow review of direct mail fundraising*. Retrieved from http://www.charityscience.com/uploads/1/0/7/2/10726656/direct_mail_pdf.pdf

Citizens United. (n.d.). *Fulfilling our mission*. Retrieved from http://www.citizensunited.org/fulfilling-our-mission.aspx

Citizens United v. Federal Election Commission. (n.d.). *Oyez*.

Connecticut Office of the State Comptroller. (2016). *Fund type: General*. Retrieved from http://openbudget.ct.gov/-!/year/2016/revenue/0/fund_type/General/0/description?vis=barChart

Davidson, C. (2015, February 3). Bundling campaign contributions is legal, but carries risks: A question of ethics. *Roll Call*.

Federal Election Commission. (2015). *Coordinated communications and independent expenditures*. Retrieved from https://transition.fec.gov/pages/brochures/indexp.shtml

Federal Election Commission. (n.d.). *Contribution limits*. Retrieved from https://www.fec.gov/help-candidates-and-committees/candidate-taking-receipts/contribution-limits-candidates/

Garrett, R. S., & Whitaker, L. P. (2016). *Coordinated party expenditures in federal elections: An overview*. Congressional Research Service.

Giving USA Foundation. (2017). *$390.05 billion (graphic)*. Retrieved from https://givingusa.org/wp-content/uploads/2017/06/Giving-USA-2017-Infographic.jpg

Hernandez, D. (n.d.). *Make a donation*. Retrieved from https://secure.c-esystems.com/diegohernandez/donation.aspx

Internal Revenue Service. (2016). *Estate tax*. Retrieved from https://www.irs.gov/businesses/small-businesses-self-employed/estate-tax

Lenkowsky, L. (2011). *Robert Payton's legacy: How to educate nonprofit leaders*. Retrieved from https://www.philanthropy.com/article/Robert-Payton-s-Legacy-How/158357

Macleod-Ball, M. W. (2014). *FEC's coordination definition is a big hot mess*. Washington Markup: American Civil Liberties Union.

Malcolm, E. R., & Unger, C. (2016). *When women win: EMILY's list and the rise of women in American politics: Mariner books*.

Malm, L., & Kant, E. (2013). *The sources of state and local tax revenues*. Retrieved from https://taxfoundation.org/sources-state-and-local-tax-revenues/

Marcus, R. (1997, September 5). 'Hard' and 'Soft' money: A crucial, sometimes fine line. *Washington Post*.

McKeever, B. (2015). *The nonprofit sector in brief 2015: Public charities, giving, and volunteering*. Urban Institutie.

Miller, M. G. (2014). *Subsidizing democracy: How public funding changes elections and how it can work in the future*. Ithica, NY: Cornell University Press.

Mutch, R. E. (2016). *Campaign finance: What everyone needs to know*. New York, NY: Oxford University Press.

Narayanswamy, A., Cameron, D., & Gold, M. (2016). Money raised as of Dec. 31. *The Washington Post*.

National Association of State Budget Officers. (2017). *Fiscal survey of the states*. Retrieved from http://www.nasbo.org/reports-data/fiscal-survey-of-states

National Conference of State Legislators. (n.d.). Contribution limits overview. Retrieved August 7, 2017 from http://www.ncsl.org/research/elections-and-campaigns/campaign-contribution-limits-overview.aspx-individual

Ostrander, R. R. (2015). School funding: Inequality in district funding and the disparate impact on urban and migrant school children. *BYU Education and Law Journal, 2015*(1), 271.

Schreiber, S. P. (2016). Social Security Administration announces large increase in 2017 wage base. *Journal of Accountancy*.

Stafford, D. (2017, July 3). Paul Ryan's House challenger launches longshot bid after viral video. *CNN Politics*.

Tax Policy Center. (2016a). *How do state and local property taxes work?* Retrieved from http://www.taxpolicycenter.org/briefing-book/how-do-state-and-local-property-taxes-work

Tax Policy Center. (2016b). *What are the sources of revenue for local governments?* Retrieved from http://www.taxpolicycenter.org/briefing-book/what-are-sources-revenue-local-governments

Tschirhart, M., & Bielefeld, W. (2012). *Managing nonprofit organizations*. San Francisco, CA: Jossey-Bass.

U.S. Census Bureau. (n.d.). *State government tax collections*. Retrieved from https://www.census.gov/govs/statetax/

University of Pittsburgh Office of Research. (2017). *Basics of federal contracting: Difference between grants and contracts*. Retrieved from http://www.research.pitt.edu/fcs-basics-federal-contracting-GrantvsContract

Watson, L. (2016). 6 years later, the impact of Citizens United still looms large. *Sunlight Foundation Blog*.

Wellstone Action. (n.d.). *Sample campaign plan*. Retrieved from http://www.wellstone.org/resources/sample-campaign-plan

Yale Investments Office. (2016). *The Yale investments office*. Retrieved from http://investments.yale.edu/

Yeager, M. (2015). The difference between super PACs and dark money groups. *Sunlight Foundation Blog*.

Budgeting and Allocating Resources

12

© Springer International Publishing AG 2018
S.R. Lane, S. Pritzker, *Political Social Work*,
https://doi.org/10.1007/978-3-319-68588-5_12

Section 1: Overview

Political social work generally takes place in electoral campaigns, public agencies, or nonprofit agencies. How we manage and spend money in each of these contexts should be aligned with our strategic planning and is a critical consideration in furthering our policy goals. This chapter builds from Chap. 11's discussion of raising revenues, focusing instead on managing these revenues once they have been received. As with the prior chapter, we provide an overview of the rules at the time of this writing and resources to help you research budgeting rules in your own political context. However, when dealing with political finances, we encourage you to *always consult experts who can help you make sure that you fully understand and follow all relevant financial laws.*

Developing Social Work Competency
The Council on Social Work Education establishes educational standards for all social work programs in the USA. Content in this chapter supports building competency in the following areas that are considered core to the practice of social work:
COMPETENCY 5: Engage in Policy Practice
COMPETENCY 8: Intervene with Individuals, Families, Groups, Organizations, and Communities
COMPETENCY 9: Evaluate Practice with Individuals, Families, Groups, Organizations, and Communities

Domains of Political Social Work	
1. Engaging individuals and communities in political processes	◄
2. Influencing policy agendas and decision-making	◄
3. Holding professional and political positions	◄
4. Engaging with electoral campaigns	◄
5. Seeking and holding elected office	◄

Section 2: Assessing Resources Needed: Budgeting for Political Social Work

Budgeting is a central component to work in any political setting. While many of the political social work interventions described in this book rely heavily on volunteers, money and/or in-kind contributions are necessary to execute these efforts. Whether we are talking about an effort as small as busing a group of community members to the state capitol for a lobby day or providing pizza to hard-working volunteers who canvass a neighborhood as part of a voter outreach effort to something as large as running a billion-dollar presidential campaign, we need to be thoughtful about what resources will be needed and how we will use these resources.

Strategic Budgeting

To be effective in political settings, budgets need to be "realistic, consistent with strategic objectives, flexible, and measurable" (Tschirhart and Bielefeld 2012). What this means is that budgeting should follow from and be led by the strategic plan of your campaign and the mission and goals of your organization. Your overall plan and your budget go hand in hand. For example, if voter contact is the focus of your campaign's strategic plan, but your electoral campaign's budget focuses just 30% of expenses on voter contact (something we do not recommend), this is a major discrepancy that needs to be resolved. Similarly, if the most important people to reach are unaffiliated voters, the majority of your budget should not be for mailers to Democrats. If you are trying to target your efforts to specific groups of voters, spending money on yard signs put up randomly around town or on pens with your name on them is not likely to further these efforts. If you are trying to convince the leadership of a key legislative committee to hold a hearing on your bill, spending money on a lobbyist without connections to committee leadership should not be part of your budget.

There is a similarly symbiotic relationship between your budget, your revenue plan, and the actual revenues you receive. Your budget and strategic plans dictate the amount of money you will need to fundraise and how and when you do so. However, creating your budget depends on assessing how much money your organization or campaign will realistically be able to raise. For example, if a single grant funds your advocacy campaign, then the realities of that grant will dictate both your strategic plan and the budget that you will be able to create. If a realistic assessment of your electoral campaign's fundraising capacity shows that you will not be able to raise all the funds you would ideally need to compete, either this is not the right election for your campaign or you need to be creative to put together a shoe-string budget. (Of course, you should continue to put in every possible effort to exceed those projected revenues.)

Tracking and Monitoring Expenditures

As you engage in your political social work efforts, track all of your spending, as well as your revenues, as meticulously as possible. The systems you use do not have to be complicated. There is no one expensive or complex piece of software that you need to use. However, your budget tracking system must be able to tell you easily how much cash you have on hand to spend on your work.

In any of the types of organizations discussed here, continually monitor your budget by comparing your projected and actual spending and your projected and actual revenues—weekly, if not daily. Monitoring is important in all settings, but even more so in an electoral campaign, where monies must be raised and spent in a fairly rapid timeline. This constant comparison enables you to know if your organization gets off target, and helps you to identify how to resolve any discrepancies.

Types of Budgets

The range of budgets for political social work varies depending on the type of agency and purpose. However, there are some core types of budgets that you will see in many of the political settings we discuss below. These include the following:

1. A **line-item budget** displays the money to be spent within specific individual categories (salaries, rent, utilities, etc.). This type of budget is used in public agency settings, campaigns, and nonprofit organizations.
2. A **program budget** categorizes expenditures by their allocation to different major activities. Within a program budget, a staff member's salary might get spread out between several different programs depending on how that person's time is allocated, while a line-item budget will list salaries separately from other expenses (Willoughby 2014).
3. The **operating budget** accounts for day-to-day activities. You will see an operations or overhead section of a public agency, campaign, or nonprofit budget. This includes resources needed to carry out the mission of the program or campaign, including such activities as employee staffing (Willoughby 2014).
4. A **capital budget** accounts for significant long-term expenses, such as a new building or significant infrastructure. We see this in public agencies and nonprofits, but not in campaigns. (A **capital campaign** is often used by a nonprofit to raise a set amount of money for capital expenses like these within a specified period of time (Nonprofit Research Collaborative 2015).)

Section 3: Electoral Campaigns

Building on the extensive discussion of campaign finance laws and practices in the last chapter, we explore how these rules inform budgeting and spending in electoral campaigns. We then discuss the process of budgeting for an electoral campaign.

Campaign Finance and Spending

Just as campaign finance rules and regulations provide restrictions on the money campaigns may receive, they also provide restrictions on how the money is spent. Federal campaign finance law defines campaign spending as disbursements. **Disbursements**, or payments from a campaign, come in two forms:

1. A campaign's **expenditures**, the "purchase, payment, distribution, loan, advance, deposit or gift of money or anything of value to influence a federal election" (Federal Election Commission n.d., para 2). Expenditures include money to fund the campaign's day-to-day work, money given to another candidate's committee, and money spent in order to fundraise, travel, advertise, and communicate with voters.

2. "**Non-expenditures**," any money a campaign spends that does not influence a federal election. Non-expenditures may include donations to charities, transfers to party committees (which support other candidates), or donations to state and local campaigns. This category may include other business-related costs not directly associated with the election, but it is never appropriate for a candidate to use funds for personal use.

At the federal level, the FEC requires extensive and regular reporting on all disbursements. Candidate campaigns must file reports on all disbursements quarterly. The FEC lays out different rules for various kinds of disbursements in terms of both spending and reporting. Any expenditure over $100 must be made by check or drawn directly from a central campaign account.

Requirements for campaign spending and disclosure can vary significantly at the state and local levels (NCSL 2015). If you are involved with a state or local campaign, we recommend that you seek out expertise to help you navigate the relevant campaign finance laws. A good place to start learning about your state's requirements is the National Conference of State Legislatures' chart of disclosure and spending requirements across states (see Resources).

FURTHER REFLECTION: The "Election-Industrial Complex."
Listen to this podcast on the "election-industrial complex": http://www.wnyc.org/story/election-industrial-complex. What are your thoughts about campaign finance and spending after listening to this? What else do you want to know?

Electoral Campaign Budgets

In an electoral campaign, your budget is essentially "your campaign plan in dollars." Accord it sufficient respect and attention (Wellstone Action n.d.). The budget is a living, breathing document that the campaign manager often has open on the computer all day every day. Create your budget at the beginning of the campaign, but be prepared to modify it throughout the campaign in reaction to changing revenue and expenses, situations, and needs. Because your campaign budget is fully dependent on the funds that you can raise, create at least two versions of the budget at the start of your campaign: (1) the budget you would realistically like and (2) a "low" version of the budget. The low version is what the budget for your campaign will look like if you do not raise all the funds you hope to raise. In campaigns, financial planning requires constant attention to the balance between the funds you need to carry out your plan and the funds you are able to raise.

It is important to be aware that in electoral campaigns, the large majority of donated funds typically come in late in the election season. This means that your budget needs to be cautious at the front end of your campaign until you know what funds you can successfully raise. It is important to save money at the beginning of your campaign, so that you can have as much money as possible to spend on reaching voters and getting them to the polls in the final weeks before the election. As we noted earlier, make sure to continually track your campaign's cash on hand. In a competitive race, you will essentially spend down all of your resources in the push to Election Day. In a primary election, you may choose to reserve some for the general election, but remember that having reserves will not do you much good if you do not get through the primary.

The size of your campaign budget will vary based on the level and location of the campaign. An electoral race for a local county or small city office might need a budget of $15,000. Campaign budgets for national races are much larger and continue to grow rapidly. In 2014, the most expensive Senate race in history was North Carolina, where together the candidates raised and spent more than $20 million, and outside groups spent $70–80 million. Just 2 years later, in 2016, approximately $175 million was spent on a Pennsylvania Senate race (The Center for Responsive Politics n.d.-a). In 2017, the most expensive House race in history took place in a runoff election for the seat in the sixth Congressional District in Georgia, costing more than $50 million (Associated Press 2017).

APPLY YOUR SKILLS: Campaign Spending in Your District
Go to www.followthemoney.org and look up the last elections in a specific district. This may be the district you used for the exercises in Chap. 7 or another district of your choice. Follow the tabs across the top of the page. How much money did candidates in that district spend in the most recent election?

Regardless of the size of the campaign budget, the same basic components are typically included. Much of your campaign budget will parallel a program budget in a nonprofit, in which you categorize expenditures by campaign activity (voter contact) rather than by category (personnel). The overhead category described below is similar to the operations budget of a nonprofit, covering the expenses needed for the campaign activities to continue. As you think about each component listed below, keep in mind the importance of efficiency in electoral campaign budgeting. One of your goals in leading a campaign is to stretch the campaign's funds as far as possible. For each of these components, seek out ways to keep costs low and/or to secure in-kind donations (e.g., office space, food for volunteers, location, and food for small fundraisers).

1. *Voter contact.* This is the campaign's most important task. In races with no paid media, voter contact typically takes up between 60 and 75% of the budget. This includes costs associated with knocking on doors or calling voters directly. This budget category might include printing and buying lists of voters and, on a bigger campaign, salaries for field or outreach staff.
2. *Paid media.* Small races are unlikely to use paid media, but races in large metropolitan areas, many state races, and most national races spend money on **paid media**. Paid media refers to TV, radio, newspaper, or digital ads created by the campaign and costs associated with producing and running these ads. Depending on the size of the campaign and paid media budget, this may be considered a subset of voter contact, or may be a stand-alone budget item. In large campaigns, especially at the federal level, this is the largest area of campaign spending.
3. *Fundraising.* While this takes up a significant chunk of your candidate and campaign's time, it generally should not be a large component of your budget. Ideally, expenses related to fundraising take up no more than 10% of the campaign's budget. Keep your fundraising costs low by focusing on fundraising techniques that do not cost a lot of money. For example, phone calls to donors have a higher rate of return than big expensive fundraising events. This is also a good way your supporters can help you without cost to the campaign. Consider asking key supporters to plan and host fundraisers in their home at their expense.
4. *Research.* Larger campaigns might spend up to 5% of their budgets on gathering information about the community or their opponents, including opposition research and polling. Smaller campaigns might gather this information through free methods: a listening tour, volunteer time, focus groups, etc.
5. *Overhead/operations.* Overhead expenses in a campaign refer to ongoing operating costs, which may include a range of expenses from pens to Internet access to rent to salaries and fringe benefits for the campaign manager and other staff. Overhead should be no more than 15–20% of your total budget. There are many creative ways to keep these costs low. For example, you might be able to use a supporter's house or an extra room in their business as an office to keep rent-related expenses to a minimum. A campaign manager one of the authors worked with always asks campaign staff and volunteers to bring their own pens. Most of us have a few pens around the house, and in aggregate, a budgetary decision like this saves the campaign money it can use for something more important to the campaign's goals. This is why you may find many campaign offices to appear run down. Many campaigns choose to spend their money on voter contact rather than on prime office rent or cleaning services.

Table 12.1 further breaks down these categories. While no specific amounts are listed for these expenses because they differ widely based on the size of the campaign, this table is intended to demonstrate the different kinds of expenses that a campaign might incur. When planning a budget for a campaign, start by looking at what spending looked like for the candidates who ran for that specific office in the last comparable election. This information generally can be found through websites like opensecrets.org, followthemoney.org, and disclosure forms filed with the FEC

Table 12.1 Campaign budget details

Category	Expense	Notes
Voter contact	Field-related salaries (field director, field staff, outreach staff)	In smaller campaigns, these may be volunteers
	Voter file	Any costs associated with securing voter data
	Direct mail (including mail consultant, mail house, printer, postage, etc.)	A consultant, mail house, and/or printer) can help you figure out who to send mail to, as well as develop the materials, mail them, etc. The cost of the consultant or mail house should include the bulk mail permit that will make mailings cheaper
	Campaign literature (walk cards, etc.)	Costs associated with printing and design. In smaller races, these can potentially be secured through in-kind donations
	Phone banking (including phones if you're providing them)	If volunteers provide their own cell phones, this can be very inexpensive
	Robocalls	Very cheap (about 7 cents per call), but very ineffective—of those who answer, about half hang up in the first 10 seconds (Philips 2008)
	Non-targeted voter contact, including lawn signs, banners, signs for visibility, etc.	Costs associated with design and printing
	Stipends for paid canvass	If you have the money, helpful to be sure you contact as many of your committed voters as possible leading up to election day
	Food for volunteers	May be donated in-kind by local businesses or volunteers
Paid media	Radio, newspaper, cable and broadcast TV production and airtime, digital	Smaller campaigns may have no paid media; for larger campaigns it may be the largest budget expenditure
Fundraising	Salaries (finance director)	
	House parties	These shouldn't cost you anything—the costs should be borne by the people hosting the parties
	Other events	Try to minimize—Involve substantial time, resource, and monetary expenses.
	Direct mail (printing, postage, paper, envelopes, return cards if used)	A consultant can help you develop the materials. For a price, will also mail them out for you. The cost of the consultant or mail house should include the bulk mail permit that will make mailings cheaper
	E-mail	The cost of sending e-mails is minimal, but someone needs to develop the message, track how it's working, and adjust
	Compliance (filing fees, legal advice)	

(continued)

Table 12.1 (continued)

Category	Expense	Notes
Research	Salaries (research director)	May be done by volunteers on a small campaign
	Polling	Smaller campaigns may do no polling, medium campaigns may benefit from polling done by parties
	Opposition research	
Operations	Salaries (campaign manager, communications director, digital director)	On a small campaign, the campaign manager may be your only paid staff member
	Fringe benefits	
	Payroll expenses	
	Rent	May be donated in-kind
	Utilities (including phone and Internet)	May be donated in-kind
	Office supplies	
	Travel	

or your state agency that oversees campaign finance. Finding the amounts that were spent in similar elections in the past can give you a starting point for what your budget might look like.

APPLY YOUR SKILLS: Campaign Expenditures

Follow this link to the FEC report filed by social worker and US Representative Kyrsten Simena (D-AZ) following her 2016 general election win: http://doc-query.fec.gov/pdf/245/201612089039944245/201612089039944245.pdf. This report includes her expenditures in the final weeks of her campaign, leading up to Election Day on November 8. The list of her campaign's itemized disbursements begins on p. 174.

As you look through this report, try to identify expenses for each of the budget categories in Table 12.1. What stands out to you about her expenditures? Does anything surprise you as you consider how her campaign spent money in its final weeks?

Section 4: Nonprofit Organizations

The ability of a nonprofit organization to spend money on political action and related work depends on its US Internal Revenue Service (IRS) classification. Before we discuss nonprofit budgeting in the political social work context, we examine the different types of nonprofits where work of a political nature takes place.

Table 12.2 Examples of nonprofit organizations in different classifications

Nonprofit classification		Examples
501(c)(3)		The Sentencing Project
		National Association of Black Social Workers (NABSW)
501(c)(4)		American Civil Liberties Union (ACLU)
		National Rifle Association (NRA)
501(c)(5)		American Federation of Labor—Congress of Industrial Organizations (AFL-CIO)
		Service Employees International Union (SEIU)
501(c)(6)		National Association of Social Workers (NASW)
		Oregon School Social Work Association
527	PAC	American Conservative Union
		Political Action For Candidate Election (PACE)
		Run for Something
	Super PAC	Americans for a Better Tomorrow, Tomorrow
		Club for Growth Action
		League of Conservation Voters
	Hybrid PAC	Correct the Record
		National Defense PAC
	Party committee	Democratic National Committee
		Republican National Committee
	527 group	EMILY's List
		New Day for America

Categories of Nonprofit Organizations and Allowable Political Activities

While many of us are most familiar with 501(c)(3) organizations, the IRS establishes several different classifications of nonprofit organizations. Each of these classifications places different restrictions on the organization's political activity, primarily in terms of how much staff time and money are spent on these activities. The differences between types of nonprofits, their tax status, and allowable activities are complicated. However, knowing what an organization is allowed to do is dependent on understanding their tax status.

In this section, we describe each of the different classifications of nonprofits that commonly engage with politics and discuss what the organization is allowed to do—and spend money on—as relates to political activity. As you read about each type of nonprofit, we encourage you to refer to Table 12.2, for examples of organizations within each classification, and Table 12.3, for highlights of allowable and restricted political activities allowed by each (Schadler 2012; Jacobs et al. 2010; Reilly and Allen 2015).

501(c)(3) Organizations

The public is most familiar with tax-exempt nonprofits, commonly called charities (Mutch 2016). These nonprofits are organized under section 501(c)(3) of the US tax code. Their income and many of their purchases are exempt from taxes. In exchange, they agree to abide by regulations on their activities, particularly restrictions on political activity. The IRS website shown in Fig. 12.1 provides guidance on what constitutes a 501(c)(3) nonprofit and what some of the restrictions are.

Table 12.3 Allowable political activities by nonprofit organizations

Nonprofit designation	An organization can …	An organization cannot …
501(c)(3)	• Advocate for an *issue stance* • *Testify on a specific bill when requested* by a legislative committee (this does <u>not</u> count as direct lobbying) • *Testify on a specific bill without request of a* legislative committee (this <u>does</u> count as direct lobbying and can constitute up to 5% of expenditures) • Advocate for *administrative regulations* • Conduct *nonpartisan voter registration and education* • *Direct grassroots lobbying, if using less than 5%* of its expenditures • *Accept tax-deductible donations* • Allow individual staff and board members to *campaign for a political candidate, <u>not</u> as representatives of the organization*	• Conduct partisan activities *on behalf of specific candidate* • *Direct or grassroots lobbying over 5%* of its expenditures • Allow individual staff and board members to *lobby <u>as</u> representatives of the organization* • Allow individual staff and board members to *campaign for a political candidate <u>as</u> representatives of the organization*
501(c)(3), with "H" election	• Advocate for an *issue stance* • *Testify on a specific bill when requested* by a legislative committee (this does <u>not</u> count as direct lobbying) • *Testify on a specific bill without request of a* legislative committee (this <u>does</u> count as direct lobbying and can constitute up to 20% of expenditures) • Advocate for *administrative regulations* • Conduct *nonpartisan voter registration and education* • *Direct lobbying, on a sliding scale, using up to 20%* of an agency's expenditures • *Grassroots lobbying, up to ¼ of amount permitted to direct lobbying* • *Accept tax-deductible donations*	• Conduct partisan activities *on behalf of specific candidate* • *Direct lobbying using over 20%* of its expenditures, based on a sliding scale • *Grassroots lobbying over ¼ of* the amount permitted for lobbying
501(c)(4)	• Conduct all policy-related activities permitted to 501(c)(3) organizations • *No-limit lobbying* related to organization's purpose • *Partisan campaign and electoral activity,* as long as it is not the primary purpose of the organization's activities • Serve as a sister organization to a 501(c)(3) organization, as long as it is not financially supported by the 501(c)(3)	• *Be financially supported by a 501(c)(3) organization* • *Accept tax-deductible donations*

(continued)

Table 12.3   (continued)

Nonprofit designation	An organization can …	An organization cannot …
501(c)(5) 501(c)(6)	• Conduct all policy-related activities permitted to 501(c)(3) organizations • *No-limit lobbying* related to organization's purpose • *Partisan campaign and electoral activity*, as long as it is not the primary purpose of the organization's activities	• *Accept tax-deductible donations*
527 (including PACs)	• Participate in *partisan campaign and electoral activity* as the sole purpose of organization's activities	• *Participate in "substantial" lobbying activities* • *Accept tax-deductible donations*

IRS

Subscriptions ∨ | Lang

Search

Filing   Payments   Refunds   Credits & Deductions   News & Events   Forms & Pubs   Help & Res

Charitable Organizations

Churches & Religious Organizations

Political Organizations

Private Foundations

Other Non-Profits

Contributors

Exemption Requirements - 501(c)(3) Organizations

♥ ✚ 🖶

To be tax-exempt under section 501(c)(3) of the Internal Revenue Code, an organization must be organized and operated exclusively for exempt purposes set forth in section 501(c)(3), and none of its earnings may inure to any private shareholder or individual. In addition, it may not be an action organization, i.e., it may not attempt to influence legislation as a substantial part of its activities and it may not participate in any campaign activity for or against political candidates.

Organizations described in section 501(c)(3) are commonly referred to as *charitable organizations*. Organizations described in section 501(c)(3), other than testing for public safety organizations, are eligible to receive tax-deductible contributions in accordance with Code section 170.

The organization must not be organized or operated for the benefit of private interests, and no part of a section 501(c)(3) organization's net earnings may inure to the benefit of any private shareholder or individual. If the organization engages in an excess benefit transaction with a person having substantial influence over the organization, an excise tax may be imposed on the person and any organization managers agreeing to the transaction.

Section 501(c)(3) organizations are restricted in how much political and legislative (*lobbying*) activities they may conduct. For a detailed discussion, see Political and Lobbying Activities. For more information about lobbying activities by charities, see the article Lobbying Issues; for more information about political activities of charities, see the FY-2002 CPE topic Election Year Issues.

Additional Information

- Application Process Step by Step: Questions and answers that will help an organization determine if it is eligible to apply for recognition of exemption from federal income taxation under IRC section 501(a) and, if so, how to proceed.
- Private foundations - requirements for exemption
- *Tax-Exempt Status*- online training available at the IRS microsite StayExempt.irs.gov.

Page Last Reviewed or Updated: 26-Jan-2017

Fig. 12.1   Internal Revenue Service guidance on 501(c)(3) nonprofit status

You may have heard the "prevailing wisdom" that nonprofit organizations cannot participate in, or spend money on, any political activities without risking their tax status. It is true that 501(c)(3) organizations have substantial restrictions on both lobbying and partisan activities on behalf of specific candidates or political parties. However, we want to underscore in this chapter that the perception of a ban on political activity is largely incorrect (Jacobs et al. 2010).

Many policy-focused activities are legally permitted under the auspices of a 501(c)(3) organization. Specifically, there are *no limits* on advocacy work or spending on this work. In this context, advocacy refers to informing and educating policymakers about issues or causes, and communicating stances on policy issues. These organizations may spend money on advocating to legislators at all levels and to executive branch agencies regarding regulations, and on nonpartisan voter outreach. Contrary to common perception, these organizations also may spend up to 5% of their expenditures on direct lobbying and/or grassroots lobbying. Direct lobbying refers explicitly to communicating with a legislator to express a view on a specific piece of legislation. Grassroots lobbying refers explicitly to communicating with the public to express a view on a specific piece of legislation, and explicitly includes a call to action.

Furthermore, if 501(c)(3) organizations want to engage in more extensive lobbying, IRS law allows them to do so while remaining tax-exempt nonprofits. Such organizations can choose to seek an "H" election in any given year, allowing them to spend up to 20% of their budget on direct lobbying, and up to ¼ of that amount on grassroots lobbying. The "H" election, described in Table 12.3, expands the scope of allowable lobbying activity. To be clear, these nonprofit organizations spend up to one-fifth of their budget on lobbying, and it is completely legal under federal law. It is important to check, however, as to whether your state places additional restrictions or responsibilities on these organizations.

501(c)(4) Organizations

Those nonprofits organized under section 501(c)(4) of the US tax code are referred to as **social welfare organizations**. These organizations differ from 501(c)(3) organizations in that many are explicitly ideological. However, like 501(c)(3) organizations, social welfare organizations may not be organized for profit and must have the exclusive purpose of promoting social welfare. In this context, social welfare is defined more broadly than you may otherwise be used to. According to the IRS (2016b), this means:

> To be operated exclusively to promote social welfare, an organization must operate primarily to further the common good and general welfare of the people of the community (such as by bringing about civic betterment and social improvements). For example, an organization that restricts the use of its facilities to employees of selected corporations and their guests is primarily benefiting a private group rather than the community and, therefore,

does not qualify as a section 501(c)(4) organization. Similarly, an organization formed to represent member-tenants of an apartment complex does not qualify, because its activities benefit the member-tenants and not all tenants in the community, while an organization formed to promote the legal rights of all tenants in a particular community may qualify under section 501(c)(4) as a social welfare organization.

501(c)(4)s are permitted greater participation in the political process than 501(c)(3) organizations. These organizations can identify seeking legislative changes as their primary purpose, and have no limits on the amount of money that they can spend on lobbying related to the organization's defined purpose. One challenge with 501(c)(4) organizations, however, is that it is often difficult for the IRS to determine their primary purpose (Mutch 2016). Unlike 501(c)(3) organizations, 501(c)(4)s may spend money on partisan activities, although the electoral campaign work cannot be their primary purpose (J. F. Reilly and Allen 2015). What this means in practice is that most 501(c)(4) organizations devote no more than 49.9% of their budget to electoral efforts (Chance 2016). Some 501(c)(3) organizations opt to set up a "sister" 501(c)(4) organization, so that they have a parallel arm that can engage in extensive lobbying and partisan activity, with fewer disclosure requirements. Planned Parenthood is one example of this: Planned Parenthood is a 501(c)(3) organization, while Planned Parenthood Action Fund is a 501(c)(4). Similarly, while the National Rifle Association is a well-known 501(c)(4) organization, its sister NRA Foundation is a 501(c)(3) organization, focused on firearms education and training.

501(c)(5) and 501(c)(6) Organizations

Two other types of nonprofit organizations share many similarities with 501(c)(4) organizations in the eyes of the IRS. 501(c)(5) organizations are those that have a primary purpose focused on improving conditions for those engaged in labor or agricultural work; labor unions are a common example. 501(c)(6) organizations are business leagues—professional or trade associations—such as the National Association of Social Workers. (Fun fact: The National Football League used to be a 501(c)(6). However, it decided to give up their nonprofit status and tax-exempt privileges in 2015 because they decided they would rather pay taxes than disclose the way they spend their money (Harwell and Hobson 2015).)

These two types of nonprofit organizations can spend unlimited amounts on political advocacy and similarly may spend as much money as they would like on lobbying that is related to the organization's primary purpose. They can spend money on political campaigns, as long as it is not the primary activity of the organization. In some cases, these organizations' expenditures for campaign activities may be taxable.

527 Organizations

Nonprofit organizations that spend money on campaigns are typically organized under section 527 of the tax code. These organizations are referred to as "political organizations." Many of the organizations that fall within this classification are regulated by campaign finance laws and must file with the FEC, including political parties, candidate committees, and **political action committees** (PACs) (The Center for Responsive Politics n.d.-b). Though they fall under this section of the tax code, they are not commonly referred to as 527s. When you hear the term 527, it is usually used to refer to a subset of political organizations that fall under this section of the tax code but are not addressed directly by campaign finance laws.

A PAC may be connected to a corporation or a labor organization, a political official (such as a "leadership PAC"), or it can be an "unconnected organization," not affiliated with any of these other players. A PAC can give money to parties and candidates, and accept money from individuals, other PACs, and political party committees, but within strict limits (The Center for Responsive Politics n.d.-b). The 527 section of the tax code also includes **Super PACs** and **hybrid PACs**. Super PACS were previously known as Independent Expenditure Committees. They have the potential to receive unlimited contributions and have no limits on how much money they can spend on elections. The one limit is that they cannot coordinate directly with a party or candidate. Hybrid PACs, sometimes called Carey Committees, have two bank accounts: one which follows all the rules of a political action committee and a second which operates like a Super PAC. This enables a hybrid PAC to have one regular PAC account that uses "hard" money; if a donor gives too much for that account, the remainder is treated as "soft" money that goes into the Super PAC account and cannot be given directly to federal candidates (Reilly 2011).

The 527 political organizations that do not fall into these categories are called "527 groups" and include those like EMILY's List. These organizations have no limits on contributions, on who can contribute, or on what they can spend (The Center for Public Integrity 2014). Taxes are not paid by 527s on the income they receive from donations. They have to disclose donors and spending (Mutch 2016).

APPLY YOUR SKILLS: Nonprofits and Tax Status
Find at least two organizations that work on issues of interest to you that are in different tax categories. You may use the following websites to do this, or other sources helpful to you.

  https://www.irs.gov/charities-non-profits/exempt-organizations-select-check

  http://www.fec.gov/pubrec/pacronyms/Pacronyms.pdf

  What are the names of these two organizations? What is the tax status of each? What political activity are they allowed to do in that tax status? What are they not allowed to do?

Nonprofit Organization and Advocacy Campaign Budgets

A nonprofit budget should have input from board members, executive staff, and program staff. This budget ideally should be created after strategic planning or other planning processes are completed so that the budget reflects the agency's priorities (Willoughby 2014). The concepts described below apply both to the budget of a nonprofit organization as a whole *and* to specific program budgets within an organization or a coalition of organizations, such as the budget of an advocacy campaign.

Nonprofit budgets are organized around a **fiscal year**. A fiscal year is the 12-month period used by a government, agency, or business, to track and record finances. Nonprofits often use either the federal government's fiscal year, October 1 to September 30, or the fiscal year used by 46 states, July 1 to June 30 (The Nonprofit Times 2012).

A nonprofit budget includes a realistic set of activities that will take place over a fiscal year and their associated expenses. In creating this budget, nonprofit organization best practices suggest using the following sources of information (Tschirhart and Bielefeld 2012):

- Previous years' budgets and any changes made to those budgets throughout the year.
- Estimates of revenue and expenses for the upcoming year: This can be challenging to do given the uncertainty of some sources of revenue and some expenses. For example, if you are not sure that the agency will receive a grant it has applied for, you might consider creating two versions of the budget: one assuming receipt of the grant, and one assuming it will not be received. Similarly, if you expect a rent increase, but do not yet know by how much, you might overestimate that cost so that you are not caught without enough funds to pay the bills.
- Forms for agency managers to request and justify specific amounts: To ensure alignment between the agency's mission and strategic plan and the budget, justifications should include explicit connections to both of these.
- A budget calendar that outlines the timetable for gathering needed information, preparing a draft budget, and getting it approved by all appropriate stakeholders.

This budget needs to be a living, breathing document that can adjust as necessary to new opportunities and challenges. A budget outlines your agency's plan for the year, and that plan will almost inevitably have to be adjusted as changes happen. Be sure to identify specific staff or board members who are responsible for monitoring the budget and reporting to the board if major changes or adjustments are needed (Tschirhart and Bielefeld 2012).

The sizes of nonprofit budgets vary, as do budgets associated with advocacy campaigns. A local advocacy campaign in a small nonprofit may cost very little, while a national advocacy campaign might require millions of dollars. In fact, the National Alliance on Mental Illness, a national advocacy organization, spends approximately $1.8 million per year on advocacy (National Alliance on Mental Illness 2016). In Table 12.4, we provide an example budget for an advocacy campaign budget within a 501(c)(3) organization. In this example, the majority of funds (78%) are allocated for personnel, including **fringe benefits**, the non-salary ways in which we pay people for their work (Internal Revenue Service 2016a). The next

Table 12.4 Sample advocacy campaign budget

Category	Expense	Spending	Source
Staffing	10% of the executive director's time	$7000 (10% of 70,000)	Grant funded
	25% of policy director's time	$12,500 (25% of 50,000)	Grant funded
	15% of communications director's time	$9000 (15% of 60,000)	Grant funded
	100% of organizer's time	$40,000 (100%) of 40,000	Grant funded
		$68,500	
	Fringe benefits, such as health insurance	$18,495 (27% of $68,500)	
Total staffing		*$86,995*	*Total grant*
Direct expenses	Travel	$10,000 (5000 miles at $0.50/mile)	Raised at house party
	Educational materials	$2000	Raised through mail solicitation
	Printing	$1000	Raised through mail solicitation
	Food at events	$1000	Raised through e-mail solicitation
Non-staffing direct expenses		*$14,000*	*Total through in-house solicitation*
Total direct		**$100,995**	
Overhead	Includes rent, utilities, etc.	$10,100 (10% of total)	Donated in-kind by agency
Total		**$111,095**	

biggest category of funds (12.6%) are allocated for direct expenses associated with implementing an advocacy campaign, such as staff member travel, food at events, and printing materials. The final category, **overhead**, essentially pays the organization for the space that the advocacy campaign takes up, such as utilities, a portion of the rent, and printers.

An advocacy campaign like this might be funded through a variety of sources. In the sample provided in Table 12.4, the majority of the money comes from a grant, while the remaining funds were raised from individual donations secured through a house party, mail solicitations, and e-mail solicitations. The overhead costs are an in-kind expense donated by the organization.

Section 5: Public Agencies

POLITICAL SOCIAL WORKER PROFILE: Natalie Powell, MSW
*Program Analyst at the US Department of Health and Human Services in the
Office of the Secretary, Assistant Secretary for Financial Resources, Office of
Budget* (Fig. 12.2).

Fig. 12.2 Natalie Powell,
MSW

Natalie remembers the specific day that she decided to start her career path
into political social work. She was a case manager and had a teenage client,
who was pregnant and also caring for an infant. After arriving for a regular
home visit, Natalie found her client on the curb with her son in her arms and
quickly learned that they were homeless. "I drove in circles around the city
with their only belongings in the back of my work van trying to find them a
place to stay. I soon realized that my client was caught in a legal loophole. At
the time there were no shelters for under-aged youth experiencing homelessness without parental consent. And because she was a few months away from
turning eighteen, Child Protective Services also could not help." Almost
immediately after this incident, Natalie dove headfirst into her MSW. "This is
just one story, but there are millions of families across the country who are
struggling."

Today, Natalie uses her field-level experiences to navigate the complex
world of federal government budgets and policymaking. "Very high level officials are looking to you every day to give them the most accurate, up to date
information so that they can make the policy decisions to move forward." In
any given day, Natalie juggles briefing senior officials, performing technical

(continued)

analyses, producing publically available documents, and crunching budget figures that soar into the billions of dollars. Timing is everything in the world of policy and budgets. Congress often looks to the executive branch to provide critical program information within a tight deadline, which informs congressional bills and makes an impact on families nationwide. "In my work, I strive to ensure that there are enough resources to serve the American people and that the policies that are implemented do not have the types of unintended consequences that withheld my client from reaching her goals."

The most difficult part of Natalie's job as a federal government employee is "working diligently on a thoughtful analysis and not having your recommendation move forward." Natalie is grateful this doesn't happen often, but understands that this is a possibility when working in political social work in a civil service setting. Despite this, Natalie is committed on moving forward, so that she can continue making positive changes that improve families' lives across the nation.

Disclaimer: Natalie Powell contributed to this statement in her personal capacity. The views expressed are her own and do not necessarily represent the views of the Department of Health and Human Services or the US Government.

Budgeting in Public Agencies

Public agencies tend to have the most limitations for raising or spending money and the most requirements for reporting where their money comes from and goes. Political social workers in public settings deal with a complex range of potential budgeting scenarios and responsibilities. Your role may include managing a budget for an agency, analyzing a state or federal budget to find its impact on your agency, developing budget recommendations for government agencies and programs, or as an elected official voting on the budget for your city, state, or country. We provide a brief overview here. Several books and websites in this chapter's Resource section provide more extensive information about budgeting processes in different areas of government.

Organizations such as the Pew Charitable Trusts' States' Fiscal Health project and the Government Finance Officers Association, listed in the Resource section, research and publicize best practices in public budgeting. Some of these best practices (Willoughby 2014) include the following:

- Look to past revenue forecasts to see if they turned out to be accurate and determine the causes for any **variance** (deviation from what was expected). In Fiscal Year 2017, 33 states received less revenue than expected, 13 received more revenue than expected, and only 4 received the amount expected (National Association of State Budget Officers 2017). Use this information to guide your budgeting decisions.

Table 12.5 Sample municipal staff budget

Category	Expense	Comments
Elected officials	Salary (Mayor, $80,000)	Set by statute
	Salaries (city council members, 9 members at $30,000 each)	Set by statute
Fringe benefits	$20,000	
Total elected officials	*$370,000*	
Appointed staff	City manager ($100,000)	
	Chief of staff ($80,000)	
	Chief financial officer ($85,000)	
	Economic development advisor ($80,000)	
	Human resource director ($80,000)	
	Purchasing director ($70,000)	
	Policy staff (5 at $40,000)	
	Communications staff (director at $70,000, 2 other staff at $40,000)	
	Outreach staff (5 at $40,000)	
	Scheduler ($50,000)	
	Other administrative staff (1 senior person at 75000, 2 general support staff at $40,000 each)	
Total staff salaries	*1,220,000*	
Fringe benefits	$305,000	May exceed this amount depending on benefits and tax rates
Total appointed staff	*$1,525,000*	
Overhead	Travel ($100,000), equipment/equipment maintenance ($400,000) Other overhead expenses such as office supplies, mailing, including printing and postage ($200,000)	These offices generally do not pay for their rent or utilities
Total overhead	*$700,000*	
Total	**$2,595,000**	

- Conduct thorough forecasts of revenue to understand the impacts of environmental changes on all potential revenue sources, in order to accurately estimate the moneys available for your current and future budgets.
- Responsibly calculate any long-term liability or debt and its budgetary impacts.
- Budget for the long term, over multiple years, to allow for long-term planning and strategy.
- Apply **result-oriented budgeting** that considers "the impacts of government spending, activities, services, and programs" (Willoughby 2014).
- Provide opportunities for public input and involvement in budgeting processes.
- Maintain balance and flexibility in both your revenue and spending plans.
- Pass the budget before the start of the fiscal year—or provide your agency's budget recommendations in a timely manner. While this may seem obvious, 10 of

the 46 states who started the 2017–2018 fiscal year on July 1 did not have final budgets by July 1 (National Conference of State Legislatures 2017).
- Make budgetary information as accessible as possible. (See the Center for Digital Government site in Resources to find out how governments in your area rate in their efforts to make information accessible.)
- Conduct efficient and equitable purchasing and contracting.
- Prepare timely financial audits using **generally accepted accounting principles (GAAP)**, a set of standard and generally accepted accounting practices released by the Financial Accounting Standards Board (FASB) or the Governmental Accounting Standards Board (GASB).

How public agencies approach their budgeting processes varies. The good news is that public budget processes often, by law, provide multiple opportunities for public input and discussion. Most states and municipalities are required to make information about their budget process public and (relatively) accessible. For example, in Wyoming, you can find the following:

- An easy-to-follow description of the budget process, on the state legislature's website (State of Wyoming Legislature n.d.-b).
- Information about legislative hearings and data gathered while the legislature was considering the budget, on the legislature's website (State of Wyoming Legislature n.d.-a).
- A detailed description from the governor of his total request for the 2-year budget term (Mead 2013). We particularly like the reader's guide (see page 21 of the Wyoming biennial budget, linked in the Resource section) which walks the reader through each category, its meaning, and how the governor's recommendation compares to agency's request for funding and the previous budget for the agency.
- Detailed information for each public agency, on the state Department of Administration and Information's website (Wyoming Department of Administration and Information n.d.).

You can find similar information online in most states, although the specific locations, detail of documentation, and ease of finding will differ significantly from state to state. A significant amount of budgetary information is online for larger cities. Even small towns will likely have information available when you visit town hall. In some towns, the residents will vote on the town budget via ballot or town meeting, providing significant motivation for town officials to clarify their budget rationale and process.

Budgeting in public agencies frequently suffers from political discord or gridlock. While the process of creating a budget at the local level might take 6 months, 12 months at the state level, or 18 months at the federal level, that timeline can change significantly if there are ideological or party disputes. In an extreme version of this, the state of Illinois went without a budget from 2015 to 2017 (O'Connor 2017).

As with the other types of political settings we describe in this chapter, budgets for public agencies range in size substantially. The smallest state budget in the country, Delaware, tops $4.1 billion in 2017–2018, while California has the largest budget, at $178 billion (Carney 2017; State of California n.d.). In Table 12.5, we provide a sample staff budget you might oversee if you were the Chief of Staff of a city with approximately $10 million in the budget for municipal administration.

FURTHER REFLECTION: State Budgets

1. For a picture of one of the more challenging scenarios possible, start at the bottom of this page and read through the timeline of the Illinois budget impasse: http://interactive.wbez.org/rauner/.

   As you read this timeline, in what ways do you think this budget impasse has impacted groups with whom social workers traditionally work?

2. Visit this tool from the Pew Charitable Trusts' States' Fiscal Health project: http://www.pewtrusts.org/en/multimedia/data-visualizations/2014/fiscal-50#ind0 and this discussion of state budgets from the National Conference of State Legislatures: http://www.ncsl.org/research/fiscal-policy/fy-2018-budget-status.aspx

   What do these data say about the fiscal health of your state? What questions would you like to ask your state legislators or executives about the budget of your state?

Section 6: Do Not Pass Go: Have Financial Experts on Board

The subtitle of this section could be "do it yourself is better for furniture than campaigns." The requirements that electoral campaigns and nonprofits face in raising and spending money are complicated. These requirements vary significantly from one state to another and from one level of campaign to another, and change often. One of the most important investments your organization or campaign can make is to consult with experts who can help you be sure to raise and spend money legally. This section focuses on the roles of experts in electoral campaigns and nonprofits. We also emphasize your responsibility to be sure that someone in your organization is familiar with the rules and laws that govern how you can raise and spend money, and has the responsibility and authority to ensure that those rules are followed. We do not cover public agencies in this section, as the processes in those agencies are so varied.

Electoral Campaigns

In an electoral campaign, the person responsible for knowing finance rules is the campaign treasurer. This person may be a paid staff member or volunteer. No candidate or issue campaign may conduct any financial transactions without a treasurer. The Federal Election Commission (2011) lays out a specific set of responsibilities of treasurers for federal election campaigns:

1. Filing the committee's registration form
2. Depositing receipts
3. Authorizing expenditures
4. Monitoring contributions
5. Keeping records
6. Signing all reports and statements
7. Filing all reports and statements on time

USE YOUR SKILLS: Your State's Campaign Finance Rules

Find your state's campaign finance disclosure and reposting requirements on the National Conference of State Legislatures web page:

http://www.ncsl.org/research/elections-and-campaigns/disclosure-and-reporting-requirements.aspx

What are the requirements for a campaign treasurer within your state? What is the name of the office in your state that oversees campaign finance? What trainings and services do they offer campaigns in your state?

Similar responsibilities are held by treasurers for electoral campaigns at all levels of government.

Typically, states have an office responsible for overseeing the campaign finance process. This office manages the ways state campaign finance rules are implemented and ensures that candidates and their campaigns understand them. As part of this process, most states will provide training for treasurers or others who are new to the process or would like a refresher. If you conduct an Internet search for "campaign finance" and your state's name, you should find the office and a list of trainings easily. Generally, the goals of these offices are to help you stay out of trouble, so take advantage of them!

Nonprofit Organizations

In a nonprofit organization, the people ultimately responsible for knowing and adhering to financial rules are the board of directors. Nonprofit board members are volunteers in a unique position. Although they are volunteers, they have **fiduciary**

responsibility for the organization; that is, they are legally responsible for the organization's financial operations and all associated filing requirements. As with campaign finance laws, financial registration and compliance rules for nonprofits vary substantially from state to state (National Council of Nonprofits 2017). The requirements can be very complicated. We have included links to the National Council of Nonprofits and the Hurwit & Associates' Nonprofit Law Resource Library in the Resource list at the end of the chapter, if you are interested in exploring these requirements in more detail. In any organization you work with, work with experts to ensure that your organization is meeting all reporting requirements. That does not mean that every member of your board needs to be a legal expert—it is often possible to bring in this expertise through staff, consultants, or membership in a collaborative group, such as a national or state council of nonprofits.

In general, nonprofit boards of directors must meet state requirements for registration and compliance in two main areas. General registration might include incorporation, application for any relevant tax exemption, providing contact information for responsible parties, and designating a **registered agent** (also called a statutory agent, agent for service of process, or a clerk) who will be notified if the organization is involved in legal action (Cullinane 2014). This is a one-time registration, but it must be updated regularly and if any of this information changes. Annual reports are often required (sometimes to multiple agencies) to verify that the nonprofit continues to do the work it set out to do and is continuing to meet state rules.

In addition to IRS reporting requirements for any political lobbying expenditures, nonprofits also have financial disclosure responsibilities. Generally, nonprofits are asked to specify in advance what types of **charitable solicitation** or fundraising activities the agency will be doing. They may need to register paid fundraisers, and, if required, pay related fees. Organizations may be required to register in the states in which potential donors live (National Council of Nonprofits n.d.). Therefore, if your organization raises money in multiple states, know whether you are required to register in all of them.

USE YOUR SKILLS: Your State's Nonprofit Registration/Fundraising Rules

1. Find your state's rules for general registration and compliance here: http://www.hurwitassociates.com/states-reporting-requirements
2. Find your state's requirements for charitable solicitation registration here. https://www.councilofnonprofits.org/tools-resources/charitable-solicitation-registration
3. Based on these resources, create a list of what the reporting requirements are specifically for new or continuing 501(c)(3) nonprofit advocacy groups in your state.

A key financial requirement for all tax-exempt organizations is to file Form 990 with the Internal Revenue Service. The 990 includes a significant amount of content about a nonprofit organization, including its mission, activities, governance, records retention, revenue, and audits. It also lists compensation for staff making over $100,000 per year, expenses, and changes in organizational assets (McLaughlin 2016). This is a critical reporting requirement to keep in mind within a nonprofit setting, but it is also an important resource as you seek to learn about, collaborate with, or work for a nonprofit organization. While the 990 will not tell you everything about an organization's finances, it offers an excellent window into the income, spending, and work of a nonprofit organization.

Since the late 1990s, the Guidestar website, linked in the Resource section, has digitized 990 forms and posted them on the Internet, so they are available for free to the public. The site currently has 1.8 million organizations represented and receives new forms from the IRS monthly. With a free account, you can look at the 990s of any organizations, generally within a few months after the forms have been filed with the government.

Review of Key Terms and Concepts

Capital budget: a type of budget that accounts for significant long-term expenses, such as a new building or significant infrastructure.

Capital campaign: a campaign often used by a nonprofit to raise a set amount of money for capital expenses within a specified period of time.

Charitable solicitation: fundraising activities performed by a nonprofit agency.

Disbursement: payments from a campaign.

Expenditure: purchase, payment, distribution, loan, advance, deposit, or gift of money or anything of value, intended to influence a federal election.

Fiduciary responsibility: legal responsibility for the organization's financial operations and all associated filing requirements.

Fiscal year: the 12-month period used by a government, agency, or business, to track and record finances.

Fringe benefits: the non-salary ways in which people are paid for their work.

Generally accepted accounting principles (GAAP): a set of standard and generally accepted accounting practices released by the Financial Accounting Standards Board (FASB) or the Governmental Accounting Standards Board (GASB).

Hybrid PAC: sometimes called Carey Committees, these PACs have two bank accounts: one which follows all the rules of a political action committee and a second which operates like a Super PAC.

Line-item budget: a type of budget that displays the money to be spent within specific individual categories (salaries, rent, utilities, etc.).

Non-expenditure: any money a campaign spends that does not influence a federal election.

Operating budget: a type of budget that accounts for day-to-day activities of an organization.

Overhead: ongoing operating costs of an organization.

Paid media: TV, radio, newspaper, or digital ads and costs associated with producing and running these ads.

Political action committee: also known as a PAC, political organizations that fall under section 527 of the US tax code. These organizations can give money to parties and candidates and accept money from individuals, other PACs, and political party committees, but within strict limits.

Program budget: a type of budget that categorizes expenditures by their allocation to different major activities.

Registered agent: a designated person (also called a statutory agent, agent for service of process, or a clerk) who will be notified if a nonprofit organization is involved in legal action.

Result-oriented budgeting: a type of budgeting that considers "the impacts of government spending, activities, services, and programs."

Social welfare organization: nonprofits organized under section 501(c)(4) of the US tax code. Many are explicitly ideological, but may not be organized for profit and must have the exclusive purpose of promoting social welfare as defined by the IRS.

Super PAC: previously known as Independent Expenditure Committees, these PACs have the potential to receive unlimited contributions and have no limits on how much money they can spend on elections.

Variance: deviation from what was expected, often used in the context of comparing intended and actual revenues.

Resources

Books

Ackerman, B., & Ayres, I. (2002). *Voting with dollars: A new paradigm for campaign finance*. New Haven, CT: Yale University Press.

Bobo, K. A., Kendall, J., & Max, S. (2010). *Organizing for social change: Midwest Academy manual for activists*. The Forum Press.

Corrado, A., Mann, T. E., & Ortiz, D. R. (2006). *The new campaign finance sourcebook*. Washington, DC: Brookings Institution Press.

McLaughlin, T. A. (2016). *Streetsmart financial basics for nonprofit managers*. Hoboken, NJ: John Wiley & Sons.

Miller, M. G. (2013). *Subsidizing democracy: How public funding changes elections and how it can work in the future*. Ithica, NY: Cornell University Press.

Mutch, R. E. (2016). *Campaign finance: What everyone needs to know*. New York, NY: Oxford University Press.

Riley, S. L., & Colby, P. W. (1990). *Practical government budgeting: A workbook for public managers*. Albany, NY: SUNY Press.

Willoughby, K. G. (2014). *Public budgeting in context: Structure, law, reform and results*. San Francisco, CA: Jossey-Bass.

Electoral Campaign Resources

Citizens United trailer: https://www.youtube.com/watch?v=BOYcM1z5fTs
Colbert Super PAC: http://www.colbertsuperpac.com/advisory/Advisory-Opinion.pdf
Federal Election Commission
  Campaign Finance Disclosure Portal: http://classic.fec.gov/pindex.shtml
  Information on Treasurers: http://www.fec.gov/pages/brochures/treas.shtml
  Hybrid PAC Information: http://www.fec.gov/law/recentdevelopments.shtml#HybridPACs
  Independent Expenditure Committee Information: http://www.fec.gov/law/recentdevelop-ments.shtml#IECommittees
Fundraising ideas for nonprofits from Fired Up Fundraising: http://www.gailperry.com/nonprofit-board-members-fundraising-ideas/
Historical article on money in American elections: http://www.motherjones.com/politics/2012/06/history-money-american-elections/
Hybrid PACs: http://talkingpointsmemo.com/muckraker/behold-the-hybrid-pac-all-the-benefits-of-a-regular-pac-with-the-super-bonuses
National Council of State Legislatures
  Campaign Finance resources: http://www.ncsl.org/research/elections-and-campaigns/campaign-finance.aspx or go to http://www.ncsl.org and in the menu under "Research" click "Elections and Campaigns" then click on "Campaign Finance".
  Disclosure and Reporting Requirements: http://www.ncsl.org/research/elections-and-campaigns/disclosure-and-reporting-requirements.aspx or go to http://www.ncsl.org and in the menu under "Research" click "Elections and Campaigns" then click on "Campaign Finance" and scroll down to click on "Disclosure and Reporting Requirements".
Super PACs: http://www.theatlantic.com/politics/archive/2016/02/super-pacs-2016/470697/
Wellstone Action
  Creating and Managing a Campaign: http://www.wellstone.org/resources/rules-and-tips-creating-and-managing-your-campaign-budget
  Sample Campaign Plan: http://www.wellstone.org/resources/sample-campaign-plan

Fundraising Resources

Certifying Fund Raising Executives: http://www.cfre.org/wp-content/uploads/2013/05/bgloss.pdf
Nonprofit Fundraising Resources: http://www.networkforgood.com/non-profit-fundraising-resources/
Nonprofit Glossary: http://grantspace.org/tools/knowledge-base/Funding-Research/Definitions-and-Clarification/glossaries
Online Fundraisers Glossary: http://www.networkforgood.com/nonprofitblog/online-fundraisers-glossary/

Nonprofit Agency Resources

How to read the new IRS 990 form: https://www.npccny.org/new990/
Guidestar website, providing nonprofit organizations' 990 forms free to the public: http://www.guidestar.org
Hurwit & Associates: http://www.hurwitassociates.com/resources
Nonprofit Finance Fund Glossary: http://www.nonprofitfinancefund.org/glossary
Sample Fundraising Plan: http://www.arts.texas.gov/wp-content/uploads/2012/05/Sample-Fundraising-Plan.pdf

State Filing Requirements for Nonprofits: https://www.councilofnonprofits.org/tools-resources/state-filing-requirements-nonprofits

Wallace Foundation Program-Based Budget Template: http://www.wallacefoundation.org/knowledge-center/Resources-for-Financial-Management/Pages/Program-Based-Budget-Template.aspx

Public Agency Resources

Budgeting and Finance: http://www.ca-ilg.org/budgeting-finance

Digital Government Achievement Awards: http://www.govtech.com/cdg/Best-of-the-Web-Digital-Government-Achievement-Awards-2016-Winners-Announced.html

Government Finance Officers Association
    Best Practices: http://www.gfoa.org/best-practices
    Publications: http://www.gfoa.org/publications

Pew Trust
    Government Performance Project: http://www.pewtrusts.org/en/archived-projects/government-performance-project
    States Fiscal Health: http://www.pewtrusts.org/en/projects/states-fiscal-health

---

References

Associated Press. (2017, June 19). Georgia's special election becomes the most expensive House race in history.

Carney, J. (2017). *Governor Carney signs fiscal year 2018 budget plan, capping General Assembly session*. Retrieved from http://news.delaware.gov/2017/07/03/governor-carney-signs-fiscal-year-2018-budget-plan-capping-general-assembly-session/

Chance, A. (2016). *Think tank and tax status: A note on the 501(c)(3) and 501(c)4 tax categories*. Retrieved from https://onthinktanks.org/articles/think-tanks-and-tax-status-a-note-on-the-501c3-and-501c4-tax-categories/

Cullinane, M. (2014). *Nonprofit Q+A: What is a registered agent?* Retrieved from https://cullinanelaw.com/what-is-a-registered-agent/

Federal Election Commission. (2011). *Committee treasurers*. https://www.fec.gov/updates/committee-treasurers-2017-record/

Federal Election Commission. (n.d.). *Making disbursements*. https://www.fec.gov/help-candidates-and-committees/making-disbursements/

Harwell, D., & Hobson, W. (2015, April 8). The NFL is dropping its tax-exempt status. Why that ends up helping them out. *The Washington Post*.

Internal Revenue Service. (2016a). *Employer's tax guide to fringe benefits*. https://www.irs.gov/pub/irs-pdf/p15b.pdf

Internal Revenue Service. (2016b). *Social welfare organizations*. Retrieved from https://www.irs.gov/charities-non-profits/other-non-profits/social-welfare-organizations

Jacobs, R., Tenenbaum, J., & Marcheski, M. (2010). *Mythbusting the top ten fallacies of 501(c)(3) lobbying*. Retrieved from http://www.acc.com/legalresources/publications/topten/mythbusting.cfm

McLaughlin, T. A. (2016). *Streetsmart financial basics for nonprofit managers*. Hoboken, NJ: John Wiley & Sons.

Mead, M. H. (2013). *Wyoming state budget 2015–2016 biennium*. Retrieved from https://drive.google.com/file/d/0BxgGvgRMOUrUSXV2UzNSSFJxaXM/view

Mutch, R. E. (2016). *Campaign finance: What everyone needs to know*. New York, NY: Oxford University Press.

National Alliance on Mental Illness. (2016). *2016 annual report*. Retrieved from https://www.nami. org/getattachment/About-NAMI/Our-Finances/Annual-Reports/2016NAMIAnnualReport.pdf

National Association of State Budget Officers. (2017). *Fiscal survey of the states*. Retrieved from http://www.nasbo.org/reports-data/fiscal-survey-of-states.

National Conference of State Legislatures. (2015). *Disclosure and reporting requirements*. Retrieved from http://www.ncsl.org/research/elections-and-campaigns/disclosure-and-reporting-requirements.aspx

National Conference of State Legislatures. (2017). *FY 2018 budget status*. Retrieved from http://www.ncsl.org/research/fiscal-policy/fy-2018-budget-status.aspx

National Council of Nonprofits. (2017). *State filing requirements for nonprofits*. Retrieved from https://www.councilofnonprofits.org/tools-resources/state-filing-requirements-nonprofits

National Council of Nonprofits. (n.d.). *Charitable solicitation registration*. Retrieved from https://www.councilofnonprofits.org/tools-resources/charitable-solicitation-registration

Nonprofit Research Collaborative. (2015). *Special report on nonprofit fundraising campaigns*. npresearch.org/images/pdf/2015-reports/NRC_Campaigns_S2015.pdf

O'Connor, J. (2017, July 16). Illinois has state budget, but no school funding plan. *Chicago Sun-Times*.

Philips, M. (2008, October 30). Politics: Do Robo-Calls work? *Newsweek*.

Reilly, R. J. (2011, August 5). Behold the 'Hybrid PAC': All the benefits of a regular PAC with the 'Super' bonuses. *Talking Points Memo*.

Reilly, J. F., & Allen, B. A. B. (2015). *Political campaign and lobbying activities of IRC 501(c)(4), (c)(5), and(c)(6) organizations*. Retreived from https://www.irs.gov/pub/irs-tege/eotopicl03. pdf.

Schadler, B. H. (2012). *The Connection: Strategies for creating and operating 501(c)(3)s, 501(c)(4)s and political organizations* (3 ed.). Washington, DC: Bolder Advocacy, Alliance for Justice.

State of California. (n.d.). *2017–18 California state budget*. Retrieved from http://www.ebudget. ca.gov/FullBudgetSummary.pdf

State of Wyoming Legislature. (n.d.-a). *Budget and fiscal information*. Retrieved from http://legisweb.state.wy.us/lsoweb/BudgetFiscal/BudgetFiscal.aspx

State of Wyoming Legislature. (n.d.-b). *Explanation of budget process*. Retrieved from http://legisweb.state.wy.us/lsoweb/BudgetFiscal/BudgetProcess.aspx

The Center for Public Integrity. (2014). *527s—Frequently asked questions*. Retrieved from https://www.publicintegrity.org/2005/11/21/5541/527s-frequently-asked-questions-5

The Center for Responsive Politics. (n.d.-a). *Most expensive races*. Retrieved from https://www.opensecrets.org/overview/topraces.php?cycle=2016&display=currcands

The Center for Responsive Politics. (n.d.-b). *What is a PAC?*. https://www.opensecrets.org/pacs/pacfaq.php

The Nonprofit Times. (2012). *Choosing your nonprofit's fiscal year*. http://nptimes.blogspot. com/2012/08/choosing-your-nonprofits-fiscal-year.html

Tschirhart, M., & Bielefeld, W. (2012). *Managing nonprofit organizations*. San Francisco, CA: Jossey-Bass.

Wellstone Action. (n.d.). *Sample campaign plan*. Retrieved from http://www.wellstone.org/resources/sample-campaign-plan

Willoughby, K. G. (2014). *Public budgeting in context: Structure, law, reform and results*. San Francisco, CA: Jossey-Bass.

Wyoming Department of Administration and Information. (n.d.). *2015–16 budget*. Retrieved from http://ai.wyo.gov/budget-division/budget-fiscal-years/2015-2016-budget

Part IV

Evaluating Political Social Work and Planning for the Future

"It is easier to spend a few months and some money electing the right people than to spend years and a lot of money trying to get the wrong people to do the right things"

–Senator Debbie Stabenow, MSW

Evaluating Political Social Work Efforts

13

© Springer International Publishing AG 2018
S.R. Lane, S. Pritzker, *Political Social Work*,
https://doi.org/10.1007/978-3-319-68588-5_13

Section 1: Overview

Is victory at the polls or successful passage of a law the only way to evaluate a campaign? This chapter considers other ways that a political strategy may be viewed to be successful, such as building candidate name recognition, facilitating the election of other candidates on a ticket, gaining credibility, and developing relationships. This chapter builds evaluation skills for advocacy and electoral campaigns through selecting appropriate metrics and methods to evaluate political social work efforts. Evaluation plans should be developed alongside your other strategic planning efforts, with benchmarks in pace before your efforts start. This helps to ensure that your evaluation efforts can inform and increase the effectiveness of your work while also ensuring that you collect the relevant data to assess the outcomes of your effort. We emphasize the ways in which evaluation can be used throughout a campaign, through both formative and summative evaluation, to assess progress and refine your strategy for success. Finally, the need for attention to monitoring implementation after a political success is discussed.

Developing Social Work Competency
The Council on Social Work Education establishes educational standards for all social work programs in the USA. Content in this chapter supports building competency in the following areas that are considered core to the practice of social work:
COMPETENCY 4: Engage in Practice-Informed Research and Research-Informed Practice
COMPETENCY 5: Engage in Policy Practice
COMPETENCY 9: Evaluate Practice with Individuals, Families, Groups, Organizations, and Communities

Domains of Political Social Work	
1. Engaging individuals and communities in political processes	◄
2. Influencing policy agendas and decision-making	◄
3. Holding professional and political positions	◄
4. Engaging with electoral campaigns	◄
5. Seeking and holding elected office	◄

Section 2: Evaluating Political Social Work

Evaluating our political campaigns is an important part of political social work practice. It is not enough for us to conduct advocacy campaigns on behalf of causes we care about or to work on behalf of good candidates. We need to make sure that the techniques we use are effective and that we are achieving our intended outcomes. The efforts we put into strategic planning are most successful when we consider how we will evaluate our political social work as part of our strategic planning. This attention to evaluating political social work practice mirrors the work we do in direct practice. Taking our clients through a planned change process involves having clear goals in mind from the beginning and identifying measures of success that help us evaluate whether those goals have been achieved. Just as we would not practice with individuals without being able to evaluate our work, we should not engage in political practice without evaluation.

Despite the importance of evaluation, many advocacy and electoral campaigns lack the resources and evaluation capacity to participate in evaluation (Whelan 2008). Some advocacy organizations are reluctant to engage in evaluation, because they perceive it as distracting from their core work. From an ethical perspective, however, if the political interventions we use are ineffective, we are obligated to consider whether we are really serving the needs of our clients and their communities. Furthermore, funders increasingly expect organizations to evaluate their advocacy efforts to ensure that their funds are being used effectively. In particular, funders are requesting evaluation measures beyond specific campaign or project outcomes. Funders are interested in methods that facilitate an organization or a community's ability to be more effective in future efforts, such as whether an advocacy campaign is building **capacity** for further political action.

At first glance, it might seem rather easy to evaluate the success of a campaign. Did your candidate win? Did your bill pass? These seem like straightforward ways to evaluate success. However, advocacy and electoral campaigns are generally not so straightforward. The complexity of political processes means that processes for conducting evaluations and identifying realistic benchmarks for measuring success are often challenging (Devlin-Foltz et al. 2012). A campaign that at first seems to have failed in reaching its desired goal may, in fact, have succeeded in moving the needle forward in important and meaningful ways.

FURTHER REFLECTION: Defining Success

Three different campaigns, both advocacy and electoral, are briefly described below. For each scenario, consider how the campaign might have defined "success" at the time. Then reflect upon what we see as the campaign's successes now, from our modern vantage point. What do *you* think ultimately constitutes success in each of these scenarios?

Scenario 1: Advocates in the USA have worked toward an Equal Rights Amendment (ERA), stating that "Equality of rights under the law shall not be denied or abridged by the United States or by any state on account of sex" since social worker Alice Paul introduced it to the Seneca Falls Convention in 1923 (Alice Paul Institute n.d.). The amendment was introduced to Congress in every session until its passage in 1972, after which it was ratified by 35

(continued)

states. Because it was not ratified by the required 38 states, however, the amendment was not added to the Constitution. To date, the amendment still has not been added to the Constitution, although efforts to do so continue. Some argue that efforts to pass and ratify the ERA set the stage for women's movements in the twentieth century. In turn, these movements led to other legislative and judicial changes that have accomplished much of the ERA's initial purpose (Teles and Schmitt 2011).

Scenario 2: In 2005, advocates in Connecticut worked with legislators to introduce a bill called "EC in the ER" to mandate that the option of emergency contraception to prevent pregnancy be offered to sexual assault survivors who came to emergency departments within 72 hours after their assault. The bill was assigned to a key legislative committee, but it never came before the full legislature for a vote. Two years later, in 2007, a revised version of this bill was signed into law by the Connecticut governor (S.B. 1343 2007). Very little about the law had changed since its introduction, but advocates shifted their approach in the intervening years.

Scenario 3: Shirley Chisolm, an educator from Brooklyn, served as a New York state legislator for 6 years. In 1968, she was the first black woman elected to the US Congress. During her second term in the House, she ran for president in the Democratic primary. Chisolm wanted to be not just the first black woman to run for president, but a viable candidate. However, she received just 151 delegate votes at that year's Democratic National Convention. She served in Congress for 14 years and cofounded the National Political Congress of Black Women. About her legacy, she said, "When I die, I want to be remembered as a woman who lived in the 20th century and who dared to be a catalyst of change. I don't want to be remembered as the first black woman who went to Congress. And I don't even want to be remembered as the first woman who happened to be black to make the bid for the presidency. I want to be remembered as a woman who fought for change in the 20th century. That's what I want" (Landers 2016). Today, her candidacy is seen as having laid the groundwork for subsequent candidacies like those of former President Barack Obama and Hillary Clinton.

Challenges in Evaluating Political Social Work Campaigns

Social work education highlights both evaluation of practice with individual clients and evaluation of service delivery, interventions, and policy on a broader scale. While many of the same themes you have learned elsewhere apply to evaluating political social work—and are discussed in this chapter—Teles and Schmitt (2011) eloquently describe some of the critical differences between evaluating service delivery and evaluating practice in the political sphere:

> *[A]dvocacy, even when carefully nonpartisan and based in research, is inherently political, and it's the nature of politics that events evolve rapidly and in a nonlinear fashion, so an effort that doesn't seem to be working might suddenly bear fruit, or one that seemed to be on track can suddenly lose momentum. Because of these peculiar features of politics, few if any best practices can be identified through the sophisticated methods that have been developed to evaluate the delivery of services. Advocacy evaluation should be seen, therefore, as a form of trained judgment—a craft requiring judgment and tacit knowledge—rather than as a scientific method. To be a skilled advocacy evaluator requires a deep knowledge of and feel for the politics of the issues, strong networks of trust among the key players, an ability to assess organizational quality, and a sense for the right time horizon against which to measure accomplishments. In particular, evaluators must recognize the complex, foggy chains of causality in politics, which make evaluating particular projects—as opposed to entire fields or organizations—almost impossible (n.p.).*

In the subsections below, we identify three of the largest challenges, aside from resource restrictions, to evaluating practice in the political sphere.

Complex Situations

As you have learned throughout this book, public policy-making is complex. It can be challenging to determine which specific forces actually lead to political change. It is similarly challenging to assess which specific forces are responsible for preventing social change from taking place. Just when we think we understand what factors cause or prevent change, we find that we might be wrong, such as when all of our predictors for an election (fundraising, polls, etc.) suggest one winner, but the opposite happens.

FURTHER REFLECTION: What Factors Cause Political Success or Failure?
Read through some of polling expert Nate Silver's analysis of why the 2016 US presidential election results turned out as they did at http://fivethirtyeight.com/features/the-real-story-of-2016/. You may know of other analyses that seek to explain Donald Trump's victory and Hillary Clinton's loss in that election. How many different factors can you name that have been identified as possible contributors to the success of the Trump campaign or to the Clinton campaign's loss?

Multiple Groups Working Simultaneously, Changing Tactics

Evaluation of political social work efforts is also complicated because often many groups work simultaneously on an effort. Sometimes this work happens intentionally together in coalition, but often it involves groups working on their own alongside one another. This makes it hard to determine the extent to which your specific organization contributed to the policy outcome. Did your one-on-one meeting with the chair of the Health and Human Services Committee stop the bill from passing, or did the bill die due to the protest on the capitol steps led by another organization? Or can you both claim some responsibility for victory?

This is further complicated by the fact that campaigns often change their tactics, making it hard to determine whether a single tactic or combination of tactics moved the needle. As Teles and Schmitt (2011) point out, advocacy is rarely achieved through a singular effort. It requires flexibility and the use of different tactics over time in order to bring about policy change. In fact, there are generally declining returns when a campaign repeatedly uses the same political tactics over time.

Systems Resist Change

By its very nature, in a political system that is designed to limit sudden policy changes, social change in the USA is rarely immediate. Often, policy changes— even some that appear immediate—are the result of years, or even decades, of efforts. In fact, well-designed and implemented tactics often fail to meet their goals even when done "correctly" because the political system is oriented toward preserving the status quo (Teles and Schmitt 2011). At the same time, politics can shift rapidly and in a nonlinear manner, throwing off what may otherwise have been successful advocacy efforts. Take, for example, climate change activism. Under President Barack Obama, efforts to address climate change were making inroads, and were expected to continue to move forward had Hillary Clinton been elected. In contrast, activists perceive that President Donald Trump's election moved those efforts in the opposite direction, particularly after his withdrawal from the international Paris climate agreement (Viscidi 2017).

Overcoming Challenges to Evaluating Political Social Work Practice

While these are all real challenges you will face in evaluating your political social work practice, there is increasing attention within the management, evaluation, and development literatures to practices that can help overcome these barriers. Consistently, these practices emphasize the need to pair evaluation efforts with assessment of the political context. This builds on the assessment skills that you have developed over the course of this book.

Acknowledge Various Definitions of Success

Experts consistently advise expanding our focus beyond policy change as the only marker of success in advocacy campaigns (Whelan 2008; Guthrie et al. 2005). Together with our funders, our boards, and our partners, we need to acknowledge explicitly that even exceptionally well-done advocacy campaigns may not yield our desired legislative goals. The political climate and other outside factors play a role in what we are able to achieve. Success in advocacy may include laying the foundation for future advocacy efforts by changing public opinion, raising awareness about the policy change among policy-makers, or building capacity to achieve your ultimate policy goal. Depending on the political context, success in advocacy may by necessity also include **playing defense** to keep bad legislation from passing—advocacy often requires advocates to act both in offensive and defensive roles (Guthrie et al. 2005). As policy conditions change, successful political efforts must continue to evaluate tactics, replicate successful ones, and change ineffective tactics to address the new realities and work toward overall social change (Teles and Schmitt 2011). Such factors should be acknowledged and measured in the evaluation process.

A similar dynamic applies to electoral campaigns. While an electoral victory is always a campaign's primary goal, it is important to acknowledge the other ways in which an electoral campaign may be successful, e.g., building name recognition for a first-time candidate, achieving a higher vote percentage than any prior candidate from the same party in your district, or creating such a formidable challenge to the incumbent that he/she spends the next 2 years in office being more responsive to the interests of your supporters.

Acknowledge Multiple Contributions to Success

As noted previously, no major policy change is solely the result of work by one person or one group (Teles and Schmitt 2011). Seeking individual claim for work done in coalition with others can fracture existing partnerships. Therefore, evaluation efforts are better spent focusing on what each organization or campaign contributed to the overall effort, rather than determining what specific part of a change is attributable to any specific actor (Devlin-Foltz et al. 2012). Focus on the process of the advocacy or electoral campaign and the ways in which participating in a particular effort may have helped an organization or a community develop the capacity to engage in future efforts.

Section 3: Evaluation Strategies

The evidence base for evaluating the effectiveness and costs of political social work efforts is limited in comparison to some other areas of social work practice (McNutt 2011). The lack of prior evidence increases the importance of introducing evaluation into your own political work. Incorporating evaluation into your practice will enable you to gauge for yourself and your organization(s) what is working and what is not and to share the results of your work to inform others.

Effective political social work, then, involves building evaluation into strategic and campaign planning from the beginning, so that all stakeholders have an agreed-upon set of benchmarks in advance (Whelan 2008; Guthrie et al. 2005). Through consistent attention to evaluating both the process of the campaign and its outcomes, a campaign can adjust its tactics, if needed (Teles and Schmitt 2011). The two approaches most commonly used in evaluating political social work practice can be defined as formative evaluation or summative evaluation.

Formative Evaluation

Formative evaluation measures the processes that are occurring within an advocacy or electoral campaign and/or within the organization(s) that is implementing the campaign. Formative evaluation can be used to measure whether we have all the resources (**inputs**) that we thought we would have access to in our campaign, and whether we are using them as effectively as intended. This approach to evaluation also measures **process indicators**, or **output measures**, that enable us to assess a campaign's "activities or efforts to make change happen" (Guthrie et al. 2005). Outputs refer to the direct products of your activities, specifically what you have directly *produced* as a result of your efforts. These may include quantitative indicators such as the number of meetings held, number of people reached by educational materials, or percentage of fundraising e-mails that are opened. These also may be qualitative in nature, such as whether all stakeholders are being included in activities or whether a campaign is staying consistent with its overall goal.

Formative evaluation allows us to monitor how our campaign is moving forward, and whether we need to adjust our strategic plan. It takes place in an ongoing fashion during the campaign. One way to continually monitor your campaign is by intentionally developing interim reports or "check-ins" that help inform your work and guide you in changing your actions as needed based on your measures of success (Whelan 2008; Guthrie et al. 2005). Such formative evaluation helps us critically assess whether we have carried out the campaign as intended, and if not, why not. For example, has the political context changed, resulting in our initial target(s) no longer being willing to meet with us? Has the media been more receptive to our campaign than we originally anticipated, suggesting a need to better integrate media-based tactics? Did our electoral campaign not reach our targeted numbers of voters during our phone banks, leaving us needing to identify new tactics for increasing turnout for our candidate? Formative evaluation and the outputs we measure can be very useful in helping us make decisions about adding, modifying, or eliminating tactics during the course of a campaign.

It is important to be clear, however, that formative evaluation and accompanying output measures are specifically focused on measuring *how a campaign is proceeding*. They are not the best approach for trying to determine whether the campaign's goals are actually being accomplished.

POLITICAL SOCIAL WORKER PROFILE: Juliana Cruz Kerker, MSW, JD

Contract Lobbyist/Legislative Advocate/Legislative Consultant (Fig. 13.1).

Fig. 13.1 Juliana Cruz
Kerker, M.S.W., J.D.

Juliana Cruz Kerker lobbies on behalf of the Texas Association of OB/GYNs and American Congress of OB/GYNs—District XI (Texas). Juliana sees her social work background as critical to her practice, giving her the skills that are required by her job on a daily basis. As a political social worker, Juliana places importance on "focusing on what my particular client needs" and practicing a client-centered approach while keeping in mind potential conflicts of interest and ethical conflicts.

Juliana began her political career as a participant in the University of Houston Graduate College of Social Work Legislative Internship Program, becoming Legislative Director for Texas State Rep. Garnet Coleman (D-147) upon graduation. Her legislative experience has taught her to always think carefully about strategy. "Working in the [Texas] Legislature, you always have to be five steps ahead of everybody"; as early as primary elections, strategy to move policy forward should be taking shape. Juliana has learned the importance of building relationships with candidates, elected officials, and their staff. She has also learned that relationships with those who may not necessarily always be on your side, but with whom you can begin to make progress, are also important. Through relationship and coalition building, Juliana says that you learn how to draw on the strengths and abilities of other allies to help make moves toward progress.

Ongoing assessment is a critical component of how Juliana approaches political strategy. She describes "testing the waters" as vital for anticipating changing environments and aiding in flexibility. She recommends preparing for the unexpected. It can be frustrating to see a well-researched and well-supported bill vetoed unexpectedly at the last minute for reasons beyond her control. Always being prepared for the unexpected has helped her to be able to quickly recover from setbacks, maintain focus on the larger goals she is trying to achieve, and move on.

(continued)

Juliana advises political social workers to be kind to yourself when working toward change on a macro level. Progress can come slowly at times, but by securing and celebrating the small incremental wins, eventually you will see a shift. For Juliana, this is best illustrated by her work with Rep. Coleman on mental health legislation nearly 10 years ago that got little traction in the Texas Legislature. During the most recent legislative session, mental health has been a priority for Texas Leadership, and a mental health bill that mirrored that earlier work has now passed the Texas House with substantial bipartisan support. What matters is the progress for people helped by the bill, not the speed at which it happens, nor the credit or thanks.

Summative Evaluation

Summative evaluation is used instead to focus on measuring the outcomes of a political campaign. This approach to evaluation collects **outcome indicators** to measure whether a change has occurred (Guthrie et al. 2005). Outcomes refer to the policy changes that accrue *as a result* of your efforts. Outcome indicators may be quantitative or qualitative. They can include indicators such as whether a bill passed, decision-makers' attitudes or behaviors on behalf of the campaign issue changed, or whether a candidate was endorsed by a major organization.

Summative evaluation is the approach that enables us to measure whether our campaign is impacting our targets in the intended way, and therefore whether it is reaching its goals. As discussed earlier in this chapter, outcome indicators often are not fully under the control of a specific campaign or organization. There may be many more factors in play, leaving it hard to discern the extent to which your specific campaign contributed to these outcomes.

As Guthrie et al. (2005) explain, summative evaluation and accompanying outcome indicators focus specifically on measuring *whether the campaign's goals are being accomplished*, rather than on measuring the campaign's activities. Belton (2001) suggests one potential method for carrying out a summative evaluation for an advocacy campaign. First, identify what policy outcome(s) would have been most likely without our campaign. Second, identify what policy outcome(s) emerged after our advocacy campaign. Third, calculate the difference between these two possible sets of outcomes. In some cases, this will be an easy calculation; in many others, it may be very difficult to discern. While political outcome measures—particularly as related to advocacy campaigns—may be harder to measure than outputs, they are a more accurate reflection of success.

A simplified illustration of Belton's method (in real life, this would have more moving parts): Let's assume we are part of an advocacy campaign to require foster care workers and foster caregivers in our state to receive training on identifying and preventing trafficking of youth in the foster care system. In step one, we consider what would have happened without our campaign. In this case, a prior bill had passed to develop training to identify youth in the foster care system at risk of becoming victims. Therefore, without our campaign, the outcome is that this training would have been developed and made available to foster care workers. In step two, we consider what outcome emerged after our campaign. In this hypothetical example, our outcome is that the state agreed to require this training of all foster care workers prior to the beginning of their employment and also of all caregivers before caring for a child in foster care. In the third step, we calculate the difference between these two outcomes. Here, we can calculate that our advocacy effort succeeded on two fronts: moving a voluntary training to a requirement for all foster care workers and adding a training requirement for caregivers.

Selecting Benchmarks

Given the challenges described above and the range of potential indicators available to a campaign, how do we choose which measures to evaluate? In using evaluation methods to determine success, it is important to identify specific **benchmarks**, which are observable, measurable standards that we use to measure how our campaign is progressing and whether it is succeeding.

Because of the challenges to measuring political work previously discussed, attention to identifying benchmarks for both output and outcome measures is critical. As Devlin-Foltz et al. (2012) note, "counting outputs such as visits to policy makers or fact sheets mailed is necessary, but not sufficient, to understand the potential impact of an advocacy effort" (p. 582). Benchmarks that track our outputs tell us what we have done, but do not provide information about how well a political social worker has influenced the decision-maker or whether engaging in these efforts has achieved the desired change. Similarly, while benchmarks that track our outcomes tell us a lot about whether our effort has been successful, they may not tell us the full story about what our campaign has accomplished—i.e., not achieving our bill's passage this year does not necessarily mean our campaign is a failure. Even if we do achieve our intended outcome, it is often not the end of a successful political effort. A policy change that passes the legislature may not be successful unless advocates continue to focus on the legislation by pushing for appropriate implementation, funding, and/or evaluation.

Section 4: Measuring Success in Political Social Work

In an ideal situation, a strategy for evaluation is discussed along with your other strategic decisions at the beginning of an advocacy or electoral campaign. We will be honest: this still rarely happens in political settings for a variety of reasons. However, we encourage you to consider ways to better integrate evaluation strategy into the political settings in which you practice—your social work training in evaluation may be one of the key skills you bring to the table. An ideal evaluation strategy incorporates the following steps:

1. Adopt an overall model for the change you are trying to create. This, at its essence, is what you are doing when you design the strategic plans we introduced you to in Part II of this book. Through this strategic planning process, you develop a clear—and logical—plan for why you expect the specific tactics you select to impact your target(s) in such a way as to enable your goals to be achieved.
2. Identify specific benchmarks that will define success for your campaign. These should match up with your campaign's long-term, intermediate, and short-term goals. In fact, you identify these when you evaluate the "M" (measurability) of your SMART goals.
3. Identify specific benchmarks for the output measures that will demonstrate that your campaign is moving forward as expected and that you are building capacity. These benchmarks should allow you to take into account changes in the political context that may influence your campaign's progress.
4. Develop a plan to collect data on these output and outcome measures.
5. Determine how you will continually report the data you collect back to key decision-makers (Guthrie et al. 2005).
6. Make changes as needed to the strategic plan to reflect these evaluation findings.

Our Code of Ethics calls on us to seek ways to meaningfully involve those who are directly affected by proposed policies both in implementing and evaluating our campaign. This is consistent with our ethical imperative for promoting empowerment and meaningful involvement in decision-making. It helps us increase our own accountability, to make sure that we do not label our work as successful when it will not result in meaningful impacts for those most directly affected (Whelan 2008).

In identifying the measures of success that your campaign will use in this strategy, it is important to acknowledge that campaigns differ widely in the types of questions they need to ask and the items they need to measure. They may pose different questions, have differing time frames, or have reasons to need different levels of rigor in the data they collect (Whelan 2008). In all cases, select benchmarks that are as rigorous as possible *and* can be feasibly collected and used with the resources you have available. Benchmarks should be clear and quantifiable, so that you know when they have or have not been reached. Care also should be taken to ensure that these benchmarks are consistent with your strategic plan or campaign plan. Bolder Advocacy, an initiative of the Alliance for Justice (see link in Resources), has played a leading role in developing benchmarks for evaluating advocacy and organizing work, and works extensively with funders to guide them in funding advocacy efforts. In the sections below, we outline some common output and outcome benchmarks, including many identified by Bolder Advocacy, which political social workers may use to evaluate their work.

POLITICAL SOCIAL WORKER PROFILE: Susan Hoechstetter, MSW
Senior Advisor for Foundation Advocacy and Evaluation, Alliance for Justice
(Fig. 13.2).

Fig. 13.2 Susan
Hoechstetter, MSW

Sue began her career path working with at-risk teens and entered her MSW program on the clinical track. As a student, she felt that working on the micro level was "going about change too slowly" for her, so she finished her clinical degree and additionally pursued a community organizing concentration at the University of Pittsburgh School of Social Work. Her last field placement was with a presidential campaign in Washington, D.C., and she says, "I just never left [DC]." Ever since, Sue has been involved in political social work working with advocates and community organizers including with the National Association of Social Workers as government relations director.

One of Sue's first post-MSW experiences was working for a migrant farmworkers group, the National Association of Farmworkers Organization (NAFO). This experience instilled in her a confidence that "people who focus on it really can get changes in the law." She was surprised at how relatively easy it was to change legislation if you can successfully organize around a specific issue. Over time, Sue explains, "what became important to me was getting people more involved in organizations and affecting policy because I could see how much we were able to get done for farmworkers."

Sue came to her current position at the Alliance for Justice with the goal of getting "foundations to not be so afraid to fund organizations that advocate to change policy." Quickly, the feedback from funders was that "we have to be responsive to our boards and show the effectiveness of the grants we're giving out, and we don't know how to evaluate that." Sue and her team at Alliance for Justice then worked to put together one of the first systems for evaluating advocacy work.

Sue realized that "there wasn't enough attention paid, in the evaluation process, to building an organization's capacity." She emphasizes that "advocacy successes are so dependent on external forces," such as who is in office, public opinion, the state of the economy, and changes in all of these factors. "Advocates and their organizations have to be ready to take advantage of opportunities" that are constantly appearing in the fluctuating political environment.

(continued)

The primary capacity assessment process that the Alliance for Justice created, the Advocacy Capacity Tool, is now used by organizations to take a snapshot of their ability and progress in building capacity for further advocacy. Sue also cited the importance of monitoring incremental progress that has been made through an advocacy effort (measuring more than just whether or not a bill passed) and noting how well an organization adapts to external changes in the evaluation process. As Sue notes, these "are now the basics in the field of advocacy evaluation."

Sue describes an example from her work coaching a group in California through the Advocacy Capacity Tool. Once they applied the tool "they realized that they had not considered what was going on in the [contemporaneous] election" and how that external force was impacting the advocacy work that they were trying to accomplish. After using the Advocacy Capacity Tool, the organization was able to recognize this gap and include nonpartisan election activities into the work that they were already doing. Sue reflects that, "having been an advocate myself, so much of what we do is intuitive, [and] I really appreciate having a tool" that helps groups and organizations have a systematic way to look at what they are doing.

Identifying Output Measures

Benchmarks used to measure the outputs of electoral and advocacy campaigns vary based on the type of campaign, goals, and tactics involved. As Devlin-Foltz et al. (2012) note, however, it is easy to make the mistake of measuring unnecessary outputs, such as the number of meetings we hold with a target, rather than whether we have built a meaningful relationship with that target:

> Advocates sometimes forget to distinguish between what can be measured and what is worth measuring …. When evaluators look at proposed measurable objectives, they must ask themselves and their clients the "so what?" question. That is, will achieving this objective tell us something we really need to know? (p. 583)

Table 13.1 lists some outputs that you might consider measuring in an electoral campaign. Others include voters contacted at each stage of the campaign process (in both voter identification and get-out-the-vote efforts), house parties held, and donor contacts made. Open rates, whether people open your campaign's e-mails, and **conversion rates**, whether people are actually completing a donation through your e-mail, can gauge the quality and utility of your e-mails. Electoral campaign outputs also may include the percentage of contacted voters who actually vote. Benchmarks focused on measuring capacity-building within electoral campaigns may include the number and level of commitment of volunteers working on behalf of the campaign. A campaign that recruits and retains a large number of volunteers may have more capacity for a subsequent run than one that does not.

There are a wide array of possible benchmarks to measure advocacy campaign outputs, as indicated in Table 13.1. Other benchmarks specifically focus on how a

Table 13.1 Example output measures for campaigns

Electoral campaign	Advocacy campaign
Number of voters contacted overall	Number of stakeholders who commit to advocacy
Numbers of 1s and 2s contacted (voters who support your candidate)	Number of legislative meetings held
Money raised	Money raised
Amount of favorable press coverage	Amount of favorable press coverage
Volunteers who come back regularly	Number of supporters who sign up to testify
Relationships built that may improve success of next run	Relationships built that may improve success of next year's advocacy campaign

campaign implements its tactics, such as the number of phone calls made, presentations or testimonies given, petitions signed, or number of asks to your network to act in support of your advocacy goal (e.g., action alerts sent), or whether your campaign has identified individuals who can serve as media spokespeople. These can tell you whether your campaign is doing what it says it will, but may not give you enough information about whether your campaign is making progress in translating these tactics into policy change. Outputs that may tell you more about how your campaign is progressing include whether a campaign has built an ongoing relationship with key decision-makers relevant to your policy issue, how often key decision-makers return your phone calls, and whether representatives of your campaign are being asked to testify at legislative hearings, or contacted by legislative staff to provide relevant, factual information (Dodson et al. 2015; Tabak et al. 2015).

Output benchmarks that focus on whether the campaign is building capacity for this specific effort may include an increase in public awareness around your issue, involvement of members of the public in your campaign, or an increase in advocacy skills among campaign participants (Belton 2001). Additionally, benchmarks may focus on the organization more broadly to assess whether it is building long-term advocacy capacity that can last beyond the current effort. Some benchmarks that Alliance for Justice (2004) has identified to assess an agency's capacity-building are presented here. Achieving these benchmarks demonstrates that an organization/campaign is developing a presence and is prepared to carry out subsequent advocacy efforts.

Benchmarks for Organizational Capacity-Building
- Maintains a consistent presence in federal, state, county, and local legislative bodies
- Can identify and has contacts in agencies that implement policies and programs related to its issue priorities
- Understands relevant agencies' deliberation and rule-making processes
- Regularly communicates with its network [of interested individuals and organizations] through e-mail, newsletters, meetings, or other means
- Regularly provides formal activities to educate and build the advocacy capacity of its network

Excerpted from *Investing in change: A funder's guide to supporting advocacy* (Alliance for Justice 2004)

In voter engagement campaigns, output-focused benchmarks might include the number of voter registration events conducted by your organization, number of new voters registered, number of candidate forums held, number of pledge cards signed, or number of brochures handed out to provide nonpartisan information about candidates. It could also include the number of social workers trained to participate in voter engagement or the level of positive response to the training.

> **APPLY YOUR SKILLS: Identifying Output Measures**
> Consider a campaign that you planned earlier in this book or a political social work campaign in which you have participated. Identify three output measures for the campaign that would be relevant, could be gathered in a fairly short period of time, and could be implemented efficiently, without placing great burden on your campaign.

Selecting Outcome Measures

Benchmarks focusing on the outcomes of political campaigns should be closely tied to the goals you have identified for your campaign. That is, you will know your campaign has been successful when you have achieved the goals you set out for the campaign.

In an electoral campaign, this commonly involves seeing your candidate elected or seeing your position reflected in the outcome of a ballot measure. Outcome measures may include those listed in Table 13.2, as well as such benchmarks as seeing a marked change in public views about your candidate (e.g., more favorable views toward your candidate, an increase in credibility as a candidate), seeing your candidate win by a specific target number of votes or achieve a specified share of the votes. Whether or not your own candidate wins, depending on your political context, an outcome that may be of interest to some campaigns is facilitating the election of other candidates on a ticket. In electoral politics, we are often interested in whether our campaign's efforts help bring out more support for other candidates who are also running. In the end, however, winning the election is the ultimate benchmark in electoral campaigns. As social worker and political trainer Kate Coyne-McCoy says, "You should enter races that you think you can win. Period" (personal communication, March 3, 2017).

Table 13.2 Sample outcome measures for campaigns

Electoral campaign	Advocacy campaign
Election victory	Successful legislative vote
Number of votes the candidate received	Bill signed by governor
Issue stances supported by the candidate that are adopted by the opponent	Regulation upheld, modified, or defeated (depending on your goal)
Increase in candidate name recognition	Public commitments to vote for future version of the bill

In an advocacy campaign, goals—and therefore desired outcome measures—may vary more widely from campaign to campaign. Typically, outcome measures focus on a change in policy, accomplishment of specific steps that indicate movement toward a policy change, or changes in the views of decision-makers. Success is often achieved when your campaign's targeted legislation passes and is signed into law, as indicated in Table 13.2.

Alliance for Justice (2004) provides a more expansive list of potential benchmarks a campaign may use to evaluate success in advocacy, beyond progress on a specific regulation of piece of legislation. Some of the benchmarks they identify are presented here.

Benchmarks for Assessing Advocacy Outcomes
- Shows that policy-makers introduce bills which reflect some or all of its interests
- Establishes that legislation representing its interests proceeds through different steps of approval in the legislative process
- Shows that policy-makers champion its issue in committee or with other legislators
- Confirms that legislation representing its interests is signed into law
- Has its comments on proposed regulations cited by the targeted administrative agency in final regulations
- Influences regular press coverage on its key issue priorities, demonstrated through quotes and issue stances reflecting its view
- Attracts media coverage of its issues

Excerpted from *Investing in change: A funder's guide to supporting advocacy* (Alliance for Justice 2004)

In voter engagement campaigns, outcome-focused benchmarks may include showing a specific increase in voter registration or voter turnout in your targeted community. It also could include measures of community empowerment connected to political engagement, such as increased expression of political voice and power.

APPLY YOUR SKILLS: Identifying Outcome Measures
Consider the campaign that you discussed in the last activity. Identify three outcome measures for the campaign that would be relevant, could be gathered in a fairly short period of time, and could be implemented efficiently, without placing great burden on your campaign. (See further discussion of these three considerations in the paragraph below.)

Data Collection

An evaluation strategy requires attention to not just what we measure, but also to how we collect our output and outcome data. There are three considerations political social workers need to keep in mind when selecting data collection methods: relevance, timeliness, and efficiency (Coffman and Reed 2009). **Relevance** of data collection asks: will the methods we are considering truly help us collect data that can inform our strategic decisions? **Timeliness** of data collection considers whether the methods can be administered and analyzed fairly quickly so that we can respond and adapt our strategy in a timely manner. Finally, given the many constraints on our time and resources, **efficiency** of data collection examines whether the data collection methods are burdensome. Can we implement them with minimal impact on our other work, given the resources at hand?

Evaluations of political social work campaigns often incorporate the same data collection methods as other types of evaluations you may have learned about in your social work education. These may include interviews, focus groups, and surveys, in order to gather information and perspectives from relevant policy stakeholders. However, given the complexities of evaluating political efforts described previously, you may find other data collection methods to be useful as well. These methods may incorporate reviews of public records, such as records of individuals' voter registrations and voter history; legislators' vote history, committee statements, and bill introduction/sponsorship; as well as the language used in bills, laws, and regulations. Some other methods for collecting data to evaluate political efforts are outlined below.

Public polling is often useful in political work, although it can be expensive to implement. For small campaigns with limited resources, partnerships with universities who conduct polling research may be one way to access this kind of data, while large electoral campaigns may incorporate polling into their campaign infrastructure. **Public polling** interviews stakeholders at random to assess their attitudes and/or behaviors. This data collection method is particularly useful for electoral campaigns interested in learning more about name recognition and favorability ratings for their candidate. However, it can also be used to gauge the knowledge, attitudes, or behaviors of advocacy stakeholders (Coffman and Reed 2009).

Legislative tracking, which we have discussed earlier in this book, is a data collection method commonly used in advocacy campaigns. Through legislative tracking, you monitor how the bill(s) or ordinance(s) you are working on is progressing through the policy-making process. As your campaign proceeds, you will also want to track companion or related proposals that are moving through the legislative process to monitor how they may be affecting your issue, and whether you need to adapt your strategy to respond to any of these. Similarly, you might track the process of proposed regulations through the *Federal Register*, or your state's equivalent publication.

At times, your evaluation strategy may require you to examine media coverage of your campaign. **Media tracking** is one method for doing this; through media tracking, you can count occurrences of your campaign, issue, or candidate being covered in various media sources. Depending on the geographical context for your campaign, you might track media on a local, state, or national level. This tracking can include print, electronic, or broadcast media sources. Through a media content analysis, you can track what the specific content related to your campaign, issue, or candidate looks like and how it is being framed.

Coffman and Reed (2009) identify several new data collection methods that have been developed for the unique characteristics associated with efforts to seek policy change. Here, we introduce two of these that may have particular relevance to the work in which readers of this book will engage. Developed by the Harvard Family Research Project, the **Policymaker Ratings** method seeks to evaluate the extent of support for a specific advocacy issue among relevant decision-makers. As part of their evaluation efforts, multiple advocates work together (or individually, and then average their ratings) to rate relevant decision-makers along a series of three scales assessing:

1. Each policy-makers' level of support for the issue, based on the policy-makers' public behaviors or actions—from 1 (not at all supportive) to 4 (extremely supportive).
2. Their level of influence over the issue, based on six criteria (member of majority party, seniority, member of a key committee, formal leadership position, relevant expertise in the content area, reputation within the legislative body)—from 1 (not very influential) to 4 (extremely influential).
3. The advocates' level of confidence around ratings #1 and #2—from 1 (not very confident) to 3 (extremely confident).

This data collection method shares similarities with the power analyses that we use to help design our strategy; however, it reminds us that such analyses are working documents. The level of support and/or influence that policy-makers hold vis-à-vis our issue can change over time, necessitating changes to our strategy. Revisiting our power analyses or conducting regular Policymaker Ratings reviews over the course of our efforts can help us identify and adapt to any shifts that occur.

The **Intense Period Debrief**, developed by the Innovation Network, responds to the extensive time constraints advocates commonly face mid-campaign by creating a very brief opportunity for advocates to pause and reflect on their campaign's progress (Coffman and Reed 2009). A **debrief interview protocol** is used either with a one-time focus group of advocates or in brief individual interviews to capture real-time information about how the campaign is proceeding and what is happening behind the scenes in the effort. This may be especially useful after a major event or shift happens in an advocacy effort. We provide sample questions provided by the Innovation Network that advocates might use as a basis for developing a one-time intensive debriefing guide.

Intense Period Debrief: Sample Questions

Excerpted from *Unique Methods in Advocacy Evaluation* (Coffman and Reed 2009)

1. What events triggered this intense period?
2. How was the organization's response determined? Who was responsible for that decision? How was that decision communicated to other partners and allies?
3. Which elements of the organization's response worked well? Which elements could have been improved?
4. What was the outcome of the intense period? Was the result positive or negative?
5. What insights will you take away from this experience that might inform your strategies going forward?

FURTHER REFLECTION: Considering Data Collection Methods

Consider the campaign that you discussed in the activities earlier in Section 3. Describe a data collection strategy you could use to gather each of those measures. Once you have identified that data collection strategy, reassess whether it is possible to collect those measures in a manner that is relevant, timely, and efficient. Is it, or do you now feel, that other measures would be more suited to the work at hand?

APPLY YOUR SKILLS: Bringing It All Together to Evaluate a Political Social Work Effort

The Nancy A. Humphreys Institute for Political Social Work has launched a campaign with the goal of engaging more social workers in electoral politics (Lane et al. 2017.; Ostrander et al. 2017). Primary tactics utilized by this campaign include presentations at conferences, meetings with interested social workers and faculty, development of relationships with elected officials and campaigns, and development of political field placements. This campaign centers around an annual Campaign School for Social Workers (www.politicalnstitute.uconn.edu). This is a 2-day training for social workers that prepares them for leadership roles in campaigns, to run their own electoral campaigns, and/or to hold careers in political social work. Over 1000 participants have attended the Campaign School over the last 21 years, from across the country.

(continued)

You have been asked to join the team responsible for evaluating the campaign's success to date. Some measures that the team has already considered are listed below.

- Creation of policy that represents social work values and ethics
- Creation of policy that prioritizes the impact on marginalized populations
- Number of social workers who run for office
- Number of social workers who hold leadership positions in electoral campaigns
- Number of social workers who volunteer on electoral campaigns
- Number of social workers who report interest in running for office
- Increase in political efficacy from the beginning of the training to the end of the training
- Number of social workers who attend the Campaign School for Social Workers

The team will be conducting both a formative and summative evaluation. Create your own set of measures that you think should be included in these evaluations, dividing the measures into output and outcome measures. You can use all or some of the measures listed here, or identify other relevant output or outcome measures that are not listed here.

Once you have identified a set of output and outcome measures to evaluate this campaign, plan your data collection. What methods would you use to collect data on each of your selected measures?

Data Analysis

How you analyze your evaluation data depends on the types of measures you select. Most of the measures we have discussed in this chapter rely on quantitative analyses that are descriptive (e.g., how many volunteers supported your campaign) or bivariate (e.g., what rates of voters contacted by your campaign voted when compared to those not contacted by the campaign) in nature. Some of the measures require qualitative analyses (e.g., have you influenced the content of press coverage). Other more advanced analytical approaches can be useful when evaluating political work, but are beyond the scope of this textbook. For example, McNutt (2011) outlines analysis methods that social workers can use to determine if their campaign is spending its funds appropriately on advocacy. These include return on investment analysis, cost-effectiveness analysis, and cost-benefit analysis.

Section 5: Win Number: The Key to Electoral Outputs and Outcomes

In an electoral campaign, your primary goal is for your candidate or issue to win, that is, to get more votes than the other side (or to get an absolute majority—more than half—in jurisdictions where a plurality is not considered enough to win an election). In advocacy campaigns, the closest analogy to this is your **whip count**, which is your estimate of how many legislators would vote the way you want them to if your issue was voted on today.

Determining your specific benchmark for reaching electoral success is not as simple as identifying how many registered voters there are in your jurisdiction and calculating the majority-plus-one. As discussed elsewhere, not all eligible voters vote, so the number of votes you win is actually dependent on the number of voters who will vote in the election, not the total number of eligible voters. How can you determine what that will be, and therefore the number of votes you will need to win the election (your "**win number**")?

One tool that is helpful in calculating a win number is the Wellstone Action "WIN Number Calculator." Here, we will use it to help us identify an outcome benchmark for the candidacy of Lisa Simpson, running for City Council in the fictional town of Springfield in November 2018.

Step 1: Determine how many candidates are in the race Fig. 13.3.

In this example, there are two candidates: our candidate, Lisa Simpson, and her opponent James Incumbent. Our example focuses on the most straightforward

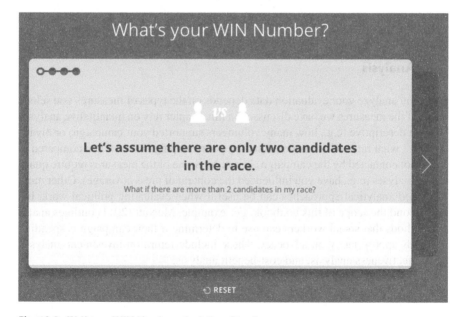

Fig. 13.3 Wellstone WIN Number calculation, Step 1

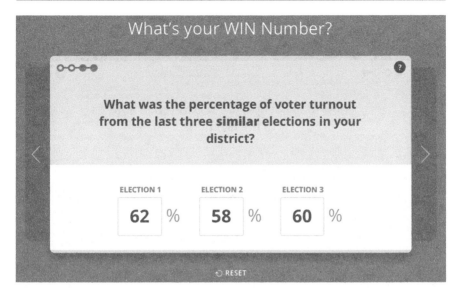

Fig. 13.4 Wellstone WIN Number calculation, Step 2

scenario—two major candidates—however, the math is slightly different if three or more candidates are in your race, or if multiple candidates are running for multiple seats (i.e., if two at-large seats are open on the City Council, and six candidates are running for these two seats) (Levy-Pollans 2013).

Step 2: Find out what the average turnout was in the last three similar elections in the district. Fig. 13.4

Our best estimate of future voter turnout is past turnout. However, it is important to be sure that we are comparing apples to apples when we make this estimate. If you are running in a midterm election year (e.g., 2018 or 2022), the turnout will be different than it was in a presidential election year (e.g., 2016 or 2020). Municipal or state elections that happen in odd number years or in times of the year other than the second Tuesday in November will have different voter turnout than federal elections. As we have discussed elsewhere in this textbook, the highest voter turnout in the USA is for presidential elections, while turnout is typically quite low for municipal and non-regular elections.

So, Lisa Simpson will want to identify the last three elections in her city that occurred in non-presidential years (e.g., 2014, 2010, and 2006). These numbers can be gathered from your state or local election officials. Lisa Simpson is running for office in a comparatively highly engaged district (in some of your own municipal elections, you may see voter turnout as low as in the single digits). In Lisa's district, the turnout for those past three elections is as follows: 62% (2014), 58% (2010), and 60% (2006). Enter these numbers into the Wellstone calculator, as shown here.

Step 3: Determine how many people are registered to vote in your district (Fig. 13.4).

Voter turnout percentages are based on the population of registered voters in a district. Remember that if individuals are not registered to vote, they cannot vote.

Fig. 13.5 Wellstone WIN Number calculation, Step 3

Therefore, campaigns typically target those individuals who are registered to vote. If your state has Election Day Voter Registration, this can change your calculations somewhat; however, for the most part, people who have never voted are hard to get to the polls to vote. (If it's still bothering you that we are not counting marginalized populations who do not participate because they do not feel they have a voice, you are not alone!) For these purposes, those who are not registered to vote may be better thought of as voters who will help us exceed, not meet, our win number (Fig. 13.5).

In Lisa's district, 1000 people are registered to vote.

Step 4: Using these variables, calculate how many votes are needed to win the election (Fig. 13.6).

So how many votes does Lisa need to win?

The calculator shows that Lisa needs 313 votes to win this election. Thus, her outcome benchmark would be "receiving 313 votes to win this City Council election."

But wait, you say, there are 1000 registered voters in Lisa's district—shouldn't we be shooting for 501 votes? Think back to our voter turnout numbers. Not everyone who is eligible to vote registers, and not everyone who is registered to vote votes. The only way we can reasonably estimate the turnout for this year is by looking to previous years that are similar to this one. Of course, no one wants to win an election by just one vote. The Resources section lists tools that can help you predict what a cushion over the last few candidates who ran in your position in this race might look like. You also can do the math yourself and calculate your **vote deficit**,

Fig. 13.6 Wellstone WIN Number calculation, Step 4

the gap between the number of people who are definitely supporting you and the number you need to win.

These calculations of course assume that turnout in this election will be consistent with other similar elections in the past. This is not always the case. There may be factors that encourage some groups to turn out or to stay home, making turnout this year higher (e.g., controversial issues on the ballot) or lower (e.g., bad weather) than prior elections. Changes in voting laws in your area also can make it easier or harder for specific groups to get to the polls. Predicting voter turnout is not an exact science, and you should assess your overall context as well as this win number as you identify your target benchmarks. However, we would not ever recommend aiming for a win number <u>lower</u> than the one that is calculated. Always aim for this number or higher to be on the safe side.

APPLY YOUR SKILLS: Selecting a Win Number
Select an upcoming election in your local municipality. Follow the four steps identified above, using the Wellstone Action "WIN Number Calculator" (http://www.wellstone.org/resources/win-number-calculator), and identify the win number for a candidate in that election. Was this process straightforward, or challenging? Why?

Section 6: Implementation

Too often, both our advocacy campaigns and our measurement of a campaign's success end when our policy goal has been reached: a bill signed in to law, a budget amendment adopted, or a local ordinance approved. Perhaps the legislature passed the bill we were supporting, or an executive agreed to change the way in which services are delivered. Unfortunately, this means that we often stop our advocacy efforts and our monitoring too soon. A similar mistake can happen after electoral campaigns. Our favored candidate wins, and we no longer pay as careful attention to the stances or actions the newly elected official takes once in office. It is critical to remember that political success only is lasting if the policy change is implemented as intended.

The **policy implementation** process is what truly brings a policy change from an idea to actuality. If they think of it at all, most people think of policy implementation as a straightforward process: A policy is approved by the relevant body and then is given to the relevant experts within that level of government to enact. This idea comes from classical Weberian models of bureaucratic decision-making, which assume that policy-makers are the ones making key decisions, and that technicians within government are merely carrying out those decisions. This makes sense in theory, but in actuality, the implementation process is a fundamental part of policy-making that has the potential to transform policy.

The policy implementation process may involve implementing policies exactly as intended by the policy-makers. It may involve developing new policies that go beyond the parameters of existing policies. It even may involve subverting the original intentions of policy-makers. The latter two options suggest a need for continued monitoring and evaluation of the implementation process, as the policies that result may do more—or less—for your policy issue than you were seeking.

In the typical implementation of a piece of legislation passed by a legislature, the responsibility for implementing the law, that is, moving the law into practice, is given to the executive branch agency or department responsible for oversight of that specific content area. This implementation process involves the agency or department developing ("promulgating") a series of written regulations (sometimes referred to as "regs," and, in final form, referred to as "rules") that explain how the law will be enacted, enforced, and evaluated by the government (Mickelson 2013). These rules or regs, subject to public comment, may include details of how a program will be staffed, what services will actually be provided, what fees (if any) will be charged, and how eligibility for services will be delivered (Mickelson 2013).

While more expansive than for many laws, a particularly complex law like the 2010 Patient Protection and Affordable Care Act (ACA) required multiple federal agencies to be involved in implementing regulations. Each agency had a role in how the law was implemented, meaning there were substantial opportunities for specific details to be determined long after the bill was signed into law. Furthermore, the ACA required a significant amount of state-level implementation decisions, creating opportunities for additional shifts to the original policy intent. From 2011 to 2014, 3702 bills and resolutions were proposed across the country related to the ACA. In 2015–2016, there were 400 relevant laws and resolutions passed across all 50 states, the District of Columbia, and Puerto Rico (National Conference of State Legislators 2017). When President Trump took office in January 2017, federal agencies substantially changed how they implemented the law (White House 2017), while legislative efforts focused on replacing it.

How a policy is ultimately carried out and communicated to clients is not just impacted by regulatory policy-making or policy-making at other levels of government. Implementation is also affected by how agency employees responsible for service delivery ("front-line workers") manage the challenges that arise in policy implementation. As Meyers et al. (1998) describe in an extensive study of the implementation of the federal Temporary Assistance to Needy Families policy, employees at the front lines working directly with welfare recipients rarely communicated to them elements of the policy that were policy-makers' priorities. This did not appear to be intentional, but rather the result of insufficient training, resources, and additional expectations being placed on already overburdened workers. Similarly, resource restrictions, large caseloads, and poor organizational culture led social workers in the UK to delay or avoid investigating allegations of elder abuse, despite enacted policy that sought to increase adult protection (Ash 2013). While political social workers may not be able to monitor all of these subsequent steps of policy implementation, we must be aware of the importance of monitoring what happens after a law is passed. Social workers are particularly well suited to see how policy implementation affects the populations we work with. Connections and networks between social workers in direct service and those engaged in policy change are a critical way to communicate problem and concerns back to policy-makers and into the policy process.

While it is beyond the scope of this chapter to go into detail about advanced policy evaluation designs and methods, we want to acknowledge the range of policy evaluation approaches that exist. These include policy content evaluation, case studies, quasi-experimental designs, and cost-benefit analyses (Centers for Disease Control n.d.). We provide some additional resources in the Resources section for readers interested in further exploring these approaches.

APPLY YOUR SKILLS: Exploring Policy Implementation
Find a bill that passed within your state within the last 2 years. Try to find information on how it is being implemented. Have any regulations been proposed related to the bill yet? Read through any proposed or final rules. In what ways do they seem consistent, or not, with what the law was originally designed to do? If the public comment period is still open, what would you want to recommending adding or modifying?

Review of Key Terms and Concepts

Benchmarks: observable, measurable standards used to measure how a campaign is progressing.

Capacity: an organization or a community's ability to achieve its goals in future efforts.

Conversion rate: the percentage of recipients who respond to a campaign's e-mail to complete a donation.

Debrief interview protocol: brief data collection process used to capture real-time information about how a campaign is proceeding and what is happening behind the scenes in the effort.

Efficiency (of data collection): the extent to which data collection methods are burdensome.

Formative evaluation: measurement of the processes occurring within an advocacy or electoral campaign and/or within the organization(s) that is implementing the campaign.

Inputs: the resources thought to be accessible during a campaign.

Intense period debrief: a very brief opportunity for advocates to pause and reflect on their campaign's progress.

Legislative tracking: monitoring how bills or ordinances are progressing through the policy-making process.

Media tracking: counting occurrences of your campaign, issue, or candidate being covered in various media sources.

Outcome indicators: measurements of success in policy changes as a result of your efforts; may be quantitative or qualitative.

Output measures: evaluation of how a campaign is proceeding. See "process indicators."

Playing defense: policy work that focuses on keeping bad things from happening.

Policy implementation: the process of moving a policy from an idea to actuality.

Policymaker Ratings: evaluating the extent of support for a specific advocacy issue among relevant decision-makers.

Process indicators: assessment of the activities a campaign is implementing and its efforts to elicit change. See the definition of output measures above.

Public polling: interviews of stakeholders at random to assess their attitudes and/or behaviors.

Relevance (of data collection): assessment of whether research methods will collect data that are able to inform our strategic decisions.

Summative evaluation: measurement of the outcomes of a political campaign.

Timeliness (of data collection): Assessment of whether research methods can be administered and analyzed fairly quickly so that we can respond and adapt our strategy in a timely manner.

Vote deficit: the gap between the number of people who are definitely supporting a campaign and the number needed to win.

Win number: the number of votes a candidate needs to win an election.

Resources

Advocacy Evaluation Resources

Alliance for Justice's Bolder Advocacy website (all free):
  Main website: http://www.bolderadvocacyorg
  ACT Quick: http://www.bolderadvocacy.org/tools-for-effective-advocacy/evaluating-advocacy/act-quick!
  Advocacy Capacity Tool: http://www.bolderadvocacy.org/tools-for-effective-advocacy/evaluating-advocacy/advocacy-capacity-tool
  International ACT: http://www.bolderadvocacy.org/tools-for-effective-advocacy/evaluating-advocacy/international-advocacy-capacity-tool
  Power Check: http://www.bolderadvocacy.org/tools-for-effective-advocacy/overview-of-evaluating-community-organizing/powercheck

Book

Alliance for Justice and the Council on Foundations. (2008). *Words to Give By.*—a book based on interviews with 23 funders about funding and evaluating advocacy. Also available at https://www.bolderadvocacy.org/wp-content/uploads/2012/01/Words_to_Give_By.pdf

Other Resources

Advocacy & Social Movements: http://www.innonet.org/index.php?section_id=3&content_id=601#resources
Calculating your win number: https://blog.ngpvan.com/running-for-local-office-you-need-this-number-to-win
Evaluation Exchange, especially volume 13, issue 11: http://www.hfrp.org/evaluation/the-evaluation-exchange/issue-archive
Evaluating Initiative: http://ctb.ku.edu/en/evaluating-initiative
Federal regulations site: https://www.regulations.gov/
http://www.hewlett.org/library/grantee-publication/elusive-craft-evaluating- advocacy
Office of Information & Regulatory Affairs: https://www.reginfo.gov/public/jsp/Utilities/faq.jsp
The Elusive Craft of Evaluating Advocacy:
Vote Deficit Calculator: http://www.wellstone.org/resources/vote-deficit-calculator

Policy Evaluation Resources from the Centers for Disease Control and Prevention

Evaluating Policy Content: https://www.cdc.gov/injury/pdfs/policy/Brief%203-a.pdf
Overview of Policy Evaluation: https://www.cdc.gov/injury/pdfs/policy/brief%201- a.pdf
Evaluating Policy Impact: https://www.cdc.gov/injury/pdfs/policy/Brief%205-a.pdf
Evaluating Policy Implementation: https://www.cdc.gov/injury/pdfs/policy/Brief%204-a.pdf

References

Alice Paul Institute. (n.d.). *The Equal Rights Amendment: Unfinished business for the Constitution.* Retrieved from http://www.equalrightsamendment.org/index.htm.

Alliance for Justice. (2004). *Investing in change: A funder's guide to supporting advocacy.* Washington, DC: Alliance for Justice.

Ash, A. (2013). A cognitive mask? Camouflaging dilemmas in street-level policy implementation to safeguard older people from abuse. *British Journal of Social Work, 43*, 99–115.

Belton, K. B. (2001). Assessing your advocacy efforts. *Association Management, 53*(2), 49–52.

Centers for Disease Control. (n.d.). Brief 1: Overview of policy evaluation. *Step by step—evaluating violence and injury prevention policies.*

Coffman, J., & Reed, E. (2009). *Unique methods in advocacy evaluation.* In Harvard Family Research Project. Innovation Network (Ed.).

Devlin-Foltz, D., Fagen, M., Reed, E., Medina, R., & Neiger, B. (2012). Advocacy evaluation: Challenges and emerging trends. *Health Promotion Practice, 13*(5), 581–586.

Dodson, E. A., Geary, N. A., & Brownson, R. C. (2015). State legislators sources and use of information: Bridging the gap between research and policy. *Health Education Researc, 30*(6), 840–888.

Guthrie, K., Louie, J., David, T., & Foster, C. C. (2005). *The challenge of assessing policy and advocacy activities: Strategies for a prospective evaluation approach.* Los Angeles, CA: The California Endowment.

Landers, J. (2016, April 25). When Shirley Chisholm ran for president, few would say: "I'm with her". *Smithsonian.com.*

Lane, S. R., Ostrander, J. A., & Rhodes Smith, T. (2017). "Politics is social work with power": Training social workers for elected office. *Social Work Education.* https://doi.org/10.1080/026 15479.2017.1366975.

Levy-Pollans, J. (2013). *What if there are more than two candidates in my race?* Retrieved from https://www.wellstone.org/blog/2014/03/what-if-theres-more-2-candidates-my-race.

McNutt, J. G. (2011). Is social work advocacy worth the cost? Issues and barriers to an economic analysis of social work political practice. *Research on Social Work Practice, 21*(4), 397–403.

Meyers, M., Glaser, B., & MacDonald, K. (1998). On the front lines of welfare delivery: Are workers implementing policy reforms? *Journal of Policy Analysis and Management, 17*, 1–22.

Mickelson, J. S. (2013). Political process. In C. Franklin (Ed.), *Encyclopedia of social work.* New York, NY: Oxford University Press.

National Conference of State Legislators. (2017). *Health innovations state law database: Tracking state laws for health care transformations, 2015–2017.* Retrieved from http://www.ncsl.org/research/health/health-innovations-database-2015.aspx

Ostrander, J., Lane, S. R., McClendon, J., Hayes, C., & Rhodes Smith, T. (2017). Collective power to create political change: Increasing the political efficacy and engagement of social workers.. *Journal of Policy Practice.*(16), 261–275

S.B. 1343. (2007). *An act concerning compassionate care for victims of sexual assault.* Retrieved from https://www.cga.ct.gov/asp/cgabillstatus/cgabillstatus.asp?selBillType=Bill&bill_num=1343&which_year=2007.

Tabak, R. G., Eyler, A. A., Dodson, E. A., & Brownson, R. C. (2015). Accessing evidence to inform public health policy: A study to enhance advocacy. *Public Health, 129*(6), 698–704.

Teles, S., & Schmitt, M. (2011). The elusive craft of evaluating advocacy. *Stanford Social Innovation Review.*

Viscidi, L. (2017, June 23). Trump's withdrawal from the Paris agreement challenges Latin America. *The New York Times.*

Whelan, J. (2008). *Advocacy evaluation: Review and opportunities.* Change Agency.

White House. (2017). *Executive order minimizing the economic burden of the Patient Protection and Affordable Care Act pending repeal.* Retrieved June 27, 2017, from https://www.whitehouse.gov/the-press-office/2017/01/2/executive-order-minimizing-economic-burden-patient-protection-and.

Making Ethical Decisions in Political Social Work

14

Table of Contents

© Springer International Publishing AG 2018
S.R. Lane, S. Pritzker, *Political Social Work*,
https://doi.org/10.1007/978-3-319-68588-5_14

Section 1: Overview

National Association of Social Workers (2017) Code of Ethics is central to political social work not just in terms of providing an imperative to engage in political social work, but also in terms of guiding practice. Many consider politics a "dirty business," so we outline specific principles in the Code of Ethics that inform social workers' decisions and actions in political social work. We discuss common ethical challenges that arise in political social work. For example, we discuss the appropriate use of opposition research of a personal nature, in view of the ethical mandate for respect of inherent dignity and worth of others. We then discuss three ethical decision-making frameworks and examine their applications to political social work practice. The chapter concludes with specific ethical dilemmas to foster discussion and reflection on ethical challenges that political social workers may face.

Developing Social Work Competency
The Council on Social Work Education establishes educational standards for all social work programs in the USA. Content in this chapter supports building competency in the following areas that are considered core to the practice of social work:
COMPETENCY 1: Demonstrate Ethical and Professional Behavior
COMPETENCY 2: Engage Diversity and Difference in Practice
COMPETENCY 5: Engage in Policy Practice

Domains of Political Social Work	
1. Engaging individuals and communities in political processes	◄
2. Influencing policy agendas and decision-making	◄
3. Holding professional and political positions	◄
4. Engaging with electoral campaigns	◄
5. Seeking and holding elected office	◄

Section 2: Code of Ethics and Political Social Work

Ethics is often not the first word that comes to mind when one thinks of working or volunteering in a political setting. We often focus on the negative, unethical things that we have seen or heard about politicians doing—lying, involvement in scandals, back-room deals, etc. Certainly, as the authors write this book, we seem to be in a political moment where there appears to be a new, major political scandal daily. It feels nearly impossible to open a newspaper, scroll through a social media feed, or to turn on the television without hearing about another political situation raising ethical concerns. Political social workers are working or volunteering in this environment every day, trying to move their policy goals forward while remaining ethical in their practice.

Fortunately, as part of a profession with a self-regulating Code of Ethics that outlines our ethical values and standards, we have some help. Regardless of what our social work practice looks like and where we practice, the National Association of Social Workers (2017) Code of Ethics applies to the behaviors and actions of all social workers. **Ethics** are critical to professional practice because they provide us with a set of standards that guide us in determining which course of action we should take. These standards help us address the reality of social work practice, which is that we face extensive and complicated ethical challenges as we practice, across domains and fields of practice (Dodd 2007).

In social work, our Code of Ethics speaks specifically, and extensively, to our professional responsibility to engage in political action to seek policies that support clients' needs and that challenge discrimination and institutional inequalities. In its preamble, the Code reminds us that "a historic and defining feature of social work is the profession's focus on individual well-being in a social context and the well-being of society" (NASW 2017). Here, the Code is telling us that we have an obligation to help individuals meet their basic needs, but that we *also* are obligated to strengthen society. As we learn in our social work education through the ecological and person-in-environment perspectives, our clients' lives are shaped by a variety of macro-level forces. Society is governed by policies—policies shape our societal institutions, they tell us what is and is not acceptable behavior in society, and they shape the well-being of the communities in which our clients live.

For example, we can work directly with a victim of intimate partner violence to help her prepare to leave her abuser. However, as Matthew Desmond (2016) describes in his book, *Evicted: Poverty and Profit in the American City*, when local ordinances fine landlords for the number of police calls that come from each property, victims of intimate partner violence avoid calling the police out of fear of being evicted from their homes. Even if we are able to help this one victim leave her situation, society as a whole continues to suffer as other victims find themselves too scared of losing their homes to reach out for protection due to this local policy. Our Code compels us to participate in changing policies such as this, as it calls on us to engage in action to "ensure that all people have equal access to the resources, employment, and opportunities they require to meet their basic human needs" (NASW 2017). In fact, social workers like Kantor and Metzger (2015), in their work in St. Louis, Missouri, have worked to address exactly this issue through municipal-level policy advocacy.

Since the Code of Ethics was first adopted in 1960, our professional obligation to strengthen society has become increasingly more explicit. When first adopted, the Code was much briefer than it is today. It specified that social workers have a responsibility to the community and broader society; however, there was no explicit mention of engaging in political action or influencing policy. A 1979 revision to the Code enumerated what these specific responsibilities to society were, including a responsibility to advocate for policy change. A substantial revision in 1996 brought us the explicit call for all social workers to participate in social and political action that exists in the Code today (National Association of Social Workers n.d.).

The Code outlines six core values and ethical principles, as well as six sections of specific ethical standards. Each of these is expected to guide practice in all arenas of social work, including political social work. It is important to note, however, that while the Code is intended to inform our practice, it is also aspirational; this means that we may not always live up to the ideals set forth in the Code. In this chapter, we examine the core values and ethical standards in detail in order to help you examine and prepare yourself for the sometimes very ethically challenging situations that you may encounter in political social work practice.

Before we do so, we feel that it is important to first share a pointed criticism of the NASW Code of Ethics and to encourage you to reflect on this criticism. Reisch and Lowe (2000) contend that "the Code assumes that the ethical issues it addresses arise primarily within the context of a clinical relationship or the administrative and supervisory environment in which that relationship occurs" (p. 24). These social work scholars argue that the Code is insufficient in speaking to the kinds of ethical challenges that arise in macro-oriented community or political settings. Hoefer (2016) similarly argues that "although social workers are called on to engage in advocacy practice…the Code is often silent on the subject of how to do so ethically" (p. 37).

> **FURTHER REFLECTION: The Code of Ethics and Political Social Work Practice**
> Re-read the NASW Code of Ethics, and reflect upon the criticism that it does not sufficiently speak to practice in macro and policy settings. Discuss this with a fellow social worker. How do you react to this criticism? Do you feel that the NASW Code of Ethics speaks to the ethical issues that may arise in political social work practice? Why or why not? What might be missing?

Core Values Expressed in the Code of Ethics

Service

It is not uncommon to hear members of the public question whether politicians have run for office for the right reasons. You may have questioned yourself whether elected officials are susceptible to changing their policy votes or stances due to financial incentives or the desire to be reelected or gain a higher office. The implication of these criticisms is that such politicians are guided perhaps by greed, but most definitely not by the value of service.

For many who work in political settings, however, a desire to work in service to the public was part of what initially brought them to this work, just as the value of service is part of what brings many students to social work as a profession. In fact, as social workers, we are explicitly obligated to "elevate service to others above self-interest" (National Association of Social Workers 2017). However, when practicing in political contexts, many challenges arise in which we may feel forced to choose between service or self-interest.

For example: Do I take a higher paying job as a lobbyist for causes I might disagree with—a job that allows me to support my family and have more financial security? Or do I take a lower-paying job where I consistently work toward policies that address the needs of vulnerable populations? As a staffer for an elected official, am I more likely to schedule a meeting for the elected official with the lobbyist who brought lunch for our office staff every day, than with a constituent who did not bring us anything? Does my human services nonprofit remain silent regarding an issue that would benefit our clients, if the issue might negatively impact a large donor to our organization? These are the kinds of decisions that make up the overall ethical application of this principle, and are faced by political social workers daily.

Social Justice

The Code of Ethics obligates social workers to pursue **social justice** as a core value. Social workers are expected to "pursue social change…strive to ensure access to needed information, services, and resources; equality of opportunity; and meaningful participation in decision making for all people" (National Association of Social Workers 2017). This emphasis on strengthening equality, ensuring equal access to rights and services, ensuring equal access to information, and prioritizing the meaningful participation of vulnerable populations is a value our profession holds strongly. It is a value that many political social workers find to be a particular guide for their practice.

Political social workers often face ethical challenges when it comes to pursuing social justice. Governments frequently have limited resources, requiring politicians (and advocates) to choose to support or advantage one group's needs over another. For example, if the state has a limited human services budget, do we promote adding funds to better support the state child welfare system, knowing that this will result in cuts to respite services for those taking care of elderly relatives?

At other times, we are forced to make decisions about whether to compromise on a bill or ordinance, potentially securing less assistance or access than what we believe is just. We must consider critically whether to accept such a compromise when the alternative, at least in the short term, is to maintain a problematic status quo. For example, a recent effort by social workers and other activists in New York advocated to "raise the age" at which juveniles are charged as adults. Prior to this effort, 16- and 17-year-olds charged with a crime were automatically charged as adults and placed into the adult correctional system. Advocates requested a "true" raise the age change, to move *all* 16- and 17-year-olds into juvenile court. Legislators instead reached a compromise. Most 16- and 17-year-olds would be moved into juvenile court; however, specific *exceptions* were outlined. These exceptions left some 16- and 17-year-olds in adult criminal court (e.g., when a "deadly weapon" was used, a victim sustained "significant physical injury," or if criminal sexual conduct was involved) (McKinley 2017).

Another common social justice issue that political social workers encounter is determining whether it is ethical to "**carve-out**" a population from a proposed policy, if doing so is believed to increase the likelihood of other vulnerable populations gaining access to rights or services they did not previously have. We face these issues both in developing campaign platforms and in trying to pass policies.

An example from Houston, Texas, demonstrates the social justice challenges involved in a carve-out. In 2014, Mayor Annise Parker sought passage of a city-wide nondiscrimination ordinance that would go beyond the federal Civil Rights Act of 1964, including race, ethnicity, religion, military status, sexual orientation, gender identity, and pregnancy as protected characteristics. The proposed ordinance included a paragraph specifically allowing individuals to use a bathroom that fit their gender identity (Smothers 2015). Referred to as the "bathroom clause," this paragraph became the focus of substantial public controversy, threatening passage of the entire ordinance. One month after introducing the ordinance, Mayor Parker removed the bathroom clause to increase the likelihood that the ordinance's other protections would pass (Fraser 2014). This carve-out removed a protection for transgender individuals in exchange for City Council's passage of the ordinance. (Despite this carve-out and City Council's passage of the ordinance, it was ultimately struck down after a long court battle.)

The value that social work places on social justice can pose challenges for social workers working within political climates or with political constituencies that do not share this value. Most political social workers work in interdisciplinary contexts where they regularly face this type of challenge. For example, during a campaign, media, donors, advisors, and/or constituents may try to steer the focus away from policy issues that address the well-being of the communities we represent. Similarly, social work legislative interns reported facing ethical challenges as they practiced in an environment that did not prioritize meaningful public participation. They also struggled with a lack of public access to accurate information about legislative proceedings (Pritzker and Barros Lane in press).

FURTHER REFLECTION: Political Social Work and Social Justice

1. New York's "raise the age" advocacy effort resulted in a bill did not meet all of the goals of the initiative, leaving some 16- and 17-year-olds in the adult criminal justice system. The compromise bill could leave some juveniles to be treated in ways the advocates defined as socially unjust. In your opinion, should the advocates have accepted the compromise legislation? Or should the advocates have held out for a more comprehensive bill, knowing that doing so might risk no change to the status quo at least in the short term?

2. The carve-out of the "bathroom clause" helped pass Houston's Equal Rights Ordinance (HERO). It granted nondiscrimination protections to many Houstonians, but left out transgender individuals. In your opinion, was continued support of the HERO ordinance on the part of many advocates and councilmembers after this carve-out consistent with the Code of Ethics? Why or why not?

Dignity and Worth of the Person

The Code of Ethics calls on social workers to "promote clients' socially responsible self-determination…to enhance clients' capacity and opportunity to change and to address their own needs" (National Association of Social Workers 2017). In political social work practice, this raises issues about how we engage with our constituencies and how we approach our advocacy work.

For example, Ezell (2001) raises questions about our clients' **self-determination** when we work on their behalf in political settings: Is it respecting the dignity and worth of individuals to advocate, or as a politician, to vote, on behalf of a vulnerable population when they haven't had the opportunity to determine on their own if the issue is in their best interests? What are our roles and responsibilities in terms of advocating alongside client populations, as opposed to advocating on their behalf? It is important to carefully consider ways that we can support clients and communities in advocating for themselves. Arnstein's (1969) participation ladder, introduced in Chap. 4, can offer guidance into supporting clients' participation. Several of the profiles and case studies we have included throughout this book offer also insight into ways that professional political social workers support communities in developing their own political voice.

What if our constituency has expressed opposition to a piece of legislation, but our policy knowledge and analyses lead us to believe that the legislation actually will help these vulnerable families? For example, what if your knowledge of the details of a health care bill tell us that it will have positive impacts on the health and well-being of low-income families in our community, but they are asking you as an elected official to oppose it? Much has been written about people who vote or advocate in ways that might be considered "against their best interest," from working class voters who vote for candidates even though their economic policies might hurt that voter's pocketbook (Frank 2007), to the "super-rich" advocating for increases in their taxes (Buffett 2011). What is our role as political social workers to determine what is in an individual or community's best interest?

Each of these questions suggests that ethical political social work practice should involve careful attention to balancing: (1) working with our constituencies to build their capacity to understand various policy choices, (2) meaningfully consulting with them and supporting their participation, and (3) utilizing our expertise to navigate complex policy choices and budgeting processes. At the same time, a reality of political social work practice is that there are often many barriers to meaningful consultation with our constituencies.

Valuing dignity and worth of the individual also incorporates cultural awareness and sensitivity in political communications and in political relationships (Ezell 2001). In political settings, too often we observe both **microaggressions** and other overt acts of discrimination and disrespect. While this is not a universal scenario by any means, a news story out of Pasadena, Texas, illustrates a blatant example of the lack of sensitivity sometimes present in political settings. During a March 2017 meeting of the Pasadena City Council, a Latino councilmember spoke up before a vote, saying, "I haven't had an opportunity to speak yet." The White mayor responded, "Well, you better speak up, boy," in a manner widely interpreted as condescending and discriminatory (Collette 2017).

It is also not uncommon to testify before a legislative committee, while observing committee members holding side conversations, walking in and out of the room, or blatantly seeming disinterested. One of the authors remembers one particular committee hearing, during which committee members kept stepping out mid-testimony for updates on "March Madness" college basketball tournament scores. This value underscores the importance of consciously reflecting on how we can prioritize respect and sensitivity toward the many individuals with whom we interact. This includes those with whom we have policy disagreements. In such situations, it is important to separate our personal values from our professional values. As discussed below, building relationships—even with those with whom we disagree—is critical to moving policy forward. We start by using social work skills such as engagement, empathy, and active listening to understand the context of others' positions before we react.

Importance of Human Relationships

The Code states that "social workers seek to strengthen relationships among people in a purposeful effort to promote, restore, maintain, and enhance the well-being of individuals, families, social groups, organizations, and communities" (National Association of Social Workers 2017). Further, it emphasizes that "relationships between and among people are an important vehicle for change" (National Association of Social Workers 2017). Building and supporting relationships is essential to social work practice in political settings.

A challenging aspect of relationships in politics, however, is that they are often **instrumental**; that is, they exist for the purpose of achieving some sort of goal(s) external to the relationship. Without relationships, we would be unable to secure donations for our campaign, to recruit campaign volunteers, to secure constituent votes for our reelection, to garner co-sponsors for a bill, to find an ally to help stop a bill we find detrimental, or to move a bill through the legislative process. As political social workers, an important consideration is how to move beyond instrumental relationships, to building relationships that are also meaningful. As Reisch and Lowe (2000) observe, this can be challenging in political and community work, as we often lack the capacity and time to build meaningful relationships with constituents and colleagues. Such relationships are important though, because they go beyond an immediate need for support or assistance and allow us to better understand a group or colleague's values and priorities. There are many opportunities to advance instrumental relationships in ways which feel ethically appropriate. For example, as an advocate or legislator, you may support issues that don't necessarily either harm or help your constituency in order to maintain instrumental relationships with other groups or policy-makers.

Social workers also need to consider the directionality of political relationships. Particularly for social work politicians and political staffers, can our constituencies count on us, as much as we rely on them? This is an essential component to **constituent services**. Constituents count on politicians' offices to hear their concerns and to be responsive to both their concerns and their needs. A recent theme in national US politics has been extensive constituent concerns over whether their Congressional representatives are willing to engage with them. This has been particularly common around health care policy. In early 2017, for example, constituents expressed public frustration at Republican members of Congress who tried to avoid engaging with angry constituents over the potential repeal of the Affordable Care Act by limiting town-hall meetings in their districts (Williams and Murphy 2017). A similar dynamic occurred in 2009 and 2010, when Democratic members of Congress canceled town hall meetings so as to not bear the brunt of frustrated Tea Party activists opposed to passage of the Affordable Care Act.

Another issue to consider in terms of relationships in political social work is **credibility**. As a staff member or campaign worker for a politician, political social workers often build on their own networks and relationships in order to mobilize support, votes, volunteers, or campaign donations. In that process, if one misrepresents the candidate or her positions, or promises things that don't materialize, your own credibility may be compromised. This connects with the next core value.

Integrity

Acting with **integrity** is a core social work value, with social workers called on to "act honestly and responsibly and promote ethical practices on the part of the organizations with which they are affiliated" (National Association of Social Workers 2017). In political environments, social workers may face many "opportunities" to act with less than full integrity. As some student legislative interns describe, working in a political setting can sometimes feel like one is in the middle of a "political game" (Pritzker and Barros Lane in press). Politicians who are known to hold one stance may vote differently due to a variety of influences (e.g., party affiliation, donor or constituent pressure, deals). Other elected officials and staffers may feel uncomfortable speaking their minds honestly for similar reasons (Pritzker and Barros Lane in press). A prominent example of this occurred during the 2016 election, as Republican leaders who indicated opposition to President Donald Trump's candidacy in off-the-record settings did not express these views publicly. In an opinion piece written during the 2016 Republican primary, Weisberg (2016) argued that these politicians opted not to express their opinions publicly because they risked losing campaign funds and votes and being publicly attacked by other Republicans if they did so.

The value of integrity also can pose challenges in electoral campaigns. If we have "dirt" on our opponent that will help us win—and therefore, our ability to pursue socially just policies—do we use it? What if this "dirt" is of a personal nature that could hurt the well-being of our opponent or his/her family? If we have access to documents related to our opponent that were illegally stolen by hackers, do we use these materials against our opponent? This exact scenario has been faced by campaigns at various levels of government. For example, in 2016, Russian hackers hacked documents from the Democratic Congressional Campaign Committee related to a set of Democratic House candidates. While the hacked material was incorporated into campaign ads in most of these candidates' Congressional races, at least one candidate, Representative Ryan Costello (R-PA) opted against using the materials against his opponent, stating, "We believed it was neither necessary nor appropriate to use information from a possible foreign source to influence the election" (Lipton and Shane 2016).

Hoefer (2016) raises another critical question of integrity that political social workers must grapple with. He asks, "Is honesty always the best policy? Is it permissible to lie if it better accomplishes social work's primary mission" (p. 28)? In practice, we are likely to come face-to-face with this question in multiple ways. For example, as social workers seeking policies that promote social justice, is it acceptable to overstate the scope or consequences of a problem if it will gain the problem more attention? Ezell (2001) makes it clear that such misrepresentation is contrary to the value of integrity. It is also evident why this might be tempting for social workers who have long struggled to get lawmakers to pay attention to their problem.

Competence

The final core social work value calls for social workers to practice with **competence**, focusing on the areas in which they are able to practice effectively and to "continually strive to increase their professional knowledge and skills and to apply them in practice..." (National Association of Social Workers 2017). The ethical demands of competence require that social workers be honest with potential employers, voters, or other constituencies about what we will be able to do, without overstating those capabilities. Ezell (2001), for example, specifically calls on social workers to only perform advocacy tasks that they are competent to do. Where necessary, he suggests partnering with others who have a skill set more appropriate to the policy goals, targets, and tactics at hand.

It can be tempting for social workers to use the call to practice competently as a justification not to spread their work into areas where they face a steep learning curve or might experience discomfort. Social workers should have a strong sense of self-awareness and a realistic understanding of their own skills. It is also important to reflect whether we are underestimating our own competence. As research on gender and candidate emergence suggests, women consistently view themselves as less qualified for running for office than do men, regardless of their objective level of qualification (Lawless 2015).

In areas that feel beyond our comfort zones, it is important to understand our strengths, their application, and areas in which we need to build strength. We can then use this knowledge to seek out situations to find meaningful opportunities to apply our skills in new ways.

Local and state level campaigns, local political offices, and small advocacy nonprofits tend to rely on limited staff, the willingness of volunteers to contribute at significant levels, and small budgets. In these situations, many on staff may be asked to be a "jack of all trades," regardless of background and prior preparation. For example, in some states, a state legislative office—even during the legislative session—may have just one staffer. This staffer might be expected to carry the representatives' bills, track and recommend votes on legislation, and handle all interactions with constituents, advocates, and lobbyists. A campaign for a local elected office or for an unlikely challenger to a popular incumbent might have just one paid staffer, or may even be completely staffed by volunteers. Such situations can pose challenges to a social worker's ability to practice according to the value of competence, especially at the beginning of a political social work career.

It is important to remember, however, that most of the people in these positions are entry-level. In many situations, social workers may be better prepared for the demands of these jobs than other candidates. Preparing carefully for these jobs, seeking out mentors and supportive networks, using supervision when available, and being willingness to ask questions and seek out assistance when needed can help social workers accomplish them with competence.

Ethical Standards in the Code of Ethics

In addition to core values, the Code of Ethics spells out ethical standards in six areas. In the sections below, we highlight some of these ethical standards and how they inform situations you are likely to encounter as a political social worker. We want to be transparent, however—neither the Code of Ethics nor this section will always tell you what to do when you face an ethical challenge. In fact, at times, this section's discussion may raise more questions than it provides answers. Ethics, unfortunately, are often complex and messy. Otherwise, we would not face so many ethical challenges in practice. Our primary goal here is to provoke your thoughts about where the Code offers guidance and where it may still leave you unsure as to how to proceed. We encourage you to reflect upon and discuss questions that arise as you read this section with fellow social workers, instructors, mentors, and other trusted members of your network. Then, in Section 3 of this chapter, we discuss some ethical decision-making tools to help you navigate these and other political social work challenges.

Ethical Responsibilities to Clients

The first set of ethical standards speaks specifically to social workers' responsibilities toward clients. In political social work, sometimes we work on behalf of individual clients, but often, we work on behalf of much larger constituencies, to whom we also have ethical responsibilities. One of the most challenging aspects of this section for political social work is the question of *who is our client?* The word "client" generally has clear meaning in direct social work practice. When we are working as an advocate, a lobbyist, an elected official, or a staffer, however, our understanding of who our client is and to whom we have professional obligations may be more complex. As an elected official, for example, our "client" might be all the constituents in our district, but these constituents might have distinct and competing interests and needs. As a staffer, our "client" is similar to that of the elected official, but at times, the elected official for whom we work may also be our "client." In fact, staffers of elected officials often talk about the priority they place on "protecting" their employer, in order to preserve their member's ability to legislate effectively.

With this in mind, we highlight several ethical standards that offer us some guidance in our work with these various clients and constituencies. Earlier in this chapter, we talked about *Sec. 1.02: Self Determination*. This standard has direct relevance to political social work practice, emphasizing the importance of respecting and incorporating the voices of each of our constituencies in our policy work.

Sec. 1.03: Informed Consent raises a related and critical issue for political social workers. This ethical standard calls on us to work with our clients "only in the context of a professional relationship based, when appropriate, on informed consent" (National Association of Social Workers 2017). This standard reminds us to be transparent about when we are acting in an official capacity, a campaign capacity, or as a private citizen. While the Code does not specify what informed consent means in a macro context, it suggests the importance of using clear language to help clients understand the purpose, risks, and limits of our work on their behalf and providing them with the opportunity to ask questions about our efforts. While political social workers may not always provide direct services, we regularly work on legislation that impacts services, as well as the rights, opportunities, and access that vulnerable populations may experience. We advocate or push for legislation and funding that we perceive as beneficial for our constituencies and oppose or stop legislation that we perceive as problematic. We take public stances on a wide range of policy issues and social problems. In doing these things, we need to be aware that we sometimes bring attention to communities affected by these issues in ways with which they might not be comfortable. See, for example, the experience of DREAMers described in the case study in Chap. 3. These young activists discovered that their messaging in order to gain rights for undocumented children was perceived as blaming parents for choosing to come to the USA.

In practical terms, seeking informed consent for our political work often may not be feasible (Ezell 2001). As *Sec. 1.14: Clients Who Lack Decision-Making Capacity* outlines, as social workers, we may find ourselves working on policy platforms or legislation that impact constituencies who are unable to provide informed consent. In these cases, the Code calls on us to take "reasonable steps to safeguard the interests and rights of those clients" (National Association of Social Workers 2017). Therefore, even when informed consent appears not to be feasible in a political context, our Code calls on us to seriously examine whether we can reach out to our clients and constituencies to make sure they are aware of the benefits and risks of our political work or of the possible policy solutions that may emerge (Ezell 2001). When we cannot do so, we should take steps to ensure that we are respecting their interests.

Sec 1.06: Conflicts of Interest is particularly relevant to practice in political settings when many competing interests are at play. Social workers clearly should not "exploit others to further their personal, religious, political, or business interests" (National Association of Social Workers 2017). While this part of the standard offers clear guidance to political social workers, other aspects of this standard raise more questions. For example, this standard also calls on social workers to "take reasonable steps to … make the clients' interests primary and protect clients' interests to the greatest extent possible" and to "take appropriate action to minimize any conflict of interest" (National Association of Social Workers 2017). Given the complexity of what "client" may mean in political social work, who takes priority when the needs of various constituencies within our district conflict? Which community members' interests do we seek to protect when multiple vulnerable populations are pitted against each other in budget decision-making? What about when community members' interests conflict with the interests of the elected official to whom we have professional obligations?

Ethical Responsibilities to Colleagues

The second set of ethical standards address our responsibilities toward our colleagues. Because of the competitive—and increasingly polarized—nature of politics, you may find some of the standards outlined in Section 2 to be particularly challenging at times. For example, *Sec 2.01: Respect* asks us to "treat colleagues with respect and ... represent accurately and fairly the qualifications, views, and obligations of colleagues…[and] avoid unwarranted negative criticism of colleagues in communications with clients or other professionals" (National Association of Social Workers 2017). This language is very clear, emphasizing the dignity and worth of those with whom we work in a political setting.

Our colleagues in a political setting may not be limited to the people who work in our office; colleagues may include the other advocates, lobbyists, staffers, and elected officials with whom we regularly engage in our work. Our colleagues include people with whom we may strongly disagree, often to the point of seeking to defeat their legislation or even to defeat them at the ballot box. This obligation to treat our colleagues with respect underscores the importance of seriously and respectfully engaging with people across political differences. Our Code suggests that we need to start where they are, seek to understand and fairly represent their stances, and to seek to promote respectful dialogue across ideological difference. At the same time, the Code indicates that if we refuse to criticize those who are hateful or promoting unjust policies because they are our colleagues, we are not serving our constituencies. When others in political settings are demeaning, derogatory, or hurtful, criticism is certainly warranted.

It is useful to understand the process by which the Code of Ethics recommends intervening with colleagues who are impaired, practicing outside of their areas of competence, or practicing unethically. We may see each of this in our political social work practice. Ethical standards in Section 2 offer specific guidance on this: for example, to respect the confidentiality of information shared with us by colleagues (*Sec 2.02: Confidentiality*), to seek to support impaired colleagues (*Sec 2.08: Impairment of Colleagues*), to help colleagues perform more competently (*Sec. 2.09: Incompetence of Colleagues*), and to avoid engaging in sexual harassment (*Sec. 2.07: Sexual Harassment*). The Code recommends that, whenever possible, a social worker engage directly with the colleague in question, and only then move through a process of sharing those concerns with others.

Sec 2.05: Consultation also raises a critical point for political social work practice, emphasizing the importance of reaching out to colleagues for "advice and counsel…when it is in the best interests of clients" (National Association of Social Workers 2017). This recalls the discussion earlier in this chapter (under "Competence") about social workers who may be expected to practice outside their competence in offices with limited staff. The explicit inclusion of consultation—or seeking out mentorship—as an ethical standard underscores its importance as a tool for political social workers asked to take on unfamiliar roles.

Ethical Responsibilities in Practice Settings

The third set of ethical standards provides guidance for engaging with the settings in which we work. Care should be taken to make sure that we act appropriately and set appropriate boundaries in supervisory roles (*Sec 3.01: Supervision and Consultation*), evaluate our employees fairly (*Sec 3.03: Performance Evaluation*), and create work assignments that encourage compliance with the Code (*Sec 3.07: Administration*).

This section has important implications for how political social workers engage with policy choices both within and outside of our organizations. *Sec. 3.07: Administration* calls on us to "advocate for resource allocation procedures that are open and fair" (National Association of Social Workers 2017). We talked previously in this chapter about the challenging—and sometimes, heart-wrenching—choices that political social workers face in influencing or determining budget and resource allocations. Here, the Code specifically guides us to be transparent and fair in that process. When we are unable to meet all of the needs of our constituencies, it expects us to develop processes to guide allocations that are "nondiscriminatory and based on appropriate and consistently applied principles" (National Association of Social Workers 2017).

Another part of this section that is especially important to highlight is part d of *Sec 3.09: Commitments to Employers*: "Social workers should not allow an employing organization's policies, procedures, regulations, or administrative orders to interfere with their ethical practice of social work." This is an important guidepost for political social workers who may at some point in their careers be asked by supervisors to act in a way that conflicts with the Code of Ethics. For example, how do we proceed when the elected official for whom we work asks us to behave in a way that is contrary to the value of integrity? Do we answer this question differently if the elected official asks us to do so as a means to furthering a social justice goal?

Ethical Responsibilities as Professionals

The fourth set of ethical standards focuses on social workers' responsibilities in professional contexts, reinforcing the core values of integrity and competence. It underscores political social workers' responsibilities to "not practice, condone, facilitate, or collaborate with any form of discrimination on the basis of race, ethnicity, national origin, color, sex, sexual orientation, gender identity or expression, age, marital status, political belief, religion, immigration status, or mental or physical disability" (*Sec 4.02: Discrimination*) (National Association of Social Workers 2017). While this standard is so elemental to political social work, it is also an example of an aspirational standard within the Code that many of us may struggle with even with the best intentions. Take a minute to think about ways that this standard might pose a challenge in your own political social work practice.

This section also extensively discusses the importance of social workers engaging in honest, unimpaired, and transparent practices. *Sec. 4.04: Dishonesty, Fraud, and Deception,* requiring that social workers "not participate in, condone, or be associated with fraud, or deception" (National Association of Social Workers 2017) is an important reminder for political social workers as we enter into practice settings in which back-door deals, trade-offs, and instrumental relationships are part of the environment, and often can be perceived as critical to achieving policy outcomes.

Sec 4.05: Impairment emphasizes not allowing our own personal challenges to interfere with our professional judgment and performance, nor with ensuring the best interests of our colleagues or constituencies. Political environments can be highly demanding and stressful at certain times, e.g., the final weeks of a political campaign, before and after a campaign kick-off or a major political debate, when challenging opposition research is made public, near a statutory budget deadline, or the last couple of months of the legislative session in a part-time legislature. When work must be completed in such situations, political social workers can find themselves struggling to balance their personal well-being and self-care with their professional responsibilities.

Ethical Responsibilities to the Profession

The Code of Ethics emphasizes our responsibilities to the social work profession as a whole in its fifth set of standards. In *Sec 5.01: Integrity of the Profession,* we are called upon to "uphold and advance the values, ethics, knowledge, and mission of the profession" (National Association of Social Workers 2017). This includes protecting and strengthening how others view the profession. Political social workers work extensively in interdisciplinary environments where social workers may be less common than other professions (though when each reader of this book enters into this work, that will certainly change this dynamic!) and where our colleagues may be unfamiliar with the profession's many strengths.

Pritzker and Barros Lane (in press) found that social work students interning in a state legislature felt like they had to justify their presence as social workers in the legislative arena, sometimes encountering questions like, "What are you doing here at the Capitol?" While working in the U.S. Senate, one of this book's authors was regularly asked—sometimes even by other social workers—why she chose to leave the social work profession. 5.01 reminds us that actively engaging others in discussions about the values, ethics, and mission of social work is, in fact, a professional obligation.

> **FURTHER REFLECTION: Integrity of the Profession**
> Some social workers in political settings choose not to identify as social workers or to use their professional credentials (BSW, MSW, LMSW, etc.). Why do you think this might be? What are your thoughts about this choice?

Another standard of particular relevance to political social workers is *Sec 5.02: Evaluation and Research.* This standard underscores our responsibility to make sure that our policy work reflects emerging research knowledge and also to inform our policy work with accurate and honest data collection. It also emphasizes our responsibility to not only ensure that strong candidates are elected to office and socially just policies are passed, but to ensure that policies and their implementation are being monitored and evaluated.

Ethical Responsibilities to the Broader Society

The final section of the Code of Ethics encapsulates much of what we have already discussed in framing both this book as a whole and this chapter in particular. It focuses on our ethical responsibilities to the broader society; that is, what we as social workers are ethically obligated to do in support of our core value of social justice. This standard most clearly delineates our roles as political social workers, including to "engage in social and political action that seeks to ensure that all people have equal access to the resources, employment, services, and opportunities they require to meet their basic human needs and to develop fully" (National Association of Social Workers 2017).

Sec 6.01: Social welfare reminds us specifically of our ethical obligation to advocate for social justice and to promote the welfare of society. This call for promoting social justice is a critical underpinning of political social work. However, as political social workers who must engage across different political ideologies to be effective in our work, it is also important than we seriously reflect upon questions such as: Whose understanding of social justice? For example, in his article, "Social justice: A conservative perspective," Bruce Thyer (2010) critiques many of his more liberal social work colleagues, arguing that "conservative social workers believe that adhering to their [conservative] principles results in a *more* socially just world via the creation of more socially just programs and policies, than the practices espoused by their more liberal colleagues" (p. 272).

In emphasizing our obligation to meet people's basic needs of people and to promote equal access to the resources people need to meet these basic needs, both *Sec 6.01* and *Sec 6.04: Social and Political Action* also raise questions about how political social workers make decisions in political and economic environments where budgetary resources are highly limited. Where limited resources are available, do we hold out for equal access to all basic needs being met, and refuse to compromise for anything less until full resources are available? Do we instead try to manage competing claims from different groups who are all seeking to have their basic needs met?

This final section of the Code of Ethics also refocuses us on our obligation to prevent discrimination against vulnerable and marginalized groups on the basis of "race, ethnicity, national origin, color, sex, sexual orientation, gender identity or expression, age, marital status, political belief, religion, immigration status, or mental or physical disability" (National Association of Social Workers 2017). It underscores the importance of self-determination in the policy process, expressly stating in *Sec 6.02: Public Participation* that we are expected to "facilitate informed participation by the public in shaping social policies and institutions" (National Association of Social Workers 2017). Not only must we engage in political action ourselves, an essential part of our political social work practice must involve helping vulnerable and marginalized groups contribute to policy-making.

EXPLORE YOUR VALUES: Ethical Challenges in *Your* Experiences as a Political Social Worker
Identify one or two ethical challenges you have encountered in a political context, whether in your personal life, your professional or volunteer experiences, or as part of your social work education. If you haven't yet had experience in a political context, identify at least one ethical challenge(s) identified in this book. Share and discuss these ethical challenges with a fellow student, colleague, or mentor. What core value(s) or ethical standard(s) might guide you in thinking about how to approach each challenge? How might it guide you?

POLITICAL SOCIAL WORKER PROFILE: Sheryl Grossman, MSW
Founder/Facilitator, Blooms Connect (Fig. 14.1).

Fig. 14.1 Sheryl Grossman, MSW

Sheryl Grossman was born in the 1970s, in "the year that the Individuals with Disabilities Education Act went into play." As Sheryl grew up, her "family had to fight for me to be included" in any activities. Her experiences from an early age made her interested in becoming a social worker. "MSW was the three letter word in the disability community…. It was typically the social worker who would take the child and put them in an institution if they had a disability… it was typically the social worker who would place a child in foster care if their parents had a disability." Sheryl herself experienced this when, at a couple months old, she was taken from her family and institutionalized in a hospital for "failure to thrive." Sheryl says, "After another few weeks it was clear that I wasn't changing, and there was something actually going on—which started the years-long process of actually getting diagnosed" with Blooms Syndrome. This trauma stayed with Sheryl's family, as is the

(continued)

experiences with many families who have dealt with disability, creating a view of the social worker as enemy.

Sheryl pursued her social work degree "to know the lingo and language of those who would be sitting across the table from me my entire life as I tried to navigate it." Early on in her social work schooling, Sheryl found her disabilities community and was able to join them in community organizing around human rights and civil rights for the disability community. As a student, "there was no [statement in the] Code of Ethics [regarding] people with disabilities." When soon after Sheryl graduated, the NASW added a statement about working with people of color, "it made me angry to no end that it could be done for one minority group, but not others. And I still saw people with disabilities as the object of pity and the need for services in social work." This led Sheryl to more closely follow the actions of NASW and advocate to have language included for people like her.

Sheryl has worked to change the way that people with disabilities are treated by the social work profession and by society as a whole. As she describes, "I saw groups of people making decisions, and I wanted to be a part of that change." She leads by example in her clinical work with people with disabilities, "helping them use their power and their voice, in whatever way, shape, or form that means." Sheryl works to empower people with disabilities to advocate for themselves, and to realize the range that this may take: from writing a letter to a representative to protesting in Senate Majority Leader Mitch McConnell's office. Sheryl reflects back on her experiences as a political social worker: "It is a 'slow as molasses' process to get people to realize that people with disabilities aren't looking for pity, or a hand out, but that they should be treated like everybody else."

Sheryl offers some advice for future political social workers. For social work students without disabilities, she advises: "Remember that you are not the disabled person" and strive to be an ally by giving the voices of those with disabilities the space to be heard. For social work students with disabilities, she suggests that "you do not have to be the lone voice" advocating for your rights; instead, finding your community and adequate outlets for support is vital to this work. She emphasizes. "We need your voice… Stick with it," but underscores, "Macro level social work and community organizing can be the channel for the rage that you're living through everyday… you can channel it into productive action. But you have to have the community and support of other disabled folks" to avoid burnout over the long term.

Section 3: Ethical Decision-Making in Political Social Work

As a political social worker, you will inevitably face ethical challenges in your practice. While substantial criticism argues that the Code of Ethics may be clearer in terms of its application to clinical or supervisory contexts than to macro contexts

(Reisch and Lowe 2000; Hoefer 2016), the ethical issues we face in political social work practice are certainly <u>not</u> any less relevant, pressing, or challenging.

Ethical issues in practice often emerge in the form of **ethical dilemmas**. In these dilemmas, we find ourselves having to choose between multiple alternatives that are "equally satisfactory or unsatisfactory" (Reisch and Lowe 2000). In some cases, dilemmas emerge when we lack sufficient time to reflect seriously on our choices between these alternatives (Reisch and Lowe 2000). In other cases, dilemmas occur when we feel forced to choose between our Code of Ethics and our employer's conflicting policies, or when we are faced with two different ethical standards or values that conflict in a given situation. When faced with these dilemmas, we must make difficult decisions about whether and how to move forward with one course of action or another.

Difficult ethical decisions are often subjective and dependent on the specific context in which the dilemma arises. Rarely are dilemmas in advocacy or other aspects of political social work clearly ethical or clearly unethical (Ezell 2001). As Gray and Gibbons (2007) note, "there are no right answers, only choices, and we are responsible for, and have to be able to live with, the decisions or choices we make" (p. 225).

The Code of Ethics is designed to serve as a resource for social workers in navigating ethical dilemmas. However, social work students and professionals alike may be hesitant to refer to the Code as they encounter these dilemmas (Dodd 2007). We encourage you to discuss and reflect upon the ethical dilemmas you encounter in practice with your colleagues, supervisors, or mentors, and to adopt a conscious process of ethical decision-making to help guide you. Through this chapter, we hope to provide you with tools that will help you use the Code more effectively in navigating practice challenges in political social work.

Approaches to Ethical Decision-Making

An **ethical decision-making framework** is a tool that takes us through a step-by-step problem-solving process to think through how we might address an ethical dilemma. To date, no ethical decision-making framework has been proposed specifically for political social work practice. However, social work literature offers several frameworks that can guide us in this work. We outline three frameworks below, and encourage you to practice using each one, with the goal of identifying a framework that can help guide your own practice as you move forward in your social work career.

Reamer's Ethical Decision-Making Process
Frederic Reamer (2002) has long been a leader in studying professional ethics in social work, and many readers of this book may already be familiar with his seven-step process of ethical decision-making. This process was intended to be applied to both micro- and macro-decision-making in social work, and can be a helpful tool

for navigating the kinds of ethical dilemmas raised in this chapter. These seven steps are as follows (Reproduced in full from Reamer 2002):

1. Identify the ethical issues, including the social work values and ethics that conflict.
2. Identify the individuals, groups, and organizations that are likely to be affected by the ethical decision.
3. Tentatively identify all possible courses of action and the participants involved in each, along with possible benefits and risks for each.
4. Thoroughly examine the reasons in favor of and opposed to each possible course of action, considering relevant
   (a) Ethical theories, principles, and guidelines
   (b) Codes of ethics and legal principles
   (c) Social work practice theory and principles
   (d) Personal values (including religious, cultural, and ethnic values and political ideology)
5. Consult with colleagues and appropriate experts (such as agency staff, supervisors, agency administrators, attorneys, ethics scholars, and ethics committees).
6. Make the decision and document the decision-making process.
7. Monitor, evaluate, and document the decision.

This process begins by asking us to identify the range of ethical issues in the specific situation, and then to explore the various parties that might be affected by any decision we might make. As we deal with issues associated with complex policy decisions, we may find that the list of entities affected by our decision is extensive. Based on this analysis, we are then asked to identify the range of actions that may be available to us to take in response to the ethical issue.

A strength of this process is the thorough critical analysis of all possible courses of action it takes us through, including reasons to support or oppose each course of action. Consistent with our earlier discussion in this chapter of the importance of consultation, this process encourages us to consult with experts prior to making a decision. It is important to realize that in political settings, individuals who hold the roles that Reamer suggests we consult with (supervisors, staff, etc.) may, in fact, have contributed to the ethical dilemma we face. This is not to say that they are necessarily behaving in a manner that society would deem as unethical, but rather that they may not share the same core values as the social work profession. This again presents an opportunity for you to seek out mentorship from other political social workers. Finally, even after you have made your decision about how to handle the ethical dilemma, Reamer (2002) indicates that the process is not complete. You must document, monitor, and evaluate what happens after your decision has been made.

Reisch and Lowe's "Ethics Work-Up"

Suggesting that there may be specific considerations when analyzing ethical dilemmas in community organizing, Reisch and Lowe (2000) developed a six-step process specifically for use in community practice, called "The Ethics Work-Up."

Community organizing and political social work share many commonalities as forms of macro social work that engage heavily with issues of power, politics, and policy; accordingly, this framework may be relevant to the kinds of dilemmas faced in political social work practice. Its six steps are as follows (Reproduced in full from Reisch and Lowe 2000):

1. Identify and articulate the facts of the ethical dilemma and their likely consequences as best as possible.
2. Identify all related value factors (personal, professional, social, or human) present for all persons involved in the case.
3. Identify and delineate the major value conflicts.
4. Set priorities for the values that have been found to be in conflict in Step 3. State the reasons that would support this priority setting.
5. Identify and set out arguments that would support the reasons advanced in Step 4 by answering the following questions:
   (a) What underlying ethical norms support this view?
   (b) Why should these norms be accepted as guides for conduct in this case?
   (c) What do these norms imply for how values should be arranged in priority order? (Revise the priority order established in Step 4 if required to do so at this point.)
   (d) What are the implications for community practice and policy development [author's note: or political social work practice] if this decision were generalized?
6. Critique the arguments given in Steps 4 and 5.

When applying this decision-making framework, your initial steps focus on clarifying the facts of the dilemma and then identifying the value conflicts at stake among all impacted constituencies. In Steps 4 and 5, you assess which are the most important values in this situation, justify this assessment, and then critically reflect even further on this assessment. This critical reflection focuses your thought process on exactly which standards matter most in this dilemma, why they matter, as well as the positive and negative implications of prioritizing these standards.

In the final step, Step 6, you engage in even more critical reflection, critiquing your own arguments. We encourage you to take into account alternative viewpoints and to evaluate your decision through a variety of other lenses in order to make sure that you can defend your stance.

Loewenbeg and Dolgoff's Ethical Rules Screen and Ethical Principles Screen

The two-part "Ethical Rules Screen" and "Ethical Principles Screen" developed by Loewenberg and Dolgoff (1996) has been previously used as a model for guiding ethical macro practice (Hardina 2004). While the "Ethics Work-Up" asks social workers to prioritize values on their own (Reisch and Lowe 2000), the Ethical Principles Screen takes a different approach, proposing a specific order to guide prioritization of ethical principles.

This process starts with the Ethical Rules Screen, which enables you to assess whether the Code sufficiently addresses your ethical dilemma. The Ethical Rules Screen involves the following three steps (slightly adapted from Dolgoff et al. 2012):

1. Are any of the rules within the Code of Ethics applicable to this dilemma? Note that these rules are expected to supersede one's personal values.
2. If one or more rules within the Code of Ethics apply, follow the rules provided in the Code.
3. If the specific dilemma is not addressed by the Code of Ethics, or conflicting guidance is provided by the Code, use the Ethical Principles Screen below.

If the Code addresses your dilemma, this screen suggests that the Code alone should guide your actions. Where the Code does not sufficiently address your dilemma, however, you would then move to the second step and apply the seven-step Ethical Principles Screen (slightly adapted from Dolgoff et al. 2012):

1. Principle: Protection of life
2. Principle: Social justice
3. Principle: Self-determination, autonomy, and freedom
4. Principle: Least harm
5. Principle: Quality of life
6. Principle: Privacy and confidentiality
7. Principle: Truthfulness and full disclosure

While each of the seven principles is important to social workers and reflected within our Code, Dolgoff et al. (2012) suggest prioritizing the more highly ranked principles over the lower-ranked principles in ethical decision-making. That is, when faced with a choice between social justice (principle 2) and truthfulness (principle 7), this screen suggests that social justice should carry more weight in your decision-making process.

As Dolgoff et al. (2012) clearly specify, however, the order of principles laid out by the Ethical Principles Screen may not always be appropriate in all contexts; instead, you may need to engage in critical reflection in order to determine whether this priority order makes sense within your practice context. Therefore, while this screen can help guide your ethical decision-making, it may serve just as a starting point, giving you a basis from which to create your own rank order of ethical principles, as applies to the specific political context in which you practice. You may also choose to add additional ethical principles that reflect your values and values that are important to the constituencies with whom you work (Hardina 2004).

Knowing Your Own Ethical Decision-Making Style

You likely already bring a preconceived orientation to ethical decision-making. The decision-maker (you!) in an ethical dilemma is a critical component of the ethical decision-making process. Our cultural background, our biases, aspects of our socialization, as well as our role in the organization and the broader context in which we practice influence how each of us approaches ethical dilemmas. Mattison (2000) terms this "**value patterning**," indicating that each of us has a specific set of priorities that we consistently apply to our own ethical decision-making processes.

Mattison (2000) and Hardina (2004) both highlight a distinction between **deontological** and **teleological** styles of ethical decision-making. A deontological style involves an absolutist approach to problem solving. For a person who adopts this style, actions are often considered "right" or "wrong," regardless of the consequences that result. For example, a political social worker who tends to subscribe to a deontological style might refuse to engage in a back-room deal to move forward a piece of legislation regardless of the legislation's substantive merits. She might argue that a back-room deal violates the core social work value of integrity and should not be entered into, regardless of any benefit that could emerge from the deal.

A teleological style, on the other hand, involves moral relativism. In this approach, the "right"-ness of an action is dependent on the consequences that are likely to result from the action. When faced with the prospect of a back-room deal to pass a piece of legislation, a political social worker who tends toward a teleological style will weigh the various consequences that could emerge from this deal. She may determine that the positive social justice impact that is likely to emerge from the bill may outweigh any concerns about the integrity of the deal. Political social workers with a teleological style are more likely to engage in political compromise to achieve what they see as the best possible outcome, even if it is not all that they hope for.

Continuous reflection on, and understanding of, your own value patterning and your ethical decision-making style can help you to make more effective decisions as you move forward as a political social work practitioner (Mattison 2000). By increasing your self-awareness of the factors that you bring personally and individually to the process of navigating challenging ethical dilemmas, you will be better equipped to adapt your approach as needed and to limit the extent to which your personal values or stylistic biases impact your decisions.

Section 4: Ethical Dilemmas in Political Social Work Practice

Many of the challenges you are likely to face in political social work—and, in fact, in all arenas of social work practice—do not have easy answers. As the Code advises us, "reasonable differences of opinion exist among social workers" (National Association of Social Workers 2017), meaning that there often is more than one appropriate way to handle a challenging ethical dilemma. What is most important, then, is that we approach these dilemmas cautiously and thoughtfully, using critical thinking to weigh alternatives.

This section provides you with an opportunity to practice and develop your own approach to ethical decision-making in political social work practice. Below we provide brief examples that illustrate common ethical dilemmas that political social workers may face in their work. Building on our discussions throughout this chapter, these examples involve challenging ethical decisions such as:

- Balancing policy "ends" versus the "means" by which you get there, particularly where the means may involve setting aside other core social work values in pursuit of moving social justice outcomes forward.
- Competing claims by different groups over limited resources.
- Ensuring self-determination and meaningful participation from constituencies.
- Achieving policy outcomes in the short-term versus the long-term sustainability of your ability to do so.

Many of the examples below illustrate complex situations that place social work values in conflict with each other. In some cases, you may find that you and fellow social workers agree on a solution. In other cases, you may find that engaging in processes of ethical decision-making lead you and your colleagues to different ways of navigating these challenges.

EXPLORE YOUR VALUES: Ethical Decision-Making
With fellow students or a colleague, apply at least one of the ethical decision-making frameworks discussed in this chapter to each of the scenarios outlined below. For each scenario, consider how our Code of Ethics might guide you in navigating the situation. Together, discuss and reflect upon alternative approaches to each scenario.

Optional follow-up activity: After you have completed this activity with a specific scenario, take on the role of another person who might be involved in the dilemma. Go through your ethical decision-making framework again. Do you end up in a similar place—why or why not?

Scenario 1: As *governor of your state*, you have proposed a substantial increase in the state's minimum wage. You and your allies have been arguing that a $15 minimum wage is an essential living wage for workers across the state. However, your proposal has faced substantial opposition on the part of the farming industry that threatens to derail this proposal. In response to this opposition, your advisors have suggested that you consider a carve-out (or exclusion) of farm workers from the minimum wage increase. The argument is that you will be more likely to be able to pass the minimum wage increase for all other workers in the state if the wages of farm workers are excluded from the proposal. Do you propose the carve-out? (Note: This scenario is directly adapted from a real-world situation in New York in 2016; McKinley 2016).

(continued)

Scenario 2: You have worked as a civil servant in a state-level executive branch agency for several years, and are the *state-wide director of a program that administers support to homeless veterans in your state*. The last gubernatorial election resulted in a change of the political party leading your state. The new governor and her political administration have come into office and have requested that each agency conduct a thorough review of every state program under their purview, with recommendations for change. There are extensive rumors—and some evidence from campaign rhetoric, as well as what is already happening in other state agencies—that this review is likely to lead to substantial cuts to state programs.

You are tasked with writing the review of the program you oversee. Your extensive experience with this program has made you aware both of its strengths and its weaknesses. You know that if you were to provide a fully honest analysis of your program and your recommendations for improvement, the administration would focus solely on the program's deficiencies and not on your recommendations for improvement. Each recommendation you make is likely to call attention to the program weaknesses you would like to improve. How do you approach your report: Do you write a fully honest report identifying the program's true strengths and weaknesses? Do you understate its weaknesses in an effort to try to protect the program? Or is there an alternative approach you would take?

Scenario 3: You are the *campaign manager for a candidate in a very tight mayoral campaign*, with the election just weeks away. Your candidate's opponent has a history of consistently opposing policies that you and the campaign believe are essential to promoting social justice in your community, and many marginalized groups in your community are concerned about the possibility of your opponent being elected.

Through opposition research, you recently discovered that two decades ago, as a college student, your campaign opponent spent several days as a patient in an inpatient mental health facility. A major issue in this campaign has been who would bring a steady hand to governance. Given the prevalence of mental health stigma in your community, releasing this information is likely to turn voters away from your opponent. Do you share this information off-the-record with a local reporter?

Scenario 4: You are the *executive director of a local nonprofit organization that provides assistance to the homeless*. Homelessness has increased in your city over the last couple of years due to broader economic factors in the state and country. As a result of these economic factors, your city government is facing major budget cuts and plans a permanent 25% cut to homelessness services directly provided by the city. As a way around this, the mayor has called you and directly asked you to support an ordinance that would revamp the city's homelessness services. The ordinance would call for the city to

(continued)

provide fewer direct services, while relying on organizations like yours to increase their service provision role.

Rather than the 25% cut, the ordinance would fund a group of local non-profits to provide these direct services at the same rate as the city currently does for the next 3 years, meaning there would not be an immediate cut to homeless services over the next 3 years. After this 3-year period, however, city funding would end, and the nonprofits would be expected to find grant funding and other means of financial support. The mayor says without support from someone who works with the homeless community, the ordinance will not pass. What do you do?

Scenario 5: As *legislative director in the office of a state legislator*, you are responsible for pushing a bill your legislator sponsored, and a corresponding appropriations request, that would provide a much-needed expansion of pre-K programs to low-income students across your state. Many advocacy groups with whom your office works closely have been working for many years on this issue, and they have counted on your legislator to be a legislative champion for this effort. You have been very heartened to discover that there seems to be more legislative support for expanding pre-K programs this year than you and the advocates have seen in prior legislative sessions.

As the state's appropriations process moves forward, however, it becomes clear that the state's revenue projections are down. While the committee chair-woman is in support of this pre-K expansion, funds for education programs are being capped below the prior budget year, and any increase in funding for one program will require substantial cuts to other programs. The chairwoman proposes that in order to expand pre-K across the state, the budget can real-locate funds that currently fund school-based programs for youth with special needs. Upon learning this information, how do you move forward with your budget proposal?

Scenario 6: You are a *policy staff member of an executive branch agency*. Your agency's budget for early intervention services for children from birth to three has been cut by the legislature. The agency has developed a proposal to redesign these early intervention services within the allocated budget. You are very uncomfortable with the direction that this work has been taking. You fear that this proposal—which substantially tightens eligibility criteria and adds cost-sharing (a system which requires families to pay for some portion of the services)—will result in the loss of services for children in the state who are most in need of services. You are asked to advocate to agency leaders that they pass the new proposal.

While you are concerned about the harm that could come from this proposal, pushing back on the proposal might derail the work that has been done so far, potentially resulting in an even more harmful policy alternative. Do you speak up about your concerns, or stay quiet?

(continued)

Scenario 7: You are a *candidate in your very first election*, and are running for an at-large seat on your local City Council. You have an extremely limited budget and have a lot of work to do to build name recognition in the city. As this is your first run for office, you are relying heavily on the advice of a campaign strategist who has advised several campaigns in your city. In prior elections, no more than 10% of the city's electorate has voted in City Council elections. Your strategist advises you to not waste very limited campaign resources on efforts to register new voters. The strategist instead advises you to limit your Get Out The Vote (GOTV) efforts to homes where residents have voted in past city elections.

As a social worker, however, you have felt strongly about expanding meaningful participation in policy on the part of vulnerable populations. In fact, that's part of what spurred your run for office. You know that people of color are less likely to be represented in policy decisions in your city, and in fact, the neighborhoods that your strategist encourages you to skip have a higher percentage of people of color than the neighborhoods that typically vote in this election. How do you proceed with your campaign?

Scenario 8: You are an *elected member of the U.S. House of Representatives*, representing a district that is struggling with the opioid crisis. Substance abuse and, in particular, opioid addiction, are tearing apart families and creating what feels in some ways like a "lost generation" in your community. You have substantial concerns about the health and well-being of your constituents and are committed to improving conditions in the communities that you represent. Based on your extensive experience with your community, review of the research that advocates and lobbyists have brought to you, and your own reading of a new health care reform bill that has been proposed in Congress, you are convinced that your constituents would greatly benefit from this bill. You are particularly pleased by the bill's specific policy and budget provisions for targeting opioid addiction in communities like yours.

However, upon learning of this bill, members of your community are concerned that it will increase their health care costs. They have been repeatedly calling your office and showing up at your town-hall meetings in opposition to this bill. Polling of your community, as well as the volume of calls in opposition, make it clear that your constituents are overwhelmingly opposed to this bill. You serve on the House Energy and Commerce Committee which has a scheduled vote on this bill in 2 weeks. What do you do?

Scenario 9: You are the *director of government affairs for a nonprofit organization*, located about 5 hours away from your state capitol. One of the top priorities of your state legislative agenda this session is the process of reshaping how mental health services are provided in schools in your state. Based on your advocacy, a bill to do exactly this has been filed, and a House committee hearing on this bill is scheduled for the end of this week.

(continued)

You and your fellow mental health advocates have worked in advocacy for over a decade each, have strong relationships with legislators, and are skilled at influencing policy. In preparing for your testimony later this week, a social work intern in your office points out that neither you nor your fellow advocates have reached out to affected populations to ask them how they feel about this bill, and whether they think it would be helpful to them. She is right. It had not occurred to you to do this, because you are confident that this bill will help vulnerable children in your state in need of mental health services. How do you respond to her criticism?

Scenario 10: You are *executive director of a local nonprofit agency* focused on community health and well-being. Your agency regularly engages in advocacy on policy issues related to health and human services, and has worked extensively on issues related to obesity. Recently, you have been asked to participate in a coalition to advocate for a local ban on sugary drinks, which you think is consistent with your agency's mission and would be beneficial for your agency's client base.

Before agreeing to participate in this coalition, you discuss it with your executive team. Your development director points out that a large portion of your agency's donors run restaurants and movie theaters that benefit from the sale of sugary drinks. Some have expressed concerns in the past about the impact of such a ban on their businesses. How does this impact your decision about whether to participate in the coalition?

Scenario 11: The governor of your state tends to surround himself with a homogenous set of policy advisors, and has been publicly criticized for doing so. The governor asks you, *a person of color, to be a member of a substantive policy advisory board*. It is clear that your invitation to this board is a "token" move, made in an overt effort to address these critiques and to make the governor look more inclusive. At the same time, accepting this invitation gets you a seat at the table to address policy decisions affecting the well-being of the state's residents. Do you accept the invitation?

Review of Key Terms and Concepts

Carve-out: to remove a population or a protection for a population from a proposed policy.

Competence: a social work value of practicing in areas in which one has appropriate abilities.

Constituent services: services offered to residents of a district by politicians in response to reported needs and concerns.

Credibility: being considered worthy of trust.

Deontological decision-making: an absolutist approach to problem solving, in which the decision-maker considers actions to be right or wrong regardless of the resulting consequences of those actions.

Ethical decision-making framework: a tool that takes us through a step-by-step problem-solving process to think through how we might address an ethical dilemma.

Ethical dilemmas: situations that arise in which we find ourselves having to choose between multiple alternatives that are equally satisfactory or unsatisfactory.

Ethics: a set of moral standards that guide us in determining which course of action we should take.

Instrumental relationship: an association that exists for the purpose of achieving some sort of external goal(s).

Integrity: the quality of acting honestly and responsibly, of having strong moral principles and promoting ethical practices.

Microaggressions: everyday slights (whether intentional or not) that communicate negative messages to marginalized groups.

Self-determination: the ability of an individual to determine the course of one's own life.

Social justice: fair access to needed information, services, and resources; equality of opportunity; and meaningful participation in decision making for all people.

Teleological decision-making: a morally relativistic approach to problem solving, in which the decision-maker perceives the rightness of an action as being dependent upon the consequences of that action.

Value patterning: the consistent application of an individual's own specific set of priorities to the ethical decision-making processes.

Resources

Book

Frederic Reamer's *Social Work Values & Ethics* (the section on "indirect practice" may be particularly useful in these contexts): https://www.amazon.com/Social-Values-Ethics-Foundations-Knowledge/dp/0231137893/ref=dp_ob_title_bk

---

References

Arnstein, S. R. (1969). A ladder of citizen participation. *Journal of the American Institute of Planners, 8*(3), 216–224.

Buffett, W. E. (2011, August 14). Stop coddling the super-rich. *The New York Times.*

Collette, M. (2017, March 28). Pasadena mayor to Hispanic councilman: "Speak up, boy". *Houston Chronicle.*

Desmond, M. (2016). *Evicted: Poverty and profit in the American city.* New York, NY: Crown Publishing Group.

Dodd, S. J. (2007). Identifying the discomfort: An examination of ethical issues encountered by MSW students during field placement. *Journal of Teaching in Social Work, 27*(1/2), 1–19.

Dolgoff, R., Harrington, D., & Loewenberg, F. (2012). *Ethical decisions for social work practice* (9th ed.). Belmont, CA: Brooks/Cole.

Ezell, M. (2001). The ethics of advocacy. In *Advocacy in the human services* (pp. 37–50). Belmont, CA: Brooks/Cole.

Frank, T. (2007). *What's the matter with Kansas? How conservatives won the heart of America.* New York, NY: Henry Holt and Company.

Fraser, J. (2014, May 14). Mayor drops bathroom provision from nondiscrimination ordinance. *Houston Chronicle.*

Gray, M., & Gibbons, J. (2007). There are no answers, only choices: Teaching ethical decision making in social work. *Australian Social Work, 60*(2), 222–238.

Hardina, D. (2004). Guidelines for ethical practice in community organization. *Social Work, 49*(4), 595–604.

Hoefer, R. (2016). *Advocacy practice for social justice* (3rd ed.). Chicago, IL: Lyceum Books.

Kantor, N., & Metzger, M. (2015). *Evicting victims: Reforming St. Louis's nuisance ordinance for survivors of domestic violence* (pp. 1–6). St. Louis, MO: George Warren Brown School of Social Work: Center for Social Development.

Lawless, J. L. (2015). Female candidates and legislators. *Annual Review of Political Science, 18,* 349–366.

Lipton, E., & Shane, S. (2016, December 13). Democratic House candidates were also targets of Russian hacking. *New York Times.*

Loewenberg, F., & Dolgoff, R. (1996). *Ethical decisions for social work practice* (5th ed.). Itasca, IL: F.E. Peacock.

Mattison, M. (2000). Ethical decision making: The person in the process. *Social Work, 45*(3), 201–212.

McKinley, J. (2016, March 25). Exemptions may color deal to lift New York State's minimum wage. *New York Times.*

McKinley, J. (2017, April 4). New York Assembly clears a major obstacle in budget talks. *The New York Times.*

National Association of Social Workers. (2017). *Code of Ethics of the National Association of Social Workers.* Washington, DC: National Association of Social Workers.

National Association of Social Workers. (n.d.). *History of the NASW Code of Ethics.* Retrieved from https://www.socialworkers.org/nasw/ethics/ethicshistory.asp

Pritzker, S., & Barros Lane, L. (in press). Supporting field-based education in political settings. *Journal of Social Work Education.*

Reamer, F. G. (2002). Eye on ethics: Making difficult decisions. *Social Work Today.*

Reisch, M., & Lowe, J. I. (2000). "Of means and ends" revisited: Teaching ethical community organizing in an unethical society. *Journal of Community Practice, 7*(1), 19–38.

Smothers, H. (2015, January 21). Houston's Equal Rights Ordinance, explained. *Texas Monthly.*

Thyer, B. A. (2010). Social justice: A conservative perspective. *Journal of Comparative Social Welfare, 26*(2), 261–274.

Weisberg, J. (2016, May 9). Why Republicans who hate Trump are afraid to say so. *Slate.*

Williams, B., & Murphy, P. P. (2017, February 23). Constituents search for 'missing' representatives. *CNN Politics.*

Political Social Work Careers and Leadership: From Jane Addams To You!

15

© Springer International Publishing AG 2018
S.R. Lane, S. Pritzker, *Political Social Work*,
https://doi.org/10.1007/978-3-319-68588-5_15

Section 1: Overview

In the first part of this book, you were exposed to an array of domains in which political social work can be practiced, and reflected on your own ideology, political knowledge, skills, efficacy, privilege, and use of power. You learned how to apply theories, assessment skills, and models in political contexts. In the second and third parts of this book, you used these knowledge and skills to design and implement effective strategies for electoral and advocacy campaigns. In the final part of this book, you have reflected on how to monitor and evaluate success within a political context and have considered how social work ethics and values apply to political practice. In this chapter, we encourage you to reflect upon all that you have learned and consider how you will integrate these skills into your own social work practice. Whether you are a student, a practitioner, or a faculty member, we hope you will find suggestions in this chapter for ways to increase your political activity. In Chap. 1 we told you to "consider yourself asked" to get involved. In this chapter, we ask you to bring all that you have learned together to develop your own specific plan for political involvement.

Developing Social Work Competency
The Council on Social Work Education establishes educational standards for all social work programs in the USA. Content in this chapter supports building competency in the following areas that are considered core to the practice of social work:
COMPETENCY 1: Demonstrate Ethical and Professional Behavior
COMPETENCY 3: Advance Human Rights and Social, Economic, and Environmental Justice
COMPETENCY 5: Engage in Policy Practice

Domains of Political Social Work	
1. Engaging individuals and communities in political processes	◄
2. Influencing policy agendas and decision-making	◄
3. Holding professional and political positions	◄
4. Engaging with electoral campaigns	◄
5. Seeking and holding elected office	◄

Section 2: Political Social Work Careers

Throughout this book, as you have explored and examined the many facets of political social work, we hope that you have reflected upon what political social work means to your professional goals. In this chapter, we come back to where we started this book, asking you to join us in prioritizing political and social change as you consider your next steps in your social work career. The competencies that you have developed through your social work education, your practice and this book can help you incorporate political social work into your career in a variety of ways. This may be in a full-time capacity, as one component of your generalist or direct practice position, or in work that is part of your personal community and civic engagement.

As you further contemplate what political social work will look like in your career, we profile social work icon Jane Addams. She offers a model of how social workers from the profession's earliest days have integrated political work into their practice across systems.

POLITICAL SOCIAL WORKER PROFILE: Jane Addams
Hull House Founder

Jane Addams is a social work icon, who laid much of the foundation of the social work profession. Her success at Hull House, her Nobel Peace Prize, and the impact she had on society can overshadow her as a person. She started as a student, a learner trying to make sense of the social issues around her, grappling with the enormity of the issues that are still prevalent today and the lack of solutions to address them. She chose to tackle social change regarding issues like poverty, education, child care, and quality of life, both within her local community and through political change. How did she go from a college graduate facing a world with little role for educated women to Hull House, a multifaceted set of services and resources for immigrants, many poor, in Chicago in the late nineteenth and early twentieth century (Harvard University n.d.)? How did she find the confidence to believe that she could make a difference in such impossible-seeming endeavors? What stirred her advocacy heart and drove her to pursue and enact tangible changes in the way social services were thought of and delivered?

(continued)

The difficulty of the challenges she faced only seemed to motivate her. As she graduated from college and looked at her options, she found few. Coming from a wealthy background, she was able to travel around Europe, where she saw social problems that are still present today in both Europe and the USA—poverty, hunger, and more. She also witnessed firsthand the settlement house model that would serve as inspiration for the Hull House and many other settlement houses in the USA. Addams' experiences led her to advocate alongside clients and not merely on behalf of them. She tried to dismantle the paternalistic model of superiority to the poor present in many agencies through a settlement house based on community, intermingling of settlers and residents, and common opportunities (Brooks 2017). Rather than a model that relegated the poor to merely surviving, while "helpers" were seen as experts, settlers and residents could learn from one another and thrive in the settlement house model.

Neither Addams nor other members of the settlement movement should be placed on a pedestal or immune from criticism, particularly of the movement's refusal to serve African-Americans in integrated settings. However, Addams leadership shows a model of serving others through both community and political change. She worked toward women's suffrage and engaged in national party politics at a time when women did not yet have the right to vote. She worked to ensure garbage collection in poor neighborhoods, key to health and hygiene, was done correctly; eventually she gained the power to compel the garbage to be removed when she was appointed to the office of garbage inspector (Jane Addams is appointed garbage inspector n.d.). She received the Nobel Peace Prize for her work as the International President of the Women's International League for Peace and Freedom in 1931. The speech honoring her with the award is available in the resource section of this chapter, along with more information about Hull House and settlement movements.

Domain 1: Careers in Engaging Individuals and Communities in Political Processes

Professional practice in this domain can take on a range of forms. In direct practice settings, social workers work within their agencies to increase voter engagement and political awareness. Other social workers practice full-time in this domain. Social workers like Tanya Rhodes Smith (profiled in Chap. 8) engage voters, train others to engage voters, and conduct research about the most effective ways to activate communities. Others conduct advocacy and legal work on behalf of populations who are denied the opportunity to vote. They may work for advocacy organizations whose work includes agendas focused on political justice, like The Sentencing Project, or may advocate to expand access to suffrage, like Jane Addams (profiled in this chapter) and Richard Cloward (profiled along with Frances Fox Piven in Chap. 8). Still others—like Sheryl Grossman (profiled in Chap. 14), Ana Rodriguez (profiled in Chap. 4), and Katie Richards-Schuster (profiled in Chap. 3)—work directly in partnership with marginalized communities, supporting them in developing their own political voices.

Domain 2: Careers in Influencing Policy Agendas and Decision-Making

Positions that provide opportunities to influence policy agendas and decision-making may be found in public agencies, nonprofit organizations, campaigns, political parties, or in organizations who lobby and advocate. In nonprofit agencies, positions with a substantial focus on this work have a wide variety of titles, including executive director, vice president of public affairs, director of governmental relations, director of public policy, program manager, organizer, policy advisor, or outreach coordinator. However, advocacy is a substantial part of the work of many macro practitioners. In their study of professional macro practitioners, with over 60 different job titles reported, Pritzker and Applewhite (2015) found that nearly 60% of respondents frequently or very frequently engage in advocacy in their current position. Over three-fourths reported that they had engaged in at least some advocacy in a prior professional position.

Across settings, positions in this domain tend to be open to professionals with a variety of degrees and therefore tend not to have "social work" in the title. Many more of these jobs may be held by social workers than is commonly realized. As one social worker, Heather Sandler, MSW, shared with the authors, "I am in a job right now that didn't previously take MSWs because I detailed my education and experience to compare with the position's [needs]." See also the advocacy careers of Constance Brooks and Nancy Amidei (both profiled in Chap. 6), Stephanie Mace (profiled in Chap. 8), and Sally Tamarkin (profiled in Chap. 5). Others like Susan Hoechstetter (profiled in Chap. 13) influence policy decision-making through work with foundations or in advising and training nonprofits to successfully work in the policy sphere. Juliana Cruz Kerker (profiled in Chap. 13) works full-time as a lobbyist. The National Association of Social Workers, idealist.org, usajobs.gov, advocacy organizations, and the professional networks you develop (see Section 4 of this chapter) are a good place to start looking for full-time jobs focused on influencing policy decisions.

In other cases, integrating this domain into your career may require that you advocate for the creation or expansion of a job beyond what is written. For example, it may be possible to infuse political content into a job that doesn't appear political on the surface. Jennifer Willett, M.S.W., Ph.D., describes:

> I couldn't get a macro job that I wanted (I was trained in community-based social work) so I took an administrative job running transition housing. It didn't require an MSW, I believe. My boss was a nurse. I then was "allowed" to be very involved in the local organizing scene. I also was constantly calling my reps, meeting with them, building coalitions, etc. Whereas my more micro peers were encouraged to run groups that clients in my program could go to. The higher-ups valued people who could do the base job but could also do other things that would make the organization better. So I found a job I could make what I wanted. I always tell my students to think about administrative jobs because, in my experience, they tend to be a bit more flexible.

Social workers also seek out volunteer opportunities, outside of their full-time position, to influence policy. Melanie Pang (profiled in Chap. 8) provides an example of this, engaging in much of her policy work outside of her full-time job.

Domain 3: Careers in Holding Professional and Political Staff Positions

Political social workers may seek full-time positions within public agencies at the local, state, or federal level, either in the civil service or as political appointees. Civil service positions are required by law to be publically advertised, so you may find open civil service positions easier to find than other political social work positions. Civil service jobs often give preference to individuals who have served in the armed services or the Peace Corps, who have disabilities, or who have previous government service. Therefore, "getting a foot in the door" with one civil service position can open up options for other opportunities. We encourage social workers interested in civil service positions to seek out advice from someone who has been through the process, or who does hiring in the civil service. Both students and alumni may have access to staff members in your college or university's career office who specialize in government positions.

The process of applying for civil service positions often can be tedious, complicated, and time intensive. (For example, one author knows a person who just got an interview for a civil service position she applied for 2 years ago.) Some civil service positions require applicants to take and pass a standardized exam, even if applicants have already passed a social work licensing test (City of New Orleans 2017). Typically, position announcements (see the USA Jobs website in Resources) indicate if an exam is required. Federal positions often require a unique form of resume (see the Partnership for Public Service's Go Government website in Resources). A few avenues for getting into civil service positions have a quicker process and are designed specifically for students and recent graduates. On the federal level, social work students are encouraged to look into positions through the Pathways and Presidential Management Fellows programs (United States Office of Personnel Management n.d.). Natalie Powell (profiled in Chap. 12) and Torey Powell (profiled in Chap. 3) both began their federal careers through the Presidential Management Fellows program.

The process to be considered for a political appointee position in a public agency varies widely by position and location. In some locations, you fill out an online application to be considered (State of California 2017). In others, you need to share your resume with someone who has connections with the hiring agency or official, or someone who knows you will need to pass along your resume. These jobs are often not posted publicly or, if they are, they are posted only briefly. As a result, networking with political allies can be particularly helpful. President Donald Trump's director of presidential personnel, Johnny DeStefano was in charge of filling up to 4000 political appointee positions in late 2016 and early 2017. In a profile in *The Washington Post,* he explained his approach to hiring political appointees:

> What I'm interested in now is, 'Why do you want the job, and more specifically, why do you want to work for this administration? … What's your vision? I want to know that myself. I'm the person who's vouching for them to the president of the United States. (Rein 2017)

Another option for full-time political staff positions is to work in the offices of elected officials. These positions range from entry-level legislative assistant positions to chief of staff. Susan Collins (profiled in Chap. 10) is chief of staff for a member of the U.S. House of Representatives. Joanne Cannon (also profiled in Chap. 10) works in the district office of a U.S. Senator as his deputy state director. These positions are often not posted. Hiring processes for legislative jobs often take place through word of mouth and in-network recommendations. In many places, new legislative job openings are often shared with legislative interns, staffers, and former staffers via a private listserv.

It is important to note that political appointments are not limited to full-time positions. Social workers also are appointed to part-time service on government policy advisory committees, councils, commissions, and boards. At the federal level, advisory committees on which social workers have served include the National Advisory Committee on Violence Against Women and the National Advisory Council for the Substance Abuse and Mental Health Services Administration. On a local level, Melanie Pang (profiled in Chap. 8) serves as an appointed co-chair of the Houston Mayor's LGBTQ Advisory Board.

Creating a network of people who know the decision makers for these positions and know that you are interested is an important first step. Depending on your area, this may mean getting to know your local elected officials, people who volunteer for your local political parties, or members of key civic groups. This is one reason why field placements and participating in volunteer opportunities are so critical to finding jobs in political settings—they allow you to build the connections necessary to find out about potential job opportunities. If you are new to your area or haven't been involved in these settings before, reach out to these folks. Get to know their work, and enable them to become aware of you and your skills. Even if you do not yet have these connections upon graduation, you can still build contacts and a reputation for working hard through political volunteer opportunities. If you have been in social work practice since you finished your education, you may find that you have already built up a network that would help you in this process if you choose to look for these jobs.

Domain 4: Careers in Engaging with Electoral Campaigns

Positions in electoral campaigns offer a wide variety of experiences, skills, and salaries, and range from entry level to senior management. If you are interested in campaign jobs, you need to be willing to start at the bottom. Joanne Cannon began her political social work career as an intern on an underdog Congressional campaign. Knocking on doors or making phone calls may seem unexpected for someone with an MSW, but remember that doing these jobs well, whether as a volunteer or entry-level staff member, generally leads to more responsibilities and opportunities on a campaign. Many organizations hire paid canvassers, especially in the summer or during the end of a campaign. These are a great way to gain experience and to begin to build relationships with people in the political community where you live. One common misconception is that if you want to work in politics, you need to work in Washington, DC. In fact campaign jobs are located all around the country.

If professional work on campaigns is the path for you, consider the following: Your social work skills prepare you well for these positions, as demonstrated by the career of Jessica Mitchell (profiled in Chap. 7). In this domain, however, you are likely to encounter many professionals who are not familiar with social work education. They may need to be educated about the strengths that you bring. As we discuss in more depth in Section 4, begin to prepare yourself by spending some time thinking about your own personal "message"—how you articulate and sell your social work skills to audiences who may not realize what those are. You also can help yourself get in the door for these positions by networking with those in the political community in your area, getting to know the players involved, and the expectations associated with the types of jobs in which you are interested.

Domain 5: Careers in Seeking and Holding Elected Office

Throughout this book we argue that social workers have a role in politics, but social workers may even have more public impact as elected officials themselves, whether as a member of a municipal commission, a local school board, state representative, the U.S. Senate, or even, one day, as president. When social workers take a seat at the table, they directly influence policies that affect the individuals and communities who are our profession's highest priorities. Across the country, we see individual social workers participating in policy decisions as elected officials. For example, Steve Kornell (profiled in Chap. 11) serves as an elected member of the St. Petersburg City Council in Florida. Kara Hahn (profiled in Chap. 2) is the elected Majority Leader of the Suffolk County Legislature in New York. Even before reading this book, you may have been familiar with the first woman to hold national elected office in the USA, social worker Jeanette Rankin (profiled in Chap. 1), and the unofficial "Dean of the [U.S.] Senate Women" for over two decades, Barbara Mikulski (also profiled in Chap. 1) (Mundy 2015).

It is our wish to see the nine social workers serving in Congress at the time of this writing and the hundreds in positions across the country be joined by more, hopefully, by you. Elected social workers identify as female, male, and transgender, white, black, Latinx, Asian, and more. They have B.S.Ws, M.S.Ws, and/or Ph.Ds, and are interested in an array of issues. They were recruited into their runs for elective office by family members, friends or acquaintances, fellow social workers, other elected officials, and political activists from their communities (Lane and Humphreys 2011).

We want you to consider joining them. All of the available research suggests that individuals are more likely to run for office if they are specifically asked. We are asking you to please consider putting your name on the ballot. From garbage collector (like Jane Addams) to the U.S. House of Representatives (like current members Barbara Lee (D-CA) and Kyrsten Sinema (D-AZ)), you can join a list of social workers who make a difference!

> **BUILD YOUR KNOWLEDGE: Political Social Work Jobs**
> Find a full-time political position in your area. As you review the position, what are your initial impressions? Could you see yourself applying to this position? Why or why not?

A Special Note: Political Social Work in Direct Practice

Social workers in direct practice have a tremendous opportunity to use political skills to help their clients. As a direct practice social worker "in the trenches," you see every day what works or fails in policy implementation. Policy-makers will not know what policies need to be changed, if they do not hear from direct practitioners and those who are directly impacted by the policies they create. By sharing this information directly with elected officials, as well as and with other social workers who hold full-time positions with policy influence, you can use your understanding of political systems to help clients on a global level at the same time as you help them one on one.

Above—and throughout this book—we have identified many ways that you can incorporate political social work into your direct service. These include, but are not limited to, participating in your organization's community or coalition work, and identifying strategies through which you can politically empower your clients or community members. They also include volunteer opportunities in each of the five domains. We encourage you to seek out mentors who can help you find ways to incorporate political content into your practice. These may include field instructors or faculty if you are a student, or employer or coworkers if you are a professional practitioner.

> **APPLY YOUR SKILLS: Political Social Work in Your Community**
> Identify an individual in your community who either practices as a full-time political social worker or who incorporates political social work into a broader social work position or into their personal work in the community. Using publically available information or an informational interview, create your own profile of this person's career path and their work.

Section 3: Preparing for Political Social Work Jobs

As you begin planning for practice in any of the five domains of political social work, this section identifies some important considerations. We hope you find these helpful in considering your potential career contexts and the path(s) you may take to get there.

Field Education

Field education can play a crucial role in preparing students for political social work practice—either directly in political settings or in agencies that engage with policy or politics in some form. Our advice in this section is for students, practitioners who serve as field instructors, and faculty members.

Students

Field education can provide you with opportunities to implement and expand the knowledge and skills that you have learned in this book and in your courses in real-world settings. In Chap. 5, you had the opportunity to read a blog post by Chenelle Hammonds, a social work student who had a field placement at the Texas Legislature. The insights that she shared in her post were all gained through her real-world experiences interning in that political setting. Field placements in political settings enable you to grapple with ethical conflicts with the support and advice of a social work field instructor. Field placements help you begin to build networks with future political allies, as well as with potential employers. Some of you may be interested in placements that are entirely focused on developing political skills; others of you might be interested in pairing your clinical education with political learning opportunities.

If you have not yet completed your field placements, we provide suggestions of some types of placements you might consider in order to strengthen your political social work skills. We map these placement settings on to the domains and contexts for political social work practice discussed throughout this book. Most of the types of agencies listed have the capacity to provide both micro and macro practice opportunities, of particular relevance for those of who are seeking generalist B.S.W. or M.S.W. generalist placements. If your school is hesitant to place students in partisan settings (a common barrier cited by field directors; Pritzker and Lane 2014), you might share this list as an example of the range of possibilities. For example, the list of options in Domain 4 can help students gather experience with electoral campaigns, with many in nonpartisan settings.

Some of these placements may already be available through your social work program; in other cases, the faculty or field staff at your school may be open to identifying new placements with political content. If these opportunities are not currently available, the following section suggests some possible opportunities to faculty. Later in this chapter, we discuss ways to advocate for changes to your social work program.

Possible options for political social work placements
Domain 1: Empowering voters and communities
Strategy 1: performing outreach to increase voting on the part of underrepresented groups
Strategy 2: registering eligible members of client systems to vote
Strategy 3: advocating for expanded political power to underrepresented groups, including increased voting rights and more just and responsive electoral processes
Settings: Any field placement

Domain 2: Influencing policy agendas and decision-making

Strategy 4: influencing the policy agendas of candidates

Settings: Local or national political parties, town committees, political leadership groups, political action committees, advocacy and professional groups (e.g., National Association of Social Workers, National Alliance for Mental Illness), think tanks, trade associations, community and grassroots organizing agencies, community development corporations, labor union chapters, issue coalitions, directly in electoral campaigns

Strategy 5: influencing policy agendas and policy decision-making by elected officials

Settings: Offices of elected officials, in public agencies with the potential to influence lawmakers (e.g., those with a legislative liaison function)

Strategy 6: influencing policy agendas and policy decision-making by government agencies

Settings: Any of those listed in 4 and 5.

Domain 3: Holding professional and political staff appointments

Strategy 7: working on policy through civil service or other professional positions

Strategy 8: serving as political appointees

Settings: Local, state, Native American tribal, or federal government offices (e.g., administrative settings within the Veterans Administration, in the legislative affairs office of an executive branch agency at the state or federal level)

Strategy 9: working for elected officials

Settings: Offices of local, state, federal, Native American tribal officials; elected officials, such as mayors, county commissioners, city council members, legislative caucuses. State and federal elected officials often have both district and capitol offices, so distance from D.C. or the state capitol doesn't preclude this work.

Domain 4: Engaging with electoral campaigns

Strategy 10: working on campaigns as volunteers or paid staff

Settings: Candidate campaigns (either as a primary placement or as a secondary placement, where an agency loans you to a campaign for part of your time).

Strategy 11: seeking passage or defeat of ballot initiatives or referenda

Settings: Issue campaigns, placements with advocacy groups that are spearheading the campaign, organizations listed in strategy 4 above

Strategy 12: educating voters about policy issues that are part of candidate or issue campaigns

Settings: Organizations that do advocacy work, organizations listed in strategy 4 above

Strategy 13: influencing which candidates run for elected office

Settings: Local or national political parties, town committees, political leadership groups, political action committees

Domain 5: Running for and holding elected office

Strategy 14: running for elected office

Strategy 15: holding elected office

Settings: In any office, particularly those in campaigns or the offices of elected officials.

Field Instructors/Practitioners and Faculty/Field Educators

The social work literature offers an array of models for implementing political content in social work internships. Schools that are successful in establishing and nurturing political social work internships report that creating a culture of social justice and advocacy within the school was helpful in increasing student interest and preparedness (Pritzker and Lane 2014). Creativity in setting up new models for field placements is a must, including use of technology, block placements, stipends, or financial supports for those who need to move or commute long distances. Many programs offer split placements or multiple placements where students can simultaneously focus on micro skills in one placement and macro skills, including political skills, in another. Engaging those who are successful in these placements to serve as field instructors for the students coming behind them is often key in making political placements stable and sustainable.

The list mentioned above provides examples of the breadth of settings that have the potential to provide political content for students. If you are a current practitioner in one of these settings, consider serving as a field instructor and introducing a student to these activities. If you are a faculty member or field educator, consider ways to make these opportunities more visible in your program.

Social Work Education: In and Out of the Classroom

Relevant coursework and the exposure available in a social work program through extracurricular opportunities can help students forge a path to a political social work career. Social work programs may offer students, faculty, staff, alumni, and community members the opportunity to learn from panel discussions, issue information seminars, visits from candidates and elected officials, general encouragement to vote and participate in advocacy, or voter registration and engagement activities. In fact, when faculty formally discuss ways to encourage students to vote, the program is more likely to encourage student participation in a range of election-focused activities (Pritzker and Burwell 2016). The range of political learning opportunities discussed in this paragraph can help students, faculty, and community participants build their political knowledge, skills, and networks.

In the authors' experiences, some students have a hard time identifying professional role models who engage in political social work, or picturing the kinds of professional positions one might pursue that focus on political social work. This is one reason that we opened this textbook with a discussion of five different domains in which political social workers regularly practice, and why we chose to incorporate profiles of political social workers practicing in an array of positions and contexts. We hope that you find these resources helpful to you in carving out your own path or in mentoring students or early career practitioners. We also encourage you to look for examples of social workers involved in political social work in your local community or state. Reach out yourself to practitioners who are creating policy change and ask them to come talk with your student groups, classes, NASW meetings, etc. Encourage them to serve as adjunct instructors or field instructors in schools of social work.

If these opportunities do not exist in your context—or you would like to see more such opportunities—advocating for them and/or jumping in to help bring them to fruition is a great way for you to build political social work skills and find others who share your interests. The Council on Social Work Education (2015) has accreditation standards that govern every social work program in the USA. Interestingly, one of these standards calls for students to be able to have opportunities to organize on behalf of their interests. This offers an important way for students to help create learning opportunities that support their future career paths. In the case study below, a group of Ohio State University College of Social Work students describe how they did exactly this in pursuit of more political social work training.

CASE STUDY: Advocacy by Ohio State University Social Work Students
As told by Nathaniel (Nate) Cindrich and Rebecca (Becky) Phillips Fig. 15.1:

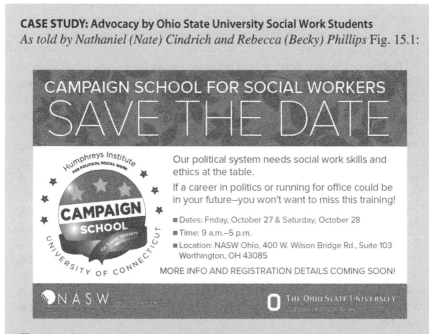

Fig. 15.1 Ohio Campaign School for social workers

In March 2016, Nate attended the 2-day Campaign School for Social Workers run by the Humphreys Institute at the University of Connecticut, along with three of our classmates, at the recommendation of Professor Njeri Kagotho. At the time Nate was a second year MSW student. By the end of the 2 days, we were convinced that this experience would benefit our classmates at Ohio State University (OSU) and strengthen our macro curriculum. We reached out to the Director of the Humphreys Institute, Tanya Rhodes Smith, who offered us guidance to bring the Campaign School to Ohio.

When Nate returned to OSU, he relayed his experience to Becky, a first year student in the MSW program also very interested in political social work.

(continued)

We decided to work together to bring the Campaign School to OSU, helped by the fact that Becky was a first year student and would remain connected to the department after Nate graduated in May. Becky and her peers reached out to the department with some suggestions for how to better meet the needs of students interested in political and advocacy social work. As a result, the department hosted several panel discussions, during which we cited the Campaign School as a specific opportunity for students. We gathered support from faculty and staff, including the Events Assistant Manager of OSU's John Glenn College of Public Affairs, and NASW's Ohio chapter Executive Director, Danielle Smith. Becky was able to leverage her position as Secretary of the College of Social Work Student Association to advocate for and subsequently plan an event focused on activism. The event was standing room only. Dean Tom Gregoire attended, highlighting the interest in and importance of this area of social work.

Becky's leadership position also helped to secure higher-level staff support for the idea of bringing the Campaign School to OSU, as well as a meeting with the Dean. In this meeting with the Dean, we asked for funding and logistical support and discussed potential barriers. One of the big concerns he raised was the importance of not appearing to have a partisan political agenda. The university's governmental affairs office would need to be on board. We assuaged these concerns by relaying that the Campaign School's goal is to prepare social workers to run for and hold public office, regardless of political party. In Becky's role as an intern at NASW Ohio, she helped facilitate communication between the Humphreys Institute, OSU, and NASW Ohio. During NASW's Advocacy Day, she specifically presented about the Campaign School as a way of getting more involved in this aspect of social work.

Ultimately, final approval for the event was given by OSU CSW (and the department of governmental affairs) in April 2017, just about a year after our advocacy started. The first (of many, we hope) Ohio State University Campaign School for Social Workers was held in October 2017, and was a great success.

We encourage other students interested in advocacy to get involved in leadership opportunities both within your department and the university in general. Working with your state's NASW chapter can be helpful if they are engaged in political/advocacy work. And don't be afraid to speak with your department's administration. As we advocated, we focused on maintaining professionalism and assuming positive intent. Talk with other classmates and bring your concerns to the department's attention as a group—there is power in collective voice. It is in our field's Code of Ethics to engage in social justice, which includes politics and advocacy—remember that and don't be afraid to point it out.

APPLY YOUR SKILLS: Creating Change Within Your Program

Thinking back to the skills you have learned throughout this book and consider how you might implement change within your social work program or university.

1. What is one change you would like to implement within your program/university? Define the long-term goal.
2. Who is the target or targets of the change effort?
3. What tactics would you use to be successful? As Nate and Becky describe above, make sure to consider who might be your allies, including fellow students, faculty, administrators, and community members or groups.
4. How would you evaluate your efforts? How would you know you have been successful?

Preparing for Political Social Work Through Continuing Education

Continuing education (CE) courses are available to social workers across the country to help them continue their learning throughout our professional careers. Continued attention to maintaining and updating skills meets the ethical requirement in the NASW Code of Ethics (2017), Section 4.01(b), which states:

> Social workers should strive to become and remain proficient in professional practice and the performance of professional functions. Social workers should critically examine and keep current with emerging knowledge relevant to social work. Social workers should routinely review the professional literature and participate in continuing education relevant to social work practice and social work ethics.

In addition to this ethical responsibility to continue to learn and develop, many social workers are also motivated to take continuing education in order to maintain licensure (Association of Social Work Boards n.d.). While the requirements vary, in general, this coursework offers an opportunity to retain and refresh your skills but also to develop competency in new areas. We encourage all practitioners, whether licensed or not, to use continuing education to develop your political social work skills. Courses offered for CE credit which may enhance your political social work skills include:

- Advocacy
- Budgeting and raising money
- Communication and social media
- Community practice
- Ethics
- Evidence base of key policies
- Issues such as environmental justice, political justice, or social justice

- Leadership
- Self-care
- Supervision
- Updates on current policies

If there are none available, we encourage you to advocate for related content with your continuing education providers. They may not know there is an audience for this content unless you request it.

Section 4: Addressing Potential Challenges

As you consider your social work career path and the role which political engagement may play in it, we also want to honestly acknowledge some possible challenges you may encounter. We do this not to intimidate you—but in the hope that through discussing these challenges, you become more prepared to navigate them successfully. Some of these challenges are more perception than reality, but even the perception that they exist can be a barrier. Overall, we expect that these challenges will lessen with more integration between social work and political work. Specifically, the increased integration we envision includes more social workers in political roles, more political social workers publicly identifying as such, and more political social workers making themselves available as role models and mentors to future social workers. These shifts can help broaden the view of the profession both inside and outside of social work (Hill et al. 2010).

> **FURTHER REFLECTION: Challenges You Might Encounter**
> Take a moment to consider your ideal career path. What are some challenges you see that might inhibit your path? What information would you like to know to help you navigate these challenges?

In this section, we reflect upon seven commonly cited challenges that students or practitioners might face in seeking a career that incorporates political engagement. These are: policy and political content in social work education, identifying potential positions, competition with those from other disciplines, issues around licensure, accessing political networks, common characteristics of the specific political positions, and issues related to supervision and interprofessional practice.

Lack of Policy and Political Content in Social Work Education

Research suggests that many social work programs have room for improvement in terms of providing hands-on opportunities for students to develop political knowledge and participation (Pritzker and Burwell 2016; Pritzker 2017). For example,

25% of social work programs that responded to Pritzker and Burwell's survey did not offer any structured election-related educational opportunities leading up to the 2012 presidential election. In another example, nearly one-third of BSW and MSW programs did not expose any of their students to voter registration efforts in a one-year period leading up to a presidential election (Pritzker 2017). When relevant opportunities are available to students, they are often done in an ad hoc way (such as discussions in classrooms led by faculty at their discretion) or when requested by student groups.

Some social work programs express concerns about offering educational opportunities specifically related to political social work. These include fears that they will be seen as violating policies such as the Hatch Act (even if it doesn't actually apply to their setting), state law, or university policy (Pritzker and Lane 2014). Faculty, administrators, and students should be mindful and specific in the ways in which they manage these opportunities. Note, for example, how the students and administration at Ohio State University in the case study earlier in this chapter navigated concerns about appearing partisan. As discussed elsewhere in this book, the legal line between partisan and nonpartisan activities leaves substantial room for engaging students in political social work. Furthermore, both the National Association of Social Workers (2017) Code of Ethics and the CSWE (2015) accreditation standards identify political ideology/political beliefs as a dimension of diversity that social workers must understand and respect. Engaging students around political social work therefore produces an additional benefit: Discussion of diverse ideologies and opinions within social work programming and curricula increases student interest, understanding, and motivation for action (Rosenwald et al. 2012; Galambos 2009).

Identifying Potential Positions

Jobs that include significant political or policy content are rarely reserved for social workers. As a result, any of the political social work positions identified earlier in this chapter, within each of the five domains, are unlikely to have the words "social worker" in the title. Without a staff member who has direct ties to the social work profession, these jobs may not be listed on social work job boards. (One exception to this is the Macro Social Work Network of the Connecticut NASW chapter.) As a result, social workers seeking full-time political social work positions need to be industrious and creative in finding potential positions.

You will often need to look for job postings in places that target not just social workers, but other disciplines as well, e.g., graduates from Masters of Public Policy, Masters of Public Administration, and law schools, or those with undergraduate majors in political science, sociology, or communications. Some good places to look for postings of political jobs might include:

- Your local NASW chapter
- Idealist.org
- usajobs.gov

- Websites of advocacy organizations and networks
- Your local political party organizations
- Organizations that help specific groups of people get elected to office

As you consider political social work positions, consider that in this realm, the duties of the job and the structure of the organization are often as important as the job title. What would you get to do in this position, and what opportunities are there to move up or to develop skills that will help you in future positions?

Competing and "Selling" Yourself as a Social Worker

As discussed in the previous section, as you enter into the application process for a political social work position, you likely will find yourself competing with people from a variety of educational backgrounds. Both within the profession and among the general public, perceptions of social work tend to emphasize the profession's role in direct practice, not its strengths in preparing policy practitioners (Hill et al. 2010). As a result, you should expect to have to describe how you have been effectively prepared by your social work education and experience. We encourage you to prepare to be able to "sell" the qualifications you bring as a social worker; that is, to connect the skills you learned in your social work education to the work at hand.

Social Work Skills as an Asset to a Political Setting

Your social work degree is an asset to a political setting, but you will need to do the hard work of helping your potential employer to realize this and to dispel some myths and misconceptions about the field. In Torey Powell's political social worker profile, he shares his experience selling his current employer on the merits of his social work degree in preparing him for his position in the federal government. You also may have to (politely) reframe a social work degree away from stereotypes that we are exclusively therapists or child welfare employees.

Through your job search process—and in your subsequent career—you have the opportunity to be an ambassador for the profession! Carmela Isabella, BSW, MSW, describes one of her experiences:

> I was [working] on a campaign and at one of the events someone asked me where I went to school for my political science degree. When I told the woman I had a bachelor and master's degree in social work, her jaw nearly dropped to the ground. She was in awe about why I was there. I explained to her that I was on the campaign because this particular candidate does not want to cut funding for veterans, senior citizens, school funds, people with disabilities, etc. I think this was a wake-up call for this woman because most people have stigmas regarding social workers. They forget that there is more to the profession than removing children from a home.

As you begin your job search process, be prepared to highlight the many ways in which a social work degree and your specific skills and experiences make you a good fit for political positions. In fact, the skills and experiences you have can,

Table 15.1 Social work skills used in campaigning and holding office

Skills	Used in campaigning		Used in holding office	
	n	%	*n*	%
Communication skills	149	60	89	39
Active listening	141	57	70	31
Forming and maintaining coalitions	49	20	43	19
Conflict management/resolution	26	11	62	27
Bargaining and compromising	15	6	54	24

better prepare you for these positions than your peers from other disciplines. Carolyn Treiss, a MSW with a law degree, tells us, "I use my social work skills more than legal skills in my legislative work." Consider, for example, what you learned in your MSW program that might not be taught in a public policy or political science or business program.

Below, we outline some examples of the assets social workers bring to political settings:

1. Social work teaches you how to consider problems and challenges differently than other disciplines do. We focus on finding strengths, assessing individual and community needs, looking at the ways policies affect individuals and communities, and working with people from diverse backgrounds.
2. Social work education is built on a liberal arts foundation, which means that you have been taught content ranging from individual development to policy, from research to working within organizations. Every social worker should come out of their BSW or generalist MSW education with a solid foundation in working with individuals, families, groups, organizations, and communities. What better preparation could there be for work in political settings?
3. Training in meeting the client where they are is very helpful in deftly working with constituents, community partners, or legislators, as well as with managing employees.
4. The depth of content on oppression, diversity, and related issues in social work education makes social workers exceptionally well prepared to engage with constituents from a variety of backgrounds, manage a diverse workforce, and communicate with stakeholders who are different in background or perspective from your own.
5. Social work education tends to heavily emphasize critical thinking, research, and writing. Highlight those skills and provide examples where needed.
6. Social work education has a heavy experiential component, so every social worker has experienced hundreds of hours of hands-on, closely supervised internships in real-world settings.
7. Social work education includes an emphasis on skills critical to success in the political arena that are not taught or emphasized in other disciplines, including active listening, engagement, communication, collaboration, etc.

8. Social workers possess an awareness of systems and how they connect, overlap, and intersect to impact individual and community well-being. Our grounding in systems theory helps us to effectively navigate politics and political systems, and prepares us well for understanding the implications of policy decisions and legislation.

One of the authors of this book has extensively studied the experiences of social workers who run for and hold office. Table 15.1 shows which skills most commonly taught in social work programs were most useful to a sample of social workers who had run for office, both as they campaigned for and held office (Lane 2011). These findings underscore how relevant the communication and active listening skills emphasized in social work education are to campaigning for office, and in some cases, also for holding elected office.

"Selling" Your Social Work Skills

We hear from social workers at all stages of their careers, from students to those who have practiced or taught for years, that it can be uncomfortable to discuss your own accomplishments. We fully understand this discomfort, but want to encourage you to practice "selling" yourself. Laura Bartok, a BSW and MSW trained social worker who has worked in many political jobs—and has run for state representative—advises political social workers: "You have to get good at telling people confidently who you are, what you've accomplished, and what you're capable of! Recognize what you've done, whether or not you want recognition for it."

Below, we identify a set of recommendations for ways to share—and sell—the assets you bring to the table, informed by our communications with political social workers who have successfully secured professional positions. You may find these recommendations helpful not only for pursuing full-time political social work positions, but also in pursuing any of the other career contexts discussed in Section 2 of this chapter.

Make sure that your written materials, especially your cover letter and resume, are understandable to potential employers who are unfamiliar with social work or social work education. Discuss internships instead of field placements, eliminate acronyms, and replace jargon with more clear language. Even if you think of some of the acronyms you use as being well-known, they may not translate to different settings. These kinds of language choices can make it easier for someone outside of social work to understand the skills you bring to the table.

Whenever possible, ask nonsocial workers and/or professional social workers already in political positions to look at your written materials to make sure they translate well to a broader audience. Keep this concern about translation in mind as you think about examples you are considering using to answer interview questions. If no one outside of the social work profession would understand them, they should not be included in your materials.

When describing the work you have done in social work and nonsocial work jobs, field placements, and volunteer opportunities, highlight this work in a way that the employer is likely to see as relevant. This is not limited to social work or direct

Table 15.2 Translating your social work experience

Before	After
Presented at weekly case conference of service providers	Created concise description of ongoing work and presented to other agency professionals on a weekly basis
Completed field placement at OASAS center	Completed 500 internship hours at a public agency that works with individuals who have substance use disorders
Completed required paperwork	Documented services provided and presented results as needed in agency and legal settings
Processed referrals to other agencies	Communicated with public and nonprofit agencies to find best services for agency clients
Completed biopsychosocial assessments	Met with new agency clients to assess their needs and fit for agency services
Provided EBP to students with ADHD, BPD, and low EQ	Researched best services for students facing a variety of barriers to their learning and implemented services to help them succeed
Built rapport with consumers utilizing the advanced generalist practice model	Created meaningful relationships with agency clients using a variety of evidence-based practices
Participated in advocacy efforts toward legislation serving the TBI community	Supported individuals who have had traumatic brain injuries by attending rallies and meeting with members of Congress to express the importance of helping this community
Acted as a case manager for individuals with an ASD diagnosis	Met with individuals with Autism Spectrum Disorder to plan and monitor their goals in order to help them live independently
Facilitated culturally competent community development through rebranding the mission of DSNI	Held meetings to encourage neighborhood residents build a network with one another
Completed program evaluations from a trauma-informed perspective	Researched the effectiveness of services offered by a nonprofit organization serving trauma survivors
Designed a DBT resource packet for the residential SMI population at PT	Constructed a resource guide of coping skill strategies and worksheets for individuals diagnosed with severe mental illness for a private residential mental health treatment center
Competent in micro, mezzo, and macro settings	Worked effectively with individuals, families, groups, and communities

policy experience. Political employers often also look for the kinds of skills and experiences, like conflict resolution and crisis management, which are critical in political settings, even if gained in other settings. For example, picture a social worker who worked for 4 years during college as a gas station attendant, handling intoxicated customers late at night. Picture another social worker who spent several years managing a busy parking lot, regularly dealing with irate people in tense situations. On first glance, these two experiences may not seem at all relevant to policy or social work, and are the kinds of experiences one might leave off of a political social work resume. However, in both cases, these social workers have clear experience demonstrating strong interpersonal relationship and communications skills, conflict management skills, and the ability to remain calm and professional in very stressful situations—each essential and easily translatable to the political realm. These work experiences, combined with social work training, can be a great package for the right political setting. Look at the job description and tailor both your resume and cover letter to the specific skills and tasks of the job description. Think back to the types of social work skills we just identified as assets to political settings. Which of these is the potential employer looking for, and how can you highlight them?

In your written materials and your interviews, discuss the work you have done in terms of the job description, using terms commonly used in that area. Table 15.2 provides some examples of ways to translate your social work experience into language relevant to jobs in political settings.

BUILD YOUR KNOWLEDGE: Political Social Work Job Application
Find a political social work position in your area. Draft a cover letter and resume tailored to that job. Trade these documents with a friend or colleague and give each other constructive feedback on ways to translate your skills to a broader audience.

APPLY YOUR SKILLS: Practice Interview
Conduct a practice interview with a friend, colleague, or mentor. Include some variation of the following challenging questions in your interview—these are questions that you may well be asked in a real interview.

- Why did you decide not to be a social worker anymore?
- Why did you decide not to use your degree?
- Why does a social worker want this job?
- What did you learn in your social work education that prepares you for this job?

When you finish, switch roles, so you both have a chance to interview and be interviewed. When both are completed, talk about which questions you felt confident answering, and which questions you need to practice.

Licensure

Social work licensure has existed since 1980, in order to accomplish a range of goals. These include protecting social work clients from mistakes and ethical lapses and reinforcing the meaning, title, and status of the social work profession (Donaldson et al. 2014). Currently all 50 states and the District of Columbia have social work licensure laws, although nationally, 38% of practicing social workers are licensed (NASW Center for Workforce Studies 2004). The requirements around licensure are varied across states, which can lead to confusion for students and professionals. The Association of Social Work Boards (ASWB), the nonprofit organization that oversees licensure in all 50 states, DC, the U.S. Virgin Islands, Guam, Northern Mariana Islands, and all 10 Canadian provinces, estimates there are 172 different license titles in 62 jurisdictions. Just three of these jurisdictions in the USA offer a license specifically for macro practice, the license most likely to encompass full-time political social work practice. Political social workers can hold a variety of other licenses, or none at all. Licensing complexity across jurisdictions creates particular complications for social workers who want to work in multiple jurisdictions, move jurisdictions, or who want to be able to move between direct and macro practice in their professional career. Some social workers may find the licensing process to be out of reach due to these complexities, its time-consuming nature, and associated costs.

Political social work practice and macro social work practice more broadly have been affected by many aspects of the licensure process (Hill et al. 2010). Many authors argue that macro social work has been marginalized in social work, in part due to the ways in which licensure emphasizes direct practice or clinical social work in many states (Donaldson et al. 2014). Social work students may take less macro coursework because of an emphasis on course content that prepares students for clinical licensure exams. Licensure exam topics are generally micro-oriented, as are the practice areas of the social workers who tend to participate on social work licensure boards. Whether deliberately or not, the content of licensure exams has the power to affect the actions of both students and the profession. Interestingly, however, despite these concerns, Pritzker and Applewhite (2015) found that 96.8% of the social workers in their sample of macro social workers passed their generalist licensure exam on their first try.

Over one-third of the macro social workers in this sample possessed no social work license. Based on this finding, Pritzker and Applewhite (2015) argue, "The aggregate impact of individual decisions not to pursue licensure may well be the reinforcement of the message that macro practice is not an essential part of the social work profession" (p. 198). While in most states, a social work education alone allows you to call yourself a social worker, in some states, one cannot identify as a social worker without a social work license (a form of title protection). As a result, macro social workers who do not pursue a license in such states are left outside of the profession, despite their social work education. Texas is one example of this, with the following language included on the Frequently Asked Questions page on the website of the Texas State Board of Social Worker Examiners:

> Licensure is required [in Texas] if you identify yourself as a social worker by using titles or initials that create the impression that you are qualified or authorized to practice social work. This includes using any title containing the words "Social Worker".... You are exempt from licensure if you do not represent yourself to the public—directly or indirectly—as a social worker and do not use any name, title, or designation indicating authorization to practice social work (Texas Health and Human Services 2013).

Unlike many direct practice positions, however, a social work license is not a professional requirement in many macro settings. In Pritzker and Applewhite's (2015) study, only one-third of the studied macro social workers worked in a position where a license of any sort was required; fewer than 50% of this subset of positions required a social work license. In some cases, individuals working in political contexts may be told that they are ineligible for licensure by licensing boards who do not see their work as social work and even explicitly challenge them as not performing social work (personal communication, K. Hill, June 13, 2017).

What do these challenges mean for social workers interested in political careers? Make sure that you are familiar with your state's licensure laws. Consider whether licensure should be a step in your career path, and if so in what form makes the most sense for you. Discuss this with your mentors and other social workers engaged in political careers. Keep in mind that in some states, licensure is necessary for you to later supervise social work students in their field placements (New York State Department of Education Office of the Professions 2010). In addition, know the rules in your state about title protection. If your state allows you to identify yourself as a social worker, please do and continue to do so as you move forward in your career! The profession needs social workers in political settings to be more visible. Finally, consider advocating for changes in your state's licensure laws that will make it easier for political social workers and other macro practitioners to thrive within the profession. Does your state need macro licensure? Would a better system of transferring licensure from one state to another be helpful? We encourage you to learn the current issues around licensure, and stay involved in the conversation (Hill et al. 2010).

> **BUILD YOUR KNOWLEDGE: Licensure Exam Content**
> Review the outlines for the four exams administered by the Association of Social Work Boards (ASWB): https://www.aswb.org/resources/?c=exam-content-outlines. What content do you see here that relates to political social work? What portion of the overall exams relate to political content? If you have already taken the licensure exam, what content was related?
>
> Once you've reviewed the exams, identify the regulatory board for your area (or the area in which you would like to practice) and its rules. What license would be appropriate for you at this stage? Do you need a license to practice as a social worker in your state?

Accessing Political Networks and Mentoring

In politics, networks are critical. They help connect you with open positions and help you identify allies who can help you achieve your campaign goals. They even may help you feel more capable of accomplishing your work and navigating difficult situations you experience in practice (Pritzker and Barros Lane in press). The challenge for social workers is that our profession is often underrepresented in political networks.

Many people discuss the process of getting jobs in the political world as a sort of an "old boys' club." It can be true that many types of political positions are shared through informal networks and recommendations as commonly as through formal job postings. While this is not the case for civil service positions, it is likely to be true for campaign positions, political appointee positions, and in the offices of elected officials. Therefore, finding ways to break into these networks is important for social workers.

In areas where political social work has a solid foundation, including the regions served by the University of Connecticut, the University of Houston, and in the District of Columbia/Maryland/Virginia area, social workers are active in the political world. As a result, social workers have to do less of the "selling" discussed above. This accomplishes two things: making the informal networking of the political world available and accessible to social workers and increasing the likelihood social workers will be considered for political positions. The early social workers who opened the door to these networks have left it open and encouraged those behind them to follow them through the door.

In many cases, these social workers have laid the groundwork for subsequent social workers through formal or informal mentoring. You may be lucky enough to have found mentors in your social work education and/or career already. These are people whose feedback you respect, and who are willing to make themselves available to you to help connect you with available opportunities, read through your application materials, and help you deal with professional dilemmas and guide career decisions. They are often key to our career advancement. Each of the authors of this book value the role that we have played in serving as mentors to new social workers exploring their potential career paths, which allows us to pay forward the mentorship that we have received (and continue to receive) ourselves. In fact, we are each incredibly honored to have each been able to help mentor some of the incredible social workers profiled in this book. If you have experienced faculty members or field instructors who have shown a particular interest in your career interests, do not be shy in reaching out to them and asking them for advice and mentorship.

Your mentors may be social workers, involved in politics, or both. Where such networks exist, one way to find mentors is through existing networks of political social workers in your area, such as the Association of Macro Practice Social Workers in Minnesota, a Macro Social Workers Network, Education and Legislative Action Network, the PACE committee of your NASW chapter, your chapter of the Macro Social Work Student Network, or another activist social work group. If these groups exist, we recommend that you get involved, introduce yourself to those in the network, invite them out for coffee, and ask their recommendations to increase your likelihood of future opportunities. If these formal networks do not exist, you may need to do the hard work of beginning to lay the groundwork for informal networks in your community or state. Through your own network building, you can help increase the networks available to future social work students and practitioners. While working in political settings, you have the opportunity to highlight ways in which social workers can contribute to political settings (Pritzker and Barros Lane in press). In addition, you can help bring other social workers into these environments; for example, by serving as a field instructor or supporting and recommending other social workers when they apply for jobs.

Position Characteristics: Salary, Job Security, and Work-Life Balance

Political social work positions vary significantly in the type of position, time requirements, and level of responsibility involved, so it is difficult to make blanket statements about salaries, job security, or work-life balance.

In some cases, salaries are quite minimal; for example, serving as a member-advocate for NASW is voluntary, with no compensation. However, while entry-level campaign positions tend to be low-paying, top-level consultants in large campaigns can make a significant amount of money. Similarly, the salaries for elected officials may range from voluntary to six-figure salaries depending on the position and geographic context. Salaries for many political social work positions in nonprofits may be comparable with other macro positions, which often are in the top tier of nonprofit jobs.

The job security of political social work positions also depends on the type of organization in which you are working, and may also be affected by whether you are a member of a union (most common in nonprofit or civil service positions). Often jobs in campaigns or political appointments lack job security. You may be concerned about this if you need to be able to plan for the future or make long-term commitments. Depending on the nature of the campaign, jobs with an advocacy or electoral campaign may come with a specific end date. However, these jobs may come also with the potential of moving on to other positions after the campaign has ended. For example, a newly-elected official is likely to choose her office staff from those who excelled on the campaign. This should be part of the discussion in your hiring process. In some cases, staff may be permitted to work a number of campaigns at once (as long as each campaign manager is aware of your commitment to each candidate), or to work for a campaign through a consulting firm. Working through a consulting firm can enable campaign staffers to have more job security as well.

Work in a part-time legislature may face a similar dynamic. While some legislative staff are year-round, full-time, others are hired on for the intense period during the legislative session. When the session ends, so does the job. At the same time, new political positions, such as on electoral campaigns, often open up soon the session ends, leading some political staff to jump from one time-limited position to another, until they seek and are hired into a more permanent position.

Jobs with elected officials or as a political appointee generally specify that your job is connected to the person who hired you. As a result, if that person is asked to step down or loses an election, your job ends too. Similarly, elected officials only serve for as long as their constituents continue to elect them, or until a term limit goes into effect. In practice, however, the power of incumbency means that these officials are likely to be re-elected. Job security then is not as tenuous as it may seem from the outside. Settings that offer more secure positions include nonprofit organizations that do advocacy work and civil service positions. Civil service positions, which encompass a significant number of political social work jobs, are among the most stable positions in the US workforce.

When considering a political social work position, like any other potential job, do your research. Positions for local, state, or federal government are generally required to publicly list salaries of officeholders. Research online and through your networks to see what an appropriate salary is and what is commonplace in terms of negotiating for moving on to another position after the one for which you are applying ends. Be sure you understand your salary, benefits, and any issues related to job security, and have these in writing. Some political social work positions are paid in nontraditional time frames (for example, a flat rate for an entire campaign, or per week), so make sure you fully know what you are agreeing to.

To be clear, these issues of salaries and job security can pose challenges when it comes to thinking about work-life balance. We know, for example, that having young families is a part of decision-making in political careers for some women (Sanbonmatsu et al. 2009). The long hours required on campaigns and in some part-time legislatures can lead to staffers who are younger, with fewer concerns about balancing long hours with their other personal commitments. It also can be challenging to balance a professional full-time direct practice job with volunteer interests in political social work.

At the same time, the authors have seen social workers across all domains (including those profiled in this book) who find ways to balance their political work with their personal obligations as partners, parents, and caretakers, and with other professional obligations. If you are interested in considering how you might incorporate any particular position—or volunteer opportunity—with your other interests and responsibilities, we recommend connecting with someone who holds that position or a similar one. Invite them for coffee, and ask how they manage these competing interests in their lives. This may even spark the beginning of a helpful mentoring relationship. You may also find the self-care section at the end of this chapter helpful in thinking about ways to promote work-life balance while engaging in political social work.

Issues Related to Supervision and Interprofessional Practice

As is true for social workers in diverse settings, in many political settings, you may find yourself the only social worker in the organization. Political social work is heavily interprofessional—you *will* be working with professionals from many different backgrounds. This may pose challenges for some of you, as you learn to work with colleagues, supervisors, and/or employees who were trained in different philosophies and different professional ethics (Pritzker and Barros Lane in press). At times, you may find that approaches to management in political settings may differ from the ideals you learned about in your social work classroom or your real-world experiences in your field placements. If this is the case for you, we encourage you to seek outside mentorship to help support you. There are several existing models of ways to do this, including as part of supervision groups or cohorts (Hill et al. 2010).

Social workers can make a difference in political settings through supervision and management that takes into account diversity and difference. As a supervisor, your social work skills can help you manage these environments effectively. As a staffer, they can guide you in helping your organization pre-empt difficult situations that may arise.

FURTHER REFLECTION: Addressing Challenges

For each of the challenges you listed in your reflection at the beginning of this section (or any others that have come to mind as you read this section), assess: (1) Is it truly a challenge? (2) What strategies can you engage in that will lessen the challenge?

Discuss your reflections with a colleague, friend, or mentor. What other ideas or assistance can they provide to guide you in navigating these challenges?

Section 5: Reassessing Yourself: How Have You Grown?

At the beginning of this book, we asked you to assess yourself as a political actor. Specifically, we asked you to assess yourself in terms of a number of key factors that inform how people behave politically: political knowledge, political skills, political ideology, prior political activity, and whether individuals have ever been recruited into political action. While these concepts are all predictors of political action, they are also all changeable. An individual can expand knowledge, skills, and activity; can shift ideology in light of new knowledge and experiences; and can be recruited into action even if this has never happened before.

We now encourage you to revisit where you stand in terms of each of these concepts. We invite you to retake six self-assessments. After you take these self-assessments, reflect back on the answers you gave at the beginning of this book and now. Has some aspect of you as a political actor changed during this course? If so, why do you think that is? If not, why not? You may wish to come back to these assessments again in a year (or five) to see whether or how your political self has changed.

SELF-ASSESSMENT: Measure Your Own Political Activity

Take the civic engagement quiz here: http://www.civicyouth.org/PopUps/Final_Civic_Inds_Quiz_2006.pdf.

Has your political activity changed over the course of the book? What would you like to do to further develop in this area?

SELF-ASSESSMENT: Test Your Political Knowledge

Take some sample questions from the U.S. Citizenship Civics Test: http://civicseducationinitiative.org/take-the-test/. Has your political knowledge changed over the course of this book? What would you like to do to further develop in this area?

SELF-ASSESSMENT: Test Your Political Skills

Take the following Political Skills Inventory (Ferris et al. 2005):

Instructions: Using the following scale, please place a number in the blank next to each item that best describes <u>how much you agree with each statement about yourself:</u>

1 = strongly disagree
2 = disagree
3 = slightly disagree
4 = neutral
5 = slightly agree
6 = agree
7 = strongly agree

1. _____ I spend a lot of time and effort at work networking with others. (NA)
2. _____ I am able to make most people feel comfortable and at ease around me. (II)
3. _____ I am able to communicate easily and effectively with others. (II)
4. _____ It is easy for me to develop good rapport with most people. (II)
5. _____ I understand people very well. (SA)
6. _____ I am good at building relationships with influential people at work. (NA)
7. _____ I am particularly good at sensing the motivations and hidden agendas of others. (SA)
8. _____ When communicating with others, I try to be genuine in what I say and do. (AS)
9. _____ I have developed a large network of colleagues and associates at work who I can call on for support when I really need to get things done. (NA)
10. _____ At work, I know a lot of important people and am well connected. (NA)
11. _____ I spend a lot of time and effort at work developing connections with others. (NA)
12. _____ I am good at getting people to like me. (II)

(continued)

13. _____ It is important that people believe I am sincere in what I say and do. (AS)

14. _____ I try to show a genuine interest in other people. (AS)

15. _____ I am good at using my connections and network to make things happen at work. (NA)

16. _____ I have good intuition or "savvy" about how to present myself to others. (SA)

17. _____ I always seem to instinctively know the right things to say or do to influence others. (SA)

18. _____ I pay close attention to peoples' facial expressions. (SA)

Has your overall score or subscale score on Networking ability (NA), Interpersonal influence (II), Social astuteness (SA), or Apparent sincerity(AS) changed over the course of the book? What would you like to do to further develop in this area?

SELF-ASSESSMENT: Explore Your Own Political Ideology
Use the Pew Research Center's Political Typology Quiz: http://www.people-press.org/quiz/political-typology/. Has your political ideology changed over the course of the book? What would you like to do to further develop in this area?

SELF-ASSESSMENT: Explore Your Experience with Political Recruitment
Over the course of the book, have you been asked by anyone to participate in political activity? Have you asked anyone else to participate in political activity? What would you like to do to further develop in this area?

SELF-ASSESSMENT: Social Work and Politics
At the very beginning of this book, we asked you to consider which political activities you planned to do in the future, and which you thought social workers were obligated to do. We encourage you to also revisit this assessment, considering which of these activities will be incorporated into your next steps.

Answer the following questions created by Rome and Hoechstetter (2010). Check the box in the first column if you plan to do this in the future, and the box in the second column if you think social workers should do this action. Tally your answers for each column.

Activity	I _plan_ to do this in the future	Social workers _should_ do this
Vote in federal elections	☐	☐
Work for pay on campaigns for candidates of my choice	☐	☐
Encourage others to vote on Election Day	☐	☐
Share my political opinions with others	☐	☐
Take an active role in relation to issues that affect me personally	☐	☐
Vote in state elections	☐	☐
Read, listen to, or watch the news	☐	☐
Refuse to vote to demonstrate dissatisfaction with certain elements of the political system	☐	☐
Volunteer for political campaigns	☐	☐
Donate money to causes that are important to me	☐	☐
Follow the progress of legislation that interests me	☐	☐
Volunteer with interest groups (NASW, EMILY's List, NRA), civic organizations (local nonprofit, community group), or a political party (Republican, Democrat)	☐	☐
Keep track of how my legislators vote on issues that interest me	☐	☐
Participate in political rallies, marches, protests, etc.	☐	☐
Voice my opinion on policy issues to media markets (radio, newspapers, TV, etc.)	☐	☐
Take an active role in relation to issues that affect my clients	☐	☐
Participate in civil disobedience when unjust laws or policies are enacted	☐	☐
Contact elected officials about issues that affect my clients	☐	☐
Use social media (Facebook, Twitter, blogs) to organize and engage in politics	☐	☐
Write/deliver testimony to elected and/or appointed political bodies	☐	☐
Vote in local elections	☐	☐
Donate money to political campaigns and/or parties	☐	☐
Discuss current policy issues with others	☐	☐
Take part in concerts or supporting events that are associated with a cause (such as "Race for a Cure") and raise awareness and donations	☐	☐
Choose to spend my money on products, organizations, or businesses that support my personal beliefs	☐	☐
Contact my local elected official(s) about issues that concern me	☐	☐
Contact my state elected official(s) about issues that concern me	☐	☐
Contact my federal elected official(s) about issues that concern me	☐	☐
Encourage and/or help others register to vote	☐	☐
Been appointed/seek appointment to a political position or government office (i.e. local commission, government board)?	☐	☐
Run for local office	☐	☐
Run for state office	☐	☐
Run for federal office	☐	☐
Total (0–33)		

Section 6: Self-Care in Political Social Work

Throughout this book, you have had the opportunity to learn about the many positive ways that engaging in political social work can benefit communities and promote social justice. In many ways, the work environment for political social workers is completely energizing. As both authors of this book, as well as the political social workers profiled here, can attest to, the work in many political social work positions is often exhilarating. No two days are ever the same, you get to engage with decision-makers and communities constantly, you often get a seat at the decision-making table, and you have the opportunity every day to engage with meaningful issues that affect real people.

At the same time, over the course of this book, we have discussed an array of challenges that political social workers face in their practice. You may work in highly stressful situations, with long hours, often in organizational cultures that don't promote self-care. You will certainly face ethical challenges, be faced with uncomfortable situations and conversations, and sometimes you may feel as if your own values are being challenged. You will have to step outside of your comfort zone, and may at times find yourself receiving critical media attention and criticism even from the people on whose behalf you are trying to work. While we hope that you have many policy wins, the reality is that you will also face losses. Some of those losses—whether in an electoral campaign or in your inability to stop a harmful piece of legislation—may feel extremely painful.

As these challenges negatively impact your physical, emotional, and mental health, self-care will be an important tool. Self-care is "the utilization of skills and strategies by social workers to maintain their own personal, familial, emotional, and spiritual needs while attending to the needs and demands of their clients" (Newell and Nelson-Gardell 2014). So often in social work, self-care is talked about in a clinical context, as a tool to help social workers protect themselves from burnout (exhaustion due to the constant demands of the work environment), compassion fatigue (emotional and psychological exhaustion that stems from regular use of empathy), and secondary traumatic stress (being vicariously traumatized through exposure to others' trauma experiences) (Newell and Nelson-Gardell 2014). As we conclude this textbook, the authors want to underscore that self-care is also critical in political social work, as we too experience these challenges. Being an effective political social worker requires that you make the time and space to take care of your own well-being. Often, this is no different than the self-care we talk about in other social work practice settings: identifying a set of activities that help keep you centered, healthy, and happy.

There is no one-size-fits-all way to carry out self-care as a political social worker, but it begins with self-awareness, which Tanya Rhodes Smith calls "the single best predictor of leadership success" (personal communication, July 11, 2017). Knowing yourself, your strengths, what sustains you, and what drains you will help you prioritize self-care in your practice. While sometimes the organizational culture in political settings makes self-care seem like a weakness, try to remember that engaging in self-care will actually help you to be more effective in your work (Saturno

2016). Identify a specific set of realistic techniques as you face difficult situations—perhaps these involve exercise, hobbies and recreational activities, religious activities, spending time outdoors, time with family and friends, alone time, or even sleep. Leave work at the office when it is at all possible to do so—this may entail silencing your phone and/or shutting off email notifications for as long as you can get away with.

Sometimes, however, the rhythms of political social work make even these techniques feel near impossible. "Budget Week" in a state legislature can require staffers to pull multiple all-nighters to prepare for votes on hundreds of amendments to the state budget. The final weeks of a campaign can require seemingly endless cross-state or cross-country travel to make sure that the candidate is making as much direct contact with voters as possible. In preparation for situations like these, reflect both on how you can act preventatively to protect yourself before these particularly stressful times come and identify specific strategies that will help you cope with these stressors when they inevitably arise (Redick 2016).

In these kinds of circumstances, self-care may no longer realistically entail long runs and a full night's sleep. Instead, keep it simple and realistic. Avoid self-care goals that you will be unable to meet, thus potentially creating another source of stress for you. Simple self-care goals could be as small as making sure you eat breakfast, whatever it may be, and taking two minutes during the day to watch a brief YouTube video that makes you laugh. For political social workers who are regularly surrounded by political news, taking even a brief break from social media can be beneficial. If you are someone who enjoys journaling, bring your journal to work with you and give yourself even just 5–10 minutes in a day to write in your journal.

Another way to take care of yourself as a political social worker is to find a support system from other social workers engaged in similar work. Where possible in your work environment, find like-minded colleagues who share your passions and commitments. For some of you, it may feel as if there aren't other social workers who can relate to your experiences, but try to widen your lens. Perhaps you are the only social worker in the South Dakota legislature—but you can connect with social workers in other state legislatures using resources like NASW PACE's list of social workers in state and local office (see Resources at the end of this chapter). The Nancy A. Humphreys Institute for Political Social Work is another helpful resource for political social workers interested in building connections with other social workers working in political settings. Your state NASW office may be a good source of support or connections. Seek out other political social workers, for consultation, mentorship, but also for a safe place to process some of your experiences with others who can relate. It also might be necessary to find a support network of people who are not connected to the political world to help create some distance between yourself and the work.

Self-care involves knowing when to say "no," drawing personal boundaries so that you have the capacity to bring your whole self to your work when it is necessary. This can feel challenging when your boss is a politician to whom you might feel uncomfortable saying "no," or when so many of your contacts during the day come from constituents to whom you or your boss are accountable. As one of the authors writes this, she thinks of a former student who was a staffer for a freshman (brand new) state legislator during his first-term. As the legislator worked late nights and weekends throughout the state's legislative session in order to keep up with the new context, the new materials, and the new demands from his district's constituents, he expected the same from his staff, leaving the exhausted staffer hesitant to ask to carve out any personal space. Another state legislator had a rule for staff in her office during the legislative session: No one goes home until the last person is finished with their work. While this created a strong sense of camaraderie and support among her staff, it also left exhausted staff feeling unable to set personal boundaries. Even at those times when maintaining boundaries seems impossible, reflect on ways to can carve out small moments for yourself. Walk extra slowly to the bathroom or water cooler, or park a little farther away from your office in the morning so that you can spend a few more minutes on your walk listening to a meditation app or music that soothes you. When you do get a day off, try to respect your own boundaries and take that time to yourself.

You also might find opportunities to practice your advocacy skills with your colleagues, in order to encourage rethinking of office policies that lead to less-than-effective work in the long-run. As a social worker in a legislative setting, one author often found herself advocating for staff on a regular basis. When you have the skills to advocate and if you are in a position with the power to do so, you can help to make workplaces as supportive of workers as possible. When you are in a position of power, you also can be mindful of the messages you send to staff members who have less power than you. If you choose to "unplug" and encourage those around you to do so, you send a message that personal self-care is important and should be prioritized. It can be a badge of honor to be the busiest, most important, most sleep-deprived person in an office, but it does not have to be.

On a final note, at several points throughout this book, we have referred to the importance of passion and motivation in guiding the work of political social workers. In Chap. 4, we discuss "the power of passion for a cause"—the power that social workers bring to political change efforts through working on behalf of causes they care deeply about. In Chap. 5, we asked you to engage with Simon Sinek's Golden Circle, and to think about your own motivations to engage in political action. We included these discussions because they are important components of making change happen, but also because regular reflection on your own motivations for the political work that you do is also an important tool for self-care. When you are faced with losses, or even just not achieving the outcomes you hoped for, it can be rejuvenating to step back and make sure that you continue to put energy behind your passions. Even when you are successful, this reflection offers a good opportunity for you to continue to consider how and why you engage in this work. Remembering why we do what we do—and the great meaning and importance attached to working toward rights and justice for vulnerable populations—can help us to refocus even on the hardest days.

BUILD YOUR SKILLS: Develop a Self-Care Plan for Your Political Social Work
Practice
Develop a realistic self-care plan, in which you address specific strategies for
preventing and managing the stressors that you may face in a future political
social work job of your choice. Think in terms of simple steps that you can
take even when stress levels are at their highest.

APPLY YOUR SKILLS: Your Political Social Worker Profile
As a final exercise, write a political social work profile of yourself in 5 years
modeled on the profiles in this book. What will you be doing? What will your
goals be?

Resources

Article

Richards-Schuster, K., Ruffolo, M. C., Nicoll, K. L., Distelrath, C., Galura, J., & Mishkin, A.
(2016). Exploring challenges faced by students as they transition to social justice work in the
"real world": Implications for social work. *Advances in Social Work, 16*(2), 372–389.

Historical Resources

Jane Addams: http://www.nobelprize.org/nobel_prizes/peace/laureates/1931/press.html
Hull House: http://hullhouse.uic.edu/hull/urbanexp/main.cgi?file=n   ew/subsub_index.
ptt&chap=82
Settlement Houses: http://socialwelfare.library.vcu.edu/settlement-houses/settlement-houses/

Jobs/Field Placements

Legislative Field Placements: http://www.socialworker.com/feature-articles/field-placement/
legislative-field-placements-social-works-impact-on-policy/
The Hill: http://thehill.com/resources/classifieds/employer
Idealist: https://www.idealist.org/en/?type=ALL
National Association of Social Workers Political Action for Candidate Election (PACE): https://
www.socialworkers.org/pace/state.asp
Partnership for Public Service's Go Government (civil service resume tips): http://gogovernment.
org/how_to_apply/write_your_federal_resume/create_your_resume.php
Political Social Work Jobs: https://www.socialworkers.org/pubs/choices/choices2.asp#Politics
Social Work Licensing Requirements: https://www.aswb.org/wp-content/uploads/2015/09/Social-
work-licensing-requirements-9.17.pdf
Social Work Today: http://www.socialworktoday.com/archive/septoct2007p44.shtml
United Nations positions: https://unjobs.org/organizations
Federal positions at USA Jobs: https://www.usajobs.gov/

Other websites

Association of Macro Practice Social Workers: http://www.ampsw.org
Ask A Manager: http://askamanager.org
Coalition for Policy Education and Practice: https://www.cswe.org/Centers-Initiatives/Initiatives/
    The-Coalition-for-Policy-Education-and-Practice-in or go to https://www.cswe.org and in the
    menu click "Centers & Initiatives" then in the right hand sidebar on the left hand side of the
    landing page click "The Coalition for Policy Education and Practice in Social Work" under
    "Initiatives."
Influencing Social Policy: http://influencingsocialpolicy.org/
Macro Social Work Student Network: http://www.mswsn.org/
Nancy A. Humphreys Institute for Political Social Work: http://politicalinstitute.uconn.edu
National Association of Social Workers Connecticut Chapter's macro group: http://naswct.org/
    about/committees-networks/
National Network for Social Work Managers: https://socialworkmanager.org/.
New Social Worker: http://www.socialworker.com
Policy Conference 2.0: http://www.influencingsocialpolicy.org/conference/

References

Association of Social Work Boards. (n.d.). *Continuing competence*. Retrieved from https://www.
    aswb.org/licensees/continuing-education/.
Brooks, D. (2017, April 25). The Jane Addams Model. *The New York Times*.
City of New Orleans. (2017). *How to apply*. Retrieved from http://www.nola.gov/civil-service/
    jobs/how-to-apply/.
Council on Social Work Education. (2015). Educational Policy and Accreditation Standards.
    Retrieved   from   https://www.cswe.org/getattachment/Accreditation/Accreditation-
    Process/2015-EPAS/2015EPAS_Web_FINAL.pdf.aspx.
Donaldson, L. P., Hill, K., Ferguson, S., Fogel, S., & Erickson, C. (2014). Contemporary social
    work licensure: Implications for macro social work practice and education. *Social Work, 59*(1),
    52–61. https://doi.org/10.1093/sw/swt045.
Ferris, G. R., Treadway, D. C., Kolodinsky, R. W., Hochwarter, W. A., Kacmar, C. J., Douglas,
    C., et al. (2005). Development and validation of the Political Skill Inventory. *Journal of
    Management, 31*(1), 126–152.
Galambos, C. (2009). Political tolerance, social work values, and social work education. *Journal
    of Social Work Education, 45*(3), 343–347.
Harvard University. (n.d.). *Jane Addams (1860–1935)*. Retrieved from http://ocp.hul.harvard.edu/
    ww/addams.html.
Hill, K., Ferguson, S. M., & Erickson, C. L. (2010). Sustaining and strengthening a macro iden-
    tity: The Association of Macro Practice Social Work. *Journal of Community Practice, 18*(4),
    513–527.
Jane Addams is appointed garbage inspector. (n.d.). Retrieved from https://worldhistoryproject.
    org/1895/jane-addams-is-appointed-garbage-inspector
Lane, S. R. (2011). Political content in social work education as reported by elected social workers.
    Journal of Social Work Education, 47(1), 53–72. https://doi.org/10.5175/jswe.2011.200900050.
Lane, S. R., & Humphreys, N. A. (2011). Social workers in politics: A national survey of social
    work candidates and elected officials. *Journal of Policy Practice, 10*, 225–244.
Mundy, L. (2015). Who will be the next Dean of the Senate women? *Politico*.
National Association of Social Workers. (2004). *Center for Workforce Studies*. Washingdon, DC:
    NASW.

National Association of Social Workers. (2017). *Code of Ethics of the National Association of Social Workers*. Washington, DC: National Association of Social Workers.

New York State Department of Education Office of the Professions. (2010). *Regulations of the Commissioner, Part 74, Social Work*. Retrieved from http://www.op.nysed.gov/prof/sw/part74.htm.

Newell, J., & Nelson-Gardell, D. (2014). A competency-based approach to teaching professional self-care: An ethical consideration for social work educators. *Journal of Social Work Education, 50*, 427–439.

Pritzker, S. (2017). A baseline assessment of policy education in social work. *Council on Social Work Education*.

Pritzker, S., & Lane, S. R. (2014). Field Note—Integrating policy and political content in BSW and MSW field placements. *Journal of Social Work Education, 50*(4), 730–739. https://doi.org/10.1080/10437797.2014.947905.

Pritzker, S., & Applewhite, S. (2015). Going 'macro': Exploring the careers of macro practitioners. *Social Work, 60*(3), 191–199.

Pritzker, S., & Burwell, C. (2016). Promoting election-related policy practice among social work students. *Journal of Social Work Education, 52*(4), 434–447.

Pritzker, S., & Barros Lane, L. (in press). Supporting field-based education in political settings. *Journal of Social Work Education*.

Redick, E. (2016). We need to prepare social work students for secondary stress in the workplace. *The New Social Worker*.

Rein, L. (2017, April 19). This Beltway insider is in charge of hiring for the Trump administration. It's taking a while. *The Washington Post*.

Rome, S. H., & Hoechstetter, S. (2010). Social work and civic engagement: The political participation of professional social workers. *Journal of Sociology and Social Welfare, 37*, 107–129.

Rosenwald, M., Wiener, D., Smith-Osborne, A., & Smith, C. (2012). The place of political diversity within the social work classroom. *Journal of Social Work Education, 48*(1), 139–158.

Sanbonmatsu, K., Carroll, S. J., & Walsh, D. (2009). *Poised to run: Women's pathways to the state legislatures*. Center for American Women and Politics, Eagleton Institute of Politics, Rutgers, The State University of New Jersey.

Saturno, S. (2016). Self-care: A social worker's guide to staying on your feet. *The New Social Worker*.

State of California. (2017). *Application for appointment*. Retrieved from https://www.gov.ca.gov/s_appointmentsapplication.php

Texas Health and Human Services. (2013). *Texas State Board of Social Worker Examiners apply for a new license—FAQs*. Retrieved from https://www.dshs.texas.gov/socialwork/sw_faqs.shtm - Must%20I%20become%20licensed?

United States Office of Personnel Management. (n.d.). *USAJOBS students & recent graduates*. Retrieved from https://www.usajobs.gov/StudentsAndGrads/.

Index

© Springer International Publishing AG 2018
S.R. Lane, S. Pritzker, *Political Social Work*,
https://doi.org/10.1007/978-3-319-68588-5

Druck:
Customized Business Services GmbH
im Auftrag der
KNV Zeitfracht GmbH
Ein Unternehmen der Zeitfracht - Gruppe
Ferdinand-Jühlke-Str. 7
99095 Erfurt